Frommer's®

Virginia

11th Edition

by Bill Goodwin

WILEY

John Wiley & Sons, Inc.

ABOUT THE AUTHOR

Born and raised in North Carolina near Hampton Roads, **Bill Goodwin** (www.billgoodwin.com) has lived in northern Virginia since 1979. He was an award-winning newspaper reporter for the *Atlanta Journal* before becoming a legal counsel and speechwriter for two U.S. senators, Sam Nunn of Georgia and Sam J. Ervin, Jr., of North Carolina. Now a full-time travel writer, Goodwin is also the author of *Frommer's South Pacific*, *Frommer's Tahiti & French Polynesia*, and *Frommer's Fiji*.

Published by:
JOHN WILEY & SONS, INC.
111 River St.
Hoboken, NJ 07030-5774

ISBN 978-1-118-11805-4 (paper); ISBN 978-1-118-22449-6 (ebk); ISBN 978-1-118-26266-5 (ebk); ISBN 978-1-118-23785-4 (ebk)

Editor: Maureen Clarke
Production Editor: Katie Robinson
Cartographer: Andy Dolan
Photo Editor: Richard Fox
Production by Wiley Indianapolis Composition Services

Front Cover Photo: Monticello ©Joe Sohm / Visions of America, LLC / Alamy Images
Back Cover Photo: Rocky Knob area, Blue Ridge Parkway ©Pat & Chuck Blackley / Alamy Images

For information on our other products and services or to obtain technical support, please contact our Customer Care Department within the U.S. at 877/762-2974, outside the U.S. at 317/572-3993 or fax 317/572-4002.

Wiley also publishes its books in a variety of electronic formats. Some content that appears in print may not be available in electronic formats.

Manufactured in the United States of America

5 4 3 2 1

CONTENTS

LIST OF MAPS

HOW TO CONTACT US

In researching this book, we discovered many wonderful places—hotels, restaurants, shops, and more. We're sure you'll find others. Please tell us about them, so we can share the information with your fellow travelers in upcoming editions. If you were disappointed with a recommendation, we'd love to know that, too. Please write to:

Frommer's Virginia, 11th Edition
John Wiley & Sons, Inc. • 111 River St. • Hoboken, NJ 07030-5774
frommersfeedback@wiley.com

ADVISORY & DISCLAIMER

Travel information can change quickly and unexpectedly, and we strongly advise you to confirm important details locally before traveling, including information on visas, health and safety, traffic and transport, accommodations, shopping, and eating out. We also encourage you to stay alert while traveling and to remain aware of your surroundings. Avoid civil disturbances, and keep a close eye on cameras, purses, wallets, and other valuables.

While we have endeavored to ensure that the information contained within this guide is accurate and up-to-date at the time of publication, we make no representations or warranties with respect to the accuracy or completeness of the contents of this work and specifically disclaim all warranties, including without limitation warranties of fitness for a particular purpose. We accept no responsibility or liability for any inaccuracy or errors or omissions, or for any inconvenience, loss, damage, costs, or expenses of any nature whatsoever incurred or suffered by anyone as a result of any advice or information contained in this guide.

The inclusion of a company, organization, or website in this guide as a service provider and/or potential source of further information does not mean that we endorse them or the information they provide. Be aware that information provided through some websites may be unreliable and can change without notice. Neither the publisher nor author shall be liable for any damages arising herefrom.

FROMMER'S STAR RATINGS, ICONS & ABBREVIATIONS

Every hotel, restaurant, and attraction listing in this guide has been ranked for quality, value, service, amenities, and special features using a **star-rating system.** In country, state, and regional guides, we also rate towns and regions to help you narrow down your choices and budget your time accordingly. Hotels and restaurants are rated on a scale of zero (recommended) to three stars (exceptional). Attractions, shopping, nightlife, towns, and regions are rated according to the following scale: zero stars (recommended), one star (highly recommended), two stars (very highly recommended), and three stars (must-see).

In addition to the star-rating system, we also use **seven feature icons** that point you to the great deals, in-the-know advice, and unique experiences that separate travelers from tourists. Throughout the book, look for:

special finds—those places only insiders know about

fun facts—details that make travelers more informed and their trips more fun

kids—best bets for kids and advice for the whole family

special moments—those experiences that memories are made of

overrated—places or experiences not worth your time or money

insider tips—great ways to save time and money

great values—where to get the best deals

The following abbreviations are used for credit cards:

AE	American Express	DISC	Discover	V	Visa
DC	Diners Club	MC	MasterCard		

TRAVEL RESOURCES AT FROMMERS.COM

Frommer's travel resources don't end with this guide. Frommer's website, **www.frommers. com**, has travel information on more than 4,000 destinations. We update features regularly, giving you access to the most current trip-planning information and the best airfare, lodging, and car-rental bargains. You can also listen to podcasts, connect with other Frommers.com members through our active-reader forums, share your travel photos, read blogs from guidebook editors and fellow travelers, and much more.

THE BEST OF VIRGINIA

H istory springs to life wherever you go in the scenic Commonwealth of Virginia. Jamestown was the first permanent English-speaking colony in North America. The American Revolution was fomented at Williamsburg and won at nearby Yorktown. Great Civil War battles raged at Manassas, Fredericksburg, Petersburg, and Richmond. Yet as much as Virginians revere history, they honor the present with the likes of two modern air-and-space museums, at **Hampton** and in the **Hunt Country** of northern Virginia. Indeed, there is something for everyone.

Sightseeing Between historic sights, Virginia's varied geological beauty unfolds. In the east are the tidal waters flanking the port city of **Norfolk,** fronting the sands of **Virginia Beach,** and surrounding the wildlife islands of **Chincoteague** and **Assateague.** To the west, the hilly Piedmont hosts cities like **Fredericksburg, Charlottesville,** and **Richmond.** Beyond, over the **Blue Ridge Mountains,** lies the splendid **Shenandoah Valley.** Straddling the Blue Ridge is **Shenandoah National Park** and its magnificent **Skyline Drive,** and southwestern Virginia sports **Mount Rogers,** Virginia's highest peak.

Eating & Drinking You can dine on all types of cuisine in Virginia, but the highlights derive from recipes handed down since Colonial times—dishes such as peanut soup and Sally Lunn bread. To this day Virginians love country ham cured the old-fashioned way, especially when crammed between hot buttermilk biscuits at breakfast. And they like their fish, oysters, and blue crabs fresh from the Chesapeake Bay. All across Virginia modern chefs are finding creative ways to use these fresh ingredients.

History Virginia abounds with buildings that rang with revolutionary oratory, small towns scarcely changed since Colonial times, and bloody Civil War battlefields. Beautifully restored **Williamsburg, Jamestown,** and **Yorktown** expertly explain America's founding. George Washington's **Mount Vernon** is one of this country's most visited homes. Thomas Jefferson lived at **Monticello,** overlooking the vibrant college town of **Charlottesville.** Less than a century later, much of the Civil War was fought on bloody battlegrounds between **Fredericksburg** and **Richmond,** the Confederate capital.

Active Pursuits Much of Virginia's wilderness looks as it did when the first English colonists settled here in 1607. Leading the list is **Shenandoah National Park** and its 500-plus miles of hiking trails. The **Shenandoah River** is a hotbed for kayaking, canoeing, and rafting.

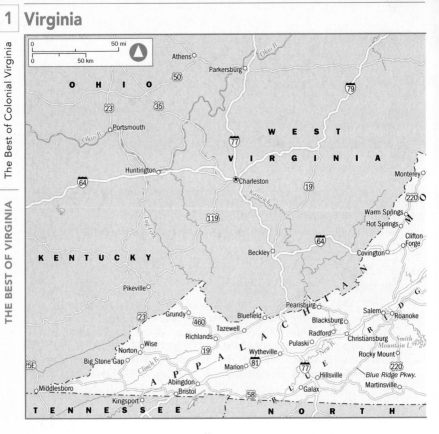

Hikers, bikers, and horseback riders will enjoy the **New River Trail** and **Virginia Creeper Trail** in Virginia's Southwest Highlands. Down east, there's plenty to do in and on the water at **Virginia Beach** and **Chincoteague** and **Assateague** islands.

THE best OF COLONIAL VIRGINIA

- o **Old Town Alexandria:** Although vibrant Alexandria is very much part of metro Washington, D.C., the historic district known as Old Town evokes the time when the nation's early leaders strolled its streets and partook of grog at Gadsby's Tavern. See "Alexandria," in chapter 4.
- o **Mount Vernon:** When he wasn't off surveying, fighting in the French and Indian War, leading the American Revolution, or serving as our first president, George Washington made his home at a plantation 8 miles south of Alexandria. Restored to look as it did in Washington's day, Mount Vernon is America's second-most-visited historic home. See p. 65.
- o **Fredericksburg:** Not only did the Fredericksburg area play a role in the birth of a nation, but it also was the boyhood home of George Washington. James Monroe,

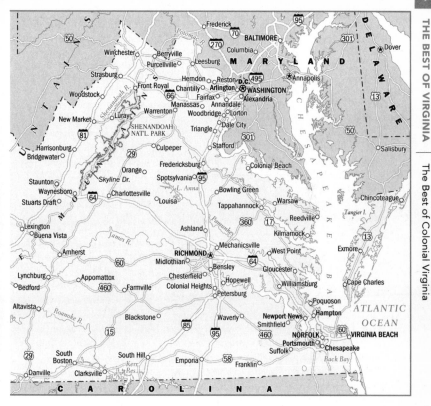

who as president kept European powers out of the Americas by promulgating the Monroe Doctrine, lived here before he moved to Charlottesville. The great Confederate leader Robert E. Lee was born beside the Rappahannock River a generation later and grew up to win great battles near Fredericksburg. Although the area is increasingly becoming part of the Washington, D.C., metropolitan area, Fredericksburg's historic Old Town retains much of the charm it possessed in those early days. See chapter 5.

○ **Charlottesville:** If Washington was the father of the United States, then Thomas Jefferson was its intellectual genius. This scholar, lawyer, writer, and architect built two monuments—his lovely hilltop home, Monticello, and the University of Virginia—that still evoke memories of this great thinker and patriot. See chapter 6.

○ **Williamsburg, Jamestown & Yorktown:** Known as the Historic Triangle, these three towns are the finest examples of Colonial America to be found. Colonial Williamsburg looks as it appeared when it was the capital of Virginia in the 18th century. The original Jamestown settlement is now a national historical park, as is Yorktown, where Washington and his French allies defeated Lord Cornwallis to end the American Revolution. See chapter 10.

3

THE best OF CIVIL WAR VIRGINIA

o **Manassas:** The first battle of the war occurred along Bull Run near Manassas in northern Virginia, and it shocked the Union (and the thousands of spectators who came from Washington to watch) when the rebels engineered a win over a disorganized Union force. They won again at the Battle of Second Manassas. See p. 79.

o **Fredericksburg:** No other town in Virginia has as many significant battlefields as Fredericksburg. Lee used the Rappahannock River as a natural line of defense, and he fought several battles against Union armies trying to advance on Richmond. You can visit the battlefields in town, and at Chancellorsville and The Wilderness, in a day. See chapter 5.

o **Appomattox Court House:** After the fall of Petersburg in 1865, Lee fled for little more than a week until realizing that continuing the war was fruitless. On April 9, he met Grant at Wilbur McLean's farmhouse and surrendered his sword. America's bloodiest conflict was over. The farmhouse is preserved as part of Appomattox Court House National Historical Park. See p. 124.

o **New Market:** While Lee and Grant were fighting in northern Virginia, other armies were battling in the Shenandoah Valley, the "bread basket of the Confederacy." On May 15, 1864, the entire teenage cadet corps of Virginia Military Institute helped the South win the Battle of New Market. They are honored at New Market Battlefield State Historical Park and its Virginia Museum of the Civil War. See p. 151.

o **Richmond:** The capital of the Confederacy, Richmond has many reminders of the war, including the magnificent Museum of the Confederacy and the White House of the Confederacy, home of Confederate President Jefferson Davis. Monument Avenue is lined with statues of the rebel leaders. The city's eastern outskirts are ringed with battle sites, part of the Richmond National Battlefield Park. See chapter 9.

o **Petersburg:** After nearly 4 years of trying to capture Richmond, Grant bypassed the Southern capital in 1864 and headed for the railroad junction of Petersburg, the lifeline of the Confederate capital. Even there, he was forced into a siege situation, but finally, in April 1865, Grant broke through and forced Lee into a westward retreat to Appomattox. See "An Easy Excursion to Petersburg," in chapter 9:

THE best OF THE GREAT OUTDOORS

o **Shenandoah National Park:** Nearly two million visitors a year venture into the Shenandoah National Park, which straddles the Blue Ridge Mountains from Front Royal to Rockfish Gap. Many visitors merely drive along the 105-mile Skyline Drive, one of America's most scenic routes, but the park has more than 500 miles of hiking trails, including 101 miles of the Appalachian Trail. Many trails start at Skyline Drive and drop down into hollows and canyons, some of them with waterfalls. Even on Skyline Drive, you are likely to encounter deer, and you might even see bear, bobcat, and wild turkey. See "Shenandoah National Park & Skyline Drive," in chapter 7.

o **Running the Rivers** (Front Royal, Luray): The South Fork of the Shenandoah River twists and turns its way between the valley towns of Front Royal and Luray, making it a perfect venue for rafting, canoeing, and kayaking—or just floating along in an inner tube. See p. 145.

- **Mount Rogers National Recreation Area:** While you won't be alone in Shenandoah National Park, you could have a hiking, biking, horseback-riding, or cross-country skiing trail all to yourself in Mount Rogers National Recreation Area. This wild land in the Southwest Highlands occupies some 117,000 acres of forest and includes its namesake, Virginia's highest peak. Two of Virginia's finest rails-to-trails hiking, biking, and riding paths serve as bookends to the 60-mile-long recreation area: the New River Trail, near Wytheville, and the Virginia Creeper Trail, from Abingdon to White Top Mountain. See "Outdoors in the Southwest Highlands," in chapter 8.
- **Back Bay National Wildlife Refuge/False Cape State Park** (Virginia Beach): You can't sunbathe on the beach of Back Bay National Wildlife Refuge, or swim in the bay, but you can hike through the dunes or take a canoe into the marshes, which are on the Atlantic Flyway for migrating birds. You can sunbathe and swim at the adjoining False Cape State Park. See "Parks & Wildlife Refuges" under "Virginia Beach," in chapter 11.
- **Assateague Island:** Of all the natural areas in Virginia, none surpasses Assateague, which keeps the Atlantic from the back bays of Chincoteague. Here you will find the famous wild ponies in Chincoteague National Wildlife Refuge and relatively tame humans strolling along some 37 miles of pristine beach. Assateague Island is also situated directly on the Atlantic Flyway, making it one of the best bird-watching sites in the country. See "Chincoteague & Assateague Islands," in chapter 11.

THE best SCENIC DRIVES

- **George Washington Memorial Parkway** (northern Virginia): Stay away during rush hour, when it becomes a major artery into and out of Washington, D.C. But any other time, the "G. W. Parkway" is a great drive along the Potomac River from I-495 at the Maryland line to Mount Vernon. The views of Washington's monuments are unparalleled. See p. 64.
- **The Presidents Route** (Va. 20; Charlottesville to Montpelier): Thomas Jefferson and James Monroe would travel the 25 miles north to visit their friends James and Dolley Madison by a winding wagon trail. Today that road is known as Va. 20, and it's still a scenic wonder through the modern vineyards and expensive horse farms of the Blue Ridge foothills. See "James Madison's Montpelier," in chapter 6.
- **Skyline Drive** (Shenandoah National Park): Few roads anywhere can top Skyline Drive, which twists and turns 105 miles along the Blue Ridge crest in Shenandoah National Park. The views over the rolling Piedmont to the east and Shenandoah Valley to the west are spectacular, especially during spring, when the wildflowers are in bloom, and in fall, when the leaves change from green to brilliant hues of rust, orange, and yellow. See "Shenandoah National Park & Skyline Drive," in chapter 7.
- **Lexington to Hot Springs:** Va. 39 runs from Lexington to Hot Springs via the Goshen Pass, a picturesque gorge cut by the Maury River. You can make a loop by continuing north from Hot Springs via U.S. 220 to the beautiful village of Monterey in "Virginia's Switzerland." From Monterey, U.S. 250 climbs over four mountains to Staunton and I-81. See chapter 7.
- **Blue Ridge Parkway:** Picking up where Skyline Drive ends, this road continues along the Blue Ridge crest south to the Great Smoky Mountains National Park in North Carolina. Of the 218 miles in Virginia, the most scenic are north of Roanoke. See "The Blue Ridge Parkway," in chapter 8.

- **Colonial Parkway:** It's not long, but the Colonial Parkway between Jamestown, Williamsburg, and Yorktown has its scenic merits, especially the views of the James River near Jamestown and of the York River near Yorktown. See chapter 10.
- **Chesapeake Bay Bridge-Tunnel:** A man-made wonder, the Chesapeake Bay Bridge-Tunnel runs for 17 miles over—and under—the mouth of the Chesapeake Bay between Norfolk and the Eastern Shore. You can barely see land when you're in the middle. See chapter 11.

THE most CHARMING SMALL TOWNS

- **Middleburg:** The self-proclaimed capital of Virginia's Hunt Country, Middleburg is small enough to be digested in an afternoon, taking up barely 6 blocks along U.S. 50. Some of the world's wealthiest individuals keep their horses near Middleburg, and the town has a host of upscale shops in buildings dating from the 1700s. See "The Hunt Country," in chapter 4.
- **Monterey:** Over Shenandoah and Bull Pasture mountains from Staunton, the village of Monterey appears more like New England than Virginia, with its white churches and clapboard homes in a picturesque valley. Thousands of visitors make the trek over the mountains to the annual Highland Maple Festival in March. See "Staunton to Warm Springs via Monterey," in chapter 7.
- **Staunton:** There's Shakespeare to be seen at the Blackfriars Playhouse in Staunton, an old railroad town that is also famous as President Woodrow Wilson's birthplace. The replica of the Bard's 17th-century indoor theater has spurred a downtown renaissance, with new restaurants and shops opening all the time. The Frontier Culture Museum is here, too. See "Staunton: A President & the Bard," in chapter 7.
- **Lexington:** One of America's best small towns, Lexington has a lively college atmosphere and a host of sights. It's home to the Virginia Military Institute (VMI), where Gen. Thomas J. "Stonewall" Jackson taught; its students went off to the Civil War at New Market. Afterward, Robert E. Lee came here as president of Washington College, now Washington and Lee University. VMI was the alma mater of Gen. George C. Marshall, who was awarded the Nobel Peace Prize for his plan to rebuild Europe after World War II. Jackson, Lee, and Marshall are buried here and have museums dedicated to them. See "Lexington: A Charming College Town," in chapter 7.
- **Abingdon:** Daniel Boone opened Virginia's Southwest Highlands to settlement in the 1770s, and a thriving town grew up at Abingdon. Homes and buildings dating to 1779 line Main Street, making it a wonderful place to stroll. The town is home to the Barter Theatre, Virginia's state stage, where you can still barter for a ticket. See "Abingdon: A Show-Stopping Town," in chapter 8.

THE best FAMILY VACATIONS

- **Shenandoah National Park:** Two lodges in the most popular part of Shenandoah National Park make this a great place for family vacations. The kids can participate in ranger programs, hike to waterfalls, or go for a pony ride in the forest. See "Shenandoah National Park & Skyline Drive," in chapter 7.

- **Colonial Williamsburg:** The Historic Area of Colonial Williamsburg is the best place for children to get a quick lesson in American history. On the streets, they might run into Thomas Jefferson (actually, an actor) and have a conversation about the Declaration of Independence, or drill and march with the 18th-century militia. As soon as they get bored, head for Busch Gardens Williamsburg or Water Country USA, two nearby theme parks, or stay at Great Wolf Lodge, whose indoor water park will keep them permanently shriveled. See chapter 10.
- **Virginia Beach:** First there's the beach, 4 miles or so of it, with lifeguards during summer—but that's not all. Rainy days can be spent at the Virginia Aquarium & Marine Science Center, the state's most popular museum. Norfolk's NAUTICUS, Hampton's Virginia Air & Space Center, and Colonial Williamsburg are all just short drives away. See chapters 10 and 11.
- **Chincoteague & Assateague Islands:** The fishing village is the setting for Marguerite Henry's classic children's book *Misty of Chincoteague,* and there are plenty of wild horses (called "ponies") in Chincoteague National Wildlife Refuge on Assateague Island, which also has a guarded beach for swimming during the summer. The best time to see the horses is during the annual pony swim the last week in July, but the kids can ride one in a small equestrian center. See "Chincoteague & Assateague Islands," in chapter 11.

THE most UNUSUAL VIRGINIA TRAVEL EXPERIENCES

- **Chimes Down Under** (Luray): One of the most fascinating caverns in the Shenandoah Valley is at Luray. Through huge subterranean rooms comes beautiful music—in the form of hammers striking million-year-old stalactites. See p. 148.
- **Ancient Hot Tubs** (Warm Springs): Since 1761, travelers have slipped their weary bodies into these natural rock pools whose waters range from 94° to 104°F (34°–40°C). You can, too. See p. 161.
- **Mounting Little Sorrel** (Lexington): After he died of wounds accidentally inflicted by his own men at the Battle of Chancellorsville, Gen. Stonewall Jackson was buried in Lexington, where he had taught at the Virginia Military Institute (VMI). His taxidermied war horse, Little Sorrel, stands in VMI's museum. Robert E. Lee's horse, Traveller, is buried outside Lee Chapel, his master's resting place. See p. 168.
- **Splashing with Harbor Seals** (Virginia Beach): Children and adults will love the Virginia Aquarium & Marine Science Center's **Harbor Seal Splash.** Accompanied by an animal care specialist, you get into a pool and splash around with the resident harbor seals and participate in a training session. See p. 297.
- **"Hoi Toide Tonoit"** (Tangier Island): Out in the Chesapeake Bay sits remote Tangier Island, whose residents have been so isolated that they still speak with the Elizabethan brogue of their forebears. Out here, "high tide tonight" is pronounced *hoi toide tonoit*—as in "hoity-toity"—and narrow 17th-century lanes barely can accommodate modern automobiles. Cruises leave from the Northern Neck and the Eastern Shore. See p. 313.

THE best COUNTRY INNS

○ **Red Fox Inn** (Middleburg): In the center of tiny Middleburg, this rambling inn maintains the romantic charm of early Virginia in its original 1728 stone structure. There's a cozy dining room downstairs. See p. 80.

○ **The Hope and Glory Inn** (Irvington): The state's most fascinating country inn occupies a converted 1890s schoolhouse, and it has cottages in the garden, but what really sets it apart is an outdoor bathroom complete with claw-foot tub. That's right: It's outdoors, albeit surrounded by a stockade fence. See p. 100.

○ **Clifton Inn** (Charlottesville): Thomas Mann Randolph, husband of Thomas Jefferson's daughter, Martha, built this clapboard house as a trading post in 1799. Today it's a luxurious but relaxed country inn. The restaurant itself is worth the trip. See p. 110

○ **The Inn at Little Washington** (Washington): For the best, you need look no further than the Blue Ridge foothill village of Washington, which everyone in Virginia calls "Little Washington." An English decorator designed the rooms here, but it's the romantic restaurant that draws the most raves. See p. 147.

○ **Fort Lewis Plantation & Lodge** (Millboro): One of Virginia's most unusual inns, the Fort Lewis Lodge occupies an old mill and rebuilt barn on a farm beside the Cowpasture River, just over the mountain from Warm Springs. A spiral staircase ascends to three rooms inside the old silo, and there are two log cabins with their own fireplaces. It's a great place to show urban kids a bit of farm life. See p. 164.

○ **The Martha Washington Hotel & Spa** (Abingdon): In Abingdon's historic district, the center portion of this Greek-revival inn was built as a private home in 1832. You can sit in wicker rocking chairs on the front porch and watch the traffic on Main Street—or imagine wolves attacking Daniel Boone's dogs nearby. See p. 198.

THE best LUXURY ACCOMMODATIONS

○ **Morrison House** (Alexandria): More like a country inn in the middle of Old Town Alexandria, this small, luxurious hotel isn't that old, but it looks exactly like the Federal-period homes surrounding it. The dining is very good. See p. 56.

○ **The Boar's Head** (Charlottesville): A 19th-century gristmill serves as the centerpiece of this lakeside resort, on the outskirts of Charlottesville, and lends ancient charm to the Old Mill dining room, one of the best places to sample Virginia wines without trekking to the vineyards. Modern amenities include a full-service spa and access to Charlottesville's best-equipped sports club. See p. 109.

○ **The Homestead** (Hot Springs): Outstanding service, fine cuisine, and a myriad of activities characterize this grand old establishment, in business since Thomas Jefferson stayed here (the first of seven presidents to do so). The Homestead offers accommodations ranging from standard rooms to plush suites. Boasting the country's oldest tee, the golf course is one of Virginia's finest. See p. 162.

○ **The Jefferson Hotel** (Richmond): A Beaux Arts landmark with Renaissance-style balconies and an Italian clock tower, the Jefferson was opened in 1895 by a wealthy Richmonder who wanted his city to have one of America's finest hotels. See p. 209.

- **Williamsburg Inn** (Williamsburg): An establishment with three fine golf courses, the Williamsburg Inn was built as part of the Colonial Williamsburg restoration but looks like it might have been here in 1750. If staying in the main inn with its superb service and cuisine won't do, you can opt for one of the restored houses and taverns that have been converted into accommodations. See p. 250.

THE best MODERATELY PRICED ACCOMMODATIONS

- **Richard Johnston Inn** (Fredericksburg): Elegant rooms lie within these two 18th-century homes across from historic Fredericksburg's visitor center. See p. 91.
- **Frederick House** (Staunton): A cross between a boutique hotel and a B&B, this collection of Victorian houses is in the heart of Staunton, a quick walk to both Woodrow Wilson's birthplace and the Blackfriars Playhouse. See p. 156.
- **Inn at Gristmill Square** (Warm Springs): A naturally warm spring used to turn the water wheel of the gristmill that makes up part of this comfortable inn. Some rooms are in an old barn and silo. See p. 163.
- **Hampton Inn Col Alto** (Lexington): No ordinary Hampton Inn, Col Alto is an 1827 manor house converted into a comfortable B&B-type hotel. Even if you stay in the modern motel buildings next door, you'll eat your continental breakfast in the period dining room. See p. 171.
- **Hotel Roanoke & Conference Center** (Roanoke): The grand, Tudor-style Hotel Roanoke stood in a wheat field when the Norfolk & Western Railroad built it in 1882. A $45-million renovation has completely restored its grand public areas to their original appearance and rebuilt all its rooms to modern standards. See p. 185.
- **Summerfield Inn** (Abingdon): Ideally situated a block behind the Barter Theatre, this bed-and-breakfast offers spacious rooms in a converted carriage house, one with a two-person hot tub and walk-in shower. See p. 198
- **The Fife & Drum Inn** (Williamsburg): Upstairs over the stores of Merchants Square, this charming bed-and-breakfast has Williamsburg's Historic Area right out its front door. For those who can't handle climbing up the stairs, owners Billy and Sharon Scruggs, themselves Williamsburg natives, have a Colonial-style cottage to rent around the corner. See p. 253.

THE best INEXPENSIVE ACCOMMODATIONS

- **Inn at the Olde Silk Mill** (Fredericksburg): Don't be surprised to see Blues and Grays toting Civil War rifles in the lobby; this place is very popular with reenactors. The rooms are laden with antiques. See p. 90.
- **Cavalier Inn at the University** (Charlottesville): The University of Virginia owns and maintains this spotless older motel, a half-mile west of the center of campus. See p. 107.
- **Big Meadows & Skyland Lodges** (Shenandoah National Park): With stunning views from atop the Blue Ridge Mountains, these two rustic but charming inns are surprisingly affordable. Just be sure to reserve as early as possible. See p. 134.
- **Llewellyn Lodge** (Lexington): This B&B within an easy walk of Lexington's many attractions is made special by owners John and Ellen Roberts, who share their knowledge of not only the town but also the surrounding wilderness. See p. 172.

- **Luray Caverns Motel West** (Luray): This old-fashioned motel with small cabins sits across the highway from the famous Luray Caverns, which owns and spotlessly maintains it. See p. 149.
- **Roseloe Motel** (Hot Springs): You don't have to pay a fortune to stay at the Homestead when you can bunk for much less at the Roseloe, a clean, 1950s-style motel across U.S. 220 from the Garth Newel Chamber Music Center. Warm Springs is a short drive, and you can pay much less than the cost of a room to use the Homestead's recreational facilities. See p. 163.
- **Colony House Motor Lodge** (Roanoke): This older but clean and very well-maintained motel is convenient to both downtown Roanoke and the Blue Ridge Parkway. Doors to the rooms have louvers to let in fresh air but not light—an unusual touch for any inexpensive hotel. See p. 185.
- **Belvedere Beach Resort** (Virginia Beach): With the Atlantic out its back door, this comfortable, clean establishment is one of the last family-owned motels among a multitude of chain properties lining the Virginia Beach oceanfront. See p. 299.

THE best OF VIRGINIA COOKING

- **Gadsby's Tavern** (Alexandria): George Washington bid goodbye to his troops from the door of Gadsby's in Alexandria's Old Town. This former rooming house and tavern looks much as it did then, and waitstaff in Colonial garb still serve chicken roasted on an open fire, buttermilk pie, and other 18th-century fare. See p. 57.
- **Mrs. Rowe's Restaurant and Bakery** (Staunton): Every town has its favorite local restaurant, where you can clog your arteries with plain old Southern favorites like pan-fried chicken, sausage gravy over biscuits, and fresh vegetables seasoned with smoked pork and cooked to smithereens. In business since 1947, Mrs. Rowe's somehow manages to cook great veggies without all that lard. See p. 158.
- **Roanoker Restaurant** (Roanoke): Another local favorite, the Roanoker regularly changes its menu to take advantage of the freshest vegetables available. And every day it serves the best biscuits in Virginia, hot from the oven. See p. 188.
- **Eley's Barbecue** (Petersburg): Like all Southerners, Virginians love their barbecue, and it doesn't get any better than at Eley's, which was formerly known as King's Barbecue. Pork, beef, ribs, and chicken roast constantly over an open pit right in the dining rooms, and the sauce is served on the side, not soaking the succulent meat and overpowering its smoked flavor. See p. 232.
- **A Chef's Kitchen** (Williamsburg): You don't merely dine at veteran chef John Gonzales's table, for he puts on an entertaining and highly informative cooking show for nearly 3 hours. See p. 257.
- **Old Chickahominy House** (Williamsburg): This reconstructed, antiques-filled, 18th-century house is one of the best places to sample traditional Virginia fare, such as Brunswick stew and Virginia ham on hot biscuits. See p. 258.

VIRGINIA IN DEPTH

Although I've lived in Virginia since 1990, I never tire of traveling its length and breadth, for my adopted home is a gorgeous land of rolling hills sandwiched between flat seashore and soaring mountains. It's so pleasing to the eye that I have trouble keeping mine on the road. This is especially true on extraordinarily scenic roads such as the winding, mountaintop Skyline Drive in Shenandoah National Park, the crown jewel of many preserved areas that beckon outdoor adventurers.

While we struggle to overcome modern problems such as urban sprawl, pollution, and unemployment, we also revere a past in which Jamestown gave birth to English-speaking America, Williamsburg fueled the fires of independence, and the American Revolution was won at Yorktown. Some 60% of all Civil War battles were fought on Virginia soil, and one of its own commanded the doomed Confederate effort. Descendants of America's early patriots and Confederate rebels still live here, and historic houses, monuments, and battlefields are a large part of the landscape.

So well preserved are our historic sites that it's easy to imagine George Washington still standing siege outside Yorktown, Thomas Jefferson still writing great political prose up at Monticello, and Robert E. Lee and Stonewall Jackson still riding at Fredericksburg and Chancellorsville. Washington's Mount Vernon, Jefferson's Monticello, the restored 18th-century village of Colonial Williamsburg, and the preserved Civil War battlefields are among our most-visited attractions.

The past is also present in our popular culture, for the mountains of Virginia were the incubator for bluegrass, old-time, and traditional country music, and many of our musicians play the tunes exactly as did their forebears. We even have an official driving route to several of country music's most revered shrines.

And let's not forget food, for dishes such as Sally Lunn bread and peanut soup have survived from Colonial times. You might say we even *eat* history here in Virginia.

VIRGINIA TODAY

Modern Virginia is a far different place than it was in Colonial times or during the Civil War. In those days only two areas—Richmond and Norfolk—were the least bit urban. Farms and small towns prevailed, along with their Jeffersonian conservatism emphasizing individual liberty and limited government (translated into modern political rhetoric: No new taxes!).

Richmond is still our capital city, but our economic dynamos are now the sprawling northern Virginia suburbs of Washington, D.C., and the mini-megapolis of Norfolk, Virginia Beach, and their Hampton Roads neighbors. Both areas rely on the federal government, which has both fueled their growth and kept them afloat during the Great Recession.

They have also given us our biggest problem: suburban sprawl and the traffic woes that go with it. The economic boom of the early 2000s saw both areas explode. The Washington suburbs have extended their tentacles west to the Blue Ridge Mountains and more than 50 miles south to Fredericksburg. In many respects we now have an urban arch stretching from Arlington south to Richmond and east to Hampton Roads—or along the corridor traced by I-95 and I-64.

As a result, both northern Virginia and Hampton Roads can be strangled by rush-hour traffic, which leads us to one of Virginia's modern conundrums: Those of us in the metropolitan areas desperately need to improve our roads and build mass transit, but other Virginians don't want to pay for it. While we gripe about wasting hours sitting in traffic, the rest of the state elects politicians who promise not to raise our taxes to solve the problem. They won't approve tax increases so that *we* can pay for it, but they will impose tolls on our heretofore free highways. (Will someone please explain to me the difference between a *toll* and a *tax*?)

Politics

On the statewide level, we Virginians have been narrowly splitting our votes between Republicans and Democrats, thanks to a growing and increasingly independent constituency in northern Virginia. In 2005 Tim Kaine was the second moderate Democrat in a row elected to the Governor's Mansion. In 2006, novelist and former Secretary of the Navy James Webb narrowly defeated Republican Senator George Allen, thus giving the Democrats control of the U.S. Senate. In 2008 we sent Democrat Mark Warner, a former governor, to the U.S. Senate, and we gave President Barack Obama a slim victory over Republican Senator John McCain. But a year later we elected conservative Republican Robert F. McDonnell to succeed Kaine as governor, and in 2011 we gave the Republicans control of the General Assembly by one seat. Gov. McDonnell has promised to fix our transportation mess without raising taxes. So far he has been doing it by imposing tolls on some of our highways. New express lanes on the Capital Beltway (I-495) in Virginia will have tolls, and he has asked the federal government for permission to impose tolls on parts of I-95 in Virginia.

The Economy

Although colonist John Rolfe is best remembered for marrying Indian princess Pocahontas, he essentially founded the tobacco industry, which for 350 years was the backbone of Virginia's economy. As tobacco wanes, the state is encouraging the planting of grapes and the building of wineries (see "Virginia's Vinos," later in this chapter).

Farm income also sprouts from apple orchards in the Shenandoah Valley; livestock, dairies, and poultry in the Piedmont; the state's famous Smithfield hams and peanuts from the Tidewater country; and seafood from the Chesapeake Bay.

Industry includes the manufacturing of clothes, chemicals, furniture, and transportation equipment, plus shipbuilding at Newport News. Mined in southwestern Virginia, coal is shipped via railroad to the world's largest coal port in Hampton Roads.

Perhaps our biggest resource is the nearby federal government, whose spending makes northern Virginia and Hampton Roads our economic dynamos. While many parts of the state have suffered severely during the recession, those two areas have not been hit as hard.

THE MAKING OF VIRGINIA

Virginia's recorded history began on April 26, 1607, when 104 English men and boys arrived at Cape Henry on the Virginia coast aboard the *Susan Constant*, the *Godspeed*, and the *Discovery*. The expedition—an attempt to compete with profitable Spanish encroachments in the New World—was sponsored by the Virginia Company of London and supported by King James I.

A Modest Beginning

Although the colonists were heartened to find abundant fish and game, if not streets paved with gold, their optimism was short-lived, for American Indians attacked them on their first day in the New World. Fleeing Cape Henry, they settled on Jamestown Island, which offered greater protection from the Spanish and the Indians but was a lousy, mosquito-infested place to live. They had also arrived in the midst of an extended drought. As one on-the-scene chronicler described it, "a world of miseries ensued." Only 50 settlers survived the first year.

The Indians captured Capt. John Smith while he was exploring the Chickahominy River and carried him to Powhatan, the paramount chief of the tribes living on Virginia's three peninsulas and Eastern Shore (see "Pocahontas & the Real First Virginians," below). According to legend, they would have killed him, but Powhatan's teenage daughter, the beautiful princess Pocahontas, interceded and saved his life. Or so Smith thought and later publicized; some experts believe it more likely that Smith misunderstood a tribal ritual.

But the colony survived that first year, and soon more men and women arrived, among them some of my ancestors.

In 1613, John Rolfe (who married Pocahontas) took the new aromatic tobacco grown in Virginia to England, where it proved to be extremely popular. The settlers had discovered not the glittery gold they expected, but the "golden weed" that would be the foundation of Virginia's fortunes and of its "first families," such as the Carters, the Hills, the Randolphs, the Lees, and the Harrisons. By midcentury, planter Robert "King" Carter of the Northern Neck was the richest man in North America.

In 1619, the Virginia Company sent a shipload of 90 women to suitors who had paid their transportation costs, and 22 burgesses were elected to set up the first legislative body in the New World. That same year, 20 Africans arrived on a Dutch ship to work as indentured servants, a precursor of slavery.

In 1699, the capital of the colony was moved from Jamestown, which had suffered a disastrous fire, to the planned town of Williamsburg. It was from Williamsburg that Colonial patriots launched some of the first strong protests against Parliament.

Unrest Grows

The French and Indian War (1754–1763) proved to be a training ground for America's Revolutionary forces, including Col. George Washington. In the field Washington acquitted himself with honor, and after General Braddock's defeat, he was appointed commander in chief of Virginia's army on the frontier.

Expenses from the war and economic hardships led the British to increase taxes in the colonies, and protests in Virginia and Massachusetts escalated. The 1765 Stamp

The American Indians who attacked the Jamestown colonists upon their arrival at Cape Henry in 1607 were members of the Kecoughtan tribe, one of more than 32 Algonquian-speaking tribes consisting of some 20,000 people living in what is now eastern Virginia and organized under several paramount chiefs. One of them, Powhatan, ruled over the area around Jamestown and eventually made temporary peace with the colonists.

Powhatan's daughter, the bright and curious Pocahontas, allegedly convinced him not to kill Capt. John Smith. She later married tobacco millionaire John Rolfe, became a Christian, and changed her name to Rebecca. In 1616, the Rolfes took their young son, Thomas, to England, where Rebecca was presented to the royal court. She died the next year in Gravesend, England.

Although wars and disease decimated the native population, the commonwealth still recognizes 11 official tribes: the **Chickahominy** (www.chickahominytribe.org), **Chickahominy Indians Eastern Division** (www.cied.org), **Cheroenhaka Nottoway** (www.cheroenhaka-nottoway.org), **Mattaponi, Monacan Indian Nation** (www.monacannation.com), **Nansemond** (www.nansemond.org), **Nottoway** (www.nottowayindians.org), **Pamunkey** (www.pamunkey.net), **Patawomeck** (www.patawomeckindians.org), **Rappahannock** (www.rappahannocktribe.org), and **Upper Mattaponi** (www.uppermattaponi.org). The Mattaponi and Pamunkey have reservations with museums and cultural centers.

The Virginia Indian Heritage Program of the **Virginia Foundation for the Humanities,** 145 Ednam Dr., Charlottesville, VA 22903 (© 434/924-2396; www.virginiafoundation.org), publishes a terrific booklet, *The Virginia Indian Heritage Trail*, about the Indians of Virginia.

Act met with general resistance. Patrick Henry inspired the Virginia General Assembly to pass the Virginia Resolves, setting forth Colonial rights according to constitutional principles. The young orator exclaimed, "If this be treason, make the most of it." The Stamp Act was repealed in 1766, but the Revenue Acts of 1767, which included the hated tax on tea, exacerbated tensions.

Ties among the colonies strengthened when Virginia's burgesses, led by Richard Henry Lee, created a committee to communicate their problems in dealing with England to similar committees in the other colonies. When the Boston Post Bill closed Boston Harbor in punishment for the Boston Tea Party, the Virginia assembly moved swiftly. Although the colonial governor dissolved the legislature, the members met at Raleigh Tavern and recommended that a general congress be held annually. Virginia sent seven representatives to the First Continental Congress in 1774, among them Lee, Patrick Henry, and George Washington.

The following year, Patrick Henry made a plea in Richmond for arming Virginia's militia. He concluded his argument with the immortal words, "Is life so dear or peace so sweet as to be purchased at the price of chains and slavery? Forbid it, Almighty God! I know not what course others may take, but, as for me, give me liberty, or give me death!"

Later in 1775, upon hearing news of the battles of Lexington and Concord, the Second Continental Congress in Philadelphia voted to make the conflict near Boston a colony-wide confrontation and chose Washington as commander of the Continental army. War had begun.

Birth of the Nation

Meeting in Williamsburg on June 12, 1776, the Virginia Convention adopted George Mason's Bill of Rights and instructed Virginia's delegates to the Continental Congress to propose independence for the colonies. Mason's document states that "all power is vested in, and consequently derived from, the people," and that "all men are created free and independent, and have certain inherent rights . . . among which are the enjoyment of life and liberty, with the means of acquiring and possessing property." He also firmly upheld the right of trial by jury, freedom of the press, and freedom of religion.

The congress meeting in Philadelphia adopted Thomas Jefferson's Declaration of Independence, based on Mason's bill, on July 4, 1776. The United States of America was born.

The Revolution was a bloody 7-year conflict marked by many staggering defeats for the patriots. Historians believe it was only the superb leadership and pertinacity of Gen. George Washington that inspired the Continental Army to continue so long in the face of overwhelming odds.

Victory at Yorktown

Virginia saw little military action until March 1781, when British General Lord Cornwallis arrived with his army at Yorktown. At the end of a long and rather fruitless march through the Carolinas, Cornwallis waited for the British navy to evacuate him and his men to New York.

While Cornwallis waited, Washington received word from the Comte de Rochambeau, commander of the French troops in America, that a French fleet was heading to the Chesapeake and would be at Washington's disposal through October 15. Washington and Rochambeau marched their 17,000-man allied army 450 miles to Virginia in hopes of trapping Cornwallis.

> ### 💬 The Brothers Lee
>
> The only brothers to sign the Declaration of Independence were Virginians Richard Henry Lee and Francis Lightfoot Lee.

On September 5, 1781, a fleet of 19 British ships appeared at the entrance to Chesapeake Bay to evacuate Cornwallis. By coincidence, French Admiral Comte de Grasse's 24 ships arrived at the same time. The naval battle ended in a stalemate, but the British returned to New York, leaving Cornwallis stranded. The French remained to block further British reinforcements or their escape by water, while Washington and Rochambeau arrived at Yorktown. The trap had worked.

After 2 weeks of bombardment, Cornwallis waved the white flag. Although the war didn't officially end until the Treaty of Paris 2 years later, the colonists and their French allies had won.

Framing the Constitution

At first the new country adopted the Articles of Confederation, which created a weak and ineffectual national government. To remedy the situation, a Constitutional Convention met in Philadelphia in 1781. Washington was elected the convention's president. He and fellow Virginian James Madison fought to have the new Constitution include a Bill of Rights and gradual abolition of the slave trade. Although both measures were defeated, the two Virginians voted to adopt the Constitution.

In 1788, Virginia became the 10th state to ratify the Constitution, and by 1791 the first 10 amendments—the Bill of Rights—had been added. Madison was author of the first nine amendments, Richard Henry Lee the tenth.

Early Virginian Presidents

George Washington was elected the first president of the new nation under the new Constitution and took office on April 30, 1789. Although he could have remained, he stepped down in 1797 after two terms, thus setting a precedent that ruled until Franklin D. Roosevelt was elected to a third term in 1940.

As the third president of the United States, Thomas Jefferson nearly doubled the size of the country by purchasing the Louisiana Territory from Napoleon.

James Madison took office as president in 1809. Unable to maintain Jefferson's peacekeeping efforts in the face of continued provocations by England, Madison was swayed by popular demand for armed response, and in 1812, Congress declared war. Although British warships attacked some coastal plantations, the only suffering Virginia witnessed was the burning of nearby Washington, D.C.

James Monroe followed, and during his two terms, the nation pushed westward, and he faced the first struggle over slavery (which resulted in the Missouri Compromise), established the Monroe Doctrine, and settled the nation's boundary with Canada.

The Civil War

It was not long before the United States became a nation divided. The issues were states' rights and the conflicting economic goals between an industrial North and an agricultural South that relied on slavery. In the election of 1860, the Republicans nominated Abraham Lincoln, whom the South vowed it would not accept; but the Democrats split and Lincoln was elected. On April 12, 1861, guns sounded at Fort Sumter in Charleston harbor. Secession had become war.

FIRST MANASSAS

In May 1861, the Confederate capital was transferred to Richmond, only 100 miles from Washington, D.C., dooming Virginia to be the major battleground of the Civil War. The Union strategy was to advance south and capture Richmond while at the same time taking the Shenandoah Valley to cut off supplies to the Confederate Army of Northern Virginia. The first of six attempts was decisively repulsed on July 21, 1861, at the Battle of First Manassas (Bull Run). Total casualties—4,828 men—made it apparent that this would be a long and very bloody conflict.

THE PENINSULA CAMPAIGN

The second major offensive against Richmond, the Peninsula Campaign, devised by Union general George B. McClellan, was the setting for a famous naval engagement.

On March 9, 1862, two ironclad vessels, the USS *Monitor* and the CSS *Virginia* (formerly the USS *Merrimack*) pounded each other with cannon. Although the battle was a draw, the advent of ironclad warships heralded a new era in naval history.

Yorktown was reduced to rubble 2 months later, and the Union army advanced up the peninsula. The Confederates retreated until taking a stand only 9 miles from Richmond. The Confederate leader, Gen. Joseph Johnson, was badly wounded during the battle. Robert E. Lee, son of Revolutionary War hero Henry "Light-Horse Harry" Lee, was appointed head of the Army of Northern Virginia. Personally opposed to secession, Lee had sadly resigned his commission in the U.S. Army when Virginia joined the Confederacy, saying, "My heart is broken, but I cannot raise my sword against Virginia." In a series of victories beginning on June 26, 1862, Lee defeated McClellan and Richmond was saved. Meanwhile, the federal government confiscated Lee's home in what is now Arlington National Cemetery (p. 61).

SECOND MANASSAS, FREDERICKSBURG & CHANCELLORSVILLE

The third Union drive against Richmond was repulsed at the Battle of Second Manassas, where Lee's 55,000 men soundly defeated 70,000 Union troops under Gen. John Pope.

On December 13, 1862, Gen. Ambrose Burnside, newly chosen head of the Army of the Potomac, crossed the Rappahannock and struck Fredericksburg while Lee's army was in northern Virginia. The Federal advance was so slow that by the time the Union armies moved, Lee's forces were entrenched on a hill overlooking the town. The result was a Union massacre, and the fourth Union drive against Richmond was repulsed.

Gen. Joseph Hooker took command of the Union army early in 1863, and, once again, Federal forces crossed the Rappahannock. Fighting raged for 4 days at Chancellorsville. The Union army retreated, and the fifth drive on Richmond failed. Among the heavy casualties, Stonewall Jackson was wounded by his own troops and died of complications resulting from the amputation of his arm. Jackson's loss was costly, as Lee learned in July 1863 at the small Pennsylvania town of Gettysburg.

A WAR OF ATTRITION

In March 1864, Gen. Ulysses S. Grant was put in command of all Federal armies. His plan for victory called for total unrelenting warfare that would put constant pressure on all points of the Confederacy. The first great confrontation between Lee and Grant, the Battle of the Wilderness, resulted in a Confederate victory, but instead of retreating back to Maryland as his predecessors had done, Grant pushed on toward Richmond. The campaign was the heaviest fighting of the Civil War. Three times Grant tried and failed to interpose his forces between Lee and Richmond. More than 80,000 men were killed and wounded.

"Like a Stone Wall"

Confederate general Thomas J. "Stonewall" Jackson acquired his nickname during the Battle of First Manassas, when Confederate brigadier general Barnard Bee, marveling at his persistence in standing his ground, exclaimed, "There stands Jackson, like a stone wall!"

LAYING SIEGE TO PETERSBURG

Lee's resistance strengthened at Richmond, and unable to capture the capital, Grant secretly moved his army across the James River toward Petersburg, an important rail junction south of Richmond and the city's main supply line. Improvised Southern forces managed to hold Petersburg until Lee arrived. Grant then resorted to an ever-tightening siege. If he left his trenches, Lee would be abandoning Petersburg and Richmond. Subjected to hunger and exposure, the Confederate will began to wane and periodic skirmishes weakened Confederate morale.

Lee, hoping to divert Grant, dispatched a small army under Jubal Early to the menaced Shenandoah Valley. Grant instructed Union General Philip Sheridan: "The Shenandoah is to be so devastated that crows flying across it for the balance of the season will have to bring their own provender." This second major valley campaign resulted in the destruction of Early's army and Lee's main source of food.

LEE'S RETREAT

Back in Petersburg, Grant launched his inevitable onslaught on April 1, 1865, when Federal forces smashed through Confederate lines at Five Forks. Petersburg fell, and Richmond was soon occupied by Federal forces and visited by Lincoln and his young son, Todd.

Lee's last hope was to rendezvous with General Joseph E. Johnston's army, which was retreating northward through North Carolina before Union General William Tecumseh Sherman's advance. However, on April 8, the vanguard of Grant's army succeeded in reaching Appomattox Court House ahead of Lee, thus blocking the Confederates' last escape route.

On April 9, 1865, the Civil War ended in Virginia at Appomattox in Wilbur McLean's farmhouse. Uncompromising in war, Grant proved compassionate in peace. Confederate soldiers were permitted to return home on parole, cavalrymen could keep their horses, and officers could retain their side arms. Rations were provided for the destitute Southerners.

Speaking to his 28,000 soldiers, the remnants of the once-mighty Army of Northern Virginia, Lee said, "I earnestly pray that a merciful God will extend to you his blessing and protection. With an unceasing admiration of your constancy and devotion to your country, and a grateful remembrance of your kind and generous consideration for myself, I bid you all an affectionate farewell."

Recovery, Renewal & Massive Resistance

Virginia was devastated by the war, and recovery was slow. Besides the physical and psychological damages, the Reconstruction era brought Virginia under federal military control until 1870.

However, by the turn of the 20th century, new railroad lines connecting remote country areas in the west with urban centers characterized Virginia's economic growth. Factories were bringing more people to the cities, and the economy, once based primarily on agriculture, now had a growing industrial base. The Hampton Roads ports enjoyed success as steamship traffic carried an increasing volume of commercial freight.

During this period, the great scholar, author, and educator Booker T. Washington, who had been born in slavery, studied at Virginia's Hampton Institute and achieved fame as an advisor to presidents.

World War I brought prosperity to Virginia with new factories and munitions plants and the expansion of military training camps throughout the state.

World War II saw a population explosion, with men and women of the armed forces flocking to northern Virginia suburbs near Washington, D.C., and the port area of Hampton Roads. Many of these people stayed after the war, and by 1955, the majority of Virginians were urban dwellers. Today, the state's population is about 8 million.

Prominent in Virginia Tidewater plantation society since the 1600s, the Byrd family dominated the state's politics from World War I until the 1980s. Under their conservative control, the "Mother of Presidents" virtually withdrew from national leadership.

Under a policy of "massive resistance" to federally mandated public school desegregation in the 1950s, the state closed the schoolhouse doors rather than admit African Americans to previously all-white institutions.

Although the old animosities still raise their ugly heads from time to time, in 1989 Virginians chose Democrat L. Douglas Wilder as the nation's first elected African-American governor, and in 2008 we cast a majority of our votes for President Barack Obama.

VIRGINIA IN POPULAR CULTURE

With so much history and so many monumental historical figures calling it home, Virginia and its citizens have been written about and filmed countless times. This is especially true of the Civil War.

The Commonwealth has also made its mark on the music scene—and not just because the Dave Matthews Band calls Charlottesville home. Country music as we know it today was born in the hollows and valleys of the Southwest Highlands.

Nonfiction

o *Mary Chestnut's Civil War* edited by C. Van Woodward (Yale University Press, 1993). Pulitzer Prize–winning autobiography of a Richmond housewife who kept a diary during the Civil War.

o *Thomas Jefferson: An Intimate History* by Fawn M. Brodie (Norton, 1998). Readable account of the third president.

o *Jefferson and His Times* by Dumas Malone (University of Virginia Press, 2007). Exhaustive, 6-volume study of Mr. Jefferson.

o *Thomas Jefferson and Sally Hemings: An American Controversy* by Annette Gordon-Reed (University of Virginia Press, 1998). Explores the affair between Jefferson and his slave.

o *The Hemingses of Monticello: An American Family* by Annette Gordon-Reed (Norton, 2008). Traces descendants of Jefferson and Sally Hemings.

o *Lee* by Douglas Southall Freeman (Macmillan, 1997). Life of Gen. Robert E. Lee.

o *Up from Slavery* by Booker T. Washington (Doubleday, 1998). The Virginia-born African American tells how he went from slavery to agricultural scientist.

o *George Washington* by Douglas Southall Freeman (Macmillan, 1948). Father of his country explained.

o *Notes on the State of Virginia* by Thomas Jefferson (Norton, 1982). Eighteenth-century Virginia through the eyes of its famous son.

- *Virginia: The New Dominion* by Virginius Dabney (University Press of Virginia, 1989). Definitive history of the Old Dominion up to 1971.
- *The Civil War* by Shelby Foote (Vintage, 1986). Slow-talking Foote became famous appearing in Ken Burns's monumental PBS series (see below).
- *The Civil War* by Geoffrey C. Ward, with Ric Burns and Ken Burns (Knopf, 1992). Don't have time for the PBS series? Read this offshoot book.
- *Witness to Appomattox* by Richard Wheeler (HarperCollins, 1991). Recaptures Lee's surrender in 1865.

Fiction

- *Traveller* by Richard Adams (Dell). About General Lee's horse.
- *Red Badge of Courage* by Stephen Crane (Bantam). A must read for Civil War buffs.
- *The Confessions of Nat Turner* by William Styron (Bantam). Based on Nat Turner's slave rebellion in 1831.

Films & Videos

- *Trail of the Lonesome Pine* (1937), with Fred MacMurray, Henry Fonda, and Sylvia Sidney, is based on John Fox's romantic tale set in an Appalachian mining village.
- *Brother Rat* (1938), with Jane Wyman and Ronald Reagan, depicts cadet life at the Virginia Military Institute.
- *Dirty Dancing* (1987), with Jennifer Grey and Patrick Swayze; filmed at Mountain Lake Resort.
- *Sommersby* (1993), with Jodie Foster and Richard Gere; filmed in Lexington, Warm Springs, and Bath County.
- *The Civil War* (1990), PBS series, Time-Life. Ken Burns's epic telling of the great tragedy.

Music

Nashville may be the modern capital of country music, but the purest forms of country music—bluegrass, old time, and traditional—trace their roots to the mountains of Virginia.

Indeed, southwestern Virginia has been central to the evolution of country music since the first European settlers arrived in these hills and valleys with few possessions other than their mandolins and fiddles. Some of the great country artists hail from here—the Carter family, Ralph Stanley, and the Stonemans, to name a few—and numerous music festivals, such as the famous Old Fiddlers Convention in Galax, take place in this area.

The area's music heritage is formally recognized by the **Crooked Road: Virginia's Heritage Music Trail,** PO Box 268, Big Stone Gap, VA 24219 (© **866/676-6847;** www.thecrookedroad.org).

This official route follows U.S. 23, U.S. 421, U.S. 58, U.S. 221, Va. 8, and Va. 40 for more than 200 miles from Breaks in the west to Rocky Mount in the east. Along the way it passes such country music shrines as the **Ralph Stanley Museum & Traditional Music Center** in Clintwood, the **Carter Family Fold** in Hiltons (p. 201), the **Birthplace of Country Music Museum** in Bristol, the **Blue Ridge**

Music Center on the Blue Ridge Parkway (p. 179), the **Rex Theater** in Galax, the **Floyd Country Store** in Floyd, and the **Blue Ridge Music Institute** in Ferrum.

EATING & DRINKING IN VIRGINIA

The late William Styron, a native of Newport News and author of *The Confessions of Nat Turner*, a novel based on Nat Turner's 1831 slave rebellion, once said that the French consider the strong, smoke-cured hams produced by Virginia to be America's prime contribution to the world's cuisine. We Virginians love our ham baked by itself, boiled with fresh vegetables, or stuffed into piping hot biscuits.

We are not as famous as Texas for our barbecue, but we know how to slow cook the shoulders of those pigs whose rumps end up as hams. While most of our barbecue joints soak the results in tomato-tinged sauce, the best are smart enough to put the red stuff on the side, thus leaving the pork to be enjoyed in all its smoky glory.

We are also crazy about rockfish (which you know as sea bass) and blue crabs, especially in their soft-shell stage, from the Chesapeake Bay. Rare is a Virginia restaurant that doesn't offer its own particular version of the crab cake. Our rivers give us bone-filled shad and rainbow trout. Our farms produce a plethora of vegetables during the summer (I've never tasted sweeter Silver Queen corn), and our Shenandoah orchards are famous for autumn apples.

And let's not forget the peanut, one of Virginia's major crops—begetting one of the state's best-loved dishes: peanut soup.

"Farm to table" restaurants are proliferating as talented young chefs turn our fresh produce into exciting variations of traditional southern fare. But when we talk of down-home-style Virginia cooking, we mean what you Yankees call "comfort food." Every small town and most big cities have at least one inexpensive, family-style

---

The Best Virginia-Style Chow

You can dine on all types of cuisine in Virginia, but we still use recipes handed down since Colonial times for dishes such as peanut soup, Sally Lunn bread, ham biscuits, and other such present-day Ole Virginny goodies. The best places to sample Virginia's own cuisine are:

o **Gadsby's Tavern,** 138 N. Royal St., Alexandria (✆ **703/548-1288; www. gadsbystavern.com**; p. 57).

o **Mrs. Rowe's Restaurant and Bakery,** 74 Rowe Rd., Staunton (✆ **540/886-1833; www.mrsrowes.com/index. html**; p. 158).

o **Roanoker Restaurant,** 2522 Colonial Ave., Roanoke (✆ **540/344-7746; www.theroanokerrestaurant.com**; p. 188).

o **Eley's Barbecue,** 3221 N. Washington St., Petersburg (✆ **804/732-5861; www.eleysbarbecue.com**; p. 232).

o **Colonial Williamsburg Taverns,** Williamsburg (✆ **800/447-8679** or 757/229-2141; **www.colonial williamsburg.com**; see chapter 10).

o **Old Chickahominy House,** 1211 Jamestown Rd., Williamsburg (✆ **757/229-4689; www. oldchickahominy.com**; p. 258).

restaurant serving simple fare such as southern fried chicken, grilled pork chops, and ham accompanied by fresh vegetables, often boiled with smoky seasoning meat.

Indeed, dining at a local restaurant in Virginia can be a real challenge for those of us on low-fat diets.

Virginia's Vinos

When Thomas Jefferson returned home to Charlottesville in 1789 after 5 years in Paris as minister to France, he brought with him a keen appreciation for fine wine. Virginians had been growing indigenous grapes and making lousy local wine since 1607, when the Jamestown colony ordered each household to cultivate 10 grapevines. Mr. Jefferson believed that European grapes, especially Italian varieties, could be grown here, and he tried seven times without success to establish a profitable vineyard winery near his home in Charlottesville.

Too bad he can't come back to life today, for Jefferson would find his beloved Virginia dotted with more than 200 vineyards. Indeed, official state policy is to encourage the growing of grapes and the production of wine. (It strikes me as ironic that the home state of tee totaling Baptist preachers Pat Robertson and the late Jerry Falwell is switching from tobacco to alcohol.)

Wineries have sprouted up like weeds all over Virginia, with the greatest concentration in the rolling hills of the Hunt Country in Northern Virginia (see chapter 4) and in the Piedmont hills surrounding Charlottesville (see chapter 6).

Many of them are small mom-and-pop operations (if this were beer, we would call them microbreweries), but together they rank Virginia with California, Washington, Oregon, and New York as one of the nation's top wine-producing states.

The climate here is too varied to produce consistently good grapes. One summer may be hot and dry, the next warm and damp. That's not to say you won't run across an excellent local vintage from an exceptional year. There just won't be much of it, simply because the state doesn't grow the quantity of grapes found in sunnier France, Italy, and California. Moderately good wines at moderate prices best describes Virginia's vinos.

Chardonnay is the most widely grown grape here, but many experts say viognier is perhaps the best suited white grape for Virginia. You'll also find Riesling in good quantity. Among the reds, cabernet sauvignon is the most widely planted grape.

Many gourmet groceries and wine and cheese shops sell Virginia wines, and occasionally you'll find them in supermarket beer-and-wine sections. Because the small vineyards don't produce enough quantity to satisfy wine distributors, from whom licensed grocers and restaurateurs are required by state law to purchase wine (that's correct: They cannot buy directly from the wineries), local vintages appear on surprisingly few restaurant lists.

Accordingly, the best places to sample them are at wine festivals or by visiting the wineries that have tasting rooms. I mention some of the better ones in the destination chapters in this book.

The **Virginia Wine Marketing Office,** 1001 E. Broad St., Ste. 140, Richmond, VA 23219 (© **804/344-8200;** www.virginiawine.org), posts "Wine Trails" (marked by wine-logo road signs) for each region in the state and publishes an annual, road-map-size "Virginia Winery Guide," which describes each winery and plots its location. Copies also are available from the Virginia Tourism Corporation, which posts the state's wine festivals on its website (see "Fast Facts: Virginia," in chapter 12.) You can download winery guides by region and get a schedule of wine festivals on the Wine Marketing Office's website. The **Virginia Wine in My Pocket** app is available from the iTunes Store (www.apple.com/itunes). *Virginia Wine Lover* magazine (www.virginiawinelover.com) is a good source of news.

WHEN TO GO

Virginia is a gorgeous place in late September and early October, during Indian summer, when our most settled period of weather gives us warm days and cool nights. It gets even more beautiful later in October, when the leaves blaze orange, red, and yellow across the state. The "leaf season" is also the most crowded time in the western part of the state, when throngs of visitors mob the mountains. (You can find out the approximate dates for peak color in the Shenandoah Valley by calling ⓒ **800/434-5323.**)

Otherwise, Virginia is busiest during summer, when the historic sites, theme parks, and beaches draw millions of visitors—and hotel rates are at their highest. The least crowded—and least expensive—time to visit is in spring. That's when the dogwoods, azaleas, and wildflowers are in a riot of bloom from one end of Virginia to the other.

The Climate

Virginia enjoys four distinct seasons, with some variations from the warmer, more humid coastal areas to the cooler climate in the mountains. Wintertime snows are usually confined to northern Virginia and the mountains. In summer, extremely hot and humid spells can last several weeks but are normally short-lived. Spring and autumn are long seasons, and in terms of natural beauty and heavenly climate, they're optimum times to visit. Annual rainfall averages 46 inches; annual snowfall, 18 inches.

Holidays

Banks, government offices, post offices, and many stores, restaurants, and museums are closed on the following legal national holidays: January 1 (New Year's Day), the third Monday in January (Martin Luther King Day), the third Monday in February (Presidents' Day), the last Monday in May (Memorial Day), July 4th (Independence Day), the first Monday in September (Labor Day), the second Monday in October (Columbus Day), November 11 (Veterans Day/Armistice Day), the fourth Thursday in November (Thanksgiving Day), and December 25 (Christmas Day). The Tuesday after the first Monday in November is Election Day, a federal government holiday in presidential-election years (held every 4 years, and next in 2012).

Virginia's Average Temperatures

	JAN	FEB	MAR	APR	MAY	JUNE	JULY	AUG	SEPT	OCT	NOV	DEC
High (°F)	44	46	56	68	75	84	90	88	81	69	57	47
High (°C)	7	8	13	20	24	29	32	31	27	21	14	8
Low (°F)	26	27	38	45	54	62	66	65	59	48	39	28
Low (°C)	–3	–3	3	7	12	17	19	18	15	9	4	–2

Virginia Calendar of Events

For an exhaustive list of events beyond those listed here, check http://events.frommers.com, where you'll find a searchable, up-to-the-minute roster of what's happening in cities all over the world.

JANUARY

Whale-Watching Boat Trips, Virginia Beach. The Virginia Aquarium & Marine Science Center sends cruise boats out looking for whales. Sightings are not guaranteed. Call ℂ **757/437-2628,** or go to www.virginia aquarium.com. January 2 to mid-March.

Lee Birthday Celebrations, Alexandria. Period music, plus house tours at Lee-Fendall House. Call ℂ **703/548-1789,** or go to www.leefendallhouse.org. Fourth Sunday in January.

FEBRUARY

George Washington Birthday Events, Alexandria, Mount Vernon, Fredericksburg. Old Town Alexandria puts on the dog to celebrate GW's birthday: walking tours; symposia; black tie or Colonial costume Saturday-evening dinner, followed by a birthnight ball at Gadsby's Tavern; a parade on Monday. Call ℂ **800/388-9119** or 703/838-4200, or visit www.visitalexandria va.com for more information. George's home at Mount Vernon also gets in on the act. Call ℂ **703/780-2000,** or go to www. mountvernon.org. Down in Fredericksburg, special activities are held at Mary Washington House and George Washington's Ferry Farm. Call ℂ **800/678-4748** or 540/373-1776, or visit www.visitfred.com. Presidents' Day weekend.

Maymont Flower and Garden Show, Richmond. A breath of spring, with landscape exhibits, vendors, and speakers at the Greater Richmond Convention Center. Call ℂ **804/358-7166,** or go to www.maymont. org. Late February.

MARCH

James Madison's Birthday, Montpelier. Ceremony at cemetery and reception at house. Call ℂ **540/672-2728,** or go to www.montpelier.org. March 16.

Highland Maple Festival, Monterey. See maple syrup produced, pour it over pancakes, and visit one of the state's largest crafts shows. Call ℂ **540/468-2550,** or go to www.highlandcounty.org. Second and third weekends in March.

Patrick Henry Speech Reenactment, St. John's Episcopal Church, Richmond. "Give me liberty or give me death" resounds once again. Call ℂ **804/648-5015,** or go to www.historicstjohnschurch.org. Closest Sunday to March 23.

APRIL

Thomas Jefferson's Birthday Commemoration, Monticello, Charlottesville. Wreath-laying ceremony at grave site, fife-and-drum corps, and a speaker. Call ℂ **434/984-9822,** or go to www.monticello.org. April 13.

Virginia Arts Festival, Williamsburg, Hampton, Newport News, Norfolk, Virginia Beach. Famous performers appear at venues from Williamsburg to Virginia Beach during this month-long festival. Call ℂ **757/282-2800,** or go to www.virginia artsfest.com. Mid-April to mid-May.

Virginia Fly Fishing Festival, Waynesboro. Anglers gather beside the South River for demonstrations, lectures, casting instruction, live music, and wine tasting. Call ℂ **703/403-8338,** or go to www.vaflyfishing festival.org. Third weekend in April.

Norfolk NATO Festival, Norfolk. Named in honor of the locally based headquarters of the North Atlantic Treaty Organization, this multihued festival celebrates both the military and the brilliant beauty of azaleas in bloom in the Norfolk Botanical Garden. Military displays include an air show, ships to visit, and aircraft exhibits. Call ℂ **757/441-1852,** or go to www.azaleafestival.org. Last week in April.

Virginia is celebrating the 150th anniversary of the Civil War (1861–65) with a plethora of activities across the state. It's being led by the **Virginia Sesquicen-** **tennial of the American** **mission (☏ 804/786-3** virginiacivilwar.org), whi events on its website.

Historic Garden Week in Virginia, statewide. The event of the year for garden lovers—a celebration with tours of the grounds and gardens at more than 250 Virginia landmarks, including plantations and other sites open only during this week. For information, contact the **Garden Club of Virginia,** 12 E. Franklin St., Richmond, VA 23219 (☏ **804/644-7776** or 804/643-7141; www.gcvirginia.org). Last full week in April.

Shenandoah Apple Blossom Festival, Winchester. Acres of orchards in blossom throughout the valley, plus music, band competitions, parades, the coronation of the queen, footraces, arts and crafts sales, midway amusements, and a carnival, with a celebrity grand marshal. Call ☏ **540/662-3863,** or go to www.thebloom.com. Ten days from late April to early May.

MAY

Virginia Gold Cup Races, Great Meadow Course, The Plains. Everyone dresses to the nines for the state's premier steeplechase event. Call ☏ **800/697-2237** or 540/347-1215 or go to www.vagoldcup.com. First Saturday in May.

Seafood Festival, Chincoteague. All you can eat—a seafood lover's dream. Get tickets in advance from **Eastern Shore Chamber of Commerce,** PO Box 460, Melfa, VA 23410 (☏ **757/787-2460;** www.chincoteague chamber.com). First weekend in May.

Jamestown Landing Day, Jamestown. Militia presentations and sailing demonstrations celebrate the arrival of the first English settlers in 1607. Call ☏ **888/593-4682** or 757/253-4838, or go to www.historyisfun. org. Early May.

Reenactment of the Battle of New Market, New Market Battlefield State Historical Park, New Market. Call ☏ **866/515-1864** or 540/740-3101, or go to www.vmi.edu/newmarket. Weekend closest to May 15.

New Market Day, Virginia Military Institute Campus, Lexington. Annual roll call for cadets who died in the Battle of New Market. Call ☏ **540/464-7000,** or go to www. vmi.edu. May 15.

Virginia Hunt Country Stable Tour, Loudon County. A unique opportunity to view prestigious Leesburg, Middleburg, and Upperville horse farms and private estates. Sponsored by Trinity Episcopal Church, Upperville. Call ☏ **540/592-3711,** or go to www.huntcountrystabletour.org. Memorial Day weekend.

Shenandoah Valley Music Festival, Orkney Springs. Music from classical to country fills the mountain air. Call **Orkney Springs Hotel** at ☏ **800/459-3396** (tickets only) or 540/459-3396, or go to www.musicfest.org. Held weekends from Memorial Day weekend through August.

JUNE

Vintage Virginia Wine Festival, Great Meadows Steeplechase Course, The Plains. Taste the premium vintages from 35 wineries, browse arts and crafts displays, eat, and listen to jazz, reggae, and pop music at this Hunt Country festival. Call ☏ **800/277-2675,** or go to www.vintagevirginia.com for information about this and many other wine festivals statewide. First weekend in June.

Harborfest, Norfolk. Tall ships, sailboat races, air shows, military demonstrations, and fireworks. Call ☏ **757/441-1852,** or go to www.festeventsva.org. Mid-June.

Boardwalk Art Show, Virginia Beach. Works in all mediums, between 14th and 28th streets on the Boardwalk. Call ☏ **800/822-3224,** or go to www.vbfun. com. Mid-June.

Opera Festival, Charlottesville.
...amount Theatre and other Charlot-
...lle settings for opera, musicals, and
...oncerts. Call ✆ **434/293-4500,** or go to
www.ashlawnopera.org. End of June to
August.

Independence Day Celebrations, statewide. Every town parties and shoots fireworks in honor of the nation's birthday.
Contact local tourist information offices.
July 4th.

Pony Penning and Carnival, Chincoteague. In this 3-day event wild horses are
herded across the Assateague Channel from
Assateague to Chincoteague and the foals
are auctioned off. The adult horses are then
herded back to Assateague. Call ✆ **757/
336-6161** or go to www.chincoteague
chamber.com. The last Wednesday, Thursday, and Friday in July.

AUGUST

Virginia Highlands Festival, Abingdon.
Appalachian Mountain culture showcase for
musicians, artists, artisans, and writers. It's
the area's largest arts and crafts show, and it
includes an antiques market and hot-air balloons. Call ✆ **888/489-4230** or 276/676-
2282, or go to www.vahighlandsfestival.org.
First 2 weeks in August.

Old Fiddler's Convention, Galax. Dating to
1935, this is one of the largest and oldest
such conventions in the world. It also coincides with the Fiddlefest street festival. Call
✆ **276/236-8541,** or go to www.oldfiddlers
convention.com. Second week in August.

Richmond Jazz Festival at Maymont, Richmond. Maymont, CenterStage, and the
Hippodrome Theater host local musicians
and international stars during this 4-day
tribute to jazz. Call ✆ **804/644-8515** or go
to www.jazzatmaymont.com. Mid-August.

Staunton Music Festival, Staunton.
Accomplished classical musicians seem to
be performing everywhere in Staunton. Call
✆ **540/569-0267** or go to www.staunton
musicfestival.com. Late August.

SEPTEMBER

American Music Festival, Virginia Beach.
Top entertainers perform on the sand. Tickets are first-come, first-served. Call
✆ **800/822-3224,** or go to www.beach
streetusa.com. Labor Day weekend.

State Fair of Virginia, Richmond Raceway
Complex, Richmond. Rides, entertainment,
agricultural exhibits, pioneer farmstead, and
flower shows. Call ✆ **800/588-3247** or
804/228-3200, or go to www.statefairva.
org. Ten days in late September.

OCTOBER

Chincoteague Oyster Festival, Chincoteague. A feast of oysters—but for advance
ticket holders only. Call ✆ **804/336-6161,**
or go to www.chincoteaguechamber.com.
Early October.

**Waterford Homes Tour and Crafts
Exhibit,** Waterford Village. This tiny Quaker
town grows to some 40,000 on this one
weekend. Call ✆ **540/882-3018,** or go to
www.waterfordva.org. First weekend in
October.

Virginia Film Festival, Charlottesville. University of Virginia pays tribute to all things
celluloid. Call ✆ **800/882-3378,** or go to
www.vafilm.com. Mid-October.

Yorktown Day, Colonial National Historic
Park, Yorktown. The British surrender in 1781
celebrated with a parade, historic house
tours, Colonial music and dress, and military
drills. Call ✆ **757/898-2410** or 898-3400, or
go to www.nps.gov/colo. October 19.

International Gold Cup, Great Meadows
Course, The Plains. Fall colors provide a
backdrop for one of the most prestigious
steeplechase races. Call ✆ **800/697-2237**
or 540/347-1215, or go to www.vagoldcup.
com. Third Saturday in October.

Marine Corps Marathon, Arlington. More
than 20,000 men and women run a 26.2-
mile course from Arlington through Washington, D.C., and back. Nicknamed
"The People's Marathon," it's open to all
(there's even a wheelchair division). Call

VIRGINIA IN DEPTH | Virginia Calendar of Events

© **800/786-8762** or 703/784-2265 or go to www.marinemarathon.com. Last Sunday in October.

NOVEMBER

The First Thanksgiving, Charles City. Reenactment at Berkeley Plantation. Call © **888/466-6018** or 804/829-6018, or go to www.berkeleyplantation.com. Early November.

Chincoteague Wildlife Refuge Week, Chincoteague. The only time of the year when visitors can drive to the northern end of Chincoteague National Wildlife Refuge on Assateague Island. Guided walks are offered for pedestrians. Call © **757/336-6122,** or go to http://chinco.fws.gov. Thanksgiving weekend.

DECEMBER

Mount Vernon by Candlelight, Mount Vernon. See Washington's mansion as he did, by the light of candles. Tickets required. Call © **703/780-2000,** or go to www.mountvernon.org. First week in December.

Grand Illumination, Williamsburg. A gala opening of the holiday season with fife-and-drum corps, illumination of buildings, caroling, dancing, and fireworks. Call © **800/447-8679** or 757/220-7645, or go to www.colonialwilliamsburg.com. First Saturday in December.

Christmas Candlelight Tour, Fredericksburg. Historic homes welcome visitors. Call © **800/678-4748** or 540/373-1776, or go to www.visitfred.com. First weekend in December.

Monticello Candlelight Tour, Charlottesville. Experience authentic Colonial decorations. Call © **804/984-9822,** or go to www. monticello.org. Early December.

Historic Michie Tavern Feast and Open House, Charlottesville. The old tavern puts on two Christmastime feasts. Reservations required. Call © **804/977-1234,** or go to www.michietavern.com. Second weekend in December.

Jamestown Christmas, Jamestown. Jamestown Settlement is all decked out 17th-century style. Call © **888/593-4682** or 757/253-4838, or go to www.historyisfun. org. Second to fourth week in December.

THE LAY OF THE LAND

Thanks to its topography, Virginia is both lovely and varied. Here in one place we have sandy beaches, one of the world's largest estuaries, mighty rivers cutting through rolling hills, and mountain ranges bordering one of America's most famous valleys.

Tidewater

The first English settlers established their beachhead on the coastal plain we call **Tidewater,** because its inland rivers and creeks rise and fall with the ocean tides. This flat land is dominated by the broad Potomac, Rappahannock, York, and James rivers, all emptying into the immense estuary known as Chesapeake Bay.

The bay cuts the rest of us off from Virginia's Eastern Shore, which is actually the southern end of the Delmarva Peninsula—so named because it is shared by the states of Delaware, Maryland, and Virginia. At the southern end of the peninsula, where the Chesapeake meets the Atlantic Ocean, sits Hampton Roads, a huge natural harbor and our country's largest naval base.

The rivers divide the Tidewater into three peninsulas, or *necks,* as we call them: The Peninsula between the James and the York; the Middle Peninsula between the York and the Rappahannock; and the Northern Neck between the Rappahannock and the Potomac.

The Piedmont

In Colonial times, the rivers were the main avenues of exploration, and later of commerce. Ships and large boats could navigate up to the "fall line," where the coastal plain gives way to the rolling hills of the **Piedmont** in central Virginia, from the North Carolina line north to the Hunt Country and suburban sprawl of northern Virginia.

> ### Take Nothing, Leave Nothing
>
> When visiting our natural areas, we should all observe the golden rule of the wilderness: Leave nothing behind, and take away only memories and photos.

The fall line saw the development of towns such as Richmond, Fredericksburg, and Alexandria, where shipborne cargos would be transferred to small river boats (we still call them by their French name, *bateaux*) or to horse-drawn wagons to be hauled west into the hill country.

The unofficial capital of the Piedmont today is Charlottesville. Presidents Thomas Jefferson, James Monroe, and James Madison all lived near Charlottesville. Theirs and other large holdings have given way to horse farms and vineyards nestled among the gorgeous hills.

The Mountains & Valleys

This Piedmont rises to meet the **Blue Ridge,** a skinny mountain chain running the entire length of Virginia.

The crest of the central Blue Ridge is preserved in its natural state by the Shenandoah National Park, whose famous Skyland Drive connects to the Blue Ridge Parkway to form one of Virginia's most scenic drives.

Those mountaintop roads look west over a series of gorgeous valleys—together known as the Great Valley of Virginia—extending from the Potomac in the north all the way to the bordering states of Tennessee and Kentucky.

The most famous is the storied Shenandoah Valley, carved by the North and South forks of the Shenandoah River from Winchester in the north to Lexington in the south.

The Roanoke River, another mighty waterway which eventually empties into North Carolina's Albemarle Sound, has cut its own valley, today home to Roanoke, the only large Virginia city completely surrounded by mountains.

Other rivers such as the New (misnamed, as it's geologically the oldest river in North America) have carved smaller valleys in Virginia's southwestern "tail." Mount Rogers is the state's highest point, but with the valley floors at 2,000 feet or more in altitude, there is little mystery in why this region is called the Southwest Highlands.

RESPONSIBLE TRAVEL

Even though Virginia has always been a pro-business state, and residential and commercial developments are eating into our green spaces, the state and federal governments have protected many thousands of acres of land in its natural condition. The Shenandoah National Park gets most of the ink, but it is dwarfed by our state parks and national forests.

Virginia Green

Virginia Green (www.virginia.org/green) is a voluntary program created by the Virginia Tourism Corporation and the state Department of Environmental Quality to promote sustainable tourism. More than 300 Virginia hotels, motels, bed-and-breakfasts, inns, cabins, and other lodging participate in the Virginia Green program by conserving water and energy, recycling their waste, reducing or eliminating the use of Styrofoam, getting us to use our linens more than once before sending them to the laundry, and sponsoring events to promote a green environment.

The Department of Environmental Quality publishes a list of Virginia Green participants on its website (www.deq.virginia.gov/p2/virginiagreen/lodging_participants. html). When making your plans, look for the Virginia Green logo.

What We Can Do

It's up to us travelers to practice **sustainable tourism,** which means being careful with the environments we explore, and respecting the communities we visit, including Virginia.

Two overlapping components of sustainable travel are **eco-tourism** and **ethical tourism.** The **International Ecotourism Society** (**TIES;** www.ecotourism.org) defines eco-tourism as responsible travel to natural areas that conserves the environment and improves the well-being of local people. TIES suggests that ecotourists follow these principles:

- Minimize environmental impact.
- Build environmental and cultural awareness and respect.
- Provide positive experiences for both visitors and hosts.
- Provide direct financial benefits for conservation and for local people.
- Raise sensitivity to host countries' political, environmental, and social climates.
- Support international human rights and labor agreements.

TOURS

Escorted tours are structured group tours, with a group leader. The price usually includes everything from airfare to hotels, meals, tours, admission to attractions, and local transportation.

Several travel companies offer escorted bus tours of historic sites in both Virginia and southeastern Pennsylvania. These 1-week or longer tours usually start in Washington, D.C, and visit Mount Vernon, Fredericksburg, Williamsburg, Richmond, Charlottesville, and Shenandoah National Park. From there they go on to Gettysburg and the Amish Country in Pennsylvania before ending in Philadelphia. You'll have to pay extra to get to Washington, D.C., and home from Philadelphia, but meals, lodging, and bus transportation are included in the tour prices.

Check out **Trafalgar Tours** (✆ **866/544-4434;** www.trafalgartours.com), **Tauck Tours** (✆ **800/788-7855;** www.tauck.com), and **Mayflower Tours** (✆ **800/323-7604;** www.mayflowertours.com) to find out what they're offering when you plan to travel.

Despite the fact that escorted tours require big deposits and predetermine hotels, restaurants, and itineraries, many people derive security and peace of mind from the structure they offer. Escorted tours let you sit back and enjoy the trip without having to drive or worry about details. They take you to the maximum number of sights in the minimum amount of time with the least amount of hassle. They're particularly convenient for people with limited mobility and they can be a great way to make new friends.

On the downside, you'll have little opportunity for serendipitous interactions with locals. The tours can be jampacked with activities, leaving little room for individual sightseeing, whim, or adventure. And they focus on the most touristy sites, so you miss out on many a lesser-known gem.

For more information on escorted general-interest tours, including questions to ask before booking your trip, see www.frommers.com/planning.

1-Day Bus Tours

During the warm months you can also take 1-day escorted bus tours from Washington, D.C., to Charlottesville with the venerable **Gray Line** (⟨ **800/862-1400** or 301/386-8300; www.graylinedc.com). The trip costs $92 for adults and $60 for children 3 to 11 and includes admission to Thomas Jefferson's Monticello home (p. 116). The company has 1-day guided tours from D.C., to Middleburg and Leesburg in the Hunt Country, and it occasionally offers 1-day excursions from D.C. to Williamsburg.

Wine Tours

Rather than risk a DUI charge, you can take tours of the Hunt Country and Charlottesville area wineries (see chapters 4 and 6, respectively). In the Hunt Country, **Reston Limousine** (⟨ **800/LIMO-141** [546-6141] or 703/478-0500; **www.reston limo.com**) goes on all-day tours on Saturday or Sunday to four local wineries for $35 per person, not including lunch or the winery tasting fees.

From Charlottesville, Erika and Chris Goddell of **Arcady Vineyard Wine Tasting Tours** (⟨ **434/872-9475; www.arcadyvineyard.com**) do the driving while you do the tasting. Their full-day tours cost about $145 per person, plus $20 per person for a silver-service picnic lunch. Reservations are required.

ENJOYING THE GREAT OUTDOORS

Although Virginia is best known for its multitude of historic sites, it's also home to a host of outdoor activities. In this section, I give you an overview of what I consider the best options available, where they are, and how to get statewide information. Please refer to the destination chapters for detailed information.

The Virginia Tourism Corporation includes a wealth of information about outdoor activities on its website (www.virginia.org) and publishes an annual *Virginia Outdoors* magazine that gives a comprehensive rundown of the activities available, a calendar of outdoor events, and a list of the many outfitters and tour companies operating in the state. Call ⟨ **800/827-3325** for a copy, or see "Visitor Information" under "Fast Facts: Virginia," in chapter 12.

Bicycling & Mountain Biking

Bicycling is popular throughout Virginia, and with good reason. Most of the state's scenic highways are open to bicycles. My favorites are the 17-mile

George Washington Memorial Parkway between Arlington and Mount Vernon (see chapter 4), the 105-mile **Skyline Drive** above the Shenandoah Valley (see chapter 7), the 218-mile **Blue Ridge Parkway** in the Southwest Highlands (see chapter 8), and the 22-mile **Colonial Parkway** between Jamestown and Yorktown (see chapter 10).

The state also has three excellent "rails-to-trails" parks, in which old railroad beds have been turned into biking and hiking avenues. I often use northern Virginia's **Washington & Old Dominion Trail,** which begins in Arlington and ends 45 miles away at Purcellville in the rolling hills of the Hunt Country (see "Alexandria," in chapter 4).

In the "Outdoors in the Southwest Highlands" section of chapter 8, I describe two dramatic trails through some of the state's finest mountain scenery. The 34-mile **Virginia Creeper Trail,** one of the country's top bike paths, begins in the Mount Rogers National Recreation Area high up on the flanks of Whitetop Mountain, Virginia's second-highest peak, and descends to Abingdon. Near Wytheville, the 55-mile **New River Trail** follows the New River, which actually is one of the world's oldest rivers. Outfitters along both trails rent bikes and provide shuttle services so you don't have to ride both ways—particularly handy on the Virginia Creeper Trail, which drops more than 3,000 feet from Whitetop Mountain to Damascus, near Abingdon.

Down on the coast, I love pedaling along the **Virginia Beach Boardwalk,** through the natural beauty of **First Landing State Park** and **Back Bay National Wildlife Refuge,** and along all of the flat Eastern Shore roads (see chapter 11).

I've never attempted them, but three major interstate bicycle routes run across Virginia. The Maine-to-Virginia **Route 1** runs 150 miles from Arlington to Richmond and connects to 130 miles of the Virginia-to-Florida **Route 17** from Richmond to the North Carolina line at Suffolk. Some 500 miles of the **TransAmerican Bicycle Trail (Rte. 76)** run from the Kentucky line to Yorktown, including a stretch through Mount Rogers National Recreation Area in the Southwest Highlands. For strip maps of these routes, contact **Adventure Cycling Association,** PO Box 8308, Missoula, MT 59802 (✆ **800/755-2453** or 406/721-1776; www.adv-cycling.org).

Mountain bikers will find plenty of trails, especially in Mount Rogers National Recreation Area and in the George Washington and Jefferson national forests, which occupy parts of the Shenandoah Valley (see chapter 7) and the Southwest Highlands (see chapter 8). For details about the latter, contact the **George Washington and Jefferson National Forests,** 210 Franklin Rd. SW, Roanoke, VA 24004 (✆ **540/265-6054;** www.southernregion.fs.fed.us/gwj).

Mountain Bike Virginia, by Scott Adams (Beachway Press, 1995), is a very handy atlas to Virginia's best trails, with excellent maps.

The **Virginia Department of Transportation's Bicycle Coordinator,** 1401 E. Broad St., Richmond, VA 23219 (✆ **800/835-1203** or 804/786-2964; www.virginia dot.org), publishes the annual *Virginia Bicycling Guide,* which describes Virginia's routes and trails and lists local bike clubs and relevant publications. Contact the department or the Virginia Tourism Corporation (see "Visitor Information" under "Fast Facts: Virginia," in chapter 12) for a free copy.

Bird-Watching

The big bird-watching draws in Virginia are waterfowl nesting in the flatlands and marshes along the coast on the Atlantic Flyway. Chincoteague National Wildlife Refuge on Assateague Island and Back Bay National Wildlife Refuge below Virginia Beach offer first-rate bird-watching. Chincoteague is especially good on Thanksgiving weekend, the only time the refuge's back roads are open to vehicles. See chapter 12.

Boating

The Chesapeake Bay and its many tributaries, including the Potomac, Rappahannock, York, and James rivers, are perfect for boating. In fact, you can come away from eastern Virginia with the impression that every other home has a boat and trailer sitting in the yard. Marinas abound on the Northern Neck (see chapter 5), and you can rent boats in Hampton Roads and over on Eastern Shore, where the back bays of Chincoteague await to be explored from a fish's-eye view (see chapter 11).

A detailed map showing public access to the Chesapeake and its tributaries is available from the **Virginia Department of Conservation and Recreation,** 203 Governor St., Ste. 302, Richmond, VA 23219 (© **804/786-1712;** www.dcr.state.va.us).

Canoeing, Kayaking & River Rafting

Kayakers and canoeists will find easy, quiet paddling on the backwater creeks of the Northern Neck (see chapter 5) and in Hampton Roads and on Eastern Shore (see chapter 11). Outfitters in Virginia Beach and Chincoteague rent both canoes and kayaks and offer guided excursions of the creeks and back bays, and you can go dolphin-watching with them off Virginia Beach.

Depending on how much rain has dropped recently, the best white-water rafting may be on the James River at Scottsville near Charlottesville (see chapter 6). White-water rafting is most likely during spring and late fall.

The best canoeing and kayaking is on the South Fork of the Shenandoah River between Front Royal Luray and Lexington (see "Rafting, Canoeing & Kayaking on the Shenandoah," p. 145). When the water is low during summer, multitudes forget canoes and rafts and lazily float down the rivers in inner tubes.

Fishing

The waters that are so great for boating are stocked with a wide array of fish. The best rivers for fishing include the South Fork of the Shenandoah near Front Royal for smallmouth bass and redbreast sunfish; the James between Richmond and Norfolk for smallmouth bass and catfish; the New near Wytheville for walleye, yellow perch, musky, and smallmouth bass; the Rappahannock from Fredericksburg to the Northern Neck for smallmouth bass and catfish; and the Chickahominy near Williamsburg for largemouth bass, chain pickerel, bluegill, white perch, and channel catfish.

The mountains have 2,800 miles of trout streams, many stocked annually. Guides are available in Lexington (see chapter 7) and Abingdon (see chapter 8).

From Virginia Beach and Chincoteague you can go deep-sea fishing on charter and party boats in search of bluefish, flounder, cobia, gray and spotted trout, sharks, and other ocean dwellers (see chapter 11).

The **Virginia Department of Game and Inland Fisheries,** 4010 W. Broad St., Richmond, VA 23230 (© **804/367-1000;** www.dgif.state.va.us), publishes an annual freshwater-fishing guide and regulations pamphlet detailing licensing requirements and regulations. Licenses, available at most sporting-goods stores, marinas, and bait shops, are required except on the first Saturday and Sunday in June, which are free fishing days.

Golf

You can play golf almost anytime and anywhere in Virginia, given the state's mild climate and more than 130 courses, but serious duffers head to **Williamsburg** and the Golden Horseshoe, Green, and Gold courses at the Williamsburg Inn, and the links at Kingsmill Resort (see chapter 10). An hour's drive away, the PGA-owned

Virginia Beach National Golf Club in **Virginia Beach** is one of the country's best upscale links (p. 292). Up in the mountains, the Homestead's beautiful course in **Hot Springs** has the nation's oldest first tee, in continuous use since 1890 (p. 162). Wintergreen Resort near **Charlottesville** also has an excellent course (p. 111), as does Lansdowne Resort near **Leesburg** (p. 75).

The best source for information is the Virginia Tourism Corporation's annual *Virginia Golf Guide,* which lists and describes the state's courses (see "Visitor Information" under "Fast Facts: Virginia," in chapter 12).

Hiking & Backpacking

The same trails that make Virginia so popular with bicyclists also make it a hiker's heaven. The state's rails-to-trails paths along old railroad beds (see "Bicycling & Mountain Biking," above) are both good and easy. Some 450 miles of the **Appalachian Trail** snake through Virginia, nearly climbing Mount Rogers and paralleling the Blue Ridge Parkway and the Skyline Drive in many places. The best backcountry trails are in **Shenandoah National Park** (see chapter 7) and **Mount Rogers National Recreation Area** (see chapter 8), with less-traveled trails in the George Washington and Jefferson national forests.

For information and maps of the Appalachian Trail, contact the **Appalachian Trail Conservancy,** PO Box 807, Harpers Ferry, WV 25425-0807 (© **304/535-6331;** www.atconf.org).

Four good books give trail-by-trail descriptions. *The Trails of Virginia: Hiking the Old Dominion,* by Allen de Hart (University of North Carolina Press, 1995), is still the most comprehensive guide. *The Hiker's Guide to Virginia,* by Randy Johnson (Falcon Press, 1992), is a slimmer, easier-to-carry volume, as is *Hiking Virginia's National Forests,* by Karin Wuertz-Schaeffer (Globe Pequot Press, 1994), which covers trails in the George Washington and Jefferson national forests in the Shenandoah Valley and Southwest Highlands. Of more recent vintage, *Hiking Shenandoah National Park,* by Bert and Jane Gildart (Falcon Press, 2006), describes and maps the park's best trails.

Horseback Riding

Equestrians will find stables with horses to rent and hundreds of miles of public horse trails on which to ride them in Virginia, the majority of them in the Shenandoah Valley and the Southwest Highlands. The **Shenandoah National Park** has its own Skyland Stables, from which you can take guided trail rides atop the Blue Ridge (see chapter 7). The granddaddy of all trails, the **Virginia Highlands Horse Trail,** runs the length of Mount Rogers National Recreation Area, which has campgrounds especially for horse owners (see chapter 8). Horses are also permitted on the Virginia Creeper Trail and the New River Trail. You can rent horses at the Mount Rogers National Recreation Area and along the New River Trail (see chapter 8). Ironically, few stables rent horses in northern Virginia's Hunt Country, where just about everyone who rides owns a horse (see chapter 4).

The **Virginia Horse Council,** 2799 Stratford Rd., Richmond, VA 23225 (© **804/330-0345;** www.virginiahorse.com), publishes a list of public horse trails and stables statewide.

Watersports

To indulge your passion for surfing, jet-skiing, wave running, sailing, or scuba diving, head for Virginia Beach, which has it all in abundance. See chapter 11.

SUGGESTED VIRGINIA ITINERARIES

Virginia is a relatively large and varied state with numerous attractions across its length and breadth. Where you go and what you see will depend on your special interests—whether you're into history or into hiking, for example. Ideally you should use chapter 1, "The Best of Virginia," to work out a route that appeals to you. I have suggested a few itineraries below that will take you throughout Virginia, to its Colonial-era attractions and its Civil War battlefields, to some of its vineyards, and up the Shenandoah, with a little Shakespeare thrown in for good measure. I've also suggested a route that will help parents travel happily with their children in Virginia.

VIRGINIA'S REGIONS IN BRIEF

First of all, you must decide where to go. I can't make that decision for you, but I can briefly tell you what the state has to offer.

Northern Virginia

My home area in northern Virginia is the fastest-growing, wealthiest, and most densely populated part of the state—with horrendous traffic to prove it. Our northern counties were once a suburban bedroom for workers in Washington, D.C., but not anymore. Areas such as Tysons Corner have become de facto cities in their own right, with employment in high-tech service industries outstripping that of the federal government. Just across the Potomac from the nation's capital, **Arlington** is best known for its national cemetery. The historic Old Town district of **Alexandria** offers fascinating daytime walks as well as good restaurants. To the south lies George Washington's **Mount Vernon** and two other Potomac plantations. To the west, I enjoy driving out to Virginia's hilly **Hunt Country,** where the first major battle of the Civil War was fought at **Manassas.**

Fredericksburg & the Northern Neck

I always look forward to visiting **Fredericksburg,** where quaint cobblestone streets and historic houses recall America's first heroes—George Washington, James Monroe, John Paul Jones—as does the quiet

Northern Neck farmland, where Washington and Robert E. Lee were born. Military buffs love to explore Fredericksburg's Civil War battlefields.

Charlottesville

Located in the rolling Piedmont hills known as "Mr. Jefferson's country," **Charlottesville** boasts President Thomas Jefferson's magnificent estate, Monticello, as well as the University of Virginia, which he designed. Drives south bring you to Poplar Forest, his beloved retreat; Patrick Henry's final home at Red Hill; and Appomattox Court House, where the Civil War ended when Robert E. Lee surrendered to Ulysses S. Grant.

The Shenandoah Valley

Some of Virginia's most striking scenic views are from the **Skyline Drive,** which follows the crest of the Blue Ridge Mountains through magnificent **Shenandoah National Park,** where you can explore a host of hiking paths, including part of the Maine-to-Georgia Appalachian Trail. Down below, charming towns like **Winchester, Front Royal, Luray, Staunton,** and **Lexington** evoke the Civil War, which flowed over the rolling countryside of the Shenandoah Valley, the South's breadbasket. In another valley high in the Allegheny Mountains to the west lie the famous mineral waters of **Warm Springs** and **Hot Springs.**

The Southwest Highlands

Beyond the vibrant railroad city of **Roanoke** rise the highlands of Virginia's southwestern extremity, a land of forests, waterfalls, and streams seemingly untouched since Daniel Boone led settlers along the Great Wilderness Road into Kentucky. The **Blue Ridge Parkway** wanders along its eastern border. Here the state's highest point, **Mount Rogers,** sits surrounded by a national recreation area teeming with trails for hiking, mountain biking, and horseback riding. Down in the Great Valley of Virginia, the beautiful town of **Abingdon** features the famous Barter Theatre, begun during the Great Depression when its company traded tickets for hams.

Richmond

The state capital has few rivals among U.S. cities for its historic associations, among them St. John's Church, where Patrick Henry said, "Give me liberty, or give me death." But it was Richmond's role as the rebel capital during the Civil War that brings visitors to the Museum of the Confederacy and the Richmond and Petersburg battlefields. Fine arts and science museums, cafes, lively concerts, and theater add to Richmond's cosmopolitan ambience, and children can get their kicks at nearby Kings Dominion amusement park.

Williamsburg, Yorktown & Jamestown

Coastal Virginia's "Historic Triangle" is one of the country's most visited areas, and with good reason. **Jamestown** is where America's first permanent English settlers arrived in 1607 (and some of my own ancestors in 1613). **Williamsburg** immaculately re-creates Virginia's Colonial capital, and **Yorktown** commemorates the last battle of the American Revolution. Adding to the triangle's allure are theme parks and world-class discount shopping. From here it's an easy excursion to see the recovered gun turret of the USS *Monitor* at one of the nation's premier maritime museums in the shipbuilding city of **Newport News.** Historic **Hampton** may be the country's oldest continuous English-speaking settlement, but it boasts a modern, high-tech air and space museum.

Norfolk, Virginia Beach & Eastern Shore

The great harbor of Hampton Roads is home to the resurgent cities of **Norfolk** and **Portsmouth.** You can play in the surf at **Virginia Beach,** whose boardwalk and 20 miles of sandy beach are lined with hotels, and commune with nature in **Back Bay National Wildlife Refuge** and remote **False Cape State Park.** Drive across the 17-mile Chesapeake Bay Bridge-Tunnel to Eastern Shore, an unspoiled sanctuary noted for the fishing village of **Chincoteague** and nearby **Assateague Island,** whose wildlife refuge and national seashore have protected the famous wild ponies and prevented any development on almost 40 miles of pristine beach.

GRAND TOUR OF VIRGINIA IN 2 WEEKS

This route takes you to all of Virginia's top attractions: the Shenandoah National Park, the Shenandoah Valley towns of Staunton and Lexington, Charlottesville, Richmond, Williamsburg, Jamestown, Yorktown, Virginia Beach, Fredericksburg, and George Washington's Mount Vernon home near Alexandria's historic Old Town district. You can expand any section of this route into a week's tour of one particular area of Virginia. For instance, you can spend a week in the Shenandoah Valley by staying 2 or more nights in, say, Winchester, Shenandoah National Park, Staunton, or Lexington. Charlottesville-Richmond-Williamsburg is another example.

This tour begins and ends at Washington Dulles International Airport in northern Virginia, the state's major air gateway, and essentially follows I-66, I-81, I-64, and I-95 to make a loop around the northern and central portions of the state. If you're driving to Virginia from the south, start in Williamsburg and work backward.

Days 1 & 2: The Hunt Country ★★

As you leave Dulles airport, first go south on Va. 28 to the National Air and Space Museum's magnificent **Steven F. Udvar-Hazy Center** (p. 73). Then head to **Leesburg,** seeing the sights in town before retiring for the night. The next morning drive to **Middleburg,** where you can browse its hip main drag and have lunch. Spend the afternoon exploring the back roads, sampling the vintages at the nearby vineyards, and crossing the mountains to **Winchester.**

Day 3: Winchester ★ to Luray

Spend the morning seeing Winchester's sights, especially the **Museum of the Shenandoah Valley** (p. 137), which provides a fine introduction to the valley. In the afternoon, drive through **Strasburg** and **Front Royal** on your way to **Luray,** where you can go underground at **Luray Caverns** (p. 148). Spend the night in Luray or drive on up into the Shenandoah National Park.

Day 4: Shenandoah National Park ★★★

From Luray, drive east on U.S. 211 to the mountaintop entrance to **Shenandoah National Park** (p. 128). Go south on **Skyline Drive** into the park's Central District, its most scenic and best equipped. Take in the views, hike the trails, or go horseback riding (be sure to call the stables in advance for riding reservations). Spend the night at the park's **Big Meadows Lodge** (p. 134) or **Skyland Resort** (p. 134).

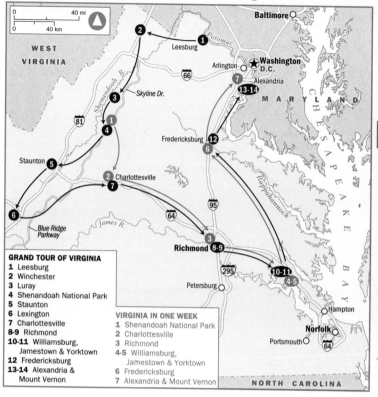

GRAND TOUR OF VIRGINIA
1 Leesburg
2 Winchester
3 Luray
4 Shenandoah National Park
5 Staunton
6 Lexington
7 Charlottesville
8-9 Richmond
10-11 Williamsburg, Jamestown & Yorktown
12 Fredericksburg
13-14 Alexandria & Mount Vernon

VIRGINIA IN ONE WEEK
1 Shenandoah National Park
2 Charlottesville
3 Richmond
4-5 Williamsburg, Jamestown & Yorktown
6 Fredericksburg
7 Alexandria & Mount Vernon

Day 5: Staunton ★★★

The next morning, take Skyline Drive south to I-64, and then west to **Staunton,** one of Virginia's best small towns. Spend the afternoon visiting the **Woodrow Wilson Presidential Library at His Birthplace** (p. 155). See Shakespeare performed at the marvelous **Blackfriars Playhouse** (p. 154).

Day 6: Lexington ★★★

Charming **Lexington** has more attractions than any other town its size in the Shenandoah Valley, so arrive in time to spend at least an afternoon visiting the **George C. Marshall Museum and Research Library** (p. 166) and Stonewall Jackson's stuffed horse in the **Virginia Military Institute Museum** (p. 168).

Day 7: Charlottesville ★★★

I-81 and I-64 will speed you to Thomas Jefferson's hometown of **Charlottesville,** or you can take the slow but much more scenic route via the **Blue Ridge Parkway** from Buena Vista to Waynesboro, and then I-64 east. Either way, spend the afternoon touring the **University of Virginia** (p. 116) and other downtown Charlottesville attractions. The next morning, beat the crowds to

Jefferson's magnificent **Monticello** (p. 116). Have lunch at nearby **Michie Tavern** (p. 115) then visit President James Monroe's **Ash Lawn–Highland** home (p. 114). When finished, take I-64 east to Richmond for the night.

Days 8 & 9: Richmond ★★

You'll have a busy 2 days seeing the sites from Richmond's days as the capital of the Confederacy. Begin at the **American Civil War Center at Tredegar** (p. 218), which expertly explains the war's origins from the Northern, Southern, and African-American perspectives. It's next door to the **Richmond National Battlefield Park's** own museum (p. 220). Next, head to the **Museum and White House of the Confederacy** (p. 219). On the second day take in **St. John's Episcopal Church** (p. 220), where Patrick Henry made his "give me liberty, or give me death" speech, and Richmond's host of specialized museums.

Days 10 & 11: Williamsburg, Jamestown & Yorktown ★★★

Two days are barely enough to scratch the surface of Virginia's "Historic Triangle." Devote one of them to the lovingly restored **Colonial Williamsburg** historic district, finishing with dinner at one of the ancient taverns. **Jamestown** will take up the next morning; **Yorktown** that afternoon. If you have children, an alternate choice for one of your days here is **Busch Gardens Williamsburg** (p. 247). If you have a few days to spare, you can spend them relaxing at **Virginia Beach.**

Day 12: Fredericksburg ★★★

Depart Williamsburg early and drive north via U.S. 17 to **Fredericksburg,** the boyhood home of George Washington, where you can spend the afternoon exploring **his mother's home** (p. 87) and the fascinating **apothecary of Hugh Mercer** (p. 86), his friend and fellow warrior. Spend the next morning at the Civil War battlefields. Then take I-95 north to Alexandria, with a stop at the **National Museum of the Marine Corps** in the town of Triangle (p. 88).

Days 13 & 14: Alexandria & Mount Vernon ★★★

George Washington, Robert E. Lee, and a host of other notables strode the cobblestone streets of **Old Town Alexandria,** the city's beautifully restored historic district beside the Potomac River. Old Town's sights will take most of a day to explore. Spend the next day south of Alexandria at Washington's home at **Mount Vernon** (p. 65). Old Town is a shuttle ride back to Dulles airport.

VIRGINIA IN 1 WEEK

Although you'll be pressing to see everything in Virginia in 2 weeks (Williamsburg, Jamestown, and Yorktown together can easily eat up a week), you can see the tip of the iceberg in a week if you really hurry and see only the top attractions. In devising this route, I have eliminated all but the best.

Day 1: Shenandoah National Park ★★★

Drive directly to the entrance of the Central District of **Shenandoah National Park** (p. 128), on U.S. 211, at Thornton Gap. Go south on the **Skyline Drive,** take in the views, hike, or go horseback riding. Spend the night at the park's **Big Meadows Lodge** (p. 134) or **Skyland Resort** (p. 134).

Day 2: Charlottesville ★★★

Drive south on Skyline Drive to U.S. 33 east, then to U.S. 29, and then south to **Charlottesville.** Spend the afternoon touring the **University of Virginia** (p. 116) and other downtown Charlottesville attractions. The next morning beat the crowds to Jefferson's magnificent **Monticello** (p. 116). Do lunch at nearby **Michie Tavern** (p. 115) before visiting President James Monroe's **Ash Lawn–Highland** (p. 114). When done, follow I-64 east to Richmond.

Day 3: Richmond ★★

It will be all you can do in one day to visit the **Museum and White House of the Confederacy** (p. 219), the **Richmond National Battlefield Park** (p. 220), **St. John's Episcopal Church** (p. 220), and the capital city's other top sights.

Days 4 & 5: Williamsburg, Jamestown & Yorktown ★★★

Spend one of these days in **Colonial Williamsburg,** the next seeing **Jamestown** and **Yorktown.**

Day 6: Fredericksburg ★★★

Depart Williamsburg early and drive north to **Fredericksburg,** where you can spend the rest of the morning exploring George Washington's boyhood home. Tour the Civil War battlefields in the afternoon.

Day 7: Alexandria & Mount Vernon ★★★

Beat the crowds by spending the morning seeing the historic sights in Old Town Alexandria and the afternoon at Washington's **Mount Vernon** plantation (p. 65).

VIRGINIA FOR FAMILIES

This 1-week route assumes you will be traveling around Virginia with children and don't want to spend most of your time cooped up with them in the same vehicle. Visiting places like George Washington's Mount Vernon and Thomas Jefferson's Monticello are great educational experiences, but the young ones won't think all that 18th-century furniture is particularly cool. Accordingly, this itinerary takes you to three areas where both you and they will be entertained.

Days 1, 2 & 3: Williamsburg, Jamestown & Yorktown ★★★

Although **Colonial Williamsburg** is a great big history lesson, it also has many activities especially for children, such as taking dancing lessons in the Governor's Mansion and marching with the local "militia." You can also keep the kids thoroughly entertained at **Busch Gardens Williamsburg** (p. 247) and **Water Country USA** (p. 247). Costumed interpreters at **Jamestown Settlement** also will keep them occupied. Should your budget allow, stay at **Great Wolf Lodge** (p. 252), which has its own indoor water park.

Days 4 & 5: Virginia Beach ★

Most kids love a day or two at the beach, and **Virginia Beach** is a good place for that. There are lifeguards on duty, and the surf usually isn't threatening. On the way from Williamsburg, stop at the **Virginia Air & Space Center** in Hampton (p. 271), where they'll love the aircraft and the IMAX movie. At the beach, don't miss taking them to the **Virginia Aquarium & Marine Science Center** (p. 297), with its touch tanks and "harbor seal splash."

Days 6 & 7: Chincoteague & Assateague Islands ★★★

A drive across the 17-mile-long **Chesapeake Bay Bridge-Tunnel** and up the Delmarva Peninsula will take you to **Chincoteague Island,** where Marguerite Henry based her children's book, *Misty of Chincoteague.* You and the kids can see the wild ponies grazing in the national wildlife refuge and national seashore on **Assateague Island,** and they can actually ride one during summer months at the **Chincoteague Pony Centre** (p. 307).

COLONIAL VIRGINIA IN 1 WEEK

This route follows the progress of Virginia's Colonial settlers in 1607 from Jamestown to Williamsburg, and then through the great tobacco plantations they built along the state's great tidal rivers to Fredericksburg and Alexandria.

Days 1, 2 & 3: Williamsburg, Jamestown & Yorktown ★★★

As noted in "Grand Tour of Virginia," above, you must hurry to see the Historic Triangle in 2 days. Even with 3 days on your hands, you'll be busy. Spend two of them in the beautifully restored **Colonial Williamsburg.** Spend the other visiting the original settlement at **Jamestown** and the great battlefield at **Yorktown,** where Lord Cornwallis surrendered to George Washington.

Day 4: The James River Plantations

This morning you can tour **Berkeley** (p. 267) and **Shirley** (p. 268), two of the great James River plantations on Va. 5 between Williamsburg and Richmond. Then head up I-295 and I-95 to Fredericksburg.

Day 5: Fredericksburg ★★★

You can spend a leisurely day on the **Fredericksburg** streets tread by George Washington, Robert E. Lee, James Monroe, and Thomas Jefferson.

Days 6 & 7: Mount Vernon & Alexandria ★★★

Take I-95 north from Fredericksburg to Woodbridge, and then U.S. 1 north and Va. 235 east to **Mount Vernon** (p. 65), Washington's magnificent plantation. It and perhaps one more Potomac plantation will take up the rest of the day. Retire to **Old Town Alexandria** via the scenic George Washington Memorial Parkway. Spend your last day exploring Old Town.

Colonial Virginia & Civil War Virginia

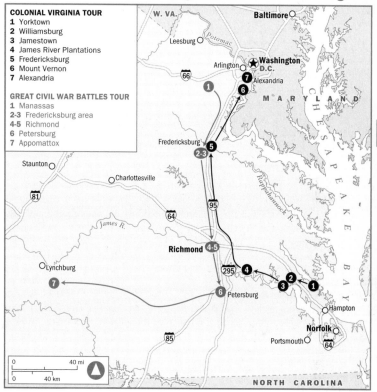

COLONIAL VIRGINIA TOUR
1 Yorktown
2 Williamsburg
3 Jamestown
4 James River Plantations
5 Fredericksburg
6 Mount Vernon
7 Alexandria

GREAT CIVIL WAR BATTLES TOUR
1 Manassas
2-3 Fredericksburg area
4-5 Richmond
6 Petersburg
7 Appomattox

THE GREAT CIVIL WAR BATTLES IN 1 WEEK

This route follows the major Union attempts to capture the Confederate capital of Richmond, about 100 miles south of Washington, D.C., between 1862 and 1865. Although the Civil War raged elsewhere in Virginia, especially in the Shenandoah Valley, the last of these Union advances put an end to the nation's bloodiest conflict when Lee surrendered his sword to Grant at Appomattox Court House.

This is a good time for this tour, as Virginia is celebrating the 150th anniversary of the Civil War between now and April 2015. The **Virginia Sesquicentennial of the American Civil War Commission** (✆ **804/786-3591;** www.virginiacivilwar.org) is organizing many events and battle reenactments. A good source for information about Civil War battlefields is the **Civil War Trust** (www.civilwar.org), which has iPhone battle apps for Manassas (Bull Run), Fredericksburg, and Chancellorsville.

Day 1: Manassas ★★

Two of the war's great battles, including its first, took place near a stream known as Bull Run, outside the town of **Manassas.** Stonewall Jackson got his nickname here when he stood his ground like a stone wall. You can spend most of a day seeing where it all took place in **Manassas National Battlefield Park** (p. 79). Plan to stay in nearby Middleburg or Leesburg in the Hunt Country.

Days 2 & 3: Fredericksburg ★★★

Sitting beside the Rappahannock River, Fredericksburg was directly in the path of the Union advances. You will need these 2 days to explore **Fredericksburg & Spotsylvania National Military Park** (p. 92), for it includes four of the Civil War's most important battles—Fredericksburg, Chancellorsville, the Wilderness, and Spotsylvania Courthouse—plus the farmhouse where Stonewall Jackson died.

Days 4 & 5: Richmond ★★★

Richmond withstood 4 years of war as the Confederacy's capital. Spend one of these days downtown at the **Museum and White House of the Confederacy** (p. 219) and at the **Richmond Civil War Visitor Center at Tredegar Iron Works** (p. 220). The latter serves as starting point for your second day's driving tour of the battlefields east of the city, now part of the **Richmond National Battlefield Park** (p. 220).

Day 6: Petersburg ★★

The war's last great action took place as Grant laid siege to **Petersburg,** then an important railway junction and the key to Richmond's supply line. After 10 months, Union forces finally broke through on April 12, 1865, forcing Lee into his final retreat. Start at downtown Petersburg's **Siege Museum** (p. 229), and then drive along the lines east of town, now part of **Petersburg National Battlefield Park** (p. 231).

Day 7: Appomattox ★★★

Lee advanced west for a week until he ran out of supplies near Appomattox Court House, about 90 miles west of Petersburg via U.S. 460, where he surrendered on April 9, 1865. The site is beautifully preserved in the **Appomattox Court House National Historical Park** (p. 124).

NORTHERN VIRGINIA

N orthern Virginia has changed immeasurably since George Washington, George Mason, and other Colonial notables lived here more than 2 centuries ago. Back then this was a land of farms, plantations, and small villages. There was no Washington, D.C., to provide government jobs driving workers to buy suburban homes across the Potomac River in Virginia.

Today Alexandria, Arlington, and other nearby northern Virginia municipalities are no longer primarily bedroom communities for D.C. workers. Thanks to burgeoning high-tech businesses and the outsourcing of government work, we are the largest economic dynamo in Virginia. Things have slowed a bit, but we continue to grow even in the teeth of today's Great Recession.

Fairfax County, which wraps around Arlington and Alexandria, is the most populous jurisdiction in Virginia, with more than one million residents—twice the population of the District of Columbia. With a median household income of more than $120,000 a year, it's also one of the richest counties in the U.S. Tysons Corner, a shopping and office complex at the junction of I-495 and Va. 7, has more office space than downtown Denver. The strip running west from there through Reston and Herndon to Washington Dulles International Airport is one of the nation's premier high-tech corridors.

Our metropolitan sprawl has extended its tentacles through Fairfax west beyond Dulles airport into the bucolic Hunt Country and as far south as Fredericksburg (see chapter 5).

All that having been said, please don't let our often congested traffic discourage you from coming, for if you avoid our rush hours, you can easily access pockets of historical charm that will take you back hundreds of years.

Washington, Mason, and Robert E. Lee would still recognize their hometown of Alexandria, where the cobblestone streets of the 18th-century Old Town still practically ring with their footsteps. On the Potomac south of Old Town, George Washington's Mount Vernon is one of our nation's most visited homes.

Out in the western part of Loudoun County and in most of Fauquier County, our crowded highways give way to the winding country roads, rolling hills, picturesque horse farms, vineyards, and Colonial-era villages that make the Hunt Country a special place to visit.

ALEXANDRIA ★★★

5 miles S of Washington, D.C.; 95 miles N of Richmond

Founded by a group of Scottish tobacco merchants, the riverfront town of Alexandria came into being in July 1749, when a 60-acre tract of land was auctioned off in ½-acre lots. As you stroll the brick sidewalks and cobblestone streets of highly gentrified **Old Town,** the city's official historic district, you'll see more than 2,000 buildings dating from the 18th and 19th centuries.

George Washington stood in the doorway of Gadsby's Tavern and reviewed his troops for the last time. Robert E. Lee spent his boyhood here. Both worshiped in the pews of Christ Church. Indeed, if they weren't instantly shocked back to death by the cars jockeying for prized parking spaces, Washington and Lee would recognize their old haunts. They may have tread the cobblestones still paving Prince Street between Union and Lee streets.

There's more than history here to explore. With its abundance of shops, boutiques, art galleries, restaurants, and tourists (not to mention hordes of older teens hanging out on Fri and Sat nights), Old Town Alexandria serves as our hip version of Georgetown over in D.C. Once you get here, you will find plenty to see, do, and eat. Give yourself a day to poke around the historic district and another to see Mount Vernon, a short drive to the south.

Essentials

VISITOR INFORMATION

The **Ramsay House Visitor Center,** 221 King St., at Fairfax Street facing Market Square (② **800/388-9119** or 703/838-4200; 703/838-5005 for 24-hr. Alexandria events recording; fax 703/838-4683; www.visitalexandriava.com), is open daily from 9am to 8pm (to 5pm Jan–Mar) except New Year's Day, Thanksgiving, and Christmas. In this 1724 house, Alexandria's oldest, you can pick up maps and brochures, find out about special events during your visit, and get information about accommodations, restaurants, sights, shopping, and whatever else. You can also get a free 1-day parking permit here (see "Getting There," below).

Be sure to pick up a free copy of *Old Town Crier* (② **703/836-9132;** www.oldtowncrier.com), a monthly magazine packed with information and news about special events, dining, shopping, and entertainment.

GETTING THERE

For more information about transportation, see "Getting There," in chapter 12.

BY PLANE   **Washington Dulles International Airport (IAD)** is about 30 miles west of Alexandria (② **703/661-2700**). **Ronald Reagan Washington National Airport (DCA)** is 2 miles north of Old Town via the George Washington Memorial Parkway (② **703/685-8000**). The website for both is **www.mwaa.com.** Washington's **Metrorail** (see "By Metrorail," below) provides easy transport from Reagan National to Alexandria via its Blue and Yellow lines. Taxis are available at both airports, and **SuperShuttle** (② **800/BLUE-VAN** [258-3826]; www.supershuttle.com) operates frequent van service.

BY CAR   All the major **car-rental firms** are based at the airports. The scenic George Washington Memorial Parkway passes through Old Town as Washington Street, Alexandria's main north-south thoroughfare. I-95 crosses the Potomac River at Alexandria; take Exit 177 and go north on U.S. 1 into Old Town. Turn east on King Street off either route to reach the heart of Old Town.

Traffic in the Washington, D.C., metro area is so bad that a columnist for the *Washington Post* writes under the pseudonym "Dr. Gridlock." Although they start earlier and run later depending on distance from D.C., weekday rush hours generally run from 6:30 to 9:30am and from 3:30 to 6:30pm, but tie-ups can occur any time, especially in construction zones. Take the area's Metrorail or other public transportation whenever possible and try to avoid the roads altogether during rush hours. WTOP (103.5 FM and 107.7 FM) gives traffic reports every 10 minutes—not that you'll understand our arcane shorthand such as the "Inner " and "Outer " Loops of the Capital Beltway.

PARKING   The first item of business is to get a **free 1-day parking permit** at the Ramsay House Visitor Center (see "Visitor Information," above), which allows you to park free for up to 24 hours at any on-street 2-hour pay spot. They do *not* apply to spaces without payment machines. You'll need your car's license plate number and the state in which it's registered—which could be other than Virginia if it's a rental.

BY TRAIN   The **Amtrak** station (© **800/872-7245** or 703/836-4339; www.amtrak.com) is at 110 Callahan Dr., at King Street.

BY METRORAIL   From Arlington or Washington, take the Blue or Yellow **Metrorail** (© **202/637-7000;** www.wmata.com) lines to the King Street station (it's next to Amtrak's Alexandria station). Metrorail operates Monday to Thursday from 5:30am to midnight, Friday 5:30am to 2am, Saturday 8am to 3am, and Sunday 8am to midnight. Fares range from $1.85 to $5.45 depending on time of day and length of ride.

From the King Street station, it's about a 15-minute walk east on King Street through Old Town's rapidly developing western section. Or you can take the free **King Street Trolley.** At other times, the DASH buses run along King Street to the visitor center at the corner of Fairfax Street. See "Getting Around," below, for more information.

CITY LAYOUT

Old Town Alexandria is laid out in a simple grid. The original town grew north-south along the Potomac River, but most of what you will want to see and do today is on, or a few blocks off, King Street, the main east-west drag, between the waterfront and the King Street Metrorail and Amtrak stations. Until a few years ago, visitors to Old Town seldom wandered west of Washington Street. But the Metro has spurred development near the station, new stores and restaurants have sprouted up all along King Street, and a large commercial real estate development known as Carlyle resides south of the station between Duke Street and Eisenhower Avenue.

GETTING AROUND

With Old Town's prime historic sites concentrated within several blocks, it's easy to park your car for the day, don comfortable shoes, and start walking—the easiest way to get around.

You can save your shoe leather for sightseeing by taking the free **King Street Trolley** (© **301/386-8300**), which runs every 15 minutes between the station and the waterfront daily between 11:30am and 10pm.

Alexandria's bus system is known as **DASH** (© **703/370-3274;** www.dashbus.com). There's no service New Year's Day, Thanksgiving, or Christmas. The visitor center gives away route maps, as does the DASH Old Town Transit Shop, 1775-C Duke St. (☎ **703/299-6227**), opposite the Embassy Suites Hotel Alexandria Old Town. Base fare is $1.50.

For a taxi, call **Alexandria Yellow Cab Company** (☎ **703/549-2500**) or **Alexandria White Top Cab Company** (☎ **703/683-4004;** www.whitetopcab.com).

Exploring Old Town

Whenever you come, you're sure to run into some activity or other—a jazz festival, a tea garden or tavern gambol, a quilt exhibit, a wine tasting, or an organ recital. But note that **many of Alexandria's main attractions are closed on Monday.**

THE TOP ATTRACTIONS

Carlyle House Historic Park   Patterned after Scottish-English manor houses, this architecturally impressive home was completed in 1753 by Scottish merchant John Carlyle for his bride, Sarah Fairfax, who hailed from one of the first families of Virginia. In April 1755, Maj. Gen. Edward Braddock, commander in chief of His Majesty's forces in North America, met five Colonial governors here and asked them to tax colonists to finance the French and Indian War. Colonial legislatures refused, in one of the first instances of serious friction between the colonies and Britain. Braddock made Carlyle House his headquarters during that war. It is now furnished with period pieces, and the original large parlor and study have survived intact. Call or check the website for special events and lectures.

121 N. Fairfax St. (near Cameron St.). ☎ **703/549-2997.** www.carlylehouse.org. Admission $5 adults, $3 children 5–12, free for children 4 and under. Tues–Sat 10am–4pm; Sun noon–4pm. 45-min. tours depart on the hour and half-hour.

Christ Church ★   In continuous use since 1773, this sturdy redbrick Georgian-style church would be an important national landmark even if its two most distinguished members were not George Washington and Robert E. Lee. You can sit in their family pews. There have, of course, been many changes since Washington's day, but for the most part, the original structure remains, including the handblown glass in the windows. The bell tower, church bell, galleries, and organ were added by the early 1800s, the "wine-glass" pulpit in 1891. The **Old Parish Hall** now houses a gift shop and an exhibit on the history of the church. Do walk in the weathered graveyard, Alexandria's first and only burial ground until 1805.

118 N. Washington St. (at Cameron St.). ☎ **703/549-1450.** www.historicchristchurch.org. Free admission; donations accepted. Mon–Sat 9am–4pm; Sun 2–4pm. Gift shop Tues–Sat 10am–4pm. Sun services 8, 9, 11:15am, and 5pm. Closed federal holidays.

Gadsby's Tavern Museum ★   The center of social life in Colonial Alexandria was Gadsby's Tavern. Consisting of two buildings—a tavern dating from about 1785 and the City Hotel (1792)—it's named for a memorable tavern keeper, Englishman

John Gadsby, whose establishment was renowned for elegance and comfort. The rooms have been restored to their 18th- and 19th-century appearance. The second-floor ballroom, with its musicians' gallery, was the scene of Alexandria's most lavish parties, including Thomas Jefferson's inaugural banquet in 1801. George Washington's birthnight ball and banquet have been an annual tradition here since 1797. Gadsby's Tavern still serves Colonial fare (p. 57).

134 N. Royal St. © **703/838-4242.** www.gadsbystavern.org. Admission $5 adults, $3 children 5–12, free for children 4 and under. Museum Apr–Oct Tues–Sat 10am–5pm, Sun–Mon 1–5pm; Nov–Mar Wed–Sat 11am–4pm, Sun 1–4pm. 30-min. tours depart 15 min. before and after the hour.

Lee-Fendall House ☺ Revolutionary War hero Henry "Light-Horse Harry" Lee sold the original lot under this house to Philip Richard Fendall (a Lee on his mother's side), who built the house in 1785. It was home to 37 Lees of Virginia until 1903. John L. Lewis, the American labor leader, was its last private owner; his estate sold it to the Virginia Trust for Historic Preservation. The trust is slowly renovating the structure with the goal of restoring it to its 1850 appearance, right down to the paint colors. It's a treasure of Lee family furniture, heirlooms, and documents. You'll see the award-winning garden with its magnolia and chestnut trees, roses, and boxwood-lined paths.

614 Oronoco St. (at Washington St.). © **703/548-1789.** www.leefendallhouse.org. Admission $5 adults, $3 children 5–12, free for children 4 and under. Wed–Sat 10am–3pm; Sun 1–3pm. Closed mid-Dec to Jan. 30-min. tours depart on the hour.

Stabler-Leadbeater Apothecary Museum Founded in 1792 by Edward Stabler, a Quaker minister and an abolitionist, the Apothecary Shop occupied these two town houses until 1933. Martha Washington ordered castor oil shortly before her death in 1802, and Robert E. Lee was shopping here in 1859 when he received orders to quash John Brown's rebellion at Harpers Ferry, West Virginia. It was more than a drugstore, however, for in addition to tinctures, elixirs, and potions such as Dragon's Blood, it also sold products such as paint (Lee bought a few gallons for Arlington House, his mansion at what is now Arlington National Cemetery; see "A Side Trip to Arlington," later in this chapter). The shop looks like it did when the Stabler-Leadbeater family closed its doors for the last time, leaving behind a collection of more than 8,000 original objects. You'll see it all on a 30-minute guided tour.

105–107 S. Fairfax St. (btw. King and Prince sts.). © **703/836-3713.** www.apothecarymuseum.org. Admission $5 adults, $3 children 5–12, free for children 4 and under. Apr–Oct Tues–Sat 10am–5pm, Sun–Mon 1–5pm; Nov–Mar Wed–Sat 11am–4pm, Sun 1–4pm. Closed New Year's Day, Thanksgiving, and Christmas.

MORE ATTRACTIONS

Alexandria Black History Museum African Americans have been part of Alexandria's history from Colonial times to the present (incumbent Mayor William D. Euille is black). The Ramsay House Visitor Center distributes a fine brochure, *A Remarkable and Courageous Journey,* which describes 23 important black-history sites, with a map showing their locations. Start at this museum, in a building constructed in 1940 as the black community's first public library after a civil rights sit-in failed to integrate the Alexandria city library. It tells the story of local African Americans from the 18th century on.

902 Wythe St. © **703/838-4356.** www.alexblackhistory.org. Admission $2. Tues–Sat 10am–4pm. Closed New Year's Day, Martin Luther King Day, Easter, July 4th, Thanksgiving, and Christmas.

The Athenaeum A handsome Greek-revival building with a classic portico and Doric columns, the Athenaeum is home to the Northern Virginia Fine Arts

Association. Art exhibits here run the gamut from Matisse lithographs to shows of East Coast artists. The building, which dates from 1851, originally contained the Bank of the Old Dominion, whose operations were interrupted when Yankee troops used the building as their headquarters during the Civil War. Today, it hosts performances by the Alexandria Ballet and, during summer, the Alexandria Classical Guitar Festival. Guided tours are available on request.

201 Prince St. (at Lee St.). ✆ **703/548-0035.** www.nvfaa.org. Free admission; donations appreciated. Sun and Thurs–Fri noon–4pm; Sat 1–4pm. Gallery shows Apr–Nov.

Fort Ward Museum and Historic Site   Civil War buffs will enjoy taking a short drive from Old Town to this museum in a 45-acre city park on the site of one of the many Union forts erected to protect Washington, D.C. The Yankees occupied Alexandria the day after South Carolina seceded from the Union and held it for 4 years. It's the best preserved of the surviving forts and the only one with a museum. About 90% of the earthwork walls are preserved, and the Northwest Bastion has been restored, with six mounted guns (facing south waiting for the Confederates who never came). The museum explains life during the occupation and shows a 12-minute orientation video. Allow about an hour.

4301 W. Braddock Rd. ✆ **703/838-4848.** www.fortward.org. Free admission. Fort daily 9am–sunset. Museum Tues–Sat 9am–5pm; Sun noon–5pm. From Old Town, follow King St. west, go right on Kenwood St., then left on W. Braddock Rd.; continue for ¾ mile to the entrance on the right.

Friendship Firehouse Museum   Alexandria's first firefighting organization, the Friendship Fire Company, was established in 1774. Today's brick building was erected to replace an earlier one destroyed by fire in 1855. The museum not only exhibits firefighting paraphernalia dating back to the 18th century, but it also documents the Friendship Company's efforts to claim George Washington as one of its own founding fathers. Tours are given by the staff on request; they take about 20 minutes.

107 S. Alfred St. (btw. King and Prince sts.). ✆ **703/838-3891** or 838-4994. http://alexandriava.gov/ FriendshipFirehouse. Free admission. Sat–Sun 1–4pm. Closed New Year's Day, Dec 24, and Christmas.

George Washington Masonic National Memorial   Visible for miles from atop Shooter's Hill, this imposing neoclassical shrine is modeled after the ancient lighthouse at Alexandria, Egypt, and dedicated to American Freemasonry's most illustrious member. The heart of the memorial is the ornate hall dominated by a colossal 17-foot-tall bronze depicting Washington as lodge master. On either side are 46-foot-long murals, one depicting him laying the U.S. Capitol cornerstone in a Masonic ceremony, another of him and his Masonic brethren attending Christ Church in Philadelphia during the Revolution. Stained-glass windows in the hall honor 16 other patriots and Freemasons associated with Washington. (No, the U.S. was not created as part of a Masonic conspiracy!) Be sure to see a Washington family Bible in the fourth-floor museum. The ninth-floor observation deck offers a 360-degree view that takes in the Potomac River, all of Washington, D.C., the Maryland shore, and northern Virginia.

101 Callahan Dr. (at King St.). ✆ **703/683-2007.** www.gwmemorial.org. 1st and 2nd floor exhibits free admission; guided tour (includes tower exhibits and observation deck) $5 per person; free for children 12 and under. Apr–Sept daily 9am–4pm; Oct–Mar Mon–Sat 9am–4pm, Sun noon–4pm. Tours Mon–Sat 10am, 11:30am, 1:30pm, and 3pm; Sun noon, 1:30, and 3pm. Closed New Year's Day, Thanksgiving, and Christmas.

The Lyceum: Alexandria's History Museum   The Lyceum tells Alexandria's story from Colonial times through the 20th century. The brick-and-stucco Lyceum itself merits a visit. Built in 1839, it was designed in the Doric temple style (with imposing white columns) to serve as a lecture, meeting, and concert hall. The first floor originally contained the Alexandria Library and natural science and historical exhibits. It was an important center of Alexandria's cultural life until the Civil War, when Union forces used it as a hospital. Today it features changing exhibits and an ongoing series of lectures, concerts, and educational programs. An adjoining non-profit shop carries books, maps, toys, and gifts.

201 S. Washington St. (℗ **703/838-4994.** www.alexandriahistory.org. Admission $2. Mon–Sat 10am–5pm; Sun 1–5pm.

Old Presbyterian Meeting House Presbyterian congregations have worshiped in Virginia since Jamestown days, when Rev. Alexander Whittaker converted the American Indian princess Pocahontas. Scottish pioneers established this congregation in 1774. Its bell tolled continuously for 4 days after George Washington's death in December 1799, and Presbyterian, Episcopal, and Methodist ministers preached memorial services from its pulpit. Buried in the church graveyard are John and Sara Carlyle; Dr. James Craik, who treated Washington and dressed Lafayette's wounds at Brandywine; and an Unknown Soldier of the Revolutionary War. The parsonage was built in the flounder style in 1787. There's no guided tour, but there are recorded narratives in the church and graveyard.

321 S. Fairfax St. (at Duke St.). (℗ **703/549-6670.** www.opmh.org. Free admission. Mon–Fri 9am–4pm. Sun services 8:30 and 11am.

THREE SPECIALIZED ATTRACTIONS

In the former headquarters of Franklin, Armfield & Co., one of America's largest 19th-century slave traders, **Freedom House Museum,** 1315 Duke St. (℗ **703/836-2858;** www.freedomhousemuseum.org), between Payne and West streets, uses first-person accounts to tell the story of the more than 1,800 enslaved persons who were bought and sold here each year. A slave compound occupied most of this city block. The museum is operated by the Northern Virginia Urban League, which shares the building. It's open Monday to Friday 9am to 5pm. Admission is free, but donations are encouraged.

Much digging has taken place to study and preserve the past in Old Town, and some of the results are on display in the **Alexandria Archaeology Museum,** 105 N. Union St. (℗ **703/838-4399;** www.alexandriaarchaeology.org), on the third floor of the Torpedo Factory Art Center. It shares space with a working laboratory. Admission is free, and it's open Tuesday to Friday 10am to 3pm, Saturday 10am to 5pm, and Sunday 1 to 5pm.

If you've ever had a clever idea for an invention you thought would revolutionize the world (and make you rich), you'll likely appreciate the **National Inventors Hall of Fame and Museum,** in the U.S. Patent & Trademark Office's Madison Building, 600 Dulany St. (℗ **571/272-0095;** www.invent.org). High-tech displays explain how inventors brought famous products into being. Admission is free. It is open Monday to Friday 9am to 5pm and Saturday noon to 5pm. From the King Street Metro station, follow Diagonal Road south to Dulany Street.

GUIDED TOURS

Though it's easy to see Alexandria on your own (see "Walking Tour: Old Town Alexandria," below), your experience will be enhanced by having a knowledgeable local guide. Take your pick among **Alexandria's Footsteps to the Past** (℗ **703/683-3451** or 703/850-7138; www.footstepstothepast.com), **Alexandria Tours of Old Town** (℗ **703/329-1122**), or the **Old Town Experience** (℗ **703/836-0694;**

www.alexandriacitywebsite.com/OldTownExperience.htm). Even if you see everything on your own during the day, you'll enjoy spooking around Old Town after dark with **Alexandria's Original Ghost & Graveyard Tours** (✆ **703/519-1749** or 703/548-0100; www.alexcolonialtours.com). They usually explore Old Town's streets and back alleys (call for the schedule and to make reservations). The Ramsay House Visitor Center (see "Visitor Information," earlier in this chapter) has their schedules and will make reservations, which are required. All three charge $15 for adults and $5 for children 7 to 13. Children 6 and under are free.

WALKING TOUR: OLD TOWN ALEXANDRIA

START:	**Ramsay House Visitor Center, King Street at Fairfax Street.**
FINISH:	**Torpedo Factory Art Center, Waterfront at Cameron Street.**
TIME:	**Allow approximately 2½ hours, not including museum and shopping stops.**
BEST TIMES:	**Anytime Tuesday through Sunday.**
WORST TIMES:	**Monday, when many historic sites are closed.**

You'll get a glimpse into the 18th century as you stroll along Alexandria's brick-paved sidewalks, lined with Colonial residences, historic houses and churches, museums, shops, and restaurants. This walk ends at the Potomac waterfront, no longer a center of commercial shipping but now home to an arts center.

Begin your walk at the:

1 Ramsay House Visitor Center

Built around 1724, the center has a Dutch barn roof and an English garden. It's located at 221 King St., at Fairfax Street, in the heart of the historic district. This is the best place to get your bearings.

Head north on Fairfax Street to:

2 Carlyle House Historic Park

This elegant 1753 manor house is set off from the street by a low wall.

Continue north on Fairfax to the corner. Turn left on Cameron Street, past the back of the old city hall, to the redbrick buildings across Royal Street, known as:

3 Take a Break 🍽

Gadsby's Tavern (p. 57) is the perfect place for a sandwich or salad during your tour of Old Town. The 18th-century complex houses a museum of 18th-century antiques, while the hotel portion is an Early American–style restaurant.

Continue west on Cameron Street and turn right on Saint Asaph Street. At Queen Street, you can see:

4 No. 523 Queen St.

At 7 feet wide, it's Alexandria's narrowest house.

Continuing north on Saint Asaph, you'll come to:

Walking Tour: Old Town Alexandria

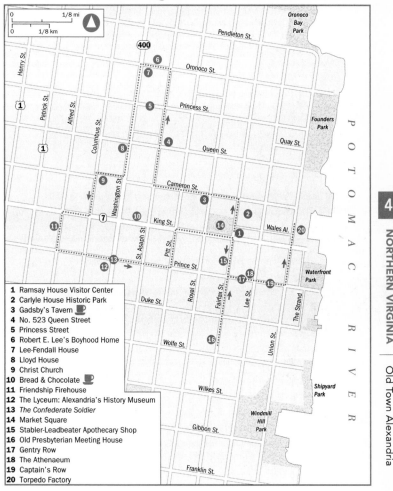

1 Ramsay House Visitor Center
2 Carlyle House Historic Park
3 Gadsby's Tavern
4 No. 523 Queen Street
5 Princess Street
6 Robert E. Lee's Boyhood Home
7 Lee-Fendall House
8 Lloyd House
9 Christ Church
10 Bread & Chocolate
11 Friendship Firehouse
12 The Lyceum: Alexandria's History Museum
13 *The Confederate Soldier*
14 Market Square
15 Stabler-Leadbeater Apothecary Shop
16 Old Presbyterian Meeting House
17 Gentry Row
18 The Athenaeum
19 Captain's Row
20 Torpedo Factory

5 Princess Street

The cobble paving stones are original (and you'll see why heavy traffic is banned here).

One block farther north on Saint Asaph, turn left at Oronoco Street. The house on your right at number 607 was:

6 Robert E. Lee's Boyhood Home

Lee's family rented this Federal-style mansion at 607 Oronoco St., where he lived from age 5 until departing for West Point in 1825. Today it's a private residence.

Across Oronoco Street, at the corner of Washington Street, is the:

7 Lee-Fendall House

This gracious white-clapboard residence was home to several generations of Lees. Enter through the pretty Colonial garden.

Head south (left) on Washington Street, a busy commercial thoroughfare, to Queen Street and cross over to:

8 Lloyd House

A beautiful late Georgian home (1797), this house is now part of the Alexandria Library and holds a fascinating collection of documents, books, and records on the city and state.

Proceed south on Washington Street to the quiet graveyard entrance behind:

9 Christ Church

The Washingtons and Lees worshiped in this Episcopal church.

Leave by the front entrance, on Columbus Street, and turn left to King Street.

10 Take a Break 🍺

A cappuccino-and-pastry pit stop at **Bread & Chocolate, 611 King St. (p. 60),** is guaranteed to revive flagging spirits. Sandwiches and salads are also available at this casual spot.

From King Street, turn left on Alfred Street, to the small but historic:

11 Friendship Firehouse

You can see an extensive collection of antique firefighting equipment here.

Exit the firehouse right, turn left on Prince for 2 blocks, and turn right on Washington.

12 The Lyceum: Alexandria's History Museum

Built in 1839 as the city's first cultural center, this is the municipal historical museum today. The shop has a lovely selection of crafts, silver, and other gift items.

Just outside the museum, at the intersection of Washington and Prince streets stands:

13 The Confederate Soldier

The sculptor modeled this dejected bronze figure after one in the painting *Appomattox* by John A. Elder. Confederate-soldier statues in Southern towns traditionally face north (in case the Yankees return), but Alexandria's looks southward, perhaps because Union soldiers occupied the city during the war.

Continue walking east on Prince Street to Pitt Street, then turn left to King Street. Turn right and you'll see the fountain in:

14 Market Square

This open space along King Street from Royal to Fairfax in front of the modern but Williamsburg-style Town Hall has been used as a town market and meeting ground since 1749. Today, the market is held on Saturday mornings.

Turn right on Fairfax Street to the quaint:

15 Stabler-Leadbeater Apothecary Shop

A remarkable collection of early medical ware and handblown glass containers is on display here.

4

NORTHERN VIRGINIA | Old Town Alexandria

Head south on Fairfax Street to Duke Street, to the:

16 Old Presbyterian Meeting House

George Washington's funeral sermons were preached in this 18th-century church in 1799. The graveyard has a marker commemorating the Unknown Soldier of the Revolutionary War.

Retrace your steps back to Prince Street and turn right. Between Fairfax Street and Lee Street you'll see:

17 Gentry Row

The local leaders who made their homes in these three-story town houses in the 18th and 19th centuries gave their name to the row.

At the corner of Prince and Lee streets is:

18 The Athenaeum

It's a handsome Greek-revival structure that now houses contemporary art shows.

Cross Lee Street to:

19 Captain's Row

This is a pretty cobblestone section of Prince Street. You're now in sight of the Potomac riverfront and may want to stroll down to the little waterfront park at the foot of Prince Street for a panoramic view of the river.

Continue north on Union Street, where you can begin your shopping expedition at:

20 Torpedo Factory Art Center

You can wander the arts-and-crafts center's studios and galleries, which are open to the public.

POTOMAC RIVER CRUISES

After you've seen Old Town's attractions on foot, you can get a view of the city from the water by taking a cruise operated by **Potomac Riverboat Company** (© **877/502-2628** or 703/548-9000; www.potomacriverboatco.com), based at the city dock behind the Torpedo Factory Art Center at the foot of King Street. Its 40-minute Alexandria Seaport Tour is fine for taking photos of Old Town from out on the river, and it's especially suitable if you are traveling with children. This tour costs $12 for adults and $6 for children ages 2 to 12. Much more scenic is the 1½-hour Washington Monuments Tour, as it goes upriver for super views of the nation's capital. This tour costs $26 for adults and $14 for children ages 2 to 12, but it's worth the extra money. All cruises run daily from June to September and weekends during May and October. Check at the dockside booth or call for information and reservations.

The company also has cruises to Mount Vernon; see p. 65.

Outdoor Activities

This part of northern Virginia has two first-rate hiking, biking, and running trails. A 17-mile paved trail starts at Memorial Bridge and borders the **George Washington Memorial Parkway** south to Mount Vernon, passing through Old Town on the way (see "A Scenic Drive Along the Potomac River," later in this chapter).

Beginning in the Shirlington area, on I-395 in neighboring Arlington, the **Washington & Old Dominion (W&OD) Trail** follows Four-Mile Run Drive and Glencarlyn Park northwest to an old railroad bed, which then proceeds 45 miles through

Leesburg to Purcellville (see "The Hunt Country," later in this chapter). **Big Wheel Bikes,** 2 Prince St., at the Strand (℘ **703/739-2300;** www.bigwheelbikes.com), rents a wide range of bikes beginning at $5 an hour. It's open Monday to Friday 11am to 7pm, Saturday 10am to 6pm, and Sunday 11am to 5pm.

Shopping

Old Town has hundreds of boutiques, antiques stores, art galleries, and gift shops selling everything from souvenir T-shirts to 18th-century reproductions. Most of the best stores are interspersed among the multitude of restaurants and offices on King Street from the waterfront to the Metrorail station. Plan to spend a fair amount of time browsing between visits to historic sites. A guide to the city's 50-plus antiques and collectibles stores is available at the visitor center (you'll pay a premium for antiques here, so you may want to wait to buy if you're going to Fredericksburg; see chapter 5).

One essential stop is the **Torpedo Factory Art Center,** 105 N. Union St., between King and Cameron streets on the Potomac River (℘ **703/838-4565;** www. torpedofactory.org). This block-long, three-story waterfront structure was built by the U.S. Navy in 1918 and operated as a torpedo shell-case factory until the early 1950s, then used as storage for artifacts from the Smithsonian Institution. Today, it houses 84 working studios where artists and craftspeople create and sell their works. The shops and galleries are open daily 10am to 5pm (to 9pm Thurs). It's closed New Year's Day, Easter, July 4th, Thanksgiving, and Christmas.

Where to Stay

The hotels recommended below are either in the heart of Old Town or near the King Street Metrorail station. Also here is **Embassy Suites Hotel Old Town,** 1900 Diagonal Rd. (www.embassysuites.com; ℘ **800/362-2779** or 703/684-5900), where every unit has a kitchen.

In the less convenient northern end of Old Town are the **Best Western Old Colony Inn,** 1101 N. Washington St. (www.bestwestern.com; ℘ **800/528-1234** or 730/739-2222); **Holiday Inn Hotel & Suites,** 625 First St. (www.holiday-inn.com; ℘ **800/465-4329** or 703/548-6300); and the **Executive Club Suites,** 610 Bashford Lane (℘ **800/535-2582** or 703/739-2582), where every unit is an apartment. Nearby, **Sheraton Suites Alexandria,** 801 N. Saint Asaph St. (www.starwood hotels.com; ℘ **800/325-3535** or 703/836-4700), provides only suites, while the high-rise **Crowne Plaza Old Town Alexandria,** 901 N. Fairfax St., at Montgomery Street (www.crowneplaza.com; ℘ **800/972-3159** or 703/683-6000), stands near the river, giving some of its 258 rooms water views.

Hampton Inn–King Street Metro   Less than a block east of the Amtrak and King Street Metro stations, this six-story hotel is a bit more upscale than most of its Hampton Inn sisters. The reasonably spacious rooms are decorated in typical Hampton fashion. The best are those on the upper floors, which have views over the city. Continental breakfast is served in the lobby, which has a 24-hour coffee and juice dispenser. The outdoor pool is open during summer.

1616 King St., Alexandria, VA 22314. www.hamptoninn.com. ℘ **800/426-7866** or 703/299-9900. Fax 703/299-9937. 80 units. $109–$289 double. Rates include continental breakfast. AE, DISC, MC, V. Self-parking $15. **Amenities:** Health club. *In room:* A/C, TV, hair dryer, Wi-Fi.

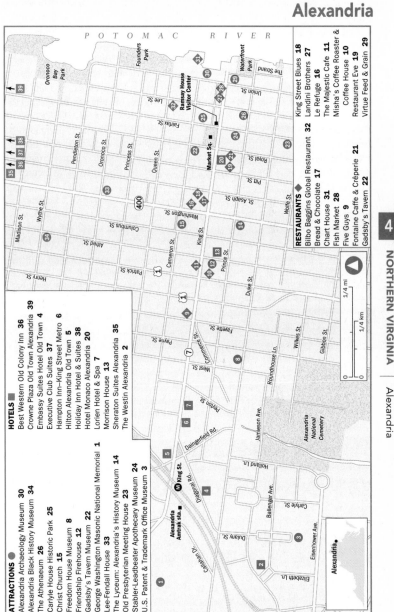

Hilton Alexandria Old Town ★   Across King Street from the Amtrak and Metro stations, this seven-story Hilton has spacious rooms furnished with antique reproductions. Those on the concierge level come equipped with marble bathrooms and feather beds. Off the lobby and with outdoor seating in warm weather, the restaurant offers seafood, prime steaks, and a little music to go with your meal. In addition, you can walk into its wine room and pick your vintage (couples can reserve a table for private dining).

1767 King St., Alexandria, VA 22314. www.hiltonalexandria.com. © **800/445-8667** or 703/837-0440. Fax 703/837-0454. 241 units. $169–$299 double; $269–$319 suite. AE, DC, DISC, MC, V. Self-parking $20. **Amenities:** Restaurant; bar; concierge-level rooms; health club; pool; room service; sauna. In room: A/C, TV, hair dryer, Wi-Fi ($13 per 24 hr.).

Hotel Monaco Alexandria ★★   This luxury hotel is ideally located in the heart of Old Town's historic district. With a Union soldier's blue uniform providing the color scheme, the spacious units evoke Alexandria's 19th-century history. Some have balconies overlooking the hotel's central courtyard. This is the most dog friendly hotel in Alexandria, with no restrictions on breed or size. The pooches get treated to twice-weekly Doggie Happy Hours and have their own water bowls in the sidewalk seating area of **Jackson 20,** the hotel's hip restaurant.

480 King St., Alexandria, VA 22314. www.monaco-alexandria.com. © **800/368-5047** or 703/549-6080. Fax 703/684-6508. 241 units. $170–$280 double; from $200 suites. AE, DC, DISC, MC, V. Parking $24. Dogs accepted. **Amenities:** Restaurant; bar; executive or concierge-level rooms; health club; pool; room service. In room: A/C, TV, hair dryer, Wi-Fi ($10/day; free for Kempton loyalty members).

Lorien Hotel & Spa ★★   A sister of the Hotel Monaco Alexandria and the Morrison House, this 2009-vintage luxurious hotel anchors a little complex built around a brick courtyard virtually hidden from busy King Street. Inside is a mix of traditional and modernist, with all the latest amenities wrapped in muted colors designed to smooth the senses. Some units have claw-foot bathtubs, and a few suites have balconies overlooking King Street. The three restaurants include the fine dining **Brabo** and its wine tasting room. The Lorien is Alexandria's only hotel with a full-service spa.

1600 King St., Alexandria, VA 22314. www.lorienhotelandspa.com. © **877/956-7436** or 703/894-3434. 107 units. $104–$240 double; $180–$240 suite. AE, DISC, MC, V. Valet parking $27; no self-parking. Pets accepted. **Amenities:** 3 restaurants; 3 bars; health club; room service; spa. In-room: A/C, TV, fridge, hair dryer, Wi-Fi ($10/day; free for Kempton loyalty members).

Morrison House ★★★   Although it was built in 1985, this boutique hotel, one of Virginia's finest, was designed after the grand manor houses of the Federal period and thus fits right into Old Town. The enchantment begins the moment you ascend the curving staircase to its white-columned portico, where a friendly butler greets you at the door of the marble foyer. It's not stuffy by any means; a polite but relaxed informality reigns here. The **Grille at Morrison House** offers fine American fare, and locals and guests alike pack the lounge on Tuesday, Thursday, Friday, and Saturday nights to hear live music. Each of the spacious, luxuriously appointed guest quarters is individually decorated and furnished with Federal-period reproductions. Some have mahogany four-poster beds, brass chandeliers, and decorative fireplaces. In your room, you'll find two phones, fresh flowers, down comforters, and robes.

116 S. Alfred St., Alexandria, VA 22314. www.morrisonhouse.com. © **800/367-0800** or 703/838-8000. Fax 703/684-6283. 45 units. $189–$399 double; $299–$499 suite. Packages available. AE, DISC, MC, V. Valet parking $25. **Amenities:** Restaurant; bar; babysitting; access to nearby health club; room service. In room: A/C, TV, hair dryer, Wi-Fi ($10/day; free for Kempton loyalty members).

The Westin Alexandria Facing the U.S. District Courthouse where 9/11 terrorist Zacarias Moussaoui and other notorious criminals were convicted, this nine-story, boomerang-shaped hotel is one of the centerpieces of the Carlyle development south of the King Street Metro station. Starting with the pendulum swinging below a sculpture-like clock standing tall in the lobby, the decor evokes inventions approved by the nearby U.S. Office of Patents and Trademarks. So does the Edison Ballroom, one of eight meeting spaces totaling 20,000 square feet. Translated: You'll find more groups and conferences than individual guests here. Rooms are high tech, both in amenities and appearance, with sleek dark furniture contrasting against stark white bedding. Upper-floor units have views of the surrounding suburbs.

400 Courthouse Sq. (at Jamieson Ave.), Alexandria, VA 22314. www.starwoodhotels.com. (✆) **800/WESTIN1** [937-8461] or 703/253-8600. Fax 703/253-8605. 319 units. $125–$500 double. AE, DC, DISC, MC, V. Valet parking $24 Sun–Thurs, $12 Fri–Sat. **Amenities:** Restaurant; bar; concierge; executive or concierge-level rooms; pool; room service. *In room:* A/C, TV, hair dryer, Wi-Fi ($9.95 per 24 hr.).

BED & BREAKFASTS

Several private Old Town homes, many of them historic properties, offer B&B accommodations under the aegis of **Alexandria & Arlington Bed & Breakfast Networks,** PO Box 25319, Arlington, VA 22202 (www.aabbn.com; (✆) **888/549-3415** or 703/549-3415), which also represents properties in adjoining Arlington and as far away as the Hunt Country. Check the website for a complete list and rates.

Where to Eat

One of the Washington area's most popular dining destinations, Old Town has many more restaurants than it does historical attractions. You'll find cuisines from around the world offered in every price range along King Street. Don't be afraid to stroll along and pick one of your own. You'll know by the number of customers who's getting nods from Old Town's affluent citizenry.

My favorite joint for coffee and pastries is **Misha's Coffee Roaster & Coffee House,** 102 Patrick St. ((✆) **703/548-4089;** www.mishascoffee.com), which hearkens back to the beatnik coffeehouses of the 1950s, with real art on the walls and thrice-read newspapers scattered about. It is open Monday to Saturday 6am to 8pm and Sunday 6:30am to 8pm.

The only place to dine beside the Potomac River is the **Chart House,** 1 Cameron St. ((✆) **703/684-5080;** www.chart-house.com), the local member of the somewhat expensive national seafood restaurant chain. It has alfresco dining in good weather. It is open daily 11:30am to 10pm.

EXPENSIVE

Gadsby's Tavern ★★ AMERICAN An essential part of the Old Town experience is to dine here, behind the portals where Washington reviewed his troops for the last time. Period furnishings and wood-plank floors re-create a Colonial atmosphere, while costumed waitstaff and balladeers make for a fun time along the lines of Colonial Williamsburg's taverns (the chow is much better here). You'll dine from the same kind of pewter and china our ancestors used, and Sally Lunn bread is baked daily. Dinner entrees usually include one of George Washington's favorites, half a duckling stuffed with fruit and served with Madeira gravy. The courtyard serves as an outdoor dining area during fine weather.

138 N. Royal St. (✆) **703/548-1288.** www.gadsbystavernrestaurant.com. Reservations recommended for dinner. Main courses $22–$24. AE, DISC, MC, V. Mon–Sat 11:30am–3pm and 5:30–10pm; Sun 11am–3pm and 5:30–10pm.

Irish-born Cathal Armstrong and his wife, Meshelle, are the brains behind several of Old Town's top restaurants. Beginning with Restaurant Eve, which they named for their daughter, they have expanded their little empire to include the Majestic, Virtual Feed & Grain, Eammon's Irish Chipper, and a 1920s speakeasy known simply as PX. In 2011 Cathal was one of five Virginia chefs named as semifinalists in the annual James Beard Restaurant and Chefs Awards. (Another was Dale Reitzer of Acacia Midtown in Richmond, p. 214).

Landini Brothers ★ ITALIAN   The classic, delicate cuisine of Tuscany is consistently fine at this rustic, almost grottolike restaurant with stone walls, a flagstone floor, and rough-hewn beams overhead. It's especially charming at night by candlelight. There's additional seating in a lovely upstairs dining room. Everything is homemade—the pasta, the crusty Italian bread, and the desserts. Things might get underway with prosciutto and melon or Top Neck clams on the half shell, followed by prime aged beef tenderloin medallions sautéed with garlic, mushrooms, and rosemary in a Barolo wine sauce.

115 King St. ✆ **703/836-8404.** www.landinibrothers.com. Reservations recommended. Main courses $23–$34; pastas $17–$19. AE, DC, DISC, MC, V. Mon–Sat 11:30am–11pm; Sun 4–10pm.

Restaurant Eve ★★★ AMERICAN   Old Town's finest restaurant, this exquisitely designed bistro was the first creation of talented chef Cathal Armstrong and his wife, Meshelle. They really have two restaurants in one here. Residing under a huge skylight, their casual Bistro serves an a la carte menu for lunch and dinner. The Chef's Tasting Room is a more formal venue featuring five-course fixed-priced dinners. In both, the menus change up to 60 times a year to make use of fresh, mostly organic produce from local farms and markets. The rich bouillabaisse with cod and clams is a constant in the Bistro. A good way to sample the fare here without filing for bankruptcy is the $15 Lickity Split-Lounge Lunch Menu, offering a choice of two items such as a salad of local asparagus and Virginia ham.

110 S. Pitt St. ✆ **703/684-4100.** www.restauranteve.com. Reservations recommended. Main courses $36–$40; 5-course tasting menu $120. AE, DISC, MC, V. Mon–Fri 11:30am–2:30pm and 5:30–9:30pm; Sat 5:30–9:30pm. Bar lounge to 12:30am Fri–Sat.

MODERATE

Bilbo Baggins Global Restaurant ★ ✦ INTERNATIONAL   Named for the lead character in *The Hobbit*, this charming restaurant has rustic wide-plank floors, wood-paneled walls, oak tables, and a brick-oven centerpiece. Upstairs is another dining room with stained-glass windows. It adjoins a skylit wine bar with windows overlooking Queen Street treetops. Candlelit at night, it becomes even cozier. The menu changes frequently to reflect seasonal specialties. At dinner, you'll enjoy entrees such as a wasabi salmon filet with a ragout of fresh asparagus and wild mushrooms. An extensive wine list is available (more than 30 boutique wines are offered by the glass and another 150 by the bottle). The bar offers lighter and less expensive fare.

208 Queen St. ✆ **703/683-0300.** www.bilbobaggins.net. Reservations accepted only for parties of 6 or more. Main courses $17–$24. AE, DISC, MC, V. Mon–Thurs 11:30am–2:30pm and 4:30–10:30pm; Fri–Sat 11am–10:30pm; Sun 10am–2:30pm and 3:30–9:30pm. Closed Christmas.

Obama Burgers

Everyone from panhandlers to Old Town's gentry can be seen hauling bags of juicy hamburgers, hot dogs, and seasoned french fries from the Old Town branch of **Five Guys Burgers and Fries,** 107 N. Fayette St. (© **703/549-7991;** www.fiveguys.com). This order-at-the-counter joint hearkens back to pre-McDonald's days when hamburgers weren't frozen beforehand and fresh potatoes were cut on the premises.

Born in nearby Arlington in 1986, the old-fashioned idea was so successful that more than 450 branches have sprung up in 30 states. Patrons at a Five Guys in Washington, D.C., were shocked when President Obama came in and took home a large sack of burgers for the White House staff. Nothing costs more than $7. The Old Town branch is open daily 11am to 10pm.

Fish Market AMERICAN Although the popular Fish Market has grown to include the building next door, its original corner location is a warehouse that's over 200 years old. Heavy beams, terra-cotta tile floors, exposed brick and stucco walls adorned with nautical antiques, copper pots over a fireplace, copper-topped bars, and saloon doors all lend an old-time ambience. If you're lucky, in fine weather you might get a table for two on a one-table-wide balcony above King Street. Although it's unexceptional, the fare is passable and reasonably priced. Offerings include Chesapeake-style (broiled, fried, or grilled) fish, shrimp, oysters, and crab. A bowl of seafood stew is warming on a cold winter's day.

105 King St. © 703/836-5676. www.fishmarketva.com. Reservations accepted for groups. Main courses $9–$25; salads and sandwiches $9–$15. AE, DISC, MC, V. Sun–Thurs 11:15am–1am; Fri–Sat 11:15am–2am (kitchen closes at 12:15am).

Le Refuge ★ 🍴 TRADITIONAL FRENCH Jean-François Chaufour's charming little restaurant, a local mainstay since 1983, is typically French country. His special three-course pre- and after-theater dinner is a great buy: It includes soup or salad; fresh catch of the day, leg of lamb, or calves' liver; and crème brûlée or peach melba for dessert. There's a lunch version, too. Regular house specialties include bouillabaisse, classic rack of lamb, rainbow trout amandine, and chicken Dijonnaise. Nightly specials feature produce fresh from the market.

127 N. Washington St. © 703/548-4661. www.lerefugealexandria.com. Reservations recommended. Main courses $19–$29; fixed-price 3-course dinner $28. AE, MC, V. Mon–Sat 11:30am–2:30pm and 5–10pm.

The Majestic ★★ AMERICAN The bright neon sign recalls the 1950s when a small town cafe occupied this storefront. Now under the same management as Restaurant Eve (Cathal and Meshelle Armstrong and their partners), it's one of Old Town's best bistros. The comfort food here is very familiar and very good: fried green tomatoes, meatloaf, calves' liver, roast chicken with gravy, New York strip steaks, and whole grilled fish. Nana's Sunday Dinner is family-style dinner on Sunday evenings for $22 per person.

911 King St. © 703/837-9117. www.majesticcafe.com. Reservations recommended. Main courses $17–$24. AE, DC, DISC, MC, V. Mon–Thurs 11:30am–2:30pm and 5:30–10pm; Fri–Sat 11:30am–2:30pm and 5:30–10:30pm; Sun 1–9pm.

Virtue Feed & Grain 🍴 Restaurant Eve's Cathal and Meshelle Armstrong and their partners, Maria Chicas and Todd Thrasher, magnificently converted a 19th-century feed-and-grain store into this stunning bistro. Except for knocking out parts of the brick walls to allow for windows and installing skylights, they preserved as much as possible of the existing structure and brought in relics from old barns and other buildings from as far away as Wisconsin. The rustic but sophisticated results include exposed wooden support beams and old-fashioned swings suspended on chains from the ceiling. There is no freezer in the kitchen, which uses only fresh vegetables, meat, and seafood culled from local farms, butchers, and fish markets. The potpourri menu ranges from unusual dishes, such as oxtail salad, to roast chicken and other familiar fare.

116 S. Union St. ⓒ **571/970-3669.** www.virtuefeedandgrain.com. Reservations accepted for ⅓ of tables. Main courses $14–$22; sandwiches $7–$10. AE, DISC, MC, V. Mon–Thurs 11:30am–3pm and 5:30–10pm; Fri–Sat 11:30am–3pm and 5:30–11pm; Sun 11:30am–2:30pm and 5:30–10pm.

INEXPENSIVE

Stalls sell inexpensive eats in the **Torpedo Factory Food Pavilion** between the Torpedo Factory Art Center, at King and Cameron streets, and the riverfront Chart House restaurant. It is open daily 11am to 9:30pm.

Bread & Chocolate CONTINENTAL/BAKERY   Part of a successful chain, this cheerful European-style restaurant offers fresh breads, croissants, napoleons, chocolate truffle cakes, Grand Marnier cakes, Bavarian fruit tarts, and other goodies. At breakfast, you can get a caffe mocha and an almond croissant, or an omelet with potatoes and a slice of melon. The rest of the day, soups, salads, sandwiches, and light main courses are available to help keep you walking.

611 King St. ⓒ **703/548-0992.** www.breadandchocolate.net. Reservations not accepted. Most items $4–$12. AE, DISC, MC, V. Mon–Wed 7am–7pm; Thurs–Sat 7am–9pm; Sun 8am–6pm.

Fontaine Caffe & Crêperie ★ 🍴 FRENCH   This little bistro-style cafe specializes in savory *ble noir* (gluten-free buckwheat) crepes from the Brittany region of France. Here the thin pancakes are wrapped around a variety of ingredients, from grilled bratwurst and Italian sausage to lentils, spinach, and tomatoes simmered in coriander coconut curry sauce. Sweet crepes are made using regular wheat flour but are even tastier. Weekend brunches add French toast and breakfast bruschetta (it's like eggs Benedict over Italian toast).

119 S. Royal St. ⓒ **703/535-8151.** www.fontainecaffe.com. Reservations not accepted. Crepes $6–$14. AE, MC, V. Mon–Fri 11:30am–2:30pm and 5:30–10pm; Sat 10am–3pm and 5–10pm; Sun 10am–3pm.

King Street Blues ★ 🍴 AMERICAN   This often-noisy and occasionally raucous (especially the first-floor bar) roadhouse is the best place in town for an inexpensive meal. It occupies all three floors of a small brick building with windows painted on its exterior brick wall. Brian McCall, a local artist, has covered almost every inch of the interior walls with papier-mâché figures and murals, all done with sly tongue-in-cheek good humor. A lively crowd packs the place for the house meatloaf (with a memorable accompaniment of garlic mashed potatoes), Southern-fried catfish, chicken-fried steak, and house-smoked baby back ribs in a sweet yet spicy sauce (you can take a bottle home).

112 N. Saint Asaph St. ⓒ **703/836-8800.** www.kingstreetblues.com. Reservations accepted. Salads and sandwiches $8–$10; main courses $10–$20. AE, DISC, MC, V. Mon–Thurs 11:30am–10pm; Fri–Sat 11:30am–11pm; Sun 11am–10pm. Bar stays open later.

Alexandria After Dark

The free weekly **City Paper** (www.washingtoncitypaper.com) and the monthly magazine **Old Town Crier** (www.oldtowncrier.com) are good sources of news about the local bar and music scene.

King Street restaurants are the center of Alexandria's ongoing club and bar scene. Especially noteworthy are **Two-Nineteen,** 219 King St. (☏ **703/549-1141;** www.219restaurant.com), which features live jazz Tuesday to Saturday nights in the Basin Street Lounge; the **Fish Market,** 105 King St. (☏ **703/836-5676;** p. 59), with either a pianist or a guitarist Thursday to Saturday nights; and **Murphy's Grand Irish Pub,** 713 King St. (☏ **703/548-1717;** www.murphyspub.com), the town's best Gaelic bar with live Irish bands to accompany corned beef and cabbage on weekends.

A modern rendition of a 1920s speakeasy, **PX** is Old Town's most refined place for a sophisticated cocktail. It's upstairs above **Eammon's Dublin Chipper,** an Irish pub at 728 King St. (☏ **703/299-8384;** www.eamonnsdublinchipper.com). PX is open Wednesday to Saturday from 6pm onward, or whenever the blue lantern is lit or the pirate flag is flying outside Eammon's. As in the Prohibition era, you must knock on the door to be admitted.

An older crowd likes to gather for live music on Tuesday, Thursday, Friday, and Saturday evenings in the cozy lounge of the **Morrison House,** 116 S. Alfred St. (☏ **703/838-8000;** p. 56). Sometimes you can hear wannabe professional singers belt out some fine jazz and even an aria or two.

Built about 1914 as a vaudeville house, the restored **Old Town Theater,** 815½ King St. (☏ **703/683-8888;** www.oldtowntheater.com), shows second-run movies. It serves hot dogs, burgers, pizzas, and a few main courses. Call or check the website for the schedule.

The **Birchmere,** 3901 Mount Vernon Ave., south of Glebe Road (☏ **703/549-5919;** www.birchmere.com), is the Washington area's prime showcase for nationally known bluegrass, country, and folk stars. Call or check the website for the schedule and reservations—which are absolutely necessary when top performers appear.

A Side Trip to Arlington

ARLINGTON NATIONAL CEMETERY ★★★

It's an easy excursion from Old Town to the famous **Arlington National Cemetery,** a cherished shrine commemorating the lives given by members of the U.S. armed forces. Its seemingly endless rows of graves mark the mortal remains of the honored dead, both the known and the unknown, who served in conflicts from the Revolutionary War to the present.

Start at the **visitor center** (☏ **703/607-8052;** www.arlingtoncemetery.mil), where you can get a free map—and if you have family buried here, find out where. Be sure to pick up the map, for it's easy to get lost in the maze of pathways. Admission to the cemetery is free. It's open daily 8am to 7pm from April through September and daily 8am to 5pm October through March, with the exceptions of Christmas and New Year's Day. You can drive here from Old Town via U.S. 1 and Va. 110, but it's easier to ride **Metrorail's Blue Line** from the King Street station. Parking in the cemetery lot costs $1.75 for the first 3 hours, $2.50 per hour thereafter.

Next door is the **Women in Military Service for America Memorial** (☏ **800/222-2294** or 703/533-1155; www.womensmemorial.org), honoring all women who have served in the military. Inside, there's a computerized registry of more than 250,000 women veterans.

This quiet expanse of green is a walker's paradise, but you can ride around via the **Tourmobile** (© 888/868-7707 or 202/554-5100; www.tourmobile.com). Service is continuous daily from 8:30am to 6:30pm April through September and 8am to 5pm October through March. Tickets cost $8.50 for adults, $7.50 for seniors, and $4.25 for children 3 to 11. At the visitor center you can also purchase Tourmobile combination tickets that include major sights in the capital, allowing you to stop and reboard when you're ready. Tourmobiles also depart here for Mount Vernon (see below).

You can spend hours looking at gravestones here, but the one you must see is the poignant **John F. Kennedy Gravesite,** marked by its eternal flame. Jacqueline Kennedy Onassis is buried next to her first husband. His brothers, Robert F. Kennedy and Edward M. Kennedy, are buried nearby. Looking north, you'll have a splendid view of the capital city across the river (during his presidency, Kennedy once remarked of this spot, "I could stay here forever").

For an even more spectacular view, walk up the ridge above the Kennedy graves to **Arlington House, The Robert E. Lee Memorial** (© 703/557-0613; www.nps. gov/arho), a plantation manse built by George Washington Parke Custis, Martha Washington's grandson by her first marriage, after his daughter married a young Virginian named Robert E. Lee. The couple lived here for 30 years before General Lee left in 1861 to join the Confederate cause. He never returned. To spite him, the federal government turned his front yard into a cemetery for slain Union soldiers. Admission is free. The mansion is open daily from 9am to 5pm (closed Christmas and New Year's Day).

Beyond the mansion, America's most distinguished honor guard slowly marches before the white-marble **Tomb of the Unknowns,** which holds the remains of unidentified combatants slain during World War I. Unknowns from World War II and the Korean War are in the crypts on the plaza in front of it. A crypt for an unknown Vietnam veteran remains vacant since modern forensic science has identified all victims of that conflict. The changing of the guard ceremony—an impressive ritual of rifle maneuvers, heel clicking, and military salutes—takes place daily every half-hour April to September, every hour on the hour the rest of the year.

Adjoining the tomb is the Greek-revival outdoor **Memorial Amphitheater,** used for holiday services, particularly on Memorial Day when the sitting president or vice president attends.

AT THE CEMETERY'S EDGES

On the northern periphery of the cemetery, just off Va. 110 about 1½ miles north of the Kennedy graves, stands the famous **United States Marine Corps War Memorial** (www.nps.gov/gwmp/marinecorpswarmemorial.htm), better known as the Iwo Jima Memorial. The iconic statue is based on news photographer Joe Rosenthal's Pulitzer Prize–winning photo of five Marines and one navy corpsman raising Old Glory on Iwo Jima in February 1945. The memorial grounds are used for military parades in summer, when there is a free shuttle from the visitor center. Call © 703/289-2500 for the schedule.

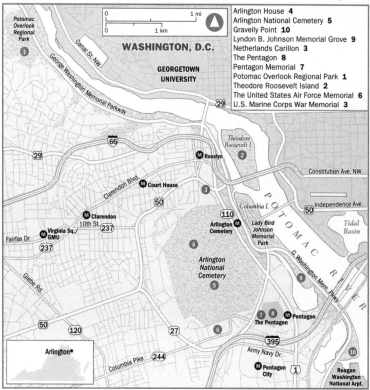

Arlington House **4**
Arlington National Cemetery **5**
Gravelly Point **10**
Lyndon B. Johnson Memorial Grove **9**
Netherlands Carillon **3**
The Pentagon **8**
Pentagon Memorial **7**
Potomac Overlook Regional Park **1**
Theodore Roosevelt Island **2**
The United States Air Force Memorial **6**
U.S. Marine Corps War Memorial **3**

Adjacent to the Iwo Jima statue, the **Netherlands Carillon** (✆ 703/289-2553; www.nps.gov/gwmp/nethcarillon.htm) was a gift from the people of Holland. Thousands of tulip bulbs are planted on the grounds surrounding the 127-foot-high open steel tower, creating a colorful display in spring. Carillon concerts are presented on Easter Sunday and every Saturday thereafter in April, May, and September, from 2 to 4pm. Concerts are held daily from 6 to 8pm June through August. You can climb the tower after the carillonneur performs and enjoy spectacular views of Washington.

Those three shiny spires curving dramatically into the air south of the cemetery come from the **United States Air Force Memorial** (✆ 7703/979-0674; www.airforcememorial.org), on Air Force Memorial Drive at Columbia Pike (Va. 244). Evoking the "bomb burst" maneuver of the Air Force's Thunderbirds precision flying team, the 270-foot-tall stainless steel spires honor the more than 54,000 American airmen who have died in combat. The memorial sits on a promontory with a panoramic view over the Pentagon and D.C. beyond (I often watch the July 4th fireworks over the National Mall from here). Admission is free. The memorial is open daily 8am to 11pm. Park free across Columbia Pike.

The terrorists who slammed American Airlines Flight 77 into the Pentagon on September 11, 2001, used a road map and followed Columbia Pike to hit the western side of the building. Facing the point of impact, the **Pentagon Memorial** (📞 **301/740-3388;** www.pentagonmemorial.org) honors the 184 lives that were lost in the Pentagon and on Flight 77 that day. Each victim is represented by a cantilevered bench extending over a small reflecting pool. Beginning with 3-year-old Dana Falkenburg and ending with 71-year-old John D. Yamnicky, they are arranged by the years in which the victims were born. The memorial is open 24 hours daily, with staff on hand 10am to 8pm. Call 📞 **202/741-1004** on your cellphone for a 24-minute audio tour. Brochures are in what looks like a 3-foot-high stainless steel lamppost near the entry. Photographs are permitted in the memorial but not elsewhere on the Pentagon grounds. There is no public parking at the Pentagon Monday to Friday 8am to 5pm. At other times you can park adjacent to the memorial in the Pentagon south lot, at the end of Columbia Pike. Your best bet on workdays is to walk 10 minutes from the Air Force memorial; take Metrorail to the Pentagon station; or park in the Pentagon visitors lot, on Army Navy Drive in Pentagon City south of I-395 (it's opposite Macy's).

A Scenic Drive Along the Potomac River

Skirting the south bank of the Potomac River for 30 miles between Mount Vernon in the south to the Capital Beltway (I-495) in the northwest, the **George Washington Memorial Parkway** ★★★ is one of Virginia's most scenic drives. It's also a major commuter route, which means lots of traffic during rush hour. Other times, you can drive the entire route in about 45 minutes without stopping. The parkway runs through Old Town Alexandria via King Street; otherwise, it's a four-lane road with neither traffic signals nor stop signs. Also, with the exception of the peaceful **Lyndon B. Johnson Memorial Grove** near the **Pentagon,** you cannot make a left turn; accordingly, if you drive it from south to north you can pull off at designated areas beside or overlooking the river. The best are **Gravelly Point Park,** on the north side of Ronald Reagan Washington National Airport (jets roar just a few feet overhead as they take off and land), and at **Potomac Overlook Regional Park,** with a great view over Georgetown in D.C.

As noted in "Outdoor Activities," earlier in this chapter, you can also run, hike, or bike along part of the parkway. **Theodore Roosevelt Island** is an 88-acre wooded preserve and bird sanctuary connected to the parkway by a footbridge just south of Rosslyn.

For more information, contact **George Washington Memorial Parkway Headquarters,** Turkey Run Park, McLean, VA 22101 (📞 **703/289-2500;** fax 703/289-2598; www.nps.gov/gwmp).

MOUNT VERNON & THE POTOMAC PLANTATIONS ★★★

Mount Vernon: 9 miles S of Old Town Alexandria

Anyone with the slightest interest in early American thought, politics, sociology, art, architecture, fashion, agriculture, or the decorative arts won't want to miss the scenic drive south along the Potomac from Alexandria to Mount Vernon, the home of George and Martha Washington. Their famous estate is on the way to two other Potomac plantations with Colonial roots—Woodlawn, which the first president gave to his

Mount Vernon & the Potomac Plantations

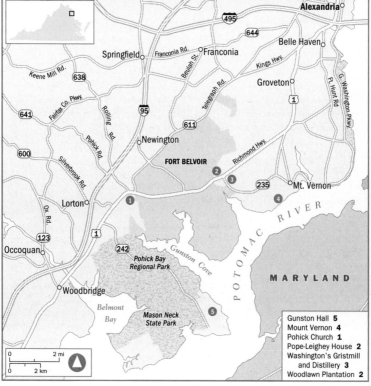

Gunston Hall **5**
Mount Vernon **4**
Pohick Church **1**
Pope-Leighey House **2**
Washington's Gristmill
  and Distillery **3**
Woodlawn Plantation **2**

adopted daughter (she was Martha's actual granddaughter via her first marriage), and Gunston Hall, where lived their creative neighbor and friend, George Mason, the most influential revolutionary you've never heard about. In between is Pohick Church, where the three worshiped.

Mount Vernon ★★★

George and Martha Washington's magnificent home overlooking the Potomac River has been one of America's most-visited shrines since 1858, when the Mount Vernon Ladies Association purchased the estate from Washington's great-grandnephew, John Augustine Washington, Jr. The association continues to own and maintain the mansion and its grounds, and it has an ongoing effort to locate and return the estate's scattered contents and memorabilia, thus enhancing its authentic appearance (ca. 1799). About 30% of its contents belonged to the Washingtons, including a key to the Paris Bastille, which Lafayette presented to Washington in 1790 via messenger Thomas Paine; the English harpsichord of Martha Washington's granddaughter, Nelly Custis; Martha's china tea service; and Washington's original globe, desk, and dressing table.

You will need at least a half-day to see Mount Vernon and the nearby gristmill and distillery. Many people show up at 8am in spring, in summer, and on weekends year-round with the idea of beating the crowds, which they inadvertently create. The guides inside the mansion do not have time to give in-depth information or answer questions when it's crowded. It's best to tour the mansion later in the day during these busy periods. Rather than stand in line, you can buy your tickets and reserve your guided audio tours online in advance at www.mountvernon.org. This is especially important during summer and on holiday weekends, when the audio tours sell out quickly. Be sure to click on "Group Tickets & Packages." Some packages include the price of the audio tour.

You will see more before reaching the mansion, thanks to the **Ford Orientation Center** and **Donald W. Reynolds Museum and Education Center,** at the estate's main gate. Life-size bronze statues of George, Martha, and her two grandchildren, Nelly and Washy Custis, welcome you to the orientation center, which features an 18-minute Hollywood-produced movie in which actors re-create important events in Washington's life. Likewise, the museum features lifelike wax models of Washington at three different ages; they were created with the help of forensic experts. The museum displays a set of false teeth Washington used (only one of his natural teeth remained intact when he assumed the presidency).

If you haven't reserved one online, rent a receiver for the guided audio tour, which is broadcast throughout the estate.

Constructed of beveled pine painted to look like stone, the house is an outstanding example of Georgian architecture. You'll enter by way of the Large Dining Room, which contains many of the original chairs, Hepplewhite mahogany sideboards, and paintings. Step outside on the long front porch and enjoy the view that prompted Washington to declare, "No estate in United America is more pleasantly situated than this." Upstairs are five bedchambers, including the Lafayette Room, where the Marquis spent a few nights, and George and Martha's bedroom, in which Washington died.

After leaving the house, tour the kitchen, smokehouse, overseer's and slave quarters, the Washingtons' graves, and the slave burial ground marked by two monuments to the African Americans who lived, worked, and died at the plantation. Down by the river, a 4-acre exhibition area explains Washington's innovative accomplishments in soil conservation and crop rotation, and his switch from tobacco to wheat, which could be planted twice a year, had a more reliable market, and did not deplete the soil as quickly as the Golden Leaf.

He ground the wheat into flour at **George Washington's Gristmill,** a 1933 reconstruction 3 miles west of the plantation on Mount Vernon Memorial Parkway (Va. 235). He put the mill's byproduct to use, making whiskey in a distillery. Costumed interpreters give 20-minute tours explaining how the mill operated, and they grind cornmeal for sale in the gift shop. They also make whiskey at the adjacent **George Washington's Distillery,** an exact reproduction of a still built in 1797–98 and burned in 1814. The mill and still are near the intersection of Mount Vernon Memorial Parkway and U.S. 1, not in Gristmill Park, a county facility you'll pass on the way.

Call or check the website for an ongoing schedule of special activities, especially in summer. Admission is free on Washington's birthday (the federal holiday of Presidents' Day, not the actual date), when a wreath-laying ceremony is held at his tomb.

3200 Mount Vernon Pkwy. (8 miles south of Old Town Alexandria and I-95). © **800/429-1520** or 703/780-2000. www.mountvernon.org. Estate admission $15 adults, $14 seniors, $7 children 6–11. Gristmill admission $4 adults, $2 children 6–11. Combination admission $17 adults, $8.50 children 6–11. Audio mansion tour rentals $6. Mount Vernon Apr–Aug daily 8am–5pm, Mar and Sept–Oct daily 9am–5pm, Nov–Feb daily 9am–4pm. Gristmill and distillery Apr–Oct daily 10am–5pm.

GETTING TO MOUNT VERNON

It's a pleasant, picturesque drive to Mount Vernon, 8 miles south of Alexandria, via the George Washington Memorial Parkway, which in some places skirts the river's edge. After passing the traffic circle in front of Mount Vernon, the same highway becomes the Mount Vernon Memorial Parkway (Va. 235), which ends at U.S. 1.

The **Tourmobile** (© 202/554-5100; www.tourmobile.com) runs from Arlington National Cemetery and from the Washington Monument in Washington, D.C., to Mount Vernon from June 15 through Labor Day daily at 11am. Tourmobile booths at the cemetery and at the Washington Monument sell tickets. The fare is $32 for adults, $16 for children 3 to 11, and free for children 2 and under, and it includes admission to Mount Vernon. The trip takes about 5 hours; reservations are required in person at least 30 minutes before departure.

The venerable **Gray Line** (© 800/862-1400 or 202/289-1995; www.grayline.com) has all-day guided bus trips from Washington, D.C., to Arlington National Cemetery and Mount Vernon. The tours depart at 8am daily except New Year's Day, Thanksgiving, and Christmas and cost $70 for adults and $45 for children 3 to 11.

From April to October, the **Potomac Riverboat Company,** at Union and Cameron streets behind the Torpedo Factory Art Center in Old Town Alexandria (© **877/511-1628** or 703/548-9000; www.potomacriverboatco.com), offers cruises down the river to Mount Vernon and back. They depart at 11am Tuesday to Sunday from Memorial Day to Labor Day and on weekends during May, September, and October for the 1-hour cruise to Mount Vernon. Round-trip fares are $40 for adults and $20 for children 2 to 11 and include admission to Mount Vernon.

While you explore the mansion, the boat goes on 40-minute **photo cruises** from the Mount Vernon wharf. Fares are $9 for adults and $5 for children 2 through 11. Kids 1 year old and under ride free on all cruises.

WHERE TO EAT AT MOUNT VERNON

At the traffic circle outside the main gate, the charming **Mount Vernon Inn** (© 703/780-0011) serves some of the Colonial-style fare George and Martha provided their guests. It's moderately priced, and the atmosphere is great—period furnishings, working fireplaces, and waitstaff in 18th-century costumes. Lunch is first-come, first-served, and reservations are highly recommended at dinner. Lunch is served daily 11am to 3:30pm except Christmas. Dinner hours are Monday to Thursday 5 to 8:30pm and Friday to Saturday 5 to 9pm. Next door, the inexpensive, mall-style **Mount Vernon Food Court** is open daily 9:30am to

5:30pm. Both are closed on Christmas. Both accept American Express, Discover, MasterCard, and Visa.

Other Potomac River Attractions

Gunston Hall ★ Although he's not well known outside Virginia (you may have heard of our university named for him but not the man), George Mason (1725–92) was one of the most liberal and creative political thinkers of his time. He wrote the Virginia Declaration of Rights, upon which Thomas Jefferson drew for the Declaration of Independence, and he helped draft the Constitution but refused to sign it because it didn't abolish slavery or initially contain a Bill of Rights. Built between 1755 and 1759, his one-and-a-half story brick house is a fine example of Colonial Georgian architecture. The restored formal gardens focus on the 12-foot-high English boxwood–lined walkway believed to have been planted by Mason. George and Ann Mason are buried here in the family graveyard. En route to the house, you'll pass a small museum of Mason family memorabilia. A nature trail goes down to the Potomac (you cannot see the river from the mansion).

10709 Gunston Rd. (Va. 242). ✆ **703/550-9220.** www.gunstonhall.org. Admission $9 adults, $8 seniors, $8 students 6–18, free for children 5 and under. Daily 9:30am–5pm. 30-min. tours every half-hour 9:30am–4:30pm. Closed New Year's Day, Thanksgiving, and Christmas.

Pohick Church This "mother church of northern Virginia" was built between 1769 and 1774 under the supervision of vestrymen George Washington and George Mason. Theirs and other prominent families paid for their own box pews, laid out opposite the pulpit. William Fitzhugh, Washington's friend who built Chatham Manor in Fredericksburg (p. 93), is buried in the graveyard. During the Civil War, Union soldiers stabled their horses in the church and stripped the interior. They did not, however, steal the English baptismal font, which dates to the 11th or 12th century and is still used today.

9301 Richmond Hwy. (U.S. 1, at Telegraph Rd.), Lorton. ✆ **703/339-6572.** www.pohick.org. Free admission; donations accepted. Mon–Fri 9am–4:30pm; Sun 12:30–4:30pm. Sun services 7:45, 9, and 11:15am (8 and 10am in summer).

Woodlawn Plantation and Pope-Leighey House ★ On a hill overlooking the Potomac River valley (but not the river), **Woodlawn Plantation** was a 2,000-acre section of Mount Vernon, of which some 130 acres remain. George Washington gave it as a wedding gift to his adopted daughter (and Martha's granddaughter), beautiful Nelly Parke Custis, and her husband (and Washington's nephew), Maj. Lawrence Lewis, when they married in 1799. Three years later, they moved into the Georgian-style brick mansion designed by William Thornton, first architect of the U.S. Capitol, and furnished it primarily with pieces from Mount Vernon (everything you see dates to before 1840, with about 30% from the Lewis' time).

On the other side of the parking lot, you leap 150 years ahead architecturally to Frank Lloyd Wright's modernistic **Pope-Leighey House,** designed in 1940 for the Loren Pope family of Falls Church. Built of cypress, brick, and glass, the flat-roofed house was created as a prototype of well-designed space for middle-income people.

Give yourself 1½ hours to explore both houses.

9000 Richmond Hwy. ✆ **703/780-4000.** www.woodlawn1805.org and www.popeleighey1940.org. Admission to each house $8.50 adults, $4 students, free for children 4 and under. Admission to both houses $15 adults, $5 students, free for children 4 and under. Admission may be higher during special events. Thurs–Mon 10am–5pm. Guided 35-min. tours depart on the hour and half-hour (last tour 4:30pm). Closed Jan–Feb, Thanksgiving, and Christmas.

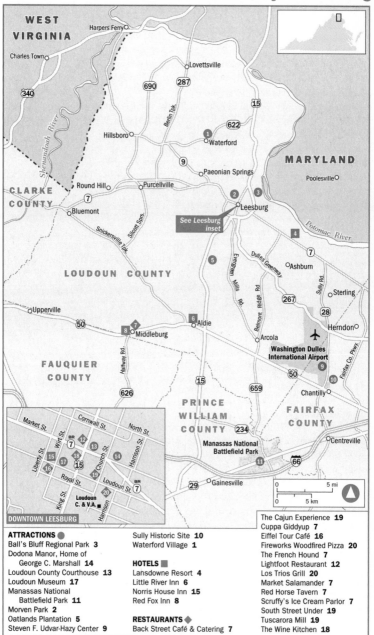

ATTRACTIONS ●
Ball's Bluff Regional Park **3**
Dodona Manor, Home of
  George C. Marshall **14**
Loudoun County Courthouse **13**
Loudoun Museum **17**
Manassas National
  Battlefield Park **11**
Morven Park **2**
Oatlands Plantation **5**
Steven F. Udvar-Hazy Center **9**

Sully Historic Site **10**
Waterford Village **1**

HOTELS ■
Lansdowne Resort **4**
Little River Inn **6**
Norris House Inn **15**
Red Fox Inn **8**

RESTAURANTS ◆
Back Street Café & Catering **7**

The Cajun Experience **19**
Cuppa Giddyup **7**
Eiffel Tour Café **16**
Fireworks Woodfired Pizza **20**
The French Hound **7**
Lightfoot Restaurant **12**
Los Trios Grill **20**
Market Salamander **7**
Red Horse Tavern **7**
Scruffy's Ice Cream Parlor **7**
South Street Under **19**
Tuscarora Mill **19**
The Wine Kitchen **18**

THE HUNT COUNTRY ★★

Leesburg: 35 miles NW of Washington, D.C., 115 miles NW of Richmond; Middleburg: 45 miles W of Washington, D.C., 95 miles NW of Richmond

Although horse farms extend southwestward from the Washington suburbs all the way to Charlottesville, the heart of Virginia's Hunt Country traditionally beats in the rolling hills between Washington Dulles International Airport and the Blue Ridge Mountains. The Colonial tradition of fox hunting still reigns out this way, and steeplechase racing occupies many a Saturday afternoon.

Beyond the rapid suburban development west of Dulles airport, the Hunt Country is studded with horse farms bordered by stone fences, plantations with elegant manses, picturesque villages, country inns, and fine restaurants. It's worth exploring the scenic country roads and getting out of your vehicle in charming little hamlets like Middleburg, Aldie, Upperville, Purcellville, and Hillsboro. Don't be surprised to see rich and famous folk strolling the streets or having a bite of lunch, for some of the world's wealthiest people keep their thoroughbreds here.

The only time when you can actually visit a few of the horse farms is during the **Virginia Hunt Country Stable Tour** (© **540/592-3711;** www.huntcountry stabletour.org), held every Memorial Day weekend.

Others with a little money have started vineyards, making the Hunt Country one of Virginia's prime wine growing areas. If you avoid getting tipsy in the tasting rooms, it's easy to wind your way through the farms and hamlets to Manassas, where the North and the South fought two major Civil War battles on the banks of Bull Run, including that conflict's first great contest. You will be following in the hoofprints of Col. John Singleton Mosby, the famous Confederate raider who made Hunt Country life miserable for the Yankees.

Essentials

VISITOR INFORMATION

For information about Leesburg and Loudoun County, contact the **Leesburg Visitor Center,** in Market Station, 112-G South St. SE, Ste. G, Leesburg, VA 20175 (© **800/752-6118** or 703/771-2170; www.visitloudoun.org). It's open daily 9am to 5pm except New Year's Day, Thanksgiving, and Christmas. In addition to the official brochure, *Touring Guide to DC's Wine Country,* ask for a copy of the walking-tour guide to Waterford Village (see "Back in Time to Waterford Village," later in this chapter).

You can follow four people around the county on the Web at **Get Lost in Loudoun** (**www.getlostinloudoun.com**), a takeoff of television reality shows.

Middleburg has an information center in the Pink Box, 12 Madison St., Middleburg, VA 22117 (© **540/687-8888;** www.middleburg.org). It's open Monday to Friday 11am to 3pm and Saturday to Sunday 11am to 4pm. Visitor information is available at www.middleburgonline.com.

For Manassas, contact the **Prince William County/Manassas Conference and Visitors Bureau,** 8609 Sudley Rd., Ste. 105, Manassas, VA 20112 (© **800/432-1792** or 703/396-7130; www.visitpwc.com). The town of Manassas has a visitor center in the Railroad Depot, 9431 West St. (© **703/361-6599;** www.visit manassas.org), that's open daily 9am to 5pm.

The Hunt Country was the stamping ground of the Confederate raider, Col. John Singleton Mosby, whose hit-and-run exploits earned him the nickname "The Gray Ghost." Today, U.S. 50 is the John S. Mosby Highway, and local residents have dubbed it the John Singleton Mosby Heritage Area. You can get a driving tour brochure explaining historic sights from local tourist info offices (see "Visitor Information," above) or directly from the **Mosby Heritage Area Association,** PO Box 1497, Middleburg, VA 20118 (© **540/687-6681;** www.mosby heritagearea.org). Tour guide Dave Goetz offers half-day **Mosby's Confederacy Tours** (© **540/351-6073** or 540/364-9086; www.mosbystours.com), which can be combined into an all-day outing. Call for prices and reservations.

For Fauquier County, contact or visit the **Warrenton-Fauquier Visitor Center,** 33 N. Calhoun St., Warrenton, VA 20186 (© **800/820-1021** or 540/341-0988; www.visitfauquier.com); it's open daily 9am to 5pm.

GETTING THERE

BY PLANE Washington Dulles International Airport is on the eastern edge of the Hunt Country, 14 miles southeast of Leesburg and 21 miles east of Middleburg. See "Getting There," in chapter 12, for details.

BY CAR You'll need a vehicle to explore the beautiful back roads of the Hunt Country. Washington Dulles airport has all the major rental firms. There are two routes from the Capital Beltway (I-495) to **Leesburg.** The free but slower way is Va. 7. Significantly faster is via the Dulles Toll Road (Va. 267) between I-495 and Washington Dulles Airport; it feeds into the Dulles Greenway (© **703/707-8870;** www.dullesgreenway.com), a privately financed toll expressway connecting the airport to Leesburg. The toll from the I-495 to Leesburg is about $6.50. *Note:* The Dulles Greenway booths accept only credit cards 11pm to 8am.

Once in downtown Leesburg, you can scout around for an on-street space or leave your vehicle in the **municipal parking garage** on Loudoun Street between King and Wirt streets, where parking is free on weekends. During the week you'll pay 50¢ an hour for the first 4 hours, $1 per hour thereafter, but no more than $5 a day. Many downtown shops will validate your ticket, so take it with you.

To **Middleburg,** you can take U.S. 50 west all the way into town or follow I-66 west to Va. 28 north to U.S. 50 west. U.S. 15 south from Leesburg intersects with U.S. 50 westbound 10 miles east of Middleburg. Park anywhere you can find a vacant on-street space in Middleburg.

Leesburg ★

Founded in 1758, Leesburg is the largest town in the Hunt Country and a good base for exploring the region. Although not as picturesque as Middleburg, it has considerable charm, with architecture ranging from pre-Revolutionary to late 19th century. The center of Leesburg and its historic district is at the intersection of Market Street (Va. 7 Business) and King Street (U.S. 15 Business), where you'll find the brick **Loudoun**

County Courthouse, built in 1895, which contains a mix of Roman-revival and classical elements. Most of what you will want to see is within 2 blocks of this key crossroads, including one of the largest collections of antiques dealers in Virginia.

EXPLORING LEESBURG

The free **Leesburg Town Service Trolley** (© 877/777-2708 or 703/777-2420; www.vatransit.org) runs between the Loudoun County Government Center (on Harrison St. in downtown Leesburg) and the Leesburg Corner Premium Outlets via Market Street (Va. 7 Business) every 30 minutes Monday to Friday 7am to 6:30pm, Saturday 10am to 9pm, and Sunday noon to 6pm. It passes the Leesburg Visitor Center.

Ball's Bluff Regional Park   On the northeastern outskirts of town, this pristine regional park is best known for a little circle of stone markers in **Ball's Bluff National Cemetery,** the nation's second-smallest national cemetery. It holds the remains of 54 Union soldiers—only one identified—who fell in the Battle of Ball's Bluff, a Confederate victory in October 1861. Many more Union troops were shot dead as they scrambled down the bluff toward the Potomac River and safety in Maryland. Many of their corpses slid into the river and floated down to Washington, bringing the grim realities of the war to the nation's capital. The park has hiking trails and interpretive displays, and volunteers lead guided tours of the battlefield on weekends from May through October. *Note:* There are no public restrooms here.

Ball's Bluff Rd. (northeast Leesburg off U.S. 15 bypass). © **703/737-7800.** www.nvrpa.org. Free admission. Daily dawn–dusk. Free walking tours Apr–Oct Sat–Sun 11am and 1pm. From U.S. 15 bypass, go east on Battlefield Pkwy. to Ball's Bluff Rd., turn left into parking lot.

Dodona Manor ★★   In 1941 Gen. George C. Marshall and his wife, Katherine, bought Dodona Manor, an early-19th-century manse, when he planned to retire from the U.S. Army. Those plans were interrupted by World War II. Marshall served as U.S. army chief of staff during the war, and after the war, he served as secretary of state (he was awarded the Nobel Peace Prize for the Marshall Plan) and secretary of defense. The house looks exactly like it did in the 1940s and 1950s, with Marshall's own bed, red-leather chair, early black-and-white television, and artwork acquired in China (Generalissimo Chiang Kai-shek, Madame Chiang, and her four maids twice were houseguests). Dodona provides a terrific view of the general's private life, while the George C. Marshall Museum in Lexington (p. 166) explains his outstanding public accomplishments.

212 E. Market St. (near east end of Loudon St.). © **703/777-1880.** www.georgecmarshall.org. Admission $10 adults, $8 seniors, $5 students 7–17. June–Aug Sat 10am–5pm, Sun–Mon 1–5pm; Sept–May Sat 10am–5pm, Sun 1–5pm. 45-min. tours depart as needed. Free parking at Shops at Dodona on E. Market St. (Va. 7).

Loudoun Museum   This small but interesting museum houses memorabilia about the county from its earliest days to the present. It distributes free visitor information and sells helpful walking-tour booklets. A 15-minute presentation sets the scene for your tour of the county. Allow another 30 minutes to explore the museum and its gift shop.

16 W. Loudoun St. (at Wirt St.). © **703/777-7427.** www.loudounmuseum.org. Admission $3 adults, $1 seniors and students 4–17, free for children 3 and under. Fri–Sat 10am–5pm; Sun 1–5pm.

Morven Park   On the northwest edge of town, this 1,200-acre estate and its mansion are requisite stops for fox hunting and horse-drawn carriage fans. The original

😊 A GRAND HOME FOR THE ENOLA GAY

When the Smithsonian Institution's magnificent National Air and Space Museum in Washington, D.C., ran out of space to house its many historic aircraft and spacecraft, it built the awesome **Steven F. Udvar-Hazy Center ★★★**, 14390 Air and Space Museum Pkwy., in Chantilly (📞 **202/633-1000**; www.nasm.si.edu/udvarhazycenter). This huge Quonset hut–like hangar is home to more than 200 planes and 135 spacecraft. Stars of the show are the *Enola Gay*, the B-29 Superfortress that dropped the first atomic bomb on Japan in 1945; the space shuttle *Enterprise*, which NASA used for approach and landing tests in the late 1970s; an SR-71 spy plane; and one of Air France's Concorde jetliners. The model spacecraft that starred in the movie *Close Encounters of the Third Kind* is on display, too (it's over in a corner by the *Enterprise*). It's worth going around with a retired

pilot on a docent tour (call 📞 **202/633-2563** for the schedule).

The center is open daily 10am to 5:30pm except Christmas (the observation tower closes at 4:30pm). Admission is free, but parking costs $15 per vehicle (there is no free parking).

The Airbus IMAX Theater shows both aviation and space films and feature movies ($9–$13 for adults, $8–$14 for seniors, $7.50–$14 for kids 2–12). Simulator rides are $7 to $8 per person. You'll need at least 2 hours here. There's a McDonald's.

The center is off Va. 28 between U.S. 50 and the Dulles Toll Road (Va. 267), near Sully Historic Site on the southeastern edge of Washington Dulles International Airport. **Virginia Regional Transit** (📞 **540/338-1610**; www.vatransit.org) provides shuttle bus service from Washington Dulles International Airport.

part of Westmoreland Davis Mansion was built as a farmhouse in 1781 but was later expanded as the home of Virginia governor Westmoreland Davis. It's now the centerpiece of an equestrian center and houses the **Museum of Hounds and Hunting.** The carriage house displays the impressive **Winmill Carriage Collection.** Allow 1½ hours to tour the house, museum, and carriages; and another 30 minutes to explore replicas of log huts built by Confederate soldiers bivouacked here prior to their victory at Ball's Bluff.

17263 Southern Planter Lane (off Old Waterford Rd.). 📞 **703/777-2414.** www.morvenpark.org. Mansion tour $5 adults, $3 children 6–12, free for children 5 and under. Carriage tour $9 adults, $5 children 6–12, free for children 5 and under. Civil War sites $3 adults, free for children 12 and under. Apr–Oct daily 11am–5pm; Nov–Mar daily 11am–4pm. Call for special events. Take Va. 7 Business west 1 mile from the center of town, turn right onto Morven Park Rd., left onto Old Waterford Rd. and park on the right.

NEARBY ATTRACTIONS

Oatlands Plantation   George Carter, a great-grandson of legendary planter Robert "King" Carter of the Northern Neck (see "Exploring the Northern Neck," in chapter 5), built this mansion in the Federal style in 1804 but later converted it to the Greek-revival manse we see today. His formal terraced garden and its 1810 propagation greenhouse—it's considered America's second oldest—are as interesting as the mansion itself. The plantation's remaining 330 acres contain unique tree species. Oatlands hosts numerous public and private events (call or check the website for the schedule). From mid-November through December, the mansion is all decked out for its annual holiday candlelight tours. You must take a tour to see the house, but you can wander the gardens on your own.

20850 Oatlands Plantation Lane (on U.S. 15, 6 miles south of Leesburg). © **703/777-3174.** www. oatlands.org. Admission $10 adults, $9 seniors and students, $1 children 5–11, free for children 4 and under. Garden and grounds $7 per person. Mar–Dec Mon–Sat 10am–5pm, Sun 1–5pm. 30- to 45-min. house tours depart on the hour (last tour 4pm). Closed Jan–Feb, Thanksgiving, Dec 24, and Christmas.

Sully Historic Site Sully Plantation, a two-and-a-half-story farmhouse, was built in 1794 by Richard Bland Lee, younger brother of Revolutionary War hero Henry "Light-Horse Harry" Lee (and thus an uncle of Robert E. Lee), who lived here with his wife, Elizabeth Collins Lee, until 1811. Washington Dulles International Airport now occupies most of the original 3,000-plus acres, leaving the main house and original stone dairy, smokehouse, and kitchen building. Unlike many Virginia plantations open to the public, this one does a fine job of demonstrating the harshness of everyday life for the plantation's slaves in its reconstructed slave quarters. You must take a tour to see the house and slave quarters, but you can wander around the grounds and look into the outbuilding windows on your own. Call or check the website for numerous special events.

3601 Sully Rd. (Va. 28). © **703/437-1794.** www.fairfaxcounty.gov/parks/sully. Main house or slave quarter tour $7 adults, $6 students, $5 seniors and children 5–15. Both tours $9 adults, $8 students, $7 seniors and children 5–15. Grounds free. Wed–Tues 11am–4pm. Grounds until sunset. Guided 45-min. tours depart on the hour. Call for holiday hours. Sully is on Va. 28, ¼ mile north of U.S. 50, 9 miles south of Va. 7 in Leesburg.

OUTDOOR ACTIVITIES

The Hunt Country's back roads and its portion of the 45-mile **Washington & Old Dominion Railroad (W&OD) Trail** (© 703/729-0596; www.nvrpa.org/park/ w_od_railroad) bring bicyclists from all over the mid-Atlantic. The W&OD follows an old railroad bed through the heart of the area, crossing South King Street in Leesburg. It's both beautiful and rigorous, on an up-and-down route that can burn your thighs.

Golfers can tee off at the Robert Trent Jones, Jr., and Greg Norman–designed links at **Lansdowne Resort** (see "Where to Stay," below). Gary Player designed the course at **Raspberry Falls Golf & Hunt Club,** 3 miles north of Leesburg on U.S. 15 (© **703/779-2555** or 703/589-1042; www.raspberryfalls.com). Less expensive are **Goose Creek Golf Club,** 43001 Golf Club Rd. (© **703/729-2500;** www.goose creekgolf.com), and the municipal **Brambleton Regional Park Golf Course,** 42180 Ryan Rd., in nearby Ashburn (© **703/327-3403;** www.nvrpa.org/park/ brambleton).

SHOPPING

Leesburg's numerous **antiques shops** are easy to find, within a block of the Market Street–King Street intersection. Check the website of the **Leesburg Antiques & Collectibles Dealers Association** (**www.leesburgantiques.com**) for its member shops.

Washington Redskins all-pro tight end Chris Cooley does more than catch footballs with his large, sensitive hands. Once an art major at Utah State, Cooley is an avid potter and painter. His and other artists' ceramics, paintings, photos, and other works are for sale at the **Cooley Gallery,** 12 S. King St. in downtown Leesburg (© **540/779-4639;** www.thecooleygallery.com). Summer hours are Wednesday to Sunday 11am to 6pm; winter hours are Thursday to Sunday 11am to 6pm.

I seldom come here without browsing at **Leesburg Corner Premium Outlets,** 241 Fort Evans Rd. (𝄐 **703/737-3071;** www.premiumoutlets.com), 2 miles east of downtown at the intersection of the U.S. 15 bypass and Va. 7. It has more than 50 stores including all of the well-known brands. Stores are open Monday to Saturday 10am to 9pm and Sunday 10am to 7pm.

WHERE TO STAY

A mansion built atop a knoll in 1773 is the centerpiece of the **Holiday Inn at Historic Carradoc Hall,** 1500 E. Market St. (Va. 7), 2 miles east of downtown (www. holidayinnleesburg.com; 𝄐 **800/465-4329** or 703/771-9200). The 122 rooms are in standard motel buildings. The newest digs in town are at the **Hampton Inn and Suites,** 117 Fort Evans Rd. (www.leesburg.hamptoninn.com; 𝄐 **800/HAMPTON** [426-7866] or 703/669-8640), and the **Comfort Suites Leesburg,** 80 Prosperity Ave. (www.comfortsuitesleesburg.com; 𝄐 **866/533-7287** or 540/669-1650), which has some Jacuzzi-equipped units. Nearby on Va. 7 is the **Best Western Leesburg-Dulles** (www.bestwestern.com; 𝄐 **800/528-1234** or 703/777-9400).

Lansdowne Resort ★★   This luxurious complex between Leesburg and Dulles airport is one of Virginia's better all-around resorts. The nine-story hotel building is surrounded by 205 acres alongside the Potomac River. Covering much of that land are 45 holes of golf on four courses, including a Greg Norman–designed 18-holer, all overseen by a clubhouse. An indoor pool off a full-service spa opens to no fewer than four outdoor pools with water slides and other contraptions to keep both adults and children thoroughly entertained. The four restaurants include a fine-dining venue, a family-style restaurant, an English pub, and a seasonal poolside snack bar. A California wine–country theme distinguishes the guest accommodations, all in the central building. Units on the top floor have marvelous views of the Potomac River Valley; the alcove suite with bay windows is the best option.

44050 Woodridge Pkwy. (off Va. 7), Lansdowne, VA 20176. www.lansdowneresort.com. 𝄐 **800/541-4801** or 703/729-8400. Fax 703/729-6096. 296 units. $179–$349 double; $279–$449 suite. Golf and other packages available. AE, DC, DISC, MC, V. Valet parking $15; free self-parking. **Amenities:** 4 restaurants; 3 bars; babysitting; children's programs; concierge; executive-level rooms; 3 golf courses; health club; Jacuzzi; 5 pools (1 indoor); room service; sauna; spa; 4 tennis courts. *In room:* A/C and fans, TV, hair dryer, Wi-Fi.

Bed & Breakfasts

While the Norris House Inn (below) is the only place to stay in downtown Leesburg, the county has a dozen or so other bed-and-breakfasts scattered among its rolling hills. Check them out through the **Loudoun County Bed & Breakfast Guild** (www.loudounbandb.com; 𝄐 **866/771-2597**).

The Norris House Inn ★   This three-story redbrick 1760 home in downtown Leesburg has a parlor and a library with oak fireplaces, among other common rooms. Guest-room furnishings are a charming mix of antiques; some rooms have four-poster beds. All have private bathrooms and nonworking fireplaces. The most interesting and private accommodations are in the atticlike third floor. Hosts Carol and Roger Healey serve full breakfasts (on the garden veranda if the weather is good).

108 Loudoun St. SW (btw. Wirt and Liberty sts.), Leesburg, VA 20175. www.norrishouse.com. 𝄐 **800/644-1806** or 703/777-1806. Fax 703/771-8051. 6 units. $110–$199 double. Rates include full breakfast. Wedding and other packages available. AE, DISC, MC, V. No children 7 or under. **Amenities:** Access to nearby health club. *In room:* A/C, hair dryer, no phone, Wi-Fi.

WHERE TO EAT

Consisting of seven restored buildings including two gristmills and a railroad freight station, **Market Square,** on Harrison Street at Loudoun Street, is home to South Street Under and Tuscaroa Mill (see below) plus **Los Tios Grill** (© 540/291-3652), serving Mexican and Salvadorean fare, and **Fireworks Woodfired Pizza** (© **703/779-8400;** www.fireworkspizza.com), whose hardwood smoke whets the appetite. Both have warm weather outdoor seating.

Spicy Louisiana cooking prevails at the **Cajun Experience,** 14 Loudon St. SE (© 703/777-6580; www.cajunexperience.biz), a branch of the Washington, D.C., restaurant of the same name.

Eiffel Tower Café ★ FRENCH   An elegant French country ambience reigns in this rambling clapboard house with large windows that let in plenty of sunlight. The menu is traditional French, including standards such as steak au poivre. Needless to say, Bastille Day (July 14) is a big event here.

107 W. Loudoun St. (btw. Wirt and Liberty sts.). © **703/777-5242.** www.eiffeltowercafe.com. Reservations recommended. Main courses $24–$32. AE, MC, V. Wed–Sun 11:30am–2:30pm and 5:30–9:30pm.

Lightfoot Restaurant ★★ AMERICAN   This fine restaurant occupies an old Romanesque-revival bank building, complete with a two-story-high oak-paneled ceiling. A round mezzanine atop the bar dominates the center of the room, which is too big and thus too noisy for intimate dining. Nevertheless, the chef puts forth an interesting mix of flavors, such as artichoke-and-cheese crusted salmon with orange-tinged couscous.

11 N. King St. (north of Market St.). © **703/771-2233.** www.lightfootrestaurant.com. Reservations recommended. Main courses $18–$30. AE, MC, V. Mon–Thurs 11:30am–11pm; Fri–Sat 11:30am–midnight; Sun 10am–10pm (brunch 10am–3pm).

South Street Under DELI/BAKERY   Operated by the Tuscarora Mill (see below), this lively bakery and deli is housed in a turn-of-the-20th-century mill, one of the six historic buildings that make up the Market Station shopping and dining complex. It's the best place in town for a breakfast of gourmet coffee and hot-out-of-the-oven pastries, or a lunch of almond-and-grape chicken salad or a made-to-order sandwich on freshly baked ciabatta bread. Order at the counter, and, in good weather, grab a table out in the sunny courtyard.

203 Harrison St. SE (in Market Station, btw. Loudoun and Harrison sts.). © **703/771-9610.** www. southstreetunder.com. Reservations not accepted. Most items $3–$8. AE, DISC, MC, V. Mon–Fri 7am–6pm; Sat 8am–6pm; Sun 8am–4pm.

Tuscarora Mill ★★ AMERICAN   "Tuskie's" brings a casual, publike ambience to this 1898 mill building. High wood-beamed ceilings, grain bins, belts, pulleys, and a scale evoke the building's past in the main dining room, while plants and skylights brighten another room to the side. Delicious luncheon fare includes sandwiches and entrees like sautéed shrimp accompanied by cheese grits and smoked country sausage, which often appears at dinner. The dinner menu changes frequently, but other nighttime standouts might include grilled rainbow trout with Cajun spices.

203 Harrison St. (in Market Station, btw. Loudoun and Harrison sts.). © **703/771-9300.** www. tuskies.com. Reservations recommended, especially on weekends. Main courses $17–$38. AE, DISC, MC, V. Mon–Thurs 11am–11pm; Fri–Sat 11am–midnight; Sun 11am–9pm (brunch 11am–2:30pm).

A favorite Sunday drive destination for us northern Virginians is the enchanting hamlet of **Waterford**, with so many 18th- and 19th-century buildings that the whole village is a National Historic Landmark. You'll feel as though you've entered an English country scene as vistas of farmland and pasture unfold behind barns and churches. A Quaker from Pennsylvania, Amos Janney, built a mill here in the 1740s. Other Quakers followed, and by 1840, most of the buildings now on Main Street and Second Street were in place. Affluent professionals who work in Washington, D.C., and the bustling northern Virginia suburbs now own many of the homes. In other words, it's a real town, not a theme park like Williamsburg, so please don't traipse through their front yards.

Many thousands of visitors descend upon this community of a few hundred people on the first full weekend in October, when local residents stage the annual **Waterford Homes Tours and Crafts Exhibit,** one of the region's best. Concerts and other events are held here throughout the year.

Be sure to get a walking-tour guide booklet at the Leesburg Visitor Center (see "Essentials" under "The Hunt Country," earlier in this chapter) or from the **Waterford Foundation, Inc.,** PO Box 142, Waterford, VA 20197 (© **540/882-3018;** fax 540/882-3921; www.waterfordva.org). The foundation's office is in the Corner Store at Main and Second streets and is open Monday to Friday 9am to 5pm. Ask the foundation about walking tours, which are given on some Sundays.

Waterford is about 6 miles northwest of Leesburg. Don't take Old Waterford Road; it's not paved. Instead, follow Va. 7 west, turn right onto Va. 9, then right on Clark's Gap Road (C.R. 662) into Waterford.

The Wine Kitchen ★★ 🍴 AMERICAN   A relaxed, homey ambience pervades this small bistro-style wine bar. The decor may be eclectic and unexciting, but there is nothing simple about the well-chosen wine list, which whimsically groups its offerings by region under such headings as "Pinot Envy" and "Whites of Fancy." A few excellent Virginia vintages appear. All are offered by the bottle, glass, or sampling floats (three glasses). Back in the kitchen, the chef doesn't allow rich sauces to overwhelm the fresh ingredients gathered from local family farms. The servings are modest, so consider ordering a salad and side along with a main course. Reservations are not accepted so arrive early on weekend evenings.

7 S. King St. © **703/777-9463.** www.thewinekitchen.com. Reservations not accepted. Main courses $9–$19. Sun and Tues–Thurs 11:30am–9pm, Fri–Sat 11:30am–10pm.

On the Loudoun Wine Trail

Loudoun County has several vineyards worth visiting. Be sure to pick up a free copy of *Touring Guide to DC's Wine Country* at the Leesburg Visitor Center. It has a map and describes each winery's specialty, location, and business hours.

Rather than risk a DUI charge, you can take tours of the Hunt Country and Charlottesville area wineries (see chapters 4 and 6, respectively). In the Hunt Country, **Reston Limousine** (© **800/LIMO-141** [546-6141] or 703/478-0500; **www.restonlimo.com**) goes on all-day tours on Saturday or Sunday to four local wineries for $35 per person, not including lunch or the winery tasting fees.

Virginia Wine Adventures LLC (© 877/VA-GRAPE [824-7273]; www.vawineadventures.com) also will tailor a tour to your specifications.

A good place to start is **Tarara Vineyard & Winery,** 13648 Tarara Lane (© **703/771-7100;** www.tarara.com), overlooking the Potomac River, where wines are aged in a 6,000-square-foot cave. Their 2002 viognier won the Virginia Governor's Cup gold medal, not that they will have any left for you to taste. The winery is open daily 11am to 5pm and to 6pm on weekends from June through December. Tours and tastings run continuously. From Leesburg, drive north on U.S. 15 to Lucketts, then east on C.R. 662.

Near Tarara and the river on Spinks Road is **Lost Creek Winery** (© **703/443-9836;** www.lostcreekwinery.com). It's open Thursday to Monday 11am to 5pm.

Northwest of Leesburg are **Loudoun Valley Vineyards,** on Va. 9 (© **540/882-3375;** www.loudounvalleyvineyards.com), which runs tours Friday from noon to 9pm and Saturday from 11am to 9pm. and **Breaux Vineyards,** north of Hillsboro on C.R. 671 (© **800/492-9961** or 540/668-6299; www.breauxvineyards.com), whose Mediterranean-style tasting room is open daily from 11am to 5pm. On C.R. 690 **Doukénie Winery** (© **540/688-6464;** www.doukeniewinery.com) is open daily from noon to 6pm.

In the southern part of the county near Middleburg, the most interesting of the local wineries is **Piedmont Vineyards,** on Halfway Road (C.R. 626) about 3 miles south of town (© **540/687-5528;** www.piedmontwines.com), a former dairy farm whose barn now houses a tasting room and gift shop. The tasting room is open daily 11am to 6pm.

Off U.S. 50 a mile east of the village, **Swedenburg Estate Vineyard,** 23595 Winery Lane (© **540/687-5219;** www.swedenburgwines.com), occupies part of Valley View Farm, founded about 1762. We can thank the late Juanita Swedenburg for bringing the lawsuit in which the U.S. Supreme Court ruled that interstate wine sales over the Internet are okay. The vineyard is open Friday to Sunday 11am to 5pm. Farther east on Champe Ford Road (C.R. 629), between Middleburg and Aldie, is **Chrysalis Vineyards** (© **800/235-8804** or 540/687-8222; www.chrysaliswine.com), noted for its Albariño variety from Spain. It's open daily 10am to 5:30pm.

Middleburg ★★★

One of Virginia's most charming small towns, Middleburg is home to those who can afford to indulge in horses, horse breeding, steeplechase racing, and fox hunting. You will see jodhpurs and riding boots worn around town here, although some locals complain they are often on "paddock princesses"—who seldom ride but who like to look the part. On weekends the village can be packed with Washington, D.C., types out for a drive in the country.

This village is so unusual that the weekly rag calls itself the *Middleburg Eccentric.* In addition to real estate notices for farms selling for multimillions, the paper carries ads for firms offering horse clipping and mane pulling. Keep an eye peeled because in addition to being very, very wealthy, the person walking next to you could be very, very famous, too.

Middleburg is included on the National Register of Historic Villages, and with 600 or so residents, it's not much larger than when it was settled in 1731. You can't get lost here, for the village occupies just 6 blocks along Washington Street (U.S. 50), with two streets—Federal and Marshall—running parallel on either side.

ATTRACTIONS

Start your tour at the **Pink Box Visitor Information Center,** on Madison Street a block north of the one traffic signal on Washington Street (see "Visitor Information" under "The Hunt Country," earlier in this chapter). The public pavilion next door is dedicated to the late Jacqueline Kennedy Onassis, in honor of the contributions she made "during her happy years in the village."

Appropriately, Middleburg is home to the **National Sporting Library & Museum,** 102 The Plains Rd. (© **540/687-6542;** www.nsl.org), a research center housing more than 16,000 books and periodicals about horse sports and fishing, some of them dating to the 17th century. It is open Tuesday to Friday 10am to 4pm and Saturday 1 to 4pm.

Drive 1½ miles north of Middleburg on C.R. 626 and you'll come to **Glenwood Park** (© **540/687-5662;** www.glenwoodpark.org), Virginia's oldest racecourse in continuous use and home to many meets during the year, including the Virginia Fall Races in early October. Follow the gravel road uphill to the bleachers (look for the gazebo) for a gorgeous view of the Blue Ridge Mountains.

Nearby wineries are worth testing (see "On the Loudoun Wine Trail," above). If you are staying in Middleburg you can crawl back to your room from Boxwood Winery's **Tasting Room Wine Bar & Shop,** 16 E. Washington St. (© **540/687-8080;** www.thetastingroomwinebar.com). It is open Thursday to Sunday 1 to 7pm.

A NEARBY CIVIL WAR ATTRACTION

Manassas National Battlefield Park ★★★ The first massive clash of the Civil War took place near a stream known as Bull Run on July 21, 1861. A well-equipped but poorly trained Union army of 35,000 marched from Washington—along with spectators who expected to see a quick Union victory. Instead of a cakewalk, the blue coats ran into the Confederate army of Gen. P. G. T. Beauregard and a fierce stand by Rebel General Thomas J. Jackson, who would thereafter be known as "Stonewall." A Confederate victory shattered any hopes that the war would end quickly.

Union and Confederate armies met here again from August 28 through August 30, 1862, in the Battle of Second Manassas, which secured Gen. Robert E. Lee's place in history as his 55,000 men soundly defeated the Union army under Gen. John Pope.

Start your tour at the Henry Hill Visitor Center, where a museum, a 45-minute video ($3 admission; shown on the hour 9am–4pm), and a 6-minute battle map program tell the story. These hills are excellent for hiking, and there are a number of self-guided walking tours that highlight Henry Hill, Stone Bridge, and the other critical areas of the two battles. Allow about 2 hours to take in the visitor center and the First Battle walking tour (it's about 1-mile long). The tour of the entire First Battle area is 6½ miles long. The Battle of Second Manassas, which raged over a much larger area, is covered in the Brawner Farm Interpretive Center.

A self-guided 12-mile driving tour will take about 1½ hours. You can download a battlefield tour app for your iPhone from the **Civil War Trust** (© **202/367-1865;** www.civilwar.org/battleapps).

6511 Sudley Rd. (Va. 234). © **703/361-1339.** www.nps.gov/mana. Admission (good for 3 days) $3 adults, free for children 16 and under. Movie $3 per person. America the Beautiful passes accepted. Battlefield daily dawn–dusk. Visitor center daily 8:30am–5pm. From Middleburg (about 11 miles), take U.S. 50 east, turn right onto U.S. 15 south, turn left at Va. 234, and continue southeast to Manassas. From I-66, take Exit 47B and go ½ mile north on Va. 234.

WHERE TO STAY

The charming **Middleburg Country Inn,** 209 E. Washington St. (www.middleburg countryinn.com; ☎ **800/262-6082** or 540/687-6082), serves as the town's sole bed-and-breakfast. About 5 miles north of town, the **Goodstone Inn & Estate,** 36205 Snake Hill Rd. (www.goodstone.com; ☎ **877/219-4663** or 540/687-4645), is much more luxurious and expensive. It has 13 rooms in a restored carriage house, two cottages, and a spring house set on a 265-acre estate.

Red Fox Inn ★★   The historic Red Fox Inn in the center of Middleburg maintains the romantic charm of early Virginia in its original 1728 stone structure. A later addition is the Stray Fox Inn. The Red Fox has three rooms and three suites, all with wide-plank floors and 18th-century furnishings; several have working fireplaces. Rooms in the Stray Fox also preserve a traditional character with hand-stenciled walls, canopy beds, hooked rugs, and original fireplace mantels. Continental breakfast is served in the dark, cozy **Red Fox Inn Restaurant,** which features a Colonial ambience—low-beamed ceilings, pewter dishes, and equestrian prints lining the walls. The seasonal menus feature staples like filet mignon, crab cakes, rack of lamb, and grilled fish, switching to venison, quail, and other game in autumn.

2 E. Washington St. (PO Box 385), Middleburg, VA 20118. www.redfox.com. ☎ **800/223-1728** or 540/687-6301. Fax 540/687-6053. 15 units. $170–$275 double; $195–$475 suite. Rates include continental breakfast. AE, DC, DISC, MC, V. **Amenities:** Restaurant; bar. *In room:* A/C, TV, hair dryer, Wi-Fi.

WHERE TO EAT

Grab a shot of caffeine at **Cuppa Giddyup,** in the basement of 8 E. Washington St., ☎ **540/687-8211**), the town's version of Starbucks, and satiate your sweet tooth at **Scruffy's Ice Cream Parlor** (☎ **540/687-3766**), which has excellent frozen yogurt.

Back Street Cafe & Catering ITALIAN   Chef Tutti Perrricone, who was born in Middleburg and worked her way up in the restaurant business, opened this little casual cafe on Federal Street in 1986. At lunch, her curried chicken salad is especially good, either by itself or in a wrap. For dinner, the menu switches to pizzas and other Italian fare. Service can be a tad inconsistent, but that's true everywhere in Middleburg.

4 E. Federal St. (btw. Madison and Liberty sts.). ☎ **540/687-3122.** Reservations accepted. Main courses $13–$17. AE, DISC, MC, V. Mon–Fri 11:30am–2:30pm and 5–9pm, Sat 5–9pm.

The French Hound ★ FRENCH   Chef de Cuisine John-Gustin Birkett is a Leesburg native who cooked in Provence before employing his skills at this relaxed bistro in a two-story house a block south of Washington Street. His menu includes familiar French fare such as leg of lamb and grilled steaks and tuna but with *Sud de France* touches like Provençal vegetable ragout and ample use of Dijon mustard in sauces, salad dressings, and crab cakes. The best tables are in the sunny front rooms.

101 S. Madison St. (at Federal St.). ☎ **540/687-3018.** www.thefrenchhound.com. Reservations recommended. Main courses $9.50–$30. AE, DISC, MC, V. Tues 5:30–9:30pm; Wed–Thurs 11:30am–2:30pm and 5:30–9:30pm; Fri–Sat 11:30am–10pm (limited menu 2:30–5:30pm); Sun 11:30am–2:30pm and 5:30–9:30pm.

Market Salamander ★ DELI   This sophisticated gourmet deli is Middleburg's top lunch spot. You can pick from delicious salads, cheeses, and cold cuts from the cooler or look up at the blackboard menu for burgers, fried chicken, pulled pork, or crab cakes cooked to order in the open kitchen. Excellent wines are available by the glass. In warm weather customers consume their purchases outside on the wrap-around porch. Locals start their day here with hot coffee and freshly baked pastries.

200 W. Washington St. (at Pickering St.). ℂ **540/687-8011.** www.marketsalamander.com. Most items $7–$10. AE, DISC, MC, V. Daily 7:30am–6pm.

Red Horse Tavern PUB FARE   Dark and cramped inside, this lively tavern more than doubles in size during warm weather months, when customers spill outside onto tables on the front porch and yard. Market Salamander across the street has much better food but the lively ambience makes this Middleburg's best place for alfresco refreshment.

112 W. Washington St. (at Pickering St.). ℂ **540/587-6443.** Reservations not accepted. Sand-wiches and burgers $6.50–$9.50; main courses $12–$17. AE, DISC, MC, V. Mon–Thurs 11am–12:30am; Fri–Sat 11am–1:30am.

Aldie

Most of the quaint hamlet of Aldie, 5 miles east of Middleburg on John Mosby High-way (U.S. 50), is a quintessential Hunt Country hamlet. Its centerpiece is **Aldie Mill Historic Park** (ℂ **703/327-9777;** www.aldiemill.org), built from 1807 to 1809, the only gristmill in Virginia powered by twin water wheels. It has been restored to grind organic grains. The mill is open for milling demonstrations from mid-April through mid-November Saturday to Sunday from noon to 5pm. Admission is free. Aldie's antiques stores and other shops merit browsing, and a visit during the annual Aldie Mill Arts Show and Sale on weekends in June, or the Aldie Harvest Festival on the third weekend in October, will be most rewarding.

Little River Inn ★ 🍴   Friendly innkeepers Tucker and Mary Ann Withers have kept this early-19th-century farmhouse in Aldie simple and authentic—like grand-ma's house—since they opened it 1982. Staying here conveys a wonderful sense of life in a small Virginia hamlet. Farm animals, a small garden, and a patio are out the back door. The main house has five bedrooms, all charmingly furnished with antique pieces; one has a working fireplace. Or you can stay in the log cabin or the Patent House, a small late-1700s domicile, both with working fireplaces. Tucker comes over every morning to cook a full breakfast to order. He and Mary Ann give a 10% discount if you book 2 nights.

39307 John Mosby Hwy. (U.S. 50; PO Box 116), Aldie, VA 22001. www.aldie.com. ℂ **703/327-6742.** 8 units, 4 with private bathroom. $125–$275 double. Rates include full breakfast. AE, DC, DISC, MC, V. **Amenities:** Pool. In room: A/C, TV (in cottages), no phone.

FREDERICKSBURG & THE NORTHERN NECK

N o journey through Virginia's storied history is complete without a stop in Fredericksburg. Sitting on the banks of the Rappahannock River, it offers both a glimpse into Colonial America and a testament to the vast amount of blood that soaked the state's soil during the Civil War.

On the way in, I-95 can be clogged with traffic resulting from suburban sprawl, which is quickly absorbing Fredericksburg within the Washington, D.C., megalopolis, and modern shopping centers are popping up like weeds around Fredericksburg. In the remarkably preserved Historic District, however, it's thrilling to walk the same streets trod by George Washington and James Monroe, both of whom lived here.

I also like to visit the home of Mary Ball Washington, the first president's mother, who raised her children on a farm across the river and who lived out her days in Fredericksburg near Kenmore Plantation & Gardens, the home of her daughter. Our First Mother is more revered in Fredericksburg than is her son.

For a bit of levity, poke your head into two of Virginia's more entertaining historic sites, the Hugh Mercer Apothecary Shop and the Rising Sun Tavern, both survivors from Mrs. Washington's time.

For a more sobering experience, look down from Marye's Heights over the killing fields where Robert E. Lee's dug-in Confederate troops literally mowed down Union forces in 1862. It was the first of four great battles that make Fredericksburg hallowed ground for Civil War buffs.

For a complete escape, drive southeast from Fredericksburg onto the bucolic Northern Neck (we call it a "neck"; you call it a peninsula) between the Potomac River on one side and the Rappahannock on the other. Large and small creeks crisscross the neck, and bald eagles, blue heron, flocks of waterfowl, and an occasional wild turkey inhabit the unspoiled marshland.

Both Washington and Lee were born on the Peninsula, and their birthplaces are easy side trips from Fredericksburg. Otherwise the Northern Neck today primarily attracts weekenders from the mid-Atlantic region who come here to get away from it all.

FREDERICKSBURG ★★★

50 miles S of Washington, D.C.; 45 miles S of Alexandria; 50 miles N of Richmond

Fredericksburg provides a lesson in American history, especially the Colonial and Civil War eras. Its quaint downtown—a 40-square-block National Register Historic District—is well worth your time. In addition to its historical attractions, the district has a college-town ambience thanks to the **University of Mary Washington** (🕾 **540/654-2000;** www.umw.edu), whose Colonial-style campus is 8 blocks west of downtown via William Street.

The town came into being in 1728 as a 500-acre frontier settlement on the banks of the Rappahannock River. George Washington spent his formative years across the river at Ferry Farm, where he supposedly tossed a coin across the Rappahannock and never told a lie about chopping down the cherry tree. His mother lived out her life in a house he purchased for her on Charles Street, and she is buried on what was then Kenmore Plantation, home of his sister, Betty Washington Lewis.

Fredericksburg was a hotbed of revolutionary zeal in the 1770s, and many of its citizens shed both blood and treasure during the War for Independence. Thomas Jefferson, George Mason, and other founding fathers met here in 1777 to draft what later became the Virginia Statute of Religious Freedoms, the basis for the First Amendment guaranteeing separation of church and state. James Monroe practiced law here before spending his final years near Jefferson at Charlottesville.

Equidistant from Richmond and Washington—the two rival capitals—the Fredericksburg area was one of the Civil War's most disputed territories. The two sides fought a major battle in town and others nearby at Chancellorsville, The Wilderness, and Spotsylvania Courthouse. Stonewall Jackson was mistakenly shot by his own men at Chancellorsville; his amputated arm is buried at Ellwood Plantation. Clara Barton and Walt Whitman nursed wounded Federal soldiers in Chatham mansion, just across the river. Cannonballs embedded in the walls of some prominent buildings, as well as the graves of 17,000 Civil War soldiers, are grim reminders of that tragic era. The battlefields are now part of a national park.

Essentials
VISITOR INFORMATION
The **Fredericksburg Visitor Center,** 706 Caroline St. (at Charlotte St.), Fredericksburg, VA 22401 (🕾 **800/678-4748** or 540/373-1776; fax 540/372-5687; www.visitfred.com), offers free maps, many restaurant menus, and walking tour brochures following the 1862 Battle of Fredericksburg and of the downtown Historic District. It also shows a 14-minute video that will get you oriented, and it sells a block ticket to the major sites (see "Money-Saving Passes," below). The center is open Monday to Saturday 9am to 5pm and Sunday 11am to 5pm. It's closed New Year's Day, Thanksgiving, and Christmas.

On the southwestern edge of town, the **Spotsylvania County Visitor Center,** 4704 Southpointe Pkwy., Fredericksburg, VA 22407 (🕾 **800/654-4118** or 540/891-6670; www.spotsylvania.org), specializes in attractions south of town. It's in the Southpoint Shopping Center on U.S. 1 at Exit 126 off I-95 and open daily 9am to 5pm.

There also is a **Virginia Welcome Center** at Mile 130 on southbound I-95.

The **Fredericksburg Visitor Center** (see "Essentials," above) sells a **Fredericksburg Timeless Pass,** which includes admission to Belmont, Fredericksburg Area Museum and Cultural Center, Hugh Mercer Apothecary Shop, James Monroe Museum and Memorial Library, Kenmore, Mary Washington House, Rising Sun Tavern, and George Washington's Ferry Farm. It does not expire and costs $32 for adults and $10 for students 6 to 18. The pass is free for children 17 and under accompanied by an adult. Or you can opt for a 1-day pass for $16 for adults and $5 for students. **Note:** Admission prices in the listings below are to the individual properties without a block ticket. Most of the block-ticket attractions are closed New Year's Day, Thanksgiving, December 24, Christmas, and December 31.

GETTING THERE

BY CAR To reach the Historic District from I-95, take Exit 130A and follow Va. 3 east. Bear left on William Street (Va. 3 Business). There are no parking meters in Fredericksburg but many on-street spaces are limited to 2 hours. The public parking lots on Sophia Street are unlimited.

BY PLANE The nearest airports are Ronald Reagan Washington National Airport, Washington Dulles International Airport (see "Getting There" under "Alexandria," in chapter 4), and Richmond International Airport (see chapter 9).

BY TRAIN Fredericksburg's **Amtrak** station (© **800/872-7245;** www.amtrak.com) is at Lafayette Boulevard and Princess Anne Street, on the southern edge of the Historic District, 3 blocks from the Fredericksburg Visitor Center.

Virginia Railway Express (© **800/743-3873** or 703/497-7777; www.vre.org) operates early-morning commuter trains from Fredericksburg's Amtrak station to Union Station in Washington, D.C., from Monday through Friday. The first southbound train departs Washington at 12:55pm, with five more between 3:35 and 7pm. Check the website for schedules and fares.

GETTING AROUND

The best ways to see the historic district are on foot or by a trolley or horse-drawn carriage tour (see below), but **Ride Fred** (© **540/372-1222;** www.ridefred.com) provides public bus service around the area Monday to Friday 8:30am to 7:30pm (daily when classes are in session at the University of Mary Washington). Most useful is the Downtown Loop (Rte. F5), which passes the Amtrak station and the university. Fares are 75¢ per person.

Exploring Fredericksburg

A majority of the Historic District attractions are along Princess Anne Street within an easy walk from the visitor center, but don't miss several notable monuments along broad **Washington Avenue** north of Kenmore Plantation & Gardens. Mary Ball Washington is buried at **Meditation Rock,** a spot where she often came to pray and meditate; there's a monument there in her honor. Just across the way is the **Thomas Jefferson Religious Liberty Monument,** commemorating Jefferson's Fredericksburg meeting with George Mason, Edmond Pendleton, George Wythe, and Thomas Ludwell Lee in 1777 to draft the Virginia Statute of Religious Freedom. The **Hugh Mercer Monument,** off Fauquier Street, honors the doctor who died fighting in the Revolutionary War and whose apothecary shop is now a museum (see below).

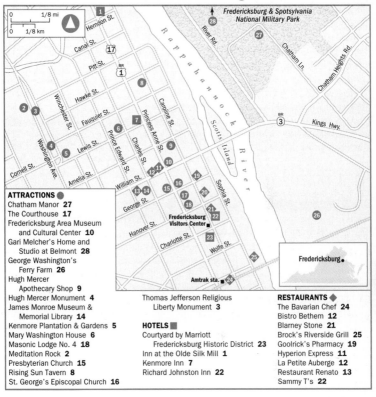

ATTRACTIONS ●
Chatham Manor **27**
The Courthouse **17**
Fredericksburg Area Museum
    and Cultural Center **10**
Gari Melcher's Home and
    Studio at Belmont **28**
George Washington's
    Ferry Farm **26**
Hugh Mercer
    Apothecary Shop **9**
Hugh Mercer Monument **4**
James Monroe Museum &
    Memorial Library **14**
Kenmore Plantation & Gardens **5**
Mary Washington House **6**
Masonic Lodge No. 4 **18**
Meditation Rock **2**
Presbyterian Church **15**
Rising Sun Tavern **8**
St. George's Episcopal Church **16**

Thomas Jefferson Religious
    Liberty Monument **3**

HOTELS ■
Courtyard by Marriott
    Fredericksburg Historic District **23**
Inn at the Olde Silk Mill **1**
Kenmore Inn **7**
Richard Johnston Inn **22**

RESTAURANTS ◆
The Bavarian Chef **24**
Bistro Bethem **12**
Blarney Stone **21**
Brock's Riverside Grill **25**
Goolrick's Pharmacy **19**
Hyperion Express **11**
La Petite Auberge **12**
Restaurant Renato **13**
Sammy T's **22**

BY GHOST TOUR   An evening option is to stroll around the historic haunts with **Ghosts of Fredericksburg Tours,** 623 Caroline St. (© **540/654-5414;** www.ghostsoffredericksburg.com). The 90-minute walks depart the visitor center parking lot at 8pm Thursday to Monday in July, Friday to Sunday in August, and Friday to Saturday September through December. They cost $11 per person (children 6 and under are free). Reservations are required.

BY TROLLEY OR HORSE-DRAWN CARRIAGE   You can sit and explore the Historic District via motorized trolley or horse-drawn carriage, both of which leave from the visitor center. **Trolley Tours of Fredericksburg** (© **540/898-0737;** www.fredericksburgtrolley.com) pass 35 historic sights. The 1¼-hour narrated tours usually leave at 10:30am, noon, 1:30, and 3:30pm from June through October. They depart at 10:30am and 1:30pm the rest of the year. Fares are $17 for adults and $8 for children 17 and under.

Or clip-clop around with the **Old Towne Carriage Company** (© **540/371-0094**), whose 45-minute narrated rides cost $17 for adults and $10 for children 4 to 10. It operates from April through December daily from 9:30am to 3:30pm.

The visitor center sells tickets for all tours.

THE TOP ATTRACTIONS

Gari Melchers Home and Studio at Belmont Situated on 27 hillside acres overlooking the falls of the Rappahannock River, Belmont began as an 18th-century farmhouse (the central six rooms of the house date to the 1790s) and was enlarged to a 22-room estate by a later owner. Although the house has historic attributes, its fame comes from being furnished with the art treasures, family heirlooms, and European antiques of famed American artist Gari Melchers, who lived here from 1916 until his death in 1932. His wife, Corinne, gave Belmont to the Commonwealth of Virginia in 1955. It takes about an hour to see the orientation video and take a guided tour of the house. You can explore the gardens and studio on your own.

224 Washington St. (C.R. 1001). © **540/654-1015.** www.garimelchers.org. Admission $10 adults, $5 children 6–18, free for children 5 and under. Thurs–Tues 10am–5pm. Closed New Year's Day, Thanksgiving, Dec 24, Christmas, and Dec 31. Guided 30-min. house tours depart on the hour and half-hour (last tour 4:30pm). From the visitor center, take U.S. 1 north across the Falmouth Bridge, turn left at the traffic light in Falmouth, and go ¼ mile up the hill; turn left on Washington St. (C.R. 1001) to Belmont.

Hugh Mercer Apothecary Shop ★★ ☺ Born in Scotland in 1726, Dr. Hugh Mercer became friends with George Washington when they were colonels during the French and Indian War (1754–63). He opened this apothecary shop in 1761 and practiced here until serving as a brigadier general in the American Revolution. He was with Washington during the famous crossing of the Delaware River on Christmas night of 1776 and died of bayonet wounds at the Battle of Princeton a few days later. (The warrior tradition continued in his family—Gen. George S. Patton was his great-great-great-grandson.) Children often let out *"Ooooos"* when hostesses in period dress show how Mercer practiced 18th-century medicine in this little shop of horrors. A garden tour explains how plants were used as medicine in those days.

1020 Caroline St. (at Amelia St.). © **800/678-4748** or 540/373-3362. www.apva.org/hughmercer apothecary. Admission $5 adults, $2 children 6–18, free for children 5 and under. Mar–Oct Mon–Sat 9am–4pm, Sun 10am–4pm; Nov–Feb Mon–Sat 10am–2pm, Sun noon–4pm. 30-min. tours depart continuously (last tour 30 min. before closing).

James Monroe Museum and Memorial Library ★ One of the most distinguished Americans of his time, James Monroe served as a U.S. senator; minister to France, England, and Spain; governor of Virginia; secretary of state; secretary of war; and fifth president of the United States (1817–25). He and Washington were the only presidents who fought in the War of Independence. As president, he promulgated the Monroe Doctrine, which kept European powers from meddling in the Western Hemisphere. Monroe practiced law in Fredericksburg from 1786 until 1789, when he moved to Charlottesville and built his home, now known as Ash Lawn–Highland (p. 114), near Monticello, the home of his close friend Jefferson. The furnishings are original Monroe possessions. You can peruse correspondence from Jefferson (don't miss the letter written partially in code), Madison, and Benjamin

> ### Giving Meaning to "Sawbones"
>
> In Dr. Hugh Mercer's Apothecary Shop you can see how he used a heated cup to remove boils and carbuncles, a knife to cut out cataracts, an ominous-looking key to extract teeth, and a saw for amputating limbs. The latter instrument gave rise to the early slang term for doctors: *sawbones.*

Franklin. Here, too, are the gun and canteen Monroe used in the American Revolution. Also on display are two Rembrandt Peale portraits of Monroe and silhouettes of the Monroes by Charles Willson Peale.

908 Charles St. (btw. William and George sts.). © **540/654-1043.** http://jamesmonroemuseum. umw.edu. Admission $5 adults, $1 children 6–18, free for children 5 and under. Mar–Nov daily 10am–5pm; Dec–Feb daily 10am–4pm. Guided 30-min. tours depart throughout the day (last tour 30 min. before closing).

Kenmore Plantation & Gardens ★★   This stately Georgian mansion was built in the 1770s for George Washington's only sister, Betty Washington, and her husband, Fielding Lewis, one of Fredericksburg's wealthiest men and a financier of the American Revolution—so much so that he had to sell Kenmore to liquidate his debts. He died a few weeks after the victory at Yorktown. Today, the house sits on three of the original plantation's 1,300 acres and has been architecturally restored to its Colonial elegance. The 40-minute tours explain the lives of the inhabitants and their servants. In addition to the elaborate molded plaster ceilings and cornices, much of the woodwork and paneling are original. Be sure to explore the famous gardens, restored and maintained according to the original plans by the Garden Club of Virginia. The George Washington Foundation owns the home and sponsors many special programs.

1201 Washington Ave. (btw. Lewis and Fauquier sts.). © **540/373-3381.** www.kenmore.org. Admission $10 adults, $4 children 6–17, free for children 5 and under. Combination ticket (admission to Kenmore Plantation & Gardens and George Washington's Ferry Farm) $15 adults, $8 children 6–17, free for children 5 and under. Mar–Oct daily 10am–5pm; Nov–Dec daily 10am–4pm. (Last tour departs 45 min. before closing). Closed Jan–Feb, Easter, Thanksgiving, Dec 24, Christmas, and Dec 31.

Mary Washington House ★   George Washington bought this white-frame house in 1772 for his mother, Mary Ball Washington, so she would be near her daughter's home at Kenmore Plantation (see above). Mary Washington was then 64 years old and had been living across the river at Ferry Farm since 1738 (see "More Attractions," below). Legend says that Lafayette found Mrs. Washington in her garden when he visited during the Revolution to pay his respects (her sundial still keeps time). Her son came in 1789 to receive her blessing before going to New York for his inauguration as president. He never saw her again, for she died later that year. Exhibits include a mirror she considered to be her "best dressing glass."

1200 Charles St. (at Lewis St.). © **540/373-1569.** www.apva.org/marywashingtonhouse. Admission $5 adults, $2 children 6–18, free for children 5 and under. Mar–Oct Mon–Sat 9am–5pm, Sun 11am–5pm; Nov–Feb Mon–Sat 10am–4pm, Sun noon–4pm. Guided 30-min. tours run continuously.

Rising Sun Tavern ★★   The Rising Sun was originally a residence, built in 1760 by Charles Washington, George's youngest brother, but beginning in the early 1790s it served as a tavern for some 30 years. You'll be thoroughly entertained during the 30-minute tours, perhaps led by a tavern wench—an indentured servant sentenced to 7 years for stealing a loaf of bread in England. The Rising Sun Tavern was a proper high-class tavern, she explains, not for riffraff. The gentlemen congregated over Madeira and cards in the Great Room or had a rollicking good time in the Taproom over multicourse meals and many tankards of ale. Meanwhile, ladies were consigned to the Retiring Room, where they would gossip and do needlework.

1306 Caroline St. (at Fauquier St.). © **540/371-1494.** www.apva.org/risingsuntavern. Admission $5 adults, $2 children 6–18, free for children 5 and under. Mar–Oct Mon–Sat 10am–5pm, Sun noon–4pm; Nov–Feb Mon–Sat 11am–3pm, Sun noon–4pm. Closed New Year's Day, Thanksgiving, Dec 24, Christmas, and Dec 31. Guided 30-min. tours run continuously.

MORE ATTRACTIONS

The Courthouse   Built in 1853, this courthouse is a fine example of Gothic-revival architecture. In fact, its architect, James Renwick, also designed St. Patrick's Cathedral in New York and the original Smithsonian "Castle" and Renwick Gallery in Washington, D.C. Exhibits in the lobby include copies of Mary Ball Washington's will and George Washington's address to the city council in 1784.

815 Princess Anne St. (Ⓒ **540/372-1066.** Free admission. Mon–Fri 9am–4pm.

Fredericksburg Area Museum and Cultural Center   This very good local museum occupies the 1816 Town Hall in Market Square, although its entry and many exhibits are in a former bank building across William Street. In existence since 1733, Market Square was the center of trade and commerce in Fredericksburg for more than a century, while Town Hall served as the city's social and legal center. Lafayette was entertained here in 1824 with lavish parties and balls, and the building continued to serve its original function until 1982. You'll see permanent exhibits about the area's history. Highlights include a Gilbert Stuart portrait of Washington and the 1668 Bible on which he took the oath to join **Masonic Lodge No. 4** (at 803 Princess Anne St.).

1001 Princess Anne St. (at William St.). (Ⓒ **540/371-3037.** www.famcc.org. Admission $7 adults, $2 children 6–18, free for children 5 and under. Apr–Oct Mon–Sat 10am–5pm, Sun 1–5pm; Nov–Mar Mon–Sat 10am–4pm, Sun 1–4pm. Closed New Year's Day, Dec 24, Christmas, and Dec 31.

George Washington's Ferry Farm   The first president was 6 years old in 1738 when his family moved to this farm across the river from Fredericksburg. It was here that George purportedly confessed to chopping down the cherry tree. He and his siblings took a ferry across the river to school in Fredericksburg. After their father,

SEMPER FI—THE U.S. MARINE CORPS MUSEUM

Rising like a beacon beside I-95 about halfway between Fredericksburg and Alexandria is the sloping steel tower atop the terrific **National Museum of the Marine Corps ★★★**, 18900 Jefferson Davis Hwy. (U.S. 1), Triangle, VA 22172 (Ⓒ **877/635-1775** or 703/784-6115; www.usmcmuseum.org). The shape of this stunning, modernistic building evokes the famous scene of leathernecks (and one navy corpsman) raising the U.S. flag on Iwo Jima during World War II—the 210-foot-tall tower slopes at the same angle as their improvised battlefield flagpole. It stands above a glass-ceiling rotunda at the museum's center, from which are suspended Marine Corps aircraft dating back to World War I. Exhibits in a labyrinth of rooms trace the corps' history since its inception in 1775. Sounds from numerous audiovisual effects can be a bit distracting, but many of the high-tech exhibits are especially good at re-creating battlefield reality. For example, a Korean War battle takes place in a chilled room to capture wintertime conditions in that conflict, while a Vietnam skirmish takes place in stifling tropical heat. You'll also feel what it was like to fly in a noisy, shaking Vietnam-era helicopter. You will need at least 3 hours to digest it all. Be sure to rent a radio tour receiver in the gift shop ($3). Two cafes are on-site, so plan to have lunch. Admission is free. The museum is open 9am to 5pm daily except Christmas. Take Exit 150 off I-95 at Triangle, go east to U.S. 1, and turn south to the museum.

Augustine Washington, died in 1743, their mother, Mary Ball Washington, stayed on the farm until 1772, when George bought her a house in town (see "Mary Washington House," above). Union soldiers camped on the farm during the Civil War. The Washingtons' 1741 house is long gone, but archaeologists continue to discover and interpret new finds, including confirmation of its foundation and cellars. Artifacts are on display in the visitor center. The George Washington Foundation, which also owns Kenmore Plantations & Gardens (see above), offers many special programs here.

268 Kings Hwy. (Va. 3). © **540/370-0732.** www.kenmore.org. Admission $8 adults, $3 children 6–17, free for children 5 and under. Combination ticket (admission to George Washington's Ferry Farm and Kenmore Plantation & Gardens) $15 adults, $8 children 6–17, free for children 5 and under. Mar–Oct daily 10am–5pm; Nov–Dec daily 10am–4pm. Closed Jan–Feb, Easter, Thanksgiving, Dec 24, Christmas, and Dec 31. Take Va. 3 east across Rappahannock River, turn right after 3rd traffic signal.

The Presbyterian Church   The local Presbyterian congregation, which dates to the early 1800s, completed this Greek-revival building in 1833. It was shelled during the Civil War, and, like St. George's Episcopal Church (below), served as a hospital where Clara Barton nursed wounded Union soldiers. Cannonballs in the front-left pillar and scars on the walls of the loft and belfry remain. The present church bell replaced one that was given to the Confederacy to be melted down for making cannons.

810 Princess Anne St. (at George St.). © **540/373-7057.** www.fredericksburgpc.org. Free admission. Sun services Sept–May 8:30 and 11am, June–Aug 8:30 and 10am. (Go to church office at other times for admission.)

St. George's Episcopal Church   Martha Washington's father and John Paul Jones's brother are buried in the graveyard of this church, and members of the first parish congregation included Mary Ball Washington and Revolutionary War generals Hugh Mercer and George Weedon. The original church on this site was built in 1732; the current Romanesque-revival structure, in 1849. During the Battle of Fredericksburg, the church was hit at least 25 times. It served as a Union hospital during the Battle of the Wilderness in 1864, when 10,000 wounded soldiers filled every available building in town. Note the three signed Tiffany windows.

905 Princess Anne St. (btw. George and William sts.). © **540/373-4133.** www.stgeorgesepiscopal. net. Free admission. Mon–Sat 8am–10pm (unless a wedding is taking place Sat), Sun 8am–8pm. Sun services 8 and 10:30am (7:45 and 10am during summer).

Shopping

Fredericksburg is one of Virginia's top treasure-troves for antiques and collectibles shoppers, as you will quickly note in the face of more than 40 stores along Caroline, Sophia, and William streets. Antiques lovers come here for lower prices than in metropolitan areas such as Alexandria, Richmond, and Norfolk. The visitor center has brochures describing each store's specialty (see "Essentials," earlier in this chapter).

River Cruises

Operated by the same company that goes to Tangier Island (p. 101) from Reedville on the Northern Neck, **Rappahannock River Cruises** (© **804/453-2628;** www. tangiercruise.com) sends the stern-wheeler *City of Fredericksburg* down the river from the city dock on Sophia Street from May through October. Most popular are the 2-hour lunch trips departing at noon Tuesday through Saturday. Fares are $25 for adults and $14 for children. The company also has dinner and Sunday brunch cruises. Call for reservations.

Where to Stay

You'll find chain hotels of every ilk off I-95. Most convenient to the Historic District is the strip along Va. 3 at Exit 130. This is also Fredericksburg's major suburban shopping area, with the Spotsylvania Mall and a multitude of other centers, plus a host of national chain restaurants. Worthy motels here include the **Best Western Fredericksburg** (✆ 800/528-1234 or 540/371-5050), **Best Western Central Plaza** (✆ 800/528-1234 or 540/786-7404), **Hampton Inn** (✆ 800/426-7866 or 540/371-0330), **Hilton Garden Inn** (✆ 877/STAY-HGI [782-9444] or 540/786-7404), **Ramada Inn–Spotsylvania Mall** (✆ 800/272-6232 or 540/786-8361), and an inexpensive **Super 8** (✆ 800/800-8000 or 540/786-8881).

The newest properties are along U.S. 1 at Exit 126 south of town, another rapidly developing commercial area known as Southpoint. These include the **Comfort Inn Southpoint** (✆ 800/228-5151 or 540/898-5550), **Days Inn Fredericksburg South** (✆ 800/325-2525 or 540/898-6800), **Fairfield Inn by Marriott** (✆ 800/228-2800 or 540/891-9100), a **Hampton Inn** (✆ 800/426-7866 or 540/898-5000), **Ramada Inn & Conference Center** (✆ 800/2-RAMADA [272-6232] or 540/898-1102), **Sleep Inn Southpoint** (✆ 877/424-6423 or 540/710-5500), and two more cheapies, the **Econo Lodge South** (✆ 800/800-55-ECONO [553-2666] or 540/898-5440) and another **Super 8** (✆ 800/800-8000 or 540/898-7100).

Courtyard by Marriott Fredericksburg Historic District ★ Across Charlotte Street from the Fredericksburg Visitor Center, this four-story hotel opened in 2009 on the site of the Indian Queen Tavern, which operated between 1771 and 1832. While the brick building seems at home in the Historic District, the decor inside is modern and high tech, beginning with a row of computer workstations just off the atrium lobby. As at all Courtyards, the spacious guest quarters are equipped for doing business, with desks and ergonomic chairs. A bistro-style restaurant serves breakfast, lunch, and dinner, while a convenience outlet is open 24 hours.

620 Caroline St., Fredericksburg, VA 22401. www.marriott.com. ✆ **800/321-2211** or 540/373-8300. Fax 540/373-8355. 98 units. $139–$219 double. Parking $10. AE, DC, DISC, MC, V. **Amenities:** Restaurant; bar; health club; Jacuzzi; pool. *In room:* A/C, TV, fridge, hair dryer, Wi-Fi.

BED & BREAKFASTS

In addition to the inns listed below, the Historic District is host to the **Schooler House Bed & Breakfast,** 1303 Caroline St. (www.theschoolerhouse.com; ✆ **540/374-5258**), an 1891 house with four fireplaces.

More convenient to the battlefields is **Stevenson Ridge,** 6901 Meeting St., Spotsylvania, VA 22553 (www.stevensonridge.com; ✆ **540/582-9041**), with rooms and suites in a restored 1812 plantation manse and other buildings, including a log cabin. It's off Courthouse Road (Va. 208) near the Spotsylvania Courthouse Battlefield.

Inn at the Olde Silk Mill ★ 🍴 Staying at this unpretentious, antiques-laden inn is like visiting your great-grandmother—provided yours owns a house with 28 bedrooms. These units evoke the Colonial and Victorian eras, with some reproductions but mostly with marble-top walnut dressers, rag rugs, canopied beds, and other antiques. It's a hub for value-conscious Civil War buffs and people participating in Civil War reenactments—don't be surprised to see musket-toting Blues and Grays in the lobby. Although amenities are scarce, the staff is friendly and helpful. The property was known as the Fredericksburg Colonial Inn until 2007, when it was renamed to reflect the original purpose of the industrial-looking building.

1707 Princess Anne St., Fredericksburg, VA 22401. www.innattheoldesilkmill.com. © **540/371-5666.** Fax 540/371-5884. 28 units. $99–$169 double. Rates include light continental breakfast. AE, DISC, MC, V. *In room:* A/C, TV, fridge, Wi-Fi.

Kenmore Inn An elegant white pediment supported by fluted columns and a front porch with wicker chairs welcome you to this late 1700s mansion in the Historic District on property originally owned by George Washington's brother-in-law, Fielding Lewis. A sweeping staircase leads to the guest rooms—a handsome assortment of both cozy and spacious accommodations furnished with antiques such as canopied four-poster beds, old chests, and walls hung with botanical prints. The house has eight working fireplaces, four in the bedrooms. The inn serves full breakfasts to its guests in the main floor dining room, which turns into a fine-dining restaurant at dinner.

1200 Princess Anne St., Fredericksburg, VA 22401. www.kenmoreinn.com. © **540/371-7622.** Fax 540/371-5480. 9 units. $130–$175 double. Rates include full breakfast. AE, DC, DISC, MC, V. **Amenities:** Restaurant; bar. *In room:* A/C, TV, Wi-Fi.

Richard Johnston Inn ★★ Two 18th-century brick row houses are joined to form this elegantly restored inn across busy Caroline Street from the visitor center. The Oriental rugs and mahogany furniture in the second-floor rooms in one house create a more formal atmosphere than in the others, which feature rockers and four-poster beds that lend a country charm. Third-floor dormer rooms are attractive, with low ceilings and dormer windows. The inn's original kitchen house also exudes charm, with brick floors, two queen-size beds, and a private entrance from the courtyard. The spacious Isabella's Suite also offers a private courtyard entrance as well as two queen-size beds, a kitchenette, and a separate living room. The Loft Suite apartment overlooking the courtyard also has a kitchenette and has a king-size bed in its loft. The two courtyard rooms here are pet-friendly. Three other units, all with Jacuzzi tubs, are in the **1890 Caroline House,** a Victorian manse a block away at 528 Caroline St.

711 Caroline St., Fredericksburg, VA 22401. www.therichardjohnstoninn.com. © **877/557-0770** or 540/899-7606. Fax 540/899-6837. 12 units. $115–$275 double. Rates include breakfast. AE, MC, V. Pet fee $25. *In room:* A/C, TV, kitchenette (in some), no phone, Wi-Fi.

Where to Eat

The swankiest restaurant in town is the **Kenmore Inn Dining Room** (see "Where to Stay," above), with an extensive wine cellar. In the restored Amtrak train station at the southern end of Caroline Street, the **Bavarian Chef,** 200 Lafayette Blvd. (© **540/371-7080;** www.thebavarianchef.com), has very good traditional German fare. Top Italian is **Ristorante Renato,** 422 William St. (© **540/371-8228**).

Hyperion Espresso (© **540/373-4882;** www.hyperionespresso.com), a college-town-style coffee shop at the corner of William and Princess Anne streets, serves the best coffee and pastries in town. The old-fashioned soda fountain still runs at **Goolrick's Pharmacy** (© **540/373-9878**), on Caroline Street at George Street.

Brock's Riverside Grill, 503 Sofia St. (© **540/370-1820;** www.brocksgrill.com), at Lafayette Boulevard beside the river, is a civilized pub with an outdoor bar where you can slake your thirst after walking around the Historic District. In cold weather the best place to tipple is the **Blarney Stone,** 715 Caroline St. (© **540/371-PINT** [7468]; www.theblarney.net).

Bistro Bethem ★★ AMERICAN The young husband-wife team of Blake and Aby Bethem (he's the chef) serve refined Southern cuisine at this art-laden bistro next door to La Petite Auberge (see below). An Italian restaurant once occupied the premises, and Blake uses the leftover clay pizza oven to finish off choices such as

Carl's Famous Frozen Custard

Listed on the National Register of Historic Places, **Carl's,** 2200 Princess Anne St. (no phone), has been making frozen custard with the same machines since 1947. The cones, shakes, and malts come in vanilla, chocolate, strawberry, and one other flavor. Carl's is open mid-February through mid-November from Sunday to Thursday 11am to 11pm, and on Friday and Saturday from 11am to 11:30pm.

rib-eye steak with onion rings, bow-tie pasta with green peas and apple-wood-smoked bacon, and seared tuna with polenta cake and braised collard greens. The Bethem's wine list has won awards. Try the homemade sorbet for dessert.

309 William St. ✆ **540/371-9999.** www.bistrobethem.com. Reservations recommended Fri–Sat. Main courses $22–$28. AE, MC, V. Tues–Sat 11:30am–2:30pm and 5–10pm; Sun 11:30am–2:30pm and 5–9pm.

La Petite Auberge ★ FRENCH   Christian Etienne Reanult's delightful restaurant was designed to look like a garden, an effect enhanced by white latticework and garden furnishings. Unpainted brick walls are hung with copper pots and cheerful oil paintings, and candlelit tables are adorned with fresh flowers. A cozy lounge adjoins. Christian and his classically trained son, Raymond, change their menu daily. They might offer salade niçoise, soft-shell crab amandine, poached salmon with hollandaise sauce, and sirloin steak with béarnaise sauce.

311 William St. (btw. Princess Anne and Charles sts.). ✆ **540/371-2727.** www.lapetiteauberge fredericksburg.com. Reservations recommended, especially at dinner. Main courses $14–$28. AE, MC, V. Mon–Fri 11:30am–2:30pm and 5:30–10pm; Sat 11:30am–2:15pm and 5:30–10pm; early-bird dinner Mon–Thurs 5:30–7pm.

Sammy T's 🍃 AMERICAN/VEGETARIAN   This popular, inexpensive pub offers a relaxed, tasteful setting and a creative health-food orientation. In fact, it's Fredericksburg's best option for vegetarians and vegans. It has a publike ambience, with large overhead fans, a pressed-tin ceiling, knotty-pine booths, and a long oak bar. Everything is made from scratch, with an emphasis on natural ingredients. The lunch and dinner menus offer many vegetarian and vegan items, such as vegetarian lasagna, a bean-and-grain burger, and a spicy black-bean cake. Entrees like burgers, fried oysters, and crab cakes are possibilities for meat and seafood eaters. You can satisfy your sweet cravings at **Sammy T's Frozen Yogurt,** around the corner on Hanover Street.

801 Caroline St. (at Hanover St.). ✆ **540/371-2008.** www.sammyts.com. Reservations not accepted. Sandwiches $4.50–$9.50; main courses $8–$23. AE, DISC, MC, V. Sun–Thurs 10:30am–9:30pm; Fri–Sat 10:30am–10pm.

THE CIVIL WAR BATTLEFIELDS ★★★

Fredericksburg has never forgotten its Civil War victories and defeats in the battles of Fredericksburg and at Chancellorsville, The Wilderness, and Spotsylvania Courthouse, 12 to 15 miles west of the city. The battles were part of three Union attempts to advance from Washington, D.C., to Richmond between December 1862 and May 1864. Only the last one succeeded. Today, the sites are beautifully preserved in the U.S. National Park Service's **Fredericksburg & Spotsylvania National Military**

Park, which also includes the Stonewall Jackson Shrine, where the great Confederate general died after being mistakenly shot by his own men.

Park headquarters are at Chatham Manor (see below), but the **Fredericksburg Battlefield Visitor Center** is at 1013 Lafayette Blvd. (U.S. 1 Business), at Sunken Road (**℃ 540/373-6122**), where you can pick up detailed tour brochures and watch a 22-minute orientation video shown on the hour and half-hour ($2 for adults, $1 for children 9 and under). The bookstore across the parking lot rents and sells the audio-tour tapes and CDs that are essential to get the most out of your visit (see "A Battle Plan for Seeing the Battlefields," below). Be sure to pick up the park service's main brochure, which has a detailed map, and pamphlets for each of the sites. In case you want more detailed information, the bookstore is packed with Civil War literature.

Admission to the battlefields is free. The Fredericksburg visitor center is open daily 9am to 5pm with extended hours in summer and on spring and fall weekends. The actual battlefields are open daily from sunrise to sunset. You can drive through the battlefields, but the visitor centers are closed New Year's Day and Christmas.

There's also a visitor center at **Chancellorsville** (see below). The Wilderness and Spotsylvania Courthouse battlefields have shelters with exhibits explaining what happened. Park rangers give **guided tours** of each battlefield daily during summer and on spring and autumn weekends. Call the visitor centers for the schedule.

For advance **information,** contact the Superintendent, Fredericksburg & Spotsylvania National Military Park, 120 Chatham Lane, Fredericksburg, VA 22405 (**℃ 540/371-0802;** www.nps.gov/frsp).

Chatham Manor

Across the river from downtown at 120 Chatham Lane, this mansion was built between 1768 and 1771 by wealthy planter William Fitzhugh, who supported the Revolution politically and financially. George Washington visited twice. During the Civil War, Chatham served as headquarters for Federal commanders—Lincoln

5

FREDERICKSBURG & THE NORTHERN NECK

Civil War Battlefields

A BATTLE PLAN FOR SEEING THE BATTLEFIELDS

Although you can drive around the battlefields in less than a day, you'll need 2 days to take the full 75-mile audio-guided auto tours of the Fredericksburg and Spotsylvania battlefields. Allow a minimum of 30 minutes at each of the two visitor centers and 3 hours for each of the four battlefield audio tours, plus driving times in between.

I strongly recommend the audio-tour CDs available at the Fredericksburg and Chancellorsville visitor centers (there's a different recording for each battle; $4.95 to rent for a day or $13 to purchase each CD). You can download a battlefield tour app for your iPhone from the **Civil War**

Trust (**℃ 202/367-1865;** www.civilwar.org/battleapps).

Although you can start at the Chancellorsville Visitor Center, it's preferable to tour the battlefields in the order in which the conflicts occurred: Fredericksburg, Chancellorsville, The Wilderness, and Spotsylvania Courthouse. Spend the first day at Fredericksburg and Chancellorsville, and the second at The Wilderness and Spotsylvania Courthouse, where the battles happened within days of each other. The Stonewall Jackson Shrine at Guinea Station is 18 miles southeast of Spotsylvania Courthouse; go there last.

visited his generals here—and as a Union field hospital where American Red Cross founder Clara Barton and poet Walt Whitman assisted the wounded. You can tour five rooms and the grounds on your own. The dining room and parlor have exhibits on Chatham's owners and the manor's role in the Civil War. National Park Service employees are on hand to answer questions and lead guided tours. Chatham is open daily 9am to 4:30pm.

Battle of Fredericksburg

The Battle of Fredericksburg took place from December 11 to December 13, 1862, when the Union army under Gen. Ambrose E. Burnside crossed the river into Fredericksburg via pontoon bridges. Burnside made a huge mistake when he sent the body of his 100,000 men uphill against Lee's 75,000 troops, most of them dug in behind a stone wall along Sunken Road at the base of Marye's Heights. The ground below the heights became a bloody killing field as Lee's cannon, firing from the hill, mowed down the Yankees.

Sunken Road—restored to look as it did in 1862—starts at the visitor center at the base of Marye's Heights. You can examine the road and follow the gently sloping pathway up the 40-foot-high heights for the fine view that turns spine chilling as you consider the lives lost on the fields below. Park rangers lead 35-minute guided tours of the road several times daily during the summer and on spring and fall weekends. The park also has summertime children's programs here.

Battle of Chancellorsville

President Lincoln fired Burnside after the Marye's Heights massacre. Under Gen. Joseph Hooker, Burnside's replacement, the Union forces crossed the river north of Fredericksburg in late April 1863 and advanced to Chancellorsville, a crossroads 10 miles west of Fredericksburg on the Orange Turnpike (now Va. 3). In a surprise attack, Stonewall Jackson flanked Hooker's line on May 2 and won a spectacular victory. Jackson was inadvertently shot by his own men that same night. He was taken 5 miles west to Ellwood Farm, where his left arm was amputated and buried in the family cemetery (see "Battle of the Wilderness," below). He was later moved to a farm near Guinea Station, where he died (see "Stonewall Jackson Shrine," below). By then, Lee had driven the Union army back across the Rappahannock.

Stop at the **Chancellorsville Visitor Center** (© **540/786-2880**), 12 miles west of Fredericksburg on Va. 3, to see another audiovisual orientation and related exhibits. Auto-tour tapes and CDs are available at the bookstore. The center is open daily 9am to 5pm, with extended hours in summer and on spring and autumn weekends. Be sure to get a pass here to see the gravestone over Jackson's arm at Ellwood Farm.

Battle of the Wilderness

A year later, under the direction of the aggressive Ulysses S. Grant, Union forces once again crossed the Rappahannock and advanced south to Wilderness Tavern, 5 miles west of Chancellorsville near what is now the junction of Va. 3 and Va. 20. Lee advanced to stop him, thus setting up the first battle between these two great generals. On May 5 and 6, 1864, the armies fought in the tangled thickets of The Wilderness. The battle was a stalemate, but instead of retreating as his predecessors had, Grant backed off and went around Lee toward his ultimate target, Richmond, via the shortest road south (now Va. 208).

The battle raged around **Ellwood Farm,** which during the Battle of Chancellorsville had served as the Confederate hospital where Stonewall Jackson's arm was

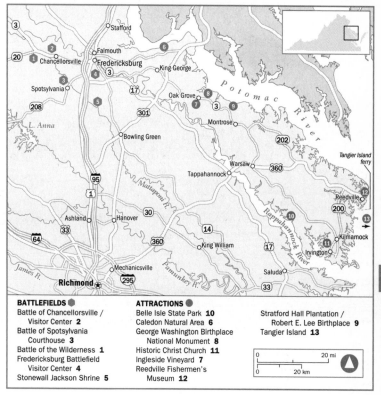

BATTLEFIELDS ●
Battle of Chancellorsville /
  Visitor Center **2**
Battle of Spotsylvania
  Courthouse **3**
Battle of the Wilderness **1**
Fredericksburg Battlefield
  Visitor Center **4**
Stonewall Jackson Shrine **5**

ATTRACTIONS ●
Belle Isle State Park **10**
Caledon Natural Area **6**
George Washington Birthplace
  National Monument **8**
Historic Christ Church **11**
Ingleside Vineyard **7**
Reedville Fishermen's
  Museum **12**

Stratford Hall Plantation /
  Robert E. Lee Birthplace **9**
Tangier Island **13**

0 ——————— 20 mi
0 ——————— 20 km

amputated and buried. You can see his arm's gravestone at Ellwood Farm, which is open Saturday and Sunday during summer. At other times you must get an Ellwood pass at the Chancellorsville Visitor Center.

Battle of Spotsylvania Courthouse

Lee quickly regrouped and tried to stop Grant 2 days later at Spotsylvania Courthouse, about 18 miles southeast of The Wilderness. Taking advantage of thick fog and wet Confederate gunpowder, Union troops breached the Southerners' line. When Lee's reinforcements arrived, the sides spent 20 hours in the war's most intense hand-to-hand combat at a site known as Bloody Angle. During the fighting, Lee built new fortifications to the rear, which he successfully defended. Instead of pushing the fight to the finish, however, Grant again backed off, flanked his entire army around Lee's, and resumed his unrelenting march toward Richmond. It was the end of major fighting in the Fredericksburg area, as the war moved south to its ultimate conclusion 11 months later at Appomattox.

There's an exhibit shelter on Grant Drive, where park rangers lead walking tours daily during summer and on weekends in spring and fall. Call the Fredericksburg or Chancellorsville visitor centers for details.

Stonewall Jackson Shrine

Now part of the park, the **Stonewall Jackson Shrine** (© **804/633-6076**) is in the wood-frame plantation office where the general spent the last 6 days of his life after being shot and mortally wounded by his own men at Chancellorsville. Jackson's doctors hoped that he would recover sufficiently to board a train at nearby Guinea Station for the ride to Richmond, but it was not to be. Jackson's body was taken to Lexington, where he was buried with full honors (see chapter 7). The office is the only structure remaining at the plantation and appears as it did when Jackson died. About half of its contents are original, including his deathbed.

The shrine is open daily 9am to 5pm from mid-June to Labor Day and Saturday to Monday 9am to 5pm the rest of the year. It's at the junction of C.R. 606 and C.R. 607, 27 miles southeast of Chancellorsville, 18 miles southeast of Spotsylvania Courthouse. From I-95, take Exit 118 at Thornburg and follow the signs east on C.R. 606.

THE NORTHERN NECK ★

The Peninsula between the Potomac and Rappahannock rivers known as the Northern Neck stretches 100 miles southeast from Fredericksburg to the Chesapeake Bay. A popular weekend getaway for residents of nearby metropolitan areas, this is a rural land of rolling hills serrated by quiet tidal creeks. Its hills are still punctuated by agricultural and small fishing villages (they speak in terms of counties here, not towns).

The Northern Neck has three areas of interest. Heading east from Fredericksburg on Va. 3, you first come to **George Washington's Birthplace National Monument,** where the first president was born in 1732 on Pope's Creek Plantation, and **Stratford Hall,** the magnificently restored plantation manse where Robert E. Lee came into this world. Nearby, the **Ingleside Vineyards** offer tours and tastings. These three sites can easily be seen on a day trip from Fredericksburg.

A left turn on Va. 202 will take you northeast to the end of the Northern Neck, at Smith Point on the Chesapeake. Here you can explore the town of **Reedville,** founded as a menhaden fishing port in 1867 by Capt. Elijah Reed, a New England seafarer. Reedville soon became rich, and its captains and plant owners built magnificent Victorian-style homes. One plant still processes the small, toothless fish, which is of little use for human consumption but valuable as meal, oil, and protein supplements used in everything from Pepperidge Farm cookies to Rustoleum paint. You can learn all about the menhaden at the local fishing museum. From Reedville you can depart on cruises to remote Tangier Island out in the bay.

Va. 200 will take you 20 miles south to the best spot on the neck, the genteel creekside hamlet of **Irvington,** home of **Christ Church,** perhaps the nation's best example of Colonial church architecture. Irvington and its neighboring villages of White Stone and Kilmarnock constitute one of Virginia's most affluent retirement communities. Irvington and the surrounding area make a good base for exploring the Northern Neck's eastern end.

Essentials

VISITOR INFORMATION   For advance information about the area, contact the **Northern Neck Tourism Council,** PO Box 1707, Warsaw, VA 22572 (© 804/333-1919; www.northernneck.org). The council's offices are at 479 Main St. (Va. 3 Business) in the Regional Center. The walk-in **Virginia's Potomac Gateway Welcome Center** (© 540/633-3205) is on U.S. 301 just south of the Potomac River Bridge. The

The First Families of Virginia

The Northern Neck is the ancestral home of some of the "First Families of Virginia," the state's oldest and most prominent clans. They were among the earliest to arrive here—in the early 1600s—and soon established large plantations beside the Rappahanock, Potomac, James, and other tidewater rivers. Here on the Northern Neck, Robert "King" Carter's vast holdings made him the wealthiest man in the colonies in the 17th century. Thomas Lee, a planter who served as governor of the Virginia Colony, built Stratford Hall in the 1730s. His son, Richard Henry Lee, made the motion for independence in the Continental Congress in 1776, and Richard and Francis Lightfoot Lee were the only brothers to sign the Declaration of Independence. Cousin Henry "Light-Horse Harry" Lee, a hero of the Revolution, coined the phrase about his friend George Washington, "First in war, first in peace, and first in the hearts of his countrymen." Light-Horse Harry and his wife, Anne Hill Carter of Shirley Plantation (p. 268) on the James River, were the parents of Robert E. Lee, who was born at Stratford Hall in 1807. The Carter family still operates Shirley Plantation, the oldest family-owned business in the United States.

Reedville Fishermen's Museum (p. 98) has information about Reedville and the Smith Point area. Information about Irvington is available at **www.irvingtonva.org**.

GETTING THERE You'll need a car to get here. From Fredericksburg, go east on Va. 3, which traverses the length of the Peninsula. Washington's birthplace is 40 miles from Fredericksburg; Irvington, 95 miles. The "fast" route from Fredericksburg to Reedville and Irvington is via U.S. 17 and U.S. 360. From Richmond, take U.S. 360; from Williamsburg, use U.S. 17 and Va. 3.

Exploring the Northern Neck

You can easily see George Washington's birthplace, Stratford Hall Plantation, and the Ingleside Vineyards on a day trip from Fredericksburg or on stops along the way to Irvington. To do this area justice, plan on at least 3 days if you go on to Reedville and Irvington, 4 days if taking an all-day cruise to Tangier Island.

George Washington Birthplace National Monument ★ Although it's a re-creation of Popes Creek Plantation, where the first president was born on February 22, 1732, this national monument shows what 18th-century farm life was like when Washington's father, Augustine, established a tobacco plantation here in 1718. The family moved to Fredericksburg when George was 3½ years old. The original site of the manor house, which burned on Christmas Day in 1779, is outlined by oyster shells. The present day Memorial House and its workshop and farm re-create a typical plantation of that era (a guide will take you through the house). You can see the site in 1½ to 2 hours. A display case in the visitor center holds Washington family artifacts uncovered during archaeological digs here. Park rangers offer talks and conduct guided tours. The graves of 32 Washington family members, including George's father, are in a small burial ground on the property.

1732 Popes Creek Rd. (Va. 204, off Va. 3), Colonial Beach. © **804/224-1732.** www.nps.gov/gewa. Free admission. Daily 9am–5pm. Closed New Year's Day, Thanksgiving, and Christmas.

Historic Christ Church ★★★ Virtually unchanged since 1735, this is the most pristine of Virginia's many Colonial-era churches. The three-tiered pulpit is in excellent condition, all 26 original pews remain, and a marble baptismal font dates to the 1660s. The church was the gift of planter and businessman Robert "King" Carter, the richest man in the colonies. His father (John Carter), four of his five wives, and two infant children are interred in the chancel (to the left as you face the Ten Commandants on the wall). King Carter's tomb is outside, on the north side of the church. His descendants include two U.S. presidents (the Harrisons) and Gen. Robert E. Lee.

The museum displays archaeological artifacts from Corotoman, King Carter's lavish plantation manse which burned down only 4 years after he finished it in 1725. Take a 30-minute guided tour through the church and graveyard.

C.R. 646, off Va. 200, 1 mile north of Irvington. © **804/438-6855.** www.christchurch1735.org. Free admission (suggested $5 donation). Church Apr–Nov Mon–Fri 8:30am–4:30pm, Sat 10am–5pm, Sun 2–5pm; Dec–Mar Mon–Fri 8:30am–4:30pm. Museum and 30-min. guided tours Apr–Nov Mon–Sat 10am–4pm, Sun 2–5pm. Worship services held in the church Sun at 8am from Memorial Day to Labor Day. Closed Dec.

Reedville Fishermen's Museum   Paying homage to Reedville's ancient way of earning a living, this museum consists of the 1875 William Walker House, the town's oldest building, which has been restored to appear as it did in 1900; the Covington Building, which houses a permanent collection and special exhibits commemorating the watermen who participate in the town's leading industry, menhaden fishing, which dates to 1874 when Capt. Elijah Reed arrived here; and the Pendleton Building, where boat building and model making take place. An 11-minute video sets the stage for a visit to the work boats out on the creek; they were refurbished in the Pendleton Building by volunteers, who also built the *Spirit of 1608*, a replica of the boat Capt. John Smith used to explore the Chesapeake region in 1608.

504 Main St., Reedville. © **540/453-6529.** www.rfmuseum.org. Admission $5 adults, $3 seniors, free for children 12 and under. Mid-Mar to Apr Sat–Sun 10:30am–4:30pm; May–Oct daily 10:30am–4:30pm; Nov to mid-Jan Sat–Sun 10:30am–4:30pm. Closed mid-Jan to mid-Mar. From Va. 3 east, take U.S. 360 east to Reedville.

Steamboat Era Museum   Although the building housing this interesting local museum looks like a railway station, inside it's devoted to the late-19th- and early-20th-century era when steamboats were the major means of transportation between Norfolk and Baltimore. The steamers stopped at waterside towns such as Irvington, which sported an opera house and several hotels and speak-easies in those days. An introductory video about the era sets the stage. Model ship lovers will especially enjoy master craftsman Bill Wright's examples showing the transition from sail to steam. Out back is the restored top deck and pilot house of the steamboat *Potomac,* which cruised the Chesapeake from 1894 until 1936.

156 King Carter Dr., Irvington. © **804/438-6888.** www.steamboateramuseum.org. Free admission ($4 suggested donation). May–Dec Thurs–Sat 10am–4pm, Sun 1–4pm; Jan–Apr by appt.

Stratford Hall Plantation ★★★   Still operated as a working farm, Robert E. Lee's birthplace is one of the great houses of the South. Magnificently set on 1,600 acres, it's renowned for its distinctive H-shaped architectural style. Brick chimney groupings flanking the roofline are some of the mansion's most striking features. The paneled Great Hall, one of the finest rooms to have survived from Colonial times, runs the depth of the house and has an inverted tray ceiling. On the same floor are bedrooms and a nursery, where you can see Robert E. Lee's crib. The fireplace in the nursery is trimmed with sculpted angels' heads.

You can enter the mansion only on 30-minute tours led by costumed guides and easily spend another 2 hours strolling the gardens, meadows, and nature trails.

One of the few places to have lunch in this area, the **Stratford Hall Dining Room** offers Virginia-style cream of crab soup, crab cake and fried oyster sandwiches, chef salads with chicken or cured ham, ham biscuits, and meals of fried chicken, crab cakes, flounder, or ham, all at reasonable prices. Rustic on the outside but comfortable inside, Stratford Hall's guesthouses and cabins, provide overnight accommodations.

483 Great House Rd. (Va. 214, 2 miles north of Va. 3), Stratford. © **804/493-8038.** www.stratford hall.org. Admission $10 adults, $9 seniors and military, $5 children 6–11, free for children 5 and under. Grounds only $5 adults, $3 children. Mar–Dec daily 9:30am–4pm; Jan–Feb Sat–Sun 9:30am–4pm (tours on the hour 10am–4pm). Dining room Tues–Sun 11am–3pm. Closed New Year's Day, Christmas, and Dec 31.

On the Wine Trail

Several Northern Neck vineyards and wineries have bound together to form the **Chesapeake Wine Trail** (© 800/393-6180; www.chesapeakebaywinetrail.com), whose website will help you plan an inebriated tour.

The oldest, largest, and most convenient to visit from Fredericksburg is **Ingleside Vineyards,** 5872 Leedstown Rd., Oak Grove (© 804/224-8687; www.ingleside vineyards.com), off Va. 3 on the Rappahannock River side of the Peninsula. You'll get here before arriving at Washington's birthplace and Stratford Hall, so go easy on tasting the Virginia Brut, a handcrafted sparkling wine. Ingleside is open Monday to Saturday 10am to 5pm and Sunday noon to 5pm, with extended summer hours.

Others are **Athena Vineyards & Winery,** 3138 Jessie Dupont Memorial Hwy., Heathsville (© 840/580-4944; www.athenavineyards.com); **Belle Mount Vineyards,** 2570 Newland Rd., Warsaw (© 804/333-4700; www.bellemount.com); the **Dog and Oyster,** 170 White Fences Dr., Irvington (© 804/438-9463; www.hope andglory.com), where rescue dogs protect the grapes from wild deer and fresh oysters are paired in the tasting room; and **Oak Crest Vineyards & Winery,** 8215 Oak Crest Dr., King George (© 540/663-2813; www.oakcrestwinery.com), near Colonial Beach.

Outdoor Activities

The country roads that wind through gently rolling hills and cross picturesque creeks make the Northern Neck a great place to ride your bicycle. One excellent route makes a loop from Reedville via U.S. 360 and C.R. 652 and C.R. 644. On C.R. 644, you'll cross the Little Wicomico River via the free Sunnybank Ferry. Some bed-and-breakfasts provide bikes for guests, but there are no places to rent them here, so bring your own.

The Northern Neck has more than 1,100 miles of shoreline and 6,500 acres of nature preserves, making it an important stop for birds migrating along the Atlantic Flyway. It also has a substantial population of bald eagles. To see the eagles, head to the **Caledon Natural Area,** on Va. 218 near King George (© 540/663-3861; www.dcr.virginia.gov/state_parks/cal.shtml), which has observation tours along the Potomac River and guided eagle-watching tours. Another fine place to view the migratory birds is at **Belle Isle State Park** (© 804/462-5030; www.dcr.state. va.us/parks/bellisle.htm), off C.R. 354 on the Rappahannock River northwest of Irvington, which has guided canoe trips and horseback riding on land. The **Northern Neck Audubon Society,** PO Box 991, Kilmarnock, VA 22482 (no phone; www. northernneckaudubon.org), runs field trips.

Another good spot for birding and much more is **Westmoreland State Park** (© 804/493-8821; www.dcr.virginia.gov/parks/westmore.htm), off Va. 3 between

George Washington's birthplace and Stratford Hall. It's the Northern Neck's largest park, with a campground, cabins, hiking trails, and boating and swimming facilities.

Golfers come here primarily to play the **Golden Eagle** course at the Tides Inn (p. 102), one of Virginia's best, and the nearby **Tartan Golf Club** (© 804/438-6200). Irvington also is home to the **King Carter Golf Club,** on Old Saint Johns Road (© **804/435-7842;** www.kingcartergolfclub.com), a fine public course where you can play for less than $50.

Reedville is the jumping-off point for fishing charters on the Chesapeake Bay, where you might hook a fighting bluefish or snag a succulent rockfish (sea bass). In Reedville call Capt. Jim Hardy of *The Ranger II* (© 804/453-6635) or **Pittman's Charters** (© **804/453-3643;** www.genepittmancharters.com). The latter operates the *Mystic Lady II,* a 25-passenger party boat.

The Hope and Glory Inn (below) uses the *Miss Ann,* a 127-foot yacht, for cruises on Carter's Creek and the Rappahannock River at sunset and other times during the day.

Where to Stay

Stratford Hall Plantation (p. 98; www.stratfordhall.org/visit/lodging; © **804/493-8038,** ext. 8039) has guesthouses and cabins for rent.

Of several bed-and-breakfasts on the Northern Neck, **Back INN Time** (www.backinntime.biz; © **804/435-2318**) is between Irvington and Kilmarnock, thus convenient to Historic Christ Church and golf at the Tides Inn. Reedville has the **Gables** (www.thegablesbb.com; © **804/453-5209**), a Victorian mansion built on the Main Street waterfront by a ship's captain who installed his schooner's wooden mast through the top two floors. Near Reedville, **Fleeton Fields Bed & Breakfast** (www.fleetonfields.com; © **800/497-8215** or 804/453-5014) sits beside a creek in the hamlet of Fleeton.

The closest motel to Irvington and Reedville is the **Holiday Inn Express,** 599 N. Main St. (Va. 3), Kilmarnock (www.hiexpress.com; © **800/465-4329** or 804/436-1500), which has an outdoor pool.

The Hope and Glory Inn ★★★ One of the most fascinating and romantic country inns in the U.S., this property occupies a three-story schoolhouse built in the 1890s. A broad center staircase leads from the lounge to seven guest rooms plus a sitting area (the latter opens to a large deck). Out back, lush gardens surround six light and airy clapboard cottages. Uninhibited guests can bathe en plein air in the gardens' outdoor bathroom complete with claw-foot tub, rainmaker shower, and pedestal sink—all surrounded by a wooden privacy fence.

The inn's own chef prepares gourmet breakfasts and evening meals, the latter served dinner-party style and shared with sharp-witted owners Dudley and Peggy Patteson. Dinners are open to the public (reservations required; $68 per person including tip). Before their meal, diners can sample vintages from the inn's own the Dog and Oyster winery as well as from Ingleside Vineyards at the cozy Detention Bar.

Note: Besides radios with CD players, none of the on-site units have telephones, TVs, or other such modern distractions, which would interfere with romance. If you need all the comforts of home, or have a family in tow, then opt for one of the inn's Tents at Vineyard Grove, on the edge of the Dog and Oyster vineyard about a mile away. These aren't tents but modern houses, each drawing its inspiration from carpenter Gothic cottages that grew out of revival "tent meetings" in the late 18th and early 19th centuries. Each has three bedrooms, three bathrooms, a full kitchen, and

A CRUISE TO TANGIER ISLAND ★★

Out in the Chesapeake Bay lies the state's most quaint and remote place to get away from it all: **Tangier Island.**

Barely above sea level and short on dry land (many deceased are buried in their loved ones' front yards), tiny Tangier was discovered by Capt. John Smith in 1608 and permanently settled in 1686. In fact, the local accent hearkens back to Elizabethan English. Unlike touristy Nantucket or Martha's Vineyard, Tangier is still a remote and authentic fishing village—the "Soft Shell Capital of the World," as evidenced by the many crab pens lining the channel into the harbor.

Tangier also has the best beach in Virginia—actually an arm of sand stretching for more than a mile south of the island. You will have all or most of this narrow peninsula to yourself once the daily cruise boats have returned to the mainland.

Weather permitting, **Tangier and Rappahannock Cruises** (*C* **804/453-2628;** www.tangiercruise.com) leaves from Buzzard Point Marina, off U.S. 360 near Reedville, daily at 10am from May 15 to October 15. The voyage takes 90 minutes. The return trip leaves Tangier at 2pm, leaving you with 2½ hours on the island. Round-trip fare is $25 for adults, $14 for children 6 to 11, and free for children 5 and under. Bicycles are $5. Reservations are required. You can also get here from Crisfield, Maryland, on the eastern shore.

Local citizens await your arrival to take you on a 10-minute island tour by oversize golf cart (there are few cars or trucks on the island). You can bring your own bicycle or rent a bike or golf cart at the wharf, although you can walk to almost every place worth seeing within 30 minutes.

A personal favorite, **Fisherman's Corner** ((*C* **757/891-2900)** serves the best fresh soft shell crabs. **Waterfront Restaurant,** at the cruise boat dock (*C* **757/891-2248),** has sandwiches. Most day-trippers opt for all-you-can-eat, family-style lunches at **Hilda Crockett's Chesapeake House** (*C* **757/891-2331;** www.chesapeakehousetangier.com).

After lunch walk up Main Street to the **Tangier Island History Museum** (*C* **302/234-1660;** www.tangierhistorymuseum.org), which has informative exhibits and free kayaks for exploring the creeks that wind through the marshes and actually cut the island in two.

You can overnight at Hilda Crockett's, although I stay at **Bay View Inn Bed and Breakfast** (www.tangierisland.net; *C* **757/891-2396),** in a 1904 Victorian house on the island's western side. The upstairs "honeymoon" room has a small balcony with a fine view of the bay. **Sunset Inn Bed & Breakfast** (www.tangierislandsunset.com; *C* **757/891-2535)** actually is closer to the mile-long beach. All three charge about $130 and up for a double and accept MasterCard and Visa.

Note: Tangier is a "dry" island, so bring your own alcoholic beverages. And be prepared to dine early since the restaurants close at 7pm.

a screened porch overlooking the headwater marshes of Carter's Creek. All guests can use a secluded outdoor pool at the Tents. Your pet can stay with you in certain cottages. You will have free use of bicycles and the town's two tennis courts across the street, and spa services are available.

65 Tavern Rd. (at King Carter Dr.; PO Box 425), Irvington, VA 22480. www.hopeandglory.com. *C* **800/497-8228** or 804/438-6053. Fax 804/438-5362. 22 units (all with private bathroom). $175–$290 double; $225–$695 cottage. Rates include full breakfast. AE, DISC, MC, V. Pet fee $40. **Amenities:** Restaurant; bar; bikes; access to nearby health club; outdoor pool. *In room:* A/C, TV (in Tents), hair dryer, kitchen (in Tents), no phone (in main building), Wi-Fi.

The Tides Inn ★ Mostly known these days for its exceptional Golden Eagle golf course, the Tides is one of Virginia's top golfing destinations. This sprawling complex consists of several low-rise buildings on the banks of Carter's Creek. In the clapboard Main Building, the dining room and Chesapeake Club lounge both have outstanding views down the creek to the Rappahannock River. Rooms in the Main Building have fine views, too, but those in the cottage like Windsor or Lancaster Houses are more spacious and feature large bathrooms, living areas, and, in some cases, balconies overlooking the creek. Otherwise only the ground floor rooms in the East, Garden, and Terrace wings have patios. The full-service spa, the marina, the golf course, and the restaurants are open to the public.

480 King Carter Dr. (PO Box 480), Irvington, VA 22480. www.tidesinn.com. ⓒ **800/843-3746** or 804/438-5000. Fax 804/438-5552. 106 units. $170–$329 double; $195–$355 suite. $25 per room daily resort fee. Golf, spa, sailing, and other packages available. AE, DC, DISC, MC, V. Valet parking free 1st night, $10 thereafter; free self-parking. From Va. 3, take Va. 200 south 2 miles to Irvington, turn right at the sign and drive to the end of King Carter Dr. Pets accepted (in some rooms), $25 per animal. **Amenities:** 3 restaurants; 2 bars; babysitting; bikes; children's programs; concierge; golf course; health club; pool; room service; spa; tennis courts; watersports equipment. *In room:* A/C, TV/DVD, hair dryer, minibar, Wi-Fi.

Where to Eat

Saturday night Chef's Table dinners are offered at both the Hope and Glory Inn and the dining rooms at the Tides Inn (see above).

The Local DELI In the same small shopping complex as Nate's Trick Dog Cafe (see below), this shop serves as Irvington's version of Starbucks in the morning and as a sophisticated sandwich-and-salad emporium after 11am. Breakfast includes a variety of coffees, teas, and pastries. Lunch and afternoon snacks include a variety of salads and panini sandwiches. Sweet teeth are drawn to the ice-cream bar, and laptop owners can surf the Web wirelessly here. Out-of-town newspapers are sold; you can linger over them at tables out on the patio.

4337 Irvington Rd., Irvington. ⓒ **804/438-9356.** www.thelocalblend.com. Reservations not accepted. Breakfast $4–$8; sandwiches and salads $6.50–$9. MC, V. Sun–Thurs 7:30am–3pm; Fri–Sat 7:30am–5pm.

Nate's Trick Dog Cafe ★ AMERICAN This casual bistro is named for a sooty statue, standing out front, of a little black dog that survived the Great Irvington Fire of 1917. A local man gave the statue to his son, telling him it was a "trick dog" because he didn't need to be fed. You, on the other hand, will be well fed from a changing menu featuring crab cakes, seared yellowfin tuna and other seafoods plus meats such as grilled filet mignon, braised lamb shanks, and bison meatloaf. Sandwiches and burgers are served at the bar.

4357 Irvington Rd. (Va. 200), Irvington. ⓒ **804/438-1055.** www.trickdogcafe.com. Reservations recommended. Main courses $18–$33; bar menu $5–$15. AE, MC, V. Tues–Sat 5–9:30pm.

Sandpiper Restaurant AMERICAN This local restaurant has been casually serving Chesapeake Bay seafood to locals and visitors alike since 1982. The star attraction: crab cakes made mostly of back fin meat. Other traditional favorites include oysters fried in a delicate batter and a platter of fried or broiled seafood. Landlubbers can opt for steaks or pork chops.

Rappahannock Dr. (Va. 3), White Stone. ⓒ **804/435-6176.** Reservations not accepted. Main courses $17–$27. DISC, MC, V. Tues–Thurs 5–9pm; Fri–Sat 5–10pm.

CHARLOTTESVILLE

S ituated in the rolling foothills of the Blue Ridge Mountains, Charlottesville is one of Virginia's most fascinating places to visit, thanks in large part to its three distinct personalities.

First, it's a quintessential college town, with the University of Virginia (UVA) predominating everyday life for a large portion of its 45,000 or so residents. UVA is one of the country's finest and most beautiful public universities—a fact most begrudgingly admitted by one who matriculated at that other fine public beauty, the University of North Carolina at Chapel Hill, one of UVA's major rivals on the playing fields.

Second, this vibrant cosmopolitan center is consistently ranked as one of America's best places to live. Its charm, the beauty of the surrounding countryside, and an extraordinary number of facilities for a town this size have attracted a number of rich and famous folk like rock star Dave Matthews, author John Grisham, and former pro football player-turned-broadcaster Howie Long. Indeed, you never know whose famous face you'll recognize on the streets and in the extraordinary number of good restaurants here. Most of the celebrities live on estates out in the surrounding horse country, giving them a high degree of privacy but also quick access to a town that takes them quite in stride.

That's not surprising because Charlottesville has always had more than its share of famous Americans, which brings up its third personality as a center of American history.

It was here that Thomas Jefferson built his famous mountaintop home, Monticello; selected the site for and helped plan the Ash Lawn–Highland home of his presidential buddy, James Monroe; rode up to Montpelier to stay with his other chum, James Madison; designed his "academical village" at UVA; and died at home 50 years to the day after Congress adopted his Declaration of Independence. "All my wishes end where I hope my days will end," he wrote, "at Monticello."

Indeed, the third president's presence is still so much in evidence here that locals call this "Mr. Jefferson's Country."

ORIENTATION & GETTING AROUND

Visitor Information

For information, contact the **Charlottesville Albemarle Convention and Visitors Bureau,** PO Box 178, Charlottesville, VA 22902

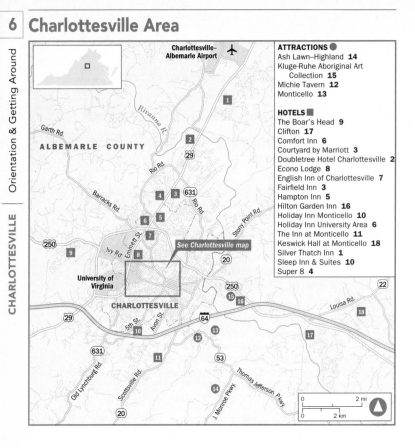

ATTRACTIONS ●
Ash Lawn–Highland **14**
Kluge-Ruhe Aboriginal Art
   Collection **15**
Michie Tavern **12**
Monticello **13**

HOTELS ■
The Boar's Head **9**
Clifton **17**
Comfort Inn **6**
Courtyard by Marriott **3**
Doubletree Hotel Charlottesville **2**
Econo Lodge **8**
English Inn of Charlottesville **7**
Fairfield Inn **3**
Hampton Inn **5**
Hilton Garden Inn **16**
Holiday Inn Monticello **10**
Holiday Inn University Area **6**
The Inn at Monticello **11**
Keswick Hall at Monticello **18**
Silver Thatch Inn **1**
Sleep Inn & Suites **10**
Super 8 **4**

(✆ **877/386-1102** or 434/293-6789; fax 434/295-2176; **www.pursuecharlottes ville.com**). The bureau's **Visitor Center** is at 610 E. Market St., on the eastern end of the Downtown Mall. It's open Monday to Saturday 10am to 5pm and closed New Year's Day, Thanksgiving, and Christmas.

Be sure to pick up copies of **The Charlottesville Guide** (www.charlottesville guide.com), a slick, advertiser-supported booklet containing maps and information about the area's attractions, hotels, restaurants, and shops; **Charlottesville Arts & Entertainment** (www.artsmonthly.com), a monthly minimagazine concentrating on the town's cultural life; and the town's two free weekly alternative newspapers, **C-Ville Weekly** (www.c-ville.com) and the **Hook** (www.readthehook.com), both packed with restaurant listings and news about what's happening. **Bites & Sites,** a C-Ville supplement, reviews every restaurant in town.

Getting There

BY CAR   Charlottesville is on I-64 from east or west and U.S. 29 from north or south. I-64 connects with I-81 at Staunton and with I-95 at Richmond. From I-64, take Exit 121 (Va. 20) south to Monticello, Ash Lawn–Highland, and Michie Tavern. To downtown from I-64, take Exit 120 and go north on 5th Street.

BY PLANE American, Delta, United, and US Airways fly commuter planes to **Charlottesville-Albemarle Airport (CHO),** 201 Bowen Loop (© **434/973-8341;** www.gocho.com), north of town off U.S. 29. The major rental car firms are here, taxis are available, and **Van on the Go** (© **866/725-0200** or 434/975-8267; www.vanonthego.com) provides shuttle service into town and to the Washington, D.C., airports.

BY TRAIN The **Amtrak** station is at 810 W. Main St. (© **800/872-7245;** www.amtrak.com), midway between the Downtown Mall and the university.

City Layout

Just as it has three personalities, Charlottesville has three centers of interest to visitors. One is on the southeastern outskirts of town, where Monticello, Ash Lawn–Highland, and Michie Tavern are within 2 miles of each other. The second is the University of Virginia, at the western end of Main Street (which morphs into University Ave. when it reaches the campus). Opposite the campus, between 13th Street and Elliewood Avenue, **The Corner** neighborhood is a typical campus enclave, with student-dominated restaurants, bookstores, and clothing stores and a dearth of parking spaces. The third area, **Historic Downtown Charlottesville,** a mile east of The Corner, is centered on the **Downtown Mall,** an 8-block, pedestrian-only strip at the eastern end of Main Street, between 2nd Street West and 7th Street East.

Getting Around

The easiest way to travel between the university and the Downtown Mall is on the **free trolley** operated by the **Charlottesville Area Transit** (**CAT;** © **434/970-3649;** www.catchthecat.org). It runs along Main Street every 10 to 15 minutes Monday to Saturday 6:40am to midnight and Sunday 8am to 5pm. In downtown, the trolley runs eastbound along Market Street, westbound along Water Street. It makes a loop on campus.

CAT also has bus service throughout the city (but not to Monticello) Monday to Saturday 6:15am to 6:30pm and Sunday 7:45am to 5:45pm. The main transit center is on the eastern end of the Downtown Mall, under the visitors center. For a taxi call **Yellow Cab** (© **434/295-4132**) or **Norm's Taxi** (© **434/327-9500**).

PARKING On-street parking is extremely limited. In the Downtown Mall area, you can park free for 2 hours with merchant validation (take your ticket with you and get it stamped) in the garages on Market Street between 5th and 6th streets NE and on Water Street between 2nd and 4th streets SE. The university's visitor parking garage is on the western side of the campus, on Emmet Street (U.S. 29 Business) a block south of University Avenue (which is the continuation of W. Main St.). On the eastern side of campus, two public garages are located opposite the University Hospital on Lee Street, off Jefferson Park Avenue. The Corner has public parking on Elliewood Avenue at 14th Street.

WHERE TO STAY

Accommodations listed here are grouped by those on the Main Street–University Avenue corridor, those convenient to Monticello, those on the outskirts of town, and those (inns) in the nearby countryside. Main Street makes a great base because a free

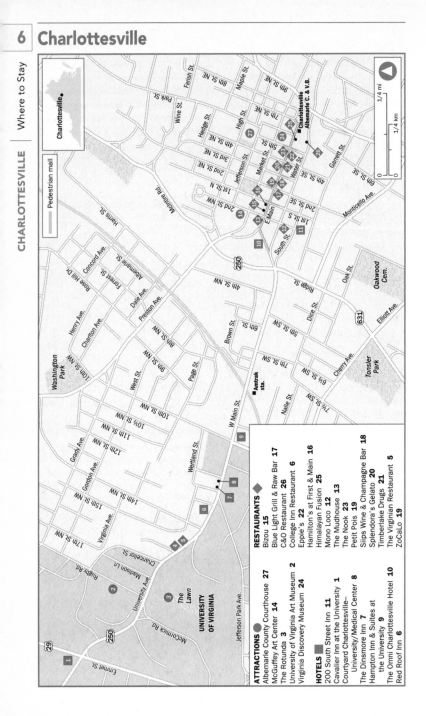

Charlottesville

Pedestrian mall

1/4 mi
1/4 km

ATTRACTIONS ●
Albemarle County Courthouse **27**
McGuffey Art Center **14**
The Rotunda **3**
University of Virginia Art Museum **2**
Virginia Discovery Museum **24**

HOTELS ■
200 South Street Inn **11**
Cavalier Inn at the University **1**
Courtyard Charlottesville–
    University/Medical Center **8**
The Dinsmore Inn **7**
Hampton Inn & Suites at
    the University **9**
The Omni Charlottesville Hotel **10**
Red Roof Inn **6**

RESTAURANTS ◆
Bizou **15**
Blue Light Grill & Raw Bar **17**
C&O Restaurant **26**
College Inn Restaurant **6**
Eppie's **22**
Hamilton's at First & Main **16**
Himalayan Fusion **25**
Mono Loco **12**
The Mudhouse **13**
The Nook **23**
Petit Pois **19**
Siips Wine & Champagne Bar **18**
Splendora's Gelato **20**
Timberlake Drugs **21**
The Virginian Restaurant **5**
ZoCaLo **19**

The visitor center operated by the **Charlottesville Albemarle Convention and Visitors Bureau** makes same-day, discounted lodging reservations (see "Orientation & Getting Around," above). It's a good way to save, provided you can live without the security of an advance reservation. Do not try this during University of Virginia events such as football games, graduation, and parents' weekends, when the town is packed and all accommodations are taken. You may not want to be in Charlottesville then anyway, but if you are, make your reservations as far in advance as possible. You will also pay premium hotel rates at these times, and some restaurants may request an advance deposit (it's their way of avoiding double bookings and no-shows). Check the schedules at www.virginia.edu.

trolley runs to the downtown and university attractions and restaurants, eliminating the need to drive and compete for a parking space.

Guesthouses Reservation Service, Inc. (✆ 434/979-7264; www.va-guest houses.com) handles bed-and-breakfast accommodations in elegant homes and private cottages.

Main Street–University Corridor

A block north of the Downtown Mall, the elegant **200 South Street Inn,** 200 South St. (www.southstreetinn.com; ✆ **800/964-7008** or 434/979-0200), occupies a stately 1856 house that has seen previous duty as a private residence, girls finishing school, and brothel. More rooms are in an 1890-vintage house next door.

Cavalier Inn at the University Owned by UVA, this five-story, glass-and-steel motel is close to Scott Stadium, University Hall, and John Paul Jones Arena, the major sports venues. Although it has been around for more than 3 decades, it is maintained in top condition. The spacious motel-style rooms are entered through external walkways bordered by wrought-iron railings, which means a dearth of privacy unless you keep the drapes drawn across the floor-to-ceiling windows. During summer you can cool off in a small outdoor pool. The hotel provides complimentary shuttle service to and from the airport and the Amtrak and bus stations.

105 Emmet St. (at W. Main St.; PO Box 5647), Charlottesville, VA 22905. www.cavalierinn.com. ✆ **888/882-2129** or 434/296-8111. Fax 434/296-3523. 118 units. $79–$119 double. Rates include full breakfast. AE, DC, DISC, MC, V. **Amenities:** Free airport transfers; outdoor pool. In room: A/C, TV, hair dryer, Wi-Fi.

Courtyard Charlottesville–University Medical Center This modern yet Colonial-style brick building fits in with the Dinsmore House Inn next door and the historic university structures nearby. Like all Courtyards, it's designed with business travelers in mind, offering well-equipped rooms and a restaurant serving a breakfast buffet daily. For the romantically inclined, six "spa king" units have two-person Jacuzzi tubs almost surrounded by floor-to-ceiling mirrors.

1201 W. Main St., Charlottesville, VA 22903. www.courtyard.com. ✆ **800/321-2211** or 434/977-1700. Fax 434/977-2600. 137 units. $129–$265 double. AE, DC, DISC, MC, V. **Amenities:** Restaurant (breakfast only); bar; health club; Jacuzzi; indoor pool; room service. In room: A/C, TV, fridge (in some), hair dryer, Wi-Fi.

The Dinsmore House Inn ★★   At the eastern edge of the university, this Federal-style house was constructed in 1817 by James Dinsmore, Thomas Jefferson's master builder. Today it is nearly surrounded by University Baptist Church and the Courtyard Charlottesville–University Medical Center, but inside is a charming bed-and-breakfast. Four-poster beds and Oriental rugs characterize the spacious rooms, four upstairs in the main house and four in an adjoining building, which holds my favorite, the Veranda Room (it opens to a private back porch). Also next door are the Monroe Room and the Jefferson Suite, both reached by very steep stairs. Full breakfast and afternoon tea are served in the formal dining room or in a bright sunroom.

1211 W. Main St., Charlottesville, VA 22903. www.dinsmorehouse.com. © **877/882-7829.** 8 units. $119–$279 double. AE, DISC, MC, V. Rates include full breakfast. **Amenities:** Access to nearby health club. *In room:* A/C, TV, DVD player, hair dryer, Wi-Fi.

Hampton Inn & Suites at the University ◢   Also well situated, this five-story brick structure is 3 blocks east of the Courtyard—far enough away from The Corner to avoid the crowds. Murals of Monticello, the Rotunda, and other local scenes overlook a gas fireplace in the center of an elegant, two-story lobby. Eight of the suites here also have gas fireplaces, and all have separate bedrooms with TVs, and kitchens with microwave ovens and dishwashers. The medium-size rooms also come well equipped. Guests are treated to an extensive breakfast in a room off the lobby.

900 W. Main St., Charlottesville, VA 22903. www.hamptonsuites.com. © **800/426-7866** or 434/923-8600. Fax 434/923-8601. 100 units. $139–$219 double; $189–$229 suite. Rates include full breakfast. AE, DC, DISC, MC, V. **Amenities:** Health club. *In room:* A/C, TV, hair dryer, kitchen (in suites), Wi-Fi.

The Omni Charlottesville Hotel ★★   You can't miss this seven-story, brick-and-glass structure with a soaring atrium lobby; its triangular shape towers above the western end of the Downtown Mall. The location is ideal because you can walk to the mall's many restaurants and shops and ride the free trolley to the university. The rooms are medium-size, and those on the upper floors have views over the city. At the street level, a fountain bubbles amid a tropical forest in the atrium lobby. The Omni has extensive meeting space and draws more conventions and groups than most hotels here. Your small pet can share your room for a fee.

235 W. Main St. (at McIntire St.), Charlottesville, VA 22901. www.omnihotels.com. © **800/843-6664** or 434/971-5500. Fax 434/979-4456. 208 units. $129–$269 double. AE, DC, DISC, MC, V. Self-parking $8. Small pets accepted ($50 fee). **Amenities:** Restaurant; bar; executive or concierge-level rooms; health club; Jacuzzi; 2 pools (indoor & outdoor); room service. *In room:* A/C, TV, fridge, hair dryer, Wi-Fi ($9.95 per 24 hr.).

Red Roof Inn   In the middle of the action and a cut above most other members of this inexpensive chain, this clean, comfortable seven-story hotel is on the eastern edge of The Corner and across West Main Street from the university. Interior hallways lead to medium-size guest rooms, which contain cherrywood furniture. Despite being a bit small, the bathrooms have surprisingly ample vanity space. The Corner's many food outlets are steps away.

1309 W. Main St. (at 13th St.), Charlottesville, VA 22903. www.redroof.com. © **800/843-7663** or 434/295-4333. Fax 434/295-2021. 135 units. $90–$209 double. AE, DC, DISC, MC, V. *In room:* A/C, TV, Wi-Fi.

Near Monticello

The most convenient chain hotels to Monticello, Ash Lawn–Highland, and Michie Tavern are the **Holiday Inn Monticello** (© **800/465-4329** or 434/977-5100), a full-service hotel with restaurant and bar, and a **Sleep Inn & Suites** (📞 **800/424-6423** or 434/244-9969). Both are on 5th Street Extended just north of I-64. The **Hilton Garden Inn,** on U.S. 250 north of I-64 (📞 **877/STAY-HGI** [782-9444] or 434/979-4442), is a recent addition to Charlottesville's hotel inventory.

The Inn at Monticello ★ This beautiful two-story stucco country house sits on 5 acres well back from Va. 20. Boxwoods, tall shade and evergreen trees, shrubs, and a bubbling brook provide a lovely setting. You enter via the front porch into a sitting room with two fireplaces and a handsome collection of antiques. Guest rooms are individually decorated and have such special features as a working fireplace, private porch, or four-poster canopy bed—but no phones. Afternoon snacks are accompanied by Virginia wine.

1188 Scottsville Rd. (Va. 20), Charlottesville, VA 22902. www.innatmonticello.com. 📞 **877/735-2982** or 434/979-3593. Fax 434/296-1344. 5 units. $175–$245 double. Rates include full breakfast. AE, MC, V. **Amenities:** Access to nearby health club. *In room:* A/C, no phone, Wi-Fi.

On the Outskirts of Town

The traffic-signal encrusted commercial strip along U.S. 29 north of the U.S. 250 bypass (Charlottesville's major suburban growth area) is lined with an ever-expanding multitude of shopping centers, chain motels, and restaurants. Here you will find the **Doubletree Hotel Charlottesville** (📞 800/494-7596 or 434/973-2121), the area's best-equipped suburban hotel, and a comfortable **Courtyard** (📞 800/321-2211 or 434/973-7100), which abuts the Fashion Square Mall. Others along U.S. 29 north include **Comfort Inn** (📞 800/228-5150 or 434/293-6188), **Econo Lodge North** (📞 800/553-2666 or 434/295-3185), **Hampton Inn** (📞 800/426-7866 or 434/978-7888), **Holiday Inn University Area** (📞 800/465-4329 or 434/293-9111), **Fairfield Inn by Marriott** (📞 800/228-2800 or 434/964-9411), and **Super 8** (📞 800/800-8000 or 434/973-0888).

The Boar's Head ★★★ Standing beside a picturesque lake, this is one of the better all-around resorts in Virginia. The focal point is a 19th-century gristmill dismantled and brought here in the early 1960s. The place is loaded with antiques and art, and its plank flooring and huge old ceiling beams give ancient charm to the **Old Mill Room,** the resort's signature restaurant offering fine dining. The innlike guest rooms upstairs in the mill are charming and romantic, but those elsewhere have more space and balconies. Some units in the Ednam Hall, which does not face the lake, have kitchenettes. In addition to the resort's own full-service spa and tennis courts, guests can play at the adjacent Boar's Head Sports Club (26 tennis courts, 2 pools, state-of-the-art fitness center) and the university's nearby Birdwood Golf Course. The Boar's Head also is one of the best places in the region to take off on a hot-air balloon ride.

200 Ednam Dr. (PO Box 5307), Charlottesville, VA 22905. www.boarsheadinn.com. 📞 **800/476-1988** or 434/296-2181. Fax 434/972-6019. 170 units. $161–$325 double; $335–$575 suite. Resort fee $8 per unit. Packages available. AE, DC, DISC, MC, V. **Amenities:** 2 restaurants; bar; bikes; concierge; golf course; health club; Jacuzzi; 4 outdoor pools (1 heated); room service; spa; 6 tennis courts. *In room:* A/C, TV, hair dryer, Internet, kitchen (in some).

English Inn of Charlottesville 🍴 Tudor-style buildings and English decor make this one of Charlottesville's most charming hotels. A wood-paneled lobby with fireplace and Oriental rugs gives it the ambience of an English country inn. Rooms are variously decorated, many with Queen Anne–style reproduction pieces. The "king suites" have bedrooms and sitting areas with sofas. In their own building enclosing a private courtyard, newer extended-stay suites offer kitchens and either one or two bedrooms. You can do laps in Charlottesville's largest indoor pool.

2000 Morton Dr. (at Emmet St.), Charlottesville, VA 22903. www.englishinncharlottesville.com. © **800/786-5400** or 434/971-9900. Fax 434/977-8008. 106 units. $90–$200 double. Rates include full breakfast. AE, DISC, MC, V. **Amenities:** Free airport transfers; health club; indoor pool. *In room:* A/C, TV, hair dryer, kitchen (in suites), Wi-Fi.

Silver Thatch Inn ★ Occupying a rambling white-clapboard Colonial-style house, a section of which dates to Revolutionary days, this charming bed-and-breakfast is on a quiet road set on nicely landscaped grounds about 8 miles north of town. Attractively decorated with authentic 18th-century pieces, the original part of the building now serves as a cozy common room, where guests are invited for afternoon refreshments. The 1812 part of the house is one of the dining rooms of the **Silver Thatch Restaurant and Pub,** one of the area's most romantic dining venues. Three guest rooms are upstairs in the main house, while four others are in the President's Cottage. Named for seven pre-20th-century Virginia-born presidents, all are lovely, with four-poster canopied beds, antique pine dressers, and carved walnut-and-mahogany armoires. Several rooms have working fireplaces. Telephones and TVs are available in the common areas.

3001 Hollymead Dr., Charlottesville, VA 22911. www.silverthatch.com. © **800/261-0720** or 434/978-4686. Fax 434/973-6156. 7 units. $170–$210 double. Rates include full breakfast. AE, DC, DISC, MC, V. 2-night minimum stay required most weekends. Take U.S. 29 about 8 miles north of town, turn right at traffic signal onto Hollymead Dr. to inn on the right. **Amenities:** Restaurant; bar; outdoor pool. *In room:* A/C, TV, hair dryer, no phone, Wi-Fi.

Two Luxurious Country Inns

Clifton Inn ★★★ You'll think you've arrived at Tara from *Gone With the Wind* when you see this stately manse, which is on the National Register of Historic Places. Thomas Mann Randolph, husband of Thomas Jefferson's daughter, Martha, built it in 1799, originally as a trading post. Although neither as physically grand nor as well equipped as Keswick Hall at Monticello (see below), this is a more intimate retreat. Guest rooms and suites upstairs in the mansion are comfortable, but for more privacy and charm, opt for the estate's whitewashed stables, old carriage house, or Randolph's law office, which have been converted into romantic outposts. The split-level carriage house sports a grand piano and Jacuzzi, while the honeymoon cottage has a glass-walled bathroom. Four more units are in Collina Farmhouse, which has its own kitchen and tennis court. The **Restaurant at Clifton** is among the best dining options in the Charlottesville area, providing international a la carte fare that lives up

---

💬 Hog Heaven

Despite a name that conjures up images of barbecue in these parts, vegetarians and vegans will find their own hog heaven 23 miles south of Charlottesville at the **White Pig Bed and Breakfast at Briar Creek Farm,** 5120 Irish Rd., Schuyler, VA 22696 (© **434/831-1416;** www.thewhitepig.com). The owners' pet white pig will never be over the coals; breakfasts and Saturday dinners at this retreat are strictly vegan.

to the inn's Relais & Château affiliation. Groups can reserve the big table for 24 in the excellent basement wine cellar.

1296 Clifton Inn Dr., Charlottesville, VA 22911. www.cliftoninn.net. © **888/971-1800** or 434/971-1800. Fax 434/971-7098. 18 units. $245–$355 double. Rates include continental breakfast and afternoon tea. AE, DC, DISC, MC, V. Minimum 2-night stay weekends. From Charlottesville take U.S. 250 east 5 miles, turn right on N. Milton Rd. (C.R. 729), go ¼ mile to Clifton Inn Dr. on left. **Amenities:** Restaurant; bar; outdoor pool; room service; tennis court. *In room:* A/C, TV, fridge (in some), Wi-Fi.

Keswick Hall at Monticello ★★★   Although it's now owned and operated by Orient Express Hotels, this superluxury estate was the creation of Sir Bernard Ashley, widower of famed designer Laura Ashley. Many of the 1912 vintage Italianate Crawford villa's rooms and suites have fireplaces, claw-foot tubs, and gorgeous views over a golf course redesigned by Arnold Palmer, but don't expect to find these in the 14 least expensive "house rooms." All guests can roam around the vast public rooms on the main level, including a lounge with fireplace, a library, and a billiards room. English afternoon tea is free to guests. **Fossett's** restaurant, also espying the links, offers a mix of fine cuisine and excellent service plus special wine tastings of the estate's own vintage. Guests can also have lunch or dinner at the bistro in the adjoining Keswick Club, a private country club whose spa, fitness center, and indoor and outdoor pools are available. All these facilities make Keswick Hall more of a resort than the nearby Clifton (see above).

701 Country Club Dr., Keswick, VA 22947. www.keswick.com. © **800/274-5391** or 434/979-3440. Fax 434/977-4171. 48 units. $260–$550 double; $485–$750 suite. Rates include afternoon tea. AE, DC, MC, V. From Charlottesville take U.S. 250 or I-64 east to Shadwell (Exit 124); then Va. 22 east and follow signs to Keswick. **Amenities:** Restaurant; bar; golf course; health club; Jacuzzi; 4 pools (1 indoor); room service; sauna; spa; 5 tennis courts. *In room:* A/C, TV, hair dryer, Wi-Fi.

A Mountain Getaway

Wintergreen Resort   About 43 miles southwest of Charlottesville, this 11,000-acre recreational real estate development offers year-round vacation activities in a Blue Ridge Mountain setting. The big draws include skiing, golf (the short, narrow fairways of Devils Knob course follow the cool summit of a 4,000-ft.-high mountain), horseback riding, mountain biking, swimming in the lake, canoeing, and an adventure center with rock climbing, skateboarding, wintertime snow tubing, and other activities. Wintergreen also has a Nature Foundation that offers guided hikes, seminars, and camps for children. The resort's focal point is the tasteful lodgelike inn, which has a huge gristmill wheel occupying the two-story registration area. Most accommodations are in small enclaves scattered throughout the property, but there are also three- to seven-bedroom homes, one- to four-bedroom condos, and studios and lodge rooms. The units are privately owned so furnishings are highly individual. There's music in the cool air as the **Wintergreen Summer Music Festival (© 434/325-8292;** www.wintergreenperformingarts.org) turns a ski slope into an amphitheater.

PO Box 706, Wintergreen, VA 22958. www.wintergreenresort.com. © **800/266-2444** or 434/325-2200. Fax 434/325-8004. 300 units. $130–$200 double; $150–$900 condos and houses. Recreational packages available. AE, DISC, MC, V. Take I-64 west to Exit 107 and follow U.S. 250 west; turn left onto C.R. 151 south, and then right on C.R. 644 for 4½ miles to resort. **Amenities:** 5 restaurants; 3 bars; babysitting; bikes; children's center or programs; concierge (winter only); 3 golf courses; health club; Jacuzzi; 5 pools (1 indoor); room service; sauna; 24 tennis courts. *In room:* A/C, TV, kitchen, Wi-Fi.

WHERE TO EAT

Locals brag that Charlottesville has more restaurants per capita than any city in Virginia. For a complete rundown, pick up a copy of **Bites & Sites,** a free restaurant guide supplement to **C-Ville Weekly** (www.c-ville.com), at the visitor center (see "Visitor Information," earlier in this chapter). Read what locals are blogging at **Mas to Millers** (www.mastomillers.com).

This area's finest, most-romantic, and most-expensive dining is in the Old Mill Room at the Boar's Head, the Restaurant at Clifton at Clifton Inn, Fossett's at Keswick Hall at Monticello, and the Silver Thatch Restaurant and Pub at the Silver Thatch Inn (see "Where to Stay," above); reservations are strongly recommended at all.

The Corner neighborhood opposite the university has several restaurants catering to the college crowd. Most are on University Avenue, including the **Virginian Restaurant** (✆ 434/984-4667; www.virginianrestaurant.com), which has been serving traditional fare since 1923, and the Greek-Italian **College Inn Restaurant** (✆ 434/977-2710; www.thecollegeinn.com), which has been around since 1950. More are on Elliewood Avenue, a block-long, alley-like street off University Avenue.

Those of us who have matriculated seldom go farther in search of a good meal than along East Main Street on the Downtown Mall, which has restaurants to suit every taste and pocketbook. All of them post their menus outside, so you can pick and choose depending on your own tastes.

For a caffeine fix, drop into the **Mudhouse,** 213 W. Main St. (✆ 434/984-6833; www.mudhouse.com), a quintessential college-town coffeehouse. For a more substantial breakfast try the **Nook,** 415 E. Main St. (✆ 434/295-6665; www.thenook cville.com), which has been serving inexpensive meals for more than half a century. Also still going strong is the soda fountain in **Timberlake Drugs,** 322 E. Main St. (✆ 434/295-9155), which has been in business since 1890. The best ice cream is at **Splendora's Gelato,** 317 E. Main St. (✆ 434/296-8555; www.splendoras.com).

Moderate

Blue Light Grill & Raw Bar AMERICAN You'll get the freshest seafood in town at this storefront restaurant on the Downtown Mall. Among the mains could be crab cakes prepared with a mustard sauce, pan-seared salmon with creamed corn, and seared sea scallops with a sweet corn salad. For the freshest catch, check the daily specials.

120 E. Main St. ✆ **434/295-1223.** www.bluelightgrill.com. Reservations recommended on weekends. Main courses $15–$28. AE, DISC, MC, V. Sun–Thurs 5–10pm; Fri–Sat 5–11pm.

C&O Restaurant ★★★ INTERNATIONAL A block south of the Downtown Mall's eastern end, this unprepossessing brick restaurant with an ancient Pepsi-Cola sign has been serving acclaimed food for more than 3 decades. From all appearances, the creaky floors in this charming old building were around in Mr. Jefferson's day. Changing monthly, the menu is basically country French but ranges across the globe—from Thailand to New Mexico and Louisiana—for additional inspiration. Many patrons stop downstairs in the Bistro, a rustic setting of exposed brick and rough-hewn barn wood, but in warm weather you can sit outdoors on the patio or in the covered garden. The C&O's wine list has won a *Wine Spectator* award for excellence. This is the best spot in town for a midnight snack, served daily until 1am.

515 E. Water St. ℗ **434/971-7044.** www.candorestaurant.com. Reservations recommended (not accepted in Bistro or patio). Main courses $15–$35. AE, MC, V. Sun–Thurs 5:30–10pm; Fri–Sat 5:30–11pm. Closed 1st week in Jan, July 4th, and Christmas.

Hamilton's at First & Main ★★ AMERICAN   Marble-top tables, crisp linen napkins, and fresh flowers let you know you're in for some high style at this urbane bistro in the Downtown Mall. It's the kind of place where you'd take a special date, but not necessarily propose marriage. The menu changes frequently, but if offered, the pan-roasted crab cakes on jasmine rice and a mango-lime barbecue sauce will demonstrate the chef's prowess. The daily vegetarian blue-plate special is very tasty, too.

101 W. Main St. ℗ **434/295-6649.** www.hamiltonsrestaurant.com. Reservations recommended. Main courses $21–$34. AE, DISC, MC, V. Mon–Sat 11:30am–3pm and 5:30–10pm.

Petit Pois ★ 🍴 FRENCH/MEDITERREAN   Next door to ZoCaLo (see below), this tiny bistro serves very good European-influenced fare and in warm weather offers ample outdoor seating under cover of umbrellas. Marinated and grilled shrimp served with white beans simmered with tomatoes makes an excellent and filling dinner appetizer or lunch entree. The vegetarian risotto is served with perfectly sautéed baby asparagus. The outdoor tables here are covered by large umbrellas.

201 E. Main St. ℗ **434/979-7947.** Reservations accepted. Main courses $19–$34. MC, V. Mon–Thurs 11:30am–2pm and 5:30–9pm; Fri–Sat 11:30am–2pm and 5:30–10pm; Sun 10:30am–2:30pm and 5:30–9pm.

ZoCaLo ★★ LATIN AMERICAN   The chef-owners at this high-energy bistro draw their culinary inspiration from Latin America, offering the likes of sea scallops dusted in Latino spices, grilled salmon with green chili, and black bean and corn relleno served with smoked tomato grits. Smoking is prohibited inside and out until the kitchen stops serving dinner.

201 E. Main St. ℗ **434/977-4944.** www.zocalo-restaurant.com. Reservations recommended. Main courses $18–$26. AE, DISC, MC, V. Tues–Sun 10:30am–2:30pm and 5:30–10pm.

Inexpensive

Bizou ★★ 🍴 AMERICAN   Don't be turned off by the greasy-spoon appearance of this narrow restaurant, whose front counter betrays a former incarnation as a diner. The tables and booths in the cramped rear dining area still have the ambience of an unpretentious small town restaurant. On the other hand, the food here is consistently good and affordably priced, especially the "classic fare" such as meatloaf, roasted chicken, and vegetable burritos. I'm fond of the "new fare" salad of yellow beets, green apples, and toasted pine nuts followed by cornmeal-breaded catfish with a jambalaya risotto. Even if you've dined elsewhere, it's worth coming here afterward for the luscious grilled banana bread with vanilla ice cream.

119 E. Main St. ℗ **434/977-1818.** Reservations not accepted. Main courses $12–$22. DISC, MC, V. Sun–Thurs 11:30am–3pm and 5–9pm; Fri–Sat 11:30am–3pm and 5–10pm.

Eppie's ★ 🍴 AMERICAN/VEGETARIAN   This busy and sometimes noisy fast-food-style restaurant is the best place on the mall for a healthy, inexpensive meal. It offers a wide range of sandwiches and salads, including very good tarragon or curry chicken salad. Other than daily specials such as turkey chili, main courses are limited to pastas (some vegetarian or vegan) and grilled chicken breast coated with lemon pepper or Jamaican jerk seasonings. The latter is both tasty and heart healthy when accompanied by a baked sweet potato and steamed fresh vegetables.

412 E. Main St. ✆ **434/963-9900.** www.eppiesrestaurant.com. Reservations not accepted. Most items $4–$11. AE, MC, V. Mon–Thurs and Sat 11:30am–8pm; Fri 11:30am–9pm. Sun brunch in summer 9am–3pm.

Himalayan Fusion ★ NEPALESE/TIBETAN/VEGAN Operated by a family from Nepal, this casual bistro serves a mix of spicy cuisines from the Himalayas. Some dishes are familiar Indian curries; others hail from Nepal, with ginger, coriander, and garlic flavors strong enough to hold their own against curry. The Tibetan-style steamed *momo* dumplings are especially good. Vegetarians and vegans will do well here.

520 E. Main St. ✆ **434/293-3120.** Reservations recommended on weekends. Main courses $10–$18. AE, DISC, MC, V. Mon and Wed–Fri 11:30am–2:30pm and 5:30–10pm; Sat noon–3pm and 5:30–10pm; Sun noon–3pm and 5:30–9pm.

Mono Loco ★ 🍴 LATIN AMERICAN This lively little bistro—10 tables indoors, a few more outside in warm weather—draws its inspiration from Latin America. Only names will be familiar, however, for creativity is on the loose here. The specials list has included a shrimp-and-bacon burrito that turned out to be a huge burrito shell from which sprang an explosion of delightful flavors. The kitchen is tiny, so don't be in a hurry on a busy night.

200 W. Water St. ✆ **434/979-0688.** www.monolocorestaurant.com. Reservations recommended on weekends. Main courses $13–$18. AE, DISC, MC, V. Mon 5–9pm; Tues–Sat 11:30am–2:30pm and 5–10pm; Sun 5–9pm.

Siips Wine & Champagne Bar AMERICAN Supplied by a local art dealer, the paintings on the walls of this sophisticated wine bar are for sale. So are glasses of wine from a very good international list, including a few of the best Virginia vintages. Wines opened the day before and properly stored overnight are discounted 30% off the regular price (50% off on Sun). Most of the menu consists of salads, sandwiches, and other light fare designed to accompany your wine tasting. A few main courses could include pizza on focaccia, or German bratwurst served with red cabbage. The tables out on the Downtown Mall are pet-friendly, and 5% of your bill is donated to the local humane society.

212 E. Main St. ✆ **434/872-0056.** www.siipswine.com. Reservations not accepted. Most items $8–$16. AE, DISC, MC, V. Mon–Wed 11:30am–10pm; Thurs–Sat 11am–midnight; Sun 10:30am–9pm. Bar later.

WHAT TO SEE & DO

See the box "Getting the Most out of Charlottesville," below, for advice on how best to use your time and money with a President's Pass to Monticello, Michie Tavern, and Ash Lawn–Highland.

The Top Attractions

Ash Lawn–Highland ★★ James Monroe's friendship with Thomas Jefferson brought him from Fredericksburg (see chapter 5) to Charlottesville, where he purchased 1,000 acres adjacent to Monticello in 1793. With Jefferson's help he built a home he called Highland (later owners added Ash Lawn in 1838 and a two-story addition in 1882). Before Monroe could settle in, Washington named him minister to France and sent him to Paris for 3 years. By the time he returned, he was suffering financial difficulties, and his "cabin castle" remained the modest house we see today. He was so in debt when he left the presidency in 1825 that he was forced to sell

Highland. He spent his final years near Leesburg and in New York City. Today the estate is owned and maintained as a working farm by his alma mater, the College of William and Mary in Williamsburg (see chapter 10). A 30-minute house tour will show you many of the family's original furnishings and artifacts. Young artists perform on the lawn here during the annual **Ash Lawn Opera Festival** in August (© 434/ 293-4500; www.ashlawnopera.org).

2050 James Monroe Pkwy. (C.R. 795), off Thomas Jefferson Pkwy. (Va. 53). © **434/293-8000.** www. ashlawnhighland.org. Admission $12 adults, $11 seniors, $6 children 6–11, free for children 5 and under. Apr–Oct daily 9am–6pm; Nov–Mar daily 11am–5pm. 30-min. tours depart every 10–15 min. Closed New Year's Day, Thanksgiving, and Christmas.

Michie Tavern ca. 1784 ★★   In 1746, Scotsman "Scotch John" Michie (pronounced "Mickey") purchased 1,152 acres of land from Patrick Henry's father, and in 1784, Michie's son, William, built this tavern on a well-traveled stagecoach route at Earlysville, 17 miles northwest of Charlottesville. A wealthy businesswoman, Josephine Henderson, had it moved to its present location and reconstructed in 1927. Included in the 30-minute living-history tours are the **Virginia Wine Museum** and reproductions of the "dependencies"—log kitchen, dairy, smokehouse, icehouse, root cellar, and "necessary" (outdoor toilet). The general store and the metalsmith shop have been re-created, along with excellent crafts and clothing shops. Behind the store is a gristmill that has operated continuously since 1797.

Plan your visit to Michie Tavern to coincide with lunchtime, when a buffet is served to weary travelers in the Ordinary, a converted log cabin with original hand-hewn walls and beamed ceilings. The fare is typical Southern dishes such as fried chicken, black-eyed peas, and corn bread. American Express, MasterCard, and Visa are accepted.

GETTING THE MOST OUT OF CHARLOTTESVILLE

Monticello, Ash Lawn–Highland, and Michie Tavern are within 2 miles of each other on or near Thomas Jefferson Parkway (Va. 53). That's off Va. 20 just south of I-64, on the southeastern outskirts of town. You'll need a full day to fully take them in.

Monticello, Ash Lawn–Highland, and Michie Tavern sell the **Presidents' Pass,** a discount pass for admission to all three. It costs $36 for adults and $18 for children 6 to 11. The attractions validate the pass when you show up, so there's no time limit on when you must use it.

You can buy Monticello tickets in advance at www.monticello.org. All tickets have specific house tour times printed on them, which has eliminated the long lines of people waiting to go through the mansion during busy periods. It's a good idea to buy your tickets as early as possible so you'll have the widest choice of tour times. Be sure to arrive at the Monticello visitor center at least 30 minutes early in order to get up to the house on time.

I would spend the morning at Monticello, then head to nearby **Michie Tavern,** where you can tour the tavern and the Virginia Wine Museum, and have lunch (expect a wait on weekends and in Oct). In the afternoon, head for Monroe's **Ash Lawn–Highland,** 2½ miles away, which will take about an hour to see.

If you have time left over, head for the **University of Virginia.** Otherwise, plan to tour the campus and see the town's other sights the next day.

683 Thomas Jefferson Pkwy. (Va. 53). © **434/977-1234.** www.michietavern.com. Admission $9 adults, $8 seniors, $4.50 children 6–11, free for children 5 and under. Buffet meals $17 adults, $11 children 12–18, $7.95 children 6–11. Daily 9am–5pm (last tour 4:20pm). Restaurant Apr–Oct daily 11:15am–3:30pm, Nov–Mar daily 11:15am–3pm.

Monticello ★★★ Pronounced "Mon-ti-*chel*-lo," the home Thomas Jefferson built between 1769 and 1809 is an architectural masterpiece and one of the most remarkable Colonial homes in the United States. Designated a UNESCO World Heritage Site, it was the first Virginia plantation manse to sit atop a mountain rather than beside a river. Jefferson rejected the British Georgian architecture that characterized his time in favor of the 16th-century Italian style of Andrea Palladio. Later, during his 5-year term as minister to France, he was influenced by the homes of nobles at the court of Louis XVI, and after returning home in 1789, he incorporated features of the Parisian buildings he so admired. The museum in the **Thomas Jefferson Visitor Center,** halfway up the mountain near Monticello's African-American graveyard, explains how he built, renovated, and remodeled Monticello over 40 years. The museum is a short course in classical architecture.

You must start at the visitor center, which also has a gift shop (surely stocked with every book in print about Jefferson), an inexpensive cafe, and the **Griffin Discovery Room,** where children can use blocks to build their own mansion and play with a version of the "polygraph" Jefferson used to make copies of his correspondence.

From there you can either walk or take a shuttle bus to the house, which has been restored as closely as possible to its appearance during Jefferson's retirement years. Nearly all the furniture and other household objects were once owned by Jefferson or his family. The vegetable garden extends to its original 1,000-foot length, and Mulberry Row—where slaves and free artisans lived and labored in light industrial shops, such as a joinery, smokehouse-dairy, blacksmith shop–nailery, and carpenter's shop—has been excavated.

Jefferson's grave is in the family burial ground.

You can tour the grounds on your own but you must take a guided tour to enter the house. See "Getting the Most out of Charlottesville," above, for advice about buying an admission pass. Optional tours of the plantation and grounds are available all year, and during summer you can send your young ones on 30-minute tours specifically designed for children.

Thomas Jefferson Pkwy. (Va. 53). © **434/984-9822** for information, 434/984-9844 on weekends, or 434/984-9800 for recorded information. www.monticello.org. Admission $22 adults, $8 children 6–11, free for children 5 and under. Mar–Oct daily 8am–6pm; Nov–Feb daily 9am–4:30pm. 30-min. tours run continuously. Closed Christmas.

The University of Virginia ★★★

One of the world's most beautiful college campuses, Jefferson's beloved **University of Virginia** is graced with spacious lawns, serpentine-walled gardens, colonnaded pavilions, and a classical Rotunda inspired by the Pantheon in Rome. Jefferson regarded its creation as one of his three greatest achievements—all the more remarkable since it was started in his 73rd year. He was, in every sense, the university's father, as he conceived it, wrote its charter, raised money for its construction, drew the plans, selected the site, laid the cornerstone in 1817, supervised construction, served as the first rector, selected the faculty, and created the curriculum. His good friends, Monroe and Madison, sat with him on the first board, and Madison succeeded him as rector, serving for 8 years.

The phrase "Renaissance man" might have been coined to describe Thomas Jefferson. Perhaps our most important founding father, he was a lawyer, architect, scientist, musician, writer, educator, and horticulturist.

After drafting the Declaration of Independence, Jefferson served as governor of Virginia, ambassador to France, secretary of state, and president of the United States for two terms, during which he nearly doubled the size of the United States by negotiating the Louisiana Purchase Treaty with France. He sent Meriwether Lewis and William Clark on their famous exploration of the territory.

Yet despite all his achievements, Jefferson ordered that his gravestone be inscribed: "Here Was Buried Thomas Jefferson/Author Of The Declaration Of American Independence/Of The Statute Of Virginia For Religious Freedom/And Father Of The University Of Virginia."

Jefferson was 83 when he died at Monticello on July 4, 1826, 50 years to the day after his Declaration of Independence was signed at Philadelphia. Ironically, his fellow revolutionary but later heated political enemy John Adams lay on his own deathbed in Massachusetts. Unaware that Jefferson had died earlier, Adams's last words were: "Jefferson survives."

The focal point of the university is the **Rotunda** (on University Ave. at Rugby Rd.), restored as Jefferson designed it. Enter on the ground level on the "village side"—that is, the side facing away from University Avenue. A student will be on duty at a desk to give you information, directions, and brochures. If you're up to it, be sure to climb the three stories to Jefferson's magnificent lecture room under the dome on the top floor. The Rotunda is open daily from 9am to 4:45pm except on holidays. Admission is free but donations are suggested.

Some 600 feet of tree-dotted lawn extends from the Rotunda's south portico to what is now Cabell Hall, designed at the turn of the 20th century by Stanford White. Pavilions on either side of the lawn are still used for faculty housing, each of a different architectural style "to serve as specimens for the Architectural lecturer." Behind each are a garden (originally used by faculty members to grow vegetables and keep livestock) and the original student dormitories, used—and greatly coveted—by students today. The room Edgar Allan Poe occupied is furnished as it would have been in 1826 and is open to visitors.

Paralleling the lawn are more rows of student rooms called the Ranges. Equally spaced within each of the Ranges are "hotels," originally used to accommodate student dining. Each hotel represented a different country, and students would have to both eat the food and speak the language of that country. Although a wonderful idea on Jefferson's part, it lasted only a short while as everyone wanted to eat French but not German.

CAMPUS TOURS When school is in session, students lead 1½-hour campus tours Monday to Saturday at 11am and 2pm. The tours are first-come, first-served, but call 📞 **434/924-3601** to make sure there will be one when you're here. Guided 1-hour historical tours of the Rotunda (📞 **434/924-1019**) take place daily at 10 and 11am, and 2, 3, and 4pm, except during the 3 weeks around Christmas (when the university is closed) and in May during graduation. Both tours are free.

The big spectator sports here are played by the University of Virginia Cavaliers, who play a full schedule of intercollegiate athletics. The UVA teams may officially be the Cavaliers, but everyone calls them the Wahoos—or 'Hoos for short. Although the nickname Wahoo comes from "Wah-hoo-wah," the school's official yell, some wags say it's from the wahoo fish, which allegedly can drink twice its own weight twice a day. And that reportedly comes from UVA's reputation as a hard-drinking party school. Call 📞 **800/542-8821** or go to www.virginiasports.com for information, schedules, and tickets.

Self-guided walking-tour brochures are available in the Rotunda and from the university's **Visitor Information Center** (📞 **434/924-0311**), which is located not on campus but in the University Police Headquarters, on Ivy Road (U.S. 250 Business) just east of the U.S. 29/U.S. 250 bypass. The visitor center is open 24 hours a day. See "Getting Around," earlier in this chapter, for parking information.

The Downtown Mall

After a morning spent seeing the university, have lunch and poke into the shops along Charlottesville's **Downtown Mall,** the pedestrian-only section of Main Street. Although the strip is the country's oldest pedestrian mall, it lacks historical charm and seems underwhelming during the cold winter months. But the mall changes character completely in warm weather, when restaurant tables line its entire length and it becomes the city's lively focal point. Fountains, park benches, shade trees, a kiosk bar, theaters, and music-making buskers enhance it all. It's especially active when nationally known artists are in concert in the **nTelos Wireless Pavilion,** on the mall's eastern end (see "Charlottesville After Dark," below).

The mall's 120-plus boutiques and art galleries make it the best place in Charlottesville to shop. You'll instinctively know the best stores when you see them. It's worth walking the entire length in one direction just to take it all in, and then going back to the most compelling shops and restaurants. The *Historic Downtown Dining, Entertainment and Shopping* brochure available at the visitor center is an invaluable aid. Go to **www.downtowncharlottesville.net** or call 📞 **434/296-8548** for mall events.

More Attractions in Town

Albemarle County Courthouse   The center of village activity in Colonial days, the courthouse in the historic downtown area features a facade and portico dating from the Civil War. There's no tour, but you can glance at Jefferson's will in the County Office Building. It's easy to imagine Jefferson, Madison, and Monroe talking politics under the lawn's huge shade trees.

501 E. Jefferson St. (at 5th St. E.). 📞 **434/296-1492.** www.albemarle.org. Free admission. Mon–Fri 9am–5pm.

The Kluge-Ruhe Aboriginal Art Collection ★   This museum, about 3 miles east of downtown, houses one of the largest public collections of Australian aboriginal art in the world. It includes the gatherings of wealthy American businessman John W. Kluge, who began collecting in 1988, and of the late Professor Edward L. Ruhe of Kansas University, who began collecting while visiting Australia as a Fulbright scholar in 1965. Kluge bought Ruhe's collection and archives and later gave it all to the University of Virginia.

400 Worrell Dr. ✆ **434/244-0234.** www.virginia.edu/kluge-ruhe. Free admission. Tues–Sat 9am–4pm; Sun 1–5pm. 40-min. guided tour Sat 10:30am.

McGuffey Art Center   Local artists and craftspeople work in their studios in this early-20th-century school building a block north of the Downtown Mall. Art is also exhibited and for sale in the center's three galleries. Shows change monthly.

201 2nd St. NW. ✆ **434/295-7973.** www.mcguffeyartcenter.com. Free admission. Tues–Sat 10am–6pm; Sun 1–5pm.

University of Virginia Art Museum   This nationally accredited museum has permanent exhibits of American and European painting, sculpture, decorative art, and photography from the 15th to the 21st centuries, ancient Mediterranean pieces, and Asian art. A highlight is its *Age of Thomas Jefferson* collection. The museum has an active temporary exhibit schedule.

In the Thomas H. Bayly Bldg., 155 Rugby Rd. ✆ **434/924-3592.** www.virginia.edu/artmuseum. Free admission; donations welcome. Tues–Sun noon–5pm.

Virginia Discovery Museum ☺   The Virginia Discovery Museum is a place of enchantment, offering numerous hands-on exhibits and programs for children ages 1 through 10. Here, they can ride a miniature carousel and dress up as firefighters, soldiers, police, and other grown-ups. The Showalter Cabin, an authentic structure that once stood on a site in Mt. Crawford, Virginia, is outfitted with the simple furnishings appropriate to an early-19th-century lifestyle. An arts-and-crafts studio, an active beehive, and a changing series of traveling and made-on-site exhibits round out the fun.

524 E. Main St. ✆ **434/977-1025.** www.vadm.org. Admission $6. Tues–Sat 10am–5pm; Sun 1–5pm. Closed New Year's Day, Easter, day before Thanksgiving, Thanksgiving, Dec 24, and Christmas.

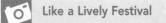

Like a Lively Festival

Don't miss strolling along Charlottesville's Downtown Mall in warm weather, when buskers make music beside the restaurant tables under the shade trees on Main Street, thus turning this pedestrian-only strip into a lively outdoor festival that sometimes erupts in the Charlottesville Pavilion, on the east end of the mall.

James Madison's Montpelier ★★★

Set on a 2,700-acre estate, facing the Blue Ridge Mountains 25 miles northeast of Charlottesville, **Montpelier** was home to President James Madison and his equally famous wife, Dolley. Madison was just 26 in 1776 when he ensured that religious freedom would be included in the Virginia Declaration of Rights, and his efforts at the federal Constitutional Convention in 1787 earned him the title "Father of the Constitution." Madison became secretary of state under his good friend Thomas Jefferson in 1801 and succeeded Jefferson as president in 1809. He and Dolley fled the White House in the face of advancing British troops during the War of 1812.

Two structures remain here from their time: the manor house and the Ice House Temple (built over a well and used to store ice). William du Pont, Sr., bought the estate in 1901 and enlarged the mansion to 55 rooms (thereby almost engulfing the Madison original) and added barns, staff houses, a sawmill, a blacksmith shop, a train station, a dairy, and greenhouses. His wife created a 2-acre formal garden, and daughter Marion du Pont Scott later built the steeplechase course in front of the mansion and initiated the **Montpelier Hunt Races,** which are still held here on the first Saturday in November.

The National Trust for Historic Preservation now owns the property and is in the process of a meticulous, multiyear restoration, which has stripped away the du Ponts' additions to the mansion, reducing it to the 22-room brick version the Madisons occupied in 1820s. The house is open to the public during the project. You can see the Constitution exhibit in the south wing and explore the basement rooms on your own, but upstairs you must take a 30-minute tour explaining the near-archaeological aspects of the restoration.

Meanwhile, the Madison's furnishings and many personal belongings (including a lock of James's hair and a bust of Dolley rendered in 1818 by John William Coffee) are on display in the visitor center. The Madisons are buried in the family graveyard.

The visitor center also shows what the house looked like during its du Pont incarnation. There's a snack bar, too, plus special children's programs during summer. Audio tours, included in the price of admission, guide you through the property.

Out on Va. 20, the small **Montpelier Train Depot** has been restored to its 1912 appearance. It's "white" and "colored" entrances will prepare you for its fascinating *In the Time of Segregation* exhibit, which explains the stark differences in how white and black travelers were treated prior to integration in the 1950s. The depot is unstaffed and admission is free. You can also explore the black experience at the **Gilmore Cabin,** built by emancipated slave George Gilmore in 1873.

You'll need at least 2 hours to see everything, and you'll do a bit of walking, so wear comfortable shoes. Also call ahead for a schedule of special events, such as the races in November, birthday celebrations for James (Mar 16) and Dolley (May 20), the Montpelier Wine Festival in May, and Constitution Day (Sept 17).

11395 Constitution Hwy. (Va. 20), Montpelier Station. (ʘ) **540/672-2728.** www.montpelier. org. Admission $16 adults, $8 children 6–14, free for children 5 and under. Apr–Oct daily 9am–5pm; Nov–Mar daily 9am–4pm. House tours every 30 min. (last tour 30-min. before closing). Closed Thanksgiving and Christmas. Take Va. 20 north for 25 miles.

Take the Scenic Route to Montpelier

Running between Montpelier and Charlottesville, Va. 20 is one of the state's most scenic drives. This 25-mile-long **Presidents Route** more or less follows the same winding road Thomas Jefferson, James Monroe, and James Madison took when they visited each other. You'll pass near Barboursville Vineyards and Burnley Vineyards on the way (see "On the Wine Trail," below).

On the Wine Trail

Thomas Jefferson's dream of producing quality wines in Virginia has come true, for along with the Hunt Country in northern Virginia (see chapter 4), the Charlottesville area today is one of the state's two top winemaking regions. Be sure to pick up a brochure for the **Monticello Wine Trail** (www.monticellowinetrail.org) at one of the visitor centers; it gives information about the 24 nearby wineries including their business hours. Five vineyards west of town have banded together on the **Appellation Trail** (www.theappellationtrail.com).

To sample all you want yet avoid driving tipsy, take a full day or afternoon excursion with **Arcady Vineyard Wine Tasting Tours** (© 434/872-9475; www.arcady vineyard.com). Erika and Chris Goddell, owners of Arcady Vineyard Bed and Breakfast, do all the driving while taking you to and from local vineyards. They do not accept marketing or trades with the wineries, and thus are free to visit the best, not those who pay the most. Their full-day tours cost about $130 per person, plus $20 per person for a silver-service picnic lunch. Reservations are required.

Most convenient of the local wineries to visit on your own is **Jefferson Vineyards,** 1353 Thomas Jefferson Pkwy. (Va. 53; © 434/977-3042; www.jeffersonvineyards. com), between Monticello and Ash Lawn–Highland. Thomas Jefferson and an Italian named Filippo Mazzei planted grapes on this property in 1774. Consider stopping for a taste after your day's sightseeing. It is open daily 10am to 6pm.

From there you can drive south on C.R. 795 to the **Trump Winery,** 100 Grand Cru Dr. (© 434/977-3895; www.klugeestate.com), the former Kluge Estate Winery and Vineyard but now owned by Donald Trump. It is open from January to February Thursday to Monday 11am to 6pm, and from March to December Wednesday to Monday 11am to 6pm (till 8pm Fri and Sat).

Near the village of Crozet, in the Blue Ridge foothills about 15 miles west of Charlottesville, **King Family Vineyards,** 6550 Roseland Farm (© 434/823-7800; www.kingfamilyvineyards.com), is one of the area's best family-owned wineries. It is open Monday to Friday 9am to 5pm and Saturday to Sunday 11am to 5pm.

Between Charlottesville and Montpelier near the intersection of Va. 20 and Va. 33, **Barboursville Vineyards,** ★★ 17655 Winery Rd., Barboursville (© 540/832-3824; www.barboursvillewine.com), is Virginia's first modern winery, established in 1976 by the largest privately owned winemaking company in Italy. It is open Monday to Saturday 10am to 5pm and Sunday 11am to 5pm. Its exceptional **Palladio** Italian restaurant (© 540/832-7848) is open for lunch Monday to Friday and for dinner Friday to Saturday, and you can stay in luxury at the winery's **1804 Inn** (© 540/832-5384). Also on the estate are the ruins of one of the five houses Thomas Jefferson designed.

Nearer to Charlottesville, **Burnley Vineyards,** 400 Winery Lane, Barboursville (© 540/832-2828; www.burnleywines.com), is one of the oldest wineries in the area. It is open from January to March Friday to Monday 11am to 5pm and from April to December daily 11am to 5pm.

OUTDOOR ACTIVITIES

If you can afford it, the best golfing is at the Arnold Palmer–redesigned links at the private Keswick Club, which guests of Keswick Hall at Monticello can pay to play (see "Where to Stay," earlier in this chapter). The University of Virginia's 18-hole **Birdwood Golf Course** (© 434/293-GOLF [4653]; www.boarshead.com), adjacent to the Boar's Head (p. 109), is one of the top 10 collegiate courses in the country. The 18-hole **Meadow Creek Golf Course,** 1400 Pen Park Rd. (© 434/977-0615; www.meadowcreekgolf.org), is a short but challenging municipal course. Call the courses to reserve tee times and get directions. Two fine courses—Devils Knob and Stoney Creek—are at Wintergreen Resort, about 43 miles away (see "A Mountain Getaway," earlier in this chapter).

You can go rafting and canoeing on the James River at Scottsville, a quaint, 19th-century town 20 miles south of Charlottesville via Va. 20. The river can run swiftly here—class I or II if it has rained recently, canoeing and tubing conditions if it hasn't.

Contact **James River Runners** (✆ **434/286-2338;** www.jamesriver.com), which has been rafting the rapids, taking adventurers on overnight canoe trips, and renting canoes and inner tubes since 1979.

Charlottesville is Virginia's prime venue for hot-air ballooning, with several companies sending their craft soaring over the foothills, depending on the direction of the wind. **Bear Ballooning** (✆ **800/932-0152** or 434/971-1757; www.2comefly.com) takes off from the Boar's Head (p. 109). Others include **Blue Ridge Balloon Company** (✆ **434/589-6213;** www.blueridgeballoon.com) and **Monticello Country Ballooning** (✆ **434/996-9008;** www.virginiahotairballoon.com). Contact them well in advance of coming here.

On the Downtown Mall, the **Main Street Arena** (✆ **434/817-2400; www.mainstarena.com**) has an indoor ice rink offering an irregular schedule of skating, skating lessons, and pickup hockey games.

CHARLOTTESVILLE AFTER DARK

This well-heeled college town has a lot going on between sunset and the wee hours. For a complete schedule, see *Charlottesville Arts & Entertainment* (www.artsmonthly. com) and the free newspapers *C-Ville Weekly* (www.c-ville.com) and the *Hook* (www. readthehook.com), all available at the visitor centers (see "Visitor Information," earlier in this chapter).

Two top performing arts centers are on the Downtown Mall. Built in 1931 and restored in 2004 after being dark for 30 years, the **Paramount Theater,** 215 E. Main St. (✆ **434/979-1922;** www.theparamount.net), has showcased the diverse likes of Bill Cosby, Vince Gill, Sir James Gallway, and Arlo Guthrie. It's also a key venue during the **Ash Lawn Opera Festival** in August (✆ **434/293-4500;** www.ashlawn opera.org).

Another restoration has brought back the 1912-vintage **Jefferson Theater,** 110 E. Main St. (✆ **434/245-4948;** www.jeffersontheater.com), which now hosts an eclectic mix of local and national entertainers.

At the mall's eastern end, the outdoor but covered **nTelos Wireless Pavilion** (✆ **877/CPAV-TIX** [272-8849] or 434/817-0220; www.thenteloswirelesspavilion. com) hosts concerts by nationally known artists as well as community events.

You can watch local theater at **Live Arts,** 123 E. Water St. (✆ **434/977-4177;** www.livearts.org), and **Old Michie Theatre for Youth and Puppetry Arts,** 221 E. Water St. (✆ **434/977-3690;** www.oldmichie.com), both near the Downtown Mall.

The University of Virginia has a constant and ever-changing parade of concerts, plays, lectures, and other events, many at the **Culbreth Theatre** and the **Helms Theatre,** both on campus at 109 Culbreth Rd. (✆ **434/924-3376;** www.virginia. edu/heritagetheatre).

The 14,500-seat **John Paul Jones Arena,** also on the UVA campus at 295 Massie Rd. (✆ **434/243-4960;** www.jonesarena.com), hosts UVA's basketball teams, traveling shows such as *Disney on Ice,* and concerts by leading artists such as Jimmy Buffett, James Taylor, and the hometown Dave Matthews Band.

To use your feet, take an entertaining **Ghosts and Mysteries Walking Tour** (✆ **434/-760-0525;** www.tellmeaboutittours.com). The 2-hour strolls cost $15 for adults and $5 for children 10 to 18. Children 9 years of age and under are free. The tours depart May to October Thursday to Saturday at 8pm from Marco & Luna

Dumpling Shop, 112 W. Main St. on the Downtown Mall. Reservations are not necessary.

Like most college towns, Charlottesville sees lesser-known bands blasting away, especially on weekends. Even if you're hard of hearing, you can feel the music coming from the student-oriented bars around The Corner. Several Downtown Mall restaurants have live music on weekends, including **Miller's,** 109 W. Main St. (© **434/971-8511;** www.millersdowntown.com), where Dave Matthews tended bar before making it big.

LYNCHBURG & ENVIRONS

When Jefferson wanted to get away from it all, he packed his bags and headed 60 miles south to Poplar Forest, his country retreat near the James River town of Lynchburg, today known as the home of the late Reverend Jerry Falwell and his fundamentalist Liberty University. Lynchburg is a base from which to explore not just Poplar Forest but one of Patrick Henry's plantation homes and the village of Appomattox Court House, where Robert E. Lee surrendered to Ulysses S. Grant. Also nearby are memorials to the great African-American leader Booker T. Washington and to the D-day invasion of World War II.

Visitor Information

The **Lynchburg Visitor Center,** 216 12th St. (at Church St.), Lynchburg, VA 24504 (© **800/723-5821** or 434/847-1811; www.discoverlynchburg.org), is open daily 9am to 5pm.

For information about adjacent Bedford County, contact the **Bedford Area Welcome Center,** 816 Burks Hill Rd. (Va. 122), Bedford, VA 24523 (© **877/447-3257** or 540/587-5682; www.visitbedford.com). The center is at the entrance to the National D-Day Memorial (see below), on Va. 122 off U.S. 460; in fact, you must buy your memorial tickets here. It is open daily 9am to 5pm.

The **Appomattox Visitor Center** is in the old train station at 214 Main St. (© **877/258-4739** or 434/352-8999; www.tourappomattox.com). It's open daily 9am to 5pm and has information about the present-day town and its restaurants, budget motels, and bed-and-breakfasts.

Exploring Lynchburg

Lynchburg has been a transportation hub since it was founded in 1786 on the banks of the James River, upon which bateaux hauled tobacco east to Richmond and merchandise west to the Shenandoah Valley. After years of neglect, the city is seriously reviving its historic downtown. Especially along Main Street you'll find renovated commercial buildings containing offices, stores, urban loft apartments, and restaurants. Sporting a huge fountain, **Riverfront Festival Park** now graces the city's waterfront.

Worth exploring during a brief stopover is **Monument Terrace,** a 139-step staircase on Court Street between 9th and 10th streets. It takes you uphill to the **Old Court House,** built in 1855 and an outstanding example of civic architecture. It's now home to the **Lynchburg Museum,** 901 Court St. (© **804/455-6226;** www.lynchburgmuseum.org), tracing the city's history. Admission is $6 for adults, $5 for seniors, $4 for students, $3 for children ages 6 to 17, and free for kids 5 and under. It is open Monday to Saturday 10am to 4pm and Sunday noon to 4pm.

I enjoy poking through the **Lynchburg Community Market,** 1219 Main St., at 12th St. (© 434/455-4485), where vendors purvey fresh farm produce and a wide range of collectibles, and having lunch at one of several food stalls, especially **Philippine Delight** (© 434/384-5654), serving *lumpia* (Philippine-style egg rolls). The market is open Tuesday to Saturday 7am to 2pm.

WHERE TO STAY IN LYNCHBURG

One of the best downtown restorations converted two warehouses of an old shoe factory into the **Craddock Terry Hotel,** 1312 Commerce St. (www.craddockterry hotel.com; © 434/455-1500), a charming, 44-room boutique hostelry. Classic posters promoting women's shoes adorn the hallways, and complimentary breakfast is delivered to the rooms in shoe-shine boxes. The hotel's Water Stone pub serves very good pizza.

Nearby Attractions

Note: Some of the following attractions are closer to Roanoke (see chapter 8) than to either Charlottesville or Lynchburg.

Appomattox Court House National Historical Park ★★★   Here, in the parlor of Wilmer McLean's home 2 miles north of Appomattox, Robert E. Lee surrendered the Army of Northern Virginia to Ulysses S. Grant on April 9, 1865, thus effectively ending the bitter Civil War. Today, the 20 or so houses, stores, courthouse, and tavern that made up the village then called Appomattox Court House have been restored by the National Park Service and are essential to any Civil War tour of Virginia. You will need at least 2 hours to visit the restored houses and walk the country lanes in the rural stillness where surrender took place. Start by picking up a map of the park and a self-guided tour booklet at the visitor center in the courthouse. Upstairs, a short video and museum exhibits include excerpts from the diaries and letters of Civil War soldiers. Then visit McLean's house, Clover Hill Tavern, Meeks' Store, the Woodson Law Office, the courthouse (totally reconstructed), the jail, and Kelly House. The Confederates laid down their arms and rolled up their battle flags on the now-restored road through the village. There's a full schedule of ranger programs during the summer. (*Note:* The park does not have a street address; on your GPS enter "Attractions," then "Appomattox Court House NHP," and be sure to spell *Appomattox* correctly.)

Va. 24 (PO Box 218), Appomattox. © **434/352-8987.** www.nps.gov/apco. Admission Memorial Day–Labor Day $4 adults, free for children 15 and under (maximum $10 per vehicle); rest of year $3 adults, free for children 16 and under (maximum $5 per vehicle). Daily 8:30am–5pm. Closed New Year's Day, Thanksgiving, and Christmas. From Lynchburg, take U.S. 460 east 22 miles to Va. 24 north.

Booker T. Washington National Monument ★   At this memorial to one of America's great African-American leaders, you can conjure up the setting of Booker T. Washington's childhood in reconstructed buildings and demonstrations of farm life and slavery in Civil War–era Virginia. Although Washington called his boyhood home a plantation, the Burroughs farm was small, at 207 acres with 11 slaves or fewer. His mother was the cook, and the cabin where he was born was also the kitchen. His family left the farm in 1865, when he was 9. He determinedly sought an education and walked most of the 500 miles from his home in West Virginia to Hampton Institute, now Hampton University (p. 270). He worked his way through school and achieved prominence as an educator, founder of Tuskegee Institute in Alabama,

Strapped for space in Richmond, the Museum of the Confederacy (p. 219) is relocating some of its exhibits to the **Museum of the Confederacy—Appomattox,** 159 Horseshoe Rd. (℮ **855/649-1861;** www.moc.org). Scheduled to open in 2012, it will portray Lee's last days and his surrender, including the sword and uniform he wore to meet Grant. Admission will be $12 for adults, $8 for seniors, $6 for children 8 to 13, and free for kids 7 and under. Combination tickets (for admission to the Museum of the Confederacy—Appomattox and the Museum of the Confederacy in Richmond or the White House of the Confederacy in Richmond) will be $15 for adults, $13 for seniors, $8 for children 8 to 13, and free for kids 7 and under. Museum of the Confederacy—Appomattox will be open daily 10am to 5pm except New Year's Day, Thanksgiving, and Christmas.

author, and advisor to presidents. Begin at the visitor center, which offers a map with a self-guided plantation tour and nature walks winding through the original Burroughs property. Call the park for guided tour times.

12130 Booker T. Washington Hwy. (Va. 122), Hardy. ℮ **540/721-2094.** www.nps.gov/bowa. Free admission. Daily 9am–5pm. Tours daily 11am and 2pm. Closed New Year's Day, Thanksgiving, and Christmas. From Lynchburg, take U.S. 460 west to Va. 122 south; park is 16 miles northeast of Rocky Mount.

The National D-Day Memorial On a hilltop with a splendid view of the Peaks of Otter up on the Blue Ridge Parkway (see chapter 8), this memorial to the American soldiers, sailors, and airmen who fought and died in the invasion of Normandy on June 6, 1944, is appropriately here in Bedford, which lost 19 of its young men during the invasion and four more during the Normandy campaign. The town of 3,200 proportionally lost more men on D-day than any other town in the United States. Stunning in its architectural symbolism, the monument recalls the landing beaches, the cliffs the soldiers climbed, and the contributions of the army, navy, and air force. Be sure to pick up a brochure or take a tour (1 hr. on foot, 45 min. by shuttle).

You must buy your tickets at the **Bedford Area Welcome Center,** near the entrance, which has a large relief map of the memorial (see "Visitor Information," under "Lynchburg & Environs," above).

1 Overlord Circle (U.S. 460 at Va. 122), Bedford. ℮ **800/352-DDAY** [3329] or 540/586-3329. www. dday.org. Admission $7 adults, $5 children 6–16, free for children 5 and under. Guided walking tours $3 per person, free for children 5 and under. Riding tours every 30 min. $2 per persons of all ages. Daily 10am–5pm. Closed New Year's Day, Thanksgiving, and Christmas.

Red Hill, Patrick Henry National Memorial In failing health, fiery orator Patrick ("Give me liberty or give me death") Henry retired to Red Hill plantation, 35 miles southeast of Lynchburg, in 1794 after serving five terms as governor of Virginia. He died here on June 6, 1799, and is buried in the family graveyard. Begin your tour at the visitor center, where you can see a 15-minute video about Henry and visit the museum with the world's largest assemblage of Henry artifacts and memorabilia. The centerpiece is Peter Rothermel's famous painting *Patrick Henry before the Virginia House of Burgesses May 30, 1765,* depicting his "If this be treason, make the most of it" speech against the Stamp Act in 1765. The site contains his actual law office, an accurate reproduction of the main house, the carriage house, and other small buildings. You'll need about an hour here. Henry also lived at Scotchtown (p. 226), north of Richmond.

1250 Red Hill Rd., Brookneal. © **800/514-7463** or 434/376-2044. www.redhill.org. Admission $6 adults, $5 seniors, $2 students. Apr–Oct Mon–Sat 9am–5pm, Sun 1–5pm; Nov–Mar Mon–Sat 9am–4pm, Sun 1–4pm. Closed New Year's Day, Thanksgiving, and Christmas. From Lynchburg, take U.S. 501 south to Brookneal, then Va. 40 east, and follow the brown signs.

Thomas Jefferson's Poplar Forest ★★ In 1806, while he was president, Jefferson himself assisted the masons in laying the foundation for this dwelling on what was then a 4,819-acre plantation and the source of much of his income. He designed the octagonal house to utilize light and airflow to the maximum in as economical a space as possible. It became his escape from the parade of visitors at Monticello, a 3-day carriage ride away. Today, his final architectural masterpiece is again a work in progress, as it is being slowly restored to the way it looked in the early 19th century. Outside, archaeologists try to discover how Jefferson landscaped the gardens. You can see artifacts from the buildings and grounds as they are brought to light and exhibited. Like James Madison's Montpelier (see above), this is a restoration in progress, not a furnished historic home. A visit to Monticello's museum will help visitors understand Jefferson's architectural intentions here.

1542 Bateman Bridge Rd. (Va. 661), Forest (6 miles southwest of Lynchburg). © **434/525-1806.** www.poplarforest.org. House tour $10 adults, $9 seniors, $5 children 12–18, $2 children 6–11, free for children 5 and under. May–Dec Wed–Mon 10am–4pm. 40-min. house tours depart on the hour and half-hour (last tour 4pm). Closed Thanksgiving and Jan–Apr. From Lynchburg, take U.S. 221 south, go south on Va. 811, turn east on Va. 661. From U.S. 460, take Thomas Jefferson Rd. (Va. 811) north, turn east on Va. 661, follow the signs.

THE SHENANDOAH VALLEY

Those of us who live in or near the Shenandoah Valley are fortunate indeed, for this is one of the most beautiful areas of the eastern United States. All we have to do is take a Sunday drive in the rolling hills dotted with picturesque small towns and well-tended farms with old stone homesteads to appreciate its grandeur.

If you're like me, you'll come here to see the view from the magnificent Shenandoah National Park atop the Blue Ridge Mountains. The park offers spectacular landscapes and a plethora of hiking and riding trails, including a portion of the Maine-to-Georgia Appalachian Trail. Skyline Drive—one of America's great scenic routes—runs the full length of the park and connects directly with the Blue Ridge Parkway, which continues south to North Carolina's Great Smoky Mountains.

Outdoor enthusiasts can ride horses and go tubing, canoeing, or rafting down on the valley floor.

As it is throughout Virginia, history is a major reason to come here. You can see where George Washington carved his initials at Natural Bridge while surveying the valley and examine the Winchester office he used during the French and Indian War.

Union and Confederate armies see-sawed up and down the valley during the Civil War, when the North tried to cut off Robert E. Lee's supplies from this "Breadbasket of the Confederacy." Stonewall Jackson left Virginia Military Institute (VMI) at Lexington to become a great Confederate general. The entire VMI Corps of Cadets fought heroically in the legendary Battle of New Market. After the war, Lee settled in Lexington as president of what is now Washington and Lee University, and both he and Jackson are buried there. As it surely must have been in their time, Lexington is one of the country's most charming college towns.

Woodrow Wilson was born in Staunton in 1856, and a museum adjoining his birthplace pays tribute to this president's peace-loving ideals. Today's artistic center of the Shenandoah, his hometown is renowned for performing Shakespeare in its exact replica of the Bard's indoor theater.

Across the mountains, take the waters in the same Warm Springs frequented by Thomas Jefferson and relax at one of the nation's premiere mountain resorts at Hot Springs.

Indeed, this 150-mile-long valley and the mountains bordering it have something for everyone.

Getting There & Getting Around

The gorgeous scenery of the Shenandoah Valley demands to be seen by private vehicle. At least part of your trip should include the park's spectacular Skyline Drive (p. 128).

The fastest way to and through the region is via I-81, which runs the entire length of the valley floor and has been designated one of America's 10 most scenic interstates. It's also a very busy truck route so drive defensively at all times.

Alongside I-81, the legendary Valley Pike (U.S. 11) is much more peaceful and is like a trip back in time at least 60 years, with its small towns and villages, old-fashioned gas stations, ancient motels, shops, and restaurants.

I-66 enters the valley from Washington, D.C., before ending at Strasburg. I-64 crosses the valley's southern end. Other major east-west highways are Va. 7 and U.S. 50, 211, 33, 250, and 60.

United Express (📞 **800/241-6522;** www.united.com) has commuter flights to and from **Shenandoah Valley Regional Airport (SHD)** off I-81 between Harrison-burg and Staunton (📞 **540/234-8304;** www.flyshd.com). Avis, Budget, and Hertz have rental cars at the airport. Call 📞 **540/234-8304** or go to the airport's website at least 24 hours in advance to arrange shuttle service. The nearest major airport is Washington Dulles International Airport, 50 miles east of Front Royal (see "Getting There," in chapter 12). There are also airports in Charlottesville (see chapter 6) and Roanoke (see chapter 8).

Amtrak (📞 **800/872-7245;** www.amtrak.com) offers direct service to Staunton.

SHENANDOAH NATIONAL PARK & SKYLINE DRIVE ★★★

Running for 105 miles atop the spine of the Blue Ridge Mountains, Shenandoah National Park is a haven for plants and wildlife. Although long and skinny, the park encompasses some 300 square miles of mountains, forests, waterfalls, and rock formations. It has more than 60 mountain peaks higher than 2,000 feet, with Hawksbill and Stony Man exceeding 4,000 feet. Unfortunately, high humidity and ozone levels frequently create obscuring smog during the summer, so spring and fall are the best seasons to catch the panoramic views from overlooks from Skyline Drive over the Piedmont to the east and the Shenandoah Valley to the west. The drive gives you access to the park's visitor facilities and to more than 500 miles of hiking and horse trails, including the Appalachian Trail.

📎 Snow, Ice & Fog

Major highways in the Shenandoah Valley are kept open during winter, but snow, ice, and fog can close secondary roads, especially Skyline Drive and other mountain roads during winter. Check with the **Virginia Department of Transportation** (📞 **800/367-7623;** www.virginiadot.org) or the **Weather Channel** (www.weather.com) for present conditions.

Today, over two-fifths of the park is considered wilderness. Animals such as deer, bear, bobcat, and turkey have returned, and sightings of deer and smaller animals are frequent; the park also boasts more than 100 species of trees.

Europeans began settling these slopes and hollows in the early 18th century. The national park came into being 200 years later, when President Franklin D. Roosevelt's Depression-era Civilian Conservation Corps built the recreational facilities, guard walls, cabins, and many hiking trails. The corps completed Skyline Drive in 1939.

To me, the park is most interesting and beautiful in the 35-mile **Central District,** between U.S. 211 at Thornton Gap and U.S. 33 at Swift Run Gap.

Just the Facts

ACCESS POINTS & ORIENTATION   Despite what your GPS may mistakenly think, the park and its Skyline Drive have only four entrances. Northernmost is at **Front Royal** on U.S. 340 near the junction of I-81 and I-66, about 1 mile south of Front Royal and 75 miles west of Washington, D.C. The entrances to the Central District are at **Thornton Gap,** 33 miles south of Front Royal on U.S. 211 between Sperryville and Luray, and at **Swift Run Gap,** 68 miles south of Front Royal on U.S. 33 between Standardsville and Elkton. The southern gate is at **Rockfish Gap,** 105 miles south of Front Royal at I-64 and U.S. 250, some 21 miles west of Charlottesville and 18 miles east of Staunton. See the map of the Shenandoah Valley inside the back cover of this book.

Skyline Drive is marked with **mile posts,** starting at zero at the Front Royal entrance and increasing as you go south, with Rockfish Gap on the southern end at Mile 105.

DISTRICTS   The access roads divide the park into three areas: **Northern District,** between Front Royal and U.S. 211 at Thornton Gap (Mile 0 to Mile 31.5); **Central District,** between Thornton Gap and U.S. 33 at Swift Run Gap (Mile 31.5 to Mile 65.7); and **Southern District,** between Swift Run Gap and I-64 at Rockfish Gap (Mile 65.7 to Mile 105).

INFORMATION   For free information and expert advice about the park's hiking trails, call or write to Superintendent, Shenandoah National Park, 3655 U.S. Hwy. 211 East, Luray, VA 22835 (© **540/999-3500;** www.nps.gov/shen). The headquarters is 4 miles west of Thornton Gap and 5 miles east of Luray on U.S. 211. The office is open Monday to Friday 9am to 4:30pm.

Aramark Virginia Sky-Line Co., the park's major concessionaire (© **888/896-3833;** www.visitshenandoah.com), maintains an informative website on which you can reserve accommodations at the park's lodges and cabins.

The **Shenandoah National Park Association** (© **540/999-3582;** www.snpbooks.org) is the best source of maps, guidebooks, and other publications about the park's cultural and natural history. It has a bookstore at park headquarters, and many of its publications are available at the visitor centers and online.

For guidebooks and detailed topographic maps of the park's three districts, write or call the **Potomac Appalachian Trail Club (PATC),** 118 Park St., Vienna, VA 22180 (© **703/242-0315** or 242-0965 for a recording of the club's activities; www.patc.net). The PATC helps build and maintain the park's portion of the Appalachian Trail, including trail cabins (see "Hiking & Other Sports," below). The PATC is part of the **Appalachian Trail Conservancy,** PO Box 807, Harpers Ferry, WV 25425-0807 (© **304/535-6331;** www.appalachiantrail.org), which covers the entire trail from Maine to Georgia.

The **National Geographic** (www.nationalgeographic.com) publishes a terrific topographic map of the park's hiking trails, showing them all on one weatherproof sheet (map no. 228). One of the best trail guidebooks is the third edition of *Hiking Shenandoah National Park* by Bert and Jane Gildart (Globe Pequot, 2006).

EMERGENCIES   In case of emergencies, call the park headquarters (© **540/ 999-3500**).

FEES, REGULATIONS & BACKCOUNTRY PERMITS   Entrance permits good for 7 consecutive days are $15 per car, $10 per motorcycle, and $8 for each pedestrian or bicyclist from March through November. These fees are $10, $10, and $5, respectively, from December through February. An annual pass ($30) is good for 1 year. Park entrance is free to holders of InterAgency passes for seniors and disabled individuals.

The **speed limit** on Skyline Drive is 35 mph, although given the number of camper vans and rubberneckers creeping along this winding, two-lane road, you'll be lucky to go that fast. This is no place to have a fit of road rage.

Plants and animals are protected; so all hunting is prohibited. Pets must be kept on a leash at all times and are not allowed on some trails. Wood fires are permitted only in fireplaces in developed areas. Skyline Drive is a great bike route, but neither bicycles nor motor vehicles of any sort are allowed on the hiking trails.

Most of the park is open to backcountry camping. Permits, which are free, are required; get them at the entrance gates, visitor centers, or by mail from park headquarters (see "Information," above). Campers are required to leave no trace of their presence. No permits are necessary for backcountry hiking, but the same "no-trace" rule applies.

RANGER PROGRAMS   The park offers a wide variety of ranger-led activities—nature walks, interpretive programs, cultural and history lectures, and campfire talks. Most are held at or near Dickey Ridge Visitor Center in the north; Byrd Visitor Center and the Big Meadows Lodge, Skyland Resort, and campground in the center; and Loft Mountain campground in the south. Schedules are published seasonally in the *Shenandoah Overlook* newspaper, available at the entrance gates, visitor centers, and from park headquarters.

SEASONS   The park's high season is from mid- to late October, when the fall foliage peaks, and weekend traffic on Skyline Drive can be bumper-to-bumper. Days also tend to be more clear in fall than in summer, when lingering haze can obscure the views. In spring, the green of leafing trees moves up the ridge at the rate of about 100 feet a day. Wildflowers begin to bloom in April, and by late May, the azaleas are brilliant and the dogwood is putting on a show. Nesting birds abound, and the normally modest waterfalls are at their highest during spring, when warm rains melt the highland snows. You'll find the clearest views across the distant mountains during winter, but many facilities are closed then, and snow and ice can shut down Skyline Drive. Also, parts of the drive are closed at night during Virginia's hunting season from mid-November to early January.

VISITOR CENTERS   There are two park visitor centers, **Dickey Ridge Visitor Center,** at Mile 4.6 in the Northern District, and **Byrd Visitor Center,** in the Central District at Mile 51 in Big Meadows. Both are open daily 8:30am to 5pm from mid-March through Thanksgiving weekend in November (to 6pm on weekends from July through Labor Day). Both provide information, maps of nearby hiking trails, interpretive exhibits, films, slide shows, and nature walks.

BE PREPARED FOR SHENANDOAH NATIONAL PARK

It was a stifling 93°F (34°C) as I drove through Luray one summer afternoon. An hour later I arrived at Big Meadows Lodge atop the Blue Ridge—where the temperature was 58°F (14°C). It's always much cooler on the mountaintops than down in the valley, especially at night, so bring suitable clothing, including comfortable walking shoes.

In addition to the magnificent map brochure the ranger will hand you, be sure to get a copy of *Shenandoah Overlook* when you enter the park or stop by a visitor center. This tabloid newspaper will be your bible during your visit as it tells you about ranger programs and everything else that's going on during your visit.

With its proximity to the Washington and Baltimore metropolitan areas, the park is at its busiest on summer and fall weekends and holidays. The fall-foliage season in October is the busiest time, and reservations for October accommodations in or near the park should be made as much as a year in advance. The best time to visit is during the spring and on weekdays from June through October.

Unless you're caught in heavy traffic on fall foliage weekends, you can drive the entire length of Skyline Drive in about 3 hours without stopping. But why rush? Give yourself at least a day, so lovely are the views from its scenic overlooks. Stop for lunch at a wayside snack bar, lodge, or one of seven official picnic grounds (or any of the overlooks will do for an impromptu picnic). Better yet, get out of your car and take at least a short hike down one of the hollows to a waterfall.

Rather than directing you to one of the park's four entry points, some GPS and Internet mapping systems may inaccurately send you via roads that are closed to the public. If so, you will have to turn around and go back.

Note: Vehicles and trailers more than 12 feet, 8 inches high cannot get through the tunnels south of Thornton Gap.

Operated by the town of Waynesboro, the **Rockfish Gap Information Center,** 130 Afton Circle, Afton, VA 22020, near U.S. 211 and Exit 99 off I-64 at the park's southern gate (✆ **540/943-5187;** www.waynesboro.va.us), has a terrific room-size topographical map of the region (and a life-size statue of Robert E. Lee). It is open daily 9am to 5pm except New Year's Day, Thanksgiving, and Christmas.

Seeing the Highlights

The **Central District,** between U.S. 211 at Thornton Gap and U.S. 33 at Swift Run Gap (that is, between Mile 31.5 and Mile 65.7), can be more crowded than the north and south districts, but it has the highest mountains, best views, nearly half of the park's 500 miles of hiking trails, and its only stables and hotels: Big Meadows Lodge and Skyland Resort. You can see the views in a day, but give it at least 2 nights if you're doing any hiking, riding, or fishing. Make your reservations for Big Meadows or Skyland as early as possible (see "Accommodations," below). If you can't get a room in one of them, try Luray, which has the nearest accommodations to the Central District (see below).

SCENIC OVERLOOKS My favorite of the 75 designated overlooks in the Central District are **Stony Man Overlook** (Mile 38.6), offering panoramas of Stony Man

Cliffs, the valley, and the Alleghenies; **Thoroughfare Mountain Overlook** (Mile 40.5; elevation 3,595 ft.), one of the highest overlooks, with views from Hogback Mountain south to cone-shaped Robertson Mountain and the rocky face of Old Rag Mountain; **Old Rag View Overlook** (Mile 46.5), dominated by Old Rag, sitting by itself in an eastern extremity of the park; and **Franklin Cliffs Overlook** (Mile 49), offering a view from atop the cliffs toward the Shenandoah Valley and Massanutten Mountain. You'll need only 10 minutes or so at each overlook, so plan to pull off at all of these. Assuming you're not smogged in, it'll be 40 minutes well spent.

If you're in the Northern District, pull off at the **Shenandoah Valley Overlook** (Mile 2.8), with views west to the Signal Knob of Massanutten Mountain across the south fork of the river; and **Range View Overlook** (Mile 17.1; elevation 2,800 ft.), providing fine views of the central section of the park, looking south. In the Southern District, **Big Run Overlook** (Mile 81.2) looks down on rocky peaks and the largest watershed in the park.

WATERFALLS   Only one waterfall is visible from Skyline Drive, at Mile 1.4, and it's dry part of the year. On the other hand, 15 other falls are accessible via hiking trails (see below).

Hiking & Other Sports

HIKING   The number-one outdoor activity here is hiking. The park's 112 trails total more than 500 miles, varying in length from short walks to a 101-mile segment of the Appalachian Trail running the entire length of the park. Access to the trails is marked along Skyline Drive. There are parking lots at the major trail heads, but they fill quickly on weekends.

Rangers at park headquarters will advise on which trails are best for you, and whether any are closed (see "Just the Facts," above).

I strongly recommend that you get maps and trail descriptions before setting out—even before leaving home, if possible. Free maps of many trails are available at the visitor centers, which also sell the topographic maps, published by the Potomac Appalachian Trail Conference, as well as a one-sheet map of all of the park's walks published by the National Geographic. See "Information," above.

An alternative to doing it yourself is to take a guided outdoor adventure organized by **Aramark Virginia Sky-Line Co.** (© **800/778-2871,** option 2; www.visit shenandoah.com). Led by mountain guides, they include short hikes from the park lodges ($10 for adults, $8 for children ages 12 and under), 1-day hikes ($123–$164 per person), and rock-climbing expeditions ($133–$174 per person). Call or check Aramark's website for schedules and reservations.

At a minimum, take one of the short hikes on trails at Dickey Ridge Visitor Center (Mile 4.6) and the Byrd Visitor Center/Big Meadows (Mile 51). There's an excellent 1.6-mile hike at Stony Man (Mile 41.7).

My gimpy knees don't necessarily agree, but I've concluded that these are the best trails in the Central District:

○ **Camp Hoover/Mill Prong ★**: Starting at the Milam Gap parking area (Mile 52.8), this 4-mile round-trip hike drops down the Mill Prong to the Rapidan River, where President Herbert Hoover, an avid fisherman, had a camp during his administration (sort of the Camp David of his day). The total climb is 850 feet; allow 4 hours.

○ **Cedar Run Falls:** Several trails begin at Hawksbill Gap (Mile 45.6). A short but steep trail leads 1.7 miles round-trip to the summit of Hawksbill Mountain, the park's highest at 4,050 feet. Another is a moderately difficult 3.5-mile round-trip hike to Cedar Falls and back. You can also connect from Cedar Run to White Oak Canyon, a 7.3-mile loop that will take all day.

○ **Dark Hollow Falls ★**: The park's most popular short hike is the 1.4-mile walk to Dark Hollow Falls, the closest cascade to Skyline Drive. The trail begins at Mile 50.7 near the Byrd Visitor Center. Allow 1¼ hours for the round-trip.

○ **Limberlost Accessible Trail:** At Mile 43 south of Skyland, Limberlost is accessible to visitors in wheelchairs. The easy 1.3-mile loop runs through an old-growth forest of ancient hemlocks. The trail has a 5-foot-wide, hard-packed surface; crosses a 65-foot bridge; and includes a 150-foot boardwalk.

○ **White Oak Canyon ★★★**: Everyone's favorite trail (especially when linked to the Cedar Run Falls trail; see above) begins at Mile 42.6 a short walk from Skyland Resort and descends into a steep gorge that is the park's scenic gem. The 7.3-mile trail goes through an area of wild beauty, passing no fewer than six waterfalls and cascades. The upper reaches to the first falls are relatively easy, but farther down the track can be rough and rocky. This not an easy trail, especially coming back up the 2,160-foot climb, a brutal ascent if you're out of shape. In other words, allow all day.

Access points to the **Appalachian Trail** are well marked at overlooks on Skyline Drive. Along the trail, five backcountry shelters for day use each offer only a table, fireplace, pit toilet, and water. The **Potomac Appalachian Trail Club,** 118 Park St. SE, Vienna, VA 22180 (℗ **703/242-0315;** www.patc.net), maintains huts and fully enclosed cabins that can accommodate up to 12 people. Use of the huts is free, but they are intended for long-distance hikers only. Cabins cost $20 to $70 on weekdays and $45 to $125 on weekends. You can reserve cabins by calling PATC Monday to Thursday 7 to 9pm or Thursday to Friday noon to 2pm (*only* during these hours). You'll have to submit a signed form (available on PATC's website), so you'll want to start the process as early as possible. PATC's website also shows cabin availabilities.

FISHING   The park's streams are short, with limited fishing, so it's hardly worth the time and effort. The park publishes a free recreational fishing brochure and an annual list of streams open for fishing, available at the Big Meadows and Loft Mountain waysides or at sporting-goods stores outside the park.

HORSEBACK RIDING   Horses are allowed only on trails marked with yellow, and only via guided expeditions with **Skyland Stables** (℗ **540/999-2211;** www.visit shenandoah.com), on the Skyland Resort grounds (Mile 41.8). Rides cost $30 per person for 1 hour and $50 for 2½ hours. Pony rides for children are $12 for 30 minutes. Children must be 4 feet, 10 inches tall to ride the horses (otherwise they can take a pony ride); an adult must accompany those 11 and under. The stables operate from April through November. Call for reservations at least 1 day in advance. *Note:* Rides can be canceled during inclement weather.

Camping

The park has four campgrounds with tent and trailer sites (but no hookups anywhere). In the middle of the park's Central District, **Big Meadows** (Mile 51.2) has the best location and sites equipped for campers with disabilities. You can reserve Big Meadows sites in advance by contacting the park service's reservation system ℗ **877/444-6777;** www.recreation.gov). "Walk to" sites cost $20 per night; those with electric hookups are $45 per night. Big Meadows campground is open from early April to the end of October.

You can reserve some sites at **Mathews Arm** (Mile 22.2) and **Loft Mountain** (Mile 79.5) at **www.recreation.gov**. Others there and at **Lewis Mountain** (Mile 57.5), are first-come, first-served. The nightly fee is $15 per site at all three. The campgrounds are open from mid-May to late October. Lewis Mountain has only 31 sites and is often full during summer and early fall. Mathews Arm and Loft Mountain have 100 and 200 sites, respectively, and usually only fill on summer and fall weekends.

Accommodations

Situated on Skyline Drive in the Central District, **Big Meadows Lodge** and **Skyland Resort** (see below) are the only hotels in the park. They are 9½ miles apart. Lodge reservations should be made well in advance—up to a year ahead for the peak fall season. You can make them through **Aramark Virginia Sky-Line Co.** (✆ **888/896-3833**; www.visitshenandoah.com), which operates both.

Aramark also manages **Lewis Mountain Cabins,** adjacent to the Lewis Mountain Campground at Mile 57.5 in the Central District. These simple abodes range from $30 for a "tent cabin" to $109 for connecting rooms. They all have private bathrooms and are supplied with towels and linens.

Big Meadows feels more historical and is convenient to many activities, but either place is worthwhile if you get a room with a view of the Shenandoah Valley.

The sections that follow later in this chapter describe accommodations in other Shenandoah Valley towns. Luray is nearest to the Central District (p. 131).

Big Meadows Lodge ★ 🍴 Built of stone and timber, this rustic building sports a large guest lounge with a roaring fireplace and window walls presenting a spectacular view over the Shenandoah Valley. Accommodations consist of small rooms in the main lodge, cabins, and multi-unit lodges with suites spread out over the premises. Request a "terrace" room in the main lodge building to have a valley view. All units have plain but comfortable furnishings and a private bathroom. Deluxe units in the Rapidan and Doubletop buildings have air-conditioning and TVs; otherwise, you won't have such modern amenities. No unit has a phone, but your cellphone should work out on the lodge terrace, and there's wireless Internet access in public areas of the main lodge. The main-lodge dining room features traditional fare such as prime rib, fried chicken, mountain trout, and pastas. Wine, beer, and cocktails are available. Live entertainment keeps the taproom busy during the season.

Skyline Dr. at Mile 51.2 (PO Box 727), Luray, VA 22835. www.visitshenandoah.com. ✆ **888/896-3833** or 540/999-2221. Fax 540/999-2011. 97 units. $109–$187 double. Highest rates charged weekends and in Oct. AE, DISC, MC, V. Closed Nov to early May. **Amenities:** Restaurant; bar; Wi-Fi. *In room:* A/C (in some), TV (in some), no phone.

Skyland Resort Skyland was built by naturalist George Freeman Pollock in 1894 as a summer retreat almost atop Stony Man Mountain, the highest point on Skyline Drive at 3,680 feet. The main building is smaller and less charming than Big Meadow Lodge's. The resort offers rooms in the main lodge as well as in rustic wood-paneled cabins and motel-type accommodations spread out over its 52 acres. Some of the buildings are dark-brown clapboard, others are fieldstone, and all nestle among the trees. More rooms have wonderful views than at Big Meadow, but again, tell the reservations clerk you want a view. The most panoramic views are from the Shenandoah building, whose air-conditioned rooms have TVs. The main building's dining room has a view, and it offers the same fare as at Big Meadows. There's a fully stocked taproom here, too.

Skyline Dr. at Mile 41.7 (PO Box 727), Luray, VA 22835. www.visitshenandoah.com. © **888/896-3833** or 540/999-2211. Fax 540/999-2231. 179 units. $129–$236 double $109–$267 cabin. Highest rates charged weekends and in Oct. Packages available. AE, DISC, MC, V. Closed Nov–early May. **Amenities:** Restaurant; bar. *In room:* A/C (in some), TV (in some), no phone.

Where to Eat

In addition to the lodges at Big Meadows and Skyland, there are daytime restaurants and snack bars at Big Meadows (Mile 51), Elkwallow Wayside (Mile 24.1), Panorama-Thornton Gap (Mile 31.5), and Loft Mountain (Mile 79.5).

Picnic areas with tables, fireplaces, water fountains, and restrooms are at Dickey Ridge (Mile 4.6) and Elkwallow (Mile 24.1) in the Northern District; Pinnacles (Mile 36.7), Big Meadows (Mile 51), and Lewis Mountain (Mile 57.5) in the Central District; and South River (Mile 62.8) and Loft Mountain (Mile 79.5) in the Southern District. As the areas are far apart, pick the one nearest to you. Big Meadows is most convenient to park activities.

WINCHESTER: A FITTING INTRODUCTION ★

76 miles W of Washington, D.C.; 189 miles NW of Richmond

To paraphrase Abraham Lincoln's Gettysburg Address, it is altogether fitting that Winchester comes first in any description of the valley's towns, for its excellent Museum of the Shenandoah Valley provides an altogether fitting introduction to this area. Especially if you're arriving by car from the north or from Washington Dulles International Airport, Winchester should be your first stop.

Winchester is also known as Virginia's Apple Capital, so-called because of the number of apple orchards in the northern end of the valley. The **Shenandoah Apple Blossom Festival** in May is one of the region's most popular events.

What is now Winchester was the site of a Shawnee Indian campground before Pennsylvania Quakers settled here in 1732. George Washington set up shop in town during the French and Indian War 20 years later, and his office is still here. Thanks to its strategic location, Winchester changed hands no fewer than 72 times during the Civil War. Both Confederate General Stonewall Jackson and Union General Philip Sheridan made their headquarters here at one time or another. It is still a major trading post, as the busy roads leading into and out of Winchester's Old Town will attest.

Give yourself at least a morning or afternoon here to visit the Museum of the Shenandoah Valley, Washington's office, and Stonewall Jackson's headquarters. If you're a country music fan, you can visit Winchester native Patsy Cline's childhood home and her gravesite.

Essentials

VISITOR INFORMATION The **Winchester/Frederick County Visitors Center,** 1400 S. Pleasant Valley Rd., Winchester, VA 22601 (© **540/542-1326;** fax 540/450-0099; www.visitwinchesterva.com), is open daily 9am to 5pm (closed New Year's Day, Thanksgiving, and Christmas). The center shows an 8-minute video about the area and a 5-minute one about the town's role in the Civil War. Take Exit 313 off I-81, go west on U.S. 50, and follow the signs.

GETTING THERE Primary access routes into Winchester include I-81, U.S. 11, U.S. 522, U.S. 50, and Va. 7.

CELEBRATING PATSY CLINE

Only die-hard country music fans know Winchester native Virginia Hensley became singer Patsy Cline. She sang "Walkin' after Midnight" on the nationally televised *Arthur Godfrey's Talent Scouts* in 1957. The record of that song sold a million copies. Other tunes like "Leavin' on Your Mind," "Imagine That," and "Crazy" (written by Willie Nelson) will forever be linked to Patsy Cline.

She was only 30 years old when she, Hawkshaw Hawkins, Cowboy Copas, and her manager Randy Hughes died in a plane crash in March 1963. Her body was brought home and buried in Shenandoah Memorial Park, 3 miles south of town on U.S. 522.

The **Patsy Cline Historic House,** 608 S. Kent St., where she lived with her mother, Hilda Hensley, from 1943 to 1953, is now a museum dedicated to her life. It has some of her personal items and a gift shop selling mementos. Guided tours take about 40 minutes. Admission is $6 for adults, $5 for seniors, $4 for children 11 to 18, and free for kids 9 and under and active-duty military. The house is open from April to October Tuesday to Saturday 10am to 4pm and Sunday noon to 4pm and from November to the first week of December Friday to Saturday 10am to 4pm and Sunday 1 to 4pm. The first week in December celebrates Patsy Cline Christmas with special events evoking her life. Closed January to March.

The Winchester/Frederick County Visitors Center (see "Essentials," above) distributes directions to Gaunt's Drug Store at Loudoun and Gerrard streets, where Cline worked; Handley High School at 425 Handley Blvd., where she studied; the house at 720 S. Kent St., where she married second husband Charlie Dick; and her grave.

For more information about the house and other facets of Cline's life, contact **Celebrating Patsy Cline, Inc. (**(C) **540/622-5555;** www.celebratingpatsycline.org).

Exploring the Town

The heart of Winchester's historic area is the **Old Town Mall,** a 4-block-long pedestrian-only stretch of Loudon Street between Piccadilly and Cork streets lined with boutiques, coffeehouses, pastry shops, and several restaurants, some of which offer outdoor seating under shade trees in warm weather (see "Where to Eat," below). Facing the mall, the imposing **Frederick County Court House** was built in 1840 and is home to the Old Court House Civil War Museum (see below).

While walking between the George Washington and Stonewall Jackson museums (see below), you can't miss the elaborate, Beaux Arts–style **Handley Regional Library,** at the corner of Braddock and Piccadilly streets ((C) **540/662-9041;** www. handleyregional.org). Built between 1907 and 1912, it's adorned with a full panoply of Classic-revival statues. A copper-covered dome covers the rotunda, which symbolizes the spine of a book, with the two flanking wings representing its open pages.

Across the street from the library is the white-columned **Elks Building,** headquarters of Union General Philip Sheridan from 1864 to 1865.

Any doubt that this northern end of the valley was fought over during the Civil War will be dispelled at **Mt. Hebron Cemetery,** on Woodstock Lane, east of downtown ((C) **540/662-4868;** www.mthebroncemetery.org). Some 8,000 men killed in the battles are buried here—the Rebels in Stonewall Confederate Cemetery on the south side of the street, the Yankees in the National Cemetery on the north side.

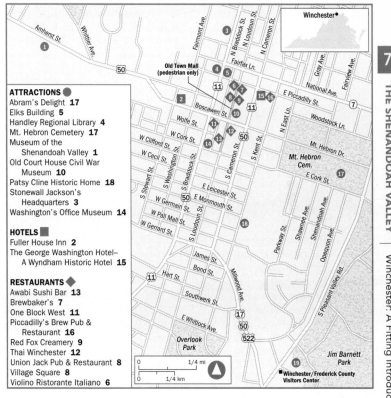

ATTRACTIONS ●
Abram's Delight **17**
Elks Building **5**
Handley Regional Library **4**
Mt. Hebron Cemetery **17**
Museum of the
  Shenandoah Valley **1**
Old Court House Civil War
  Museum **10**
Patsy Cline Historic Home **18**
Stonewall Jackson's
  Headquarters **3**
Washington's Office Museum **14**

HOTELS ■
Fuller House Inn **2**
The George Washington Hotel–
  A Wyndham Historic Hotel **15**

RESTAURANTS ◆
Awabi Sushi Bar **13**
Brewbaker's **7**
One Block West **11**
Piccadilly's Brew Pub &
  Restaurant **16**
Red Fox Creamery **9**
Thai Winchester **12**
Union Jack Pub & Restaurant **8**
Village Square **8**
Violino Ristorante Italiano **6**

Abram's Delight   If you're here between April and October, walk across the lot from the visitor center to this native-limestone residence built beside a lake in 1754 by Quaker Isaac Hollingsworth. The oldest house in Winchester, it served as the town's first Quaker Meeting House. Today, it's fully restored and furnished with 18th- and 19th-century pieces. Guided tours are available.

1340 S. Pleasant Valley Rd. ℰ **540/662-6519.** www.winchesterhistory.org. Admission (without block ticket) $12 family, $5 adults, $4.50 seniors, $2.50 students 7–18, free for children 6 and under. Apr–Oct Mon–Sat 10am–4pm, Sun noon–4pm. 45-min. house tours depart when a guide is available. Closed Nov–Mar.

Museum of the Shenandoah Valley ★★★   A visit to this terrific museum will enrich your tour of the valley by explaining in a nutshell its geography and history. The museum is on the western side of town at the site of **Glen Burnie,** a redbrick plantation home standing on the original homestead of Winchester founder James Wood. With sections dating to 1755, Glen Burnie is surrounded by magnificent formal gardens, which shouldn't be missed (many couples have held weddings among the flowers). You should allot at least 2 hours to see the museum and the gardens. (The Glen Burnie mansion is closed until 2014 for massive renovations.) Begin in the modern museum building, where a huge topographic map of the entire valley introduces exhibits tracking the

Saving with a Block Ticket

You can buy a **block ticket** to visit Abram's Delight, Washington's Office Museum, and Stonewall Jackson's Headquarters for $20 for a family, $10 adults, $9 seniors, $4 students 7 to 18, and free for children 6 and under. Tickets are available at the museums or the Winchester/Frederick County Visitors Center (see "Essentials," above).

Shenandoah's development from prehistoric times to the present. The museum also houses the remarkable collection of 18th-century furniture and art—including paintings by Rembrandt Peale and Gilbert Stuart—and miniature houses. The museum's tearoom serves soups, salads, and sandwiches from 11am to 4pm.

801 Amherst St. (U.S. 50 W). ⓒ **888/556-5799** or 540/662-1473. www.shenandoahmuseum.org. Admission to museum $8 adults, $6 seniors and students 7–18; museum and gardens $10 adults, $9 seniors and students 7–18; gardens only $6 adults, $5 seniors and students 7–18, free for children 6 and younger. Garden audio tours $2. Museum Tues–Sun 10am–4pm. Gardens Mar–Oct Tues–Sun 10am–4pm. Closed New Year's Day, Thanksgiving, Dec 24, and Christmas.

Old Court House Civil War Museum   Housed in the 1840 Frederick County Court House, this new museum tells of Winchester's role in the Civil War, when it see-sawed between Union and Confederate hands. Both sides used the courthouse as a hospital and prison. The museum's most interesting exhibit is upstairs where upwards of 500 prisoners were detained. Many of them carved graffiti into the walls, which you can see through windows.

20 N. Loudon St. (on Old Town Mall). ⓒ **540/542-1145.** www.civilwarmuseum.org. Admission $5 per person, free for children 5 and under. Wed–Sat 10am–5pm; Sun 1–5pm.

Stonewall Jackson's Headquarters ★   Stonewall Jackson used this Victorian home, once owned by a great-grandfather of actress Mary Tyler Moore, as his headquarters in the winter of 1861 to 1862. It's filled with maps, photos, and memorabilia. As you aren't allowed to just walk through, plan on taking a guided tour. Two guides are usually on hand, so there's seldom a wait.

415 N. Braddock St. (btw. Peyton St. and North Ave.). ⓒ **540/667-3242.** www.winchesterhistory. org. Admission (without block ticket) $12 family, $5 adults, $4.50 seniors, $2.50 students 7–18, free for children 6 and under. Apr–Oct Mon–Sat 10am–4pm, Sun noon–4pm. 30-min. house tours depart as needed. Closed Nov–Mar.

Washington's Office Museum ★★   George Washington used this small log cabin (since covered with clapboard) as his office in 1755 and 1756 when he was a colonel in the Virginia militia, charged with building a fort to protect the colony's frontier from the French and the Indians. The building itself is the highlight of this charming little museum, whose exhibits explain Washington's career from 1748 to 1758. You can see it all in 30 minutes. Informative staff members are on hand to answer questions and lead guided tours.

32 W. Cork St. (at Braddock St.). ⓒ **540/662-4412.** www.winchesterhistory.org. Admission $12 family, $5 adults, $4.50 seniors, $2.50 students 7–18, free for children 6 and under. Apr–Oct Mon–Sat 10am–4pm, Sun noon–4pm. Closed Nov–Mar.

Where to Stay

If you decide to stay over, the area along Millwood Avenue (U.S. 50) at I-81 (Exit 313), on the southeast side of town, has Winchester's major shopping mall and several chain restaurants and motels. About half the rooms at the **Holiday Inn Historic Gateway** (℃ 800/465-4329 or 540/667-3300) face a courtyard with outdoor pool; the hotel's restaurant is one of the town's more popular lunch spots. Also nearby are the venerable **Best Western Lee-Jackson Motor Inn** (℃ 800/528-1234 or 540/662-4154), a **Fairfield Inn & Suites** (℃ 800/228-2800 or 540/665-8881), a **Wingate by Wyndham** (℃ 800/676-4283), and an inexpensive **Red Roof Inn** (℃ 866/386-4682 or 540/667-5000).

Among the local bed-and-breakfasts is **Fuller House Inn & Carriage House,** 229 W. Boscowen St. (www.fullerhouseinn.com; ℃ **877/722-3976** or 540/722-3976), in the historic district.

The George Washington Hotel—A Wyndham Historic Hotel ★★ In its heyday this 1924-vintage Colonial-revival hotel hosted Lucille Ball and other famous Apple Blossom Festival queens. Betty Crocker held an apple pie baking contest in the ballroom one year. But it fell on hard times, and in the 1970s the George Washington became an assisted living facility. After a masterful renovation, it is once again Winchester's premier hotel. Appropriately, a Gilbert Stuart portrait of the first president oversees the lobby, off which the Half Note bar sports a large mural of jazz musicians at work (it hosts the real thing on weekends). Downstairs, the Dancing Goat restaurant offers inventive American fare and outdoor seating in warm weather. You can swim around Grecian columns in the Roman bath–like indoor pool. Of the guest quarters, the Extended King models add a sitting area, and some of the 10 suites have fireplaces. Most units have walk-in showers with multiple heads.

103 Piccadilly St., Winchester, VA 22601. www.wyndham.com/hotels/DCAGW. ℃ **800/WYNDHAM** [996-3426] or 540/678-4700. Fax 540/678-1228. 90 units. $119–$139 double; $169–$289 suite. Valet and self-parking $4. AE, DISC, MC, V. **Amenities:** Restaurant; bar; executive or concierge-level rooms; health club; Jacuzzi; pool; room service. In room: A/C, TV, fridge (in suites), hair dryer, Wi-Fi.

A NEARBY COUNTRY INN WITH A FRENCH FLAVOR

L'Auberge Provençale ★★ 🍴 Executive chef Alain Borel and his vivacious wife, Celeste, have re-created the look, feel, and cuisine of Provence in this 1750s fieldstone farmhouse set on a hilltop with a view of the Blue Ridge. Three of the 11 guest rooms are in this building; antiques and beautiful fabrics complement the Colonial farmhouse's fine features. The remaining cozy accommodations, in an adjoining gray-clapboard addition, are individually decorated with Victorian and European pieces and lovely French Provincial–print fabrics. Exceptional works of fine art adorn the guest rooms. Alain uses the finest-quality ingredients from his own garden and local farmers to create his superb five-course prix-fixe dinners ($88 per person; reservations required). Even breakfast is a splendid repast, and Alain will provide a gourmet picnic lunch on request. Children ages 10 or over are welcome.

U.S. 340 (PO Box 190), White Post, VA 22663. www.laubergeprovencale.com. ℃ **800/638-1702** or 540/837-1375. Fax 703/837-2004. 14 units. $170–$350 double. Rates include full breakfast. AE, DC, MC, V. From I-81, take U.S. 50 east 7 miles, turn right on U.S. 340; L'Auberge is 1 mile on the right. No children 9 or under. **Amenities:** Restaurant; Jacuzzi; pool. In room: A/C, CD player.

Where to Eat

The Old Town Mall along Loudon Street in the heart of downtown has a number of coffeehouses, bakeries, and restaurants, most between Boscawen and Piccadilly streets. All of them have seating on the mall during warm weather. See **www.oldtownwinchesterva.com** for a full list.

For informal fare, there's the pub like **Brewbaker's** (*(C)* **540/667-0429;** www.brewbakersrestaurant.com), where the big front windows are pushed open in warm weather. The British-style **Union Jack Pub & Restaurant** (*(C)* **540/722-2055;** www.theunionjackpub.com) occupies two stories of the old Union Bank building. For ethnic fare, **Thai Winchester** (*(C)* **540/678-0055;** www.thaiwinchester.com) serves a very good beef salad, and **Awabi Sushi Bar** (*(C)* **540/686-7432**) has authentic Japanese cuisine. For old fashion ice cream, cookies, and cakes head to **Red Fox Cremery** (*(C)* **540/545-8630**).

One Block West ★★ AMERICAN You'll find some of Winchester's most refined dining in this small building almost hidden on Indian Alley, which runs north-south 1 block west of the Loudon Street mall (hence, the name of the restaurant). Although he changes the menu daily to take advantage of fresh produce, chef-owner Ed Matthews always puts the grill to excellent use on steaks, tuna, lamb chops, pork loin, and bison. You can dine outside in warm weather.

25 S. Indian Alley (btw. Boscawen and Cork sts.). *(C)* **540/662-1455.** www.oneblockwest.com. Reservations recommended, necessary on weekends. Main courses $20–$26. AE, MC, V. Tues–Sat 11am–2pm and 5–10pm.

Piccadilly's Brew Pub & Restaurant AMERICAN A sports pub atmosphere prevails in this busy restaurant occupying a warehouse built in 1900. This is especially true on warm evenings, when tables spill out to both a long side porch and a vacant lot next door, and ball games are projected on the wall of an adjacent building. Slaked down with pints of the house brew, the bill of fare contains a wide selection of bar snacks, salads, sandwiches, and main courses emphasizing meatloaf, steaks, grilled chicken, and other comfort foods. This is one of Winchester's top nightspots during summer when live bands play in the vacant lot Friday and Saturday evenings.

125 E. Piccadilly St. *(C)* **540/535-1899.** www.freewebs.com/piccadillys. Salads and sandwiches $7–$12; main courses $13–$24. AE, DISC, MC, V. Sun–Wed 11:30am–11pm; Thurs–Sat 11:30am–1am.

Village Restaurant ★ AMERICAN/MEDITERRANEAN The best place for romance on the Old Town Mall, this bistro serves cuisine from Virginia to the Mediterrean. From home comes crab cakes with roasted corn and pepper relish and fried chicken with braised collard greens and blackeye peas. From beyond Gilbratar you may see vegetarian moussaka or grilled scallops Oscar with couscous pilaf. The adjoining **V² Lounge and Piano Bar** is a fine place to relax with a Virginia vintage.

103 N. Loudon St. *(C)* **540/667-8961.** www.villagesquarerestaurant.com. Reservations recommended. Main courses $18–$28. AE, DISC, MC, V. Mon–Thurs 11:30am–10pm; Fri–Sat 11:30am–midnight; Sun 11:30am–3pm.

Violino Ristorante Italiano ★ ITALIAN I know people in Leesburg who will drive across the mountain for lunch or dinner at this restaurant, the domain of Italian natives Franco and Marcella Stucco and their son, Riccardo. This is not the place for spaghetti and meatballs, for their style leans toward ravioli filled with swiss chard and fresh goat ricotta cheese in a walnut sauce, braised rabbit cooked in the style of Ligura, and other more sophisticated dishes.

181 N. Loudon St. *(C)* **540/667-8006.** www.violinorestaurant.com. Reservations recommended. Main courses $15–$30. AE, DISC, MC. V. Mon–Fri 11:30am–2pm and 5–9pm; Sat noon–2pm and 5–9pm.

MIDDLETOWN & STRASBURG: ANTIQUES GALORE

Middletown: 13 miles S of Winchester, 174 miles NW of Richmond, 76 miles W of Washington, D.C.; Strasburg: 6 miles S of Middletown

On U.S. 11, essentially flanking the intersection of I-81 and I-66, the hamlet of Middletown and the small town of Strasburg are collectively one of the best places in Virginia to browse for antiques and collectibles. This is especially true of Strasburg, which justifiably calls itself the "Antiques Capital of Virginia." The sprawling **Great Strasburg Antiques Emporium** is one of the state's largest collections of dealers. Both towns have exceptional country inns offering antiques-filled accommodations and fine dining, and Middletown's Wayside Theatre will entertain anyone who loves live theater.

Between Middletown and Strasburg stands Belle Grove Plantation, the 18th-century home of President James Madison's sister and later the site of a fierce Civil War battle. The house and battlefield now comprise a national historic site. Also in the Civil War, Gen. Stonewall Jackson rolled the railroad locomotives he stole from the Union during his daring Great Train Raid on Martinsburg, West Virginia, down the Valley Pike to the existing station at Strasburg, which is now a local museum.

Except for Belle Grove Plantation, the museums here are not as interesting as are others in the valley. Consequently, stop in Middletown and Strasburg either to hunt for antiques and collectibles or to stay in one of two inns in order to catch a show at the Wayside Theatre.

Essentials

VISITOR INFORMATION For information contact the **Strasburg Chamber of Commerce,** 157 N. Holliday St. (PO Box 42), Strasburg, VA 22657 (℗ **540/465-3187;** www.strasburgvachamber.com). Walk-in information is available at the **Gateway to Shenandoah Visitor Center,** which shares space with Hupp's Hill Cedar Creek Museum (see below). The center is open Friday to Tuesday 9am to 5pm.

GETTING THERE From I-81, take Exit 302 west to U.S. 11 into Middletown. Take Exit 298 or 300 into Strasburg.

The Top Attractions

Belle Grove Plantation and Cedar Creek Battlefield are part of **Cedar Creek & Belle Grove National Historical Park,** PO Box 700, Middletown, VA 22645 (℗ **540/868-9176;** www.nps.gov/cebe). It's an unusual national park in that it relies heavily on the National Trust for Historic Preservation, which owns Belle Grove, and the Cedar Creek Battlefield Foundation, which maintains a large portion of the battle site and operates Hupp's Hill Cedar Creek Museum (see below).

Belle Grove Plantation ★★ One of the finest homes in the Shenandoah Valley, the beautiful Belle Grove stone mansion was built in 1797 by Maj. Isaac Hite, whose grandfather, Joist Hite, first settled here in 1732. Major Hite's wife was Nelly Madison Hite, sister of President James Madison. At Madison's request, Thomas Jefferson was actively involved in Belle Grove's design. The columns and Palladian-style front windows are just two examples of Jefferson's influence. The mansion is owned and operated by the National Trust for Historic Preservation. The interior is furnished with period antiques.

336 Belle Grove Rd. (off U.S. 11), Middletown. ☏ **540/869-2028.** www.bellegrove.org. Admission $10 adults, $8 seniors, $6 children 6–12, free for children 5 and under. Apr–Oct Mon–Sat 10am–4pm (last tour starts at 3:15pm); Sun 1–5pm (last tour starts at 4:15pm). Nov–Dec hours vary; call for details. Closed Dec 31–Mar 31 except some weekends, including Thanksgiving. From Winchester, take U.S. 11 south or I-81 south to Exit 302 at Middletown, then U.S. 11 south 1 mile.

Cedar Creek Battlefield Belle Grove was at the epicenter of the Battle of Cedar Creek, fought on 4,000 acres surrounding the manor house on October 19, 1864, when Confederate General Jubal Early surprised Union forces under Gen. Philip Sheridan, who had been ordered to cut off Gen. Robert E. Lee's supplies by razing the Shenandoah Valley. Despite early Southern successes, the North prevailed thanks to a 10,000-horse calvary charge led by Gen. George Armstrong Custer. The battlefield visitor center explains what happened and distributes the U.S. National Park Service's battlefield brochure. The battle is reenacted each year on the weekend closest to October 19.

8437 Valley Pike (U.S. 11), Middletown. ☏ **540/869-2064.** www.ccbf.us. Free admission. Apr–Oct Mon and Fri–Sat 10am–4pm, Sun 1–4pm; Nov–Mar by appt. only. From Winchester, take U.S. 11 south or I-81 south to Exit 302 at Middletown, then U.S. 11 south 1 mile.

Hupp's Hill Cedar Creek Museum Formerly dedicated to Stonewall Jackson, this museum got new life in 2011 when the Cedar Creek Battlefield Foundation took it over and, in effect, incorporated it into the Cedar Creek & Belle Grove National Historical Park. Park rangers lead walking tours through the breastworks, which both sides used as an artillery emplacement (call for times). Exhibits inside explain the entire Valley Campaign of 1864. On display are bullets, swords, shells, canteens, and other relics.

33229 Old Valley Pike (U.S. 11; 1-mile north of Strasburg). ☏ **540/465-5884.** www.ccbf.us. Admission $5 per person, free for children 10 and under. Fri–Tues 9am–5pm.

Antiquing

Antiques lovers will want to hunt in nearby Strasburg, which has a bevy of fine outlets at the intersection of U.S. 11 and Va. 55. The **Great Strasburg Antiques Emporium ★★**, 110 N. Massanutten St. (☏ **540/465-3711**), is one of the state's largest shops, an enormous warehouse with vendors selling both antiques and a plethora of collectibles (I have become lost wandering around this labyrinth). It's open Sunday to Thursday 10am to 5pm, and Friday to Saturday 10am to 6pm. A coffee shop serves sandwiches and salads for lunch.

You can't buy them, but there are plenty of antiques at the **Strasburg Museum,** 440 E. King St. (Va. 55; ☏ **540/465-3175;** www.strasburgmuseum.org), just 2 blocks east of the emporium. It occupies the old train station where Stonewall Jackson brought his stolen locomotives. Admission is $3 for adults, $1 for teenagers, and 50¢ for children ages 11 and under. It is open May to October daily 10am to 4pm.

Where to Stay & Eat

Out in the hills northwest of Middletown, the serene **Inn at Vaucluse Spring,** 231 Vaucluse Spring Lane, Stephens City, VA 22655 (www.vauclusespring.com; ☏ **800/869-0525** or 540/869-0200), offers a romantic retreat from life's pressures. It has 15 guest rooms in six buildings, including cottages and a Federal-style mansion house, the inn's centerpiece. A stay includes a three-course breakfast, and the inn is open for dinner Friday to Saturday.

Chain motels include the **Ramada Strasburg** (www.ramada.com; ℂ **888/288-4982** or 540/465-2444) and **Fairfield Inn & Suites Shenandoah Valley** (www.marriott.com/hotels/travel/iadst-fairfield-inn-and-suites-strasburg-shenandoah-valley; ℂ **888/236-2427** or 540/465-1600). Both are on U.S. 11 about 1 mile north of Strasburg.

Hotel Strasburg ★   Built as a hospital in 1902, this Victorian hotel is furnished with an impressive collection of period pieces, many for sale. Most units are in the main building, but three suites and a room are in the Chandler House, while the Taylor House holds four suites. Ten rooms have Jacuzzis. Known for excellent international fare, the dining room is Strasburg's best place for breakfast, lunch, or dinner. A first-floor pub offers friendly conversation and libation.

213 S. Holliday St., Strasburg, VA 22657. www.hotelstrasburg.com. ℂ **888/763-8327** or 540/465-9191. Fax 540/465-4788. 29 units. $89–$115 double; $129–$190 suite. Weekend and other packages available. AE, DC, DISC, MC, V. From I-81, take Exit 298 and go south on U.S. 11 for 1½ miles and turn right on King St., then turn left onto Holliday St. **Amenities:** Restaurant; bar. In room: A/C, TV, Wi-Fi.

Wayside Inn ★   This rambling roadside inn first offered libation to Shenandoah Valley travelers in 1797, and it has continued to function ever since. The rooms are beautifully decorated with an assortment of 18th- and 19th-century pieces. Each room's decor reflects a period style, from Colonial to elaborate Victorian Renaissance-revival. Expect to find canopied beds, armoires, highboys, writing desks, antique clocks, and stenciled or papered walls adorned with fine prints and oil paintings. Southern-style home cooking is served in seven antiques-filled dining rooms. Cocktails and light fare are served in **Larrick's Tavern.**

7783 Main St., Middletown, VA 22645. www.alongthewayside.com. ℂ **877/869-1797** or 540/869-1797. Fax 540/869-6038. 22 units. $99–$169 double. AE, DC, DISC, MC, V. From I-81, take Exit 302 to U.S. 11 (Main St.). **Amenities:** Restaurant; bar. In room: A/C, TV, Wi-Fi.

Middletown After Dark

Since 1961, the **Wayside Theatre,** 7853 Main St. (U.S. 11) in Middletown (ℂ **540/869-1776;** www.waysidetheatre.org), has staged fine productions by contemporary dramatists. The late actor Peter Boyle and actresses Susan Sarandon and Donna McKechnie began their careers here. The venue, however, has been having financial difficulties, so check the website before showing up for a play. The box office is open Monday to Friday 10am to 5pm.

FRONT ROYAL: A SPY'S HOME

20 miles SE of Strasburg; 174 miles NW of Richmond; 70 miles W of Washington, D.C.

At the northern end of Skyline Drive, Front Royal has the valley's widest array of outdoor activities: golfing; horseback riding; and canoeing, rafting, kayaking, and inner tubing on the sometimes lazy, sometimes rapid South Fork of the Shenandoah River (see "Rafting, Canoeing & Kayaking on the Shenandoah," below). And if you didn't disappear into the caverns in Luray, you can go underground here.

   Strategically located on a flat plain near a pass in the Blue Ridge and at the juncture of the north and south forks of the Shenandoah River, Front Royal was named for a royal oak that stood in the town square during the Revolutionary War. In those days, it was a wild and woolly frontier way station at the junction of the two trails that later became U.S. 340 and Va. 55. During the Civil War, it was home to the infamous Confederate spy Belle Boyd, whose close contact—to say the least—with Union officers led to Stonewall Jackson's surprise victory at the Battle of Front Royal in 1862.

Essentials

VISITOR INFORMATION   Contact the **Front Royal/Warren County Visitors Center,** 414 E. Main St., Front Royal, VA 22630 (✆ **800/338-2576** or 540/635-5788; www.discoverfrontroyal.com). It occupies the old train station and is open daily from 9am to 5pm except New Year's Day, Thanksgiving, and Christmas. From I-66, follow U.S. 340 into town and turn left on Main Street at the Warren County Courthouse.

GETTING THERE   From I-66, take Exit 6, U.S. 340/U.S. 522 south; it's 5 minutes to town. Front Royal is also easily reached from I-81 by taking I-66 east to Exit 6.

Exploring the Town & the Caverns

Civil War enthusiasts should pick up a free driving tour brochure from the visitor center (see "Essentials," above). It will lead you to the key sites of the Battle of Front Royal, which Stonewall Jackson won in May 1862. He directed his troops from atop a knoll in **Prospect Hill Cemetery,** on Prospect Street, where the remains of 276 soldiers from all 13 Confederate states are buried.

In downtown, you'll find two mildly fascinating Civil War attractions on Chester Street, 2 blocks north of the visitor center. You should be able to see them both in 1½ hours.

Operated by the United Daughters of the Confederacy, the **Warren Rifles Confederate Museum,** 95 Chester St. (✆ **540/636-6982;** http://vaudc.org/museum. html), memorializes the great conflict with a collection of Civil War firearms, battle flags, uniforms, letters, diaries, and other personal items. Admission is $5 for adults, free for students and children accompanied by adults. It's open April 15 through November 1 Monday to Saturday from 9am to 4pm and Sunday noon to 4pm, and by appointment the rest of the year.

Next door behind **Ivy Lodge Museum,** home to the Warren Heritage Society (✆ **540/636-1446;** www.warrenheritagesociety.org), is the 1819 **Belle Boyd Cottage,** in which the Confederate spy pillow talked with her unsuspecting Union lovers. The white, house-size cottage now houses the society's archives. It's open Monday to Saturday from noon to 4pm. Admission is $3 per person and free for children 9 and under. Or you can buy a combination ticket for $5 and visit the **Balthis House,** built in 1788 and the oldest remaining house on Chester Street.

Skyline Caverns ☺   Although not as varied as those in Luray Caverns (see below), the highlights here are rock formations called anthodites—delicate white spikes that spread in all directions from their positions on the cave ceiling. Their growth rate is about 1 inch every 7,000 years. A sophisticated lighting system enhances formations like the Capitol Dome, Rainbow Trail, Painted Desert, and Fairy Land Lake, which mirrors the stalactites suspended above it. A miniature train covering about a half-mile is a popular attraction for kids. The cave temperature is a cool 54°F (12°C) year-round, and the tours take an hour, so bring a sweater, even in summer. Back on the surface, the kids can ride a miniature train and wander through the Enchanted Dragon Mirror Maze.

RAFTING, CANOEING & KAYAKING ON THE SHENANDOAH

The streams flowing west down from Shenandoah National Park end up in the South Fork of the Shenandoah River, which winds its way through a narrow valley between the Blue Ridge and Massanutten mountains. The switchbacks between Front Royal and Luray are the region's main center for river rafting, canoeing, and kayaking from mid-March to mid-November. The amount of recent rain will determine whether you go white-water rafting, canoeing, kayaking, or floating downstream in an inner tube.

About 5½ miles of the river skirts the **Raymond R. "Andy" Guest, Jr. Shenandoah River State Park,** 8 miles south of Front Royal on U.S. 340 (✆ **540/622-6840;** www.dcr.state.va.us/parks/andygues.htm). The park has 5½ miles of river frontage, 13 miles of hiking trails, fishing, horseback riding, picnic areas, and a primitive campground (✆ **800/933-PARK** [7275] or 804/225-8367 to reserve a site). The park is open daily 8am to dusk. Admission is $3 per vehicle weekdays and $4 on weekends and holidays.

Several rafting and canoe outfitters are based along U.S. 340, which parallels the river between Front Royal and Luray. All require advance reservations, and all are closed from November through April.

- **Front Royal Canoe Company** (✆ **800/270-8808** or 540/635-5440; www.frontroyalcanoe.com) provides equipment and guides from its location on U.S. 340 south of Front Royal.
- In Bentonville, a small village about 8 miles south of Front Royal, you'll find **Downriver Canoe Company** (✆ **800/338-1963** or 540/635-5526).
- Near Luray, you can go with **Shenandoah River Outfitters** (✆ **800/622-6632** or 540/743-4159; www.shenandoah-river.com).

10344 Stonewall Jackson Hwy. (U.S. 340). ✆ **800/296-4545** or 540/635-4545. www.skylinecaverns.com. Admission $16 adults, $8 children 7–13, free for children 6 and under. Train rides $3 per person, free for children 2 and under. Mirror Maze $5 per person, free for children 4 and under. June 15 to Labor Day daily 9am–6pm; Mar 15–June 14 and day after Labor Day to Oct 31 Mon–Fri 9am–5pm, Sat–Sun 9am–6pm; Nov 1–Mar 14 daily 9am–4pm. Mandatory 1-hr. tours run continuously. Entry is 2 miles south of downtown Front Royal, 1 mile south of the Shenandoah National Park's northern entrance.

Sports & Outdoor Activities

GOLF Front Royal has more golf courses than any other valley town. Duffers are welcome at the 27-hole **Shenandoah Valley Golf Club** (✆ 540/635-3588; www.svgcgolf.com), the 36-hole **Bowling Green Country Club** (✆ 540/635-2095; www.bowlinggreencountryclub.net), the 18-hole **Jackson's Chase** (✆ 540/635-7814; www.jacksonschase.com), the 18-hole **Blue Ridge Shadows Golf Club** (✆ 866/631-9661 or 540/631-9661; www.blueridgeshadows.com), and the 9-hole **Front Royal Country Club** (✆ 540/636-9062). Call for directions, starting times, and greens fees.

HORSEBACK RIDING The Front Royal area also offers more horseback riding than anywhere else in the valley. The 4,500-acre **Marriott Ranch,** 5305 Marriott

Lane, Hume, VA 22639 (✆ **877/278-4574** or 540/364-2627; www.marriottranch. com), offers 1½-hour guided trail rides, buggy rides, summer sunset rides, and full-moon rides. Serious equestrians can stay over in the **Inn at Fairfield Farm,** the ranch's bed-and-breakfast inn (✆ **540/364-3221**), which has 10 rooms (7 with bathrooms). Hume is on the eastern side of the Blue Ridge, about 15 minutes from Front Royal via U.S. 522, C.R. 635, and C.R. 726.

Another stable is **Highlander Horses,** 5297 Reliance Rd., Front Royal (✆ **540/636-4523;** www.highlanderhorses.com).

Where to Stay

The top chain hotel here is the **Holiday Inn & Suites at Front Royal Blue Ridge Shadows** (www.holidayinn.com/frontroyalva; ✆ **800/465-4329** or 540/631-3050, in the rapidly developing stretch of U.S. 522/U.S. 340 north of I-66. It's adjacent to the Blue Ridge Shadows Golf Club (see "Sports & Outdoor Activities," above). Nearby is a **Hampton Inn** (✆ **800/426-7866** or 540/635-1822), on U.S. 340 south of I-66.

Within walking distance of the visitor center and museums is the recently reno-vated **Quality Inn Skyline Drive** (✆ **800/228-5151** or 540/635-3161), on U.S. 522 east of U.S. 340. An inexpensive **Super 8** (✆ **800/800-8000** or 540/636-4888) is at the junction of U.S. 340 and Va. 55.

My favorite bed-and-breakfast here is **Killahevlin,** 1401 N. Royal Ave. (www. vairish.com; ✆ **800/847-6132** or 540/636-7335), occupying a hilltop mansion built by William Edward Carson, an Irishman who came to the United States in 1885 when he was 15 years old and amassed a fortune in the limestone business. The house is listed on the National Register of Historic Places. Among its luxurious ame-nities is an Irish pub just for guests.

Another good choice is the cozy **Woodward House on Manor Grade,** 413 S. Royal Ave./U.S. 340 South (www.acountryhome.com; ✆ **800/635-7011**), 7 blocks south of the visitor center.

Where to Eat

Main Street Mill Restaurant and Pub AMERICAN   Occupying a pictur-esque 1922 mill building next door to the visitor center, this establishment has mas-sive supporting columns and ceiling beams of chestnut. Local artist Patricia Windrow executed the distinctive *trompe l'oeil* murals representing Front Royal's pioneer and 19th-century eras. Lunch fare includes soups, spicy chili, salads, and overstuffed deli sandwiches. Main courses range from pastas to bacon-wrapped filet sirloin steak.

500 E. Main St. (next to visitor center). ✆ **540/636-3123.** Reservations not needed. Salads and sandwiches $7–$8.50; main courses $11–$18. AE, MC, V. Sun–Thurs 10:30am–9pm; Fri–Sat 10:30am–10pm.

Soul Mountain Café ★ 🎒 INTERNATIONAL   A porcelain Buddha oversees this lively storefront bistro, where a crew of young chefs turn out wide-ranging fare. The mesclun salad with roasted tomato and tossed with pesto was very good and large enough for a light meal. Andouille sausage sautéed with peppers over penne pasta was almost too cayenne laden to eat, but the slow-roasted Jamaican jerk chicken with coconut cream went down easy. The lunch menu adds delicious wraps.

300 E. Main St. (at Chester St.). ✆ **540/636-0070.** Reservations accepted. Main courses $13–$22. MC, V. Wed–Sun noon–3:30pm and 5:30–9pm.

Over the Mountains to "Little Washington"

A more scenic alternative to taking the short route via U.S. 340 south from Front Royal to Luray is U.S. 522 across the Blue Ridge, then U.S. 211 west across Thornton Gap. This route takes you into the eastern Blue Ridge foothills, which are a southern extension of the Hunt Country described in chapter 4. The northern entry to the Shenandoah National Park's Central District is on U.S. 211.

Going this way will give you a chance to tipple the vintages at **Rappahannock Cellars,** on Hume Road (C.R. 635) between U.S. 522 and the village of Hume (*©* **540/635-9398;** www.rappahannockcellars.com), whose owners moved their winery here from California. It is open Sunday to Friday from 11:30am to 5pm and Saturday 11:30am to 6pm.

Just off U.S. 211 you'll come to the two-street village of **Washington,** better known in these parts as "Little Washington." George Washington, then a surveyor's assistant, helped lay it out in 1749. Today it's dominated by the Inn at Little Washington (see below), but we common folk can walk across the street and grab a bite at the plain and inexpensive **Country Cafe** (*©* **540/675-1066**). It's open Monday to Thursday 8am to 8pm and Friday to Saturday 8am to 9pm. We can also catch chamber music, jazz, drama, or a film at the **Theatre at Washington** (*©* **540/675-1253;** www.theatre-washington-va.com).

Rather than forking over a king's ransom to stay at the Inn at Little Washington, we can retire at the **Heritage House Bed & Breakfast** (www.heritagehousebb.com; *©* **888/819-8280**) or the more expensive **Foster Harris House** (www.fosterharris.com; *©* **800/874-1036** or 540/675-3757), whose owner, John MacPherson, has written a cookbook with his breakfast recipes. Both are on Washington's Main Street.

The Inn at Little Washington ★★★ One of America's finest country inns, this marvelous establishment is not so much an outstanding inn with a restaurant as it is an outstanding restaurant with outstanding rooms. Owner/chef Patrick O'Connell makes inventive use of regional products—trout, Chesapeake Bay seafood, wild ducks, local cheeses—for his fabulous fixed-price dinners (if you have to ask how much, your credit limit likely isn't high enough). For a real treat, reserve one of the two fireside tables back in the kitchen, where you can watch the master and his crew at work. The extraordinary 14,000-bottle wine cellar may leave you pondering before selecting from its 40-page list (trust the waiters; they know what they're doing even if you don't). Dinner reservations are essential.

English decorator Joyce Evans magnificently appointed the inn's rooms, and her original sketches are framed and hanging in the upstairs hallways. The two bi-level suites have loft bedrooms, balconies overlooking the courtyard garden, and bathrooms with Jacuzzi tubs. Antiques and Oriental rugs add warmth to the rooms, distinguished by extravagantly canopied beds and hand-painted ceiling borders. Some rooms are across the street atop the inn's shops: The old Mayor's House has been turned into a suite with a garden, and five other houses provide accommodations, including the Rose Cottage, which has hosted former Vice President Al Gore and his ex-wife, Tipper.

Middle and Main sts. (PO Box 300), Washington, VA 22747. www.theinnatlittlewashington.com. *©* **540/675-3800.** Fax 540/675-3100. 18 units. $425–$770 double; $870–$2,645 suite. Add $245 for Sat, $145 for Fri, $75 for Sun. Rates include continental breakfast and afternoon tea. MC, V. From Front Royal, take U.S. 522 south 16 miles, then west on U.S. 211 to Washington. **Amenities:** Restaurant; bar; room service. *In room:* A/C, TV, Wi-Fi.

LURAY: AN UNDERGROUND ORGAN

6 miles W of Shenandoah National Park; 91 miles SW of Washington, D.C.; 135 miles NW of Richmond

Established in 1812, this small town is home to the famous Luray Caverns, the most visited caves in the eastern United States. It also has a very good historical museum and a sensitive zoo, where rescued animals await to be visited. Luray's accommodations are the closest to the Shenandoah National Park's popular Central District, making it the most convenient base in the valley if you can't get a room at one of the park's inns. The park headquarters and the Thornton Gap entry are up U.S. 211 a few miles east of town. Luray also is near the South Fork of the Shenandoah River, making it a center of watersports (see "Rafting, Canoeing & Kayaking on the Shenandoah," above).

Essentials

VISITOR INFORMATION Located in the town's restored train station, the **Luray–Page County Chamber of Commerce,** 18 Campbell St., Luray, VA 22835 (© **888/743-3915** or 540/743-3915; www.luraypage.com), is a good source of information about Shenandoah National Park. Be sure to see the center's model railroad exhibit. From Main Street (Business U.S. 211) go south on Broad Street (Business U.S. 340) and bear left. Open daily 9am to 5pm.

GETTING THERE Luray occupies the junction of U.S. 211 and U.S. 340. From Shenandoah National Park, take U.S. 211 west. From I-81, follow U.S. 211 East (this scenic road goes up and over Massanutten Mountain). From Front Royal, take U.S. 340 south. While U.S. 211 bypasses Luray to the north, Business U.S. 211 goes through town as Main Street. Business U.S. 340 goes through downtown as Broad.

Exploring the Town

You can get out of your vehicle and go for a pleasant stroll on the **Hawksbill Greenway,** a paved pedestrian path following Hawksbill Creek between downtown and the U.S. 211 bypass.

Luray Caverns ★★★ ☺ This U.S. Registered National Natural Landmark is the Shenandoah Valley's most interesting and entertaining cave. In addition to monumental columns in rooms more than 140 feet high, you'll see beautiful cascades of natural colors on the interior walls. Humanity and nature join forces in an unusual organ that produces music when rubber-tipped plungers tap the stalactites. There are no guided tours; instead, audio tours will lead you through a system of brick-and-concrete walkways. It's about 55°F (13°C) down here, so bring a jacket or sweater.

You get more for your money here, for admission to the caverns includes the **Luray Valley Museum.** Housed in a log cabin across the parking lot from the cave, it contains an extraordinary collection of historic items gathered by Rob Graves, whose family owns the caverns. It's the most comprehensive display in the valley. Especially notable is a Bible printed in 1536 and brought here in the 1700s by a Menonite settler from Switzerland. Outside the cabin are living history exhibits.

Also on the grounds is the **Car and Carriage Caravan Museum,** a collection of antique carriages, coaches, and cars—including actor Rudolph Valentino's 1925 Rolls-Royce. The complex also contains a snack bar, gift shop, and fudge kitchen. Separate admission is charged to get thoroughly confused in the outdoor **Garden Maze.**

Across U.S. 211 stands the **Luray Singing Tower,** a stone carillon with 47 bells. It was given to the town of Luray in 1937 as a memorial to one of its residents. Free concerts are given spring through autumn (pick up a schedule at the Luray visitor center or at the caverns).

U.S. 211 west (2 miles west of downtown). ✆ **540/743-6551.** www.luraycaverns.com. Admission to caverns and museums $23 adults, $21 seniors, $11 children 6–12, free for children 5 and under; Garden Maze $7 adults, $6 children 6–12, free for children 5 and under. Apr–June 14 daily 9am–6pm; June 15 to Labor Day daily 9am–7pm; day after Labor Day to Oct daily 9am–6pm; Nov–Mar Mon–Fri 9am–4pm, Sat–Sun 9am–5pm.

Luray Zoo ★ ☺ Various "wild animal parks" and even a "Dinosaur Land" vie for your attention in the Shenandoah. If you're traveling with children, this small zoo is worth a stop. It's a rescue facility, which means owners Mark and Christine Kilby take in unwanted or abused exotic animals, including tigers, monkeys, lemurs, crocodiles, and alligators. The snake collection is one of the largest on the East Coast. Best times to visit are the 11:30am animal encounter show and venomous snake demonstration from Memorial Day to Labor Day (call for times).

1087 U.S. Hwy. 211 W. (2½ miles west of downtown). ✆ **540/743-4113.** www.lurayzoo.com. Admission $10 adults, $5 children 3–12, free for children 2 and under. Apr–Oct daily 10am–5pm; Nov–Mar Sat–Sun 10am–5pm. Closed New Year's Day, Thanksgiving, and Christmas.

Where to Stay

The **Days Inn,** on the U.S. 211 bypass north of town (✆ **800/325-2525** or 540/743-4521), is surrounded by acres of farmland, giving most rooms mountain views. The **Best Western,** on West Main Street/U.S. 211 Business (✆ **800/528-1234** or 540/743-6511), is an older motel opposite the Mimslyn Inn in town. Both have outdoor swimming pools.

The Cabins at Brookside 🔱 Owners Bob and Cece Castle remodeled this 1940s service station/motel into a collection of log-looking cabins with comfortable Williamsburg-style furnishings throughout. These are the closest accommodations to the Shenandoah National Park's Central District. Although located along busy U.S. 211, the rear of the cabins open to decks or sunrooms overlooking a bubbling brook, and road noise dies down after dark. Five "honeymoon" units have whirlpool tubs or hot tubs, four have gas fireplaces, and one has a kitchen (the others, fridges only). None has a TV or phone, but three newer cabins about 2 miles away do.

2978 U.S. 211 E., Luray, VA 22835. www.brooksidecabins.com. ✆ **800/299-2655** or 540/743-5698. Fax 540/743-2413. 12 units. $85–$200 double. DISC, MC, V. From Luray, go east 4½ miles on U.S. 211. From Shenandoah National Park Headquarters, go west ½ mile on U.S. 211. **Amenities:** Restaurant. *In room:* A/C, fridge, no phone.

Luray Caverns Motel 🔱 Sitting opposite Luray Caverns, which owns and spotlessly maintains it, this older motel is dated, but the spacious rooms and small cabins are very good value. The motel sends its overflow in busy times to the equally clean **Luray Caverns Motel West,** a short distance west on U.S. 211, where the choice unit is an apartment with full kitchen.

U.S. 211 W. (PO Box 748), Luray, VA 22835. www.luraycaverns.com. ✆ **888/941-4531** or 540/743-4536. 19 units. $72–$95 double; $144–$178 apt. AE, DISC, MC, V. **Amenities:** Pool. *In room:* A/C, TV, hair dryer, Wi-Fi.

The Mimslyn Inn ★★ Built in 1931 on 14 acres of lawns and trees, this three-story Colonial-style inn has morphed into a luxury hotel equipped with a full-service

The "Cabin Capital of Virginia"

Just as bed-and-breakfasts once spread like wildfire across Virginia, **mountain cabins** are hot these days. There are so many of them for rent in these parts that Luray calls itself the "Cabin Capital of Virginia," and the local Chamber of Commerce sponsors **www.cabincapital. com**, with links to rental cabins. Because many are rented by the week, cabins and vacation homes are mostly taken by city folk on break from Washington and Baltimore metropolitan areas. The easiest way to rent is through **Allstar Lodging** (www.allstarlodging.com; © **866/ 780-STAR** [7827] or 540/843-0606), an agency representing many cabin owners.

spa. High-back rockers behind tall white columns on the front porch have Blue Ridge vistas, as do most of the guest rooms and the Skyline Terrace, a light-filled third-floor sunroom and rooftop patio with fireplace. (It's used for functions.) Almost hidden behind the lobby fireplace, curving stairs lead up to the guest rooms and down to the spa and to the lively **Speakeasy Bar & Restaurant** (p. 151). While it serves excellent fare, the elegant **Circa '31** dining room off the lobby plays second fiddle to the Speakeasy. Each of the guest rooms is individually decorated, some with a European flair, others tending to Colonial Americana. The top-floor suites are by far the largest, with spa tubs and separate living rooms boasting gas fireplaces.

401 W. Main St., Luray, VA 22835. www.mimslyninn.com. © **800/296-5105** or 540/743-5105. Fax 540/743-2632. 45 units. $115–$155 double; $235–$325 suite. AE, DISC, MC, V. **Amenities:** 2 restaurants; 2 bars; health club; Jacuzzi; pool; room service; spa. *In room:* A/C, TV, fridge (in some suites), hair dryer, Wi-Fi.

BED & BREAKFASTS

Woodruff Inns ★ Three charming Victorian houses make up this collection of B&Bs. The star is the **Victorian Inn,** on Main Street (www.victorianinnluray.com; © **540/860-4229**), which has three romantic, Jacuzzi-equipped suites. The suites have sun-filled sitting rooms and balconies with private entries so you don't have to go through the house to get to your room. The master suite also has a decorative fireplace in the bathroom. Less expensive but nonetheless charming are rooms in the nearby **Woodruff House** and the **Victorian Rose.** They both have hot tubs in their gardens. All three houses are furnished with mid- to late-19th-century antiques.

138 E. Main St., Luray, VA 22835. www.woodruffinns.com. © **866/937-3466** or 540/743-1494. Fax 540/743-1722. 9 units. $139–$189 double. Rates include breakfast. AE, DISC, MC, V. **Amenities:** Jacuzzi. *In room:* A/C.

Where to Eat

Artisans Grill AMERICAN This casual restaurant occupies a storefront strategically located on Main Street (Business U.S. 211) at its junction with Broad Street (Business U.S. 340) in the center of town. The menu offers a wide selection of salads, burgers, and sandwiches throughout the day, while dinnertime sees consistently good chargrilled steaks, chicken, ribs, and fish.

2 Main St. (at Broad St.). © **540/743-7030.** www.artisansgrill.com. Reservations accepted. Sandwiches and salads $7.50–$9.50; main courses $18–$24. Sun and Wed–Thurs 11am–9pm; Fri–Sat 11am–10pm.

Gathering Grounds Patisserie & Café AMERICAN   This charming café occupies a converted Victorian-era hardware store, which still has its pressed tin ceiling, oak counter, nail and screw drawers, and rolling ladder. It's the business district's favorite place for morning coffee, bagels and croissants, or for a lunch of freshly made salads and sandwiches, all fresh and reasonably healthy.

55 E. Main St. ⓒ **540/743-1121.** www.ggrounds.com. Most items $6–$10. DISC, MC, V. Mon 11am–3pm; Tues–Thurs 7am–7pm; Fri–Sat 8am–7pm.

The Restaurant at the Victorian Inn AMERICAN   At night the first floor of this member of the Woodruff Inns (see "Where to Stay," above) turns into a romantic fine-dining venue. The menu varies by season and availability of local produce. One autumn evening saw pork tenderloin with pineapple salsa and Cornish hen with an apple cider sauce. Summer might see salmon baked in a garlic-wine sauce. Virginia vintages appear on the wine list. Best tables in warm weather are on the front porch.

138 E. Main St. ⓒ **540/743-1494.** www.woodruffinns.com. Reservations accepted. Main courses $17–$27. AE, DISC, MC, V. Tues–Sat 5–9pm.

The Speakeasy Bar & Restaurant AMERICAN   I've been to Luray many times, but until recently there was little in the way of entertainment. That changed with the renovation of the Mimslyn Inn and the opening of this downstairs restaurant, the most sophisticated pub in town. It can be very busy when musicians perform

NEW MARKET: STUDENTS AT WAR

Between Luray and Staunton at the intersection of I-81 and U.S. 211, the village of **New Market** holds a hallowed place in Civil War history, for it was here that 257 Virginia Military Institute cadets charged the veteran Union lines on May 15, 1864, won the day, and returned to campus victorious. A descendant of Thomas Jefferson and nine other students were killed and 47 were wounded. Hearing of the battle, Union General Ulysses S. Grant exclaimed, "The South is robbing the cradle and the grave."

Today the cadets are honored by the **New Market Battlefield State Historical Park** and the **Virginia Museum of the Civil War ★★★**, 8895 Collins Dr. (ⓒ **540/740-3101;** www2.vmi.edu/museum/nm). The museum is one of the state's best. Explaining the military strategies, the museum's circular display of photos and newspaper headlines is the best chronological account of the war in Virginia I've seen. It begins with a wall-size painting of Richmond before the war and ends with a photo of the burned-out city in 1865. The award-winning film *Field of Lost Shoes* (45 min.), tells the cadets' story.

Outside on the rolling, grassy fields, you can take a self-guided 1-mile walking tour along the final Confederate assault on the Union line. The Bushong farmhouse, which served as a battlefield hospital, is now a museum of 19th-century valley life.

Admission is $10 for adults, $9 for seniors and active-duty military, $6 for children 6 to 12, and free for kids 5 and under. The museum is open daily 9am to 5pm except New Year's Day, Thanksgiving, December 24, and Christmas. The battle is reenacted in May on the weekend after Mother's Day.

While here you can explore New Market's many antiques and collectibles stores along Congress Street (U.S. 11) and sample good home cooking at the inexpensive **Southern Kitchen,** 9576 Congress St. (ⓒ **540/740-3514**), ½ mile south of the I-81 interchange. It's open daily 7am to 9pm.

from Thursday to Saturday nights. The chow is good pub fare such as nachos, burgers, wraps, fish and chips, and pan-fried mountain trout.

In the Mimslyn Inn, 401 W. Main St. © **540/743-5105.** www.mimslyninn.com. Reservations not accepted. Sandwiches $8–$10; main courses $14–$27. AE, DC, DISC, MC, V. Sun–Mon 4–9pm; Tues–Thurs 4–10pm; Fri–Sat 4–11pm.

7 A Mountain Resort with Golf & Skiing

Primarily a timeshare operation, **Massanutten Resort,** PO Box 1227, Harrisonburg, VA 22801 (www.massresort.com; © **800/207-6277** or 540/289-9441), offers year-round outdoor activities. The property has 27 holes of golf, tennis courts, indoor and outdoor swimming pools, a half-dozen downhill ski slopes, and areas for snowboarding and snow tubing (riding inner tubes down a gentle slope). The 140 hotel rooms have a queen-size or two double beds, sitting areas, and balconies. Most of the 800-plus timeshare units are equipped with kitchens, fireplaces, and decks, and many have whirlpools. There's a restaurant, pizzeria, bar, and grocery store on-site. From I-81, take Exit 247A and follow U.S. 33 east 10 miles to the resort entrance on the left.

STAUNTON: A PRESIDENT & THE BARD ★★★

42 miles S of New Market; 142 miles SW of Washington, D.C.; 92 miles NW of Richmond

The birthplace of Woodrow Wilson, our 28th president, Staunton (pronounced "Stanton") is equally proud today of its Blackfriars Playhouse, a stunning replica of one of Shakespeare's theaters, which brings the Bard to the Shenandoah and has led to Staunton becoming the valley's foremost performing-arts center. Along with Wilson's first home, many 19th-century downtown buildings in Staunton's revitalized historic district have been refurbished, including the train station and its adjacent **Wharf District,** now a shopping and dining complex. The mostly female **Mary Baldwin College,** whose pastoral campus lies across the street from the Wilson birthplace, lends a university atmosphere to this downtown in renaissance.

Settled well before the Revolution, Staunton was a major stop for pioneers on the way west. The Frontier Culture Museum on the outskirts of town explains the origins of the unique Shenandoah Valley farming communities. In the early 1800s, this was the eastern terminus of the Staunton-Parkersburg Turnpike (now U.S. 250), a major mountain road linking the Shenandoah Valley and the Ohio River. When the Central Virginia Railroad arrived in 1854, Staunton became even more of a regional center.

Plan to spend at least a full day exploring one of Virginia's best small towns and an evening at the theater.

Essentials

VISITOR INFORMATION The **Staunton Visitors Center,** 35 S. New St. (at Johnson St.), Staunton, VA 24401 (© **540/332-3971;** www.visitstaunton.com), provides information, free maps, and walking-tour brochures to the historic district. It's open April to October daily 9am to 6pm and November to March daily 9:30am to 5:30pm.

You can also get general information from the **Staunton/Augusta County Travel Information Center** (© **800/332-5219** or 540/332-3972) at the Frontier Culture Museum, on U.S. 250 west of Exit 222 off I-81. It is open daily 9am to 5pm except New Year's Day, Thanksgiving, and Christmas.

Staunton

ATTRACTIONS ●
Blackfriars Playhouse **11**
The R.R. Smith Center for
   History and Art **10**
The Woodrow Wilson
   Presidential Library at
   His Birthplace **13**

HOTELS ■
Frederick House **7**
Howard Johnson Express Inn
   Staunton **1**
Stonewall Jackson Hotel &
   Conference Center **12**

RESTAURANTS ◆
Aioli Mediterranean Cuisine **4**
Byers Street Bistro **14**
Cranberry's Grocery & Eatery **9**
The Depot Grille **15**
Emilio's Italian Restaurant &
   Pompeii Lounge **6**
Mill Street Grill **16**
Shenandoah Pizza **5**
The Split Banana **3**
Staunton Grocery **2**
Wright's Dairy Rite **17**
Zynodoa Restaurant **8**

GETTING THERE   Staunton is at the junctions of I-64 and I-81 and U.S. 11 and U.S. 250. I-81 and Va. 262 form a beltway around the town. **Shenandoah Valley Regional Airport** (SHD; ☏ **540/234-8304;** www.flyshd.com) is off I-81 between Harrisonburg and Staunton, but the nearest major airports are at Roanoke and Richmond.

Amtrak trains serve Staunton's station at 1 Middlebrook Ave. (☏ **800/872-7245;** www.amtrak.com). The station is unstaffed except when trains arrive.

GETTING AROUND   The **Downtown Staunton Trolley's Green Line** (☏ **800/ 305-0077;** www.staunton.va.us/community/transportation) is free and runs around town every 30 minutes (May–Dec Mon–Sat 10am–10pm; Jan–April Mon–Sat 10am–6pm). The Red and Silver Lines go farther afield and are mainly useful to local residents. Pick up a route map at the Staunton Visitors Center, the trolley's first stop at 15 and 45 minutes after the hour (see "Visitor Information," above). There's no narration, but riding the Green Line will give you a 30-minute overview of the town.

Exploring the Town

Downtown Staunton is a treasure trove of Victorian architecture, from stately residences to the commercial buildings downtown and in the adjacent Wharf District

7

THE SHENANDOAH VALLEY   Staunton: A President & the Bard

153

(actually along the railroad, not a river). Pick up a walking-tour brochure from the visitor center (see "Essentials," above), and set out on your own. The brochure describes five tours, but be sure to take the "Beverly" and "Wharf" tours, which cover all of historic downtown. Whether you do it yourself or go with a guide (see Guided Tours," below), be prepared to work up a sweat: Staunton is built on the side of a steep hill, a la San Francisco.

Blackfriars Playhouse ★★★ 🎭 Home to the **American Shakespeare Center,** this stunning re-creation of the first indoor theater in the English-speaking world, which William Shakespeare and his colleagues built on part of London's Blackfriars Monastery in 1642, is, in itself, a reason to visit Staunton. As in the Bard's time, the audience sits on three sides of the stage, most on benches (don't worry; you can rent cushions and seat backs). Members of the theater's acclaimed resident company as well as touring troupes perform Shakespeare's masterpieces, but the theater also hosts other classic plays. Be sure to take an actor-led guided tour, which sheds light on the theater and performance conventions in the Bard's day.

10 S. Market St. (btw. Beverley and Johnson sts.). ☏ **877/682-4235** or 540/851-1733. www.american shakespearecenter.com. Tour $5 per person; performances $12–$42. Box office Mon–Sat 9:30am–5pm. 1-hr. tours Apr–Oct Mon–Wed and Fri–Sat 11am and 2pm, Thurs 2pm; Nov–Mar Mon–Wed and Fri 2pm, Sat 11am.

Frontier Culture Museum ☺ In light of its history as a major stopping point for pioneers, Staunton is a logical location for this museum, which consists of 17th-, 18th-, and 19th-century working farmsteads representing the Old World origins of the Shenandoah's early settlers—Northern Irish, English, and German—and explaining how aspects of each were blended into a fourth farm, a typical Colonial American homestead. Staff members in period costumes plant fields, tend livestock, and do domestic chores. An 8-minute video will set the stage for your self-guided exploration, which will take about 2 hours to thoroughly cover. Children will love seeing the animals, but bring them in warm weather as many exhibits are outdoors. The museum store sells marvelously smooth fudge freshly made by the dairy farm.

1290 Richmond Ave. (U.S. 250; ½ mile west of I-81). ☏ **540/332-7850.** www.frontiermuseum.org. Admission $10 adults, $9.50 seniors, $9 students, $6 children 6–12, free for children 5 and under. Mid-Mar to Nov daily 9am–5pm; Dec to mid-Mar daily 10am–4pm. Closed New Year's Day, Thanksgiving, and Christmas.

The R.R. Smith Center for History and Art This beautifully restored Victorian hotel is now home to the Staunton-Augusta Art Center, the Augusta County Historical Society, and the Historic Staunton Foundation. They use the three galleries to display paintings, photographs, and other works by local artists as well as traveling exhibits, such as a show on maps and illustrations drawn by Jed Hotchkiss, Stonewall Jackson's mapmaker during the Civil War. The museum store is especially good during its Arts for Gifts sale from November through Christmas.

> ### 💬 Mr. Jefferson on the Run
>
> Staunton served as Virginia's capital for 17 days during June 1781, when then-Governor Thomas Jefferson fled Richmond to avoid advancing British troops.

20 S. New St. ☏ **540/885-2028.** www.rrsmithcenter.org. Free admission; donations encouraged. Mon–Fri 10am–5pm; Sat 10am–4pm; Sun 1–4pm.

The Woodrow Wilson Presidential Library at His Birthplace ★★★ A National Historic Landmark, this handsome home, built in 1846 by a Presbyterian congregation as a manse for their ministers, stands beside an excellent library and museum detailing Wilson's life. The future president was born here on December 28, 1856, but the family left Staunton when he was only 2. The house is furnished with many family items, including Wilson's crib and the chair in which his mother rocked him. The galleries of the museum next door trace Wilson's Scots-Irish roots, his academic career as a professor and president at Princeton University, and, of course, his 8 presidential years (1913–21), which spanned World War I. Don't overlook the beautiful Victorian garden or Wilson's presidential limousine, a shiny Pierce-Arrow. You must take the 35-minute guided tour of the house, but you can wander through the museum and gardens on your own. About 1½ hours will be required to see it all.

24 N. Coalter St. (at Frederick St.). ✆ **888/496-6376** or 540/885-0897. www.woodrowwilson.org. Admission $14 adults, $12 seniors, $7 students, $5 children 6–12, free for children 5 and under. Mid-Mar to mid-Nov Mon–Sat 9am–5pm, Sun noon–5pm; Mid-Nov to mid-Mar Mon–Sat 10am–5pm, Sun noon–4pm.

GUIDED TOURS

The **Historic Staunton Foundation** (✆ **540/885-7676**; www.historicstaunton.org) has free 2-hour **guided tours** of downtown at 10am May to October from the Emily Smith House, 24 N. Coalter St., next to the Woodrow Wilson Presidential Library at His Birthplace. Reservations are not necessary.

Local native Marney Gibbs of **Staunton Guided Tours** (✆ **540/885-2430**; www.stauntonguidedtours.com) will provide narration as you ride the trolley around town followed by a 10-block walking tour of downtown. Tours run June to October Tuesday to Saturday at 11am and November to May Saturday at 1:30pm. She charges $10 for adults and $7 for children 7 to 13. Reservations are requested.

Shopping

Beverley Street between Lewis and Market streets—downtown Staunton's main drag—is a fine place to browse a number of art galleries and antiques stores. I'm always left astounded by the vast collection of old stuff crammed into **Worthington Hardware Co.,** 26 W. Beverley St. (✆ **540/885-0891**), which once was a hardware store. The **Wharf District,** along Middlebrook Avenue and Byers Street, has more antiques shops.

The museum store at the R.R. Smith Center for History and Art (see above) is a fine place to shop for works by local artists and artisans. Even better is **Co-Art Gallery,** 22 W. Beverley St. (✆ **540/886-0737**; www.coartgallery.com), where more than 40 artists display their works. One gallery belongs to the Beverley Street Studio School, which is upstairs.

Down in the Wharf District, you can watch a skilled glass blower working at **Sunspot Studios,** 202 S. Lewis St. (✆ **540/885-0678**; www.sunspots.com), which carries a wide range of glass products. Across the intersection is **Ox-Eye Vineyards Tasting Room,** 44 Middlebrook Ave. (✆ **540/849-7926**; www.oxyeyvinyards.com), where you can sample this local vineyard's vintages and walk home.

Fans of the singing Statler Brothers, who grew up here, can buy their albums and souvenirs at their **Statler Brothers Gift Shop,** 1409 N. August St. (✆ **540/885-7297**; www.statlerbrothers.com).

The town of Waynesboro, 15 miles east of Staunton via I-64, is home to the **Artisans Center of Virginia,** 801 W. Broad St. (U.S. 340; ✆ **877/508-6069** or

540/946-3294; www.artisanscenterofvirginia.org), which represents more than 200 skilled artisans from throughout Virginia, each chosen by a jury. You can both browse and buy their work in the center's gallery. Also in Waynesboro is the **P. Buckley Moss Museum,** 150 P. Buckley Moss Dr. (☎ **800/343-8643** or 540/949-6473; www.pbuckleymoss.com), which displays her endearing paintings, many inspired by the valley's Amish and Mennonite communities. She has been a full- or part-time resident of Waynesboro since 1964.

Where to Stay

The budget-priced **Howard Johnson Express Inn,** 268 N. Central Ave. (www.hojo.com; ☎ **800/446-4656** or 540/886-5330), is downtown's only chain motel. The four-story building faces a parking lot, but rooms are moderately spacious and comfortable. Three rooms have Jacuzzi tubs, and there's an outdoor pool.

Near Exit 225 off I-85 (Woodrow Wilson Parkway) north of town, the **Holiday Inn Golf & Conference Center** (☎ **800/465-4329** or 540/248-6020; www.histaunton.com) is adjacent to the Country Club of Staunton, where guests can play. Staunton's largest concentration of motels is on U.S. 250 at Exit 222 off I-81, where you'll find the **Best Western Staunton Inn** (☎ 800/528-1234 or 540/885-1112), a **Comfort Inn** (☎ 800/228-5150 or 540/886-5000), an above-average **Econo Lodge** (☎ 800/446-6900 or 540/885-5158), a **Hampton Inn** (☎ 800/426-7866 or 540/886-7000), and a **Super 8** (☎ 800/800-8000 or 540/886-2888).

Frederick House ★★   The best place to stay in the area, these seven town houses dating from 1810 are now a European-style hotel—that is, a cross between an inn and a bed-and-breakfast. The rooms and suites are individually decorated with authentic antiques and reproductions from the Victorian era. Most have gleaming hardwood floors below Oriental rugs, and seven units have decorative fireplaces. All suites have separate living rooms, and three of them have two bedrooms. If you don't mind bright light at the crack of dawn, my favorite unit here is the Harmon Suite, whose bedroom once was a sun porch extending across the rear of one of the houses. With an oversize king-size bed, it's understandably the honeymoon suite. Frederick House is across the street from Mary Baldwin College and just 2 blocks from Woodrow Wilson's birthplace and the Blackfriars Playhouse. Hosts Joe and Evy Harmon know their hometown like the backs of their hands.

28 N. New St., Staunton, VA 24401. www.frederickhouse.com. ☎ **800/334-5575** or 540/885-4220. Fax 540/885-5180. 23 units. $109–$189 double; $159–$219 suite. Rates include full breakfast. Theater and other packages available. AE, DISC, MC, V. **Amenities:** Access to nearby health club. In room: A/C, TV, hair dryer, Wi-Fi.

Stonewall Jackson Hotel & Conference Center   Next door to the Blackfriars Playhouse, this classic downtown hotel first opened in 1924 and served as Staunton's special-occasions center until the 1960s, when it fell on hard times and was turned into an assisted-living facility. Thanks to a $21-million restoration, it's back in business as the town's prime commercial hotel and conference center. Be sure to walk up on the mezzanine and check out the 1924 Wurlitzer organ. It overlooks the bright lobby whose walls showcase some of the hotel's original silverware, dishes, and other 1920s mementos. The main dining room off the lobby provides breakfast daily, while the lobby lounge serves dinner. Rooms in the original building were expanded and updated but are still a tad smaller than those in a modern wing added during the restoration. They all have antique-looking furniture, writing desks, two phones, and bathrooms with ample granite vanities. There's an indoor pool here.

24 S. Market St., Staunton, VA 24401. www.stonewalljacksonhotel.com. © **866/880-0024** or 540/885-4848. Fax 540/885-4840. 124 units. $99–$189 double; $210–$410 suite. AE, DC, DISC, MC, V. **Amenities:** Restaurant; bar; health club; Jacuzzi; pool; room service. *In room:* A/C, TV, hair dryer, Wi-Fi.

Where to Eat

Staunton probably runs second only to Charlottesville in restaurants per capita, and it keeps adding more as the town's renaissance continues. In fact, there are so many that I wonder if the local residents know how to cook for themselves.

DOWNTOWN RESTAURANTS

Staunton Station, the town's old railway depot on Middlebrook Avenue between Augusta and Lewis streets in the Wharf District, is now a dining/entertainment complex. The train station is home to the family-oriented **Depot Grille** (© **540/885-7332;** www.depotgrille.com). Nearby, **Byers Street Bistro** (© **540/887-8100;** www.byersstreetbistro.com) is a popular restaurant-bar with warm-weather outdoor tables fronting a municipal parking lot on Byers Street at Central Avenue. All are moderately priced.

A nearby pub with good food and ambience is **Mill Street Grill,** 1 Mill St. (© **540/886-0656;** www.millstreetgrill.com), south of Johnson Street. Occupying the basement of the old White Star mill, which produced Melrose flour from 1890 to 1963, it offers barbecue ribs, steaks, prime rib, seafood, and some vegetarian dishes. Heavy beams and backlit stained-glass windows help to make it warm and cozy.

Staunton's top restaurants (see below) are along Beverly Street, the main drag, where you'll also find excellent pies at **Shenandoah Pizza** (© **540/213-0008;** www.shenandoahpizza.com) and rich, smooth homemade ice cream at the **Split Banana** (© **540/908-2962;** www.thesplitbanana.com).

Aioli Mediterranean Cuisine MEDITERRANEAN/TAPAS   A native of Casablanca, chef-owner Said Rhafiri refined his cooking skills in the South of France before immigrating to the U.S. and eventually landing in this brick-walled bistro. His excellent tapas (an unfilling choice before a play at Blackfriars) include the likes of mussels steamed with herbs, sea scallops with lemon-garlic aioli, and grilled jumbo shrimp. The Mediterrean main courses include some interesting twists, such as his version of seafood paella in which clams, mussels, shrimp, and fish were served over a tomato and herb risotto instead of being simmered in rice.

29 N. New St. © **540/885-1414.** Reservations recommended. Tapas $6–$10; main courses $17–$24. Mon–Tues 5–9pm; Wed–Thurs 5–9:30pm; Fri–Sat 5–10pm.

The 1950s Live

The 1950s are still very much alive at **Wright's Dairy Rite,** 346 Greenville Ave. (U.S. 11), a block south of Richmond Road (© **540/886-0435;** www.dairy-rite.com), a classic drive-in that has had car-hop service since it opened in 1952. Even if you dine inside this brick building or outside on the patio, you must lift a phone to place your order, and then wait for it to be delivered to your leatherette booth. Nothing here costs more than $8.50. MasterCard and Visa are accepted. It is open Sunday through Thursday from 10am to 10pm and Friday and Saturday from 10am to 11pm (until 9 and 10pm, respectively, during winter).

Cranberry's Grocery & Eatery ★ 🍴 HEALTH/VEGETARIAN Walk through this gourmet natural-foods grocery to the counter in the rear, where you can order the healthiest breakfast or lunch in Staunton. Fresh fruit, freshly baked muffins, and yeast or malt waffles lead the morning list. Lunch brings sandwiches, salads, and huge wraps, some with meat or chicken but most vegetarian. Wash it down with a freshly squeezed veggie juice.

7 South New St. 🕐 **540/885-4755.** www.gocranberrys.com. Reservations not accepted. Breakfast $3–$10; salads and sandwiches $5–$10. MC, V. Apr–Nov Mon–Wed 7:30am–5:30pm, Thurs–Sat 7:30am–7:30pm; Dec–Mar Mon–Sat 7:30am–5:30pm.

Emilio's Italian Restaurant and Pompeii Lounge ★ ITALIAN This pleasant establishment is run by accomplished cooks who moved here from Italy. You'll enter through a nondescript foyer in front of a small bar, but French doors lead to sophisticated L'Italia, with modern art hung in lighted alcoves. Ceiling spotlights highlight the black tables and chairs set far apart for privacy. Upstairs, the Pompeii Lounge presents outdoor dining on its rooftop patio, which hosts live music Thursday to Saturday nights during summer. The well-prepared offerings at both institutions range from Sicilian-style veal parmigiana to northern Italian veal piccata in a sauce of white wine, lemon, and capers.

23 E. Beverly St. 🕐 **540/885-0102.** www.emiliositalianrestaurant.com. Reservations recommended. Pasta $14–$18; main courses $18–$28. AE, DISC, MC, V. Tues–Thurs 11am–10pm; Fri–Sat 11am–11pm; Sun 11am–9pm. Lounge till later Fri–Sat.

Staunton Grocery ★★ AMERICAN Until another establishment opens and robs it of its perch, chef Ian Boden's bistro is Staunton's top restaurant. Although bistro style, it's more formal and intimate than its main competitor, Zynodoa Restaurant (see below), as its candles and white-linen tablecloths attest. The menu, which changes frequently depending on what the chef has corraled from local farms, is expressed for foodies. One recent offering: "Roasted monk fish + house cured bacon + hominy stew + fried pork belly + garlic kale." That's a lot of olde Virginny ingredients, but it was anything but down-home cooking. Yummy!

105 W. Beverly St. 🕐 **540/886-6880.** www.stauntongrocery.com. Reservations recommended. Main courses $17–$26. AE, MC, V. Tues 5–9pm; Wed–Sat 11am–2pm and 5–9pm.

Zynodoa Restaurant ★★ AMERICAN This casual bistro in a converted storefront takes its name from the American Indian pronunciation of *Shenandoah*. You can converse with local professionals at the friendly bar before retiring to a booth or table to pick from an eclectic menu that changes seasonally. Appetizers such as seared sea scallops with steamed asparagus and shaved Romano cheese are smallish though artistically presented, whereas the main courses are more substantial.

115 E. Beverley St. 🕐 **540/885-7775.** www.zynodoa.com. Reservations recommended. Main courses $21–$28. AE, MC, V. Wed–Sat 5–11:30pm; Sun noon–8pm.

A COUNTRY RESTAURANT IN THE SUBURBS

Mrs. Rowe's Restaurant and Bakery ★★ 🍴 AMERICAN Opened in 1947 by the late Mrs. Mildred Rowe and still run by her family, this is one of the better home-style restaurants in Virginia. Made from recipes from Mrs. Rowe's own cookbook, dishes here are very much in the Southern tradition but lighter than the usual fare cooked with prodigious portions of salt and lard. Grilled steaks, country ham, and pork chops lead the regular items, and you can also choose from daily specials such as meatloaf and gravy or fried flounder filet (though this is not the best place for fried chicken). The vegetable plate is popular, including good corn pudding, spoon bread, baked tomatoes, and cucumber-and-onion salad. Locals order slices of pie along with their main courses, just to make sure they get their favorite flavors.

74 Rowe Rd. (U.S. 250, just east of I-81). ℂ **540/886-1833.** www.mrsrowes.com/index.html. Reservations not accepted. Sandwiches $4–$7.50; main courses $8–$15. DC, DISC, MC, V. Mon–Sat 7am–8pm; Sun 7am–7pm. Breakfast daily 7–10:45am.

Staunton After Dark

Staunton has more going on after sunset than any town its size in Virginia. For a list follow the "Stanton on Tap" link on the Staunton Visitor Center's website (www.visitstaunton.com), or pick up a hard copy of the page at the center. See "Visitor Information," earlier in this chapter.

Staunton's showpiece is the **Blackfriars Playhouse** (see above), where you can see performances of Shakespeare's plays as well as other plays and concerts.

Music rules the roost during July and August when the Heifetz International Music Institute (www.heifetzinstitute.org) brings young talent to town for the annual **Staunton Music Festival** (ℂ **540/569-0267;** www.stauntonmusicfestival.com). Concerts take place all over town, some of them impromptu.

For art-house movie fans, the restored **Visulite Cinemas,** 12 N. Augusta St. (ℂ **540/885-9958;** www.visulitecinemas.com), showcases offbeat films such as Michael Moore's *Capitalism: A Love Affair,* which the mall cinemas won't touch in these Republican-leaning parts. The Visulite dates from 1937. The owners have also taken over the **Dixie Theater,** 125 E. Beverly St. (ℂ **540/885-8445**).

The top venue for live music is **Mockingbird Roots Music Hall,** 123 W. Beverly St. (ℂ **540/213-8777;** www.mockingbird123.com), a restaurant whose food plays second fiddle to national and regional bands performing in the backroom music hall.

The pubs in and around **Staunton Station,** the old railway depot on Millwood Avenue (see "Where to Eat," above), as well as the Pompeii Lounge on East Beverly Street, have live bands playing on weekend nights.

The city has a summertime program of free outdoor concerts in Gypsy Hill Park and the Wharf District. Check with the visitor center for a schedule.

You can wander the streets, ride the trolley, or explore spooky Thronrose Cemetery at night with **Ghosts of Staunton** (ℂ **540/448-2743;** www.ghostsofstaunton.com). Call for the schedule and prices.

Staunton to Lexington via Raphine

The rural area around the tiny hamlet of Raphine, about halfway between Staunton and Lexington, is quintessential Shenandoah Valley, with country roads winding among farms blanketing steep hills. This gorgeous area makes an easy excursion from either of the two towns or as a stop between them. The quick way is via I-81, but Va. 252 is much more scenic. However you get here, follow Raphine Road (C.R. 606) between the Interstate and Va. 252.

Starting at Exit 205 off I-81, take Va. 56 east toward Steele's Tavern and follow the signs to the picturesque **Cyrus McCormick Farm** (ℂ **540/377-2255;** www.arec.vaes.vt.edu/shenandoah-valley). Now part of a Virginia Tech agricultural research facility, it's in a lovely rural setting with a small blacksmith shop, a gristmill, and other log cabins, where exhibits include a model of Cyrus McCormick's 1831 invention, the first reaper, which revolutionized American agriculture and made him a fortune. This is an excellent place to spread out a picnic and take a half-mile walk along Mad Creek to the mill pond. It's open daily 8:30am to 5pm; admission is free.

Now backtrack west on Va. 56, go under I-81, and follow C.R. 606 for 1 mile through Raphine to the award-winning **Rockbridge Vineyard** (✆ **888/511-9463** or 540/377-6204; www.rockbridgevineyard.com). The tasting room is open Sunday to Monday noon to 5pm and Tuesday to Saturday 10am to 6pm.

Four miles west of I-81 is the 1882-vintage **Wade's Mill** (✆ **540/348-1400;** www.wadesmill.com), which grinds whole grains into flour, cornmeal, polenta, semolina, and an herb beer mix for pancakes (the mill supplies the area's top restaurants). The shop sells high-quality kitchen gear, and occasional cooking events feature guest chefs. The mill is open April to mid-December, Wednesday to Saturday 10am to 5pm, and Sunday 1 to 5pm June to August.

Another interesting stop is **Clark's Olde Time Music Center,** at Clark's Lumber Company, 1288 Ridge Rd., Raphine (✆ **540/377-2490**), where artists play old-style country music on Friday nights, except in July. Admission is $8. Call for the schedule.

Most of this area is in northern Rockbridge County, so contact the **Lexington & Rockbridge Area Visitor Center** for more information (see below).

You can stay in this area at **Fox Hill Bed & Breakfast,** 4383 Borden Grant Trail, Fairfield, VA 24435 (www.foxhillbb.com; ✆ **800/869-8005** or 540/377-9922), which sits on rolling pastureland with a fine view of the Blue Ridge about 13 miles north of Lexington. Fox Hill is no Victorian home full of frilly lace and antiques, for it was built during the 1990s as an equestrian inn. The architecture is more German than Virginian, with lots of knotty pine and a big stone fireplace in the guest lounge.

Staunton to Warm Springs via Monterey

Another scenic alternative to I-81 from Staunton to Lexington is via U.S. 250 West across the mountains into Highland County, whose rugged beauty has given it the nickname "Virginia's Switzerland." In fact, U.S. 250 from Staunton to the town of **Monterey** is one of the state's most scenic excursions. Carved out of the rocks in the early 1800s as the Staunton-Parkersburg (W. Va.) Turnpike, the two-lane highway climbs steeply over four mountains on its way to Monterey. Don't be in a hurry: the 50-mile drive can take 1½ hours.

Plan to stop a few moments atop Shenandoah Mountain at the breastwork remains of **Confederate Fort Edward Johnson,** 25 miles west of Staunton. Rebel Gen. Edward Johnson built the fort in the winter of 1862 to protect the Shenandoah Valley from Union forces advancing from the west. It was abandoned a few months later without ever seeing action. There is an interpretive trail and a tremendous view.

Later Gen. Stonewall Jackson led his army across the mountain and won the Battle of McDowell, in the Bullpasture River valley. Today you'll pass through the village of McDowell, which explains the battle in the **Highland Museum and Heritage Center** (✆ **540/396-4478;** www.highlandcountyhistory.com). The museum is behind the funeral home on U.S. 250 and is open from mid-March through October Thursday to Saturday 11am to 4pm and Sunday 1 to 4pm. Admission is free. Next door, members of the local Mennonite community sell homemade maple syrup and candy in the **Sugar Tree Country Store & Sugar House** (✆ **800/396-2445** or 540/396-3469), which still has its pot-belly stove. It's open Monday to Saturday 10am to 5pm.

MONTEREY

Seen from U.S. 250 as it descends into the valley, Monterey's white clapboard churches and Victorian homes conjure up images of New England hamlets. At more than 2,500 feet elevation, it enjoys a refreshing, springlike climate during summer. Information is available in the Highland Inn on Main Street (see below). Stroll along Main Street (U.S. 250) past the likes of **H&H Cash Store,** a holdover from the days when general stores sold a little bit of everything. You can also poke your head into arts-and-crafts stores.

The best (and most crowded) time is on the second and third full weekends in March, when Monterey hosts the **Highland Maple Festival,** one of Virginia's top annual events (see "Virginia Calendar of Events," in chapter 2). A smaller version, the **Hands and Harvest Festival,** is held on the second weekend in October.

Accommodations are available at the charming **Highland Inn,** on Main Street (www.highland-inn.com; Ⓒ 888/466-4682 or 540/468-2143; fax 540/468-3143), a 16-unit, veranda-fronted hotel built in 1904, renovated and improved in the 1990s. The inn serves dinner Wednesday to Saturday and brunch on Sunday.

Fresh deli sandwiches and salads are available on Main Street at **Evelyn's Pantry** (Ⓒ **540/468-3663**), where you can shop the pantry for local maple syrup and candies. It's open Monday to Friday 7:30 to 5:30pm and Saturday 7:30 to 4pm. Famous hereabouts for its peanut butter pie, **High's Restaurant,** also on Main Street (Ⓒ **540/468-1600**), serves inexpensive, down-home Southern fare Monday to Saturday 6am to 8pm and Sunday 7am to 6pm.

For more information contact the **Highland County Chamber of Commerce,** PO Box 223, Monterey, VA 24465 (Ⓒ **540/468-2550;** www.highlandcounty.org). It's open Monday to Friday 10am to 5pm.

From Monterey, U.S. 220 takes you 30 miles south through the narrow, pastoral Jackson River Valley—one of the most idyllic in Virginia—to Warm Springs (see below). From there, you can drive 42 miles across the mountains to Lexington via Va. 39 and the Goshen Pass, a marvelously scenic drive.

WARM SPRINGS & HOT SPRINGS ★★

Hot Springs: 220 miles SW of Washington, D.C., 160 miles W of Richmond; Warm Springs: 5 miles N of Hot Springs

At temperatures from 94° to 104°F (35°–40°C), thermal springs rise in appropriately named Bath County. This little highlands valley has been a retreat since the 18th century, when Thomas Jefferson and other notables stopped at Warm Springs to "take the waters." The Homestead was founded in 1766 and is still one of the nation's premier spas and golf resorts (it has the nation's oldest tee). After you've soaked in the waters, played the links, and had your pedicure, you can hear small ensembles making music at the Garth Newel Music Center.

Warm Springs today is a charming little hamlet that serves as the Bath County seat. The even smaller village of Hot Springs, 5 miles to the south, is virtually a company town: It lives to serve The Homestead. Hot Springs' Main Street begins where U.S. 220 circles around the resort and runs for 2 blocks south; here you'll find a deli and several upscale art and clothing dealers, some in the old train depot.

Granted, there is a whole lot of moneyed folk visiting and living in this valley, including the Rev. Pat Robertson, who has a mansion up on the mountaintop. Fortunately we of the tax-paying classes don't have to spend a fortune to enjoy it for a day or two; there are relatively inexpensive places to stay and eat here.

Essentials

VISITOR INFORMATION The **Bath County Chamber of Commerce,** 169 Main St. (PO Box 718), Hot Springs, VA 24445 (✆ **800/628-8092** or 540/839-5409; www.discoverbath.com), operates a visitor center (with free Wi-Fi) on Main Street south of the Homestead. It's open Monday to Saturday 9am to 5pm. There's an information kiosk in Warm Springs at the Jefferson Pools, on U.S. 220 just south of the Va. 39 junction. It usually has copies of a walking-tour brochure to the little village.

GETTING THERE U.S. 220 runs north and south through Hot Springs and Warm Springs, with access to I-64 at Covington, 20 miles of winding mountain road south of Hot Springs. (*Note:* Some GPS devices do not give the best route from Covington; rely on a real map and stay on U.S. 220.) The scenic route is via Va. 39 from Lexington, a 42-mile drive following the Maury River through the canyonlike **Goshen Pass.** You can also take the scenic route from Staunton via Monterey, described earlier in this chapter.

The nearest regular air service is at **Roanoke Regional Airport** (p. 181). Clifton Forge has an **Amtrak** station (✆ **800/872-7245;** www.amtrak.com).

Taking the Waters & Classical Music ★★★

The most famous of the thermal springs are the **Jefferson Pools,** in a grove of trees in Warm Springs, just south of the intersection of U.S. 220 and Va. 39 (✆ **540/839-5346;** www.thehomestead.com). The crystal-clear, 98°F (37°C) waters of these natural rock pools circulate gently and offer a wonderfully relaxing experience. The octagonal white clapboard bathhouse covering the men's pool was built in 1761, and the women's building dates to 1836, and they've been little changed since. The only luxuries you'll get at the pools are a clean towel and a rudimentary changing room. Use of the pools costs $17 an hour. Reservations aren't taken for the pools—just walk in. They are open June to October daily 10am to 5pm. Bathing suits are required during coed family time from 10am to 1pm. They are optional, but men and women cannot bathe together, from 1 to 5pm. Call for winter hours.

There's music in the mountain air on summer weekends at the **Garth Newel Music Center,** on U.S. 220 between Warm Springs and Hot Springs (✆ **877/558-1689** or 540/839-5018; www.garthnewel.org). The center's summer-long music festival has been drawing critical acclaim since the 1970s, and concerts now go into the autumn months. Long known for classical music, it now features jazz, blues, and other varieties—all performed by small ensembles. Garth Newel also sponsors a series of Music Holiday Weekend Retreats in spring, fall, and winter. Accommodations and dining at the on-site **Manor House** are part of the package. Call, write, or check the website for details.

Where to Stay

Bed-and-breakfasts include **Vine Cottage Inn** (www.vinecottageinn.com; ✆ **800/410-9755** or 540/839-2422), a block from the Homestead.

The Homestead ★★★ ☺ Dating back to 1766, this venerable spa and golf resort has hosted presidents since Thomas Jefferson, plus innumerable social elites. Guests enter across a porch adorned with white rockers into the Great Hall, lined with 16 Corinthian columns and a 211-foot floral carpet. It's worth stopping in here just to see this magnificent room. Guests have a variety of accommodations in rooms and suites with a Virginia country-manor ambience and custom-designed mahogany furniture. Most units offer spectacular mountain views. Best are the suites in the South Wing, which have working fireplaces, private bars, sun porches, two TVs, and two phones.

Making this an excellent family resort, a multitude of diversions for all ages include three outstanding golf courses, 12 tennis courts, bowling, fishing, hiking, horseback and carriage rides, ice skating on an Olympic-size rink, lawn bowling and croquet, billiards, sporting clays and skeet trap, and downhill and cross-country skiing mid-December to March. Then you can ease the aches and pains in the springs-fed indoor pool or the full-service spa, which also takes advantage of the hot springs.

The historic **Main Dining Room** is a lush palm court, in which a trio performs during six-course dinners and for dancing afterward (coat and shirt with collar required after 6pm). The Homestead's signature restaurant, the **1766 Grille,** is more casual, as is the **Casino Club,** with seating out on the lawn in warm weather. Even **Martha's Market,** the coffee and ice cream shop, is a bit rich for my plastic, but I have splurged across Main Street at **Sam Snead's Tavern,** a casual pub serving traditional American fare (open for dinner only). Or you can dine at the golf clubs or at the ski slopes.

7697 Sam Snead Hwy. (U.S. 220; PO Box 2000), Hot Springs, VA 24445. www.thehomestead.com. © **800/838-1766** or 540/839-1776. Fax 540/839-7670. 483 units. $175–$550 double; $350–$900 suite. Resort fee 15% per day. Packages available. AE, DC, DISC, MC, V. **Amenities:** 5 restaurants; 3 bars; babysitting; bikes; children's center or programs; concierge; 3 golf courses; health club; Jacuzzi; indoor and outdoor pools; room service; sauna; spa; 12 tennis courts. *In room:* A/C, TV, hair dryer, Wi-Fi.

Inn at Gristmill Square ★ 🍴   Five restored 19th-century buildings, including an old mill, make this unique hostelry in Warm Springs seem like a small village. It includes the Blacksmith Shop, which houses a country store; the Hardware Store, with seven guest units; the Steel House, with four units; the Miller's House, with four rooms; and the old silo, with two rooms that have curving walls. Furnishings are period pieces, with comfortable upholstered chairs, brass chandeliers, four-poster beds, and marble-top side tables, and many units have working fireplaces. Breakfast is served in your room in a picnic basket. Other facilities include an outdoor pool and three tennis courts, and you can wade in the warm stream winding through the property. The rustic **Waterwheel Restaurant** (see "Where to Eat," below) and **Simon Kenton Pub** are cozy spots in the old mill building.

124 Old Mill Rd. (C.R. 645; PO Box 359), Warm Springs, VA 24484. www.gristmillsquare.com. © **540/839-2231.** Fax 540/839-5770. 16 units, 1 suite. $110–$145 double. Rates include continental breakfast. DISC, MC, V. From U.S. 220 N., turn left onto C.R. 619 and right onto C.R. 645. **Amenities:** Restaurant; bar; outdoor pool; room service. *In room:* A/C, TV, fridge, hair dryer, Wi-Fi.

Roseloe Motel 🍴   At the opposite extreme from the Homestead, this brick-fronted motel offers inexpensive, well-maintained, and clean rooms near the Garth Newel Music Center, between Warm Springs and Hot Springs. Four units have full kitchens, 2 have kitchenettes, and all have microwave ovens and refrigerators. It's very popular with cost-conscious leaf watchers and deer hunters during fall, so book early.

10849 Sam Snead Hwy. (U.S. 220 N.), Hot Springs, VA 24445. © **540/839-5373.** Fax 540/839-4625. 14 units. $70–$85 double. AE, DISC, MC, V. From Hot Springs, go north 3 miles on U.S. 220. *In room:* A/C, TV, fridge, kitchen (in some), Wi-Fi.

Warm Springs Inn 🍴   Directly across the road from the Jefferson Pools, this comfortable inn occupies three buildings—the former Bath County courthouse, the former county jail, and the former county clerk's office (the latter still has the original vault for keeping the government's loot). The courthouse is now home to Elliott's at Warm Springs Inn (see "Where to Eat," below), while guests stay in the converted jail and clerk's office. The rooms lack luxuries but they are charming and comfortable. Everyone gets to enjoy lounging on the wraparound porches.

12968 Sam Snead Hwy. (U.S. 220), Warm Springs, VA 24484. www.warmspringsinnva.com. © **540/ 839-5351.** Fax 540/839-5352. 23 units (all with private bathroom). $79–$150 double. Rates include full breakfast. AE, DISC, MC, V. **Amenities:** Restaurant; bar. *In room:* A/C, TV, no phone, Wi-Fi (in most).

AN UNUSUAL COUNTRY INN

Fort Lewis Plantation & Lodge ★★ ☺ You'll discover one of Virginia's most remote and unusual country inns at this farm beside the Cowpasture River, across the mountain from Warm Springs. About half the guest quarters are in a reconstructed barn, from which an outside spiral staircase leads to three rooms with curved walls inside the silo. One end of the rough-looking barn is now a comfortable lounge with stone fireplace and large windows looking out over a Jacuzzi-equipped deck to the farmland and mountains beyond. Other guests stay in hand-hewn log cabins, each with a fireplace, or in a restored farmhouse. Activities include mountain biking, hiking, and taking a cool dip in one of Virginia's best swimming holes (it has a rock wall on one side). You can fish for trout in the Cowpasture River, but don't count on eating your catch; you must throw it back into the river.

6300 Old Plantation Way, Millboro, VA 24460. www.fortlewislodge.com. © **540/925-2314.** Fax 540/925-2352. 19 units. $215 double; $230–$310 cabin. Rates include breakfast and dinner. MC, V. Closed early Nov through Mar. From Warm Springs, go 14 miles east on Va. 39, turn left on Indian Draft Rd. (C.R. 678) and drive north 11 miles, then turn left on River Rd. (C.R. 625) to entrance. **Amenities:** Restaurant; bar; bikes; Jacuzzi; swimming hole. *In room:* A/C.

Where to Eat

Part of a gasoline station 3½ miles north of Hot Springs, **Cucci's at the Varsity** (© **540/839-4000**) provides inexpensive pizza, spaghetti, and other Italian fare. It's open Monday to Thursday 11am to 10pm and Friday to Saturday 11am to 11pm.

On an alley off Main Street in Hot Springs, **Lindsay's Roost Bar and Grill** (© **540/839-2142**) caters to the working class with inexpensive country-style breakfasts, sandwiches, burgers, and main courses such as fried mountain trout. It's open Monday to Saturday 9am to 8pm. Also in Hotsprings is the **Duck-In Deli & Subway** (© **540/839-3000**), a convenience store with a coffee shop. It is open daily 7am to 8pm.

Country Cafe AMERICAN I've seen Rev. Pat Robertson munching on fried chicken here at Hot Springs' favorite country restaurant. It's good Southern fare like my mother used to cook. All is not fried, however, including the broiled, sautéed, or chargrilled mountain trout, the best meal here. Finish it off with a slice of delicious homemade cream pie. Beer and wine are served but not spirits.

6156 Sam Snead Hwy. (U.S. 220 S.; 1 mile south of the Homestead). © **540/839-2111.** Reservations not accepted. Main courses $7.50–$16. MC, V. Tues–Sat 7am–9pm; Sun 8am–2pm.

Elliott's at Warm Springs Inn ★ INTERNATIONAL Chef Josh Elliott owned a small storefront bistro in downtown Hot Springs when I started writing this book many moons ago. He went away to make some real money but is now back home plying his trade in the Warm Springs Inn (see above). Some tables are in the old courtroom, and during pleasant weather some spill out on the wraparound porch.

Josh combs the globe for culinary influences, with the likes of sesame seared tuna served over a pine nut risotto with an orange and ginger sauce. He is an excellent pastry chef, so save room for dessert. The setting alone is worth an evening here.

At Warm Springs Inn, 12968 Sam Snead Hwy. (U.S. 220). © **540/839-5351.** www.warmsprings innva.com. Reservations strongly recommended. Main courses $17–$25. AE, DISC, MC, V. Wed– Sat 6–9pm.

The Waterwheel Restaurant ★ INTERNATIONAL   This charmer occupies the old mill building at the Inn at Gristmill Square in Warm Springs (see "Where to Stay," above), thus is its name derived from the huge water wheel that once powered the grist. The signature dish here is mountain trout lightly breaded with cornmeal and black walnuts; it's a tasty twist on Southern cooking. There's an extensive wine cellar, from which you can partake premeal or après meal in the tiny, one-table pub.

In the Inn at Gristmill Square, 124 Old Mill Rd. (C.R. 645), Warm Springs. © **540/839-2231.** www. gristmillsquare.com. Reservations highly recommended. Main courses $24–$31. DISC, MC, V. Sept–April daily 6–8:30pm; May–Oct daily 6–9pm. Sun brunch 11am–2pm.

LEXINGTON: A CHARMING COLLEGE TOWN ★★★

36 miles S of Staunton; 180 miles SW of Washington, D.C.; 138 miles W of Richmond

A college atmosphere prevails in Lexington, one of America's most charming small towns. Fine old homes line tree-shaded streets, among them the house where Stonewall Jackson lived when he taught at Virginia Military Institute. A beautifully restored downtown looks so much like it did in the 1800s that scenes for the movie *Sommersby* were filmed on Main Street (Richard Gere's character was hanged behind Stonewall's house). After the Civil War, Robert E. Lee came to Lexington to serve as president of what was then Washington College; he and his horse, Traveller, are buried here. And Gen. George C. Marshall, winner of the Nobel Peace Prize for his post–World War II plan to rebuild Europe, graduated from VMI, which has a fine museum in his memory.

Washington and Lee University has one of the oldest and most beautiful campuses in the country. Built in 1824, Washington Hall is topped by a replica of an American folk art masterpiece, an 1840 carved-wood statue of George Washington. Lee reputedly planted some of the massive trees dotting the campus.

Sometimes called the West Point of the South, VMI opened in 1839 on the site of a state arsenal, abutting the Washington and Lee campus (W&L's buildings are like brick Southern manses; VMI's look like stone fortresses). VMI's big moment in history took place during the Civil War at the Battle of New Market on May 15, 1864, when the corps of cadets helped turn back a larger Union army (p. 151). A month later, Union General David Hunter got even, bombarding Lexington and burning down VMI. He spared Washington College because it was named for the first president.

Essentials

VISITOR INFORMATION   The **Lexington Visitor Center,** 106 E. Washington St., Lexington, VA 24450 (© **877/453-9822** or 540/463-3777; fax 540/463-1105; www.lexingtonvirginia.com), is a block east of Main Street. Begin your tour of Lexington at this excellent source of information, with museum-like displays about the town's history, an accommodations gallery for making same-day reservations, and free walking-tour brochures (you can park in the center's lot while touring the town). The center is open daily 8am to 6pm June through August and 9am to 5pm the rest of the year. It's closed New Year's Day, Thanksgiving, and Christmas.

GETTING THERE   Lexington is at the junction of I-81 and I-64. U.S. 60 and U.S. 11 go directly into town. The nearest regular air service is at **Roanoke Regional Airport** (p. 181). Staunton has the nearest **Amtrak** station (© **800/872-7245;** www.amtrak.com).

Exploring the Town

Be sure to pick up a free **walking-tour** brochure at the visitor center. It explains Lexington's historic buildings and contains one of the best maps of downtown. Beginning at the visitors center, there are free **guided walking tours** at 3pm Friday from April through October. No reservations are required; just show up.

During the school year, VMI cadets lead walking tours of their campus, departing the Virginia Military Institute Museum lobby daily at noon.

For a good overview, take a ride with **Lexington Carriage Company** (© **540/463-5647**), whose horse-drawn carriages depart from the visitor center for 45-minute narrated tours daily 10am–5:30pm during the summer and 11am to 5:30pm during April, May, September, and October. Fares are $13 for adults, $6 for children 4 to 12, and free for kids 3 and under.

Haunting Tales of Historic Lexington (© **540/464-2250;** www.monsters anddinosaurs.com) conducts 1½-hour nighttime walks through the streets, back alleys, and Stonewall Jackson Cemetery from Memorial Day weekend to Halloween. The cost is $12 for adults, $6 for children 4 to 12, and free for children 3 and under. Reservations are strongly recommended, so call ahead.

George C. Marshall Museum and Research Library ★★   Facing the Virginia Military Institute parade ground, this impressive stone structure houses the personal archives of General of the Army George C. Marshall, a 1901 graduate of VMI. As army chief of staff in World War II, Marshall virtually directed that conflict (he chose Gen. Dwight D. Eisenhower to command all Allied forces in Europe). After the war he served as secretary of state and secretary of defense under President Truman. He is best remembered for the Marshall Plan, which fostered the economic recovery of Western Europe after the war. For his role in promoting postwar peace, he became the first career soldier to be awarded the Nobel Peace Prize, in 1956. His Nobel medal is on display. An electronic map charts the war and Marshall's decisions. Allow an hour to explore the museum on your own.

> ### Presidential Prototype
>
> The George C. Marshall Museum and Research Library is the prototype for modern presidential libraries, starting with President Truman's in Independence, Missouri.

1600 VMI Parade. © **540/463-7103.** www.marshallfoundation.org. Admission to museum $5 adults, $4 seniors, free for students and children; free admission to research library. Museum Tues–Sat 9am–5pm; Sun 1–5pm. Library Mon–Fri 9am–4:30pm.

Lee Chapel and Museum ★★★   This magnificent Victorian-Gothic chapel on the Washington and Lee campus was built of brick and native limestone in 1867 at the request of General Lee. Begin on the auditorium stage and the striking white-marble sculpture *Lee Recumbent*, which Edward Valentine carved shortly after Lee's

Lexington

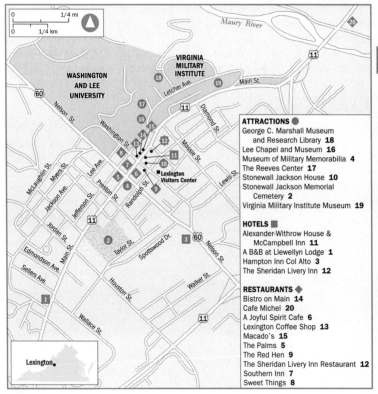

ATTRACTIONS ●
George C. Marshall Museum
  and Research Library **18**
Lee Chapel and Museum **16**
Museum of Military Memorabilia **4**
The Reeves Center **17**
Stonewall Jackson House **10**
Stonewall Jackson Memorial
  Cemetery **2**
Virginia Military Institute Museum **19**

HOTELS ■
Alexander-Withrow House &
  McCampbell Inn **11**
A B&B at Llewellyn Lodge **1**
Hampton Inn Col Alto **3**
The Sheridan Livery Inn **12**

RESTAURANTS ◆
Bistro on Main **14**
Cafe Michel **20**
A Joyful Spirit Cafe **6**
Lexington Coffee Shop **13**
Macado's **15**
The Palms **5**
The Red Hen **9**
The Sheridan Livery Inn Restaurant **12**
Southern Inn **7**
Sweet Things **8**

death in 1870. Flanking it are Charles Willson Peale's 1772 portrait of George Washington and Theodore Pine's painting of Lee. The remains of the general and many other members of the Lee clan (including "Light-Horse Harry" Lee of Revolutionary War fame) are entombed in the basement, where Lee's office remains just as he left it. His beloved horse, Traveller, is buried outside the museum. The museum includes the impressive Washington-Custis-Lee collection of American portraits. Allow 30 minutes to see the statue, the crypt, and Lee's office, another 30 in the museum.

At Washington and Lee University. 📞 **540/458-8768.** http://chapelapps.wlu.edu. Free admission. ($5 donation suggested.) Apr–Oct Mon–Sat 9am–5pm, Sun 1–5pm; Nov–Mar Mon–Sat 9am–4pm, Sun 1–5pm. Limited free parking on Jefferson St., opposite west end of Henry St. Follow signs from parking lot.

Museum of Military Memorabilia   This small museum displays a collection of military uniforms and various bits of soldiers' gear, with the oldest dating from 1740 in Prussia and the newest from the War in Iraq. The uniforms come from several different countries and represent a number of conflicts. You'll also see insignia, flags, a few weapons, trench art from World War I, and a piece of the Berlin Wall. If you miss the beginning, you can join the 45-minute guided tours in progress.

122½ S. Main St. (in the driveway next to the Presbyterian Church). ℂ **540/464-3041.** Admission $3 per person. Apr–Oct Wed–Fri noon–5pm, Sat 9am–5pm; Nov–Mar by appt. 45-min. tours run continuously.

The Reeves Center This former professor's residence contains a collection of more than 4,000 pieces of hand-painted Chinese export porcelain, one of the top five such collections in the United States. Highlights are the porcelain place sets used by the Robert E. Lee family and an armorial piece commissioned by George Washington. The latter is one of several hundred pieces painted with family coats of arms.

At Washington and Lee University.ℂ **540/458-8034.** www.wlu.edu. Free admission. Mon–Fri 9am–4pm.

Stonewall Jackson House ★★ Maj. Thomas Jonathan Jackson came to Lexington in 1851 to teach natural philosophy (physics) and artillery tactics at VMI. Jackson lived in this Federal-style house with his second wife, Mary Anna Morrison, their daughter, and five slaves from early 1859 until he was summoned to Richmond in 1861; it was the only house he ever owned. Exhibits tell the story of the Jacksons' stay here, and many of the Jacksons' personal effects duplicate the items on the inventory of Jackson's estate made shortly after he died near Chancellorsville in 1863. His body was returned to Lexington and buried in Stonewall Jackson Memorial Cemetery (see below). Also have a look at the backyard vegetable garden and the carriage house, which protects a Rockaway model Jackson owned.

8 E. Washington St. (btw. Main and Randolph sts.). ℂ **540/463-2552.** www.stonewalljackson.org. Admission $6 adults, $3 children 6–17, free for children 5 and under. Mar–Dec Mon–Sat 9am–5pm, Sun 1–5pm. Call for winter hours. Guided 30-min. tours depart on the hour and half-hour (last tour 30 min. before closing). Closed New Year's Day, Easter, Thanksgiving, and Christmas.

Stonewall Jackson Memorial Cemetery An Edward Valentine statute of Jackson stands tall over the general's grave in the center of this peaceful cemetery. Jackson's two wives, his two daughters, his son-in-law, and two Virginia governors are interred around him. Also here are the remains of 144 confederate foot soldiers and Gen. E. F. Paxton, who, like Jackson, was killed at Chancellorsville. John Mercer Brooke, who designed the Confederate ironclad CSS *Virginia,* formerly the USS *Merrimack,* is here. The cemetery office, on its northern boundary, distributes a guide to the gravesites.

314 S. Main St. (at White St.). ℂ **540/436-2931.** Free admission. Daily dawn–dusk.

Virginia Horse Center Sprawling across nearly 400 acres, the Virginia Horse Center offers educational seminars and sales of fine horses, and it has a coliseum for concerts as well as horse shows. Annual events include draft pulls, rodeos, various competitions, and competitive breed shows. Call or check the website for the schedule.

Va. 39 (1 mile west of U.S. 11 and north of I-64). ℂ **540/463-7060.** www.horsecenter. org. Admission varies by event; most are free. Daily, hours vary by event. From downtown, take U.S. 11 north, turn left on Va. 39 ⅒ mile north of I-64; the center is 1 mile on the left.

Impressions

Let us cross the river and rest under the shade of the trees.
—Stonewall Jackson's last words,
May 10, 1863

Virginia Military Institute Museum ★★ This museum tracing VMI's history is well worth a visit, especially to see the raincoat Stonewall Jackson was wearing when his own men accidentally shot him at Chancellorsville (the bullet hole is in the upper left shoulder) and—thanks to taxidermy—Jackson's unflappable war horse, Little Sorrel. Also here is one of Gen. George S. Patton's shiny helmet liners. Patton graduated from VMI in 1907. The museum resides in the basement of **Jackson Memorial Hall,** the school's auditorium, which was built in 1915 with federal funds paid in partial compensation for the Union army's burning the school after its cadets helped defeat Federal troops at the Battle of New Market in May 1864. Be sure to step into the auditorium, where B. West Clinedinst's oversize oil painting of the cadets' heroic Civil War charge looms over the stage.

In Jackson Memorial Hall at the Virginia Military Institute, 415 Letcher Ave. $©$ **540/464-7334.** www.vmi.edu/museum. Free admission; $5 donation suggested. Daily 9am–5pm. Closed New Year's Day, Thanksgiving, and Christmas week.

The Natural Bridge ★★★

Thomas Jefferson called this hugely impressive limestone formation "the most sublime of nature's works . . . so beautiful an arch, so elevated, so light and springing, as it were, up to heaven." The bridge was part of a 157-acre estate Jefferson acquired in 1774 from King George III. In the early 1750s it was included in the survey of western Virginia carried out by George Washington, who carved his initials into the face of the sheer stone wall and beside Cedar Creek at the base of the gorge. This geological oddity dramatically rises 215 feet above the creek; its span is 90 feet long and spreads at its widest to 150 feet. The Monacan Indian tribes worshiped it as "the bridge of God." Today, it is also the bridge of man, as U.S. 11 passes over it.

The bridge itself and its **Monacan Indian Living History Village** are worth seeing, but the surroundings seem like a borderline tourist trap. That's not to say you and the children can't eat up a day here, or that the youngsters won't thoroughly enjoy themselves in the deepest caverns on the East Coast (45-min. tours depart every 30 min.), at the toy, wax, and monster museums, as well as exploring Dinosaur Kingdom. There's also an independently operated zoo up the road, but the nearby Virginia Safari Park (see "On Safari in Virginia," below) is more fun. Also here: a department store–size souvenir shop, a restaurant, and a hotel.

There are no guided tours, but there are interpreters under the bridge and in the Monacan village. The bridge is a steep ¼-mile downhill walk from the visitor center, but shuttle buses will take you down and back up. From there, the 1-mile-long **Cedar Creek Trail** descends past a cave and a waterfall. During summer, a 45-minute sound-and-light show begins at dusk beneath the bridge.

Admission to the bridge, Monacan village, the show, the caverns, and the wax and toy museums is $28 for adults and $16 for children 5 to 12. Tickets without the caverns cost $18 for adults and $10 for children 5 to 12. Caverns-only tickets are $14 adults and $9 for kids 5 to 12. The bridge is open daily from 8am to dusk. The attractions are open daily 8am to sunset during summer and 8am to 5pm the rest of the year. You can see the bridge itself until dusk.

The bridge is 12 miles south of Lexington on U.S. 11. For more information, or to book a hotel room or campsite here, contact **Natural Bridge,** 15 Appledore Lane (PO Box 57), Natural Bridge, VA 24578 ($©$ **800/533-1410** or 540/291-2121; fax 540/291-1896; www.naturalbridgeva.com).

Outdoor Activities

The Lexington Visitor Center's website (www.lexingtonvirginia.com; see "Essentials," above) has an outdoor section with a complete rundown of the area's active pursuits.

On Safari in Virginia

It's a far cry from the real Serengeti, but the **Virginia Safari Park ★★★**, 8 miles south of Lexington at Exit 180 off I-81 (© **540/291-3205;** www.virginiasafari park.com), has zebras, giraffes, antelopes, monkeys, emus, deer, elk, and bison among the more than 1,000 animals roaming the hills between Lexington and Natural Bridge. There's even a petting area with giraffes, goats, lambs, and pigs. Tigers, cheetahs, serval cats, and other predators live in cages. The best way to see the grazing beasts is on a 1-hour wagon ride that's offered at 11:30am, 1pm and 3pm daily during summer and on weekends during spring and autumn. At other times you merely drive your own vehicle through the park. Admission is $15 for adults, $14 for seniors, and $10 for children 3 to 12. The park is open from mid-March to Thanksgiving weekend daily 9am to 5pm.

An avid outdoorsman, co-host John Roberts at **Llewellyn Lodge** runs fly-fishing trips and hiking expeditions into the hills and mountains (see "Where to Stay," below).

CANOEING, KAYAKING & RAFTING The Maury River, which runs through Lexington, provides some of Virginia's best white-water rafting and kayaking, especially through the Goshen Pass, on Va. 39 northwest of town. The visitor center has info on several put-in spots, or you can rent gear or explore the Maury and James rivers with **Wilderness Canoe Company,** 631 James River Rd., Natural Bridge Station, VA 24579 (© **540/291-2295;** www.wildernesscanoecampground.com). Call, write, or check the website for schedules and reservations.

HIKING Two linear parks connect to offer hikers and joggers nearly 10 miles of gorgeous trail between Lexington and Buena Vista, a railroad town 7 miles to the southeast. The major link is the **Chessie Nature Trail,** which follows an old railroad bed along the Maury River between Lexington and Buena Vista. No vehicles (including bicycles) are allowed, but you can cross-country ski the trail during winter. The Chessie trail connects to **Woods Creek Trail,** which starts at the Waddell School on Jordan Street and runs down to the banks of the Maury. Both trails are open from dawn to dusk. The visitor center has maps and brochures.

There are excellent hiking, mountain-biking, horseback-riding, and all-terrain-vehicle trails in the **George Washington National Forest** (www.fs.fed.us), which encompasses much of the Blue Ridge Mountains east of Lexington. Small children might not be able to make it, but the rest of the family will enjoy the 3-mile trail up to **Crabtree Falls,** a series of cascades tumbling 1,200 feet down the mountain (it's the highest waterfall in Virginia). Heartier hikers can scale up to the Appalachian Trail on the mountaintop. Crabtree Falls is on Va. 56 east of the Blue Ridge Parkway; from Lexington, go north on I-81 to Steeles Tavern (Exit 205), then east on Va. 56.

Shopping

Lexington's charming 19th-century downtown offers more than a dozen interesting shops and art galleries, most of them on Main Street and on the blocks of Washington and Nelson streets between Main and Jefferson streets. Among the best is **Artists in Cahoots,** a cooperative venture run by local artists and craftspeople in the 1789 Alexander-Witherow House, at the corner of Main and Washington streets (© **540/464-1147;** www.artistsincahoots.com). It features an outstanding selection of paintings, sculptures, wood and metal crafts, hand-painted silk scarves, handblown glass, Shaker-style furniture, photographs, prints, decoys, stained glass, and jewelry. **Virginia Born & Bred,** 16 W. Washington St. ((?) **540/463-1832**), has made-in-Virginia gifts. Collectibles hunters will find an amazing array of old and not-so-old stuff literally crammed into the **Second Hand Shop,** 7 S. Jefferson St. ((?) **540/463-7559**), between Washington and Nelson streets.

Where to Stay

Wherever you choose to stay, rooms will be difficult to find, and rates will be highest, during football weekends, graduation, and other activities at Washington and Lee University and at Virginia Military Institute, as well as during major shows at the Virginia Horse Center.

Lexington has several chain motels, especially at the intersection of U.S. 11 and I-64 (Exit 55), 1½ miles north of downtown. The 100-unit **Best Western Inn at Hunt Ridge,** 25 Willow Springs Rd./Va. 39 (www.dominionlodging.com; (?) 800/464-1501 or 540/464-1500), is the only full-service hotel among them, offering a restaurant, bar, limited room service, indoor-outdoor pool, and fine mountain views. Try to get one of its six rooms with balconies.

Nearby are **Best Western Lexington Inn** (www.dominionlodging.com; (?) 800/780-7234 or 540/458-3020); **Comfort Inn–Virginia Horse Center** (www.dominionlodging.com; (?) 800/628-1956 or 540/463-7311), **Country Inn & Suites** (www.countryinns.com; (?) 800/456-4000 or 540/464-9000), **Econo Lodge** ((?) 800/446-6900 or 540/463-7371), **Holiday Inn Express** (www.dominionlodging.com; (?) 800/465-4329 or 540/463-7351), **Super 8** (www.super8.com; (?) 800/800-8000 or 540/463-7858); and **Wingate by Wyndham** (www.wingatehotels.com; (?) 800/228-1000).

Hampton Inn Col Alto ★★ This is no ordinary Hampton Inn: Col Alto is an 1827 manor house built on a plantation that was once on the outskirts of town. The carefully renovated mansion now houses 10 bedrooms comparable to deluxe country inns or B&Bs. An interior designer individually decorated these luxurious quarters with made-in-Virginia linens and reproduction antiques. Accommodations range from huge, light-filled rooms on the front of the house to smaller, more private ones in the rear. One unit even has a semi-round "fan" window of the style favored by Thomas Jefferson. Manor house guests can choose to have breakfast and the morning newspaper delivered to their rooms. Rooms in the L-shaped motel wing are somewhat larger than average and have microwave ovens, coffeemakers, robes, and irons and ironing boards; some have balconies overlooking a courtyard with outdoor swimming pool and whirlpool. Guests in both wings get complimentary breakfasts in the original dining room.

401 E. Nelson St., Lexington, VA 24450. www.hamptoninn.com/hi/lexington-historic. (?) **800/426-7866** or 540/463-2223. Fax 540/463-9707. 86 units. $139–$169 double motel room; $215–$265 double manor house. Rates include breakfast. AE, DC, DISC, MC, V. **Amenities:** Health club; Jacuzzi; pool. In room: A/C, TV, hair dryer, Wi-Fi.

The Sheridan Livery Inn This downtown inn occupies a large barn-size structure built in 1887 by John Sheridan to house his stable and carriage business. The architecture has dictated spacious rooms, very high ceilings, tall windows, and 25 steps leading to the second floor (there is no elevator, so request a first-level unit if you have trouble climbing stairs). Although traditional furniture creates comfort and elegance in the units, this is not an antiques-laden inn. Seven of the 12 units have both a queen- and full-size bed, while two others have a king bed and sofa. Three suites have separate living rooms with sleeper sofas, and two of these also have tiny wrought-iron balconies. There are no public areas here; instead, guests are diverted to the **Sheridan Inn Restaurant** (see below).

35 N. Main St., Lexington, VA 24450. www.sheridanliveryinn.com. ℂ **540/464-1887.** Fax 540/464-1817. 12 units. $89–$170 double. Rates include continental breakfast. AE, DISC, MC, V. **Amenities:** Restaurant; bar. *In room:* A/C, TV, fridge (in some), hair dryer, Wi-Fi (in most).

BED & BREAKFASTS

In addition to the one mentioned below, Lexington has several other B&Bs; the visitor center offers a complete list.

A B&B at Llewellyn Lodge ★ ✦   A brick Colonial-style house, John and Ellen Roberts' Llewellyn Lodge is within easy walking distance of all of Lexington's historic sites. On the first floor are a cozy sitting room with working fireplace and a TV room. Guest rooms are decorated in exceptionally attractive color schemes. All rooms have ceiling fans, and four have TVs. A screened gazebo out back has a fan, too. Co-host John has hiked every trail and fished every stream in the Blue Ridge Mountains; he organizes fly-fishing and hiking expeditions (see "Outdoor Activities," above).

603 S. Main St., Lexington, VA 24450. www.llodge.com. ℂ **800/882-1145** or 540/463-3235. Fax 540/463-3235. 6 units (all with private bathroom). $89–$199 double. Rates include full breakfast. AE, DISC, MC, V. *In room:* A/C, TV (in most), Wi-Fi.

Where to Eat

If your sweet tooth starts aching while you're walking around town, stop at **Sweet Things,** 106 W. Washington St., between Jefferson Street and Lee Avenue (ℂ **540/463-6055**), for a cone or cup of "designer" ice cream. It's open Monday to Thursday noon to 9:30pm, Friday to Saturday noon to 10pm, and Sunday 2 to 9:30pm.

The **Lexington Coffee Shop,** 9 W. Washington St. (ℂ **540/464-6586**), is a quintessential, college-town coffeehouse with a selection of exotic brews plus bagels and pastries. It's open Monday to Friday 7am to 5:30pm, Saturday 8am to 5pm, and Sunday 8am to 3pm.

You can't miss noticing **Macado's,** 30 N. Main St. (ℂ **540/463-8200**), occupying the Willson-Walker House, an 1820 Greek-revival building with big front porches both upstairs and down. It's an incongruous home for this casual and often noisy sports bar. It's open daily 8pm to 1am.

Bistro on Main ★ AMERICAN   High-quality photographs—all for sale—decorate the walls of this storefront bistro offering a mix of cuisines. A light-fare list ranging from burgers to a four-cheese lasagna is available after 9pm, while the wide-ranging regular dinner menu offers shrimp and grits in a low-country wine-and-cream sauce, chicken or steak fajitas, grilled New York steak, and vegetarian grilled Portobello mushrooms with tomato, spinach, and Monterrey jack with a roasted pepper sauce. The crab cakes are unimpressive.

8 N. Main St. ℂ **540/464-4888.** www.bistro-lexington.com. Reservations recommended. Main courses $12–$24; light fare $9–$12. MC, V. Tues–Sat 11:30am–2:30pm and 5–9pm (light fare to 10pm Tues–Thurs, to 11pm Fri–Sat); Sun brunch 11am–2pm.

Blue Sky DELI/BAKERY   Everything is made from scratch at this deli, which is the outlet for a local artisan bakery. The focaccia is excellent for sandwiches or as accompaniment for fresh salads and very good soups. Breakfast features pastries, bagels, and gourmet coffees and teas. Vegetarians have several choices here. Order at the counter in the art-filled room.

125 W. Nelson St. ✆ **540/463-6546.** Most items $6–$9. MC, V. Daily 7:30am–4:30pm (to 3:30pm in summer).

Healthy Foods Coop & Counter Culture Café VEGETARIAN/VEGAN
This store has been selling natural and organic groceries since 1976. Some of the fresh produce is turned into vegetarian and vegan lunches by the cafe in the rear. The daily menu might offer a hummous plate or black bean curry with vegetables. It's all very fresh and tasty.

110 W. Washington St. ✆ **540/463-6954.** www.healthyfoodscoop.org. Most items $6–$7.50. AE, DISC, MC, V. Cafe Mon–Sat 11am–2pm. Store Mon–Fri 9am–6pm, Sat 9am–5pm.

A Joyful Spirit Cafe 🍴 DELI   This bright, lively, order-at-the-counter restaurant is one of the best places in town for a joyful combination of flavors for salads, sandwiches, and wraps. Most ingredients are fresh, many right from the farm. If you're lucky you can claim one of the two tables out on the sidewalk. There's often live music during weekend evening hours.

26 S. Main St. ✆ **540/463-4191.** Reservations not accepted. Sandwiches and salads $3.50–$7. AE, DISC, MC, V. Mon–Wed 11am–3pm; Thurs 11am–3pm and 6–10pm; Fri–Sat 9:30am–3pm and 6–10pm; Sun 11am–3pm.

The Palms AMERICAN   With neon palms in its storefront window, this popular pub draws town and gown residents alike with its substantial (if uninspired) fare, sports TVs, and friendly bar. At lunch or dinner, the hearty burgers will not disappoint. Deli sandwiches run the gamut from roast beef to smoked turkey. Dinner entrees include choices like baby back ribs, in-house cut steaks, steamed shrimp, and pastas. The building was constructed in 1836 as a debating hall and public library. You can still get into lively debates at the friendly bar.

101 W. Nelson St. ✆ **540/463-7911.** Reservations not accepted. Sandwiches, burgers, and salads $7–$9; main courses $9–$20. AE, DISC, MC, V. Mon–Sat 11:30am–1am; Sun noon–11pm.

The Red Hen ★ AMERICAN   This charming establishment, in a small red building dating to 1898, was Lexington's first farm-to-table restaurant. Founder John Blackburn requires his executive chef to use fresh ingredients culled from some of the top local farms. As a result, the menu changes nightly, featuring dishes such as local duck breast served with grits from Wades Mill and local pumpkin, wax beans, and cherry tomatoes. There are 26 indoor seats plus more outside in warm weather.

11 E. Washington St. ✆ **540/464-4401.** www.redhenlex.com. Reservations recommended. Main courses $20–$25. AE, MC, V. Tues–Sat 5–9pm.

The Sheridan Livery Inn Restaurant AMERICAN   Other than Macado's sports bar (see above), the big covered patio of this restaurant at the rear of the Sheridan Livery Inn is downtown's only place with outdoor dining. The kitchen had been limping along until young chef Franky Benincasa (son of co-owners Ugo and Gina Benincasa) and his wife, Meredith, sold their restaurant in Charlottesville and returned home to take over here. Frankie's main courses are best when he's cooking in the South Carolina Low Country style, such as shrimp and sausage over cheese grits. The grilled rainbow trout was accompanied by tasty braised collards over hopping John (that's black-eyed peas and rice). Sandwiches, burgers, and salads are available all day.

In the Sheridan Livery Inn, 35 N. Main St. ✆ **540/464-1887.** www.sheridanliveryinn.com. Sandwiches $7.50–$13; main courses $16–$26. AE, DISC, MC, V. Daily 11am–9pm.

Southern Inn ★ AMERICAN   Crisp linen adorns the plain wooden booths at this former down-home-style Southern restaurant (note the 1950s neon sign out front). You can order excellent sandwiches such as Dijon and tarragon chicken salad, and the regular menu features comfort food such as an excellent rendition of Mom's meatloaf, but the real stars here are specials like sea scallops sautéed with garlic and herb butter, and braised lamb shanks with herb risotto. There's an excellent wine list featuring Virginia vintages. The small but lively pub next door serves the same fare and attracts a more affluent crowd than the Palms (see above).

37 S. Main St. ℂ **540/463-3612.** www.southerninn.com. Reservations recommended. Sandwiches $11–$13; main courses $17–$32. AE, MC, V. Mon–Tues 5–10pm; Wed–Sat 11:30am–10pm; Sun 11:30am–9pm.

Lexington After Dark

The ruins of an old limestone kiln provide the backdrop for the open-air **Theater at Lime Kiln ★★**, 607 Borden Rd., off U.S. 60 W. (ℂ **540/436-7088;** www.theater atlimekiln.com), which presents concerts from March through September.

Join W&L students and faculty on campus for famous visiting artists in concerts, plays, and recitals in the **Lenfest Center for the Performing Arts** (ℂ **540/458-8000;** http://lenfest.wlu.edu). The schedule is released prior to each school year.

You can also relive the 1950s at **Hull's Drive-In,** 4 miles north of downtown on U.S. 11 (ℂ **540/436-2621;** www.hullsdrivein.com), one of the nation's few remaining outdoor movie theaters. It shows double features Friday, Saturday, and Sunday nights from April through October.

ROANOKE & THE SOUTHWEST HIGHLANDS

Y ou soon notice after leaving the art-loving, railroad-oriented city of Roanoke that I-81 begins climbing into the mountains as it heads into the Southwest Highlands, Virginia's increasingly narrow "tail" hemmed in by West Virginia, Kentucky, Tennessee, and North Carolina. You don't come down on the other side of the mountains, however, for I-81 deposits you instead in the Great Valley of Virginia, whose floor averages 2,000 feet in altitude. Just as they delineate the Shenandoah Valley, the Blue Ridge Mountains form the eastern boundary of the Southwest Highlands. And just as Skyline Drive follows the crest of those mountains east of the Shenandoah, here it's the Blue Ridge Parkway.

I should say the parkway follows the mountains, not their crest, for while peaks above 4,000 feet are rare in the Shenandoah National Park, here they regularly exceed that altitude, with Mount Rogers reaching 5,729 feet, the highest point in Virginia.

Mount Rogers National Recreation Area rivals the Shenandoah National Park with 300 miles of hiking and riding trails, including a stretch of the Appalachian Trail. On its edges, the Virginia Creeper and New River trails take hikers and bikers along old railroad beds.

The region's history includes Daniel Boone following the Wilderness Road through the mountains, plateaus, and hollows to Cumberland Gap and on into Kentucky. Gorgeous Abingdon and other small towns still have log cabins from those days.

The Highlanders have preserved their traditional arts, crafts, and renowned mountain music. Abingdon hosts both Virginia's official state theater and the Virginia Highlands Festival, one of America's top annual arts-and-crafts shows. The famous Carter family makes mountain music at tiny Maces Spring, and fiddlers from around the world gather every August for their old-time convention at Galax.

Whether you love history, drama, music, arts, crafts, the great outdoors, or all of the above, you will likely be enchanted with Virginia's beautiful Southwest Highlands.

Getting There & Getting Around

As is true in most parts of Virginia, traveling by **car** is the only way to go. Truck-infested I-81 runs the entire length of the highlands and is its major thoroughfare. U.S. 11 follows I-81, and the Blue Ridge Parkway parallels it to the east. I-77 cuts north-south through the center of the region (the section from Wytheville north to Bluefield, West Virginia, is one of America's most scenic interstates). Otherwise, most byways in the region are mountain roads—narrow, winding, and sometimes steep—so give yourself ample time to reach your destination.

The area's air gateway is **Roanoke Regional Airport.** The nearest **Amtrak** (© **800/872-7245;** www.amtrak.com) stations are in Lynchburg and Clifton Forge, each about 50 miles from Roanoke. See "Getting There" under "Roanoke: City Below a Star," below.

THE BLUE RIDGE PARKWAY ★

Maintained by the U.S. National Park Service, the Blue Ridge Parkway is in some respects a continuation of the 105-mile-long Skyline Drive. Taking up where the Shenandoah National Park ends, it runs another 469 miles southwest through Virginia's Blue Ridge Mountains to the Great Smoky Mountains National Park in North Carolina, thus linking these scenic wonders. Magnificent vistas and the natural beauty of the forests, wildlife, and wildflowers combine with pioneer history and mountain music to make this a beautiful and fascinating route.

Unlike Skyline Drive, which is surrounded by wilderness for its entire length, in many places the parkway runs through mountain meadows and farmland as well as forests (some, but not all, national forests). Nature hikes, camping, and other activities are largely confined to the visitor centers and to more than 200 overlooks. There are about 100 **hiking trails** along the route, including the Appalachian Trail, which parallels the parkway from Mile 0 to about Mile 103.

In Virginia, the 62-mile stretch between Otter Creek and Roanoke Mountain is the most dramatically scenic part. It crosses the James River Gorge and climbs Apple Orchard Mountain, the highest parkway point in Virginia (elevation 3,950 ft.). At times, the road here runs along the ridgeline, rendering spectacular views down both sides of the mountains at once. It also passes the peaceful Peaks of Otter Lodge, the only hotel actually on Virginia's share of the parkway (p. 179).

South of Roanoke, the parkway runs through the rolling hills of an agricultural plateau, with more meadows and less mountain scenery.

Just the Facts

ACCESS POINTS & ORIENTATION   Unlike Skyline Drive, which has only four entry points, you can get on and off the Blue Ridge Parkway at numerous places. The northern entrance is at the southern end of Skyline Drive, near Waynesboro on U.S. 250 at Exit 99 off I-64. The major access points in Virginia are U.S. 60 east of Buena Vista; U.S. 501 between Buena Vista and Lynchburg (Otter Creek and the James River Gorge); U.S. 460, Va. 24, U.S. 220, and the Mill Mountain Spur near Roanoke; U.S. 58 at Meadows of Dan; and I-77 at Fancy Gap. You can also get up here from Buchanan or Bedford via Va. 43, but note that trucks and trailers (including RVs) are not permitted on the very steep portion of Va. 43 between Buchanan and the parkway.

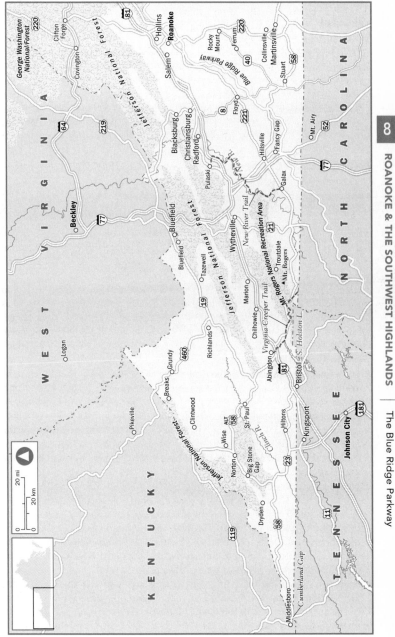

Mile Posts on the west side of the parkway begin with Mile 0 at the northern Rockfish Gap entry and increase as you head south. The North Carolina border is at Mile 218.

INFORMATION For general information, contact the **U.S. National Park Service (NPS),** 199 Hemphill Knob Rd., Asheville, NC 28801 (© **828/298-0398;** www.nps.gov/blri). Ask for a copy of the NPS's brochure with an excellent map of the parkway and the *Parkway Milepost,* a quarterly tabloid newspaper with articles about the parkway and a schedule of events. Both are available at the visitor centers, which also sell books about the parkway.

You can also get an information packet, including a copy of the indispensable *Blue Ridge Parkway Directory & Travel Planner,* from the **Blue Ridge Parkway Association,** PO Box 2136, Asheville, NC 28802-2136 (© **828/298-0398;** www.blueridge parkway.org).

EMERGENCIES Call the National Park Service at © **800/727-5928** in case of emergencies anywhere along the parkway.

FEES, REGULATIONS & BACKCOUNTRY PERMITS There is no fee for using the parkway. The maximum speed limit is 45 mph in rural areas and 35 mph in built-up zones. Bicycles are allowed on paved roads and parking areas, but not on any trails. Camping is permitted in designated areas (see "Camping," below). Fires are permitted in campgrounds and picnic areas only. Hunting is prohibited. Pets must be kept on a leash. No swimming is allowed in parkway ponds and lakes.

VISITOR CENTERS Several visitor centers along the parkway are the focal points of most visitor activities, including ranger programs. Operated by the town of Waynesboro, the **Rockfish Gap Visitor Center** (© **540/943-5187;** www. waynesboro.va.us), at the northern end (Mile 0), is open year-round. Others are closed from November through March. Hours for all are daily 9am to 5pm. Here's a rundown heading south:

○ **Humpback Rocks Visitor Center** (Mile 5.8) has picnic tables, restrooms, and a self-guiding trail to a reconstructed mountain homestead.

○ **James River Visitor Center** (Mile 63.6), near U.S. 501 northwest of Lynchburg, is worth a stop. It has a footbridge that crosses the river to restored canal locks, exhibits, and a nature trail. The nearby Otter Creek wayside has a daytime restaurant and campground.

○ **Peaks of Otter** ★★ (Mile 86), at Va. 43 northwest of Bedford, is the most picturesque visitor center. It has a 2-mile hike to the site of a historic farm, wildlife and Native American exhibits, restrooms, and the Peaks of Otter Lodge (p. 179), which sits beside a gorgeous lake wedged between two cone-shaped mountains—the Peaks of Otter. A trail leads to the top of Sharp Top, the taller of the two at 3,875 feet. Weather permitting, **Sharp Top Bus** runs to within 1,500 feet of the peak. It's a strenuous 1.6-mile hike to the summit, so allow 2½ hours for the total excursion. Needless to say, wear comfortable walking shoes and bring water. The bus runs from early June through October Wednesday to Sunday every hour on the hour from 10am to 4pm. Buy your tickets and water at the camp store (© **540/586-1066**) beside the visitor center. Round-trip fares are $8 for adults and $6 for children ages 12 and under.

○ **Virginia's Explore Park** (Mile 115) is on the grounds of a former living history museum on the outskirts of Roanoke.

- **Rocky Knob** (Mile 167), southeast of Va. 8, has some 15 miles of hiking trails (including the Rock Castle Gorge National Recreational Trail), a comfort station, and a picnic area.
- **Mabry Mill** (Mile 176), between Va. 8 and U.S. 58, has a picturesque gristmill with a giant wheel spanning a little stream. Displays of pioneer life, including crafts demonstrations, are featured and the restored mill still grinds flour. A restaurant, open May through October, adjoins it.

SEASONS   The parkway is at its best during spring, when the wildflowers bloom and leaves are multihued green, and during mid-October, when changing leaves are at their blazing best (and traffic is at its heaviest). Winter is not a good time because most facilities are closed, and snow, ice, and fog can close the road.

ON THE WINE TRAIL   At Mile 171.5, between Va. 8 and U.S. 58 north of Mabry Mill, you can turn off on C.R. 726 and follow the signs to **Château Morrisette,** 287 Winery Rd. SW, Floyd, VA 24091 (✆ **540/593-2865;** www.chateaumorrisette. com), one of the three largest vineyards in Virginia. It produces Black Dog and Our Dog Blue, two of the state's best-known red wines. It's open for tastings and sales Monday through Thursday 10am to 5pm, Friday and Saturday 10am to 6pm, and Sunday 11am to 5pm. A restaurant is open for lunch Wednesday to Sunday April through December and Friday to Saturday from January through March. It serves dinner on Friday and Saturday all year.

MOUNTAIN MUSIC   At Mile 213, the **Blue Ridge Music Center** (✆ **276/236-5309;** www.blueridgemusiccenter.org) celebrates fiddle and banjo music of the sort you can hear at the annual Old Fiddler's Convention in Galax, 6 miles to the north (see "Virginia Calendar of Events," in chapter 2). The center is open daily 9am to 7pm in summer and Wednesday to Sunday 9am to 5pm in spring and autumn. It's closed from November through April. You can stop here during summer and hear mountain music Sunday to Thursday 10am to 4pm. The center also hosts nighttime concerts by local musicians in its amphitheater.

Camping

The visitor centers at **Otter Creek,** Mile 61 (✆ **804/299-5125**); **Peaks of Otter,** Mile 86 (✆ **540/586-4357**); **Roanoke Mountain,** Mile 120 (✆ **540/982-9242**); and **Rocky Knob,** Mile 167 (✆ **540/745-9664**), all have campgrounds. The **Roanoke Mountain campground** is actually on Mill Mountain, about 1 mile west of the parkway above Roanoke (see "Roanoke: City Below a Star," below).

Campgrounds are open from about May 1 to early November, depending on weather conditions. Drinking water and restrooms are available, but shower and laundry facilities are not. There are tent and trailer sites, but none have utility connections. Sites cost $16 a night. Interagency Senior Pass holders get a 50% discount. Daily permits are valid only at the campground where purchased.

Cabins are available at **Rocky Knob Cabins,** Meadows of Dan, VA 24120 (✆ **540/593-3903**).

You can call or make reservations at www.recreation.gov.

Accommodations

Peaks of Otter Lodge ★ 🍴   Split-rail fences and small footbridges add to the picturesque beauty of this serene, lakeside lodge nestled in a gorgeous valley between the two Peaks of Otter. On a grassy slope overlooking the lake, accommodations are in motel-like units a 600- to 900-foot walk from the main building (bring an umbrella and insect repellent). Virtually identical, the rooms have private balconies or terraces to maximize the splendid view. Only the lodge rooms equipped for guests with disabilities have TVs, and none has a phone. The lodge has no Wi-Fi, and cellphone reception is spotty, so you really are away from it all up here. Reservations are accepted beginning October 1 for the *next* year's fall foliage season. The casual, family-style Lakeview Restaurant is open daily from 7:30am to 8:30pm. The parkway's Peaks of Otter visitor center, with its ranger programs and shuttle bus up Sharp Top Mountain, is within walking distance (see "Just the Facts," above).

Milepost 86 (PO Box 489), Bedford, VA 24523. www.peaksofotter.com. © **800/542-5927** or 540/586-1081. Fax 540/586-4420. 63 units. $90–$140 double. MC, V. **Amenities:** Restaurant; bar. *In room:* A/C, TV (in rooms equipped for those w/limited mobility).

ROANOKE: STAR CITY ★

54 miles SW of Lexington; 74 miles NE of Wytheville; 193 miles SW of Richmond; 251 miles SW of Washington, D.C.

Sprawling across the floor of the Roanoke Valley and surrounded by mountains, Virginia's largest metropolitan area west of Richmond likes to call itself the "Capital of the Blue Ridge." It's also known as "Star City," for the huge lighted star overlooking the city from Mill Mountain, which stands between it and the Blue Ridge Parkway.

There was no star on the mountain when Colonial explorers followed the Roanoke River gorge through the Blue Ridge Mountains in the 18th century. They established several settlements in the Roanoke Valley, including one named Big Lick. When the Norfolk and Western Railroad arrived in the 1880s and laid out a town for future development, it decided that *Roanoke*—a Native American word for "shell money"— was a more prosperous-sounding name for the new city.

Roanoke is still a major railroad junction, as the busy tracks cutting through downtown will attest. It honors this iron-horse heritage at two excellent museums, one full of extraordinary photographs capturing the last days of the steam locomotive, the other displaying steam engines, cabooses, and other railway cars from that bygone era. An informative "Railwalk" follows the tracks between the two museums. When seen together, surely these two railroad museums are among the very best in the country.

Nearby is the ultramodern Taubman Museum of Art, the newest addition to a downtown that launched itself on a renaissance long before Norfolk and other Virginia cities undertook to reclaim their central areas. Notable to visitors is the restored Market Square, where farmers sell fresh produce—and everyone else comes to wine and dine.

Essentials

VISITOR INFORMATION

Contact the **Roanoke Valley Visitors Center,** 101 Shenandoah Ave. NE, Roanoke, VA 24016 (© **800/635-5535** or 540/342-6025; fax 540/342-7119; www.visit roanokeva.com), in the restored Norfolk & Western Railway Passenger Station (which it shares with the O. Winston Link Museum; p. 182). The station sits across the tracks from Market Square in front of the Hotel Roanoke & Conference Center. The bureau's visitor center is the best place to pick up maps and brochures for walking and biking tours before exploring Roanoke, and you can make same-day hotel reservations

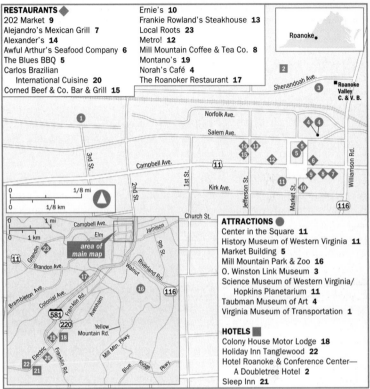

RESTAURANTS ◆
202 Market **9**
Alejandro's Mexican Grill **7**
Alexander's **14**
Awful Arthur's Seafood Company **6**
The Blues BBQ **5**
Carlos Brazilian
    International Cuisine **20**
Corned Beef & Co. Bar & Grill **15**
Ernie's **10**
Frankie Rowland's Steakhouse **13**
Local Roots **23**
Metro! **12**
Mill Mountain Coffee & Tea Co. **8**
Montano's **19**
Norah's Café **4**
The Roanoker Restaurant **17**

ATTRACTIONS ●
Center in the Square **11**
History Museum of Western Virginia **11**
Market Building **5**
Mill Mountain Park & Zoo **16**
O. Winston Link Museum **3**
Science Museum of Western Virginia/
    Hopkins Planetarium **11**
Taubman Museum of Art **4**
Virginia Museum of Transportation **1**

HOTELS ■
Colony House Motor Lodge **18**
Holiday Inn Tanglewood **22**
Hotel Roanoke & Conference Center—
    A Doubletree Hotel **2**
Sleep Inn **21**

here. Be sure to go behind the staff desk for a look at a one-eighth-scale model of steam locomotive No. 1218. The center is open daily 9am to 5pm.

GETTING THERE

BY PLANE **Roanoke Regional Airport** (ROA; ⓒ **540/362-1999;** www. roanokeairport.com), 5½ miles northwest of downtown off Hershberger Road (Exit 3E off I-581), is served by Allegiant Air, Delta, United, and US Airways. The major car-rental units have booths on-site. **Roanoke Airport Transportation Service** (ⓒ **800/228-1958** or 540/345-7710; www.roanokeats.com) runs vans to downtown, to Blacksburg, and to other highland points as far away as Abingdon (see "Abingdon: A Show-Stopping Town," later in the chapter) and throughout the Shenandoah Valley (see chapter 7). If you're not in a hurry, catch the **Smartway Bus** (ⓒ **800/388-7005** or 540/982-6622; www.smartwaybus.com), an express service that stops at the airport nine times a day Monday through Saturday on its way between Roanoke and Blacksburg. The one-way fare to downtown is $3.

BY CAR From I-81, take I-581 (Exit 143) south into the heart of Roanoke. I-581 becomes U.S. 220; together, they form an expressway through town. The Blue Ridge Parkway runs along the top of the mountains east of the city; the major Roanoke exits are at U.S. 460, Va. 24, the Mill Mountain Spur Road (at Mile 120), and U.S. 220.

8

ROANOKE & THE SOUTHWEST HIGHLANDS

Roanoke: Star City

BY TRAIN The nearest **Amtrak** (📞 **800/872-7245;** www.amtrak.com) stations are at Lynchburg and Clifton Forge, each about 50 miles from Roanoke. It's easiest to connect from Lynchburg by the **Smartway Connection** (📞 **800/388-7005** or 540/982-6622; www.smartwaybus.com), an express bus service between the Lynchburg Amtrak station and the Roanoke Civic Center. The one-way fare is $4, exact change required. Reservations are not required but call for schedules.

GETTING AROUND

Yellow Cab (📞 **540/345-7711**) is the largest taxi company here. **Valley Metro** (📞 **540/982-2222;** www.valleymetro.com) provides public bus service Monday to Saturday 5:45am to 8:45pm. The downtown transfer point is Campbell Court, 17 W. Campbell Ave. Its free **Star Line Trolley** travels along Jefferson Street south to the Carilion Roanoke Memorial Hospital complex every 15 minutes Monday to Friday 7am to 7pm. The visitor center distributes free route maps.

Exploring Market Square

Market Square, in the center of downtown at Market Street and Campbell Avenue, is Roanoke's answer to Alexandria's Old Town and Richmond's Shockoe Slip. As they have for more than a century, stands and shops at the **Historic City Market** display plants, flowers, fresh fruits and vegetables, dairy and eggs, and farm-cured meats (Sat morning is the best time to visit). Nearby, restored Victorian-era storefronts house an eclectic mix of trendy restaurants, gift shops, art galleries, antiques dealers, and an Orvis store.

At the center is the **Market Building.** Constructed of redbrick in 1922 and recently renovated, it now houses fast-food restaurants and specialty shops. It's open Monday to Thursday 11am to 7pm, Friday to Saturday 11am to 9pm, and Sunday noon to 3pm.

Once the Shenandoah Hotel, on Market Square at Campbell Avenue, the **Center in the Square** is another renovation project (📞 540/342-5700; www.centerinthesquare.org). When it reopens in 2013 after a complete overhaul, it will once again be home to the **History Museum of Western Virginia** (📞 540/342-5770; www.history-museum.org), the **Science Museum of Western Virginia** (📞 540/342-5710; www.smwv.org), the **Harrison Museum of African American Culture** (📞 540/857-4395; www.harrisonmuseum.com), and the **Mill Mountain Theatre** (www.millmountain.org). Meanwhile, most of their exhibits are in storage or limited temporary quarters.

An enclosed walkway leads over the railroad tracks from Market Square to the visitor center and the O. Winston Link Museum, both in the city's restored train station which sits in front of the Hotel Roanoke & Conference Center, itself a sightseeing attraction (p. 185).

Also from Market Square, you can follow the **David S. and Susan S. Goode Railwalk** beside the tracks to the Virginia Museum of Transportation.

The Top Attractions

O. Winston Link Museum ★★★ In the restored Norfolk & Western Railway Passenger Station, this marvelous museum displays the extraordinary black-and-white railroad photography of the late O. Winston Link. Born in Brooklyn, Link took his first photos of N&W locomotives in 1955, and for the next 5 years, he traced the railroad's tracks, taking thousands of pictures of smoking locomotives just before the end of the era of steam. The museum, which he helped design, is both art gallery and

Built in 1905, Roanoke's Norfolk & Western Railway Passenger Station not only houses the visitor center and the O. Winston Link Museum, but it's also home to the **Raymond Loewy Gallery.** Known as "the father of industrial design," Loewy remodeled the station in 1949 but is better known for the slenderized Coca-Cola bottle, the Studebaker Avanti automobile, and logos for Exxon, Shell, and Nabisco, all displayed here. Admission to the gallery is free; it's open daily 9am to 5pm.

railroad museum, for many items, such as an original 1930s gasoline pump and parts of a country store, are on display in front of the photos in which they appear. This juxtaposition of art and history makes for one of the most fascinating museums in Virginia. Come here first, and then follow the **David S. and Susan S. Goode Railwalk** along the tracks to the actual locomotives and railway cars on display at the Virginia Museum of Transportation (see below).

101 Shenandoah Ave. (in old train station). ✆ **540/982-5465.** www.linkmuseum.org. Admission $5 adults, $4.50 seniors, $4 children 3–11, free for children 2 and under. Includes admission to History Museum of Western Virginia. Combination tickets (for admission to O. Winston Link Museum and the Virginia Museum of Transportation) $12 adults, $10 seniors, $8 children 3–11, free for children 2 and under. Mar–Dec daily 10am–5pm; Jan–Feb Mon–Sat 10am–5pm, Sun noon–5pm.

Taubman Museum of Art ★★ This strikingly modern structure of metal and glass stands in stark contrast to the redbrick facades dominating downtown Roanoke. It was designed by Los Angeles–based architect Randall Stout, who said he wanted to "evoke rolling mountains in the roof forms, river gorges in the circulation zones, and rock strata in the facades." Some traditional-minded Roanokers probably see no more mountains and river gorges than some Sydney residents see sails in their famed opera house down under. Those local controversies notwithstanding, the building itself is worth a visit. Inside, children will enjoy the interactive Art Venture, where they can perform in their own puppet show. Upstairs, the Fralin Center for American Art hosts visiting exhibitions and houses the museum's own collection, including John Singer Sargent's 1888 portrait of Mrs. George Gribble, affectionately known as "Norah"—also the name of the museum's fine cafe (p. 187). The museum store is excellent.

110 Salem Ave. ✆ **540/342-5760.** www.taubmanmuseum.org. Admission $7 adults, $6 seniors, $3.75 children 5–13, free for children 4 and under. Tues–Sat 10am–5pm, Sun noon–5pm.

Virginia Museum of Transportation ★★ ☺ In a restored freight depot, this wide-ranging museum has aviation and automotive exhibits, but its best feature is an extraordinary collection of vintage locomotives, passenger and mail cars, and cabooses on display out back. Everyone can climb aboard some of them, and kids can ride model trains, cars, and a helicopter in the playground. Inside, they will get a kick out of a gargantuan and very real model railroad. The oral history exhibit featuring African Americans talking about working on the railroad is worth an adult stop. You'll need 1 to 2½ hours to thoroughly digest all the exhibits.

303 Norfolk Ave. (at 3rd St.). ✆ **540/342-5670.** www.vmt.org. Admission $8 adults, $7 seniors, $6 children 3–11, free for children 2 and under. Combination tickets (for admission to Virginia Museum of Transportation and O. Winston Link Museum) $12 adults, $10 seniors, $8 children 3–11, free for children 2 and under. Mon–Sat 10am–5pm; Sun 1–5pm. Rail yard closes 30 min. earlier.

Attractions on Mill Mountain

Situated between the city and the Blue Ridge Parkway, Mill Mountain offers panoramic views over Roanoke Valley. The two main attractions are in **Mill Mountain Park,** on the Mill Mountain Parkway Spur, a winding road that leaves the Blue Ridge Parkway at Mile 120. Local citizens know they're home when they see the red, white, and blue neon **Roanoke Star** on the mountain. Erected in 1949 as a civic project, it stands 89 feet tall, uses 2,000 feet of neon tubing, and is visible from most parts of the city. Stop at the base for a magnificent view over the city and valley.

Also here is the **Discovery Center** (✆ **540/853-1236;** www.roanokeva.gov/outdoors), which explains the wildlife and history of the mountain. Its honeybee exhibit is worth seeing. Admission is free. It's open from April to October Monday to Saturday 10am to 5pm. Call for winter hours.

From downtown, take Jefferson Street south and turn left on Walnut Avenue, which becomes the J.P. Fishburn Parkway and intersects the Mill Mountain Parkway Spur at the entry to Mill Mountain Park.

Mill Mountain Zoo ☺   This small zoo is home to more than 50 animal species, including snow leopards, monkeys, prairie dogs, hawks, red pandas, and Japanese macaques. The animals are caged, so don't come up here if that bothers you. An open-air, narrow-gauge train runs around the periphery, giving access to red wolves and deer. You'll need about 1½ hours up here. The zoo is about a 5-minute walk from the parking lot. It's much more scenic and shady to take the pathway through the wildflower garden than the paved road.

In Mill Mountain Park, Mill Mountain Pkwy. Spur. ✆ **540/343-3241.** www.mmzoo.org. Admission $7.50 adults, $5 children 3–11, free for children 2 and under. Train rides $2. Apr–Nov 10am–4:30pm. Call for winter hours. Closed New Year's Day, Thanksgiving, and Christmas.

Where to Stay

The most convenient chain hotel choices to the Blue Ridge Parkway include the **Holiday Inn Tanglewood-Roanoke** (www.holidayinn.com; ✆ 800/465-4329 or 540/774-4400) and a **Sleep Inn Tanglewood** (www.sleepinn.com; ✆ 800/628-1929 or 540/772-1500). They are in a large commercial area centered around Tanglewood Mall and are near Carlos Brazilian International Cusine and Montano's International Restaurant (see "Where to Eat," below)

The area around the airport and Valley View Mall has many chain hotels in all price ranges. Among the best is the recently renovated, California-style **Sheraton Roanoke Hotel & Conference Center** (www.sheraton.com/Roanoke; ✆ 540/563-9300).

Bed-and-breakfasts near downtown include the **Black Lantern Inn,** 1526 Franklin Rd. SW (www.blacklanterninn.com; ✆ 540/206-3441), and **The King George Inn,** 315 King George Ave. (www.kinggeorgeinnbandb.com; ✆ 757/675-4034).

Cambria Suites Roanoke ★   Opened in 2010, this sleek structure stands across Reserve Avenue from a park and near the Carilion Roanoke Memorial Hospital complex. The free Star Line Trolley running along nearby Jefferson Avenue makes it convenient to downtown from 7am to 7pm weekdays, and the hotel provides a free shuttle at other times (you're on your own on weekends). About a third larger than most hotel rooms, every unit has a bedroom and separate living room, both with TVs, and each has a microwave oven. Furnishings are all modern, high-tech style. The lobby level bistro and bar feature Wolfgang Puck products, including complimentary coffee and tea in the lobby. There's a guest laundry, and bikes are for rent.

301 Reserve Ave., Roanoke, VA 24016. www.cambriasuitesroanoke.com. © **888/822-62742** or 540/400-6226. Fax 540/400-6279. 127 units. $99–$189 double. AE, DISC, MC, V. **Amenities:** Restaurant; bar; bike rentals; health club; Jacuzzi; indoor pool; room service (dinner only). *In room:* A/C, TV, fridge, hair dryer, Wi-Fi.

Colony House Motor Lodge ★ 🐾   The same family has owned and operated this clean, well-maintained motel since it was built in 1959. A series of peaked roofs creates cathedral ceilings in some upstairs rooms. All have louvered screen doors that let in fresh air without sacrificing privacy. About half the units are at the rear of the property; they face a steep hillside and get less light but also less traffic noise. All have refrigerators and microwave ovens, and two suites have whirlpool tubs. A roadside outdoor swimming pool has a view of the Kmart across Franklin Road. Continental breakfast is served here. Carlos Brazilian International Cuisine (p. 187), Montano's International Restaurant (p. 187), and other restaurants are nearby.

3560 Franklin Rd. (U.S. 220 Business), Roanoke, VA 24014. www.colonyhousemotorlodge.com. © **866/203-5850** or 540/345-0411. Fax 540/345-1137. 72 units. $70 double. Rates include continental breakfast. AE, DC, DISC, MC, V. From I-581/U.S. 220, exit at Franklin Rd. (U.S. 220 Business), turn left at traffic signal to motel on right. From Blue Ridge Pkwy., take U.S. 220 Business west, exit on Franklin Rd. north to motel on right. **Amenities:** Pool. *In room:* A/C, TV, fridge, Wi-Fi.

Hotel Roanoke & Conference Center—A DoubleTree by Hilton Hotel ★★★   The Norfolk & Western Railroad built this grand Tudor-style hotel in 1882 on a hill overlooking its new town. Heated by steam from the railroad's maintenance shops and cooled by America's first hotel air-conditioning system (using circulating ice water), it became a resort as well as a stopover. Virtually every celebrity passing through Roanoke stayed here. For the locals, it was—and is—*the* place for wedding receptions, reunions, beauty pageants, and other special events. After a magnificent restoration financed in part by the Virginia Tech Foundation and local residents, it is once again *the* place for wedding receptions, reunions, beauty pageants, and other special events. Given the odd shape of the structure, there are 92 room configurations, many with sloping ceilings and gable windows. Some have windows on two sides, while a few others seem like small cottages. The elegant **Regency Room** restaurant is famous for its peanut soup and crab cakes, and pub fare is available in the knotty **Pine Room Pub,** which has a large bar, a TV, and a billiards table.

110 Shenandoah Ave., Roanoke, VA 24016. www.hotelroanoke.com. © **800/222-8733** or 540/985-5900. Fax 540/853-8264. 332 units. $119–$229 double; $239–$750 suite. Packages available. AE, DC, DISC, MC, V. Valet parking $12; self-parking $7. From I-581 south, take Exit 5, cross Wells Ave. into parking lot. **Amenities:** 2 restaurants; 2 bars; concierge; executive or concierge-level rooms; health club; pool; room service. *In room:* A/C, TV, hair dryer, Wi-Fi ($9.95 per 24 hr.).

Where to Eat

Roanoke is one of Virginia's more interesting dining scenes. While you can still get good country cooking here (including wonderful biscuits), young chefs are using flavors their Southern ancestors never imagined, much less tasted.

Many restaurants pay to publish their menus in the *Menu* (www.themenuroanoke. com), published by the *Roanoker Magazine.* Look for copies at the visitor center.

DOWNTOWN RESTAURANTS

Market Square (see "Exploring Market Square," above) is Roanoke's dining center, with the 3 blocks of Campbell Avenue between Williamson Road and Jefferson Street, and the contiguous block of Jefferson Street, offering a host of restaurants catering to many tastes and all pocketbooks. Most post their menus outside, so take a stroll and see what's happening.

A *très* cool bistro and wine bar, **202 Market,** 202 Market Sq. (🕻 540/343-6644; www.202market.net), competes head-to-head with Metro! (see below) as coolest downtown restaurant. The Market Square branch of **Awful Arthur's Seafood Company,** 108 Campbell Ave. (🕻 540/344-2997; www.awfularthursseafood.com), has surprisingly good fish, is open on Sunday, and has sidewalk tables during warm weather. **Alejandro's Mexican Grill,** 125 Campbell Ave. (🕻 540/206-2611; www. alejandrosmexicangrill.com), offers authentic Latin food from a big blackboard menu. For something more down home, the **Blues BBQ Company,** 107 Market Sq. (🕻 540/344-5683; www.bluesbbqco.com), serves a passable version of the vinegary North Carolina version. Sweet tooths are filled with frozen yogurt at the local branch of **Frogurt,** 118 Campell Ave. (🕻 540/857-0007; www.frogurtusa.com).

A block to the west, **Frankie Rowland's Steakhouse,** 104 S. Jefferson St. (🕻 540/527-2333; www.frankierowlandssteakhouse.com), is Roanoke's swankiest purveyor of tender beef. It's across the street from Alexander's (see below).

To check e-mail and get a caffeine fix, try **Mill Mountain Coffee & Tea Co.,** 117 Campbell Ave. (🕻 540/342-9404; www.millmountaincoffee.com), which has fresh salads and deli sandwiches for lunch. If your arteries can handle it, take your morning lard at **Ernie's,** 210 Market St. (🕻 540/342-7100), which opens at 6am Monday through Saturday. Ernie's does not accept credit cards.

Alexander's ★★ AMERICAN   Alexander's was the first trendy restaurant to open, in 1979, during downtown's Renaissance, and it's still one of the best. The pinkish lighting, widely spaced tables, and extraordinarily attentive waitstaff make it a great place for special occasions. Using organic meats, vegetables, and cheeses, the New American menu blends the classics with flavors from Louisiana, Asia, and the Mediterranean.

105 S. Jefferson St. 🕻 **540/982-6983.** www.alexandersva.com. Reservations recommended. Main courses $20–$38. AE, MC, V. Wed 11am–2pm and 5–9pm; Tues and Thurs 5–9pm; Fri–Sat 5–10pm.

Corned Beef & Co. Bar and Grill AMERICAN   A block west of Market Square, this lively sports-bar emporium—the largest one of its kind I've ever seen—occupies half a city block. There's a sophisticated billiards parlor and beaucoup TV screens for watching every game being televised at the moment. You can even watch from a rooftop patio during warm weather. Having a good time may be the main reason to come here (it literally overflows with young folk on weekend nights), but the chow is better than average pub fare: deli sandwiches (including the namesake corned beef), salads, wood-fired pizzas, and main courses such as chicken *diablo* (a breast piqued with Texas Pete hot sauce). I'm fond of the shrimp and asparagus quesadillas.

107 Jefferson St. ℂ **540/342-3354.** www.cornedbeefandco.com. Reservations accepted. Salads, sandwiches, burgers $8–$9; pizzas $9–$14; main courses $10–$19. AE, DISC, MC, V. Mon–Sat 11:30am–midnight (bar till 2am).

Metro! MODERN AMERICAN/SUSHI   This sophisticated, high-energy bistro and lounge brings the big city to Roanoke. You can watch the chefs scurrying around the open kitchen through the big storefront windows on Campbell Avenue, but wander on in for a drink and some sushi at the large martini bar, which dominates the main dining room. An ample sampling of the city's well-heeled young professionals will be here, especially on weekend nights when Metro! turns into a South Beach–style lounge. Beforehand, the kitchen provides a wide range of exciting fare, from sushi and sashimi to Maryland-style crab cakes.

14 Campbell Ave. SE. ℂ **540/345-6645.** www.metroroanoke.com. Reservations recommended, especially on weekends. Sushi $8–$17; main courses $19–$29. AE, DISC, MC, V. Mon 5–10pm; Tues–Sat 11:30am–2pm and 5–10pm (bar to 2am).

Norah's Cafe ★ 🍴 AMERICAN   The Taubman Museum of Art's cafe is an excellent place for lunch even if you don't go upstairs to see its namesake, John Singer Sargent's portrait of Mrs. George Gribble. You can watch the trains rumble by outside the glass walls, which make it seem like you're lunching alfresco. The limited menu features out-of-the-ordinary salads, sandwiches, wraps, and desserts. The Cobb salad with steamed shrimp is excellent. This is a free Wi-Fi spot.

In Taubman Museum of Art, 110 Salem Ave. ℂ **540/204-4122.** www.taubmanmuseum.org. Sandwiches and salads $7–$10. AE, DISC, MC, V. Tues–Thurs and Sat 10am–3pm; Fri 10am–8pm; Sun 11:30m–3pm.

RESTAURANTS NEARER THE BLUE RIDGE PARKWAY

Carlos Brazilian International Cuisine ★★ BRAZILIAN   It's worth taking a ride out to Brazilian-born chef Carlos Amaral's fine restaurant, across from the Tanglewood Mall, not only for the excellent food but also for the view over the Roanoke Valley. Most tables here have no view at all, so reserve as soon as possible for one in the semicircular Olinda Room, whose window walls offer an unimpeded vista (and be sure to tell them you want the Olinda Room). Best view of all is from patio tables out front; they are first-come first-served. The food highlights are obviously Brazilian, and include my favorite, *moqueca mineira*, a blend of shrimp, clams, and fish in a slightly spicy tomato sauce. Vegetarians can pick from pastas, Brazilian black beans served with collard greens, or a meatless version of paella Valenciana.

4167 Electric Rd. (U.S. 220 Business; south of I-581/U.S. 220). ℂ **540/342-6455.** www.carlosbrazilian. com. Reservations recommended. Main courses $10–$30. AE, MC, V. Mon–Fri 11:30am–2pm and 5–10pm; Sat 4–10pm. From downtown, take I-581/U.S. 220 south to 1st Franklin Rd. exit, turn right, go uphill on Electric Rd., make U-turn after Ogden Rd.; restaurant is up hill on right. From Blue Ridge Pkwy., take U.S. 220 west to 1st Franklin Rd. exit, turn left, go uphill on Franklin Rd., which becomes Electric Rd., make U-turn after Ogden Rd.; restaurant is up hill on right.

Montano's International Restaurant INTERNATIONAL   Entry into this busy, casual restaurant is through a market whose chiller cases are stuffed with excellent cold cuts, cakes, and chocolates, and whose shelves are packed with wines and beers from around the world. Likewise, the lengthy menu spans the globe from Chesapeake crab cakes to Spanish paella, from Italian veal parmigiana to Brazilian *moqueca*. All of it is good (although I prefer the *moqueca* at Carlos's, above) and served in prodigious portions. More than 20 sandwiches and 15 salads appear, and vegetarians have half a dozen choices. One side of the big room is devoted to a sports bar, where musicians appear on weekends. Montano's is very popular with locals of every age and taste.

In Townside Festival Center, 3733 Franklin Rd. ⓒ **540/344-8960.** www.montanos.net. Reservations recommended on weekends. Sandwiches and salads $9–$14; main courses $11–$27. AE, DISC, MC, V. Mon 10am–10pm; Tues–Sat 10am–10:30pm.

Roanoker Restaurant ★ 🍴 AMERICAN   A popular local restaurant since 1941, the Roanoker occupies a Colonial-style building surrounded by much-needed parking lots. Several dining rooms offer booth seating arranged to provide privacy. Antique signs from Roanoke businesses adorn the walls. At breakfast, the fluffy biscuits are the best I've ever eaten, either plain, sandwiching country ham or sausage, or covered in sausage gravy. Lunch and dinner specials change daily, depending on available produce. If you're lucky, the fresh vegetables will include skillet-fried yellow squash and onions, a mouthwatering Southern favorite.

2522 Colonial Ave. (south of Wonju St.). ⓒ **540/344-7746.** www.theroanokerrestaurant.com. Reservations not accepted. Breakfast $4–$8.50; sandwiches $5.50–$7; main courses $7.50–$13. MC, V. Tues–Sat 7am–9pm; Sun 8am–9pm. From downtown, go south on Franklin Rd., turn right on Brandon Ave., left on Colonial Ave. From I-581/U.S. 220, go south to Colonial Ave. exit, turn left at traffic light on Colonial Ave. to restaurant on left.

RESTAURANTS IN GRANDIN VILLAGE

Grandin Village, at the intersection of Grandin Road and Memorial Avenue, is one of Roanoke's trendiest close-in suburban neighborhoods. It's a fun place to have a meal and join the locals out for a stroll. You might even see students of the Roanoke Ballet Theatre, Roanoke's only nonprofit school of dance, practicing in its storefront studio. To get here from downtown, take Campbell Avenue west and bear left when it morphs into Memorial Avenue.

Flanking the **Grandin Theater,** 1310 Grandin Rd., SW (ⓒ **540/345-6177**), several good restaurants feed the village's affluent residents. Among the most interesting are the **Issac's Mediterranean Restaurant,** 1910 Memorial Ave. (ⓒ **540/904-5002;** www.theisaacsrestaurant.com); **Norberto's Italian Ristorante,** 1908 Memorial Ave. (ⓒ **540/342-1611;** www.norbertos.com); **Rockfish Food & Wine,** 1402 Grandin Rd. (ⓒ **540/904-5454;** www.rockfishfood.com), which carries an extensive wine list; and **Surf N Turf Grill,** 1329 Grandin Rd. (ⓒ **540/342-4995**), whose seafood is better than its steaks. None is expensive.

It's easy to get on a sugar high at **Pop's Ice Cream & Soda Bar,** 1916 Memorial Ave. (ⓒ **540/345-2129**) and **Viva la Cupcake,** 1302 Grandin Rd. (ⓒ **540/204-3100;** www.vivalacupcakes.com). On the other hand, owner Al Hubbard of **Healthy Stuff Cakery/Cafe,** 1731 Grandin Rd. (ⓒ **540/345-2407**), uses squash, zucchini, and oatmeal but no processed sugar in his luscious cakes and cookies.

Owner Michelle Bennett of **Cups Coffee & Tea,** 1402 Grandin Rd. (ⓒ **540/339-9675;** www.cupscoffeeandtea.com), jokes that she serves her brew in "D cups."

Local Roots ★ AMERICAN   Few farm-to-table restaurants work as hard at acquiring fresh produce from local farmers than does this pleasant bistro, the best in Grandin Village. In fact, it even grows herbs and vegetables in its own garden. Consequently the menu changes frequently depending on what's available, and the daily specials are definitely worth considering, such as local farm-raised trout accompanied by chicken of the woods mushrooms, a variety that grows on the side of trees and actually looks like breast of chicken. The three- and five-course chef's tasting menus are good value.

1314 Grandin Rd. ✆ **540/206-2610.** www.localrootsrestaurant.com. Reservations recommended. Main courses $19–$25; 3- and 5-course tasting menus $45–$60. AE, MC, V. Tues–Fri 11:30am–2pm and 5–10pm; Sat 5–10pm; Sun 11am–2:30pm and 5–9pm.

Roanoke After Dark

Available at the visitor center (see "Essentials," earlier in this chapter) and at many hotels and restaurants, the free *City Magazine* (www.citymagazineonline.com) has a rundown of what's going on around town.

The **Roanoke Civic Center,** 710 Williamson Rd. NE (✆ **540/853-5483;** www.roanokeciviccenter.com), hosts visiting performers and concerts by the **Roanoke Symphony** (✆ **540/343-9127;** www.rso.com).

When the Center in the Square reopens it will once again host the **Mill Mountain Theatre** (✆ **540/342-5749;** www.millmountain.org) and performances by the **Roanoke Ballet Theatre** (✆ **540/345-6099;** www.roanokeballet.org), whose studio is at 1318 Grandin Rd.

Baseball fans can see the Class A **Salem Red Sox** (✆ **540/389-3333;** www.minorleaguebaseball.com), an affiliate of the big-league Boston Red Sox, play in Salem, Roanoke's sister city.

The Market Square area running along Campbell Avenue to Jefferson Street is Roanoke's pub-crawling scene, especially on weekends when many restaurants and pubs have music and dancing. **Metro!** and **202 Market** attract the well-heeled young professional set, while **Corned Beef & Company** gets the sometimes rowdy masses; don't be surprised to see cops across Jefferson Street. (See "Where to Eat," above, for details about all three.) The **Regency Room** and the **Pine Room** in the Hotel Roanoke & Conference Center (p. 185) have live music and dancing on weekends.

A Nearby Mountain Resort

Mountain Lake Hotel   Surrounded by 2,600 acres, this rustic mountaintop resort consists of a stately, rough-cut-stone lodge with clusters of small, white-clapboard summer cottages nearby. The spacious, stone-walled dining room has large windows offering panoramic lake views—a romantic evening setting. More than 20 types of accommodations are available in the main hotel, cottages, and the Blueberry Ridge Complex (units in the latter are more sizeable and modern, and they're open year-round). The popular parlor suites have Jacuzzis and fireplaces, and some rooms offer lake views. Cottages are more simply furnished, although guests enjoy kitchens and porches with rockers. Chestnut Lodge is a three-story gray-clapboard building set on the side of a hill. Rooms here are decorated in country style, with fireplaces and balconies. Your unit will not have a TV, but there's plenty of swimming, boating, fishing, hiking, and tennis to keep you busy.

Pembroke, VA 24136. www.mountainlakehotel.com. ✆ **800/346-3334** or 540/626-7121. Fax 540/626-7172. 101 units. $150–$250 double; $150–$310 suite; $150–$920 cabin or cottage. Rates include breakfast and dinner. AE, DISC, MC, V. Hotel closed Nov–Apr. From I-81, take Exit 118B, U.S. 460 west; turn right onto C.R. 700 and go 7 miles to Mountain Lake. **Amenities:** Restaurant; bar; bikes; children's programs; Jacuzzi; outdoor pool; sauna; tennis court; watersports equipment/rentals. *In room:* Kitchen (in some cottages), Wi-Fi.

> 💬 *Dirty Dancing*
>
> Mountain Lake played the part of the Catskills resort in the movie *Dirty Dancing,* starring Jennifer Grey and the late Patrick Swayze.

OUTDOORS IN THE SOUTHWEST HIGHLANDS

The Southwest Highlands are great for getting outdoors and experiencing nature, especially if you're into hiking, biking, and horseback riding. Mount Rogers National Recreation Area (NRA), one of Virginia's prime locales for backcountry activities, runs for 60 miles along the mountaintops south of I-81 between Wytheville and Abingdon. Adding to the allure are two old railroad beds turned into excellent biking-and-hiking trails on its northern and southern flanks: the New River Trail State Park to the north and the Virginia Creeper Trail to the south.

Mount Rogers National Recreation Area

Noted for its 400 miles of hiking, mountain-biking, cross-country-skiing, and horse trails, including part of the Appalachian Trail, Mount Rogers NRA includes 117,000 forested acres. Included is its namesake, Virginia's highest peak at 5,729 feet. Nearby White Top is the state's second-highest point at 5,520 feet. Most of the land, however, flanks Iron Mountain, a long ridge running the area's length. Ranging the extensive upland meadows are wild ponies, introduced to keep the grasses mowed.

Not all of this expanse is pristine; as part of the George Washington and Jefferson national forests, it's subject to multiple uses such as hunting and logging. Nevertheless, you'll find three preserved wilderness areas and plenty of backcountry to explore, with mountain scenery that's some of the best in Virginia.

JUST THE FACTS

ACCESS POINTS & ORIENTATION   Access roads from I-81 are U.S. 21 from Wytheville, Va. 16 from Marion, S.R. 600 from Chilhowie, Va. 91 from Glades Spring, and U.S. 58 from Damascus and Abingdon. S.R. 603 runs 13 miles through beautiful highland meadows from Troutdale (on Va. 16) to Konnarock (on U.S. 58).

INFORMATION   Because the area is so vast and most facilities widespread, it's a good idea to get as much information in advance as possible. Contact the **Mount Rogers National Recreation Area,** 3714 Hwy. 16, Marion, VA 24354 (© **800/628-7202** or 276/783-5196; www.fs.fed.us/r8/gwj/mr).

Another good source is the **Wytheville Visitor Center,** 975 Tazewell St., Wytheville, VA 24382 (© **877/347-8307** or 276/223-3355; www.visitwytheville.com). It is open daily 9am to 5pm. Take Exit 70 off I-81 and follow the signs.

FEES, REGULATIONS & BACKCOUNTRY PERMITS   There is no charge to drive through the area, but parking fees of $3 per vehicle apply to specific recreational areas, payable on the honor system. Except for the Appalachian Trail and some others reserved for hikers, mountain bikes are permitted but must give way to horses. Cyclists and horseback riders must walk across all bridges and trestles. Hikers must not spook the horses. Fishing requires a Virginia license. The "leave no trace" ethic applies: Leave nothing behind, and take away only photographs and memories.

VISITOR CENTER   The area headquarters is at 3714 Va. 16, about 6 miles south of Marion (take Exit 45 off I-81 and go south on Va. 16). Exhibits describe the area, and there's a bookstore with maps and other publications for sale. The center is open Memorial Day through October Monday to Friday 8am to 4:30pm and Saturday 9am to 4pm. The rest of the year, it's open only Monday to Friday 8am to 4:30pm. It's closed on federal holidays.

SEASONS The area gets the most visitors on summer and fall weekends and on holidays. Spring is punctuated by wildflowers in bloom (the calendars published by the Blue Ridge Parkway are generally applicable here), while fall foliage is at its brilliant best in mid-October. Cross-country skiers use the trails during winter. Summer thunderstorms, winter blizzards, and fog any time of the year can pose threats in the high country, so caution is advised.

THE TOP SCENIC DRIVES

You can enjoy the scenery without getting out of your car. From Marion on I-81, take Va. 16 south 16 miles to the country store at Troutdale. Turn right on S.R. 603 and drive 13 miles southwest to U.S. 58. Turn right there and drive 20 miles down Straight Branch—a misnomer if ever there was one—through Damascus to I-81 at Abingdon.

An alternative route is to continue on Va. 16 south past Troutdale and turn west on U.S. 58. This will take you past **Grayson Highlands State Park.** After the park, turn right on S.R. 600 north. This road climbs almost to the summit of White Top Mountain. Up there, a dirt track known as Spur 89 branches off for 3 miles to the actual summit; it's the highest point in Virginia to which you can drive a vehicle and has great views. S.R. 600 then descends to a dead end at S.R. 603; turn right there and drive down to U.S. 58, then west to Damascus and Abingdon, as described above.

OUTDOOR PURSUITS

CAMPING In addition to the horse camps mentioned below, the recreation area has several other campgrounds, all open from mid-April through December. A limited number of sites can be reserved in advance by calling © **877/444-6777** or going to www.recreation.gov.

On S.R. 603 between Troutdale and Konnarock, **Grindstone** serves as a base camp for hikers heading up Mount Rogers. It has 109 sites with campfires, drinking water, a .5-mile nature trail, and weekend ranger programs during summer. **Beartree Recreation Area,** a popular site 7 miles east of Damascus on U.S. 58, features a sand beach on a 12-acre lake stocked with trout for fishing. Both Grindstone and Beartree have flush toilets and warm showers. Grindstone has electric and water hookups; Beartree does not. Fees range from $3 to $19 per night.

HIGH-COUNTRY HIKING Almost two-thirds of the area's 400 miles of trails are on these routes: the local stretch of the **Appalachian Trail** (64 miles), the **Virginia Highlands Horse Trail** (66 miles), and the **Iron Mountain Trail** (51 miles). Many of the other 67 trails connect to these routes, and many can be linked into circuit hikes.

You can walk for days on the white-blaze Appalachian Trail without crossing a paved road, especially on the central stretch up and down the flanks of Mount Rogers between S.R. 603 and S.R. 600. A spur goes to the top of the mountain. The blue-blaze **Mount Rogers Trail,** a very popular alternate route, leaves C.R. 603 near Grindstone Campground; a spur from that track heads down into the pristine Lewis Fork Wilderness before rejoining the Appalachian Trail.

Running across the southern end of the area, the **Virginia Creeper Trail** offers a much easier yet beautiful, hike and bike ride. See "The Virginia Creeper Trail," below.

HORSEBACK RIDING Riders can use 150 miles of the area's trails, including Iron Mountain, New River, and the Virginia Highlands Horse Trail, which connects Elk Garden to Va. 94. Horse camps are at Fox Creek, on Va. 603; Hussy Mountain, near Speedwell; and Collins Cove, about 4 miles east of Cripple Creek. They have toilets, and drinking water for horses (but no water for humans).

The Virginia Creeper Trail ★★★

The fabulously beautiful **Virginia Creeper Trail** is a 34-mile hiking, biking, and horseback-riding route following an old railroad bed between Abingdon and White Top Station, at the North Carolina line on the southern flank of White Top Mountain, just inside Mount Rogers National Recreation Area. The name comes from the fact that steam locomotives had such a slow time on the grade that they became known collectively as the Virginia Creeper. If you can ride a bike, this is one of Virginia's top outdoor excursions.

The trail starts at an elevation of 2,065 feet in Abingdon, drops to 2,000 feet at Damascus (11 miles east on U.S. 58), then climbs to 3,675 feet at White Top. No one in his or her right mind would ride a bike *up* that mountain, but if you stay in Abingdon, you can take a shuttle up and coast for 17 of the 23 gorgeous miles downhill to Damascus.

Beginning 2 miles east of Damascus, the stretch between Green Cove Station and Iron Bridge crosses High Trestle (about 100 ft. high) and has swimming holes in the adjacent stream. Green Cove is a seasonal forest service information post with portable toilets and a snack bar. It was at Green Cove that O. Winston Link took one of his most famous photographs, of a mare bowing her head as the Virginia Creeper crawled past. It's on display at the O. Winston Link Museum in Roanoke and the Abingdon Passenger Train Station in Abingdon (see "O. Winston Link Museum," earlier and "Exploring Abingdon," below).

Outfitters in Damascus renting bikes and operating shuttles to the top of the trail include **Blue Blaze Bike & Shuttle Service,** 226 W. Laurel Ave. (© 800/475-5905 or 276/475-5095; www.blueblazebikeandshuttle.com); the **Bike Station,** 501 E. 3rd St. (© 276/475-3629; www.thebike-station.com); and **Shuttle Shack,** 744 N. Beaver Dam (© 276/475-3773; www.shuttleshack.com). In Abingdon, **Virginia Creeper Trail Bike Shop** (© 888/245-3648 or 276/676-2552; www.vacreepertrailbikeshop. com) is on Pecan Street near the trail head. All charge about $13 per person for the shuttle; or $24 for both shuttle and rental. Reservations are advised, so call ahead.

For more information contact the Abingdon Convention & Visitors Bureau (see "Essentials" under "Abingdon: A Show-Stopping Town," below) or the website of the **Virginia Creeper Trail Club,** PO Box 2382, Abingdon, VA 24212 (www.vacreepertrail.org).

> ### Trail Town, USA
>
> The village of **Damascus** (www.damascus.org) makes so much of its living off the Virginia Creeper that it calls itself "Trail Town, USA." Its **Trail Days** festival in mid-May draws hikers and cyclists from far and wide (**www.traildays.us**).

New River Trail State Park ★★

The exceptional **New River Trail** runs for 57 miles between Galax and Pulaski. The trail follows an old railroad bed beside the New River (in geologic terms one of the oldest rivers in the United States—it predates the Appalachian Mountains). The river flows toward the Mississippi, on its way carving the New River Gorge in southeastern West Virginia, the best white-water rafting spot in the eastern U.S.

The park's headquarters are at **Foster Falls,** a restored mining hamlet on Foster Falls Road (C.R. 608), about 20 miles northeast of Wytheville, or 2 miles north of U.S. 52 (take Exit 24 off I-77 and follow the signs). From April through November you can enter the trail here daily 8am to dusk. Parking costs $2 per vehicle during the week, $3 on weekends and holidays.

Other entries to the trail are at **Shot Tower Historical State Park** (see below); **Draper,** near Exit 92 off I-81; **Allisonia** and **Hiwassee,** both on C.R. 693; **Barren Springs,** on Va. 100; **Austinville,** on Va. 69; **Ivanhoe,** on Va. 94; **Byllesby Dam,** on C.R. 602; and **Galax,** on U.S. 58. There's also a branch trail to **Fries,** on Va. 94.

Foster Falls River Company (✆ 276/699-1034) rents bicycles, canoes, kayaks, and inner tubes at Foster Falls. Bikes cost $5 per hour or $18 per day. Canoes and kayaks start at $7 an hour or $30 per day. Tubes go for $18 per day. The company also provides shuttle service between the key points along the trail, so you don't have to walk, ride, or paddle back to your car.

The adjacent **Foster Falls Horse Livery** (✆ 276/699-2460) rents horses and has guided horse and pony rides along the trail starting at $20 per person for short rides.

For more information, call **New River Trail State Park,** 176 Orphanage Dr., Foster Falls, VA 24360 (✆ 276/699-6778; www.dcr.virginia.gov/state_parks/new. shtml). The office is open Monday to Friday 8am to 4:30pm.

While in this area, you can stop at **Shot Tower Historical State Park,** on U.S. 52 near Exit 5 off I-77, which features a stone shot tower built about 1791. Molten lead, poured from the top of the tower, fell 150 feet into a kettle, thus cooling and turning into round shot. The lead was mined at nearby Austinville, birthplace of Stephen Austin, the "Father of Texas." (There's a monument to Austin at the New River Trail State Park in Austinville.) Park admission is free, but parking costs $2 per vehicle during the week, $3 on weekends and holidays. The park is open daily 8am to dusk.

Where to Stay

There are no accommodations within Mount Rogers National Recreation Area. Marion is the closest town to the area's center. Tops there is the **General Francis Marion Hotel & Conference Center** (✆ 877/783-4802 or 276/793-4800; www. gfmhotel.com), a lovingly restored 1927 commercial hotel on Main Street (U.S. 11) in the center of Marion's business district. On U.S. 11 north of downtown is the **Econo Lodge Marion** (✆ 800/553-2666 or 540/783-6031). While overnighting you can take in a play or concert in the restored **Lincoln Theater** (✆ 276/783-6093; www.thelincoln.org).

The Virginia Creeper Trail ends in Abingdon, which has several hotels and bed-and-breakfasts (see "Where to Stay," p. 198).

At the strategic intersection of I-81 and I-77 close to New River Trail State Park, Wytheville has more than 1,200 motel rooms, most in national chain establishments along the interstates. The largest concentration is at Exit 73 off I-81 (U.S. 11), where the **Holiday Inn Wytheville** (✆ 800/465-4329 or 276/228-5483) has its own restaurant. Also at Exit 73 is a **Days Inn** (✆ 800/325-2525 or 276/228-5500), **Motel 6** (✆ 800/446-8356 or 276/228-7988), and **Red Carpet Inn** (✆ 800/251-1962 or 276/228-5525). Some rooms in the Days Inn, Motel 6, and Red Carpet Inn are virtually beside I-81 and are subject to traffic noise. You can also take Exit 73 to reach a parking lot–surrounded **Econo Lodge** (✆ 800/424-4777 or 276/228-5517), about 1 mile to the south on U.S. 11.

ABINGDON: A SHOW-STOPPING TOWN ★★★

49 miles SW of Wytheville; 133 miles SW of Roanoke; 315 miles SW of Richmond; 437 miles SW of Washington, D.C.

While on his first expedition to Kentucky in 1760, Daniel Boone tramped across the 2,000-foot-high Holston Valley and camped at the base of a hill near a small settlement known as Black's Fort. When wolves emerged from a cave and attacked his dogs, Boone named the place Wolf Hill. Boone and other pioneers opened the area for settlement, and by 1778, a thriving community named Abingdon had grown up around Black's Fort and Wolf Hill. The Washington County Courthouse has replaced the fort, but Boone's cave is still there, behind one of the historic buildings on Main Street.

Indeed, Abingdon today looks much as it did in those early years, making it one of Virginia's most picturesque and rewarding small towns to visit. Its beauty and historical charm have attracted more than its share of actors, artists, craftspeople, and even a few writers. Visitors drive hundreds of miles to attend shows at the Barter Theatre, Virginia's official state stage, and they pull off I-81 to visit Heartwood, a new center celebrating the region's arts, crafts, and music. Best time to be here is during the first 2 weeks of August when Abingdon hosts the popular Virginia Highlands Festival, a display of the region's best arts and crafts.

Essentials

VISITOR INFORMATION   Contact the **Abingdon Visitor Center,** 335 Cummings St., Abingdon, VA 24210 (© **800/435-3440** or 276/676-2282; fax 276/676-3076; www.abingdon.com), located in a gorgeous Victorian house on the left as you drive into town on U.S. 58. It's open daily 9am to 5pm.

GETTING THERE & GETTING AROUND   **Tri-Cities Regional Airport** (© **423/ 325-6000;** www.triflight.com) is near I-81 about 30 miles southwest of Abingdon between Bristol and Kingsport, Tennessee. You can rent a car there.

Abingdon is at the junction of I-81 and U.S. 11, U.S. 19, and U.S. 58. From I-81, take Exit 17 and follow U.S. 58 West directly into town. U.S. 11 runs east-west along Main Street (which has a phenomenal amount of traffic for such a small town). The local **taxi depot** is at 495 W. Main St. (© **276/628-4409**).

Exploring Abingdon
A WALKING TOUR OF MAIN STREET

Pick up a walking-tour brochure and map at the visitor center (see "Essentials," above), and head north on Cummings Street. To your left as you cross the railroad bridge is the open-air **Abingdon Farmer's Market,** where farmers sell their produce April to October, Tuesday 3 to 6pm and Saturday 7am to noon.

At the top of the hill you'll come to the **Field-Penn 1860 House Museum** (see "The Top Attractions," below). From there head west on Main Street through Abingdon's 3-block-long business district. Several antiques and collectibles emporia will vie for your attention, but keep going to Depot Square. Turn left there to the restored **Abingdon Passenger Train Station,** now home to the **Historical Society of Washington County** (© **276/628-8761;** www.hswcv.org). Don't miss the small collection of dramatic railway photographs by O. Winston Link, whose work is also

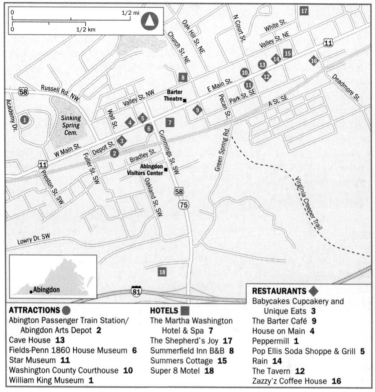

ATTRACTIONS ●
Abington Passenger Train Station/
  Abingdon Arts Depot **2**
Cave House **13**
Fields-Penn 1860 House Museum **6**
Star Museum **11**
Washington County Courthouse **10**
William King Museum **1**

HOTELS ■
The Martha Washington
  Hotel & Spa **7**
The Shepherd's Joy **17**
Summerfield Inn B&B **8**
Summers Cottage **15**
Super 8 Motel **18**

RESTAURANTS ◆
Babycakes Cupcakery and
  Unique Eats **3**
The Barter Café **9**
House on Main **4**
Peppermill **1**
Pop Ellis Soda Shoppe & Grill **5**
Rain **14**
The Tavern **12**
Zazzy'z Coffee House **16**

showcased in his museum in Roanoke (p. 182). The station is open April to October, Tuesday to Saturday 10am to 4pm.

The freight depot next door is now the **Abingdon Arts Depot** ★ (© 276/628-9091), where you can see artists at work Thursday to Saturday 11am to 3pm.

Now backtrack east along Main Street and cross Cummings Street to the Martha Washington Hotel & Spa, the Barter Theatre, and 30 other buildings and homes—with birth dates ranging from 1779 to 1925.

At the bottom of the hill, a right turn on Pecan Street will take you to the western head of the **Virginia Creeper Trail** (see above). Parked under a shed there is "Abingdon's Mollie," or officially Norfolk & Western Engine No. 433, similar to the steam locomotives that had such a tough time with the grade that they became facetiously and collectively known as the "Virginia Creeper."

Stop at the top of the hill and look up at the Tiffany stained-glass windows in the **Washington County Courthouse,** built in 1869 to replace an earlier version burned during the Civil War. Spectacular when seen at night, the windows were added as a memorial to World War I veterans. From here you'll head downhill again past the **Tavern,** considered the oldest building in town. Built around 1779 and used as a stagecoach inn and tavern, it's now home to one of the town's better restaurants

After walking over Abingdon's second hill—where the 1869 Washington County Courthouse stands—you'll come to the **Cave House.** Behind it is the actual cave whence emerged the wolves that attacked Daniel Boone's dogs. It's not marked, but to find it, take the alley to the left of the house to a stop sign, and turn right. You can peer through lattice into the mouth of the cave, which is below a rickety old barn.

(see "Where to Eat," below). You can still see the mail slot in the original post office in an addition on the east side of the building.

A few more blocks will bring you to well-earned refreshment at **Zazzy'z Coffee House.** On the way home stop and look at the local arts and crafts for sale in **Holston Mountain Artisans** (see "Shopping," below).

THE TOP ATTRACTIONS

Fields-Penn 1860 House Museum   This 1860 manse depicts how Abingdon's upper class lived in the mid–19th century. James Fields, who built it, was a bricklayer and building contractor; George Penn, who bought it in the 1890s, was a lawyer. It's operated by the William King Museum (see below). Docents aren't always available so don't be disappointed if it isn't open.

208 W. Main St. © **276/676-0216.** Free admission. Apr–Dec Wed 11am–4pm, Thurs–Sat 1–4pm. Closed Jan–Mar.

Heartwood—Southwest Virginia's Artisan Gateway ★★   Looking like a barn cut in two, this modern facility promotes and preserves the crafts, music, food, and culture of the 19 counties comprising the Southwest Highlands. All rolled into one, it's an information center, a high-quality crafts shop, a record store, a performing arts venue, and a restaurant (see "Where to Eat," below). Only master artisans, all members of the 'Round Mountain network (www.roundthemountain.org), can sell their works here. In the music area, which belongs to the Crooked Road (see "Country Music's Crooked Road," below), you can listen to and buy old-time, bluegrass, gospel, or handcrafted musical instruments. Musicians perform on a stage in the center of the large building. It's an educational experience and a chance to shop for unique souvenirs and gifts.

At Virginia Highlands Community College, 1 Heartwood Circle (near Exit 14 off I-81). © **276/492-2400.** www.heartwoodvirginia.org. Free admission. Mon–Sat 10am–9pm; Sun 10am–3pm. From downtown go south on Main St. (U.S. 11) and follow signs.

Star Museum   Abingdon native Robert Weisfeld now uses this storefront building, which once housed his family's newspaper, to display his huge collection of celebrity memorabilia, much of it garnered while he lived in New York City for 16 years. Marilyn Monroe's red cocktail dress, Errol Flynn's swim trunks, and a copy of Michael Jackson's first Motown single ("I Want You Back") are well hidden among the items. None of them are labeled, so call in advance to arrange a guided tour by Weisfeld.

170 E. Main St. © **276/608-7452**. Admission $10 adults, $3 children 12 and under. Tues–Sat 1–6pm.

William King Museum   In a refurbished school building on the west side of town, this museum is very good at showcasing the region's cultural heritage, and does it in more detail than does Heartwood (see above). In addition to the visiting exhibits in the school building, the museum displays its collection of O. Winston Link photographs in the Abingdon Passenger Train Station (see "A Walking Tour of Main Street," above), and it administers the Fields-Penn 1860 House Museum. There's a good museum shop.

415 Academy Dr. (©) **276/628-5005**. www.williamkingmuseum.org. Admission $5 adults, $3 seniors and students. Tues–Wed and Fri 10am–5pm; Thurs 10am–9pm; Sat–Sun 1–5pm.

A Nearby Gristmill & a Winery

A scenic 4¼-mile drive leads from Valley Street in Abingdon through a picturesque valley to **White's Mill** ((©) **276/628-2960;** www.whitesmill.org), built in 1790 and now on the National Register of Historic Places. It's owned by a nonprofit foundation, which is slowly restoring it and its 22-foot-diameter steel wheel and original grinding stone. Admission is by donation, and it's open Wednesday to Sunday 10am to 5pm. It is closed January to March. You can buy meal from the mill's grinders at a shop across the road.

In rolling hills about 7½ miles east of town, **Abingdon Vineyard & Winery** ((©) **276/623-1255;** www.abingdonwinery.com) is open for tasting its reds and whites from March 15 to December 15, Tuesday to Saturday 10am to 6pm and Sunday noon to 6pm. Follow U.S. 58 east 5 miles past I-81, turn right on Oseola Road (S.R. 722), and follow the grape cluster signs 2½ miles to the winery.

Shopping

In addition to those for sale at Heartwood—Southwest Virginia's Artisan Gateway (see "The Top Attractions," above)—outstanding mountain arts and crafts are available at **Holston Mountain Artisans ★★**, 214 Park St., at South Court St.

COUNTRY MUSIC'S CROOKED ROAD

Southwestern Virginia has been central to the evolution of country music since the first European settlers arrived in these hills and valleys with few possessions other than their mandolins and fiddles. Some of the great country artists hail from here—the Carter Family, Ralph Stanley, the Stonemans—and numerous music festivals, such as the famous Old Fiddler's Convention in Galax, are part of the weekend fun.

The area's music heritage is formally recognized by the **Crooked Road: Virginia's Heritage Music Trail** ((©) 276/492-2085; www.thecrookedroad.org). This official route follows U.S. 23, U.S. 421, U.S. 58, U.S. 221, Va. 8, and Va. 40

for more than 200 miles from Breaks in the west to Rocky Mount in the east. Along the way it passes such country music shrines as the **Ralph Stanley Museum & Traditional Music Center** in Clintwood; the **Carter Family Fold** in Hiltons; the **Birthplace of Country Music Museum** in Bristol; the **Blue Ridge Music Center** on the Blue Ridge Parkway; the **Rex Theater** in Galax; the **Floyd Country Store** in Floyd; and the **Blue Ridge Music Institute** in Ferrum.

Rather than drive all that way, you can do a virtual tour, listen to the music, and buy the artists' CDs at Heartland—Southwest Virginia's Artisan Gateway (see "The Top Attractions," above).

(© **276/628-7721;** www.holstonmtnarts.com), a 130-member cooperative. The handmade quilts here are extraordinary. The shop is open April to October, Monday to Saturday 10am to 5:30pm and Sunday 1 to 5pm.

Main Street has several **antiques shops,** which you will pass during your walking tour. **Note:** Most are closed on Sunday, some on Monday.

Where to Stay

Abingdon has several chain motels adjacent to I-81. **Hampton Inn** (© 800/426-7866 or 276/619-4600) and **Super 8** (© 800/800-8000 or 276/676-3310) are most convenient to downtown at Exit 17. **Quality Inn & Suites** (© 877/676-9090 or 276/676-9090) and **Holiday Inn Express** (© 800/465-4329 or 276/676-2929) are at Exit 19, at the north end of town. **Best Western Abingdon Inn & Suites** (© 800/800-8000 or 276/676-3310) and **Comfort Inn** (© 800/221-2222 or 276/676-2222) are at Exit 14.

The Martha Washington Hotel & Spa ★★★ The center portion of this Greek-revival structure was built in 1832 as a private residence and later served as a girls school. White-wicker chairs give the front porch the look of an old-time resort. With loudly creaking floors, the lobby and adjoining parlors are elegantly decorated, with original marble fireplaces and crystal chandeliers. Choose from regular or deluxe rooms, the latter larger and more lavishly appointed with fine antiques. Two premium suites have two fireplaces, whirlpool tubs, and steam showers. Another suite has a small private balcony overlooking Main Street. The **dining room** serves good American fare amid Victorian elegance at breakfast and dinner, and **Martha's Gourmet Market** offers made-to-order sandwiches and salads Monday to Saturday 10am to 3:30pm. You can pamper yourself in the full-service spa, swim all year in the indoor pool, and soak in two hot tubs out in a pleasingly landscaped garden.

150 W. Main St., Abingdon, VA 24210. www.marthawashingtoninn.com. © **888/999-8078** or 276/628-3161. Fax 276/628-8885. 61 units. $225–$275 double; $395–$595 suite. Resort fee $10. AE, DC, DISC, MC, V. **Amenities:** Restaurant; bar; babysitting; health club; Jacuzzi; indoor pool; room service; spa; tennis court. *In room:* A/C, TV, hair dryer, Wi-Fi.

BED & BREAKFASTS

In addition to the Summerfield Inn listed below, Abingdon has more than 15 B&B accommodations. Among them, the **Shepherd's Joy** (www.shepherdsjoy.com; © **276/628-3273**) is a working sheep farm.

You can rent **Summers Cottage,** 309 W. Main St. (www.abingdoncottage.com; © **2767/628-5556**), a small Victorian house built in 1909 and meticulously restored in 2009 by Ramsey and Betsy White, who also own Zazzy'z Coffee House, about 100 yards away (see "Where to Eat," below). The cottage has two bedrooms, two baths, a kitchen, and a screened back porch. Betsy is the former curator of the William King Museum and has decorated the walls with works by local artists and artisans. Rates range from $100 to $200 depending on the day of the week and the season.

Summerfield Inn ★★ Ideally located just 1 block from the Barter Theatre, this 1920s Colonial-revival residence is the top pick in the area. Guests can sit for a spell on wicker rockers and an old-fashioned swing on the wraparound front porch. The living room is furnished with a player piano, plush Regency-style sofas flanking the fireplace, and 13 clocks—the latter collected by helpful hosts Janice and Jim Cowan. The guest rooms offer both the ambience of a private home and the luxurious comfort of a fine hotel. Especially nice are the three private units in the Carriage House next to the main building, especially the Rose Room with its two-person hot tub and walk-in shower. In fact, five of the seven units here have jetted tubs.

101 W. Valley St., Abingdon, VA 24210. www.summerfieldinn.com. © **800/668-5905** or 276/628-5905. Fax 276/628-7515. 7 units. $170–$200 double. Rates include full breakfast. AE, MC, V. *In room:* A/C, TV, Wi-Fi.

Where to Eat

Don't forget the dining room and Martha's Gourmet Market in the Martha Washington Inn (see above). The dining room is Abingdon's most elegant place to dine, while the daytime market provides excellent salads and sandwiches.

Babycakes Cupcakery and Unique Eats Natalie Shortridge was so successful baking cupcakes for children's birthday parties that she and husband Nick opened this little bakery-restaurant. They soon expanded their menu to include the likes of gourmet coffee and waffles for breakfast. At lunch they add sandwiches and an excellent chicken salad with blueberries, bacon, and lemon. Their cupcakes come in 20 flavors.

134 Wall St. © **276/623-0018.** www.babycakescupcakery.vpweb.com. Reservations not accepted. Most items $2–$9. AE, DISC, MC, V. Mon–Thurs 8am–6pm; Fri–Sat 8am–8pm.

The Barter Café ★ 🍴 DELI Big window walls let lots of light into this delightful, gardenlike room attached to the Barter Theatre's Stage II. Theater posters add an artsy touch, while easy chairs and sofas make this seem like a coffeehouse. In fact, you can get your morning latte or espresso here, plus high-cholesterol pastries. Big deli sandwiches, paninis, and wraps are both lunchtime and evening specialties. Everything is made from scratch, so don't be in a rush. Order at the counter and they'll call an actor's name when your order is ready (I did love being called Harrison Ford). Notice the *Book of Fantasies* sculpture out front.

110 Main St. (actually on Church St.). © **276/619-5462.** www.bartertheatre.com. Reservations not accepted. Salads and sandwiches $6.50–$7.50. AE, DISC, MC, V. Mon–Tues 11am–4pm; Wed–Sat 11am–11pm; Sun 11am–10pm.

Heartwood—Southwest Virginia's Artisan Gateway SOUTHERN AMERICAN You can smell the smoke wafting from the barbecue pit as you approach this regional arts and crafts center (see "The Top Attractions," above). One of the crafts on display is traditional Southern cooking such as farm fresh scrambled eggs and applewood smoked bacon and barbecued pork, chicken, and beef from the pit. It's all locally sourced, as are the wines, beers, ciders, and mead. There's also lamb, goat cheese ravioli, and chicken marsala, and you'll probably enjoy the chef's version of Low Country shrimp and grits. Southwest Highlanders go to dinner early, so note the 7pm bewitching hour.

At Virginia Highlands Community College, 1 Heartwood Circle (near Exit 14 off I-81). © **276/492-2400.** www.heartwoodvirginia.org. Reservations not accepted. Most items $5–$10. AE, DISC, MC, V. Mon–Sat 7–10am and 11:30am–7pm; Sun 10am–3pm (brunch). From downtown go south on Main St. (U.S. 11) and follow signs.

House on Main INTERNATIONAL This charming restaurant resides in a large house built in 1909 and stands behind two huge shade trees in the middle of the business district. Top tables in warm weather are out on the front porch, and the former dining room and study are adorned with antiques and original oak paneling. The chef uses local ingredients such as White's Mill grits to accompany shrimp, and cornmeal to bread catfish raised in nearby North Carolina.

231 W. Main St. ✆ **276/619-0039.** www.houseonmain.com. Reservations recommended. Main courses $19–$28. AE, DISC, MC, V. Mon–Wed 5–9pm; Thurs–Sat 11am–2pm and 5–9pm; Sun 11am–2pm.

Pop Ellis Soda Shoppe & Grill 🍴 AMERICAN   President Obama has been known to unexpectedly jump out of his limousine, run into a local joint, and order a burger and fries—as he did here while campaigning for the White House in 2008. He came into this former pharmacy, whose soda fountain harkens back to the days when every drugstore had one. "Hand-jerked" sodas, sundaes, and banana splits are as good as they come. The menu also offers burgers and a wide range of sandwiches and salads. Vegetarians have several choices.

217 W. Main St. ✆ **276/623-8187.** www.ellissodashoppe.com. Reservations not accepted. Sandwiches, burgers, and salads $8–$10. AE, MC, V. Mon 11am–4pm; Tues–Sat 11am–9pm.

Rain ★★★ NEW AMERICAN   Ben Carroll, a talented young chef who toiled at the Tavern before opening this casual restaurant in 2010, cooks some of the best food you will have in Virginia. From immaculate presentation to exciting tastes, everything shows his attention to detail. To start, an incredible version of bruschetta features toasted thin slices of Tennessee prosciutto (that is, local country ham) and a mayonnaise tinged with red-eye gravy (made with country ham drippings) over a baguette. Ahi tuna is flown in from Hawaii, seared, and served with a honey wasabi sauce. The blackened rib-eye steak under a creamy bleu cheese sauce is accompanied by delicious fried spinach that is lighter than air. There are outdoor tables in warm weather, and an indoor bar has its own light-fare menu.

283 E. Main St. ✆ **276/739-2331.** www.rainabingdon.com. Reservations recommended. Light fare $4.50–$9; main courses $18–$27. DISC, MC, V. Tues–Sat 11am–2pm and 5–9pm.

The Tavern ★★ INTERNATIONAL   Set aside a night for the Tavern, for having dinner in the town's oldest building is an essential part of the Abingdon experience. The Tavern was built in 1779 as an inn for stagecoach travelers. Exposed brick-and-stone walls, log beams, and hand-forged locks and hinges make it seem little changed since then. Despite the indoor charm, choice warm-weather tables are on an upstairs porch and on the brick terrace under a canopy of towering trees. The menu reflects gregarious German-born owner Max Hermann's well-traveled background but the best choices are excellent Wiener schnitzel and other German fare.

222 E. Main St. ✆ **276/628-1118.** www.abingdontavern.com. Reservations recommended for outdoor seating. Main courses $25–$36. AE, MC, V. Mon–Sat 5–10pm. Closed New Year's Day, Thanksgiving, and Christmas.

Zazzy'z Coffee House ★ 🍴 COFFEE SHOP/DELI   When failing eyesight made Dr. Ramsey White stop filling cavities, he converted this Victorian house from dental offices into a charming coffee shop. One room is set aside for Internet access (two computer terminals plus wireless access, all complimentary). In addition to house-ground coffee, the snack bar in the rear serves breakfast and lunches of deli-style sandwiches, salads, and soups.

380 E. Main St. ✆ **276/698-3333.** www.zazzyz.com. Reservations not accepted. Most items $3–$7. AE, DISC, MC, V. Mon–Fri 7:30am–6pm; Sat 8am–6pm; Sun 9am–3pm.

Abingdon After Dark

During summer you can take in a movie at the **Moonlite Drive-in,** on U.S. 11 South (✆ **276/628-7881;** www.moonlitetheatre.com). It's one of a handful of drive-in movie theaters left in Virginia.

The career of an aspiring, Virginia-born actor named Robert Porterfield came to a halt during the Great Depression. Giving up on Broadway, he and 22 other unemployed actors came to Abingdon in the summer of 1933 and began putting on plays and shows. Their first production was John Golden's *After Tomorrow*, for which they charged an admission of 40¢, or the equivalent in farm produce—thus did their little operation become known as the Barter Theatre.

Playwrights who contributed—among them Noel Coward, Thornton Wilder, Robert Sherwood, Maxwell Anderson, and George Bernard Shaw—were paid with a Virginia ham. Shaw, a vegetarian, returned the smoked delicacy and requested spinach instead; Porterfield and his crew obliged.

Barter Theatre ★★★ Official policy still permits barter for admission (with prior notice), but theatergoers now pay with cash or plastic to attend the State Theater of Virginia, America's longest-running professional repertory theater. The building was constructed around 1832 as a Presbyterian church and was the town hall and opera house from 1876 until 1933, when Robert Porterfield brought his unemployed actors here (see "Hams for Hamlet," above). Recent productions, now performed by a professional company, have included *Forever Plaid* and *Of Mice and Men*. The theater's alumni include Patricia Neal, Ernest Borgnine, Gregory Peck, Ned Beatty, and Kevin Spacey. Across Main Street, the **Barter's Stage II** specializes in the classics. The season for both stages runs from February through December. 127 W. Main St. (at College St.). ✆ **276/628-3991.** www.bartertheatre.com. Tickets $20–$40, depending on show and time.

The Carter Family Fold Music Shows ★★ Anyone with the slightest interest in country or traditional mountain music will make the 78-mile round-trip from Abingdon to Maces Spring, a hamlet in the Poor Valley, where you will see and hear established and aspiring artists every Saturday night at the Carter Family Memorial Music Center. This is the ancestral home of country music royalty A. P. Carter, wife Sara, and Maybelle Addington Carter (Maybelle was Sara's cousin, A. P.'s sister-in-law, and mother of June Carter, who married Johnny Cash). Their descendants won't allow today's performers to use any electric equipment, so the music is as pure as it was when the Carters cut their first record in 1927. Come early to visit the log cabin in which A. P. Carter was born in 1891 and to see the Carter Family Museum in the country store he operated from 1943 until his death in 1960. C.R. 614, Maces Spring. ✆ **276/386-9480.** www.carterfamilyfold.org. Music show tickets $10–$20 adults, $1–$5 children 6–11, free for children 5 and under. Museum and cabin admission 50¢ per person. Shows Sat 7:30pm; doors and museum open 6pm. From Abingdon take I-81 south 17 miles to Bristol, U.S. 58 west 19 miles to Hiltons, then C.R. 614 east 3 miles to auditorium.

8

ROANOKE & THE SOUTHWEST HIGHLANDS

Abingdon: A Show-Stopping Town

RICHMOND

N ow a sprawling metropolitan area flanking the James River in the center of the state, Richmond has been Virginia's capital since 1780 and has been the stage for much history. It was in Richmond's St. John's Church that Patrick Henry concluded his address to the second Virginia Convention with the stirring words "Give me liberty, or give me death!" During the Revolution, turncoat Gen. Benedict Arnold led British troops down what is now Main Street in 1781 and set fire to many buildings, including tobacco warehouses—in those days, the equivalent of banks. Cornwallis briefly occupied the town, and Lafayette came to the rescue.

Richmond is an essential stop for every Civil War enthusiast, for it was as capital of the Confederate States of America that the city left an indelible mark on American history. Jefferson Davis lived in the Confederate White House here while presiding over the rebel government, and it was in the mansion that Robert E. Lee accepted command of the Army of Northern Virginia. For 4 years, the Union army tried unsuccessfully to capture the city. Troops often battled on its outskirts; its tobacco warehouses overflowed with prisoners of war, its hospitals with the wounded, and its cemeteries with the dead. Richmond didn't fall into Union hands until Grant chased Lee out of Petersburg—an easy excursion to the south—a week before the surrender at Appomattox.

Richmond has changed in many ways since then, not the least in its demographics. Many descendants of the white Confederate soldiers have fled to the sprawling suburbs, leaving the African-American descendants of the slaves those soldiers fought to keep in bondage to make up a majority of the municipality's population—and the city council.

Racial tensions ran high for many years. For example, the city council created a stir by voting to place a statue of the late Arthur Ashe—the great African-American tennis star and Richmond native—among those of Civil War heroes lining Monument Avenue.

But local residents have come together lately to launch a rebirth of Richmond's downtown area, including construction of a sparkling performing arts center and the conversion of an abandoned department store into a fine hotel. Jackson Ward, the historic black neighborhood, is showing signs of rebirth despite the recession.

In addition to its Civil War battlefields and museums, Richmond has splendid historic homes, an excellent fine arts museum, a hands-on science museum with a state-of-the-art planetarium, and a charming botanical garden.

ORIENTATION & GETTING AROUND

Visitor Information

The **Richmond Visitors Center,** 401 N. 3rd St. (btw. Clay and Marshall sts.), Richmond, VA 23219 (🕿 **888/742-4666;** www.visitrichmondva.com), provides information and operates a same-day discounted hotel reservation service. It also shows a 10-minute orientation video. The center is in the Greater Richmond Convention Center and is open daily 9am to 5pm. There is free 20-minute parking in spaces by the serpentine brick wall on 3rd Street between Clay and Marshall streets.

In addition, the **Richmond International Airport Visitors Center** (🕿 **804/236-3260**) is open Monday to Friday 9:30am to 4:30pm and Saturday to Sunday noon to 5pm.

Approaching from the north via I-95, there's an information booth in the **Bass Pro Shop,** 11550 Lakeridge Pkwy., in Ashland. It is open Thursday to Monday 10am to 6pm.

The state operates a visitor information center in the **Bell Tower** (🕿 **804/786-4485**) on the State Capitol grounds, off 9th Street between Grace and Marshall streets. It's open Monday to Friday 9am to 5pm. The small gift shop is a good place to stock up on "Virginia Is for Lovers" gear.

Another comprehensive source of information is **www.discoverrichmond.com**, a community site operated by the *Richmond Times-Dispatch* newspaper (www.timesdispatch.com).

As soon as you see one, grab a copy of Richmond's free alternative newspaper, **Style Weekly** (www.styleweekly.com), available in boxes throughout town. It is a very good source of what's going on while you're here.

Getting There

BY PLANE   American, Continental, Delta, JetBlue, Southwest, United, and US Airways fly to **Richmond International Airport (RIC),** Airport Drive off I-64, I-295, and Williamsburg Road (U.S. 60; 🕿 **804/226-3052;** www.flyrichmond.com), about 15 minutes east of downtown. The major car-rental companies have desks at the airport, and taxis are available. **Groome Transportation** (🕿 **800/552-7911** or 804/222-7222; www.groometransportation.com) offers 24-hour van service to Richmond, Petersburg, Fredericksburg, and Williamsburg. One-person fares range from $24 to downtown Richmond to $46 to Williamsburg. Public bus service is available during weekday morning and evening rush hours (see "Getting Around," below), but frankly, if you can afford to fly into Richmond, forget the local bus system.

BY CAR   Richmond is at the junction of **I-64,** traveling east-west, and **I-95,** traveling north-south. **I-295** bypasses both Richmond and Petersburg on their east sides. **U.S. 60** (east-west) and **U.S. 1** and **U.S. 301** (north-south) cross here.

BY TRAIN & BUS   Several daily **Amtrak** (🕿 **800/872-7245;** www.amtrak.com) trains pull into two stations here. The main terminal is at 7519 Staples Mill Rd. (U.S. 33), north of I-64. There is no shuttle service from the Staples Mill Road station into tourist areas, so a better choice is the **Main Street Station** at 1500 E. Main St. in Shockoe Bottom. This restored French Renaissance–style building served as the city's transportation hub from 1901 until 1959 and is itself worth a look.

As in any city, it's wise to stay alert and be aware of your surroundings, whatever the time of day. Ask at the visitor center or at your hotel desk if a neighborhood you intend to visit is safe. Most neighborhoods described in this chapter are generally safe during the day, and Shockoe Slip, Shockoe Bottom, The Fan, and Carytown are safe during the evening when their restaurants are open. Nevertheless, avoid all deserted streets after dark. Most hotels have free shuttles in the downtown area, so take them when going out in the evening.

The **Greyhound/Trailways** bus terminal is at 2910 N. Boulevard (✆ **800/231-2222;** www.greyhound.com).

City Layout

Richmond is located at the fall line of the James River. Several bridges cross the river, and there's access to Brown's Island and Belle Isle from the **Richmond Riverfront Canal Walk,** a promenade extending along the downtown riverfront beside the **James River & Kanawha Canal** (see "What to See & Do," later in this chapter).

Instead of growing away from the river, the original city spread westward on the hills along the north shore. Thus, the main streets run east-west for several miles from the original settlement, in today's Shockoe Bottom, to Carytown.

Foushee Street divides street numbers east and west, while **Main Street** divides them north and south.

The Neighborhoods in Brief

As you explore the neighborhoods described below (moving from east to west), you'll get a good sense of Richmond's history.

Church Hill Named for St. John's Church, its major landmark, this east Richmond neighborhood is largely residential, with many 19th-century Greek-revival residences.

Tobacco Row Bordering Church Hill and paralleling the James River for some 15 blocks between 20th and Pear streets, this is an urban redevelopment area. Handsome redbrick warehouses are being turned into apartment homes. The Edgar Allan Poe and Virginia Holocaust museums are here.

Shockoe Bottom Roughly bounded by Dock and Broad streets and 15th and 20th streets, Shockoe Bottom was Richmond's first business district. It once encompassed tobacco factories, produce markets (farmers still sell produce at the **17th Street Farmer's Market** btw. E. Main and E. Franklin sts.), slave auction houses, warehouses, and shops, and it retains much of its original character. Today, old-fashioned groceries with signs in their windows for fresh chitterlings stand alongside trendy shops, restaurants, and noisy nightclubs aimed primarily at 20-somethings.

Shockoe Slip Bordering downtown roughly between 10th and 14th streets and Main and Canal streets, this warehouse and commercial area was reduced to rubble in 1865 and rebuilt as a manufacturing center after the war. With its cobblestones restored and old-fashioned streetlamps providing light, East Cary Street features renovated warehouses containing restaurants, galleries, nightspots, shops, and two major hotels. The Richmond Riverfront Canal Walk boat rides begin here.

Downtown West and north of Shockoe Slip, downtown is Richmond's governmental and financial center. It includes the old and new city halls, the state capitol, and the government buildings of **Capitol Square** and the historic homes and museums of the **Court**

Richmond Overview

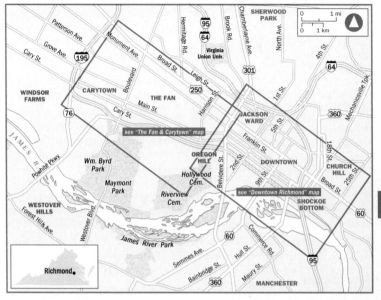

End area, notably the Valentine Richmond History Center, the Museum and White House of the Confederacy, and the John Marshall House. On its western edges it encompasses the Coliseum, the city's convention center, and several blocks of East Broad Street, which was once home to Richmond's grand department stores and is being redeveloped, including Richmond Center-Stage, the city's new performing arts venue.

Jackson Ward North of Broad Street, the National Historic District of Jackson Ward was home to many free African Americans before the Civil War ended slavery. Its famous residents have included the first woman bank president in the United States, Maggie Walker, and legendary dancer Bill "Bojangles" Robinson, who donated a stoplight for the safety of children crossing the intersection of Leigh Street and Chamberlayne Avenue (where a monument to him stands today). Notable, too, is the fine ornamental ironwork gracing the facades of many Jackson Ward residences. The area

around the Hippodrome Theater, on North Second Street is rapidly being redeveloped.

The Fan Just west of downtown, The Fan is named for the shape of the streets, which more or less "fan" out from downtown. Bordered by West Broad, Boulevard, West Main, and Belvidere, this gentrified area of turn-of-the-20th-century town houses includes Virginia Commonwealth University and many restaurants and galleries. The main drag is on West Main Street between South Harrison and South Lombardy streets. Monument Avenue's most scenic blocks, with the Civil War statues—and one of African-American tennis star Arthur Ashe—down its median strip, are in The Fan.

Carytown Just west of Boulevard, affluent Carytown has been called Richmond's answer to Georgetown. Cafes, restaurants, boutiques, antiques shops, and the Byrd Theater, a restored 1928-vintage movie palace, bring weekend crowds to West Cary Street between Boulevard and Nasemond Street.

9 RICHMOND | The Neighborhoods in Brief

205

Getting Around

BY PUBLIC TRANSPORTATION Of little use to visitors, the **Greater Richmond Transit Company** (GRTC; © 804/358-GRTC [4782]; www.ridegrtc.com) operates the **public bus** system throughout the metropolitan area. Base bus fare is $1.50 (exact change only).

The Quick Route Across Town

To drive across town quickly, use **Main Street,** which is one-way going west (it changes into **Ellwood Ave.**); and the parallel **Cary Street,** one-way going east. Avoid two-way **Broad Street** because you cannot make left turns at many of its intersections.

Much more useful is the free **To the Bottom and Back Bus** (© 804/239-8180; www.2bnb.org), operated by a nonprofit organization devoted to reducing the amount of drunk driving in the city. The buses operate Thursday to Saturday 6pm to 3am between Shockoe Bottom and Carytown, following Main Street/Ellwood Avenue westbound and Cary Street eastbound. The buses are equipped with GPS tracking devices so you can find where one is on the website or on your smart phone.

BY TAXI Call **Richmond Checker Taxi** (© 804/245-9457; www.richmondcheckertaxi.com), **Veterans Cab Association** (© 804/329-1414; www.veteranscabrichmond.com), or **Deb's Taxi Service** (© 804/439-2232; www.debstaxiservice.com). Fares are approximately $2.50 per mile.

WHERE TO STAY

The **Richmond Visitors Center** (© 888/742-4666; www.visitrichmondva.com) has a reservations service on its website, and it makes same-day reservations for walk-in visitors, often at a discount (see "Visitor Information," above). **Note:** Inexpensive rooms can be scarce here on race weekends at Richmond International Raceway (see "Sports & Outdoor Activities," later in this chapter).

Chain motels of every description are scattered throughout the suburbs. Most convenient to the key attractions is the campuslike Executive Center area, on West Broad Street (U.S. 33/250) at I-64 (Exit 183), about 5 miles west of downtown. Among its hotels is the California-style **Ramada Plaza Richmond West** (© 888/288-4982 or 804/285-2000), which until recently was the Sheraton Richmond West; the **Courtyard by Marriott Richmond West** (© 800/321-2211 or 804/282-1881); an **Econo Lodge** (© 800/553-2666 or 804/672-8621); the **Hampton Inn West** (© 800/426-7866 or 804/747-7777); and the **Holiday Inn Richmond I-64 West End** (© 800/465-4329 or 804/285-9951).

The hotels listed below provide **free shuttle service** to attractions and restaurants within a 3-mile radius, which covers all of Shockoe Slip and downtown.

Hotels in or near Shockoe Slip

The Berkeley Hotel ★★ At this elegant inn, a handsome redbrick facade opens into a seemingly old-world interior. Although established in 1988, the hotel creates the illusion that it was built long ago. A cozy ambience and attentive service prevail. Some of the luxuriously appointed guest quarters have whirlpool tubs and balconies. The Berkeley's **Dining Room** is one of Richmond's most refined hotel dining rooms. **Nightingale's Lounge** adjoins.

Downtown Richmond

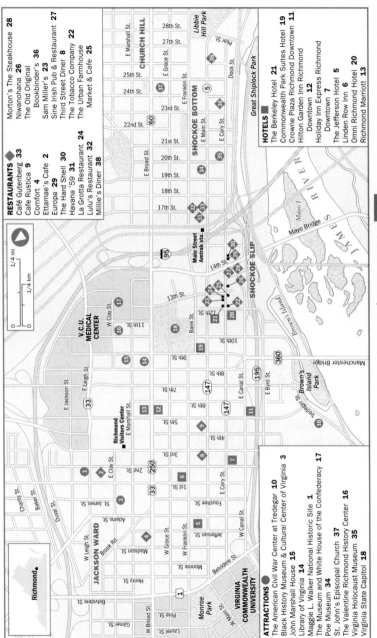

RESTAURANTS ◆
Café Gutenberg **33**
Cafe Rustica **9**
Comfort **4**
Ettamae's Cafe **2**
Europa **29**
The Hard Shell **30**
Havana '59 **31**
La Grotta Restaurant **24**
Lulu's Restaurant **32**
Mille's Diner **38**
Morton's The Steakhouse **28**
Niwanohana **26**
The Old Original
    Bookbinder's **36**
Sam Miller's **23**
Sine Irish Pub & Restaurant **27**
Third Street Diner **8**
The Tobacco Company **22**
The Urban Farmhouse
    Market & Cafe **25**

HOTELS ■
The Berkeley Hotel **21**
Commonwealth Park Suites Hotel **19**
Crowne Plaza Richmond Downtown **11**
Hilton Garden Inn Richmond
    Downtown **12**
Holiday Inn Express Richmond
    Downtown **7**
The Jefferson Hotel **5**
Linden Row Inn **6**
Omni Richmond Hotel **20**
Richmond Marriott **13**

ATTRACTIONS ●
The American Civil War Center at Tredegar **10**
Black History Museum & Cultural Center of Virginia **3**
John Marshall House **15**
Library of Virginia **14**
Maggie L. Walker National Historic Site **1**
The Museum and White House of the Confederacy **17**
Poe Museum **34**
St. John's Episcopal Church **37**
The Valentine Richmond History Center **16**
Virginia Holocaust Museum **35**
Virginia State Capitol **18**

9

RICHMOND | Where to Stay

207

1200 E. Cary St., Richmond, VA 23219. www.berkeleyhotel.com. ✆ **888/780-4422** or 804/780-1300. Fax 804/648-4728. 55 units. $209–$239 double; $269–$400 suite. Packages available. AE, DC, DISC, MC, V. Valet parking $21; no self-parking. **Amenities:** Restaurant; bar; room service. *In room:* A/C, TV, hair dryer, Wi-Fi.

Commonwealth Park Suites Hotel 🏊 All but 10 of the 59 units in this 11-story hotel are spacious, two-room suites. Some features, such as bidets in the bathrooms and handcrafted armoires hiding the living room TVs, hearken back to its days as a luxury boutique hotel. Most of the furniture is now more Scandinavian than Virginian, however, and it seems to me the bright blue bedspreads with gold brocade are a tad gaudy for Richmond. Nevertheless, you get a lot of room for the money, and the location on Bank Street opposite the Virginia State Capitol, just 4 blocks from Shockoe Slip, is superb.

910 Bank St., Richmond, VA 23219. www.commonwealthparksuites.com. ✆ **888/343-7301** or 804/343-7300. Fax 804/343-1025. 59 units. $89–$114 double, $92–$128 suites. Packages available. AE, DISC, MC, V. Valet parking $12; no self-parking. **Amenities:** Restaurant; exercise room, sauna. *In room:* AC, TV, fridge, hair dryer, Wi-Fi.

Omni Richmond Hotel ★ Along with the Berkeley Hotel (see above) across the street, the Omni enjoys a terrific location next to Shockoe Slip's boutiques, restaurants, and clubs. It boasts a handsome pink-marble lobby, with green velvet–upholstered chairs and sofas around a working fireplace. Rooms are decorated in soft pastels, and some have spectacular views of the nearby James River. Club-floor rooms offer access to a private lounge, where a complimentary continental breakfast and afternoon refreshments are served on weekdays. **Trevi's,** the hotel's casual Italian restaurant, opens to the James Center office tower's atrium. *Note:* Self-parking here is on an hourly in-out rate, so if you're going to use your vehicle, the valet service can be less expensive.

100 S. 12th St., Richmond, VA 23219. www.omnirichmond.com. ✆ **800/843-6664** or 804/344-7000. Fax 804/648-6704. 361 units. $159–$199 double; $350–$750 suite. Packages available. AE, DC, DISC, MC, V. Valet parking $20; self-parking $21 maximum (in-out hourly rate applies). **Amenities:** Restaurant; bar; concierge-level rooms; access to nearby health club; pool; room service. *In room:* A/C, TV, fridge, hair dryer, Wi-Fi ($9.95 per 24 hr.).

Downtown Hotels

Crowne Plaza Richmond Downtown You won't mistake this Crowne Plaza for any other building in town—it's a starkly modern, triangular 16-story high-rise with reflecting glass windows. Most of the rooms offer stunning river and city views, especially the Point Suites in the sharp corners of the building (their windows render 270-degree views). Some suites are bi-level, with sleeping lofts upstairs. It's less expensive than the Berkeley and the Omni Richmond, and it's only a few blocks to Shockoe Slip. The mezzanine-level **Pavilion Cafe** serves all three meals, while the **Great Room** off the lobby offers Starbucks coffee, drinks, and light fare with a view of Canal Walk.

555 E. Canal St., Richmond, VA 23219. www.crowneplaza.com/ric-downtown. ✆ **800/227-6963** or 804/788-0900. Fax 804/788-7087. 299 units. $99–$229 double; $250–$880 suite. AE, DC, DISC, MC, V. Valet parking $14; self-parking $10. **Amenities:** Restaurant; bar; executive or concierge-level rooms; health club; pool; room service. *In room:* A/C, TV, fridge (in most), hair dryer, Internet, Wi-Fi (in some).

Hilton Garden Inn Richmond Downtown ★ For generations the Miller & Rhoads department store was such a landmark that its prominent clock (now in the Valentine Richmond History Center; see review later in this chapter) was everyone's favorite spot to rendezvous—as in, "Meet me under the clock." But suburban stores stole its clientele, and M&R closed its doors for the last time in 1990. The building sat empty until 2009, when it reopened with 133 apartments above this unusual hotel. The large rectangular building wraps around a glass-roof-covered courtyard, and it can be quite a hoof from the elevators to some of the guest rooms. Although the building was gutted, the architecture dictated that some units have very high ceilings and monstrous window walls. Otherwise, they are typical Hilton fare. Both the lobby and the **Great American Grill** are adorned with photos of Richmond when everyone met under the clock, a replica of which now hangs in the lobby here.

501 E. Broad St., Richmond, VA 23219. www.hiltongardeninn.com. ✆ **800/HILTONS** [445-8667] or 804/344-4300. Fax 804/344-4375. 250 units. $119–$259 double. AE, DC, DISC, MC, V. Valet parking $25; no self-parking. **Amenities:** Restaurant; bar; health club; Jacuzzi; pool; room service. *In room:* A/C, TV, fridge, hair dryer, MP3 docking station, Wi-Fi.

Holiday Inn Express Richmond Downtown   It's worth paying extra for a two-room suite at this modest but comfortable hotel, since five of them have two-person Jacuzzis in their living rooms. There is no restaurant on premises, but full breakfast is complimentary, and every unit has a microwave oven and a fridge. Although the hotel fronts Cary Street, you must enter the parking garage off Second Street between Cary and Canal streets and take the elevator to "PL," which is the lobby level.

201 E. Cary St., Richmond, VA 23219. www.hiexpress.com. ✆ **888/465-4329** or 804/788-1600. Fax 804/788-1661. 100 units. $109–$129 double; $119–$139 suite. Rates include full breakfast. AE, DC, DISC, MC, V. **Amenities:** Health club. *In room:* A/C, TV, fridge, hair dryer, Wi-Fi.

The Jefferson Hotel ★★★   One of Virginia's finest hotels, this stunning six-story Beaux Arts building is the creation of Maj. Lewis Ginter, a founder of the American Tobacco Company who also founded the Lewis Ginter Botanical Garden (see "What to See & Do," later in this chapter). The magnificent limestone-and-brick facade is adorned with Renaissance-style balconies, arched porticos, and an Italian clock tower. Two-story faux-marble columns, embellished with gold leaf, encircle the soaring rotunda—the original lobby—which has a small museum explaining the hotel's history. From there, the marble grand staircase leads up to today's reception desk in the Palm Court lobby. There Edward Valentine's magnificent statue of Thomas Jefferson stands directly under a stained-glass-domed skylight, 9 of its 12 panes original Tiffany glass.

Furnished with custom-made 18th-century reproduction pieces, the well-equipped rooms come in 57 different configurations, including two-room suites. It's worth paying extra for one of the Deluxe rooms, which have more space and charm—some have their original fireplace mantels—than the Superior models. A few Deluxe King rooms have balconies, as does the presidential suite.

Lemaire, the hotel's prime dining room, specializes in Chesapeake-style seafood. The **Rotunda** (as in the University of Virginia) is put to use for outstanding Sunday jazz brunches (about $55 for adults, $20 for children, including champagne, tax, and tip; reservations are required). Off the Rotunda, **T.J.'s** (as in Thomas Jefferson, who else?) offers good Mediterranean-inspired fare in a relaxed setting. The hotel's bar is almost hidden behind the Rotunda's original reception windows. Across the way, the gift shop serves freshly brewed coffees and teas. Other notable amenities include a state-of-the-art health club and a resortlike indoor pool under a skylight. Your dog can enjoy the luxuries here, too.

Mr. Jefferson's Ascot

Take a close look at Edward Valentine's stunning statue of Thomas Jefferson standing in the middle of the Palm Court in the Jefferson Hotel. In an effort to save it during a 1902 fire, Valentine and others lassoed the statue and pulled it down on some mattresses. Unfortunately the fall decapitated Mr. Jefferson. Hotel legend says the sculptor added the ascot to conceal T. J.'s scar.

101 W. Franklin St., Richmond, VA 23220. www.jeffersonhotel.com. © **800/484-8014** or 804/788-8000. Fax 804/225-0334. 262 units. $365–$395 double; $435–$795 suite. Packages available. AE, DC, DISC, MC, V. Valet parking $16; self-parking $12. Pet fee $50/day (dogs only). **Amenities:** Restaurant; bar; concierge; executive or concierge-level rooms; health club; indoor pool; room service. *In room:* A/C, TV, hair dryer, Wi-Fi.

Linden Row Inn 🌢 The facades of this row of seven mid-19th-century Greek-revival town houses and their garden dependencies (small, separate buildings) have remained intact. Original interior features, such as fireplaces, marble mantels, and crystal chandeliers, grace the town houses, which the National Trust for Historic Preservation has officially designated a Historic Hotel of America. Rooms in the houses, all with windows nearly reaching the 12-foot ceilings, have a mix of late-Empire and early-Victorian pieces, with marble-top dressers. Less charming, the garden rooms overlook a walled garden and patio, and those in the carriage houses offer contemporary-looking furniture. Entry to the town house units is from wooden steps and walkways, so you may have to pull your shades for privacy.

100 E. Franklin St., Richmond, VA 23219. www.lindenrowinn.com. © **800/348-7424** or 804/783-7000. Fax 804/648-7504. 70 units. $99–$169 double; $250 suite. Rates include continental breakfast. AE, DISC, MC, V. Valet parking $11. **Amenities:** Access to nearby YMCA. *In room:* A/C, TV, fridge (in parlor suites), hair dryer, Wi-Fi.

Richmond Marriott Adjacent to the convention center, this Marriott has extensive meeting space of its own, and it offers more amenities than the Hilton Garden Inn across Broad Street. Many of its spacious accommodations offer panoramic city views. Those on the top three floors have their own concierge lounge offering breakfast and afternoon refreshments. A bar, coffee shop, and sports bar and restaurant are off the lobby. Other amenities include a health club with a shallow indoor swimming pool.

500 E. Broad St., Richmond, VA 23219. www.marriott.com. © **800/228-9290** or 804/643-3400. Fax 804/788-1230. 402 units. $139–$269 double; $300–$600 suite. Packages available. AE, DC, DISC, MC, V. Valet parking $25; self-parking $17. **Amenities:** Restaurant; bar; concierge-level rooms; health club; Jacuzzi; indoor pool; room service. *In room:* A/C, TV, hair dryer, Wi-Fi ($13 per 24 hr.).

Bed & Breakfasts in the Fan

A few of the Victorian homes in The Fan have been turned into luxurious bed-and-breakfasts. They have an umbrella organization, **Historic Richmond Inns** (www.historicrichmondinns.com), upon whose website you can see all of them and make reservations with your choice. Like most Fan houses, they have front porches for sitting in a rocking chair and watching the neighbors stroll by.

Museum District Bed & Breakfast, 2811 Grove Ave. (www.museumdistrictbb.com; © **804/359-2332**), and the **Kensington Bed and Breakfast,** 2926 Kensington Ave. (www.thekensingtonbedandbreakfast.com; © **8a04/358-9901**), flank the joint campus of the Virginia Museum of Fine Arts and the Virginia Historical Society/ Museum of Virginia History. See "'Boulevard' Museums," later in this chapter.

Both **Maury Place at Monument,** 3101 W. Franklin St. (www.mauryplace.com; *©* **804/353-2717**), and **Grace Manor Inn,** 1853 W. Grace St. (www.thegrace manorinn.com; *©* **804/3353-4334**), are just steps from Monument Avenue.

The **William Miller House,** 1129 Floyd Ave. (www.williammillerhouse.com; *©* **804/254-2928**), at the edge of the Virginia Commonwealth University campus, is nearer Main Street and the commercial heart of The Fan.

WHERE TO EAT

The city has hundreds of restaurants. Beyond those recommended here, you won't go wrong following the "Critics' Picks" in Richmond's free alternative newspaper, *Style Weekly* (www.styleweekly.com), available in boxes throughout town. *Richmond Magazine* (www.richmondmagazine.com) also reviews local restaurants.

Church Hill/Tobacco Row

Millie's Diner ★★ INTERNATIONAL Once Millie's really was a diner, and although it's been renovated, the counter, booths with jukeboxes, and open kitchen from those days are still here. It hasn't been a diner since 1989, when talented chefs started turning out a variety of tasty dishes at the gas stove. My favorite, the spicy Thai shrimp, is usually on the menu, which changes every few weeks. Whatever you order, it will be made from scratch—as you watch, if you grab a counter seat. You can dine outside at lunch or brunch during warm weather but not at dinner.

2603 E. Main St. (at 26th St.). *©* **804/643-5512.** www.milliesdiner.com. Reservations accepted only for seating before 6:30pm. Main courses $20–$31. AE, DC, DISC, MC, V. Tues–Fri 11am– 2:30pm and 5:30–10:30pm; Sat 10am–3pm (brunch) and 5:30–10:30pm; Sun 9am–3pm (brunch) and 5:30–9:30pm.

The Old Original Bookbinder's ★★ AMERICAN On the first floor of River Lofts, one of the old Tobacco Row warehouses converted into condos, this branch of the Philadelphia institution is Richmond's best place for both seafood and steaks. The warehouse's brick walls and the exposed air ducts overhead add a certain rustic charm to this chic but casual spot. The chef takes his own approach to traditional Chesapeake dishes such as jumbo crab cakes served with rémoulade and Chinese pepper sauces. For landlubbers, steaks range from 8 to 24 ounces. There's free validated parking in the lot across the street, plus valet parking Friday and Saturday evenings.

2306 E. Cary St. (btw. 23rd and 24th sts.). *©* **804/643-6900.** www.bookbindersrichmond.com. Reservations highly recommended. Main courses $20–$40. AE, MC, V. Sun–Thurs 5–9pm; Fri–Sat 5–10pm.

Shockoe Bottom

Like Shockoe Slip and Carytown, "The Bottom" has several restaurants offering a variety of cuisines.

Café Gutenberg *🍴* AMERICAN/VEGETARIAN The chefs at this casual bistro raid the Farmer's Market across 17th Street for their "local vegetable fondue," actually steamed fresh vegetables served with a Vermont cheese "gravy" on a French baguette. I'm fonder of their homemade corncakes, which can be ordered plain, with a mixed berry compote, topped with regular country or vegan sausage, or served with lox, cream cheese, and scrambled eggs. The top main course is a mixed grill with a choice of beef, shrimp, and chicken, or with vegetarian mock duck and tofu. You can watch the Bottom scene from sidewalk tables in warm weather.

1700 E. Main St. (at 17th St.). ℭ **804/497-5000.** www.cafegutenberg.com. Reservations recommended on weekends. Sandwiches and salads $7–$9; main courses $13–$17. AE, DISC, MC, V. Wed–Fri 11am–11pm; Sat–Sun 8am–11pm.

Havana '59 CUBAN   This lively theme restaurant presents a strange sight across the street from the covered stalls of the Farmer's Market, especially during warm weather when its big, garage-style storefront windows roll up to let fresh air in. Then you might swear you're in Havana in 1959 when Fidel Castro marched into town. Fake palms, ceiling fans, string lights, Cuban music, and adobe walls with gaping holes (where plaster ought to be) set a festive scene. The Cuban-accented cuisine lives up to the ambience. The menu changes frequently, so you never know what will be marching into Havana on any given day. There's validated parking in the lot at Franklin and 17th streets.

16 N. 17th St. (btw. Main and Franklin sts.). ℭ **804/780-2822.** www.havana59.net. Reservations recommended. Main courses $16–$25. AE, DC, DISC, MC, V. Mon–Thurs 5–10pm; Fri–Sat 5–11pm.

Lulu's Restaurant ★ AMERICAN/VEGETARIAN   A casual bistro with mostly booth seating, Lulu's specializes in refined comfort food for both vegetarians and carnivores. The menu even denotes gluten-free choices. Vegetarians can opt for such items as meatless spaghetti, herbed potato gnocchi, and spicy Indian-style samosas. The rest of us can go for meatloaf, fried catfish, grilled lamb chops, and a very rich version of chicken and dumplings. There's a list of very good wines.

21 N. 17th St. ℭ **804/343-9771.** www.lulusrichmond.com. Reservations recommended. Main courses $17–$27. AE, MC, V. Mon–Thurs 11:30am–2:30pm and 5:30–9:30pm; Fri 11:30am–2:30pm and 5:30–10pm; Sat 10am–2:30pm and 5:30–10pm; Sun 10am–3pm.

Shockoe Slip

With a bevy of good-to-excellent restaurants, East Cary Street between 12th and 15th streets is Richmond's premier dining mecca, especially for tourists and conventioneers. On-street **parking** is always at a premium in this busy area, but you can resort to the municipal garage on East Cary Street at 14th Street.

You can get fresh if not inspired sushi at **Niwanohana,** 1309 E. Cary St. (ℭ 804/225-8801); excellent Italian at **La Grotta Restaurant,** 1218 E. Cary St. (ℭ 804/644-2466; www.lagrottaristorante.com); Chesapeake Bay seafood at the **Hard Shell,** 1411 E. Cary St. (ℭ 804/643-2333; www.thehardshell.com); upscale American at **Sam Miller's,** 1210 E. Cary St. (ℭ 804/643-1301; www.sammillers.com); and Italian pasta and Spanish tapas at **Europa,** 1409 E. Cary St. (ℭ 804/643-0911; www.europarichmond.com).

Steak lovers can grill their extra cash at a branch of **Morton's The Steakhouse** at 111 Virginia St. (ℭ **804/648-1662;** www.mortons.com/richmond), a block south of East Cary Street.

Consistently popular as a professionals' watering hole, **Siné Irish Pub & Restaurant,** 1327 E. Cary St. (ℭ **804/649-7767;** www.sineirishpub.com), is anything but a typical Irish pub, offering a wide selection of seafood, steaks, and chicken in addition to the usual corned beef and cabbage. In warm weather you can dine and drink on the deck out back.

The Tobacco Company AMERICAN   Appropriately, this dining-entertainment complex is in a former tobacco warehouse converted to a sunny, plant-filled three-story atrium. It was a pioneer in Shockoe Slip's renaissance and still draws so many tourists and expense-account types that many locals consider it a tourist trap. It's a fun place, nonetheless. An antique elevator carries you from the first-floor Atrium Lounge to the two dining floors above. Nostalgic touches abound—brass chandeliers, Tiffany-style lamps, a cigar-store Indian. Contemporary American cuisine is featured. You might opt for a 12-ounce cut of slow-roasted prime rib. There's live music and dancing in the Atrium Lounge beginning at 9:30pm Wednesday through Saturday.

1201 E. Cary St. (at 12th St.). (©) **804/782-9431.** www.thetobaccocompany.com. Reservations accepted. Main courses $19–$36. AE, DISC, MC, V. Mon–Thurs 11:30am–2:30pm and 5:30–10pm; Fri 11:30am–2:30pm and 5:30–10:30pm; Sat 5:30–10:30pm; Sun 5:30–9:30pm. Lounge Mon–Fri 11:30am–2am.

The Urban Farmhouse Market & Café ★ 🏠 DELI/COFFEEHOUSE This urban deli is a great spot for breakfast, especially when the big storefront doors swing open in warm weather, letting Cary Street into the comfortable dining room filled with both tables and sofas. Freshly baked artisan breads are used for breakfast and lunch sandwiches, and you Yankees can get your fill of lox and bagels. The Surry country ham is stacked so high it's hard to eat it all, yet vegetarians and vegans have choices, too, including vegetable sausage and vegan hummus with sweet peppers. The Thai tuna salad is worth taking home. The evening board is limited to cheese plates and other light fare.

1217 E. Cary St. (©) **804/325-3988.** www.theurbanfarmhouse.net. Reservations not accepted. Most items $5–$12. AE, DISC, MC, V. Mon–Fri 6:30am–8pm; Sat 7:30am–9pm; Sun 7:30am–8pm.

Jackson Ward

Ettamae's Cafe ★ AMERICAN Although this little charmer is in predominately African American Jackson Ward, it's the creation of the Caucasian brother-sister team of Laura Bailey and Matthew Morand, who named it for their grandmother. You will pass them busily at work in the kitchen before climbing the stairs to their bright, cheerful dining room and a few wrought iron tables out on the roof overlooking the street. Lunch sees an interesting collection of sandwiches, several of them vegetarian. The sweet and spicy pulled pork flavored with cumin and served with peppers and *queso manchego* (Spanish sheep's milk cheese) is a standout. A few sandwiches find their way on the dinner menu, which features the likes of Creole-style steak and shrimp, fennel-dusted sea scallops with crisp prosciutto and a blackberry malbec glaze, and baked vegetarian pasta with cheeses, roasted tomatoes, and asparagus.

522 N. 2nd St. (©) **804/888-8058.** www.ettamaescafe.com. Reservations recommended. Salads and sandwiches $5–$12; main courses $15–$30. DISC, MC, V. Tues–Fri 11am–3pm and 5–10pm; Sat 10am–3pm and 5–10pm; Sun 10am–3pm.

Downtown

Cafe Rustica ★★ 🍴 INTERNATIONAL You can't make a reservation but it's worth waiting for a table at this tiny, seven-table bistro to sample its "European comfort" food served in generous portions at very reasonable prices. After a tasty salad of thick-sliced fresh beets served with bleu cheese, candied walnuts, and crispy greens, I went on to a huge, tender, and luscious pork chop rubbed Spanish style with sour orange, cumin, garlic, and oregano. Vegetarians can run off to Mykonos with grilled vegetables topped with *tzatziki* (tangy cucumber yogurt dip). For dessert, the fried pound cake with lemon sauce and fresh berries is worth a repeat visit. On Sunday night, the three-course supper is an excellent value; one week there may be roast chicken, another may see pot roast.

414 E. Main St. (✆) **804/225-8811.** www.caferustica.com. Reservations not accepted. Main courses $15–$18; Sun supper $15. AE, DISC, MC, V. Mon 11am–3pm; Tues–Fri 11am–3pm and 5–10pm; Sat 5–10pm; Sun 5–9pm.

Comfort AMERICAN   This old storefront with a pressed-tin ceiling is home to some of Richmond's best comfort food, which one local wag described as "soul food for white folks." Very good versions of meatloaf, fried catfish, and pulled pork barbecue appear, all in substantial portions. Nightly specials sometimes include a smoky pork tenderloin in a bourbon-and-molasses sauce served with braised collard greens and cheese grits. My Southern mother never cooked anything this good.

200 W. Broad St. (at N. Jefferson St.). (✆) **804/780-0004.** www.comfortrestaurant.com. Reservations recommended. Main courses $16–$26. AE, MC, V. Mon–Thurs 11:30am–2:30pm and 5:30–10:30pm; Fri 11:30am–2:30pm and 5:30–11pm; Sat 5:30–10:30pm.

The Fan

Acacia Midtown ★★ *◢* AMERICAN   I first met chef Dale Reitzer and his wife, Aline, more than a decade ago when they were operating the first version of Acacia, in the 19th-century First Baptist Church, now a Carytown shopping center. They've moved on and up since then, with Dale twice being a semifinalist for the prestigious James Beard Foundation's Outstanding Chef Award. He is still plundering local farms for the fresh produce he uses for what might be called refined comfort food. Depending on the season, you might have Chincoteague oysters on the half shell with pickled jalapeño and a lime-basil ice. Main courses could see sautéed rockfish from the Chesapeake Bay served with celery root purée. The fixed-priced three-course dinner is an excellent value.

2601 W. Cary St. (✆) **804/562-0138.** www.acadiarestaurant.com. Reservations recommended. Main courses $22–$28; fixed-price dinner $24. AE, MC, V. Mon–Thurs 5:30–9pm; Fri–Sat 5:30–10pm.

Joe's Inn *◢* ITALIAN   This consistently popular neighborhood hangout has been serving inexpensive Greek-accented Italian fare since 1952, including veal parmigiana, fish, pizzas, and pasta. The house specialty is gargantuan portions of spaghetti. Two can easily share an order of somewhat rubbery spaghetti à la Joe, which is served steaming hot en casserole, bubbling with a layer of baked provolone between the pasta and heaps of rich meat sauce. Soups, salads, omelets, and sandwiches are also options.

205 N. Shields Ave. (btw. Grove and Hanover sts.). (✆) **804/355-2282.** www.joesinn.com. Reservations not accepted. Breakfast $4.50–$14; sandwiches $4–$8; main courses $9–$16. AE, MC, V. Mon–Thurs 9am–midnight; Fri–Sat 8am–2am; Sun 8am–midnight.

Strawberry Street Café ★ *◢* AMERICAN   Another neighborhood favorite, this casual cafe is decorated in turn-of-the-20th-century style, with a beautiful oak bar and a gorgeous stained-glass room divider. At lunch or dinner, you can help yourself

---

A Sobering Experience

Richmond's favorite spot for after-the-bars-close sobering-up meals is the **3rd Street Diner**, 218 E. Main St., at 3rd Street ((✆) **804/788-4750**), which stays open 24 hours daily. It's a noisy diner with less-than-lightning-fast service, but nothing on the menu costs more than $12.

The Fan & Carytown

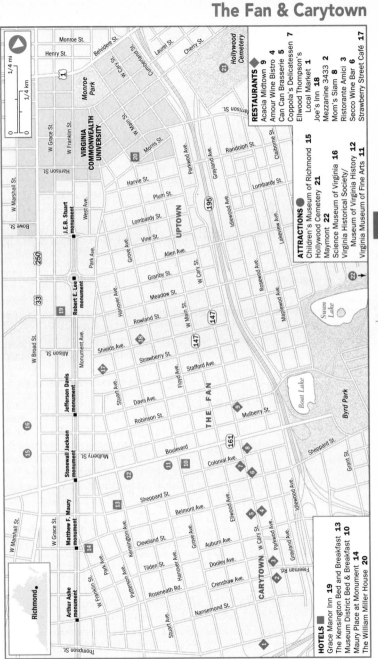

RESTAURANTS ◆
Acacia Midtown **9**
Amour Wine Bistro **4**
Can Can Brasserie **5**
Coppola's Delicatessen **7**
Ellwood Thompson's
  Local Market **1**
Joe's Inn **18**
Mezzanine 3433 **2**
Mom's Siam **8**
Ristorante Amici **3**
Secco Wine Bar **6**
Strawberry Street Café **17**

ATTRACTIONS ●
Children's Museum of Richmond **15**
Hollywood Cemetery **21**
Maymont **22**
Science Museum of Virginia **16**
Virginia Historical Society/
  Museum of Virginia History **12**
Virginia Museum of Fine Arts **11**

HOTELS ■
Grace Manor Inn **19**
The Kensington Bed and Breakfast **13**
Museum District Bed & Breakfast **10**
Maury Place at Monument **14**
The William Miller House **20**

Monroe St.
Henry St.
Monroe Park
VIRGINIA COMMONWEALTH UNIVERSITY
Hollywood Cemetery
UPTOWN
THE FAN
CARYTOWN
Byrd Park
Boat Lake
Swan Lake

Richmond

to unlimited offerings from an extensive salad bar partially nestled in a claw-foot bathtub. Summer sees fried green tomato sandwiches. The dinner menu offers pastas plus steaks, pork chops, and homemade chicken potpie with a flaky crust.

421 N. Strawberry St. (btw. Park and Stuart aves.). (C) **804/353-6860.** www.strawberrystreetcafe. com. Reservations needed for large groups. Sandwiches and burgers $7–$13; main courses $11–$17. AE, MC, V. Mon–Thurs 11am–10:30pm; Fri 11am–11pm; Sat 10am–11pm; Sun 10am–10:30pm.

Carytown

You and a few other travelers will find a wide variety of cuisine along the 7 blocks of West Cary Street between Boulevard and Nasemond Street. Among them are four Thai restaurants, of which **Mom's Siam,** 2811 W. Cary St. ((C) **804/359-7607**), at Colonial Avenue, has plentiful outdoor seating.

Two chic wine bars let you snack while partaking of the grape. **Amour Wine Bistro,** 3129 W. Cary St. ((C) **804/353-4020;** www.amourwinebistro.com), pairs the food style and wine of a different region of France each week. **Secco Wine Bar,** 2933 W. Cary St. ((C) **804/353-0670;** www.seccowinebar.com), has Italian-influenced food but a wide-ranging list.

After dinner you'll find me standing in line at the Carytown branch of **Sweet Frog Premium Frozen Yogurt,** 3137 W. Cary St. ((C) **804/213-3089;** www.sweetfrog yogurt.com).

Can Can Brasserie FRENCH   This chic Parisian-style bistro and wine bar would be right at home on the Avenue des Champs-Elysées. Lots of dark wood and etched room dividers carry out the theme, and a long steel-topped bar to one side is a good place to sample both wine and *fruits de mer crus* (that is, a raw bar). It's a lively, fun joint. The roasted red snapper atop chickpea polenta was so-so, but the accompanying vegetables were terrific. From now on I'm sticking to steak and fries, sole meunière, or a very good burger.

3120 W. Cary St. (btw. Belmont and McCloy sts.). (C) **804/358-7274.** www.cancanbrasserie.com. Reservations recommended. Burgers $13–$14; main courses $23–$26. AE, MC, V. Mon–Thurs 7:30am–10pm; Fri–Sat 7:30am–11pm; Sun 9am–3pm and 5:30–10pm.

Mezzanine 3433 ★ AMERICAN   This lively bistro's tiny kitchen does a fine job with such modern Southern standards as Low Country shrimp and grits under a surprisingly spicy cream sauce. The main plates are relatively small, so I started with a small mountain of fried green tomatoes. The blackboard menu changes daily depending on what's available from local farms and markets. Noisy 30-somethings can pack the small dining room and front porch, especially on Friday and Saturday evenings.

3433 W. Cary St. (btw. N. Crenshaw Ave. and N. Nansemond St.). (C) **804/353-2186.** www. mezzanine3433.com. Reservations accepted for parties of 4 or more. Main courses $12–$29. AE, DISC, MC, V. Tues–Thurs 5–10pm; Fri–Sat 5–11pm; Sun 10:30am–11pm. Bar open later.

Ristorante Amici ITALIAN   This delightful restaurant has been serving consistently good northern Italian cuisine since 1991. On the street level is a small bar and seating in an enclosed sidewalk patio whose windows are open during fine weather. The owners hail from Cervinia, a resort in the Italian Alps, where they perfected their craft. Their menu changes seasonally, but you might begin with thinly sliced buffalo (as in, bison) Carpaccio. Among the entrees could be buffalo saltimbocca. You get it: The chef plays with traditional Italian favorites. The wine list, with many Italian vintages, is surprisingly affordable.

3343 W. Cary St. (btw. Freeman Rd. and S. Dooley St.). © **804/353-4700.** www.amiciristorante.net. Reservations recommended. Main courses $17–$38. AE, DISC, MC, V. Mon–Sat 11:30am–2:30pm and 5:30–10pm; Sun 5–9pm.

PICNIC FARE

Coppola's Delicatessen, 2900 W. Cary St., at South Colonial Avenue (© **804/359-NYNY** [6969]; www.coppolasdeli.com), evokes New York's Little Italy with an aromatic clutter of cheeses, sausages, olives, pickles, pasta salads, antipasti, cannoli, specialty sandwiches, and pasta dinners. It is open Monday to Wednesday 10:30am to 8pm, Thursday to Saturday 10:30am to 9pm, and Sunday 11am to 7pm. There's a branch a block north of Shockoe Slip at Main and 12th streets (© **804/225-0454**), which is open Monday to Friday 10am to 4pm.

Carytown's version of Whole Foods is **Ellwood Thompson's Local Market,** 4 N. Thompson St. (© **804/359-7525;** www.ellwoodthompsons.com), carrying a wide range of homegrown produce and bakery goods. One part of the store is devoted to **Ellwood's Cafe,** which turns the goodies into salads and sandwiches. The vegan muffins are delicious. The store is open daily 7am to 9pm.

WHAT TO SEE & DO

Well worth taking is a 2-hour walking tour of downtown given by **Historic Richmond Tours** (© **804/649-0711,** option 4; www.richmondhistorycenter.com), a service of the Valentine Richmond History Center (see "Top Historical Attractions," below). They depart from the Richmond Visitors Center May to October Monday to Saturday at 10:30am and cost $10 per person, including admission to the Valentine Richmond History Center.

The center helps **Segway of Richmond,** 1301 E. Cary St. (© **804/343-1850;** www.segwayofrichmond.biz), in Shockoe Slip, to develop a variety of 2-hour guided historical tours via two-wheeled, motorized Segways. Reservations are a must.

Richmond Riverfront Canal Walk ★

George Washington envisioned a system of canals that would link America's eastern seaboard with the Ohio and Mississippi rivers in the west. In Richmond, construction began in 1789 on the James River & Kanawha Canal, which was to run alongside the James River and connect it to the Kanawha River. It reached as far as Buchanan, Virginia, before the railroads made canal transportation obsolete in the early 19th century. (Its towpath was later sold to the Richmond and Allegheny Railroad, which laid tracks along it.)

The city has restored more than 1 mile of the canal between Tobacco Row and the Tredegar Iron Works, at the foot of 5th Street, and turned it into the **Richmond Riverfront Canal Walk** (© **804/648-6549;** www.venturerichmond.com).

The ends of the walk are the most interesting parts. Near the eastern end, at the foot of Virginia Street in Shockoe Slip, you can take a 35-minute ride on the canal in a bateau operated by **River District Historic Canal Cruises** (© **804/649-2800** or 804/788-6466). Weather permitting, the motorized passenger boats run from mid-June to mid-August Wednesday through Saturday from noon to 7pm and Sunday from noon to 5pm. Spring and fall schedules are usually Thursday through Saturday from noon to 7pm and Sunday from noon to 5pm, but call to confirm. Rides are $6 for adults, $5 for seniors and children 5 to 12, and free for kids 4 and under. Buy tickets at the booth at the south end of Virginia Street.

At the western end of the walk, at the foot of 5th Street, the **Tredegar Iron Works** on Brown's Island was the South's largest industrial complex during the Civil War, producing about half of the Confederacy's armaments. The restored brick building now houses the National Park Services' **Richmond Civil War Visitor Center at Tredegar Iron Works** and the American Civil War Center at Tredegar (see "Top Historical Attractions," below). Opposite the visitor center, **Brown's Island** is the scene of festivals and free outdoor concerts and movies sponsored by Venture Richmond (see the box, "Fun Freebies," later in this chapter).

Top Historical Attractions

The American Civil War Center at Tredegar ★★ Before visiting Richmond's other Civil War sites, it helps to go through this museum, next door to the Richmond National Battlefield Visitor Center at Tredegar Iron Works. (See "Richmond National Battlefield Park," below.) Using films, photos, contemporary quotations, and other sources, it explains the buildup to the war (1775–1860), its causes, and its legacies from three perspectives: the North, the South, and the African American. At the end you'll have a chance to vote on what you think it was all about. The museum occupies an 1861 gun foundry building. More than 150 artifacts are on display, including life masks of Abraham Lincoln and Robert E. Lee. Get your parking ticket validated here.

500 Tredegar St. ② **804/780-1865.** www.tredegar.org. Admission $8 adults, $6 seniors, $2 children 6–17, free for children 5 and under. Parking $3/hr., free with validation. Daily 9am–5pm.

John Marshall House ★ This is the restored home of John Marshall, a giant in American judicial history, serving as chief justice of the U.S. Supreme Court from 1801 to 1835. In 1803, Marshall ruled in *Marbury v. Madison* that federal courts can overturn acts of Congress, thus establishing the doctrine of judicial review. Earlier, Marshall served in the Revolutionary army, argued cases for his close friend George Washington, served as ambassador to France under John Adams, and had a brief term as secretary of state. He was a political foe of his cousin, Thomas Jefferson. Largely intact, the house he built between 1788 and 1790 is remarkable for many original architectural features—exterior brick lintels, interior wide-plank pine floors, wainscoting, and paneling. Period antiques and reproductions supplement Marshall's own furnishings and personal artifacts. If you have to wait for a tour, spend the time checking out the museum shop and the gardens.

818 E. Marshall St. (at 9th St.). ② **804/648-7998.** www.apva.org/marshall. Admission $10 adults, $7 seniors, $5 students, free for children 3 and under. Admission includes Valentine Richmond History Center and 1812 Wickham House. Mar–Dec Fri–Sat 10am–4pm, Sun noon–5pm. Guided 1-hr. house tours on the hour and half-hour.

Saving with a Court End Passport

You can save with a Court End Passport, which includes admission to the John Marshall House, the Valentine Richmond History Center, and the Black History Museum and Cultural Center of Virginia. The passports are available at the three attractions and cost $10 for adults and $7 for seniors and children 4 to 18. They are free for children 3 and under.

Maggie L. Walker National Historic Site 🏛 The daughter of a former slave, Maggie L. Walker was a gifted woman who achieved success in the world of finance and business and rose to become the first African-American woman bank president in the country. Originally a teacher, Walker, after her marriage in 1886, became involved in the affairs of a black fraternal organization, the Independent Order of St. Luke, which grew under her guidance into an insurance company, then into a full-fledged bank, the St. Luke Penny Savings Bank. The bank continues today as the Consolidated Bank and Trust, the oldest surviving African-American-operated bank in the United States. Walker also became editor of a newspaper and created and developed a department store. Her residence from 1904 until her death in 1934, this house remained in her family until 1979. The National Park Service has restored it to its 1930 appearance. Park rangers lead 30-minute guided tours.

600 N. 2nd St. (btw. Lee and Jackson sts.). ℂ **804/771-2017.** www.nps.gov/malw. Free admission. Mar–Oct Mon–Sat 9am–5pm; Nov–Feb Mon–Sat 9am–4:30pm. Closed New Year's Day, Thanksgiving, and Christmas. 30-min. tours depart as necessary.

The Museum and White House of the Confederacy ★★★ A required stop for all Civil War buffs, this excellent museum houses some 20,000 artifacts, the largest Confederate collection in the country, much contributed by veterans and their descendants. All the war's major events and campaigns are documented. The 1818 mansion next door was the wartime home of President Jefferson Davis. As the White House of the Confederacy, it was the center of social and political activity in Richmond. Formal dinners, luncheons, and occasional cabinet meetings were held in the dining room, a Victorian chamber with ornate ceiling decoration; some of the furniture in this room is original to the Davis family. Guests were received in the center parlor, interesting now for its knickknacks produced by captured Confederate soldiers and for an 1863 portrait of Davis. You can explore the museum on your own, but you must take a guided tour to see the house. Allow at least 2 hours for both. There is validated parking in Virginia Commonwealth University's medical center parking deck next door. (Completely surrounded by the medical center and thus unable to expand, the museum is moving some of its collection to the **Museum of the Confederacy—Appomattox;** p. 125.)

1201 E. Clay St. (at 12th St.). ℂ **804/649-1861.** www.moc.org. Admission to museum or White House $10 adults, $8 seniors, $6 children 7–18, free for children 6 and under. Combination ticket (admission to both museum and White House) $15 adults, $13 seniors, $8 children 7–18, free for children 6 and under. Daily 10am–5pm. White House tours 11:30am–4pm; 45-min. tours depart continuously. Closed New Year's Day, Thanksgiving, and Christmas.

Poe Museum ★ As a young man, poet Edgar Allan Poe worked as an editor, critic, and writer for the *Southern Literary Messenger*. The desk and chair he used are among the memorabilia, photographs, portraits, and documents that tell the story of his rather sad life and career. The museum complex centers on the Old Stone House, the oldest building in Richmond; it dates to about 1737. Poe didn't live here, but as a 15-year-old he was part of a junior honor guard that escorted Lafayette here when the aging general visited in 1824. The other buildings were added to house the collection of Poe artifacts and publications, the largest in existence. Most fascinating is the Raven Room's illustrations by Edouard Manet and James Carling to Poe's poem, "The Raven."

The Poe Museum is only a block from the Virginia Holocaust Museum (p. 225), so park once to see both attractions.

1914–1916 E. Main St. ✆ **888/213-2763** or 804/648-5523. www.poemuseum.org. Admission $6 adults, $5 seniors and students, free for children 6 and under. Tues–Sat 10am–5pm; Sun 11am–5pm.

Richmond National Battlefield Park ★★★   As the political, medical, and manufacturing center of the South and the primary supply depot for Lee's Army of Northern Virginia, Richmond was a prime Union target throughout the Civil War. In 1862 Gen. George McClellan's Peninsula Campaign attacked from the southeast, and in 1864 Gen. Ulysses S. Grant advanced from the north. Neither succeeded in capturing Richmond, but Grant won the war by laying siege to Petersburg, thus cutting off Richmond's supplies from the south. The bloody battlefields of those campaigns ring Richmond's eastern side, now mostly suburbs, for some 80 miles.

Stop first at the **Richmond Civil War Visitor Center at Tredegar Iron Works,** at the foot of 5th Street on the Richmond Riverfront Canal Walk (see above). Here, a 22-minute video about the battles will get you oriented. Upstairs, the *Richmond Speaks* exhibit poignantly tells the city's story with photos, artifacts, and readings from letters soldiers wrote to their families. Outside stands a touching statue of President Abraham Lincoln and son Todd, a depiction of their visit to Richmond shortly after it fell in 1865. The visitor center and Chimborazo Medical Museum (see below) are open daily 9am to 5pm; they are closed New Year's Day, Thanksgiving, and Christmas.

Before driving around the battlefields, be sure to get the free park service brochure, which has an excellent map outlining the route, and buy a CD tour ($16) at the bookshop, which also carries a wide array of Civil War books. You will need at least an hour at the visitor center and another three to complete the battlefield tour without stops, so give yourself at least half a day, more to do it in comfort.

Your first stop heading out of town will be the **Chimborazo Medical Museum,** on East Broad Street at 33rd Street (open daily 9am–5pm). This was the site of one of the Confederacy's largest hospitals (about 76,000 patients were treated here). Park headquarters are located here.

There are visitor centers at **Cold Harbor** to the northeast and at **Fort Harrison** and **Glendale/Malvern Hill** to the southeast. Cold Harbor was the scene of a particularly bloody 1864 encounter during which 7,000 of Grant's men were killed or injured in just 30 minutes. Programs with costumed Union and Confederate soldiers reenacting life in the Civil War era take place during the summer. The Cold Harbor Visitor Center is open daily 9am to 5pm, and rangers lead walking tours of the battlefield during summer. The Fort Harrison and Glendale/Malvern Hill visitor centers have seasonal hours.

✍ **Keep Going**

It's convenient to combine a tour of the Civil War battlefields east of Richmond with the James River plantations (see chapter 10), as the Fort Harrison and Glendale/Malvern Hill visitor centers are near Va. 5, the Plantation Route.

3215 E. Broad St. (at 33rd St.), Richmond, VA 23223. ✆ **804/226-1981.** www.nps.gov/rich. Free admission to all visitor centers. Parking (in the Tredegar Iron Works lot) $3/hr.; free 1-hr. validation.

St. John's Episcopal Church ★★   Although St. John's dates to 1741, its congregation was established in 1611. Alexander Whitaker, the first rector, instructed Pocahontas in Christianity, baptized her, and married her to John Rolfe. It was here at the second Virginia Convention in 1775 when Thomas Jefferson, George Mason, George Washington, Richard Henry Lee, and other soon-to-be revolutionaries heard Patrick Henry deliver his incendiary words: "Is life so dear, or peace so sweet, as to be purchased at the price of chains or slavery? Forbid it, Almighty God! I know not what course others may take; but as for me, give me liberty, or give me death!" Henry's speech is reenacted on Sunday at 2pm from Memorial Day through Labor Day (admission is free but donation plates are passed). Purchase tour tickets at the gift shop behind the church.

2401 E. Broad St. (at 24th St.). (C) **804/648-5015.** www.historicstjohnschurch.org. Free admission; donations accepted. Tours $7 adults, $6 seniors, $5 children 7–18, free for children 6 and under. Open to the public Mon–Sat 10am–4pm, Sun 1–4pm (to 5pm in summer). 20-min. tours Mon–Sat 10am–3:30pm and Sun 1–3:30pm (to 4:30pm in summer). Sun services 8:30 and 11am.

Valentine Richmond History Center ★ This museum takes its name from Mann S. Valentine II, a 19th-century businessman and patron of the arts whose fortune was based on a patent medicine called Valentine's Meat Juice, and his brother, the noted sculptor Edward Valentine, whose extraordinary image of Thomas Jefferson adorns the Jefferson Hotel (p. 209). Documenting the history of Richmond, it includes the Federal-style **1812 Wickham House,** built by attorney John Wickham, who helped defend Aaron Burr against treason charges in 1807. Highlights include spectacular wall paintings, perhaps the rarest and most complete set in the nation. Even more interesting to me is the **Edward Valentine Sculpture Studio,** in a carriage house behind the Wickham House. It contains Edward Valentine's personal effects and plaster models of his work, including an early version of *Lee Recumbent,* now at the Lee Chapel and Museum in Lexington (p. 166). Café Richmond is a good place to refresh during your walking tour.

> ### 💬 A Lifelike Washington
>
> The Houdon statue of George Washing-ton in the rotunda of the Virginia State Capitol is the only one ever made of the first president from life. "That is the man, himself," said Lafayette. "I can almost realize he is going to move."

1015 E. Clay St. (C) **804/649-0711.** www.richmondhistorycenter.com. Admission $8 adults; $7 seniors, students, and children 7–18; free for children 6 and under. Tues–Sat 10am–5pm; Sun noon–5pm. 30-min. Wickham House tours depart on the hour 11am–4pm.

Virginia State Capitol ★★ In continuous use since 1788, this is the second-oldest working capitol in the United States. Thomas Jefferson patterned the Classical-revival building on the Maison Carrée, a Roman temple built in Nîmes, France, during the 1st century A.D. As with so many of his designs, Jefferson created a magnificent rotunda, whose dramatic focal point today is Houdon's life-size statue of George Washington. A marble bust of Lafayette by Houdon is also here, along with busts of the seven other Virginia-born presidents. Washington Irving took notes here in 1807 when John Marshall tried and acquitted Aaron Burr of treason. The Confederate Congress also met in the Hall of the House of Delegates, which resembles an open courtyard.

Visitors must enter the capitol's modern welcome center under the south lawn. From there you can wander through the building, but I highly recommend the 1-hour guided tour. To the east is the **Executive Mansion,** official residence of the governor of Virginia since 1813. Another historic building is the old **Bell Tower,** built in 1824, which now houses a state visitor center.

1000 Bank St. (at 10th St.). (C) **804/698-1788.** www.virginiacapitol.gov. Free admission. Mon–Sat 8am–5pm; Sun 1–5pm. 1-hr. guided tours Mon–Sat 9:30am–4pm, Sun 1:30–4pm.

9

RICHMOND

What to See & Do

"Boulevard" Museums

The Virginia Historical Society/Museum of Virginia History and the Virginia Museum of Fine Arts share a campus on Boulevard between Grove and Kensington avenues, and a **parking garage** at Sheppard Street and Stuart Avenue.

Standing between them is the **Robinson House,** a two-story farm house built in the mid-1850s by Anthony Robinson, Jr. When Robert E. Lee's army deserted Richmond in 1865, Robinson's widow, Rebecca, asked Union soldiers to occupy the farm in exchange for protecting her against rampaging looters. It was a Confederate soldier's home until the last veteran died in 1941.

Virginia Historical Society/Museum of Virginia History ★   Housed in the neoclassical Battle Abbey, built in 1913 as a shrine to the state's Civil War dead, the South's oldest historical society (founded in 1831) has the world's largest collection of Virginia artifacts. Touring it is like rummaging through the state's attic: You'll see gold buttons from Pocahontas's hat, Patrick Henry's eyeglasses, and much more. Long-term and changing exhibits cover a range of subjects, from Colonial armaments to archaeologists solving Virginia historical mysteries. Genealogists will find a treasure-trove of family histories in the library of some 125,000 volumes, 7 million manuscripts, and a database of slave names.

428 N. Boulevard (at Kensington Ave.). © **804/358-4901.** www.vahistorical.org. Free admission. Museum Mon–Sat 10am–5pm, Sun 1–5pm. Library Mon–Sat 10am–5pm. Closed New Year's Day, Easter, July 4th, Thanksgiving, Dec 24, and Christmas.

Virginia Museum of Fine Arts ★★   This splendid art museum possesses more than 20,000 works of art. Among its gems is the largest public Fabergé collection outside Russia—more than 300 objets d'art created at the turn of the 20th century for tsars Alexander III and Nicholas II. Other highlights include the Goya portrait *General Nicholas Guye,* a life-size marble statue of Roman emperor Caligula, Monet's *Iris by the Pond,* and six magnificent Gobelin *Don Quixote* tapestries. That's not to mention the works of de Kooning, Gauguin, van Gogh, Delacroix, Matisse, Degas, Picasso, Gainsborough, and others; antiquities from China, Japan, Egypt, Greece, Byzantium, Africa, and South America; art from India, Nepal, and Tibet; and an impressive collection of contemporary American art. Plan to stay for lunch for the museum also has two very good and inexpensive cafeterias.

200 N. Boulevard (at Grove Ave.). © **804/340-1400.** www.vmfa.state.va.us. Free admission; $5 donation suggested. Admission fee for some special exhibitions. Sat–Wed 10am–5pm; Thurs–Fri 10am–9pm. Closed New Year's Day, July 4th, Thanksgiving, and Christmas.

Houses, Gardens & Cemeteries

Agecroft Hall   In an elegant neighborhood overlooking the James River, Agecroft Hall is a late-15th-century Tudor manor house that was built in Lancashire, England, and brought here piece by piece in the 1920s. Today it serves as a museum portraying the social history and material culture of an English-gentry family of the late-Tudor and early-Stuart eras. Typical of its period, the house has ornate plaster ceilings, massive fireplaces, rich oak paneling, leaded and stained-glass windows, and a two-story great hall with a mullioned window 25 feet long. Furnishings authentically represent the period. Adjoining the mansion are a formal sunken garden, resembling one at Hampton Court Palace; and a formal flower garden; an Elizabethan knot garden; and an herb garden. Visitors see a brief video about the estate before taking the tour. Plan some time to explore the gardens as well. Appropriately, the **Richmond Shakespeare**

Festival (✆ **804/323-4000;** www.richmondshakespeare.com) plays here each June and July.

4305 Sulgrave Rd. ✆ **804/353-4241.** www.agecrofthall.com. Admission $8 adults, $7 seniors, $4 students; half price for gardens only. Tues–Sat 10am–4pm; Sun 12:30–5pm. Guided 30-min. house tours depart on the hour and half-hour.

Hollywood Cemetery　Perched on the bluffs overlooking the James River not far from Maymont (see below), Hollywood Cemetery is the serenely beautiful resting place of presidents Monroe and Tyler; Confederate president Jefferson Davis; six Virginia governors; and 18,000 Confederate soldiers, including James Ewell Brown (Jeb) Stuart and 21 other Confederate generals. Designed in 1847, it was conceived as a place where nature would remain undisturbed. A 90-foot granite pyramid, a monument constructed in 1869, marks the Confederate section. A 20-minute film about the cemetery is shown in the office. The best way to see it from April through October is on a 90-minute walking tour by **Historic Richmond Tours** (✆ **804/649-0711,** option 4; www.richmondhistorycenter.com), Monday through Saturday at 10am and once a month on Sunday. The tours cost $7 per person. Reservations are required.

412 S. Cherry (at Albemarle St.). ✆ **804/648-8501.** www.hollywoodcemetery.org. Free admission. Cemetery daily 8am–5pm (to 6pm during daylight saving time). Office Mon–Fri 8:30am–4:30pm.

Lewis Ginter Botanical Garden ★★　In the 1880s, self-made Richmond millionaire, philanthropist, and amateur horticulturist Lewis Ginter (a founder of the American Tobacco Company and creator of the Jefferson Hotel) built the Lakeside Wheel Club as a playground for the city's elite. The resort boasted a lake, a 9-hole golf course, cycling paths, and a zoo. After Ginter's death in 1897, his niece, Grace Arents, converted the property to a hospice for sick children. An ardent horticulturist herself, she imported rare trees and shrubs and constructed greenhouses. Now owned by the city, it's one of the finest botanical gardens in Virginia. The **Conservatory** is the only such classical, domed facility in the state. Give yourself plenty of time to walk through the 40 acres of gardens, tour the Bloemendall House, visit the conservatory and library-education complex, have lunch at the **Garden Cafe** or refreshments in the **Robins Tea House,** and browse the garden shop.

1800 Lakeside Ave. (at Hilliard Rd.). ✆ **804/262-9887.** www.lewisginter.org. Admission $11 adults, $10 seniors, $7 children 3–12, free for children 2 and under. Daily 9am–5pm (to 9pm Thurs in Apr and July–Sept). Take I-95 N. to Exit 80 (Parham Rd.) and turn left on Parham Rd., right on Lakeside.

Maymont ★ ☺　In 1886, Maj. James Henry Dooley, another of Richmond's many self-made millionaires, purchased a 100-acre dairy farm and built this 33-room Romanesque revival–style mansion surrounded by beautifully landscaped grounds. Maymont is elaborately furnished with pieces from many periods chosen by the Dooleys—Oriental carpets, an Art Nouveau swan-shaped bed, marble and bronze sculpture, porcelains, tapestries, and Tiffany vases. The **Nature & Visitor Center** has interactive exhibits interpreting the James River. There are outdoor animal habitats for birds, bison, beavers, deer, elk, and bears. At the **Children's Farm,** youngsters can feed farm animals. A collection of late-19th- and early-20th-century horse-drawn carriages is on display at the **Carriage House.** Carriage and hayrides are a weekend afternoon option during summer. You can see everything else on your own, but you must take a guided tour in order to visit the mansion's upstairs rooms.

2201 Shields Dr. (north of the James River btw. Va. 161 and Meadow St.). ✆ **804/358-7166.** www. maymont.org. Free admission; $5 donation suggested. Carriage, tram, and hay wagon rides $3

Richmond has plenty to keep children busy, such as the **Children's Farm** at **Maymont,** where they can feed chickens, piglets, goats, peacocks, cows, donkeys, and sheep (see "Houses, Gardens & Cemeteries," above.)

There are few DO NOT TOUCH signs in the **Science Museum of Virginia,** 2500 W. Broad St. ((✆ **800/659-1727** or 804/864-1400; www.smv.org), with tons of hands-on educational exhibits aimed at children. Even adults will enjoy seeing a movie in the 250-seat Ethyl Corporation IMAX Dome & Planetarium, which shows IMAX films as well as sophisticated special-effects multimedia planetarium shows. The building itself merits attention: It's the Beaux Arts former Broad Street Station, designed in 1919 by John Russell Pope (architect of the Jef-

ferson Memorial, the National Archives, and the National Gallery of Art) as the city's train station. Admission is $11 for adults and $10 for seniors and children 4 to 12. Tickets to films cost $9. Admission to both costs $16 for adults and $15 for seniors and children 4 to 12. The exhibits are open Tuesday to Saturday 9:30am to 5pm, Sunday 11:30am to 5pm, and some Mondays. Call or check the website for IMAX showtimes.

Nearby, the **Children's Museum of Richmond,** 2626 W. Broad St. ((✆ **877/295-2667** or 804/424-2667; www.c-mor.org), has more innovative hands-on exhibits for kids ages 6 months to 12 years. Admission is $8 for everyone ages 1 to 59 and $7 for seniors. It is open Tuesday to Saturday (daily in summer) 9:30am to 5pm and Sunday noon to 5pm.

adults, $2 children. Grounds daily 10am–5pm. House Tues–Sun noon–5pm. Guided 25-min. house tours depart every half-hour (last tour 4:30pm). Go south to the end of Boulevard; follow signs to the parking area.

Wilton House Museum   Originally built on the James River about 14 miles below Richmond, this 1753 Georgian mansion was painstakingly dismantled and reconstructed on this bluff overlooking the river in 1933. Most of the original brick, flooring, and paneling were saved. Wilton's design has been attributed to Williamsburg architect Richard Taliaferro. It was part of a 2,000-acre plantation where William Randolph III entertained many of the leading figures of the day, including George Washington, Thomas Jefferson, and Lafayette. The house has a fine collection of period furnishings based on an 1815 inventory. All rooms feature pine paneling, some with fluted pilasters and denticulate cornices.

215 S. Wilton Rd. (off W. Cary St.). (✆ **804/282-5936.** www.wiltonhousemuseum.org. Admission $10 adults, $8 seniors and students, free for children 5 and under. Mar–Jan Tues–Sun 1–4:30pm; Feb by appt. only. Tours depart continuously every 45 min. Closed national holidays. Take Va. 147 (W. Cary St.) west and turn south on Wilton Rd.

Special-Interest Museums

The lobby of the **Library of Virginia,** 800 Broad St. ((✆ **804/692-3919;** www.lva.lib.va.us), has changing exhibits of state documents and published works, some of them more than 400 years old. Containing papers going back to the 1600s, the library's records are a treasure-trove for genealogists. It's open Monday to Saturday 9am to 5pm; admission is free.

Black History Museum & Cultural Center of Virginia   In Jackson Ward, this museum houses documents, limited editions, prints, art, and photos emphasizing the history of the state's African-American community. It's in a Federal-and-Greek-revival-style house built in 1832 and purchased a century later by the Council of Colored Women under the leadership of Maggie L. Walker. See "Top Historical Attractions," earlier in this chapter.

00 Clay St. (at Foushee St.). ✆ **804/780-9093.** www.blackhistorymuseum.org. Admission $5 adults, $4 seniors, $3 children 11 and under. Tues–Sat 10am–5pm.

Virginia Aviation Museum   Although it is minuscule when compared to the National Air and Space Museum's monstrous Steven F. Udvar-Hazy Center in the Hunt Country (p. 73) or the fine Virginia Air & Space Center in Hampton (p. 271), the Virginia Aviation Museum, on the grounds of Richmond International Airport, does have some beautifully restored craft dating from 1916 to 1946 plus a SR-71 Blackbird spy plane. The museum is a division of the Science Museum of Virginia (see "Cool Richmond Stuff for Kids," above).

5701 Huntsman Rd. ✆ **804/236-3622.** www.vam.smv.org. Admission $6.50 adults, $5.50 seniors and children 4–12. Tues–Sat 9:30am–5pm; Sun noon–5pm. Closed Thanksgiving and Christmas.

Virginia Holocaust Museum   Built by Richmond's Jewish community, one of the oldest in the United States, this Tobacco Row museum honors those who died in or lived through the Holocaust. Local survivors tell their stories in the moving Survivors' Room. There's also a mock ghetto surrounded by barbed wire and a model of an underground hiding place.

2000 E. Cary St. ✆ **804/257-5400.** www.va-holocaust.com. Free admission; donations encouraged. Mon–Fri 9am–5pm; Sat–Sun 11am–5pm.

Nearby Attractions

About 14 miles north of Richmond via I-95, the neighboring communities of **Ashland** (on U.S. 1) and **Hanover** (on U.S. 301) have deep historical roots. Patrick Henry once tended bar at Hanover Tavern, built in 1723, and argued cases in the **Hanover County Courthouse,** dating from 1735. For more information contact the **Ashland/Hanover Visitor Center,** 112 N. Railroad Ave. in Hanover (✆ **800/897-1479** or 804/752-6766; www.town.ashland.va.us). Hours are daily 9am to 5pm except major holidays.

Kings Dominion ☺   This 400-acre fanciful facility is one of the most popular theme parks on the East Coast. Although it offers a wide variety of attractions, it's principally known for its thrill rides and water park. It's especially famous for having one of the largest roller coaster collections on the East Coast (you can spend all day here just being jolted up and down). Almost like its own theme park, the splash-happy **WaterWorks** features two monstrous wave pools and White Water Canyon, a wet-and-wild ride simulating white-water rafting. Most rides are included in the price of admission but some cost extra, which can throw a wrench into a well-planned budget. See "Getting Your Money's Worth in Kings Dominion," below, for advice from two veteran visitors.

   Best Western Kings Quarters, 16102 Theme Park Way, Doswell, VA 23047 (✆ **804/876-3321;** www.bestwesternkingsquarters.com), offers accommodations on-site.

Doswell, VA. ✆ **804/876-5000.** www.kingsdominion.com. Admission $59 adults, $37 seniors and anyone under 48 in. tall, free for children 2 and under. Season and multiday passes available. Some rides cost extra. Memorial Day to Labor Day daily 10:30am to 9 or 10pm; Apr to day before Memorial Day and day after Labor Day to late Oct Sat–Sun 10:30am–8pm. Take Va. 30 (Exit 98) off I-95.

My friend Tatyana Hillock and her daughter, Jennifer, have visited **Kings Dominion** several times and give this advice: The park is huge, so arrive early and spend all day to get your money's worth, but wear comfy shoes or sandals as you will be on your feet most of the day. Lines for the rides are shorter on weekdays and after 7pm on weekends; it's also cooler after 7pm in summer. Food, drinks, and bottled water are costly inside the park, but there are inexpensive fast-food outlets across the parking lot, and you can refill empty water bottles at any park restaurant. The park's coin-operated vending machines don't always work properly. Spectacular July 4th fireworks are best seen from the parking lot, where no crowds or buildings block your view. Tatyana closes her eyes to avoid fright on the coasters, but Jennifer says she keeps hers wide open!

Scotchtown ★   One of Virginia's oldest plantation houses, Scotchtown is a charming one-story white-clapboard home built around 1719. It's best known as a residence of Patrick Henry, who lived here from 1771 to 1778 with his wife, Sarah, and their six children. Henry served as governor of Virginia during those years, but sadly, Sarah was mentally ill during much of that time and eventually confined to a room in the basement. Although Henry last lived at Red Hill near Lynchburg (p. 125), this is the only house he ever occupied that is still standing. His mahogany desk still bears his ink stains, and bookshelves hold his law books. Dolley Madison, whose mother was a first cousin to Patrick Henry, and her mother lived here while their family moved back to this area from North Carolina. Unlike so many historic houses, none of the rooms here are roped off.

16120 Chiswell Lane, Beaverdam. © **804/227-3500.** www.apva.org/scotchtown. Admission $8 adults, $6 seniors, $4 students 6–18, free for children 5 and under; grounds only $3 per person. Mar–Nov Fri–Sat 10am–5pm, Sun 1–5pm; Dec–Feb by appt. only. 1-hr. house tours depart on demand. Closed Easter, Mother's Day, July 4th. From Ashland follow Va. 54 west, turn right on Scotchtown Road (C.R. 671) north, take right fork on C.R. 685.

SPORTS & OUTDOOR ACTIVITIES

Spectator Sports

AUTO RACING   See NASCAR racing at **Richmond International Raceway,** between Laburnum Avenue and the Henrico Turnpike/Meadowbridge Road (© **804/329-6796;** www.rir.com). The raceway is Virginia's largest sports facility, attracting crowds of 70,000 or more. Unless you're a NASCAR fan, check the website and avoid being in Richmond on race weekends, when accommodations are scarce.

BASEBALL   The **Richmond Flying Squirrels** (© **804/359-3866;** www.squirrels baseball.com), a Class AA affiliate of the San Francisco Giants, play their summertime games at the Diamond, 3011 N. Boulevard.

COLLEGE SPORTS   **Virginia Commonwealth University's** Rams, who surprised sports fans by making it to the Elite Eight of the NCAA basketball tournament in 2011, play at the **Coliseum** (📞 **804/282-7267;** www.vcuathletics.com). The **University of Richmond's** Spiders play football and basketball in the Colonial Athletic Association (📞 **804/289-8388;** www.richmondspiders.com).

HORSE RACING   Virginia's only parimutuel racetrack, **Colonial Downs,** is on Va. 155, between I-64 (Exit 205) and U.S. 60 in New Kent County, 25 miles east of Richmond (📞 **888/482-8722** or 804/966-7223; www.colonialdowns.com). Call or check the website for schedules and ticket prices.

Outdoor Activities

GOLF   Golf courses abound in the Richmond area. Among them are the public **Belmont Park Recreation Center,** 1800 Hilliard Rd. (📞 **804/266-4929;** www. co.henrico.va.us/rec/belmont-golf-course), and semiprivate **Glenwood Golf Club,** Creighton Road (📞 **804/226-1793**).

RIVER RAFTING, CANOEING & KAYAKING   Depending on the amount of water in it at any given time, the James River is good for rafting, canoeing, and kayaking. The best way to experience it is with **Riverside Outfitters,** 6836 Old Westham Rd. (📞 **804/560-0068;** www.riversideoutfitters.net), which rents equipment and has guided rafting, canoeing, and kayaking trips.

SHOPPING

Richmond's neighborhoods have a number of specialty shops, including those mentioned below. The visitor centers provide brochures that cover these and many other stores around the city and out in the suburbs.

For distinctive souvenirs, don't forget museum gift shops, especially those at the Science Museum of Virginia, the Virginia Museum of Fine Arts, the Museum and White House of the Confederacy, Valentine Richmond History Center, and the Children's Museum of Richmond.

There are upscale shops along East Cary Street in Shockoe Slip, but the best place in town for a pleasant shopping stroll is in **Carytown,** the 7 blocks of West Cary Street between Boulevard and Nasemond Street that are lined with a mix of interesting stores. **Ten Thousand Villages,** 3201 W. Cary St. (📞 **804/358-5170;** www. richmond.tenthousandvillages.com), carries international handcrafts, with lots of baskets and primitive pottery.

You'll also find gourmet food shops, ethnic restaurants, secondhand clothing stores, and the landmark **Byrd Theater,** which shows second-run films at discount prices.

RICHMOND AFTER DARK

Richmond is no New York or London, so you won't be attending internationally recognized theaters and music halls. Nevertheless, you might be able to catch visiting productions and artists at several venues. The city has its own ballet company and theater groups, and pierced-set bands rock Shockoe Bottom.

Current entertainment schedules can be found in the Thursday "Weekend" section of the *Richmond Times-Dispatch* (www.timesdispatch.com), the city's daily newspaper. The free tabloid *Style Weekly* (www.styleweekly.com) has details on theater productions, concerts, dance performances, and other happenings. It's widely available at the visitor centers and in hotel lobbies.

The Performing Arts

The city's version of the Lincoln and Kennedy centers in New York and Washington, respectively, is the dazzling **Richmond CenterStage ★★**, 600 E. Grace St., between 6th and 7th streets (📞 804/327-5755; www.richmondcenterstage.com). Occupying the original Thalhimers downtown department store building and the renovated **Carpenter Theatre,** the complex hosts Broadway shows, touring artists, and performances by the **Richmond Ballet** (📞 804/359-0906; www.richmondballet.com), the **Virginia Opera** (📞 804/643-6004; www.vaopera.org), the **Richmond Symphony** (📞 804/788-1212; www.richmondsymphony.com), and the **Richmond Philharmonic** (📞 804/673-7400; www.richmondphilharmonic.org).

Built in 1914 as a vaudeville venue and for many years the center of African-American entertainment in Richmond, Jackson Ward's **Hippodrome Theater,** 528 N. 2nd St. (📞 **804/266-2021**), was slated to reopen soon after we went to press.

Next to the Greater Richmond Convention Center, the **Richmond Coliseum,** 601 E. Leigh St. (📞 **804/780-4970;** www.richmondcoliseum.net), presents everything from the Ringling Bros. and Barnum & Bailey circus to rock concerts. It seats about 12,000. Major sporting events—wrestling, ice hockey, and basketball—are also scheduled.

In the summer months, Richmond goes outdoors to **Dogwood Dell Festival of the Arts** in Byrd Park, at Boulevard and Idlewild Avenue (📞 **804/646-3355;** www.dogwooddell.net), for free music and drama under the stars in this tiered grassy amphitheater. Bring the family, spread a blanket, and enjoy a picnic.

Fun Freebies

A nonprofit organization called **Venture Richmond** (📞 **804/788-6466;** www.venturerichmond.com) keeps Richmond hopping with a series of free outdoor concerts, beer blasts, and street festivals from May through September. Check the website for what's happening.

The nonprofit **Theatre IV** (📞 **804/344-8040;** www.theatreiv.org) stages family-oriented performances in the **Empire Theater,** 114 W. Broad St., at Jefferson Street. Dating from 1911, the Empire is the oldest theater in Virginia.

Virginia Commonwealth University presents a wide range of performances at its **W. E. Singleton Center for the Performing Arts,** 922 Park Ave., at Harrison Street (📞 **804/828-6776;** www.vcumusic.org). Likewise at the University of Richmond's **Modlin Center for the Arts** (📞 **804/289-8980;** www.modlin.richmond.edu), which does not have a street address but is on Crenshaw Way off Westhampton Way.

Tickets for most events are available through **Ticketmaster** (📞 **804/262-8003;** www.ticketmaster.com).

The Club & Music Scene

Shockoe Bottom is the city's funky nightlife district, although the usual weekend revelers are more likely to have pierced eyebrows than packed wallets. It occupies the square block beginning with the 17th Street Farmer's Market going east along East Main and East Franklin streets to 18th Street. Its joints attract the "let's see your ID" crowd, and they go up and down in popularity. If you can find a parking space, you can see for yourself what's going on by barhopping around Shockoe Bottom's busy block (but *do not* wander off onto deserted streets). ***Note:*** Many Shockoe Bottom establishments are closed on Sunday and Monday.

Up Cary Street in the more affluent (and well-behaved) Shockoe Slip, several restaurants and pubs have live music, including the **Tobacco Company,** 1201 E. Cary St. (℃ **804/782-9555;** www.thetobaccocompany.com), which has acoustic jazz upstairs Tuesday to Saturday and dancing downstairs Wednesday to Saturday 8pm to 1am.

Many other restaurants and bars have live music, especially on weekends.

AN EASY EXCURSION TO PETERSBURG ★★

After his frontal assaults failed to capture Richmond in 1864, Gen. Ulysses S. Grant turned his attention to Petersburg, a vital rail junction on the Appomattox River 23 miles south of the Confederate capital. Moving his troops south across the James River at Hopewell southeast of Richmond, he advanced on Petersburg, hoping thus to cut off Gen. Robert E. Lee's supplies and starve him into submission. The ever-wily Lee quickly countered, however, and the tragic 10-month Siege of Petersburg ensued. Finally, on April 2, 1865, a Union assault smashed through Lee's right flank, at what is now a privately funded memorial park. Lee retreated west that very night and surrendered a week later at Appomattox Court House (see "Lynchburg & Environs," in chapter 6).

Sitting at the strategic junction of I-95 and I-85, Petersburg today is a quiet Southern city. Although much of its downtown business district has a down-on-its-heels appearance, the Old Town section near the river is undergoing a restoration and has antiques stores, restaurants, and two Civil War–era museums. The major sights, however, are on Petersburg's eastern and southern outskirts, where the battle lines were drawn.

VISITOR INFORMATION When you arrive, take Washington Street (Exit 52) west and follow the Petersburg Tour signs to the **Petersburg Visitor Center,** 19 Bollingbrook St., Petersburg, VA 23804 (℃ **800/368-3595** or 804/733-2430). There you can get maps and literature and buy a block ticket to local museums (see below). The center is open Monday to Saturday 9am to 5pm and Sunday 1 to 5pm.

Information also is available from **Petersburg Area Regional Tourism,** PO Box 1776, Petersburg, VA 23805 (℃ **877/730-7278;** www.petersburgarea.org).

Exploring Old Town Petersburg

The visitor center (see above) shares space, a telephone number, and business hours with the **Farmers Bank Museum** (www.apva.org/FarmersBank). Constructed in 1817, the building was the Petersburg branch of the Farmers Bank of Virginia, which printed its own money (the presses and printing plates are still here) during the Civil War. Some of the Confederate States of America currency is on display. At night the bank's cash was lowered into a vault in the basement.

Old Town's top attraction is the **Siege Museum,** 15 W. Bank St. (℃ **804/733-2404;** www.craterroad.com/siegemuseum.html), occupying the old Merchant Exchange, a magnificent Greek-revival temple-fronted building. It tells the story of everyday life in Petersburg up to and during the siege in displays and an interesting 18-minute film narrated by the late actor Joseph Cotten, a Virginia native whose ancestors lived in Petersburg during the Civil War. The film is shown on the hour and half-hour. Give yourself another 30 minutes to see the museum.

Centre Hill Mansion, 1 Centre Hill Circle (📞 **804/733-2401**), between Adams and Tabb streets, is a nicely restored 1823 mansion furnished with Victorian pieces. You'll have to take a 30-minute tour (departing every hour 10:30am–4:30pm).

The Siege Museum and Centre Hill Mansion are open April to September Monday to Saturday 10am to 5pm. Call for winter hours.

The visitor center sells **block tickets** to the Siege Museum, Centre Hill Mansion, and Old Blandford Church (see below) for $11 for adults and $9 for seniors and children 7 to 12. Otherwise, admission to each is $5 for adults and $4 for seniors and children 7 to 12. Active-duty military personnel pay the seniors/children rate.

The Civil War Battlefields

Together, the sites below will take most of a day to tour. After a look around Old Town, drive out to the national battlefield's visitor center east of the city and follow the one-way tour to The Crater. You'll come out of the national battlefield at Crater Road (U.S. 301); Old Blandford Church is a quarter-mile north. Have lunch at King's Barbecue, which is on Crater Road south of I-95 (see "Where to Stay" and "Where to Eat," below). Spend the afternoon at Pamplin Historical Park.

Old Blandford Church ★   About 2 miles south of downtown, this ancient church boasts one of the largest collections of Tiffany-glass windows in existence and is noted for the first observance of Memorial Day. The church was constructed in 1735 of imported English brick but abandoned in the early 1800s. During the Civil War, the building became a hospital for wounded soldiers. Many were later buried in the 189-acre graveyard, whose oldest gravestone dates from 1702. The 13 Confederate and border states each sponsored one of the Tiffany windows as a memorial to its Confederate dead. The local Ladies Memorial Association commissioned the 14th window. The artist himself, Louis Comfort Tiffany, gave the church the 15th window, a magnificent "Cross of Jewels" that is thrillingly illuminated at sunset. You can visit the parklike graveyard on your own, but the only way to see inside the church is on a 45-minute guided tour.

319 S. Crater Rd. (U.S. 301; at Rochelle Lane). 📞 **804/733-2396.** www.craterroad.com/oldbland fordchurch.html. Admission $5 adults, $4 seniors and children. Apr–Sept Mon–Sat 10am–5pm, Sun 1–5pm; Oct–Dec Tues–Sat 10am–5pm, Sun 1–5pm; Jan–Mar Tues 1–5pm, Sun 1–5pm. 30-min. tours depart every 45 min. From downtown take Bank St. east and turn right on Crater Rd. (U.S. 301).

Pamplin Historical Park & The National Museum of the Civil War Soldier ★   The Petersburg Breakthrough Battle, where Union troops ended the siege by breaking through the Confederate lines on April 2, 1865, occurred on the grounds of this privately owned park, home to some of Virginia's best-preserved Confederate earthwork fortifications. There's a re-created Military Encampment with costumed interpreters and a Battlefield Center with artifacts and exhibits about the battle. Guides lead 30- to 45-minute walking tours of the battlefield at least once a day; call for times since the

> ### 📷 The First Memorial Day
>
> After the Civil War, a group of Petersburg schoolgirls and their teacher came to Old Blandford Church to decorate the graves of the soldiers buried in the churchyard. The ceremony inspired Mary Logan, wife of Union General John A. Logan, who was head of the major organization of Union army veterans, to campaign for a national Memorial Day, which was first observed in 1868.

tours will add immeasurably to your visit. The nearby **Banks House** served as Grant's headquarters. One of Virginia's few remaining slave dwellings is behind the house. You start all this at the **National Museum of the Civil War Soldier,** which is dedicated to the common foot soldier (no famous generals need apply). The Field Quarter interprets what slave life was like in the 19th century.

6125 Boydton Plank Rd. (U.S. 1). ℂ **804/861-2408.** www.pamplinpark.org. Admission $12 adults, $7 children 6–12, free for children 5 and under. Summer daily 9am–5pm. Off-season hours vary. Closed New Year's Day, Thanksgiving, and Christmas. Park is 6 miles south of downtown, 1 mile south of Exit 61 off I-85.

Petersburg National Battlefield Park ★★★ Wrapping around the city's eastern and southern flanks, this park preserves the key sites of the siege that lasted from mid-June 1864 to early April 1865. The main visitor center (on Va. 36) displays exhibits and artifacts, while a one-way 4-mile battlefield driving tour has wayside exhibits; some stops have short walking trails. The last and most fascinating is the site of The Crater, literally a depression in the ground where a group of miners from Pennsylvania dug a passage beneath Confederate lines and exploded 4 tons of powder, creating the 170-foot by 60-foot crater. The explosion killed 278 Confederates, and, during the ensuing battle, thousands more men on both sides were killed or wounded. To get a fuller perspective, follow the entire siege line from the Eastern Front visitor center 26 miles south to Five Forks Battlefield in Dinwiddie County. Admission includes an extremely helpful audio tour of the battle lines.

Also part of the park is **Grant's Headquarters at City Point,** at present-day Hopewell, 26 miles to the east via Va. 36. City Point was the largest Union supply base during the war. Abraham Lincoln spent 2 of the last 3 weeks of his life there.

5001 Siege Rd. (Va. 36; 2½ miles east of downtown via E. Washington St.). ℂ **804/732-3531.** www.nps.gov/pete. Admission $5 per vehicle, $3 per pedestrian or bicyclist. Park daily 8am–dusk. Museum daily 9am–5pm. Closed New Year's Day, Martin Luther King Day, Thanksgiving, and Christmas.

Attractions at Fort Lee

Fort Lee is home to the U.S. Army Quartermaster Corps and its **Quartermaster Museum,** 1201 22nd St. (ℂ **804/734-4203;** www.qmmuseum.lee.army.mil), which has uniforms and equipment from all of America's wars. Stars of the show are the World War II jeep with a Mercedes car seat specially installed for Gen. George S. Patton and one of the armored "Circus Wagons" in which Gen. Dwight D. Eisenhower lived when on the road in Europe during the war. The museum is open Tuesday to Friday 10am to 5pm and Saturday to Sunday 11am to 5pm. Admission is free.

Next door, the **U.S. Army Women's Museum** (ℂ **804/734-4327;** www.awm.lee.army.mil) is the only facility in the world dedicated to army women. It traces their contributions from the Revolution to the present. If you, a relative, or another woman you know was in the army, especially during World War II, then this is a poignant stop. It's open Tuesday to Friday 10am to 5pm and Saturday 11am to 5pm. Admission is free.

As part of the Pentagon's base realignment program, Fort Lee will someday become home to the **U.S. Army Ordnance Museum** (www.ordmusfound.org).

The gate into Fort Lee is a mile east of the national battlefield visitor center on Va. 36. This is an active U.S. army post, so you must show valid photo identification, and you and your vehicle are subject to being searched. Tell the guards at the gate that you want to visit the Quartermaster Museum and the U.S. Army Women's Museum, and they'll tell you how to get there.

Where to Stay

Several motels on South Crater Road (U.S. 301) include **Comfort Inn Petersburg** (© 804/732-2000), **Days Inn Petersburg-Fort Lee/South** (© 804/733-4400), **Econo Lodge South** (© 804/862-2717), **Hampton Inn Petersburg-Fort Lee** (© 804/732-1400), **Holiday Inn Express Hotel & Suites Petersburg-Fort Lee** (© 804/518-1800), **Howard Johnson Inn Petersburg** (© 804/733-0600), and **Quality Inn Petersburg** (© 804/732-2900).

Where to Eat

As you tour Old Town, you can fuel up on pastries and caffeine at **Java Mio,** 322 N. Sycamore St. (© **804/861-1646**), a trendy coffeehouse offering sandwiches and salads for lunch plus dinner and live music on Friday night.

Worthy Old Town restaurants include the **Brickhouse Run,** 407–409 Cockade Alley (© **804/862-1825**; www.brickhouserun.com), a British pub which is open Tuesday to Saturday, and **Andrade's International Restaurant,** 7 Bollingbrook St. (© **804/862-1365**; www.andradesinternational.com), with a wide-ranging menu and patio dining in warm weather. Andrade's is open daily.

Near The Crater and Old Blandford Church, **King's Famous Barbecue,** 2910 S. Crater Rd. (© **804/732-0975**; www.kingsfamousbarbecue.com), has the same offerings and prices as Eley's Barbecue (below).

Eley's Barbecue ★★ ◢ AMERICAN   Formerly known as King's Barbecue, this Petersburg institution has been supplying some of Virginia's best barbecue since 1946. The setting is a pine-paneled room adorned with an extraordinary collection of pig dolls and figurines. Pork, beef, ribs, and chicken smoke constantly in an open pit right in the dining room. Unlike most other barbecue emporia, the meat is served just as it comes from the pit. Aficionados can enjoy the smoked flavor au naturel or apply vinegary sauce from squeeze bottles. The menu also offers such Southern standbys as crispy fried chicken, ham steak, and seafood items like salmon cakes and fried oysters.

3221 W. Washington St. (U.S. 1 S.). © **804/732-5861.** www.eleysbarbecue.com.Sandwiches $3–$7; main courses $6–$19. AE, MC, V. Mon–Fri 11am–8:30pm; Sat–Sun 7–10:30am and 11am–8:30pm. Follow U.S. 1 S. to the city limits, 3 miles from downtown.

WILLIAMSBURG, JAMESTOWN & YORKTOWN

Virginia's Historic Triangle saw not just the establishment of English-speaking Colonial America at Jamestown in 1607; it watched as its citizens gathered in Williamsburg to help foment the Revolution, which ended here with the deciding battle at Yorktown. Hampton, America's oldest continuously English-speaking town, is now home to a very modern air-and-space museum. In Newport News, a fine maritime museum displays part of the USS *Monitor,* whose Civil War battle with the CSS *Merrimack* on Hampton Roads was the first engagement between ironclads.

Sightseeing A visit to this area is a big history lesson. You might have a sidewalk conversation with "Thomas Jefferson" in beautifully restored 18th-century **Colonial Williamsburg.** At **Historic Jamestowne** you will see where the first English colonists landed, and at **Jamestown Settlement** visit re-creations of the ships they came in and the village they built. At **Yorktown Battlefield** you will walk the ramparts from which Washington bombarded Cornwallis into submission, and see how his troops lived at **Yorktown Victory Center.**

Eating & Drinking Even dining in Williamsburg is like a trip back in time. This is especially so at **Christiana Campbells's Tavern, Josiah Chowning's Tavern, King's Arms Tavern,** and **Shields Tavern.** Restored or rebuilt to their 18th-century appearance, they present Colonial fare, staff dressed in period costume, and entertainment from the time of George Washington and Thomas Jefferson. Modern Virginia fare is served nearby at the **Old Chicamominy House** and **Pierce's Pitt Bar-B-Que.** You see how it's cooked at **A Chef's Kitchen.**

Active Pursuits The Historic Triangle is modern Virginia's golf mecca. Two of the area's seven courses are among the nation's best: Colonial Williamsburg's **Golden Horseshoe** and Kingsmill Resort's famous **River Course,** which espies the James River and hosted the LPGA Michelob Ultra Open for several years. When not on the links you can **bike** the scenic Colonial Parkway from Williamsburg to Jamestown and Yorktown.

Shopping Williamsburg is one of the best places to shop in Virginia. After seeing how merchandise was made in the late 1700s at Colonial

Williamsburg's reconstructed crafts and trade shops, you can browse the modern stores in **Merchants Square,** then drive out to see porcelain dolls being made at **Williamsburg Doll Factory.** On the way, **Prime Outlets Williamsburg** is one of the state's largest outlet malls. You can sample the wares at the **Williamsburg Winery,** Virginia's first modern vineyard.

GETTING THERE & GETTING AROUND

Getting There

BY PLANE Newport News/Williamsburg International Airport (PHF), 14 miles east of Williamsburg (© 757/877-0221; www.nnwairport.com), is served by Allegiant, AirTran, Delta, Frontier, and US Airways. The major car rental firms have desks at the airport, and taxis await each incoming flight.

More flights arrive at **Richmond International Airport** (see chapter 9), about 45 miles west of town via I-64. **Norfolk International Airport** (see chapter 11) is about the same distance to the east, but traffic on I-64 can cause delays in ground transport to Williamsburg during rush hours, especially on summer weekends when beach traffic funnels through the Hampton Roads Bridge Tunnel.

BY CAR The main drag is **I-64,** which runs down the center of the Peninsula between Richmond and Hampton. When traffic on I-64 comes to a standstill, as it often does on summer weekends, you can take the mostly four-lane **U.S. 60,** which parallels it. The two-lane John Tyler Highway (Va. 5) also runs between Richmond and Williamsburg, passing the James River plantations (see "James River Plantations," later in this chapter). The scenic **Colonial Parkway** connects Williamsburg, Jamestown, and Yorktown. Va. 199 runs around the southern side of Williamsburg, and when combined with I-64 forms a beltway around the town.

For the Historic Area, take Exit 238 (Va. 143) off I-64 and follow the signs south to Va. 132 and Colonial Williamsburg. The visitor center will be on your left as you approach the town. Va. 199, which forms a beltway around the southern side of the city, joins I-64 at Exit 242 east of town; this is the quickest way to get to Busch Gardens Williamsburg and Water Country USA. The scenic Colonial Parkway runs through a tunnel under the Historic Area; you can get on and off at the Colonial Williamsburg Visitor Center.

BY TRAIN & BUS Both **Amtrak** trains (© 800/872-7245; www.amtrak.com) and **Greyhound** buses (© 800/231-2222; www.greyhound.com) arrive at the local **Transportation Center** (© 757/229-8750), at Boundary and Lafayette streets within walking distance of Williamsburg's Historic Area.

Cab service is provided by **Historic Taxi** (© 757/258-7755), **Williamsburg Taxi Service** (© 757/221-0004), and **Triangle Taxi** (© 757/594-6969).

Getting Around

THE HISTORIC AREA Because cars are not allowed into the Historic Area between 8am and 10pm, you must park elsewhere. The Colonial Williamsburg Visitor Center (see "Exploring the Historic Area," below) has ample free parking. After you have bought your tickets to the Historic Area, you can use them to ride Colonial Williamsburg's shuttle buses from the visitor center to and around the

Historic Area (only ticket holders are allowed on these buses). The buses will take you between the visitor center and the **Gateway Building,** behind the Governor's Palace, where guides conduct a 30-minute Orientation Walk. It's a good way to get an overview of the village. From there, the buses make a circle around the circumference of the Historic Area. The buses begin operating at 8:50am, with frequent departures until 10pm.

You can also walk from the visitor center to the Historic Area, a 20-minute stroll via a footpath.

WILLIAMSBURG AREA The easiest way to get around outside the Historic Area is by trolley and public buses operated by **Williamsburg Area Transport** (**WAT;** ✆ **757/259-4093;** www.williamsburgtransport.com). The newest addition to the fleet is the **Williamsburg Trolley,** which runs from Merchants Square west on Richmond Road to High Street, then southwest to the New Town shopping area on Ironbound Road at Monticello Avenue near Va. 199. Fare is 50¢ for adults, 25¢ for seniors and travelers with disabilities, and free for children 12 and under. Exact change is required.

Not to be confused with Colonial Williamsburg's shuttles in the historic area, WAT's buses run around the town and surrounding area Monday to Saturday about every hour 6am to 8pm and 6am to 10pm during the summer months. Bus fare is $1.25. Exact change is required. The **Blue Line** runs west from the Transportation Center and passes a majority of the area's motels, chain restaurants, and shopping centers on Richmond Road (U.S. 60 W.). The **Gray Line** operates east from the Transportation Center to Busch Gardens Williamsburg via Lafayette Street and Pocahontas Trail (U.S. 60 E.). The **Yellow Line** links the Colonial Williamsburg Visitor Center to the Transportation Center and Busch Gardens Williamsburg from Memorial Day to Labor Day.

Bike rentals are available from Easter through October at the **Spa of Colonial Williamsburg,** 307 S. England St., between the Williamsburg Inn and the Williamsburg Lodge (✆ **757/220-7720;** see "Where to Stay," later in this chapter). The land is flat here, so getting around via bicycle is a great idea.

Historic Taxi (✆ **757/258-7755**), **Williamsburg Taxi Service** (✆ **757/254-2190**), and **Yellow Cab of Williamsburg** (✆ **757/722-1111**) are based at the Transportation Center.

TO JAMESTOWN & YORKTOWN Besides driving, the easiest way to get from Williamsburg to Jamestown and Yorktown from April 15 through October 31 is via the free **Historic Triangle Shuttle** (✆ **757/898-2410**), which follows the Colonial Parkway. The buses depart the Colonial Williamsburg Visitor Center daily every 30 minutes from 9am to 3:30pm, with the final return trips departing Jamestown and Yorktown at 5:15pm. (**Note:** The shuttle is funded by the federal government, so it may not be operating, or not be free when you get here.)

WILLIAMSBURG ★★★

150 miles S of Washington, D.C.; 50 miles E of Richmond

You'll never have a better opportunity to examine Virginia's past than in Colonial Williamsburg, as the town's restored Historic Area is known. Unlike most other historical attractions in Virginia, Williamsburg has not just been meticulously re-created to look exactly as it did in the 1770s, when the town served as Virginia's capital. Today,

Williamsburg's Historic Area is, for all practical purposes, one of the world's largest and best living-history museums.

Here the British flag flies most of the year over the Capitol building. Women wear long dresses and ruffled caps, and men don powdered wigs. Taverns serve Colonial fare, blacksmiths and harness makers use 18th-century methods, and the local militia performs drills on Market Square. Clip-clopping horses draw carriages just as their ancestors did when George Washington rode these streets. Your impromptu banter with "Thomas Jefferson" in the King's Arms Tavern will seem so authentic you just might forget it's Bill Barker, an actor/interpreter who has been bringing Jefferson to life since 1993.

Youngsters tend to like watching a musket being fired and being locked up in the town's stocks, but they might otherwise become a bit bored with all the talk about history and start badgering you to get on to Busch Gardens Williamsburg. But it's worth the effort, for both you and they will come away with an understanding and appreciation of life in 18th-century Virginia, before the advent of running water and video games.

Essentials

VISITOR INFORMATION

For advance information specific to the Historic Area, contact the **Colonial Williamsburg Foundation,** PO Box 1776, Williamsburg, VA 23187 (© **800/447-8679** or 757/220-7645; www.colonialwilliamsburg.com). Open 365 days a year, the foundation's visitor center is a font of information, worthy of being the first stop on any exploration of Williamsburg (see "Exploring the Historic Area," below). The on-site regional information desk is also helpful.

The next-best source for general information about hotels, restaurants, and activities in the area is the **Greater Williamsburg Chamber & Tourism Alliance,** 421 N. Boundary St., Williamsburg, VA 23187 (© **800/368-6511** or 757/229-6511; www.williamsburgcc.com), between Lafayette and Scotland streets, 2 blocks north of the Historic Area. The alliance sells one of the best local maps, and you can search for money-saving package deals on its website. The office is open Monday to Friday 8:30am to 5pm.

The **Williamsburg Hotel and Motel Association** (© **800/211-7165;** www.gowilliamsburg.com) publishes its own visitors guide and operates a hotel and motel reservation service in conjunction with the Greater Williamsburg Chamber & Tourism Alliance (see "Where to Stay," later in this chapter).

ORIENTATION

The restored, 1-mile-long-by-half-mile-wide **Historic Area** is at the center of Williamsburg. The 99-foot-wide **Duke of Gloucester Street** is this area's principal east-west artery, with the Capitol building at the eastern end and the Wren building of the College of William and Mary at the west end. **Merchants Square** shops and services are on the western end of Duke of Gloucester Street, next to the college. The visitor center is north of the Historic Area.

Richmond Road (U.S. 60 W.), running northwest from the Historic Area, is Williamsburg's main commercial strip, with numerous motels, restaurants, and shopping centers, including the area's outlet malls. On the east side of town, **York Street/Pocahontas Trail** (U.S. 60 E.) runs out to Busch Gardens Williamsburg. **Bypass Road** joins these two highways on the north side of the Historic Area.

Williamsburg Area

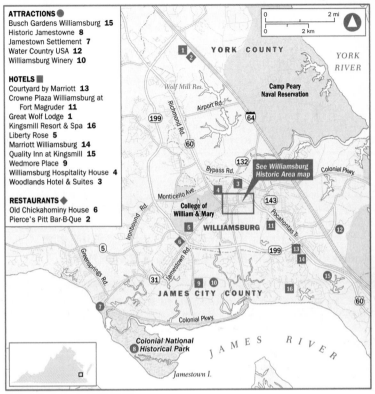

ATTRACTIONS ●
Busch Gardens Williamsburg **15**
Historic Jamestowne **8**
Jamestown Settlement **7**
Water Country USA **12**
Williamsburg Winery **10**

HOTELS ■
Courtyard by Marriott **13**
Crowne Plaza Williamsburg at
  Fort Magruder **11**
Great Wolf Lodge **1**
Kingsmill Resort & Spa **16**
Liberty Rose **5**
Marriott Williamsburg **14**
Quality Inn at Kingsmill **15**
Wedmore Place **9**
Williamsburg Hospitality House **4**
Woodlands Hotel & Suites **3**

RESTAURANTS ◆
Old Chickahominy House **6**
Pierce's Pitt Bar-B-Que **2**

History & Background

In 1699, after nearly a century of famine, fevers, and battles with neighboring American Indian tribes, the beleaguered Virginia Colony abandoned the mosquito-infested swamp at Jamestown for a planned city 6 miles inland and about halfway to Yorktown, which had developed as a major seaport. They named it Williamsburg for the reigning British monarch, William of Orange.

In typical English fashion of the time, royal Governor Francis Nicholson laid out the new capital on a grid with public greens and a half-acre of land for every house on the main street. People used their lots to grow vegetables and raise livestock. Most houses were whitewashed wood frame (trees being more abundant than brick), and kitchens were in separate structures to keep the houses from accidentally burning down. A "palace" for the royal governor was finished in 1720.

The town prospered and became the major cultural and political center of Virginia. The government met here four times a year during "Publick Times," when rich planters and politicos (one and the same, mostly) converged on Williamsburg, and the population (normally about 1,800) doubled. Shops displayed their finest wares, and there were balls, horse races, fairs, and auctions.

10

WILLIAMSBURG, JAMESTOWN & YORKTOWN

Williamsburg

237

You'll see a familiar face in *Williamsburg—the Story of a Patriot*, the 35-minute film shown at the Colonial Williamsburg Visitor Center—and on TVs in hotels operated by the Colonial Williamsburg Foundation. It's Jack Lord, who later became famous as Detective Steve McGarrett in the 1970s TV show *Hawaii 5-0*. Students at the College of William and Mary consider the 1950s film so campy that they learn every one of Lord's lines by heart.

Williamsburg played a major role as a seat of royal government and later as a hotbed of revolution until the government moved to Richmond in 1780 to be safer from British attack. Many of the seminal events leading up to the Declaration of Independence occurred here. Thomas Jefferson and James Monroe studied at the College of William and Mary, the nation's second-oldest university behind Harvard. Jefferson was the second state governor and last occupant of the Governor's Palace before the capital moved to Richmond (Patrick Henry was the first). During the Revolution, Williamsburg was the headquarters of first Cornwallis, then Washington and Rochambeau, who planned the siege of Yorktown in George Wythe's house.

A REVEREND, A ROCKEFELLER & A REBIRTH

Williamsburg ceased to be an important political center after 1780 but remained a charming Virginia town for another 150 years or so. As late as 1926, the Colonial town plan was virtually intact, including numerous original buildings. Then the Reverend W. A. R. Goodwin, rector of **Bruton Parish Church** (and no known relation to yours truly), envisioned restoring the entire town to its Colonial appearance as a symbol of our early history. He inspired John D. Rockefeller, Jr., who during his lifetime contributed some $68 million to the project and set up an endowment to help provide for permanent restoration and educational programs. Today, gifts and bequests by thousands of Americans sustain the project Goodwin and Rockefeller began.

The Historic Area now covers 301 acres of the original town. A mile long, it encompasses 88 original buildings and several hundred reconstructed houses, shops, taverns, public buildings, and outbuildings, most on their original foundations and reflecting extensive archaeological, architectural, and historical research.

Williamsburg set a very high standard for other Virginia restorations. Researchers investigated international archives, libraries, and museums and sought out old wills, diaries, court records, inventories, letters, and other documents. The architects studied every aspect of 18th-century buildings, from paint chemistry to brickwork. Archaeologists recovered millions of artifacts excavating 18th-century sites to reveal original foundations.

The Historic Area also includes 90 acres of gardens and greens, and 3,000 surrounding acres serve as a greenbelt against commercial encroachment.

The Colonial Williamsburg Foundation, a nonprofit organization, owns most of the Historic Area, conducts the ongoing restoration, and operates the Historic Area and its visitor center. A profit-making subsidiary owns and operates the foundation's hotels and taverns. Needless to say, "CW" exerts enormous influence over tourism, the town's main source of income.

Exploring the Historic Area

FIRST STOP: THE VISITOR CENTER

Begin your visit at the **Colonial Williamsburg Regional Visitor Center,** on Va. 132 south of U.S. 60 Bypass (📞 **800/447-8679** or 757/220-7645; www.colonial williamsburg.com). Watch for the signs pointing the way from all access roads to Williamsburg. The center and Historic Area attractions are open daily 9am to 5pm (to 9pm in summer). Some attractions are closed on specific days, and hours can vary, so check the *This Week* brochure (available at the visitor center) for current information.

The visitor center has a bookstore, a gift shop, a regional information desk, and two **reservations services:** one for Colonial Williamsburg Foundation **hotels** (📞 **800/ 447-8679** or 757/220-7645; www.colonialwilliamsburg.com), the other for two of its four Colonial **taverns** (📞 **800/828-3767** or 757/229-2141). It's advisable to make tavern reservations well in advance anytime, and it's essential every day during the summer and on weekends during spring and fall (see "The Early Bird Gets the Reservation," later in this chapter).

The center continuously shows a free 8-minute video about Williamsburg, and once you've bought your ticket to the Historic Area, you can watch the 35-minute orientation film, *Williamsburg—The Story of a Patriot,* which also runs throughout the day.

Parking at the visitor center is free. You can park for an hour for free, and then pay, in the public lots and garages near **Merchants Square** at the western end of Duke of Gloucester Street. But be careful: Spaces labeled "P2" are restricted to 2 hours; those marked "P1" and "P6" are long-term.

Tickets

It costs nothing to stroll the streets of the Historic Area and perhaps debate revolutionary politics with the interpreters pretending to be Thomas Jefferson or Patrick Henry, but you will need a **ticket** to enter the key buildings and the museums, see the 35-minute orientation film at the visitor center, use the Historic Area shuttle buses, and take a 30-minute Orientation Walk through the restored village.

The Colonial Williamsburg Foundation changes its system of tickets and passes so frequently that I'm almost wasting ink telling you what they are as of this writing. You should *definitely* call the visitor center or check the Colonial Williamsburg website

📎 PLANNING YOUR TIME IN WILLIAMSBURG

There is so much to see and do in the Historic Triangle that you can easily spend a week in this area and still not see everything. Colonial Williamsburg itself requires a minimum of 2 days to explore, preferably three. It will take at least another day to see Jamestown and Yorktown. If you have kids in tow, they'll want to spend a day at Busch Gardens Williamsburg or Water Country USA, although you can satisfy them by visiting the parks after dark during the summer months.

Spend ample time planning your visit at the Colonial Williamsburg Visitor Center. Historic Area programs change frequently, so it's imperative to pick up a copy of **This Week,** the single most valuable tool in planning the best use of your time. It provides opening hours for attractions and schedules for the week's presentations, exhibits, plays, and events. It also has a detailed map.

You can buy tickets to Colonial Williamsburg, Busch Gardens Williamsburg, Water Country USA, Colonial Historical National Park, and other Historic Triangle attractions separately and pay full price, or you can do some shopping and come up with money-saving combination deals.

For example, ask about the **America's Historic Triangle Ticket,** which includes admission for 7 consecutive days to Colonial Williamsburg, Historic Jamestowne, Jamestown Settlement, Yorktown Battlefield, and Yorktown Victory Center. It cost $79 for adults and $34 for children 6 to 17. Another option is the **Jamestown-Yorktown Four Site Value Ticket,** granting admission to

Historic Jamestowne, Jamestown Settlement, Yorktown Battlefield, and Yorktown Victory Center for $30 for adults, $20 for teenagers 13 to 18, and $10 for children 6 to 12. Both passes are available at the attractions.

Some hotels and motels offer guests discounted ticket prices to local attractions; it's worth asking when you call to make your reservation. **Colonial Williamsburg** (📞 800/447-8679 or 757/220-7645; www.colonialwilliamsburg.com) almost always offers packages including tickets and discounted rates at its hotels. The **Williamsburg Hotel & Motel Association** (📞 800/211-7164; www.gowilliamsburg.com) also has hotel-ticket deals.

(www.colonialwilliamsburg.com) for the latest information. With that caveat, this was the admission structure at press time:

A **Single-Day Ticket** allows access to all Historic Area exhibition buildings and museums and costs $38 for adults and $19 for children ages 6 to 17. It is free for children 5 and under. You can add the Governor's Palace for $10 for adults and $5 for children (good for the day you buy it, regardless of the time you purchased it).

The **Multiday Ticket** also allows access to all Historic Area exhibitions and museums, but it is good for 3 consecutive days. It costs $46 for adults and $23 for children 6 to 17.

For longer stays, it's worth buying an **Annual Pass** for $59 for adults and $30 for children ages 6 to 17. It's good for 1 year and includes a 25% discount on most evening performances (See "Williamsburg After Dark," below).

Tickets are available at the Colonial Williamsburg Regional Visitor Center, a **ticket booth** at the Merchants Square shops on Henry Street at Duke of Gloucester Street, and **Lumber House Ticket Office** on Duke of Gloucester Street opposite the Palace Green (open daily 8:45am–9pm).

American Express, Diners Club, MasterCard, and Visa are accepted at Colonial Williamsburg ticket outlets, attractions, hotels, and taverns.

THE COLONIAL BUILDINGS
Bassett Hall

Built between 1753 and 1766, Bassett Hall was the mid-1930s residence of Mr. and Mrs. John D. Rockefeller, Jr., and it is restored and furnished to reflect their era. The name derives from the ownership of Martha Washington's nephew Burwell Bassett, who lived here from 1800 to 1839. Despite changes the Rockefellers made, much of the interior is original, including woodwork, paneling, mantels, and yellow-pine flooring. Much of the furniture is 18th- and 19th-century American in the Chippendale, Federal, and Empire styles. There are beautifully executed needlework rugs made by

Williamsburg Historic Area

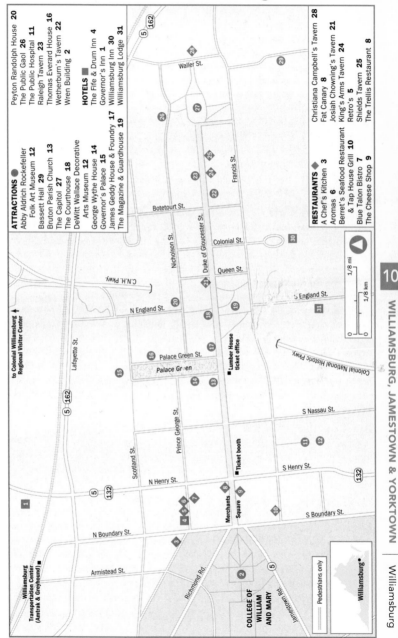

ATTRACTIONS ●
Abby Aldrich Rockefeller
  Folk Art Museum **12**
Bassett Hall **29**
Bruton Parish Church **13**
The Capitol **27**
The Courthouse **18**
DeWitt Wallace Decorative
  Arts Museum **12**
George Wythe House **14**
Governor's Palace **15**
James Geddy House & Foundry **17**
The Magazine & Guardhouse **19**

Peyton Randolph House **20**
The Public Gaol **26**
The Public Hospital **11**
Raleigh Tavern **23**
Thomas Everard House **16**
Wetherburn's Tavern **22**
Wren Building **2**

HOTELS ■
The Fife & Drum Inn **4**
Governor's Inn **1**
Williamsburg Inn **30**
Williamsburg Lodge **31**

RESTAURANTS ◆
A Chef's Kitchen **3**
Aromas **6**
Berret's Seafood Restaurant
  & Tap House Grill **10**
Blue Talon Bistro **7**
The Cheese Shop **9**

Christiana Campbell's Tavern **28**
Fat Canary **8**
Josiah Chowning's Tavern **21**
King's Arms Tavern **24**
Retro's **5**
Shields Tavern **25**
The Trellis Restaurant **8**

10

WILLIAMSBURG, JAMESTOWN & YORKTOWN | Williamsburg

241

Mrs. Rockefeller, and early-19th-century prayer rugs adorn the morning room. Hundreds of examples of ceramics and china are on display, as are collections of 18th- and 19th-century American and English glass, Canton enamelware, and folk art. It's open Wednesday, Thursday, and Saturday from 9am to 5pm.

Bruton Parish Church ★★

Named to honor Colonial Governor Sr. William Berkeley and the prominent Ludwell family, whose ancestral homes were in Bruton, England, this Anglican parish has been around since at least 1674. Now numbering about 1,800 members, the parish (and not Colonial Williamsburg) owns this impressive brick church, which opened its doors to worshipers in 1715. It was the first cruciform-shaped church built in Virginia. The pews bear the names of famous and not-so-famous vestrymen. Unless services, weddings, or other ceremonies are taking place, the church is open Monday to Saturday 10am to 4pm and Sunday 12:30 to 4:30pm. Admission is free but $1 donations are encouraged. Sunday services are at 7:30, 9, and 11:30am and 5:30pm. The church often hosts candlelight concerts. For more information contact Bruton Parish at ☎ **757/229-2891** or www.brutonparish.org.

The Capitol ★★★

Virginia legislators met in the H-shaped Capitol from 1704 to 1780. America's first representative assembly, it had an upper house—His Majesty's Council of State—consisting of 12 members appointed for life by the king. Freeholders of each county elected members of the lower House of Burgesses (there were 128 burgesses by 1776). The Burgesses became a training ground for patriots such as George Washington, Thomas Jefferson, Richard Henry Lee, and Patrick Henry. As 1776 approached, the Burgesses passed resolutions against Parliament's Stamp Act and levy on tea ("taxation without representation," to quote the immortal words of Patrick Henry that became a motto of the Revolution).

The Capitol burned down in 1747, was rebuilt in 1753, and succumbed to fire again in 1832. This reconstruction is of the 1704 version, complete with Queen Anne's coat of arms adorning the tower and the Great Union flag flying overhead. The Secretary's Office next door is original. You must take a 30-minute **tour** to get inside the Capitol.

The Courthouse ★★★

Dominating Market Square, the courthouse is an intriguing window onto Colonial criminal justice. An original building, the courthouse was the scene of proceedings ranging from criminal trials to the issuance of licenses. Wife beating, pig stealing, and debtor and creditor disputes were among the cases tried here. You can participate in the administration of Colonial justice at the courthouse by sitting on a jury or acting as a defendant. In Colonial times, convicted offenders were usually punished immediately after the verdict. Punishments included public flogging at the whipping post (conveniently located just outside the courthouse) or being locked in the stocks or pillory, where the offenders were subjected to public ridicule. Jail sentences were rare—punishment was swift and drastic, and the offenders then returned to the community, often bearing lifelong evidence of their conviction.

George Wythe House ★

On the west side of the Palace Green is the elegant restored brick home of George Wythe (pronounced "with"), classics scholar, noted lawyer and teacher (Thomas Jefferson, Henry Clay, and John Marshall were his students), and member of the House

Standing at the western end of Duke of Gloucester Street, the stately **Sir Christopher Wren Building** may not be part of Colonial Williamsburg, but it is the oldest restored structure here. Believed to have been designed by Sir Christopher Wren, it's America's oldest academic building. Constructed between 1695 and 1699, even before there was a Williamsburg, it's the campus centerpiece of the **College of William and Mary,** the country's second-oldest college behind only Harvard University. King William III and Queen Mary II chartered the school in 1693, and over the next century it was the alma mater of many of the country's early leaders, including Thomas Jefferson. (Its most famous modern alumni are actresses Glenn Close and Linda Lavin and comedian Jon Stewart of *The Daily Show.*) Fire gutted the Wren building in 1705, 1859, and 1862. Its exterior walls remained intact, and in 1928 John D. Rockefeller, Jr., restored it to its Colonial appearance. The college still uses its upstairs classrooms and offices, but the first-floor Grammar School, Great Hall, and Wren Chapel (site of many a campus marriage) are open to the public Monday to Friday 10am to 5pm, Saturday 9am to 5pm, and Sunday noon to 5pm. Admission is free. The college's **visitor information office** in the rear of the building (© **757/221-3278;** www.wm.edu/visitors) has campus maps.

of Burgesses. A close friend of royal governors, Wythe nevertheless was the first Virginia signer of the Declaration of Independence. Wythe did not sign the Constitution, however, because it did not contain a Bill of Rights or antislavery provisions. His house was Washington's headquarters prior to the siege of Yorktown and Rochambeau's after the surrender of Cornwallis.

Governor's Palace ★★★

This meticulous reconstruction is of the Georgian mansion that was the residence and official headquarters of royal governors from 1714 until Lord Dunmore fled before dawn in the face of armed resistance in 1775, thus ending British rule in Virginia. The palace now portrays the final 5 years of British rule. Though the sumptuous surroundings, nobly proportioned halls and rooms, 10 acres of formal gardens and greens, and vast wine cellars all evoke splendor, the king's representative was, by that time, little more than a functionary of great prestige but limited power. He was more apt to behave like a diplomat in a foreign land than an autocratic Colonial ruler.

Tours, given continuously through the day, end in the gardens, where you can explore the elaborate geometric parterres, topiary work, bowling green, *allées,* and a holly maze patterned after the one at Hampton Court. Plan at least 30 minutes to wander the stunning grounds and visit the kitchen and stable yards.

James Geddy House & Foundry ★

This two-story L-shaped 1762 home (with attached shops) is an original building where you can see how a comfortably situated middle-class family lived in the 18th century. Unlike the fancier abodes, the Geddy House has no wallpaper or oil paintings; a mirror and spinet from England, however, indicate relative affluence.

James Geddy, Sr., was a gunsmith and brass founder who advertised in the *Virginia Gazette* of July 8, 1737, that he had "a great Choice of Guns and Fowling Pieces, of several Sorts and Sizes, true bored, which he will warrant to be good; and will sell them as cheap as they are usually sold in England." A younger son, James, Jr., became the town's foremost silversmith and was a member of the city's Common Council involved in furthering the patriot cause. Craftsmen cast silver, pewter, bronze, and brass items at a foundry here.

The Magazine & Guardhouse ★★

Another original building, this octagonal brick structure was constructed in 1715 to house ammunition and arms for the defense of the colony. In Colonial Williamsburg, every able-bodied freeman belonged to the militia from the ages of 16 to 60 and did his part in protecting hearth and home from attack by local tribes, riots, slave uprisings, and pirate raids. The high wall and guardhouse were built during the French and Indian War to protect the magazine's 60,000 pounds of gunpowder. Today the building is stocked with 18th-century equipment—flintlock muskets, cannons, barrels of powder, bayonets, and drums, the latter for communication purposes. Children can join the militia here during the summer (see "Especially for Kids," below).

Peyton Randolph House ★

The Randolphs were one of the most prominent and wealthy families in Colonial Virginia. Sir John Randolph was a respected lawyer, speaker of the house of Burgesses, and Virginia's representative to London, where he was the only Colonial-born Virginian ever to be knighted. When he died, he left his library to 16-year-old Peyton, "hoping he will betake himself to the study of law." When Peyton Randolph died in 1775, his cousin, Thomas Jefferson, purchased his books at auction; they eventually became the nucleus of the Library of Congress. Peyton Randolph followed in his father's footsteps, studying law in London after attending the College of William and Mary. Known as the great mediator, he was unanimously elected president of 1774's First Continental Congress in Philadelphia, and though he believed in nonviolence and hoped the colonies could amicably settle their differences with England, he was a firm patriot.

Carriage Rides

A fun way to see the Historic Area is on horse-drawn carriage rides, which depart from a horse post in front of the Magazine & Guardhouse (see above). Check with the visitor center or the John Greenhow Store on Duke of Gloucester Street for schedules and prices.

The house (actually, two connected homes) dates to 1715. It is today restored to reflect the period around 1770. The house is open to the public for self-guided tours with period-costumed interpreters in selected rooms.

The Public Gaol ★

As noted above, imprisonment was not the usual punishment for crime in Colonial times, but persons awaiting trial and runaway slaves sometimes spent months in the Public Gaol. In winter, the cells were bitterly cold; in summer, they were stifling. Beds were piles of straw; leg irons, shackles, and chains were used frequently; and the daily diet consisted of "salt beef damaged, and Indian meal." In its early days, the gaol doubled as a madhouse, and during the Revolution, redcoats, spies, traitors, and deserters swelled its population.

The gaol opened in 1704. Debtors' cells were added in 1711 (though the imprisoning of debtors was virtually eliminated after a 1772 law made creditors responsible for their upkeep), and keeper's quarters were built in 1722. The thick-walled redbrick building served as the Williamsburg city jail through 1910. The building today is restored to its 1720s appearance.

The Public Hospital ★

Opened in 1773, the Public Hospital for Persons of Insane and Disordered Minds was America's first mental asylum. From 1773 to about 1820, "treatment" involved solitary confinement and a grisly course of action designed to "encourage" patients to "choose" rational behavior (it was assumed back then that patients willfully chose a life of insanity). So-called therapeutic techniques included the use of drugs, submersion in cold water for extended periods, bleeding, blistering salves, and an array of restraining devices. On a self-guided tour, you'll see a 1773 cell, with a straw-filled mattress on the floor, ragged blanket, and manacles. The hospital is also the entry for Colonial Williamsburg's art museums (see below).

Raleigh Tavern ★★

This most famous of Williamsburg taverns was named for Sir Walter Raleigh, who launched the "Lost Colony" that disappeared on Roanoke Island in North Carolina some 20 years before Jamestown was settled. After the Governor's Palace, it was the social and political hub of the town, especially during Publick Times. Regulars included George Washington and Thomas Jefferson, who met here in 1774 with Patrick Henry, Richard Henry Lee, and Francis Lightfoot Lee to discuss revolution. Patrick Henry's troops gave their commander a farewell dinner here in 1776.

The original tavern was destroyed by fire in 1859. Reconstructed on the original site in 1932, the current structure includes two dining rooms; the Apollo ballroom, scene of elegant soirees; a clubroom that could be rented for private meetings; and a bar where ale and hot rum punch were the favored drinks.

In the Raleigh Tavern Bakery, you can buy 18th-century confections like Sally Lunn bread, sweet potato muffins, and ginger cake as well as soups and sandwiches from 9am to 5pm daily.

R. Charlton's Coffeehouse

In the 1760s Richard Charlton opened this coffeehouse near the Capitol, where it soon became a stylish gathering place for the social elite, who read 3-month-old newspapers from London and engaged in heated political discussion. Charlton dispensed China tea imported via England, coffee from the West Indies, and chocolate from the West Indies. You'll have a chance to sample the liquids but not linger; admission is by tour only.

Thomas Everard House ★

One of the oldest buildings in Williamsburg, the Thomas Everard House was built in 1717 as a residence-cum-shop by public armorer and master gunsmith John Brush. The most distinguished owner was Thomas Everard, two-time mayor of Williamsburg.

Stocks & Bondage

The punishments meted out in 18th-century Williamsburg included public ridicule. The convicted had their neck, arms, and legs bound in stocks and pillories. Passersby added to the ridicule by tossing rotten tomatoes at the convicts. Modern visitors are more likely to have a laugh; in fact, millions of us have had our photos taken with our heads and hands dangling from the stocks.

Though not as wealthy as George Wythe and John Randolph, he was in their elite circle. He enlarged the house, adding the two wings that create a U shape. Today, the home is restored and furnished to its Everard-era appearance. The smokehouse and kitchen out back are original. (The Thomas Everard is open Tues, Wed, and Fri 9am–5pm.)

Wetherburn's Tavern

Though less important than the Raleigh Tavern, Wetherburn's also played an important role in Colonial Williamsburg. George Washington occasionally favored the tavern with his patronage. And, like the Raleigh, it was mobbed during Publick Times and frequently served as a center of sedition and as a rendezvous of Revolutionary patriots. The heart-of-yellow-pine floors are original, so you can actually walk in Washington's footsteps. Windows, trim, and weatherboarding are a mixture of old and new; and the outbuildings, except for the dairy, are reconstructions. **Twenty-five-minute tours** are given throughout the day. The tavern is open Monday, Tuesday, Thursday, and Saturday.

THE ART MUSEUMS OF COLONIAL WILLIAMSBURG ★★

From the central hallway of the Public Hospital (see above), an elevator descends underground to Colonial Williamsburg's two fine museums.

The 62,000-square-foot **DeWitt Wallace Decorative Arts Museum** houses some 10,000 objects representing the highest achievement of American and English artisans from the 1640s to 1800. You'll see period furnishings, ceramics, textiles, paintings, prints, silver, pewter, clocks, scientific instruments, mechanical devices, and weapons. Don't miss Charles Willson Peale's 1780 portrait of George Washington, which he patterned after the coronation portrait of George III of England, in the Masterworks Gallery.

Go through the Weldon Gallery on the upper level to the **Abby Aldrich Rockefeller Folk Art Museum** with more than 2,600 folk-art paintings, sculptures, and art objects. Mrs. Rockefeller was a pioneer in this branch of collecting in the 1920s and 1930s. Her collection includes household ornaments and useful wares (hand-stenciled bed covers, butter molds, pottery, utensils, painted furniture, boxes), mourning pictures (embroideries honoring departed relatives and national heroes), family and individual portraits, shop signs, carvings, whittled toys, calligraphic drawings, weavings, quilts, and paintings of scenes from daily life.

A cafe here offers light fare, beverages, and a limited luncheon menu.

SHOPS, CRAFTS & TRADE EXHIBITS

Numerous 18th-century crafts demonstrations occur throughout the Historic Area. Such goings-on were a facet of everyday life in the preindustrial era. Dozens of crafts are practiced by more than 70 master craftspeople at 21 sites. They're an extremely skilled group, many having served up to 7-year apprenticeships. The program is part of Williamsburg's efforts to present an accurate picture of Colonial society, portraying the average man and woman as well as more illustrious citizens.

You can see a cabinetmaker, a wig maker, a silversmith, a printer and bookbinder, a blacksmith, a shoemaker, a gunsmith, a milliner, a wheelwright, and carpenters—all carrying on, and explaining, their trades in the 18th-century fashion.

Especially for Kids

In addition to Busch Gardens Williamsburg and Water Country USA (see below), families can enjoy many hands-on activities in the Historic Area. A fun activity is at the **Governor's Palace,** where the dancing master gives lessons. During the summer kids can "enlist" in the militia and practice marching and drilling at the **Magazine and Guardhouse** (I still have a snapshot of myself holding a flintlock when I was a boy). If they get unruly, you can lock them in the stocks in front of the **Courthouse.** Inquire at the visitor center for special themed tours in areas of your children's specific interests.

THE THEME PARKS

Busch Gardens Williamsburg ☺ At some point you may need a break from early American history, especially if you have kids in tow, so head over to Busch Gardens Williamsburg, a 360-acre family entertainment park. Little mental effort is required to enjoy the shows, festivities, and more than 50 rides, including the world-class roller coasters Apollo's Chariot and Alpengeist. Young children will especially enjoy the Sesame Street Forest of Fun, which has rides their own size.

Arrive early—but try not to come when it's raining, as some rides may not operate. Bring comfortable shoes; and, remember, you will get wet on some of the rides, so wear appropriate clothing. As soon as you're through the turnstiles, pick up a copy of the park map and the day's activity schedule, which tells what's showing and when at the entertainment venues. Then take a few minutes to carefully plan your time—it's a big park with lots to see and do. Busch Gardens changes every year, so be on the lookout for new attractions.

1 Busch Gardens Blvd. (3 miles east of Williamsburg on U.S. 60). ℂ **800/343-9746.** www.busch gardens.com. Admission and hours vary, so call ahead, check website, or get brochure at visitor center. Admission $67 adults, $57 children 3–9, free for children 2 and under for unlimited rides, shows, and attractions. Parking $13. Mid-May to Labor Day daily; late Mar to mid-May and day after Labor Day to Oct Fri–Sun. Closed Nov to late Mar.

Water Country USA ☺ Virginia's largest water-oriented amusement park features exciting water slides, rides, and entertainment set to a 1950s and 1960s surf theme. The largest ride—Big Daddy Falls—takes the entire family on a colossal river-rafting adventure. Or you can twist and turn on giant inner tubes through flumes, tunnels, water "explosions," and down a waterfall to "splashdown." And there's much more, all of it wet and sometimes wild. It's a perfect place to chill out after a hot summer's day in the Historic Area.

176 Water Country USA Pkwy. (off Va. 199, north of Exit 242 off I-64). ℂ **800/343-7946.** www. watercountryusa.com. Admission and hours vary, so call ahead, check website, or get brochure at visitor centers. Admission $47 adults, $40 children 3–9, free for children 2 and under. Parking $12. Late May to Labor Day daily. Closed day after Labor Day to late-May. Take Va. 199 north of I-64 and follow signs.

Outdoor Activities

BICYCLING Not only is a bike the easiest way to get around the Historic Area, but the 23-mile-long **Colonial Parkway** between Jamestown and Yorktown is also one of Virginia's most scenic bike routes. There is no dedicated bike path, but vehicular traffic usually is light enough that you'll have the road virtually to yourself. You'll pedal along the banks of the James and York rivers (where there are picnic areas) and through a tunnel under Colonial Williamsburg. The 7 miles between Williamsburg and Jamestown are flat, but you'll have more car traffic to contend with than on the rolling 13-mile journey to Yorktown. Rentals are available at the **Spa of Colonial Williamsburg,** 307 S. England St., between the Williamsburg Inn and the Williamsburg Lodge (ℂ **757/220-7720;** see "Where to Stay," below).

GOLF   The Williamsburg area is *the* place to play golf in Virginia—if you can afford it; a round here can cost $100 and up during the prime summer months. It all started in 1947 with Colonial Williamsburg's noted 18-hole **Golden Horseshoe** course (📞 **757/220-7696**) and a 9-hole course for guests of the Williamsburg Inn. On the James River, **Kingsmill Resort** (www.kingsmill.com; 📞 **800/832-5665** or 757/253-3998) has three top-flight 18-hole courses of its own, including the world-famous River Course, which hosted the LPGA Michelob Ultra Open from 2003 to 2009. See "Where to Stay," below, for more about the Williamsburg Inn and Kingsmill Resort.

Ford's Colony (📞 **800/334-6033** or 757/258-4130; www.fordscolony.com) has two Dan Maples–designed courses, the challenging Blue-Gold (12 of 18 holes bordered by water) and the more forgiving White-Red. Another Maples-designed course is in the works. **Williamsburg National Golf Club** (📞 **800/826-5732** or 757/258-9642; www.wngc.com) has Virginia's only Jack Nicklaus–designed course, which *Golf Digest* magazine considers one of the state's top 10 links.

Royal New Kent Golf Club (📞 **888/253-4363** or 804/966-7023; www.traditionalclubs.com/royal) has "a succession of you've-never-seen-this-before holes," according to *Golf Digest*. Its sister course at **Stonehouse Golf Club** (📞 **888/253-4363** or 757/566-1138; www.traditionalclubs.com) is more like a mountain course, with great vistas to please your eyes and deep bunkers to test your skills. Also pleasing to the eye, **Kiskiack Golf Club** (📞 **800/989-4728** or 757/566-2200; www.traditionalclubs.com) has two lakes nestled among its rolling hills.

Call the courses for current greens fees, directions, and tee times.

HORSEBACK RIDING   One- and 3-hour rail rides are available at **Stonehouse Stables** (📞 **757/566-9633**; www.stonehousestables.com) in Toano, off U.S. 60 west of Williamsburg. Call for prices and reservations, which are required.

Shopping
IN THE HISTORIC AREA

Duke of Gloucester Street is the center for 18th-century wares created by craftspeople plying the trades of our forefathers. The goods include hand-wrought silver jewelry from the Sign of the Golden Ball, hats from the Mary Dickinson shop, handwoven linens from Prentis Store, books bound in leather and hand-printed newspapers from the post office, gingerbread cakes from the Raleigh Tavern Bake Shop, and everything from foods to fishhooks at Greenhow and Tarpley's, a general store. In fine weather, check out the outdoor market next to the Magazine.

Run by the Colonial Williamsburg Foundation, the **Craft House,** on Duke of Gloucester Street at Henry Street in Merchants Square (📞 **757/220-7747**), features Williamsburg's own branded dinnerware, flatware, glassware, pewter, silver, folk art, jewelry, and ceramics. Its sister store, **Williamsburg At Home** (📞 **757/220-7749**), carries high-end furniture and housewares.

Other "shoppes" in **Merchants Square** offer a wide range of merchandise: antiques, antiquarian books and prints, 18th-century-style floral arrangements, candy, toys, handcrafted pewter and silver items, needlework supplies, country quilts, Oriental rugs, and everything Virginian, including hams and peanuts. It's not all of the "ye olde" variety, however, for national chains such as Chico's, Williams-Sonoma, and Barnes & Noble (disguised as the William and Mary Bookstore) are here, too. Merchants Square has free 2-hour parking for its customers.

ON RICHMOND ROAD

Shopping in the Historic Area is fun, but the biggest draws are along Richmond Road (U.S. 60) between Williamsburg and Lightfoot, an area 5 to 7 miles west of the Historic Area. If you like outlet shopping, Richmond Road is for you.

Most of the action is at **Williamsburg Premium Outlets ★★**, between Airport and Lightfoot roads (© **877/466-8853** or 757/565-0702; www.premiumoutlets. com/williamsburg). The largest and best outlet mall here, it dwarfs its competition by a mile, which is about how far you will walk from one side to the other. I always drive through it first and spot my favorite shops before hunting down a parking space. You'll find an ever-growing array of the top brands here. The mall is open Monday to Saturday 10am to 9pm and Sunday 10am to 7pm with extended hours on major shopping weekends.

Among the major stores in residence at the much smaller **Williamsburg Outlet Mall** (© **888/746-7333** or 757/565-3378; www.williamsburgoutletmall.com), at the intersection of U.S. 60 and Lightfoot Road (C.R. 646), are Bon Worth, Dress Barn, L'eggs, Pendleton, Lee/Wrangler, and Totes. It's enclosed in an air-conditioned mall, a saving grace on sweltering summer days. It's open Monday to Saturday 10am to 9pm and Sunday 10am to 6pm.

Across the highway you can browse for collectibles and perhaps find a priceless piece of antiquity at the **Williamsburg Antique Mall,** 500 Lightfoot Rd. (© **757/ 565-3422;** www.antiqueswilliamsburg.com), with 45,000 square feet of dealer space. It's open Monday to Saturday 10am to 6pm and Sunday noon to 5pm.

Continue west 1½ miles on U.S. 60, and you'll come to the **Williamsburg Doll Factory** (© **757/564-9703;** www.dollfactory.com), with limited-edition porcelain collector's dolls. You can observe the doll-making process and buy parts to make your own. Other items available are stuffed animals, dollhouses and miniatures, clowns, and books on dolls. It's open Monday to Saturday 9am to 5pm and Sunday 10am to 4pm.

ON THE WINE TRAIL

In 1623, the Jamestown colonists were required to plant "20 vines for every male in the family above the age of 20." By doing so, it was thought, the fledgling colony would develop a profitable wine industry. As it turned out, the profitable industry was tobacco, not grapes, and winemaking didn't take off until the 1980s, when the **Williamsburg Winery,** 5800 Wessex Hundred (© **757/229-0999;** www.williamsburg winery.com), proved that good grapes could be grown on the Peninsula. Its Governor's White is one of the most widely purchased of Virginia's wines, although you may like the John Adlum blended chardonnay much better. Tastings and 45-minute tours cost $10 per person.

Time your visit to have a bite of lunch along with your Two Shilling Red in the winery's **Gabriel Archer Tavern.** Freshly baked French bread accompanies imported cheeses, interesting salads, and sandwiches. It's reasonably priced, too, with lunch items running $8 to $17 and dinner main courses from $16 to $21. A combined tasting tour and lunch costs $30.

The winery is open Monday to Saturday 10am to 5pm and Sunday 11am to 5pm (Apr–Oct daily to 6pm). The tavern serves lunch Monday to Friday and dinner Thursday to Monday. From the Historic Area, take Henry Street (Va. 132) south, turn right on Va. 199, left on Brookwood Drive, and another left on Lake Powell Road to the winery.

Where to Stay

COLONIAL WILLIAMSBURG FOUNDATION HOTELS

The Colonial Williamsburg Foundation operates four hotels in all price categories: Williamsburg Inn (very expensive), Williamsburg Lodge (expensive), Woodlands Hotel & Suites (moderate), and the Governor's Inn (inexpensive), plus a collection of tavern rooms and houses known as the Colonial Houses. Guests at all except the Governor's Inn can use most of the sports facilities at the Williamsburg Inn and Williamsburg Lodge.

For advance reservations, call the **visitor center reservations service** (℃ **800/ 447-8679;** www.colonialwilliamsburgresort.com). You also can make walk-in reservations at the Colonial Williamsburg Visitor Center.

Governor's Inn ★ 🔧   Least expensive of the foundation's hotels, the extraordinarily well-maintained Governor's Inn is a two- and three-story, 1960s-vintage brick motel, most of whose rooms open to outdoor walkways. This is not your ordinary inexpensive motel, for the rooms come stocked with thick towels and Gilchrist & Soames toiletries. Williamsburg posters on the walls remind you where you are. My only complaint was that my heating and air-conditioning unit was a bit noisy. There's an outdoor pool for cooling off. The inn is on the northwestern edge of the Historic Area near the Transportation Center, which means that trains come by during the night. On the other hand, you can walk from here to everything in the historic area.

506 N. Henry St. (Va. 132; at Lafayette St.), Williamsburg, VA 23185. www.colonialwilliamsburg.com. ℃ **800/447-8679** or 757/229-1000. Fax 757/220-7480. 200 units. $59–$99 double. Rates include continental breakfast. AE, DC, DISC, MC, V. **Amenities:** Access to health club at Williamsburg Woodlands; pool. *In room:* A/C, TV, hair dryer, Wi-Fi.

Williamsburg Inn ★★★   One of the nation's most distinguished hotels, this rambling white-brick Regency-style inn has played host to U.S. presidents and heads of state including Queen Elizabeth II (both in 1957 for Jamestown's 350th anniversary

---

🏷 Just for Guests

There are advantages to staying at one of the Colonial Williamsburg Foundation's hotels. For example, you can purchase discounted Colonial Williamsburg admission tickets valid for the length of your stay ($30 for adults, $15 for children 6–17). You also get breaks on other fees and can use your room keys to charge Historic Area expenses to your hotel bill.

Another perk is use of the **Spa of Colonial Williamsburg,** 307 S. England St., between the Williamsburg Inn and the Williamsburg Lodge (℃ **757/220-7720**). In addition to a wide range of treatments, it has gourmet cuisine and rents bikes.

Like most hotels these days, room rates at the foundation's accommodations vary widely depending on the season and how many guests may be booked on a given night. Try to reserve as far in advance as possible for the busy summer season and for spring and fall weekends. You might get a bargain during other times, especially if business is slow. You also can make walk-in reservations at the Colonial Williamsburg Visitor Center—at discounted rates if the hotels have rooms to spare (don't expect to get a deal on weekends and holidays). Also be sure to ask about holiday, golf, family, and other package deals.

and in 2007 for the 400th). This is also a great golf resort, with three top-flight courses to play, including the noted Golden Horseshoe (see "Outdoor Activities," above). With giant floor-to-ceiling windows overlooking the renowned Golden Horseshoe golf course, the **Regency Dining Room** features classic American cuisine (coats and ties are required after 6pm). The champagne Sunday brunch is worth a go (reservations are required). All of the spacious accommodations are exquisitely furnished with reproductions, books, and photos. Rooms in a modern building called **Providence Guesthouses,** adjacent to the inn, are furnished in a contemporary blend of 18th-century and Oriental styles, with balconies or patios overlooking tennis courts and a beautiful wooded area. The inn's fitness center is in Colonial Williamsburg's full-service spa, between here and the Williamsburg Lodge (below).

136 Francis St., Williamsburg, VA 23187. www.colonialwilliamsburg.com. © **800/447-8679** or 757/229-1000. Fax 757/220-7096. 62 units. Main inn $319–$579 double, $439–$799 suite; Providence Guesthouses $199–$339 double. AE, DC, DISC, MC, V. **Amenities:** Restaurant; bar; concierge; 3 golf courses; health club; Jacuzzi; pool; room service; sauna; spa; tennis courts. *In room:* A/C, TV, fridge, hair dryer, Wi-Fi.

Williamsburg Lodge ★★ Across the street from the Williamsburg Inn, the foundation's second-best hotel has been restored to its original 1930s appearance, albeit with modern conveniences. The original structures were gutted, and Colonial Williamsburg's state-of-the-art conference center was added. Only the existing Tazewell Wing, a 1970s-vintage structure whose rooms have balconies facing landscaped courtyards, escaped serious surgery. The other more luxurious rooms are in four Colonial-style "Guest Houses" linked to the main building by covered brick walkways. The new units are notable for their Colonial Williamsburg–designed furniture and their retro 1930s bathrooms. Guests here share all of the Williamsburg Inn's facilities, including the luxurious **Spa of Colonial Williamsburg** across the street. Large suites occupy the second floor of the main building, which houses a restaurant and comfy bar.

310 S. England St., Williamsburg, VA 23185. www.colonialwilliamsburg.com. © **800/447-8679** or 757/229-1000. Fax 757/220-7685. 323 units. $129–$299 double; $199–$469 suite. AE, DC, DISC, MC, V. **Amenities:** Restaurant; bar; children's programs; concierge; health club; Jacuzzi; pool; room service; spa; tennis courts. *In room:* A/C, fridge, hair dryer, Wi-Fi.

Woodlands Hotel & Suites ★ ☺ Located beside the visitor center, this is the foundation's third-best hotel. A separate building with a peaked roof and skylights houses the lodgelike lobby, where guests are treated to continental breakfast in a room with a fireplace. Interior corridors lead to the guest quarters in a U-shaped building around a courtyard. The more expensive suites have separate living and sleeping rooms divided by the bathroom and a wet bar with coffeemaker, fridge, and microwave oven (you won't have a fridge or microwave in the moderately spacious rooms). All units have Colonial-style pine furniture and photos of the Historic Area on their walls. Huzzah BBQ Grille is on the premises. There's plenty to keep kids occupied around the complex. Couple that with the pullout sofa beds in the suites, and it's a good choice for families of moderate means.

105 Visitors Center Dr. (PO Box 1776), Williamsburg, VA 23187. www.colonialwilliamsburg.com. © **800/447-8679** or 757/229-1000. Fax 757/229-7079. 300 units. $69–$159 double; $119–$209 suite. Rates include continental breakfast. AE, DC, DISC, MC, V. **Amenities:** Restaurant; bar; babysitting; bikes; children's programs; concierge; health club; outdoor pool. *In room:* A/C, TV, fridge (in suites), hair dryer, Wi-Fi.

COLONIAL HOUSES ★★

My favorite way to experience Colonial Williamsburg up close and personal is to stay in one of the foundation's **Colonial Houses.** In fact, they are the only way to actually stay in the Historic Area mere steps from the main attractions. Scattered throughout the district, these former laundries, workshops, small homes, and stand-alone kitchens have been converted into one- and two-bedroom bungalows. Others are rooms in taverns, some of which have as many as 16 units. Some rooms are tiny; tell the reservation clerk precisely what size and bed configuration you'd like. For example, I have stayed in the Robert Carter Kitchen, a two-story converted cookhouse just off the Palace Green. It has a downstairs living room and Pullman kitchen, and a winding staircase leads to a bedroom and bathroom. The sloping upstairs ceiling under a dormer roof was head-knockingly low on the sides.

Tastefully furnished with 18th-century antiques and reproductions, all the houses are variously equipped with kitchens, living rooms, and fireplaces—and in some cases, sizable gardens. They all have air-conditioning, TVs, phones with dial-up dataports, and coffeemakers. The Williamsburg Inn, which manages the houses, provides room service, and guests here can use the facilities there. Each house has its own parking space. Tavern rooms range from $149 to $269, while houses go for $189 to $459 per night. Reserve through the visitor center's **reservations service (☏ 800/ 447-8679;** www.colonialwilliamsburg.com).

OTHER HOTELS & MOTELS

I have room in these pages to mention but a few of this area's more than 80 chain hotels and motels. You can book rooms, buy tickets, and search for money-saving package deals on **www.visitwilliamsburg.com**, operated jointly by the Greater Williamsburg Chamber & Tourism Alliance and the Williamsburg Hotel and Motel Association (see "Visitor Information" under "Essentials," earlier in the this chapter). Or you can call the association's reservations service at ☏ **800/899-9462.**

The majority of hotels and motels are west of the Historic Area on Richmond and Bypass roads. None of them is within walking distance of the Historic Area, but you can take the local buses (see "Getting Around," earlier in this chapter).

Closest to Busch Gardens Williamsburg are the **Marriott Williamsburg,** 50 Kingsmill Rd. (☏ **800/442-3654** or 757/220-1500), the **Courtyard by Marriott Williamsburg,** 470 McLaws Circle (☏ **800/321-2211** or 757/221-0700), and the **Quality Inn at Kingsmill** (☏ **877/424-6423** or 757/220-1100). All are in an office park off U.S. 60 East at the entry to the Kingsmill complex.

Sitting on U.S. 60 between the Historic Area and Busch Gardens Williamsburg, the **Crowne Plaza Williamsburg at Fort Magruder,** 6545 Pocahontas Trail (☏ **800/333-3333** or 757/220-2250), draws lots of conventions and meetings but is also a good choice for families with children.

Great Wolf Lodge ★ ☺   About 7 miles west of the Historic Area, this large theme hotel built of logs to resemble a rustic Rocky Mountain lodge is geared to families with children. A whimsical theme prevails (the cafeteria-style restaurant is named Loose Moose Bar & Grille), but despite the rusticity, the star of the show is a monstrous indoor water park featuring a plethora of pools and water slides. Adults can spend their leisure hours being pampered in the full-service spa. While a few guest rooms have hot tubs and fireplaces geared to grown-ups, most carry on the family theme, with log cabin–like areas set aside for bunk beds in some units. Only the hotel's guests can use the water park, whose admission is included in the room rates.

549 E. Rochambeau Dr., Williamsburg, VA 23188. www.greatwolflodge.com. © **800/551-9653** or 757/229-9700. Fax 757/227-9780. 405 units. $199–$699 per unit. AE, DC, DISC, MC, V. **Amenities:** 5 restaurants; 2 bars; babysitting; children's programs; health club; Jacuzzi; pool; room service; spa; watersports equipment. *In room:* A/C, TV, fridge, hair dryer, Wi-Fi.

Wedmore Place ★ The owners of the Williamsburg Winery accomplished what they set out to do when designing this hotel: Make it seem as if you are staying in Europe. In fact, the fountain in the cobblestone courtyard at the center of the old-brick building seems ancient despite dating to 2007. The rooms and public areas are loaded with Eurocentric art and other items, including a full set of body armor standing by the lobby fireplace. Named and decorated in the style of various European provinces, the luxurious guest quarters have wood-burning fireplaces. I'm fond of the charming top-floor units with dormer windows. Opening to the outdoor pool, Café Provencal serves breakfast to guests and Mediterranean-influenced fare to anyone at dinner. You can walk to Gabriel Archer Tavern at the winery (see "On the Wine Trail," above) for lunch or dinner.

5819 Wessex Hundred, Williamsburg, VA 23185. www.wedmoreplace.com. © **866/933-6673** or 757/941-0310. Fax 757/941-0318. 28 units. $165–$395 double; $300–$750 suite. AE, DISC, MC. V. **Amenities:** Restaurant; bar; health club; pool. *In room:* A/C, TV, hair dryer, Wi-Fi.

Williamsburg Hospitality House On Richmond Road about a half-mile west of the Historic Area and opposite the College of William and Mary's football stadium, this four-story brick hotel is as convenient to the major sights as any large nonfoundation, nonchain hotel. It's built around a central courtyard with flowering trees, plants, and umbrella tables. Spacious guest rooms and public areas are appointed with a gracious blend of 18th-century reproductions. You can open the windows in some units, to let in fresh air. Meetings rather than families make up the bulk of the business here, but couples will fit right in.

415 Richmond Rd., Williamsburg, VA 23185. www.williamsburghosphouse.com. © **800/932-9192** or 757/229-4020. Fax 757/220-1560. 296 units. $89–$139 double; $250–$475 suite. AE, DC, DISC, MC, V. **Amenities:** 2 restaurants; bar; health club; outdoor pool; room service. *In room:* A/C, TV, hair dryer, Wi-Fi ($9.95 per 24 hr.).

BED & BREAKFASTS

Williamsburg has more than 20 B&Bs, including **Liberty Rose,** 1022 Jamestown Rd. (www.libertyrose.com; © **800/545-1825** or 757/253-1260), in a charming white-clapboard home sitting on a wooded hilltop 1¼ miles from the Historic Area. Closer in is **Williamsburg Sampler,** 922 Jamestown Rd. (www.williamsburgsampler.com; © **800/722-1169** or 757/253-0399), a 1976-vintage replica of an 18th-century plantation manse. For more choices, go to **www.bandbwilliamsburg.com,** official site of the Williamsburg Bed & Breakfast Network (no phone). You can book online.

The Fife & Drum Inn ★★ 🏠 Occupying upstairs quarters in one of the Merchants Square buildings, this charmer is the only privately owned inn in the Historic Area. "Colonial Williamsburg is your front yard," say owners Billy and Sharon Scruggs, who grew up here and put out a full breakfast every morning, including Virginia country ham biscuits. A sky-lit hallway with faux-brick floor and clapboard siding (it looks like a street) leads to the seven medium-size rooms and two suites, some of which have dormer windows. The suites open to a narrow porch out back. Whimsical features such as birdhouses hide a few of the TVs. The Conservancy Room is the most romantic, with a canopied double bed and a claw-foot bathtub. The inn does not have an elevator, but you can opt for a street-level Colonial cottage around the corner and avoid the 17 steps in the main building. The cottage can sleep up to six.

441 Prince George St., Williamsburg, VA 23185. www.fifeanddruminn.com. © **888/838-1783** or 757/345-1776. Fax 757/345-3433. 9 units. $119–$199 double or suite; $285–$295 cottage. Rates include full breakfast. AE, DISC, MC, V. Free parking. *In room:* A/C, TV, Wi-Fi.

A NEARBY RESORT WITH CHAMPIONSHIP GOLF

Kingsmill Resort & Spa ★★★ Nestled on beautifully landscaped grounds beside the James River, this luxurious, country club–like resort is the centerpiece of a 2,900-acre residential development. It's one of Virginia's most complete resorts, offering three golf courses, a sports complex with 15 tennis courts, and a full-service spa. The highlight is the world-famous River Course, which has hosted PGA and LPGA tournaments in its storied past. Accommodations consist of guest rooms and one-, two-, and three-bedroom suites in gray clapboard buildings overlooking the James River, golf-course fairways, or tennis courts. The suites have complete kitchens and living rooms with fireplaces. Daily housekeeping service, including fresh linens, is included. Kingsmill's main dining room offers fine cuisine with a terrific view of the James, while the golf club's restaurant overlooks the River Course. You can have a snack and sip a cold one down at the marina. Guests can take a complimentary shuttle to Colonial Williamsburg, Busch Gardens Williamsburg, and Water Country USA.

1010 Kingsmill Rd., Williamsburg, VA 23185. www.kingsmill.com. © **800/832-5665** or 757/253-1703. Fax 757/253-3993. 425 units. $189–$269 double; $349–$699 suite. Golf, tennis, and spa packages available. AE, DC, DISC, MC, V. From I-64 take Exit 242 and follow Va. 199 west past U.S. 60 to sign for Kingsmill on the James. **Amenities:** 5 restaurants; 6 bars; babysitting; children's programs; concierge; 3 golf courses; health club; Jacuzzi; pool (indoor & outdoor); room service; sauna; spa; 15 tennis courts; water sports equipment. *In room:* A/C, TV, hair dryer, kitchen (in suites), Wi-Fi.

Where to Eat

Williamsburg abounds in restaurants catering to tourists. Most national chain, fast-food, and family restaurants have outlets on Richmond Road (U.S. 60) west of town.

COLONIAL WILLIAMSBURG FOUNDATION TAVERNS ★★

The Colonial Williamsburg Foundation runs four reconstructed 18th-century "ordinaries" or taverns. They aim at authenticity in fare, ambience, costuming of the staff, and entertainment by wandering balladeers. Dinner at one of the taverns is a necessary ingredient of the Williamsburg experience. Their seasonal hours and menus change often, so what I write here may be inaccurate by the time you arrive. Current bills of fare are posted out front, at the ticket booth on Henry Street at Duke of Gloucester Street, and available at the visitor center, so you can see what's being served before making your reservations.

The Early Bird Gets the Reservation

Advance reservations for dinner at Christiana Campbell's and King's Arms taverns are essential during the summer and on weekends during spring and fall. You can book tables up to 60 days in advance by dropping by or calling the visitor center (© **800/447-8679** or 757/229-2141). Lunch reservations are accepted only for major holidays.

You don't need a reservation to buy soups, sandwiches, and baked goods at the bakery in the **Raleigh Tavern** (p. 245), which is open daily from 9am to 5pm.

Christiana Campbell's Tavern   One block behind the Capitol, Christiana Campbell's Tavern is "where all the best people resorted" around 1765. George Washington recorded in his diary that he dined here 10 times over a 22-month period. After the capital moved to Richmond, business declined and operations ceased. In its heyday, the tavern was famous for seafood, and today that is once again the specialty. Campbell's is an authentic reproduction with 18th-century furnishings, blazing fireplaces, and flutists and balladeers to entertain diners. Dinner here is a sit-down affair, and the menu leans toward fish and fowl. Reservations are highly recommended. There's a parking lot in the rear.

101 S. Waller St. ⓒ **800/447-8679** or 757/229-2141. Reservations required at dinner. Main courses $23–$35. AE, DC, DISC, MC, V. Tues–Sat 5–9pm.

Josiah Chowning's Tavern   In 1766, Josiah Chowning announced the opening of a tavern "where all who please to favour me with their custom may depend upon the best of entertainment for themselves, servants, and horses, and good pasturage." It's charming, with low-beamed ceilings, raw pine floors, and country-made furnishings. There are two working fireplaces, and at night you dine by candlelight. These days it's once again operated like a boisterous 18th-century pub, with plenty of ale and Virginia-style barbecue ribs. One of the best things to do here after 9pm is to take in the 18th-century music, magic, and games in Gambols Pub.

109 E. Duke of Gloucester St. ⓒ **800/447-8679** or 757/229-2141. Reservations required for dinner. Main courses $25–$30. AE, DC, DISC, MC, V. Daily 11:30am–3pm and 5–9pm.

King's Arms Tavern   On the site of a 1772 establishment, King's Arms Tavern is a re-creation of the tavern and an adjoining home. Stables, a barbershop, laundry, smokehouse, kitchen, and other outbuildings have also been reconstructed. The original proprietress, Mrs. Jane Vobe, was famous for her fine cooking, and her establishment's proximity to the Capitol made it a natural meeting place during Publick Times. Today, the 11 dining rooms (8 with fireplaces) are painted and furnished following early Virginia precedent. The Queen Anne and Chippendale pieces are typical appointments of this class of tavern, and the prints, maps, engravings, aquatints, and mezzotints lining the walls are genuine examples of period interior decorations. Balladeers wander the rooms during dinner. There's outdoor dining in the garden during warm weather.

409 E. Duke of Gloucester St. ⓒ **800/447-8679** or 757/229-2141. Reservations required at dinner. Main courses $31–$37. AE, DC, DISC, MC, V. Thurs–Mon 11:30am–2:30pm and 5–9pm.

Shields Tavern 🍴   With 11 dining rooms and a garden under a trumpet-vine-covered arbor that seats 200, Shields is the largest of the Historic Area's tavern/restaurants. It's named for James Shields who, with his wife, Anne, and family, ran a much-frequented hostelry on this site in the mid-1700s. Based on a room-by-room inventory of Shields' personal effects, the tavern has been furnished with items similar to those used in the mid–18th century, and many rooms have working fireplaces. The modern bill of fare features Southern comfort food such as barbecue and seafood gumbo.

422 E. Duke of Gloucester St. ⓒ **800/447-8679** or 757/229-2141. Reservations required at dinner. Main courses $24–$27. AE, DC, DISC, MC, V. Tues–Sat 11:30am–2:30pm and 5–7:45pm.

RESTAURANTS IN MERCHANTS SQUARE

Aromas Coffeehouse, Café & Bakeshop 🍴 AMERICAN   Attracting both the town and gown crowd, this well-worn, often noisy restaurant is both Williamsburg's favorite coffeehouse and one of its best choices for light, inexpensive meals. I often start my day here with a fresh pastry and a cup of gourmet coffee or tea, although the morning fare also includes sausage biscuits, brie-stuffed French toast, and bagels with lox and cream cheese. Lunch switches to sandwiches, wraps, salads, and several vegetarian selections. A limited menu of main courses appears after 5pm, headlined by Low Country barbecued shrimp over cheese grits. Order at the counter and wait for your number to be called, and be prepared to dine with plastic utensils. Beer and wine are served by the glass.

431 Prince George St. © **757/221-6676.** www.aromasworld.com. Reservations not accepted. Breakfast $4–$8.50; sandwiches and salads $6–$9; main courses $11–$15. MC, V. Mon–Thurs 7am–10pm; Fri–Sat 7am–11pm; Sun 8am–8pm.

Berret's Seafood Restaurant & Tap House Grill ★ AMERICAN   A congenial, casual place, Berret's has a popular outdoor Tap House Grill, where you will find me quenching my thirst after schlepping around the Historic Area all day. It has heaters, so you can sit out here well into autumn. In the adjoining restaurant, canvas sailcloth shades, blue-trimmed china, and marine artifacts on the walls make an appropriate backdrop for the traditional Chesapeake Bay seafood. Oysters or clams raw or steamed on the half shell do nicely as starters. For a main course, the crab cakes are pan-fried and served over a thin slice of Virginia ham—a pleasant combination of flavors. The Tap House serves sandwiches and main courses (the latter are not in the same league as those inside the dining room). There's a good selection of Virginia microbrews and wines by the glass.

199 S. Boundary St. © **757/253-1847.** www.berrets.com. Reservations recommended for dinner. Sandwiches and salads (Tap House Grill only) $9.50–$15; main courses $19–$30. AE, DISC, MC, V. Restaurant Mon–Sat 11:30am–3:30pm and 5–10pm, Sun 11am–3:30pm and 5–9:30pm. Tap House Grill daily 4–10pm.

Blue Talon Bistro ★★ 🍴 FRENCH/AMERICAN   Serious comfort food is the motto at this lively French-style bistro, the domain of chef David Everett and his talented team and Williamsburg's third-best restaurant behind A Chef's Kitchen and the Fat Canary (below). Although much of the comfort food has a decidedly French flair, the menu ranges from American-style rotisserie chicken and cedar-roasted salmon to *salade Niçoise*, a meal in itself. You can also order a fat hamburger here anytime. Order-at-the-bar breakfast here is *très* French, with hot-out-of-the-oven croissants and other pastries.

420 Prince George St. © **757/476-2583.** www.bluetalonbistro.com. Reservations recommended. Breakfast $6–$10; burgers $11; main courses $16–$28. DISC, MC, V. Daily 8–10:30am (breakfast only) and 11am–9pm.

The Cheese Shop 🗡 DELI   This gourmet deli is the best place in Williamsburg for takeout salads, sandwiches, and other fixings. Head to the rear counter and place your order for ham, roast beef, turkey, chicken, and barbecue sandwiches on a choice of fresh bread. The cheese counter has a wide selection of domestic and imported brands plus fresh salads. You can eat your meal at wrought-iron umbrella tables out front. The marvelous Fat Canary adjoins (see below). The wine shop in the basement carries more than 4,000 bottles from around the world.

410 Duke of Gloucester St. ☎ **757/220-0298.** www.cheeseshopwilliamsburg.com. Most items $5–$7. AE, DISC, MC, V. Mon–Sat 10am–8pm; Sun 11am–6pm.

A Chef's Kitchen ★★★ 🗡 INTERNATIONAL   Veteran chef John Gonzales, who has authored two cookbooks and appeared on several TV shows, says he started this fascinating cooking school–cum–restaurant because he "felt sorry for the audiences on the Food Network" who never get to eat the meals they watch being prepared. Here, you will not only watch this entertaining chef at work, but you will also enjoy the fruits of his labors over the course of a 3-hour evening. The restaurant is designed like a culinary classroom, with 25 seats at three tables arranged stadium style so that all can watch him at the kitchen up front. The one nightly seating begins at 6:30pm with champagne and hors d'oeuvres. Then John prepares and serves at least four more courses, each paired with an inexpensive "great find" wine (available in the gourmet store at the front of the building). The menu changes completely every few weeks but is announced in advance on the restaurant's website. The fixed price includes wine and the tip, making this a good value. Make your reservations as early as possible. John also teaches hands-on daytime classes.

501 Prince George St. ☎ **757/564-8500.** www.achefskitchen.biz. Reservations required. Fixed-price menu $85 per person, including tip. DISC, MC, V. Wed–Sat 6:30pm seating.

Fat Canary ★★★ AMERICAN   This high-energy bistro is consistently Williamsburg's best restaurant. The sophisticated but relaxed dining room sports a long bar down one side—a favorite local watering hole—and an open kitchen that uses fresh local and other ingredients for its creative American fare. Both the full and the more-limited and less-expensive menus are offered on the patio out front during warm weather. Reservations are not accepted at the outdoor tables, but it's worth the wait. Everything is excellent here. The restaurant's name comes from Colonial-era poet John Lyly's line, "Oh for a bowl of fat Canary, rich Palermo, sparkling sherry." By that he meant wines from the Canary Islands as well as Italy. Today's wine list is very good, with more than a dozen vintages available by the glass.

410 Duke of Gloucester St. ☎ **757/229-3333.** www.fatcanarywilliamsburg.com. Reservations recommended indoors, not accepted outdoors. Main courses $29–$39; outdoor light menu $13–$20. AE, DISC, MC, V. Daily 5–10pm.

The Trellis Restaurant AMERICAN/SEAFOOD   Formerly owned by Marcel Desaulniers, author of *Death by Chocolate* dessert cookbook, this restaurant is now under the aegis of chef David Everett of the Blue Talon Bistro (see above). Here the emphasis is on seafood, from sautéed barramundi (Australian white fish) with salsify puree to seared yellow fin tuna on a watermelon, radish, and arugula salad. The breakfast menu runs from Virginia ham biscuits to Sally Lunn French toast with bourbon vanilla syrup, all in large serving sizes. If the weather is fine, you can dine out on the brick terrace.

Duke of Gloucester St. ☎ **757/229-8610.** www.thetrellis.com. Reservations recommended at dinner. Breakfast $6–$10; main courses $19–$26. AE, DC, DISC, MC, V. Daily 8–10:30am (breakfast only) and 11am–9pm.

NEARBY COUNTRY-STYLE DINING

Old Chickahominy House ★★ TRADITIONAL SOUTHERN   One of the great places to sample traditional, down-home Virginia cooking, the Old Chicka-hominy House is a reconstructed 18th-century house with mantels from old Glouces-ter homes and wainscoting from Carter's Grove Plantation. Floors are bare oak, and walls, painted in traditional Colonial colors, are hung with gilt-framed 17th- and 18th-century oil paintings. The adjoining rooms house an antiques/gift shop. The entire effect is cozy and charming. Before making my rounds, I often opt for the plantation breakfast of real Virginia ham with two eggs, biscuits, cured country bacon and sausage, grits, and coffee or tea. At lunch, Miss Melinda's special is a cup of Brunswick stew with Virginia ham on hot biscuits, canned fruit salad, homemade pie, and tea or coffee. Also check out the Shirley Pewter Shop next door.

1211 Jamestown Rd. (at Va. 199). © **757/229-4689.** www.oldchickahominy.com. Reservations not accepted. Most items $4.50–$10. MC, V. Mon–Thurs 8:30–10:30am and 11:30am–2:30pm; Fri 7:30–10:15am and 11:30am–2:30pm; Sat–Sun 7:30–10:15am and 11:45am–2:15pm. Closed 2 weeks in Jan, July 4th, Thanksgiving, and Christmas.

Pierce's Pitt Bar-B-Que BARBECUE   Visible from I-64, this gaudy yellow-and-orange barbecue joint has been dishing up pulled pork, chicken, and smoked ribs since 1961, as the walls hung with old photos of the owners and their family and staff will attest. The pulled pork is better than the ribs here; it comes soaked in a smoky-flavored, tomato-based sauce. Order at the counter and take your meal (served in plastic containers) to a table inside or outdoors under cover. No alcoholic beverages are served here.

447 E. Rochambeau Dr., Lightfoot (beside I-64). © **757/565-2955.** Reservations not accepted. Sandwiches $4–$5; main courses $7–$20. MC, V. Daily 10am–9pm. Closed New Year's Day, Thanks-giving, and Christmas. From Historic Area go west on Richmond Rd. (U.S. 60), right on Airport Rd. (C.R. 645) 2 miles toward I-64, follow signs to restaurant on Rochambeau Dr., about 2 miles.

Williamsburg After Dark

You should spend at least one evening taking in a little 18th-century nightlife in Colonial Williamsburg. The Colonial taverns have evening entertainment, especially **Gambols Pub,** into which Josiah Chowning's Tavern morphs after 9pm (see "Where to Eat," earlier).

Colonial Williamsburg also conducts nighttime tours and other activities in the Historic Area. Check the schedule in *This Week,* the weekly brochure. Copies are available at the visitor center (see "Exploring the Historic Area," earlier in this chapter).

Another fun way to spend a warm-weather evening is spooking around the Historic Area, either with one of Colonial Williamsburg's official tours or with the **Original Ghosts of Williamsburg Tours** ★★ (© **877/62-GHOST** [624-4678] or 757/565-4821; www.theghosttour.com), which entertainingly blends ghost stories and local folklore with historical fact. Children will enjoy them, too. The candlelight tours are based on L. B. Taylor's bestselling 1983 book, *The Ghosts of Williamsburg.* The tours cost $11 per person (free for kids 5 and under) and take place nightly March through December and on Saturday in January and February. Call for reservations, which are essential.

The **Kimball Theatre,** on Duke of Gloucester Street in Merchants Square (© **757/565-8588;** www.kimballtheatre.com), hosts concerts, special lectures by College of William and Mary professors, puppet shows, second-run movies, and other events. Call or drop by the theater to see what's going on. William and Mary Drama Department students refine their skills in the **William and Mary Theater** (📞 **757/221-2676;** www.wm.edu). The college also has an active calendar of concerts and lectures. Its athletic teams participate in a full schedule of intercollegiate contests (📞 **757/221-3340;** www.tribeathletics.com).

Don't be surprised to see bands playing after dark in summer on Duke of Glouster Street in **Merchants Square.**

For more ideas pick up a copy of *Williamsburg* magazine or check its website at www.williamsburgmag.com.

JAMESTOWN: THE FIRST COLONY ★★

9 miles SW of Williamsburg

The story of Jamestown, the first permanent English settlement in the New World, is documented here in a national park on the Jamestown Island site where the colonists landed. You'll learn the exploits of Capt. John Smith, the colony's leader, rescued from execution by the American Indian princess Pocahontas; the arrival of the first African-American slaves; and how life was lived in 17th-century Virginia. Archaeologists have excavated more than 100 building frames, evidence of manufacturing ventures (pottery, winemaking, brick making, and glass blowing), wells, and roads. The fascinating Archaearium museum displays hundreds of thousands of artifacts of everyday life—tools, utensils, ceramic dishes, armor, keys, and the like—uncovered during the digs.

Next door at Jamestown Settlement, a state-run living-history museum complex, you can see re-creations of the three ships in which the colonists arrived in 1607, the colony they built, and a typical American Indian village of the time.

Allow at least half a day for your visit and consider packing a lunch. There is a cafe at Jamestown Settlement, but you may want to take advantage of the picnic areas at the U.S. National Park Service site.

GETTING THERE & GETTING AROUND   The scenic way here from Williamsburg is via the picturesque Colonial Parkway, or you can take Jamestown Road (Va. 31).

An alternative to driving from Williamsburg from April 15 through October 31 is the free **Historic Triangle Shuttle** (see "Getting Around," earlier in this chapter). Once you're here, the free **Jamestown Area Shuttle** (📞 **757/898-2410**) runs continuously between Historic Jamestowne and Jamestown Settlement.

Historic Jamestowne ★★★   Now part of the Colonial National Historical Park and jointly administered by the National Park Service and the Association for the Preservation of Virginia Antiquities (APVA; www.apva.org), this is the site of the actual colony. It was an island then; now an isthmus separates it from the mainland. After passing the main gate, proceed to the **visitor center** and buy your ticket. While there, you can watch a 15-minute video telling the story of Jamestown from its earliest days to 1699, when the capital of Virginia moved to Williamsburg. Inquire at the reception desk about audiotape tours, ranger-led walking tours, costumed interpretive programs, and other programs offered during your visit.

From the visitor center it's a 5-minute walk via boardwalk across a marsh to the river and **James Cittie,** as the colonists called their new village. The brick foundations outside aren't original, but they do stand on the actual locations of the 17th-century homes as determined by extensive and very much ongoing archaeological work. You're welcome to view the digging, and APVA archaeologists and volunteers will answer your questions. Most of what's left of James Cittie is now about 18 inches below ground, but the tower of one of the first brick churches in Virginia (1639) still stands. Behind the tower, **Memorial Church** is a 1907 re-creation built by the Colonial Dames of America on the site of the original structure (note the glass panels along the sides of the floor, which show some of the original foundation). In 1619, the church housed the first legislative assembly in English-speaking North America. A wooden stockade fence stands above the triangular borders of the 1607 **James Fort,** part of which has eroded into the James River.

> ### 💬 A Shiny Hand
>
> The statue of Pocahontas standing beside the old church at Historic James-towne is green, well-weathered brass— except her outstretched right hand. Legend says you'll have good luck if you shake her hand, which hundreds of people do every day, thus keeping it perpetually bright and shiny.

A short walk along the seawall past Confederate breastworks—built during the Civil War to protect this narrow part of the river—will take you to the fascinating **Archaearium,** which artfully displays the results of the archaeological digs, including the skeleton of one of the colonists and a resin cast reproduction of another belonging to a young man who apparently died of a musket shot to the right knee, giving rise to the theme of the interactive display: "Who Shot J. R.?"

A fascinating **5-mile loop drive** begins at the visitor center parking lot and winds through 1,500 wilderness acres of woodland and marsh that have been allowed to return to their natural state in order to approximate the landscape as 17th-century colonists found it. Illustrative markers interpret aspects of daily activities and industries of the colonists—tobacco growing, lumbering, silk and wine production, pottery making, farming, and so on.

Back near the main gate stands the reconstructed **Glasshouse,** where costumed interpreters make glass in the ancient way used by the colonists in 1608 during their first attempt to create an industry (it failed). Remains of the original glass furnaces are nearby.

Allow at least 2 hours for this special attraction.

Southern end of Colonial Pkwy., at Jamestown Rd. (Va. 31). © **757/898-2410** or 757/229-1773. www.nps.gov/colo. Admission $10 adults, free for children 15 and under. Includes admission to Yorktown Battlefield, good for 7 days. InterAgency passes accepted. Main gate daily 8:30am–4:30pm. Visitor center daily 9am–5pm. Closed New Year's Day and Christmas.

Jamestown Settlement ★★ ☺ Established in 1957 by the Commonwealth of Virginia to celebrate Jamestown's 350th anniversary, this living-history museum shows you what the colonists' three ships, their colony, and a typical Powhatan Indian village looked like, and costumed interpreters demonstrate how the colonists lived back then.

The entrance building shows a 20-minute film about Jamestown, *1607: A Nation Takes Root,* and has museum galleries featuring artifacts, documents, decorative objects, dioramas, and graphics relating to the Jamestown period. Don't miss the exact reproduction of the deerskin-and-seashells cape worn by Powhatan, father of Pocahontas (the Ashmolean Museum in Oxford, England, has the original).

Leaving the museum complex, you'll come directly into the **Powhatan Indian Village,** representing the culture and technology of a highly organized chiefdom of 32 tribes that inhabited coastal Virginia in the early 17th century. There are several mat-covered lodges, which are furnished as dwellings, as well as a vegetable garden and a circle of carved ceremonial posts. Historical interpreters tend crops, tan animal hides, and make bone and stone tools and pottery. The exhibits are interactive, and visitors may participate in such activities as using a shell to scrape the fur off deerskin. Children are more likely to enjoy a visit here than to Historic Jamestowne.

Triangular **James Fort** is a re-creation of the one constructed by the Jamestown colonists in the spring of 1607. Inside the wooden stockade are primitive wattle-and-daub structures with thatched roofs representing Jamestown's earliest buildings. Interpreters are engaged in activities typical of early-17th-century life, such as agriculture, military activities (including firing muskets), carpentry, blacksmithing, and meal preparation.

A short walk from James Fort are reproductions of the three **ships,** the *Susan Constant, Godspeed,* and *Discovery,* that transported the 104 colonists to Virginia. Boarding and exploring the ships will give you an appreciation of the hardships they endured even before they reached the hostile New World.

A guided 1½-hour tour is the best way to take all this in. They are given several times a day.

Jamestown Rd. (Va. 31), at James River. ⓒ **888/593-4682** or 757/253-4838. www.historyisfun.org. Admission $16 adults, $7.25 children 6–12, free for children 5 and under. Combination ticket (admission to Jamestown Settlement and Yorktown Victory Center) $20 adults, $10 children 6–12, free for children 5 and under. Daily 9am–5pm (to 6pm June 15–Aug 15). Closed New Year's Day and Christmas.

YORKTOWN: REVOLUTIONARY VICTORY ★★★

14 miles NE of Williamsburg

Although the 13 American colonies declared their independence from England on July 4, 1776, their dream of freedom from King George III came to fruition here at Yorktown in October 1781, when Gen. George Washington and his French allies won the last major battle of the American Revolution. "I have the Honor to inform Congress that a Reduction of the British Army under the Command of Lord Cornwallis is most happily effected," Washington wrote to the Continental Congress on October 19, 1781. Though sporadic fighting would continue for 2 years before a treaty was signed, the Revolutionary War, for all intents and purposes, was over.

Today, the decisive battlefield is a national park, and the Commonwealth of Virginia has built the Yorktown Victory Center, an interpretive museum explaining the road to revolution, the war itself, and the building of a new nation afterward.

Predating the Revolution and overlooking the picturesque York River, the old town of Yorktown itself is worth exploring, especially its re-created Colonial-era seaport village at **Yorktown Riverwalk Landing,** on Water Street almost beneath the Coleman Bridge, which carries U.S. 17 over the York River. Here you'll find shops, a restaurant, and a museum dedicated to the Chesapeake Bay's famous "watermen."

You'll need at least half a day to digest all this history. Plan to spend a morning or afternoon seeing the sights and having lunch.

Essentials

VISITOR INFORMATION For advance information, contact **York County Tourism Development,** 301 Main St. (PO Box 523), Yorktown, VA 23690 (*©* **757/890-3300;** www.visityorktown.org).

GETTING THERE & GETTING AROUND The easiest and most scenic way here from Williamsburg is via the picturesque Colonial Parkway. From Norfolk or Virginia Beach, take I-64 West to U.S. 17 North and follow the signs to Yorktown. Park free in the garage at the Yorktown Riverwalk Landing on Water Street.

A good alternative to driving here from Williamsburg from April 15 through October 31 is the free **Historic Triangle Shuttle** (see "Getting Around," earlier in this chapter).

Once you're here, the free **Yorktown Trolley** makes nine stops along the waterfront and in the village from mid-March through October, every 20 to 25 minutes daily.

History

Yorktown's history dates to 1691, when the General Assembly at Jamestown passed the Port Act creating a new town on the York River, which unlike the James River, has a shoal-free, deepwater channel to the Chesapeake Bay. Yorktown quickly became a principal mid-Atlantic port and a center of tobacco trade. By the time of the American Revolution, it was a thriving town with several thousand planters, innkeepers, seamen, merchants, craftsmen, indentured servants, and slaves. Water Street, paralleling the river, was lined with shops, inns, and loading docks.

The Victory at Yorktown After a rather fruitless and exhausting march through the Carolinas, Cornwallis brought his weary army to Yorktown in hopes of being evacuated to New York by the British navy. Marching quickly from the north, George Washington's army of 17,600 American and French troops (the latter under the Comte de Rochambeau) laid siege to Yorktown on September 28, 1781. Meanwhile, a French fleet sailed up from the Caribbean and held the British navy away from the Virginia Capes, thereby preventing Cornwallis's escape.

On October 9, the Americans and the French began bombarding the British positions. Washington personally fired the first American round. At 8pm on October 14, the French stormed Redoubt 9 while the Americans made short work of Redoubt 10.

Just 2 days later, a desperate Cornwallis tried to escape with his troops across the York River to Gloucester Point, but a violent storm scattered his boats. On October 17 at 10am, a British drummer appeared on the rampart and beat out a signal indicating a desire to discuss terms with the enemy. A cease-fire was called, and a British officer was led to American lines where he requested an armistice. On October 18, commissioners met at the house of Augustine Moore and worked out the terms of surrender.

At 2pm on October 19, 1781, the French and Continental armies lined Surrender Road, each stretching for over a mile on either side. About 5,000 British soldiers and seamen, clad in new uniforms, marched out of Yorktown to a large field, where they laid down their weapons and battle flags. Gen. Charles O'Hara of the British Guards represented Cornwallis who, pleading illness, did not surrender in person.

The Top Attractions

Yorktown Battlefield ★★★ Today, most of Yorktown and the surrounding battlefield areas are included in this 4,300-acre section of the Colonial National Historical Park. You can drive around the key battle sites, which have interpretive

You'll enjoy the 90-minute audio driving-tour tape or CD of the Yorktown battlefield, available in the battlefield gift shop for $4.95. Narrated by "British and American colonels" whose polite hostilities to each other are most amusing, the taped commentary further elucidates the battlefield sites. Listen to the introduction in the parking lot; it will tell you when to depart. Tape or not, drive the Battlefield Route first; then if time permits, the Encampment Route.

markers, but begin at the visitor center, where the 16-minute documentary film *Siege at Yorktown* is shown on the hour and half-hour. Not to be missed among the museum displays is Washington's actual sleeping and dining tent, now preserved in a hermetically sealed room (it's really cool to actually walk into his tent without entering the glass-enclosed room). There's also a replica (which you can board and explore) of the quarterdeck of HMS *Charon;* additional objects recovered during excavations; exhibits about Cornwallis's surrender and the events leading up to it; and dioramas detailing the siege. Upstairs, an on-the-scene account of the Battle of Yorktown is given by a 13-year-old soldier in the Revolutionary army, his taped narrative accompanied by a sound-and-light show.

National Park Service rangers are on hand to answer questions. They give free **tours** of the British inner defense line seasonally (call the visitor center for times).

To make it easy to follow what happened, the park is divided into two routes. You won't stay in your car the whole time; it's frequently necessary to park, get out, and walk to redoubts and earthworks. A lot of the drive is very scenic, winding through woods and fields abundant with bird life. The Encampment Route is especially beautiful.

On the 7-mile **Battlefield Route,** you'll see the **Grand French Battery,** where French soldiers manning cannons, mortars, and howitzers fired on British and German mercenary troops; the **Moore House,** where British and American representatives hammered out the surrender on October 18, 1781; and **Surrender Field,** where the British laid down their arms at the end of the siege.

Note: The Moore House is usually open daily 1 to 4:30pm during summer and on weekends 1 to 4pm in spring and autumn, but check with the visitor center to be sure. The 10-mile **Encampment Route** takes you to the sites of Washington's and Rochambeau's headquarters, the French cemetery, Artillery Park, and the American and French encampments.

North end of Colonial Pkwy. ✆ **757/898-2410** or 898-3400. www.nps.gov/colo. Admission $10 adults, free for children 15 and under. Includes admission to Yorktown Battlefield, good for 7 days. InterAgency passes accepted. Audio CD $4.95. Battlefield daily 8:30am–dusk. Visitor center daily 9am–5pm. Closed Christmas.

Yorktown Victory Center ★ This state-operated multimedia museum offers an excellent orientation to Yorktown, and coming here first will prepare you for your battlefield tour. You'll start with an open-air timeline walkway known as the Road to Revolution, which illustrates the relationship between the colonies and Great Britain beginning in 1750. Aspects of the American Revolution are explored in its gallery exhibits. *Witnesses to Revolution* focuses on ordinary individuals who recorded their observances of the war and its impact on their lives. The Converging on Yorktown gallery and the film, *A Time of Revolution,* focus on the military campaign. *Yorktown's*

Sunken Fleet uses artifacts recovered from British ships sunk during the siege of Yorktown to describe shipboard life. *The Legacy of Yorktown: Virginia Beckons* examines how people from many different cultures shaped a new American society.

Outdoors, costumed interpreters in the Continental army encampment re-create the lives of men and women who took part in the American Revolution. There are presentations on weaponry, military drills and tactics, medicine, and cookery. Nearby, an 18th-century farm site demonstrates how "middling" farmers—no wealthy plantation owners here—lived and worked.

Colonial Pkwy. (½ mile west of Yorktown). ✆ **888/593-4682** or 757/253-4838. www.historyisfun. org. Admission $9.50 adults, $5.25 children 6–12, free for children 5 and under. Combination ticket (admission to Yorktown Victory Center and Jamestown Settlement) $20 adults, $10 children 6–12, free for children 5 and under. Daily 9am–5pm (to 6pm June 15–Aug 15). Closed New Year's Day and Christmas.

Touring the Town

Though it is doubtful that Yorktown would have recovered from the destruction and waste that accompanied the Siege of 1781, it received the coup de grâce in the Great Fire of 1814 and declined steadily over the years, becoming a quiet rural village. Although it remains the seat of York County, it never regained its prominence as a seaport and has, like Williamsburg, changed so little that many of its picturesque old streets and buildings (whose walls escaped the fire) have survived intact to this day.

Self-guided or ranger-led walking tours of historic Yorktown—which includes some places of interest not related to the famed battle—are available at the Yorktown Battlefield visitor center (call for times; see listing above). From the visitor center, take the path to:

THE VICTORY MONUMENT   News of the victory by American and French forces at Yorktown reached Philadelphia on October 24, 1781. Five days later, Congress resolved "that the United States . . . will cause to be erected at York, in Virginia, a marble column, adorned with emblems of the alliance between the United States and his Most Christian Majesty; and inscribed with a succinct narrative of the surrender of Earl Cornwallis to his excellency General Washington, Commander in Chief of the combined forces of America and France."

So much for government intentions: The cornerstone of the symbolic 98-foot marble shaft with Lady Liberty atop was laid a century later to open the Yorktown Centennial Celebration. The podium is adorned with 13 female figures hand in hand in a solemn dance to denote the unity of the 13 colonies; beneath their feet is the inscription "One Country, One Constitution, One Destiny"—a moving post–Civil War sentiment.

A footpath leads from the monument into town, where you can explore Cornwallis Cave.

CORNWALLIS CAVE   According to legend, Cornwallis lived here in two tiny "rooms" during the final days of the siege when he hoped to cross the river and escape overland to New York. Various occupants of the cave—which may at one time have included the pirate Blackbeard—carved out the two rooms. Confederate soldiers later enlarged the shelter and added a roof. The cave is at the foot of Great Valley Road, right on the river.

From here you can follow Water Street along the river and Yorktown's white-sand beach (locals like to sunbathe and swim here) to **Yorktown Riverwalk Landing,** the town's waterfront dining-and-shopping complex.

On Water Street adjacent to the Yorktown Riverwalk Landing, the **Watermen's Museum** (📞 **757/887-2641;** www.watermens.org) displays a bug-eye, a skipjack, a dug-out canoe, and other working boats unique to the Chesapeake Bay, plus oyster harvesting tools and other equipment used by the region's famous "watermen" to earn their living. Admission is $5 for adults, $2 for students, and free for kids 5 and under. It's open April to December,

Tuesday to Saturday 10am to 4pm and Sunday 1 to 4pm.

While at the Yorktown Riverwalk, you can get out on the York River on the **Alliance** (📞 **800/979-3370**), a 105-foot-long, three-mast-tall schooner that makes three cruises daily between May and October. The 2-hour voyages cost $35 for adults and $30 for children 12 and under. It also has sunset cruises for $35 per person.

THE DUDLEY DIGGES HOUSE   This 18th-century weatherboard house on Main Street at Smith Street is the only wood-frame house to survive the siege. Owner Dudley Digges was a Revolutionary patriot who served with Patrick Henry, Benjamin Harrison, and Thomas Jefferson on the Committee of Correspondence. After the war, he was rector of the College of William and Mary. It's still a private residence, not open to the public.

THE NELSON HOUSE   Scottish merchant Thomas Nelson made three voyages between Great Britain and Virginia before deciding to settle in Yorktown in 1705. He became co-operator of a ferry, charter member of a trading company, builder of the Swan Tavern, and a large-scale planter. In 1729, he built this house, at Main and Nelson streets, which is considered one of the finest examples of Georgian architecture in Virginia. His grandson, Thomas Nelson, Jr., signed the Declaration of Independence, served as governor of Virginia during the war, and marched the 3,500-man state militia to Yorktown to help Washington win the victory. The Revolution ruined his health and fortune, however, and he died in 1789. Though damaged (cannonballs remain embedded in the brickwork), the house survived the Battle of Yorktown, and the Nelson family continued to live in it until 1907. The National Park Service acquired the house in 1968 and restored it to its original appearance. It's open daily 10am to 4:30pm in summer and daily 1 to 4pm the rest of the year.

THE SESSIONS HOUSE   Just across from the Nelson House, this is the oldest house in Yorktown, built in 1692 by Thomas Sessions. At least five U.S. presidents have visited the house, today a private residence.

THE CUSTOM HOUSE   Dating to 1720, this brick building at the corner of Main and Read was originally the private storehouse of Richard Ambler, collector of ports. It became Gen. J. B. Magruder's headquarters during the Civil War.

GRACE EPISCOPAL CHURCH   On Church Street near the river, Grace Church dates to 1697 and has been an active house of worship since then. Its first rector, Rev. Anthony Panton, was dismissed for calling the secretary of the colony a jackanapes. Gunpowder and ammunition were stored here during the siege of Yorktown. During the Civil War, the church served as a hospital. It's open to visitors daily 9am to 5pm. The communion silver, made in England in 1649, is still in use. Thomas Nelson, Jr., is buried in the adjacent graveyard.

THE SWAN TAVERN For over a century the Swan Tavern, at the corner of Main and Ballard streets (✆ **757/898-3033;** www.antiquesatswantavern.com), was Yorktown's leading hostelry. Originally owned by Thomas Nelson, it was in operation 20 years before Williamsburg's famous Raleigh Tavern. The Swan was destroyed in 1863 by an ammunition explosion at the courthouse across the street, rebuilt, and destroyed again by fire in 1915. Today it is reconstructed as per historical research, and the premises house a fine 18th-century antiques shop. It's open Monday to Saturday 10am to 5pm and Sunday 12:30 to 5pm.

THE POOR POTTER Constructed on the site of Yorktown's original pottery factory on Read Street, inland from the Custom House, this reconstruction shows how the locals produced pottery of better quality than the wares their English cousins were making back home.

Where to Eat

Carrot Tree Yorktown CAFE Occupying the Cole Diggs House, Yorktown's oldest brick residence (ca. 1720), this sandwich shop is a good place for refreshment during your walking tour of town. The house was restored by the National Park Service, which won't allow a stove inside for safety reasons. Consequently, many items are prepared in Williamsburg and heated in a microwave oven here. It's good stuff nevertheless. Check out the pastries in the chiller box by the front door; they make a fine snack. Lunch sees salads, barbecue, Brunswick stew, and made-to-order sandwiches.

411 Main St. (at Read St.). ✆ **757/246-9559.** www.carrottreekitchens.com. Reservations recommended for dinner. Most items $6–$15. AE, DISC, MC, V. Sun–Thurs 11:01am–3:29pm; Fri–Sat 11:01am–3:29pm and 5–8:30pm.

Nick's Riverwalk Restaurant ★ AMERICAN The main tenant in Yorktown Riverwalk Landing, this interesting if not gourmet restaurant stretches across the waterfront side of the complex, affording excellent views of the river and the Coleman Bridge almost overhead. It really is two restaurants, each with its own kitchen. One is the more-refined **Riverwalk Restaurant;** the other is the casual and somewhat less-expensive **High Tide Bar & Grill.** The latter has outdoor seating in fine weather. Both feature all-American fare, including my favorite, grilled fresh tuna.

In Yorktown Riverwalk Landing, 323 Water St. ✆ **757/875-1522.** www.riverwalkrestaurant.net. Reservations recommended in dining room. Dining room main courses $17–$29; bar & grill sandwiches $9–$13. AE, DISC, MC, V. Dining room daily 11:30am–2:30pm and 5–9pm. Bar & grill daily 11:30am–9pm. Closed Mon Sept–Mar.

JAMES RIVER PLANTATIONS

While Williamsburg was the political capital of Virginia during the 18th century, its economic livelihood depended on the great tobacco plantations beside the James River. Several of the mansions built during that period of wealthy landowners still stand today between Williamsburg and Richmond, some occupied to this day by the same families that have produced generals, governors, and two presidents. Two of them are open to the public, providing an authentic feel for 18th-century plantation life.

Seeing the Plantations

Plantations are on both sides of the James River, but the easiest to visit are on John Tyler Highway (Va. 5) between Williamsburg and Richmond. From Williamsburg,

Garden Week in Virginia, during the last week in April, is the ideal time to visit the plantations. All the grounds are at their magnificent, full-bloom best then. It's also the only time that the manor house at **Westover,** which shares a lane with the Berkeley Plantation off Va. 5 (ⓒ **804/829-2882**), is open to the public. Richmond's founder, William Byrd II, built this beautiful Georgian manor house in the 1730s directly on the banks of the James River. You can walk around the grounds and gardens year-round, daily 9am to 6pm. Admission is an honorary $2 for adults and 50¢ for children 15 and under. The grounds at **Sherwood Forrest Plantation,** 14501 John Tyler Hwy./Va. 5 (ⓒ **804/282-1441;** www. sherwoodforest.org), also are open to the public daily 9am to 5pm. Admission is $5 for adults and free for children 15 and under. Sherwood Forrest, the longest wood-frame house in the U.S., was the home of U.S. President John Tyler, whose descendants still live here.

take Jamestown Road and bear right on Va. 5. From Richmond, take Main Street east, which becomes Va. 5. This so-called Plantation Route covers a distance of 55 miles between Williamsburg and Richmond and makes an excellent scenic driving tour between the two cities. You can easily see the plantations in half a day.

See **www.charlescity.org** for information about bed-and-breakfast accommodations and dining in this area.

Berkeley Plantation ★   The aristocratic Harrison family bought Berkeley in 1691. Benjamin Harrison III made it a prosperous operation, and in 1726 his son, Benjamin Harrison IV, built the three-story Georgian mansion. Benjamin Harrison V was a signer of the Declaration of Independence and thrice governor of Virginia. The next generation produced William Henry Harrison, the frontier fighter whose nickname "Old Tippecanoe" helped him get elected as our ninth president. His grandson, another Benjamin Harrison, took the presidential oath 47 years later. George Washington was a frequent guest, and every president through Tyler enjoyed Berkeley's gracious hospitality.

Berkeley was twice occupied by invading troops. During the American Revolution, a British army under Benedict Arnold burned the family portraits, practiced target shooting on the cows, and went off with 40 slaves. During the Civil War, Gen. George McClellan's Union army trampled the gardens and chopped up the elegant furnishings for firewood.

The Harrisons never returned to live at Berkeley after the Civil War. John Jamieson, a Scottish-born New Yorker who had served as a drummer in McClellan's army, purchased the disfigured manor house and 1,400 acres in 1907. His son, Malcolm, completely restored the house and grounds to their appearance in the early days of the Harrisons' tenure. Allow 1½ hours to see a 10-minute audiovisual presentation, take a 45-minute guided tour of the house, and explore the magnificent grounds and gardens.

12602 Harrison Landing Rd. (off Va. 5; 30 miles west of Williamsburg). ⓒ **888/466-6018** or 804/829-6018. www.berkeleyplantation.com. Admission $11 adults, $7.50 children 13–16, $6 children 6–12, free for children 5 and under. Mid-Mar to Dec daily 9:30am–4:30pm (last tour 4:30pm); Jan to mid-Mar daily 10:30am–3:30pm (last tour 3:30pm). Closed Thanksgiving and Christmas.

10

WILLIAMSBURG, JAMESTOWN & YORKTOWN | James River

The First Thanksgiving

On December 4, 1619, 38 English colo- nists sent by the Berkeley Company put ashore in Virginia after a 3-month voy- age. They fell on their knees in a prayer of thanksgiving. If you're here the first Sunday of November, you can participate in the annual commemoration of that first Thanksgiving in the New World.

Shirley Plantation ★★★   Described by one architectural historian as "the most intact 18th-century estate in Virginia," Shirley was founded beside the James River in 1613, making it Virginia's oldest plantation. The plantation manse was built between 1723 and 1738 by Shirley heiress Elizabeth Hill and her husband, John Carter, eldest son of Robert "King" Carter, the richest man in the colonies (it was King Carter who financed Historic Christ Church in Irvington on the Northern Neck; p. 97). Their granddaughter, Anne Hill Carter, was born, grew up, and married Virginia governor and Revolutionary War hero Henry "Light-Horse Harry" Lee here. Their son, Robert E. Lee, made his own place in history. The extraordinarily well-preserved mansion is noted for its carved "flying staircase"—it rises three stories with no visible means of support—and Queen Anne forecourt flanked by the kitchen and other dependent buildings, both the only remaining examples of this architectural style in America. Now in its 11th generation, the Carter family continues to operate Shirley as a work- ing plantation, making it America's oldest family-owned business. After the 30-min- ute tour, allow at least another 30 minutes to explore the grounds and dependencies of this National Historic Landmark.

501 Shirley Plantation Rd. (off Va. 5), Charles City (35 miles west of Williamsburg). © **800/232- 1613** or 804/829-5121. www.shirleyplantation.com. Admission $11 adults, $10 seniors, $7.50 chil- dren 6–18, free for children 5 and under. Daily 9:30am–4:30pm (last tour 4:30pm). 30-min. house tours depart every half-hour. Closed Thanksgiving and Christmas.

A DAY TRIP TO HAMPTON & NEWPORT NEWS

Jamestown was barely 2 years old when Capt. John Smith sent a contingent of men to build a fort on the Hampton River, strategically located on the western shore of Hampton Roads. The colony's first seaport, the town was founded in 1610, making Hampton the nation's oldest continuously English-speaking settlement. It was here in 1718 that British troops displayed the head of Edward Teach, better known as Blackbeard the Pirate, whom they killed during a furious battle on North Carolina's Outer Banks. His captured crew was dispatched to the gallows in Williamsburg.

Unfortunately, few structures remain from those early days besides **Fort Monroe.** During the Civil War a Confederate general ordered the town burned to the ground to prevent Union forces from holding the fort and quartering troops and former slaves here. You can visit the Fort Monroe room where Confederate president Jefferson Davis was imprisoned after the war, the fine museum at Hampton University, and the very modern Virginia Air & Space Center, a smaller but excellent rendition of the Smithsonian Institution's National Air and Space Museum in Washington, D.C.

Named for Christopher Newport, skipper of the *Discovery,* one of the three ships that brought the Jamestown colonists to Virginia, Newport News also dates back to the early 1600s and has a long maritime tradition. The city is home to the Mariners' Museum, the largest maritime museum in the Western Hemisphere, and to the remains of the USS *Monitor*.

Hampton has enough interesting sights to take up most of a day trip from Williamsburg. The Mariners' Museum is on the way to Hampton, so you can spend part of the morning there on the way. You can also visit both cities on day excursions from Norfolk and Virginia Beach (see chapter 11).

Essentials

VISITOR INFORMATION   For advance information, contact the **Hampton Convention and Visitor Bureau,** 1919 Commerce Dr., Hampton, VA 23666 (© **800/800-2202** or 757/727-1102; fax 757/727-6712; www.hamptoncvb.com).

For information about Newport News, contact the **Newport News Tourism Development Office,** 700 Town Center Dr., Ste. 320, Newport News, VA 23606 (© **888/493-7386** or 757/926-1400; fax 757/926-1441; www.newport-news.org). The walk-in **Newport News Visitor Center** is in Newport News Park, 13560 Jefferson Ave., south of Fort Eustis Boulevard near Exit 250 off I-64 (© **888/493-7386** or 757/886-7777). It's open daily 9am to 5pm except Thanksgiving and Christmas.

With 8,000 acres, **Newport News Park,** 13560 Jefferson Ave. (© **757/888-3333;** www.nnparks.com), is the largest municipal park east of the Mississippi River and has one of the best campgrounds in Virginia.

GETTING THERE   From Williamsburg, take I-64 East. To reach downtown Hampton, take Exit 267 and turn right on Settlers Landing Road and cross the Hampton River to the visitor center (a left turn at the exit will take you to Fort Monroe and the Casemate Museum via the town of Poquoson). To reach the Mariners' Museum, take Exit 258 and follow J. Clyde Morris Boulevard (U.S. 17) south; the museum is at the southern end of the boulevard. From Norfolk and Virginia Beach, take I-64 West through the Hampton Roads Bridge Tunnel to these exits. In Hampton there's **free parking** in the municipal garage on Settlers Landing Road 1 block west of the Virginia Air & Space Museum.

Newport News/Williamsburg International Airport (PHF; © **757/877-0221;** www.nnwairport.com) is here, and **Amtrak** (© **800/872-7245;** www.amtrak.com) has daily service to its station in Newport News.

Attractions in Hampton

The Hampton Convention and Visitor Bureau shares quarters with the **Hampton History Museum,** 1919 Commerce Dr. (© **757/727-1610;** www.hampton1610.com), where you can learn of the city's past. The visitor center is open Monday to Saturday 9am to 5pm and Sunday 1 to 5pm; the museum is open Monday to Saturday 10am to 5pm and Sunday 1 to 5pm. Both are closed New Year's Day, Thanksgiving, and Christmas. Admission to the museum is $5 for adults, $4 for seniors and children 4 to 12, and free for kids 3 and under.

In its own air-conditioned pavilion next to the Virginia Air & Space Center (see below), the **Hampton Carousel** (© **757/727-6381**) is a painstakingly restored 1920s merry-go-round that anyone of any age will enjoy riding. The 48 original horses—so intricately carved you can see their veins—go up and down to the sounds of organ music. Rides cost $2. The carousel is open in summer daily noon to 5pm. Off-season hours are Friday to Sunday noon to 5pm.

The Casemate Museum   Located at Fort Monroe, Casemate Museum is a must see for Civil War buffs; Confederate president Jefferson Davis was imprisoned in the bowels of **Fort Monroe** in 1865 after being captured in Georgia. The accusation that he had participated in Lincoln's assassination was disproved, and Davis was released in 1867. Located at the tip of a peninsula and surrounded by a moat, the fort was built between 1819 and 1834 and is the largest brick fort in the United States. Robert E. Lee served as second in command of the construction detachment in 1831 when he was a young officer in the Army Corps of Engineers. Edgar Allen Poe spent 16 months here in 1828 and 1829 as an enlisted man. During the Civil War, it became known as Freedom Fortress as escaped slaves who entered its gates were considered to be "contrabands of war" and thus free. The dungeonlike casemates, where Davis was held, were designed as storage for seacoast artillery. After 1861, they were modified to serve as living quarters for soldiers and their families. You'll need about 45 minutes in the museum to view displays of military memorabilia and Davis's sparsely furnished quarters (his intricately carved pipe—an egg-shaped bowl clenched in an eagle's claw—is outside the door). Tours can be arranged in advance by contacting the museum.

Note: Fort Monroe was decommissioned as a federal installation in 2011. The Fort Monroe Authority is developing plans for its future use.

151 Bernard Rd., Fort Monroe. ✆ **757/788-3391.** www.fmauthority.com. Free admission. Daily 10:30am–4:30pm. Closed New Year's Day, Thanksgiving, and Christmas. From I-64 take Exit 267. From downtown Hampton, take Settlers Landing Rd. east across Hampton River bridge and under I-64 into Phoebus, take right fork onto County St., turn right on Mallory St., left on Mellen St., straight into Fort Monroe. Follow signs to museum.

Hampton University Museum ★   Across the river from downtown, Hampton University was founded in 1868 to provide an education for newly freed African Americans. Its graduates include Booker T. Washington, who founded Tuskegee Institute in Alabama and whose birthplace is preserved near Lynchburg (see chapter 6). Near the campus entrance stand the Emancipation Oak Trees, where the Emancipation Proclamation was read to the people of Hampton for the first time in 1863. Four other landmarks are nearby, including the imposing Memorial Chapel (1886). The museum is noted for its fine collection of African-American art, including a significant number of Harlem Renaissance paintings. Don't miss the works by Henry O. Tanner, including his renowned *The Banjo Lesson.* It also has notable holdings of African art, including one of the world's first collections of Kuba art from the Democratic Republic of the Congo. Rivaling the African collection is the Native American collection, which includes works from 93 tribes; it was established in 1878, when the federal government began sending Native Americans from reservations in the West to be educated at Hampton.

In the Huntington Building at Hampton University. © **757/727-5308.** http://museum.hamptonu. edu. Free admission. Mon–Fri 8am–5pm; Sat noon–4pm. Closed major holidays. From downtown Hampton, take Settlers Landing Rd. across the Hampton River and follow signs to the university and museum.

Virginia Air & Space Center ★★★ ☺ A stunning glass-fronted futuristic structure on the edge of Hampton's riverfront, this museum chronicles the history of aviation and space travel and also serves as the official visitor center for NASA's Langley Research Center and Langley Air Force Base. There's a 3-billion-year-old rock brought back from the moon by *Apollo 17.* In the main gallery, about 10 air vehicles are suspended from the 94-foot vaulted ceiling, and below sits the *Apollo 12* command module—complete with reentry burn marks. The Riverside 3-D IMAX Theater shows 45-minute films about flying and space as well as full-length features such as the Harry Potter movies. There are no guided tours; allow at least 2 hours to explore it all on your own, more if you see a movie.

600 Settlers Landing Rd. (at King St.). © **757/727-0900.** www.vasc.org. Admission $12 adults, $11 seniors and active military, $9.50 children 3–18 and students, free for children 2 and under. 45-min. IMAX film $9 adults, $8 seniors, $7 children 3–18 and students, free for children 2 and under. Combination ticket (admission to center and 45-min. IMAX film) available. Memorial Day to Labor Day Mon–Wed 10am–5pm, Thurs–Sun 10am–7pm; off season Mon–Sat 10am–5pm, Sun noon–5pm.

Harbor Cruises

The most popular harbor cruises in Virginia are on the **Miss Hampton II,** 764 Settlers Landing Rd. (© **888/757-2628** or 757/722-9102; www.misshamptoncruises. com), a 65-foot passenger boat that sails across Hampton Roads and within sight of the huge U.S. naval base at Norfolk. You'll pass Blackbeard's Point, where the pirate's head was displayed in 1718, and the pre–Civil War **Fort Wool,** on a 15-acre island out in the Chesapeake. The narrated 3-hour cruises depart from the town dock, on Settlers Landing Road beside the Crowne Plaza Hampton Marina hotel. Departures are usually Tuesday to Saturday at 10am and 2pm from Memorial Day through Labor Day and Tuesday at 10am in April, May, September, and October but call ahead to be sure. Fares are $23 for adults, $21 for seniors and military, $12 for children 6 to 12, and free for kids 5 and under.

A Maritime Museum in Newport News

The Mariners' Museum ★★★ This is the largest maritime museum in the Western Hemisphere. The highlight today is its **USS *Monitor* Center,** which houses the remains of the famous Union ironclad. The *Monitor* sank off Cape Hatteras after a stalemate battle with the CSS *Virginia* (formerly the USS *Merrimack*) on Hampton Roads in 1862. Divers in the 1990s recovered the ship's round, one-gun turret, which is kept here in a perpetual bath of saltwater to prevent it from rusting. You can actually walk into a remarkable, full-size reproduction of the turret exactly as it was found, lying upside down, on the floor of the Atlantic Ocean, a crewman's skeleton clearly visible. Hundreds of other artifacts—including handwritten letters—are also on display.

100 Museum Dr., Newport News. © **757/596-2222.** www.mariner.org. Admission $12 adults, $11 seniors, $10 students, $7 children 6–12, free for children 5 and under. Wed–Sat 10am–5pm; Sun noon–5pm. Closed Thanksgiving and Christmas. From I-64, take Exit 258A, follow J. Clyde Morris Blvd. (U.S. 17) south to intersection with Warwick Blvd. (U.S. 60), go straight on Museum Dr.

NORFOLK, VIRGINIA BEACH & THE EASTERN SHORE

T he Jamestown colonists first set foot in the New World at Cape Henry on April 26, 1607. Although they stayed just long enough to plant a cross in the sand and give thanks for their safe passage from England, later generations did decide to live here—lots of them, including some of my close relatives.

Today, the cities of Norfolk, Virginia Beach, Portsmouth, and Chesapeake comprise a megalopolis of nearly a million people sprawling along the southern shores of Hampton Roads, one of the world's largest natural harbors.

Norfolk and Portsmouth have been important seaports since being founded in 1682 and 1752, respectively. They were fought over often during the Civil War, including the famous battle between the first ironclads, USS *Monitor* and CSS *Virginia* (nee *Merrimac*), out on Hampton Roads.

Indeed, the navy still rules here, for this area has America's largest concentration of naval bases, which add enormously to its economy.

The sailors once made Norfolk a bawdy seaport, but the city has rebuilt its downtown into a vibrant center of shopping, dining, and sightseeing. Norfolk's attractions include Virginia's best art museum, a marvelous botanical garden, and the state zoo.

A brief ferry ride across the Elizabeth River takes you on an easy excursion to Portsmouth's gentrified Olde Towne, whose rich architecture may remind you of Charleston and Savannah.

A sprawling suburb for most of the year, Virginia Beach sees its population more than double during the summer, when 20 miles of uninterrupted sand and surf draw vacationers from around the globe. With a host of outdoor activities, a multitude of hotels, and close proximity to the other cities, it's no mystery why most visitors make "VaBeach" (as locals refer to the oceanfront area) their base for exploring this area.

From Virginia Beach, the 17-mile engineering marvel known as the Chesapeake Bay Bridge-Tunnel will whisk you north to a different world: Virginia's rural Eastern Shore. Here you will visit Chincoteague Island, home of an ancient fishing village, and its neighbor, Assateague Island, site of a magnificent national seashore and a wildlife refuge teeming with birds and the famous wild ponies of Assateague.

NORFOLK ★

190 miles SE of Washington, D.C.; 93 miles E of Richmond; 17 miles W of Virginia Beach

Downtown Norfolk was once notorious for its sailor bars; for many years, in fact, residents from surrounding towns didn't go into downtown Norfolk. That's not true now, for the rowdy joints have been replaced by a vibrant, modern downtown of high-rise offices, condominiums, marinas, museums, shops, nightspots, a 12,000-seat minor league baseball park, and a downtown cruise-ship terminal. The MacArthur Center, a shopping mall just a few blocks from the riverfront, now dominates downtown.

Also here are Virginia's finest art museum, the state's official zoo, and a botanical garden that comes ablaze with springtime azaleas. After dark, the state's symphony, opera, and stage company add highbrow culture. Hot restaurants bring exciting tastes and foodies to downtown and the hip residential neighborhood known as Ghent. Interspersed among the modern ingredients are reminders of Norfolk's past, such as historic houses and the old City Hall, now a museum and memorial to World War II hero Gen. Douglas MacArthur.

Indeed, this Southern star is one of the more diverse and fascinating Virginia cities in which to spend a day or two.

Essentials

VISITOR INFORMATION

For advance information, contact **VisitNorfolk,** 232 E. Main St., Norfolk, VA 23510 (© **800/368-3097** or 757/441-1852; www.visitnorfolktoday.com), which dispenses walking-tour brochures and other information at its offices (Mon–Fri 8:30am–5pm), across Main Street from the Norfolk Marriott. There's a small information center at NAUTICUS (p. 279).

Arriving from the west via I-64, there's an **Ocean View Visitor Center** on Fourth View Street at Exit 273 in the Ocean View section (© **757/441-1852**). It's open daily 9am to 5pm.

The **Norfolk Police & Fire-Rescue Museum,** 401 E. Freemason St. (© **757/441-1526**), next to the Moses Myers House also has visitor information (p. 280).

GETTING THERE

BY PLANE **Norfolk International Airport (ORF),** on Norview Avenue 1½ miles north of I-64 (© **757/857-3351;** www.norfolkairport.com), is served by American, Delta, Southwest, United, and US Airways. The major car-rental firms have desks here. Taxis await all flights (see "Getting Around," below), and **Airport Connection–Norfolk** (© **866/823-4626** or 757/963-0433; www.onetransportation solution.com) runs shuttles to points between Williamsburg and Virginia Beach.

BY CAR From the west, I-64 runs from Richmond to Norfolk, then swings around the eastern and southern suburbs, where it meets I-664 to form the Hampton Roads Beltway around the area. U.S. 460 also runs the length of Virginia to Norfolk and is a good way to avoid the backups that often plague the bridge-tunnels on I-64 and I-664, especially on summer weekends. U.S. 13 and U.S. 17 also pass through the area. From Virginia Beach, I-264 goes through downtown and Portsmouth.

Hampton Roads has some of Virginia's most congested traffic. Lengthy backups can occur anytime on I-64 at the Hampton Roads Bridge-Tunnel between Norfolk and Hampton, especially during weekday rush hours and all day on summer weekends. If you're approaching on I-64 from the west, an alternative is to take I-664 and the Monitor-Merrimac Memorial Bridge-Tunnel, then Va. 164 east to Portsmouth and the Midtown Tunnel (U.S. 58) into Norfolk. On summer weekends take U.S. 460 from Petersburg to Norfolk, thus avoiding both bridge-tunnels. U.S. 13 is another alternate route from the northeast. Tune your radio to 610 AM or call ✆ **800/792-2800** on your cellphone to check on current conditions.

BY TRAIN & BUS   A connector bus serves downtown Norfolk from the **Amtrak** station in Newport News (✆ **800/872-7245;** www.amtrak.com). **Greyhound** (✆ **800/231-2222;** www.greyhound.com) has bus service to downtown Norfolk.

CITY LAYOUT

Norfolk occupies two peninsulas formed by the Chesapeake Bay and the Elizabeth and Lafayette rivers. **Downtown** is on the southern side of the city, on the north bank of the Elizabeth River. Centered on Freemason Street and within walking distance to the northwest, **Freemason** is Norfolk's oldest residential neighborhood, with most of its 18th- and 19th-century town houses restored as private homes, businesses, and restaurants. You'll still find a few cobblestone streets here.

Northwest of Freemason, across a semicircular inlet known as the Hague, **Ghent** was the city's first subdivision and is now its trendiest enclave. Most houses in "old" Ghent, near the Hague and the Chrysler Museum of Art (p. 276), were built between 1892 and 1912. Now thoroughly gentrified, it's home to everyone from well-heeled professionals to writers, artists, and college students. The heart of Ghent's business district runs along **Colley Avenue** between Baldwin Avenue and 21st Street, and along **21st Street** from Colley Avenue east to Granby Street. Here you'll find antiques shops, restaurants, and the artsy NARO Cinema.

GETTING AROUND

The easiest way to get around downtown Norfolk is on foot, but it also has one of Virginia's best public transportation systems.

BY CAR   A car is the easiest way to get around the spread-out metro area. Be careful when driving in downtown Norfolk to observe restrictions along the route of the Tide light rail (see below). **Parking** is available downtown at the MacArthur Center and in municipal garages (the most convenient is on Atlantic Ave. btw. Waterside Dr. and Main St.). The city posts a downtown map showing its parking garages at **www. norfolk.gov/parking**. Visitors to the Douglas MacArthur Memorial (p. 278) can have their tickets validated for 3 hours of free parking.

BY LIGHT RAIL   Norfolk's light rail system, the **Tide** (✆ **757/222-6100;** www. gohrt.com/services/the-tide), runs 7½ miles between the Eastern Virginia Medical Center (west of downtown at Brambleton Ave. and Hampton Blvd.), and Newtown Road (near Princess Anne Rd. on the city's eastern outskirts). Designed primarily to get workers into and out of the city, it has only four downtown stops: **York**

Street/Freemason, on York Street west of Duke Street; **Monticello,** on Monticello Avenue between Freemason and Charlotte streets; **MacArthur Square,** in front of the Douglas MacArthur Memorial (p. 278); and **Civic Plaza,** on Plume Street east of St. Paul's Boulevard. A nearby stop is at **Harbor Park,** the baseball stadium on the Elizabeth River east of downtown. The trains run Monday to Thursday 6am to 11pm, Friday to Saturday 6am to midnight, and Sunday and holidays 11am to 9pm. The fare is $1.50 per ride or $3.50 for all day.

BY BUS The **NET Connector** (© 757/222-6100; www.gohrt.com/services/the-net) is an easy way to get from downtown to the Ghent neighborhood. The buses operate every 30 minutes Monday to Friday 7am to 10am and 4:05 to 9pm, Saturday 10am to midnight, and Sunday noon to 9pm. The fare is $1.50 with exact change required. The routes are shown on NET's website and on city maps distributed at the visitor centers (see "Essentials," above).

To go farther afield, **Hampton Roads Transit** (**HRT;** © 757/222-6100; www.gohrt.com) provides public bus service throughout the region. Although it can take as long as 2 hours each way, the Route 20 bus goes from Monticello Avenue and Charlotte Street to the Virginia Beach oceanfront. Fares start at $1.50 for adults, 75¢ for seniors and persons with disabilities, $1 for children 18 and under, and free for kids shorter than 38 inches tall. Exact change is required.

BY TAXI For taxis, call **Andy's Cab Co.** (© 866/840-6573 or 757/622-3232; www.andystaxigroup.com), **Black and White Cabs** (© 757/855-4444), or **Norfolk Checker** (© 757/855-3333; www.norfolkcheckertaxi.com).

Seeing the Sights

Downtown Norfolk's centerpiece is the **MacArthur Center,** a 1-million-square-foot shopping mall covering the 9 square blocks bordered by Monticello and City Hall avenues, Freemason Street, and St. Paul's Boulevard (© 757/627-6000; www.shopmacarthur.com). The main entrance is on Monticello Avenue at Market Street.

SEEING NORFOLK ON FOOT AND SEGWAY

Two self-guided walking tours of downtown will take you through 400 years of Norfolk's history. Beginning at the Freemason Street Reception Center, 401 E. Freemason St., sidewalk inlays and medallions mark the route of the **Cannonball Trail** through downtown, along the waterfront, and through the historic Freemason neighborhood. The local version of Virginia's **Civil War Trails** follows much the same route but with an emphasis on Norfolk in 1862. Pick up maps and brochures at the visitor centers.

Norfolk Walkabouts (© 757/641-7968; www.norfolkwalkabouts.com) has 90-minute guided historic tours from Town Point Park through the historic Freemason neighborhood Wednesday to Sunday at 10am and 1pm. They cost $15 per person. Reservations are required.

You will also have a guide as you follow the Cannonball Trail with **Segway Tours of Hampton Roads** (© 757/412-9734; www.segwayofhamptonroads.us), 90-minute rides on the stand-up Segway machines. They cost $60 per person. Reservations are essential. The office is in the Waterside Festival Marketplace.

In downtown Norfolk stick to the busy main streets between the MacArthur Center and the Waterside, and don't take unnecessary risks like wandering off into deserted or ill-lit side streets. Police on bicycles and volunteer **Downtown Ambassadors** patrol the streets; they will answer questions about the area, give directions, and escort you back to your car (☎ **757/478-7233**).

Anchored by Nordstrom and Dillard's department stores, it has most of the mall regulars, an 18-screen cinema, a food court, and full-service restaurants.

Built in 1983 between Waterside Drive and the Elizabeth River, the **Waterside Festival Marketplace** (☎ 757/627-3300; www.watersidemarketplace.com), which everyone calls simply the Waterside, was the catalyst for downtown Norfolk's revitalization, like Baltimore's Inner Harbor or Boston's Faneuil Hall. The ferries and harbor cruises leave from the dock outside this glass-and-steel pavilion. With so much of its shopping business now going to the MacArthur Center, the Waterside is now primarily a dining and entertainment venue. Some local interests would like to replace it with a convention center.

In **Town Point Park,** to the west of the Waterside, don't miss *The Homecomer,* a statue of a returning sailor greeted by his wife and child, and the moving **Armed Forces Memorial,** where letters written home by fallen sailors and marines, created in bronze, litter the ground. The park's amphitheater features a full schedule of free events all year—concerts, children's theater, magic shows, puppetry, and more. Beyond the park stand the riverfront's most conspicuous buildings, the huge gray **NAUTICUS,** an interactive science and technology center, and the glass-enclosed, semicircular **Half Moone Cruise and Celebration Center,** the city's modern cruise-ship terminal (www.cruisenorfolk.org).

East of the Elizabeth River bridges and I-264, **Harbor Park,** a 12,000-seat stadium, is home to the **Norfolk Tides,** a Class AAA International League baseball team affiliated with the Baltimore Orioles (☎ 757/622-2222; www.norfolktides.com).

Chrysler Museum of Art ★★★ This imposing Italian Renaissance building on the Hague inlet is Virginia's finest art museum. It spans artistic periods from ancient Egypt to the present and includes one of the finest and most comprehensive glass collections in the world. Also here is an outstanding collection of Art Nouveau furniture. Other first-floor galleries exhibit ancient Indian, Islamic, Asian, African, and pre-Columbian art. Most second-floor galleries are devoted to painting and sculpture, particularly Italian baroque and French, including works by Monet, Renoir, and Matisse. American art holdings include paintings by Charles Willson Peale, Benjamin West, John Singleton Copley, Thomas Cole, Thomas Hart Benton, Calder, Kline, and Warhol. A permanent gallery is devoted solely to photography. An audio tour will explain some of the key items as you see them. Allow at least 2 hours here, half a day to do it complete justice.

The museum runs the Moses Myers House and the Norfolk History Museum (see below).

245 W. Olney Rd. ☎ **757/664-6200.** www.chrysler.org. Free admission; donations encouraged. Wed 10am–9pm; Thurs–Sat 10am–5pm; Sun noon–5pm. Closed New Year's Day, July 4th, Thanksgiving, and Christmas.

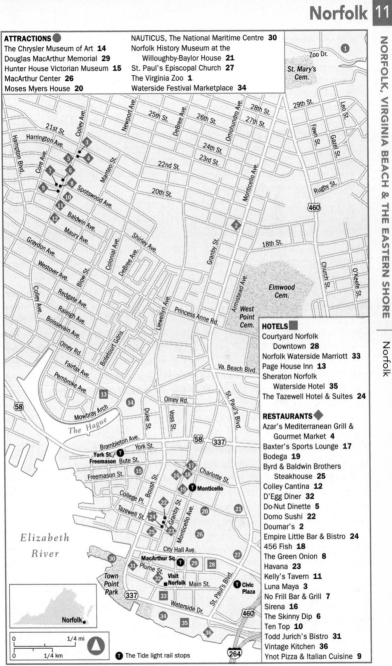

ATTRACTIONS ●
The Chrysler Museum of Art **14**
Douglas MacArthur Memorial **29**
Hunter House Victorian Museum **15**
MacArthur Center **26**
Moses Myers House **20**

NAUTICUS, The National Maritime Centre **30**
Norfolk History Museum at the
  Willoughby-Baylor House **21**
St. Paul's Episcopal Church **27**
The Virginia Zoo **1**
Waterside Festival Marketplace **34**

HOTELS ■
Courtyard Norfolk
  Downtown **28**
Norfolk Waterside Marriott **33**
Page House Inn **13**
Sheraton Norfolk
  Waterside Hotel **35**
The Tazewell Hotel & Suites **24**

RESTAURANTS ◆
Azar's Mediterranean Grill &
  Gourmet Market **4**
Baxter's Sports Lounge **17**
Bodega **19**
Byrd & Baldwin Brothers
  Steakhouse **25**
Colley Cantina **12**
D'Egg Diner **32**
Do-Nut Dinette **5**
Domo Sushi **22**
Doumar's **2**
Empire Little Bar & Bistro **24**
456 Fish **18**
The Green Onion **8**
Havana **23**
Kelly's Tavern **11**
Luna Maya **3**
No Frill Bar & Grill **7**
Sirena **16**
The Skinny Dip **6**
Ten Top **10**
Todd Jurich's Bistro **31**
Vintage Kitchen **36**
Ynot Pizza & Italian Cuisine **9**

● The Tide light rail stops

Built in 1932 as the Norfolk Museum of Arts and Sciences, the imposing Italian Renaissance building on the Hague inlet was a nondescript city museum until 1971. Then Walter P. Chrysler, Jr., idiosyncratic son of the motor company's founder, brought a large portion of his enormous art collection to Norfolk. Previously he had displayed it in the Chrysler Building in New York City, then in Provincetown, Massachusetts. When his relationship with Provincetown soured, he looked south to Norfolk, hometown of his second wife, Jean Outland Chrysler. At the time his collection was worth about $65 million. Today it's valued at $1 billion. Chrysler, Jr., lived here until his death in 1988, whereupon he bequeathed the collection to the city. Author Peggy Earle tells the fascinating yarn in *Legacy: Walter Chrysler Jr. and the Untold Story of Norfolk's Chrysler Museum of Art* (University of Virginia Press).

Douglas MacArthur Memorial ★★ General Douglas MacArthur's immortal words "I shall return" are engraved on a bronze plaque, along with excerpts from his other speeches, at his final resting place in Norfolk's old City Hall, whose soaring dome towers over the side-by-side marble crypts of the general and his wife, Jean. Shown every half-hour in a theater next door, a 25-minute film will give you a perspective on MacArthur's life and help you understand the exhibits. Filled with his corncob pipe, sunglasses, and other personal memorabilia, the chronologically arranged galleries trace U.S. history during MacArthur's life and his role in events up to his ringing Old Soldiers Never Die speech to Congress after President Truman fired him during the Korean War. There's a replica of the plaque marking the spot on the USS *Missouri* where MacArthur presided over the surrender of Japan. The memorial will validate your city garage tickets for 3 hours of free parking.

MacArthur Sq. (btw. City Hall Ave. and Plume St., at Bank St.). ☎ **757/441-2965.** www.macarthur memorial.org. Free admission; donations encouraged. Tues–Sat 10am–5pm; Sun 11am–5pm. Closed New Year's Day, Thanksgiving, and Christmas.

Hunter House Victorian Museum This redbrick and stone-trimmed Romanesque-revival-style house in the historic Freemason neighborhood was built by prominent banker and merchant James Wilson Hunter in 1894 from plans designed by Boston architect W. P. Wentworth. Hunter and his wife, Lizzie Barnes Hunter, had three children, none of whom ever married and all of whom spent their entire lives here. They bequeathed the house as a museum of Victorian architecture and decorative arts, the role it plays today. Their original furnishings and decorative arts are still here, along with pieces donated by others. It's a fascinating look at how life was lived in Victorian Norfolk. You must take a tour, which departs on the hour and half-hour.

240 W. Freemason St. ☎ **757/623-9814.** www.hunterhousemuseum.org. Admission $5 adults, $4 seniors, $1 children. Wed–Sat 10am–3:30pm; Sun 12:30–3:30pm. Tours on the hour and half-hour (last tour 3:30pm).

Moses Myers House It has the MacArthur Center looming over its backyard these days, but this handsome early-Federal brick town house was in Norfolk's oldest residential neighborhood when it was built by Moses Myers and his wife, Eliza, who moved from New York City to Norfolk in 1787. They were the first Jews to settle here, and programs in observance of Jewish holidays are among the museum's annual events. Some 70% of the furniture and decorative arts displayed belonged to the first generation of the family, which lived here until 1930. Two Gilbert Stuart portraits of Mr. and Mrs. Myers hang in the drawing room, which contains some distinctive Empire pieces. The fireplace surround has unusual carvings depicting a sun god—with the features of George Washington.

A block away is the **Norfolk History Museum at the Willoughby-Baylor House,** 601 E. Freemason St. (✆ 757/441-1526), which is also administered by the Chrysler Museum of Art. The Willoughby-Baylor House was built in 1794 by Capt. Thomas Willoughby, whose ancestor, Capt. Thomas Willoughby I, received a royal grant of 200 acres in 1636, of which 50 acres became the city of Norfolk. The museum uses objects from the Chrysler Museum of Art's collections to explain Norfolk's history. Its garden is designed like Colonial gardens at the time it was built.

331 Bank St. ✆ **757/441-1526.** www.chrysler.org/about-the-museum/historic-houses. Free admission; donations recommended. Fri–Sun noon–4pm. Last 30-min tour 3pm. Closed New Year's Day, Memorial Day, July 4th, Thanksgiving, and Christmas.

NAUTICUS ☺   The large gray waterfront building designed like an artist's rendering of a futuristic battleship is an interactive science and technology center dedicated to the U.S. Navy and the sea over which it rules. It's actually three attractions in one. On the third-floor is a very good children's museum with a plethora of movies and hands-on interactive exhibits aimed at families with kids ages 8 to 14. After a morning here, your school-age kids may be ready to enlist.

On the second floor is the **Hampton Roads Naval Museum ★** (✆ **757/444-8921;** www.hrnm.navy.mil), in which the U.S. Navy tells the story of its presence here. The exhibit describing the Civil War battle between the ironclads USS *Monitor* and CSS *Virginia* out on Hampton Roads is worth seeing.

To navy veterans like me, the star of this show is the ***Battleship Wisconsin* ★★★**. Berthed alongside the museum, this mighty 888-foot-long decommissioned battleship launched in 1943 and saw duty in the Pacific during World War II. It was recalled from mothballs to fight in the Korean and gulf wars. It now belongs to the City of Norfolk. You can go inside and see where the ship's officers lived, and walk outside on the teak decks. Stare up at the enormous 16-inch guns; it's quite a sight. (There's a spectacular view of the bow framed by a tile archway on Boush St. at the end of Plume St.)

The ***Victory Rover*** cruises to the naval station leave from here (see "Harbor Cruises to Where the Ironclads Fought," below). You can buy tickets combining admission to NAUTICUS and a cruise.

1 Waterside Dr. ✆ **800/664-1080** or 757/664-1000. www.nauticus.org. Free admission to 1st deck and naval museum; admission to NAUTICUS exhibits, theaters, and parts of battleship $14 adults, $13 seniors and military; $9.50 children 4–12, free for children 3 and under. Combination tickets (admission to NAUTICUS exhibits, theaters, and parts of battleship and a topside tour of battleship) $29 adults, $24 children 4–12; (admission to NAUTICUS exhibits, theaters, and parts of battleship and 2-hr. cruise on *Victory Rover* Mar–Dec) $28 adults, $19 children 4–12. Memorial Day to Labor Day daily 10am–5pm; rest of year Tues–Sat 10am–5pm, Sun noon–5pm. Entire complex closed New Year's Day, Thanksgiving, Dec 24, and Christmas. Battleship closed during inclement weather.

Norfolk Botanical Garden ★★   The grounds of this botanical garden, on Lake Whitehurst about 4 miles northeast of downtown and adjacent to Norfolk International Airport, are brilliantly abloom in April with one of the East Coast's largest display of azaleas—the best time to visit. This quiet beauty can be seen from a

25-minute tram tour, from a 45-minute pontoon boat tour, or by foot over more than 12 miles of floral pathways. The Statuary Vista is a beautiful setting for Moses Eze-kiel's heroic-size statues of great painters and sculptors including Rembrandt, Rubens, Dürer, and da Vinci. Notable, too, are the rose garden, with more than 450 varieties among its 3,000 bushes; a classic Japanese hill-and-pond garden; a fragrance garden; an Italian Renaissance garden; and a WOW Children's Garden. In April the queen of the Norfolk NATO Festival is crowned in the Hofheimer Camellia Garden and Renaissance Court. Garden lovers can easily spend half a day here. You can grab a bite at the Azalea Café.

6700 Azalea Garden Rd. (off Norview Ave., near airport). © **757/441-5385.** www.nbgs.org. Admission $9 adults, $8 seniors and military, $7 children 3–18, free for children 2 and under. Boat tours $5 per person, free for children 2 and under. Gardens Apr to mid-Oct daily 9am–7pm; mid-Oct to Mar daily 9am–5pm. Tram tours Apr to mid-Oct daily 10am–4pm; mid-Oct to Mar Mon–Fri 10am–4pm, Sat–Sun 10am–4:30pm. Boat tours Memorial Day to Labor Day daily 10:30am–4:45pm; Apr to day before Memorial Day and day after Labor Day to Oct 15 Mon–Fri 11:45am–3:30pm, Sat–Sun 10:30am–4:45pm. Take I-64 to Exit 279 (Norview/Airport), go east on Norview Ave., turn left on Azalea Garden Rd.

The Norfolk Police Museum and the Fire-Rescue Museum
After visiting the Moses Myers House next door (see above), you can spend a few minutes examin-ing uniforms, equipment, firearms, a motorcycle, a jail door, and other items dis-played in honor of Norfolk's police and firefighters. Located at the same address, these two museums are a good source of information on weekends when the city's downtown visitor center is closed.

401 E. Freemason St. © **757/441-1526.** www.norfolk.gov/police/museum.asp. Free admission. Wed–Sat 10am–4pm, Sun noon–4pm.

St. Paul's Episcopal Church ★
Although severely damaged when the British shelled Norfolk on January 1, 1776, this lovely brick Anglican church survived and is the only pre-Revolution building in downtown. A cannonball from one of Lord Dun-more's ships remains lodged in the southwest wall. The main chapel was constructed in 1739 to serve a parish that had been in existence since about 1636. The tower was added in 1902, and the interior was restored to its Colonial-revival form in 1913. This is a serene respite in bustling downtown, so take a moment to reflect inside the church, and then examine the ancient tombstones in the shady churchyard. Graves date to the 1600s, although the earliest original stone is from 1748; three others dat-ing from 1673, 1687, and 1681 were brought here.

201 St. Paul's Blvd. © **757/627-4353.** www.saintpaulsnorfolk.com. Free admission; donations suggested. Mon–Fri 9am–5pm. Services Wed noon, Sun 8 and 10:30am.

The Virginia Zoo ★ ☺
Your children will be entertained and educated at Vir-ginia's state zoo, on 53 acres adjacent to Norfolk's Lafayette Park and bordered by the Lafayette River. You can take them on a miniature train ride to scope it all out, then on a boardwalk safari to see rhinos, giraffes, and baboons in the noted African plains exhibit (lions are nearby but understandably are not allowed near the grazing animals, their natural prey). Tigers, monkeys, elephants, red pandas, reptiles, and colorful birds are also among the nearly 400 animals here. Be sure to ask in advance about the zoo's behind-the-scenes tours and animal encounters.

3500 Granby St. (at 35th St.). © **757/441-2374.** www.virginiazoo.org. Admission $11 adults, $10 seniors, $9 children 2–11. Train rides $2 per person. Daily 10am–5pm. Train rides every 30 min. daily 10:30am–4:30pm. Closed New Year's Day, Thanksgiving, and Christmas. From downtown, go north on Monticello Ave., which merges with Granby St., to the zoo on the right.

A FERRY RIDE TO OLDE TOWNE PORTSMOUTH

Across the Elizabeth River from downtown Norfolk, Portsmouth's **Olde Towne** section traces its roots back to 1752. Like those in Charleston and Savannah, its homes present a kaleidoscope of architectural styles: Colonial, Federal, Greek revival, Georgian, and Victorian. Plaques mounted on imported English street lamps point out their architectural and historical significance.

Ferries were the main means of getting across the river until the 1950s, and paddlewheel ferries (© **757/222-6100;** www.gohrt.com) still makes the short but picturesque trip. During summer they depart the Waterside marina every 30 minutes Monday to Friday from 7:15am to 11:45pm and on weekends from 10:15am to 11:45pm. Off-season service ends at 9:45pm Sunday through Thursday and 11:45pm Friday and Saturday. The fare is $1.50 for adults and 75¢ for children, seniors, and passengers with disabilities (exact change required). There is no ferry service on Thanksgiving or Christmas.

Get off at the second stop, Portsmouth's **North Landing Visitor Center,** on Harbor Court (© **800/767-8782** or 757/393-5111; www.visitportsva.com), and pick up a walking-tour brochure and map. The center is open daily 9am to 5pm.

Worth seeing are the **Portsmouth Naval Shipyard Museum,** 2 High St., and the nearby **Lightship Portsmouth Museum** (for both: © **757/393-8591;** www.portsnavalmuseums.com), in Riverfront Park at the foot of London Boulevard. The Lightship Portsmouth Museum is the lightship *Portsmouth,* built in 1915 and anchored offshore until the 1980s to warn mariners of the dangerous shoals on the approach to Hampton Roads. The shipyard museum is open Tuesday to Saturday 10am to 5pm and Sunday 1 to 5pm. The lightship is open Friday to Saturday 10am to 5pm and Sunday 1 to 5pm. Admission to both Friday to Sunday is $4 for adults, $3 for seniors and military, and $2 for children 2 to 17; Tuesday to Thursday is half price.

Tree-lined High Street, the main drag running inland from the harbor, has several restaurants and coffee shops, including the **Bier Garden** (© **757/393-6022**) and **Cafe Europa** (© **757/399-6652**).

Harbor Cruises

Three cruise boats docked at the Waterside or NAUTICUS offer cruises on the Elizabeth River, Hampton Roads, and the Chesapeake Bay. You will pass the naval base with nuclear subs and aircraft carriers and cross the site of the Civil War battle between the USS *Monitor* and the CSS *Virginia.*

The best for the money is the 2-hour *Victory Rover* (© **757/627-7406;** www. navalbasecruises.com) cruise from NAUTICUS to the Norfolk Naval Station—or as close thereto as security will permit. It has summertime trips departing at 11am, 2pm, and 5:30pm, and at least one trip a day (usually departing at 2pm) the rest of the year. Fares are $20 for adults and $12 for children. Combination tickets (for the cruise and admission to NAUTICUS) cost $28 for adults and $19 for children.

From April to October, cruises run Wednesday to Saturday on the *American Rover* (© **757/627-7245;** www.americanrover.com), a graceful schooner modeled after 19th-century Chesapeake Bay schooners. Prices for the 1½-hour midday cruise and the 2-hour 3pm cruise along the Elizabeth River are $10 and $16 for adults and

$8 to $10 for children 11 and under, respectively. The *American Rover* also offers sunset voyages and adults-only Saturday night party cruises. Call for times and reservations.

Also departing from the Waterside, the sleek *Spirit of Norfolk* (© 866/304-2469 or 757/625-3866; www.spiritofnorfolk.com) is like an oceangoing cruise ship, complete with dancing, good food, and entertainment. Call for prices and the schedule and to make reservations.

Shopping for Antiques ★★

Norfolk is one of the better places in Virginia to search for antiques, with at least 32 shops selling a range of furniture, decorative arts, glassware, jewelry, and other items from both home and overseas. The best place to look is in Ghent, where several shops sit along the 4 blocks of West 21st Street between Granby Street and Colonial Avenue, especially at the corner of Llewellyn Avenue. Granby Street has more than a dozen shops of its own. The visitor centers have a list of the shops.

Where to Stay

Downtown Norfolk seems to have festivals and reunions going on every weekend, when hotel rooms can be scarce and the rates are the highest.

Courtyard Norfolk Downtown ★ ✦   Compared to its suburban sisters, this breed of city-center Courtyards has a larger lobby with fireplace, a bar open nightly, and a restaurant serving breakfast and dinner but not lunch. The comfortable rooms and suites are typical Courtyard, with big desks, high-speed Internet, and other amenities aimed at business travelers. Unlike the other downtown hotels, here you can open the windows to let in fresh air. This is downtown's best moderately priced hotel.

520 Plume St. (btw. Court St. and St. Paul Blvd.), Norfolk, VA 23510. www.courtyard.com. © **800/ 321-2211** or 757/963-6000. Fax 757/963-6001. 140 units. $99–$189 double; suites $199–$289. AE, DC, DISC, MC, V. Valet and self-parking $18. **Amenities:** Restaurant; bar; free health club; Jacuzzi; indoor pool; room service. *In room:* A/C, TV, fridge, hair dryer, Wi-Fi.

Norfolk Waterside Marriott ★★   One of Norfolk's two convention hotels (the Sheraton, below, is the other), and its most elegant, this 24-story high-rise is connected to the Waterside via a covered skywalk. Its mahogany-paneled lobby is a masterpiece of 18th-century European style, with fine paintings, a crystal chandelier, potted palm trees, comfortable seating areas with gleaming lamps, and one-of-a-kind antiques. A magnificent staircase leads to a breakfast-only restaurant, a piano lounge, and meeting rooms on the second floor. There's a branch of Don Shula's 347 Steakhouse and sports bar downstairs off the lobby. Guest rooms are sumptuously furnished with dark-wood pieces. Although the rooms do not have balconies, odd-numbered upper-floor units do have a river view. The indoor pool here opens to a sun deck overlooking the river.

235 E. Main St. (btw. Atlantic St. and Martins Lane), Norfolk, VA 23510. www.marriott.com. © **800/ 228-9290** or 757/627-4200. Fax 757/628-6452. 405 units. $169–$259 double; $375–$700 suite. AE, DC, DISC, MC, V. Valet parking $26; self-parking $19. **Amenities:** Restaurant; bar; concierge; concierge-level rooms; health club; Jacuzzi; outdoor pool; room service; Wi-Fi (free in public areas). *In room:* A/C, TV, hair dryer, Wi-Fi ($9.95 per 24 hr.).

Sheraton Norfolk Waterside Hotel ★★   Next door to the Waterside and overlooking busy Norfolk Harbor, this contemporary 10-story hotel has a more modern ambience than its main competition, the traditionally styled Marriott 2 blocks away. A three-story, light-filled atrium lobby gives way to a restaurant with outdoor seating and a bar with 30-foot windows overlooking the river. About a third of the spacious units facing the river have small balconies (they're allotted on a first-come, first-served basis). Although the Sheraton draws groups and conventions, its location and facilities also make it a good choice for individuals, couples, and families.

777 Waterside Dr., Norfolk, VA 23510. www.sheraton.com. © **800/325-3535** or 757/622-6664. Fax 757/625-8271. 445 units. $109–$189 double; $400–$600 suite. AE, DC, DISC, MC, V. Valet parking $22; self-parking $12. Small pets accepted. **Amenities:** Restaurant; bar; concierge; concierge-level rooms; health club; Jacuzzi; outdoor pool; room service; Wi-Fi (free in public areas). *In room:* A/C, TV, Internet ($10 per 24 hr.).

The Tazewell Hotel & Suites   Built in 1906, this hotel underwent a renovation that was intended to restore it to boutique-hotel status. The two-story lobby with floor-to-ceiling paned windows and the brass elevator doors were repaired to resemble their former grand-hotel status. Although the rooms are improved, they are more like those in a suburban chain hotel than a luxurious historic property. As is the case with most hotels built at the turn of the 20th century, some of the rooms are tiny by today's standards. Services and amenities are scarce, too. The hotel's best feature is its location, in the midst of Granby Street's restaurant row.

245 Granby St., Norfolk, VA 23510. www.thetazewell.com. © **757/623-6200.** Fax 757/623-6123. 58 units. $99–$199 double. Rates include continental breakfast. AE, DISC, MC, V. Parking $15. **Amenities:** Access to nearby health club. *In room:* A/C, TV, fridge (in some), hair dryer, Wi-Fi.

BED & BREAKFASTS

Page House Inn ★   Across the street from the Chrysler Museum of Art in the Ghent district, this grand three-story brick Colonial-revival mansion with an expansive veranda was built in 1899. You will find a plethora of golden oak here—paneling, sliding doors, and moldings, plus a hand-carved fireplace in the living room and a soaring staircase ascending to the rooms upstairs. In the basement, a billiards room boasts a big-screen TV. Guest quarters are beautifully furnished with four-poster beds and one-of-a-kind antiques. Five units have gas-log fireplaces. The grandest also sports a sunken hot tub and a walk-in steam room/shower big enough for two. Gourmet breakfasts are served in your room if you like. Your small pooch is welcome here.

323 Fairfax Ave. (at Mowbray Arch), Norfolk, VA 23507. www.pagehouseinn.com. © **800/599-7659** or 757/625-5033. Fax 757/623-9451. 7 units. $145–$230 double. Rates include full breakfast. AE, MC, V. Free parking. Pet fee $25 (small dogs only). **Amenities:** Bikes; health club; room service. *In room:* A/C, TV, hair dryer, Wi-Fi.

Where to Eat

To sample the bills of fare at several restaurants, take a 90-minute food tour with **Norfolk Walkabouts** (© **757/641-7968;** www.norfolkwalkabouts.com). Its downtown tasting tours take place Wednesday and Saturday at 11am, while a Ghent tour departs Saturday at 2pm. They each cost $38, which is nonrefundable. Reservations are required.

DOWNTOWN

The downtown renaissance has turned **Granby Street** from Main to Charlotte streets into Norfolk's Restaurant Row, as hip new dining rooms open all the time (and a few disappear). Here you'll find a wide range of restaurants and pubs.

   The swanky **Byrd & Baldwin Brothers Steakhouse,** 116 Brooke Ave. (© **757/222-9191;** www.byrdbaldwin.com), in a restored 1906 building half a block west of

Granby Street, has the best steaks. **Bodega,** 422 Granby St. (☎ **757/622-8577;** www. bodegaongranby.com), serves tapas along with the street's best Spanish and Italian fare. **Domo Sushi,** 273 Granby St. (☎ 757/628-8282), serves just that, plus other Japanese offerings. **Havana,** 255 Granby St. (☎ 757/627-5800), serves Cuban-influenced fare. **Sirena,** 455 Granby St. (☎ 757/623-6622), is tops for Italian fare.

> ### Dining Beside the River
>
> **Joe's Crab Shack** (☎ **757/625-0655;** www.joescrabshack.com), is the only locally owned Norfolk restaurant with outdoor tables overlooking the Elizabeth River.

Late-night fare is available at the fast-paced **Empire Little Bar & Bistro,** 245 Granby St. (☎ **757/626-3100;** www.littlebarbistro.com), which specializes in tapas and is open daily 5pm to 1:30am, and at **Baxter's Sports Lounge,** 500 Granby St. (☎ **757/622-9837;** www.baxterssportslounge.com), a monstrous sports bar with pool tables and good pub fare (daily 11am–2am). They are two of Granby Street's liveliest joints on weekends and are good for getting into conversations with local residents.

The MacArthur Center, on Monticello Avenue at Market Street, has a very good and inexpensive **food court** up on the third floor.

My favorite downtown breakfast spot is **D'Egg Diner,** 404 E. Main St. (☎ **757/626-3447**), opposite the Norfolk Marriott. It serves inexpensive eggs, waffles, pancakes, bagels, and healthier fare such as fruit salads. It's open daily 7am to 3pm. (For you Starbucks addicts, there's a branch next door to D'Egg.)

456 Fish ★★ 🖋 AMERICAN   This casual but sophisticated restaurant is tops on the Granby Street strip for fish. You might want to start with fried green tomatoes with a lobster rémoulade, then select from pan-seared salmon, crab-stuffed tilapia, seared rare tuna coated with sesame, or macadamia-crusted mahimahi. Also check the daily specials, which usually are the freshest fish available.

456 Granby St. ☎ **757/625-4444.** www.456fish.com. Reservations recommended. Main courses $14–$30. AE, DISC, MC, V. Sun–Thurs 5–10pm; Fri–Sat 5–11pm.

Todd Jurich's Bistro ★★★ AMERICAN   Executive chef Todd Jurich's urbane bistro is one of the finest restaurants in Hampton Roads. You'll see why when you partake of Todd's creative twists on Southern traditions, such as his all-lump-meat crab cakes—a far cry, indeed, from the fried cakes dispensed at many Chesapeake Bay seafood shacks. Todd uses only fresh produce, drawn whenever possible from local farms. For lunch, you can choose from salads, sandwiches, or smaller portions of the dinner mains. Vintages from the award-winning wine list go on sale during cocktail hour (4:30–6:30pm) at the wine bar.

150 Main St. (entry on Boush St., opposite NAUTICUS). ☎ **757/622-3210.** www.toddjurichsbistro. com. Reservations recommended. Main courses $18–$40. AE, DC, DISC, MC, V. Mon–Fri 11:30am–2pm and 5:30–10pm; Sat 5:30–10pm.

Vintage Kitchen ★★★ AMERICAN   Todd Jurich had a monopoly on fine downtown dining until French-trained chef Phillip Craig Thomason, a Portsmouth native, opened this restaurant on the ground level of the Bank of Hampton Roads skyscraper. His is the only really good downtown restaurant with a river view, which almost alone makes it a fine choice. Like his teachers in Paris, Chef Thomason uses fresh-from-the-farm ingredients. These show up first in his exquisite pumpkin soup with cinnamon croutons and his spicy Caesar salad. From there pay attention to the specials, which always feature a fresh fish of the day. Weekday lunches offer the best burgers in Hampton Roads. Vegetarians will always find something tasty here. Unlike most Virginia restaurants, this one actually specializes in Virginia wines.

In Dominion Towers, 999 Waterside Dr. (© **757/625-3370.** www.vintage-kitchen.com. Main courses $24–$28. AE, DISC, MC, V. Mon–Wed 11am–2pm; Thurs–Fri 11am–2pm and 5:30–10pm; Sat 5:30–10pm. Cocktails Mon–Fri 2–6pm

IN GHENT

The heart of Ghent lies along Colley Avenue between Maury and Harrison avenues, flanking the artsy Naro Theatre. It's pleasant to stroll these short blocks and take in the busy scene, especially on warm weekend evenings when the restaurants are busy and their sidewalk tables are packed. In addition to Luna Maya, No Frill Bar and Grill, and the Green Onion (below), several good restaurants satisfy a variety of tastes.

Azar's Mediterranean Grill & Gourmet Market, 2000 Colley Ave. (© 757/664-7955; www.azarfoods.com), serves an international menu and purveys gourmet groceries. **Colley Cantina,** 1316 Colley Ave. (© 757/622-0033; www.colleycantina.com), proffers very good Tex-Mex. **Ynot Pizza & Italian Cuisine,** 1517 Colley Ave. (© 757/624-9111; www.ynotpizza.com), delivers on its name in a comfortable setting. **Kelly's Tavern,** 1408 Colley Ave (© 757/623-3216; www.kellystavern.com), dishes up reasonably good fish and chips and other pub fare. Vegetarians and vegans will be at home at tiny, laidback **Ten Top,** 748 Shirley Ave. (© 757/622-5422; www.thetentop.com), in a three-store shopping center.

At the **Skinny Dip,** 1619 Colley Ave. (© 757/383-6400; www.ilovetheskinnydip.com), you can pour your own regular, nonfat, kosher, or vegan frozen yogurt.

Best place for an artery-clogging cooked breakfast is the **Do-Nut Dinette,** 1917 Colley Ave. (© 757/625-0061).

The Green Onion INTERNATIONAL This bistro-style storefront restaurant with a display kitchen in the rear isn't the fanciest place to dine, but the chef mixes flavors in exciting combinations, such as sautéed scallops finished with a sweet corn and snow pea sauce. Meat lovers can opt for steaks, and vegetarians always have choices here. There are a few tables out front on the sidewalk.

Cones & Carhops

Some of the waffle-like ice-cream cones made at **Doumar's,** an old-fashioned drive-in with carhops and curb service at 19th Street and Monticello Avenue (© **757/627-4163;** www.doumars.com), come from the original cone-making machine invented by Abe Doumar, who introduced it to the world at the St. Louis Exposition in 1904. Abe's descendants keep his invention oiled and working, and descendants of his North Carolina–style barbecue sandwiches (a steal at $2.50 apiece), burgers, hot dogs, sundaes, and milkshakes round out the inexpensive menu. Doumar's has been around since the 1930s, which makes it a hip historical attraction. It is open Monday to Thursday 8am to 11pm and Friday to Saturday 8am to 12:30am.

1603 Colley Ave. ⓒ **757/963-6100.** www.thegreenonionrestaurant.com. Reservations recommended. Main courses $16–$33. AE, DISC, MC, V. Mon–Fri 10am–3pm and 5–10:30pm; Sat–Sun 10am–3pm and 5pm–midnight.

Luna Maya ★★ 🍴 LATIN AMERICAN/VEGETARIAN/VEGAN   This creation of Bolivian-born sisters Karla and Vivian Montano brings the delightful flavors of Latin America to Ghent. Although burritos and tamales outnumber dishes from Bolivia and Argentina, this is no refried-beans joint. Try a spicy shrimp or chorizo burrito to see what I mean. Vegetarians and vegans get at least four choices here daily. You won't get linens and silver, but the food is interesting and good.

2010 Colley Ave. ⓒ **757/622-6986.** www.lunamayarestaurant.com. Reservations accepted for groups. Main courses $12–$18. AE, MC, V. Tues–Sat 4:30–10pm.

No Frill Bar & Grill ★ AMERICAN   Don't expect romance at this always-busy neighborhood favorite. Families as well as couples will find something appealing on the extensive menu of large salads (with or without meat or fish), pita wraps, sandwiches, burgers, and "platters" ranging from home-style meatloaf to Low Country shrimp and grits. I found the nightly specials appealing and opted for a huge salad with fried scallops, country ham, jalapeño poppers, and numerous vegetables, all topped with toasted almonds and a red wine vinaigrette. Each bite presented distinct flavors depending on what came up on my fork. I went away full and quite pleased.

806 Spotswood Ave. ⓒ **757/627-4262.** www.nofrillgrill.com. Sandwiches and burgers $7–$12; main courses $14–$19. AE, MC, V. Sun–Thurs 11am–10pm; Fri–Sat 11am–11pm; Sun 10am–3pm.

Norfolk After Dark

Pick up a copy of **Veer Magazine** (www.veermag.com), a weekly paper free at the visitor information centers, most hotel lobbies, and the Waterside. The "Daily Break" section in the local rag, the **Virginian-Pilot** (www.pilotonline.com), is also a good source of local information.

THE PERFORMING ARTS

From opera to riverside rock concerts, Norfolk has a wider array of performing arts than any city in the state, and the choices keep growing. For what's playing, check the website of **Visit Norfolk** (www.visitnorfolktoday.com) and move your cursor onto "Play" and then select from the choices under "Arts & Entertainment" in the drop-down menu.

If your brow is high, visit the **Virginia Stage Company** (ⓒ 757/627-1234; www.vastage.com), which performs dramas and musicals from October through April in the **Wells Theatre,** 110 Tazewell St. (ⓒ **757/627-6988**), at Monticello Avenue opposite the MacArthur Center. Built in 1913, this restored Beaux Arts gem is on the National Register of Historic Places.

The **Virginia Symphony** (ⓒ **757/892-6366;** www.virginiasymphony.org) often plays at **Chrysler Hall,** Charlotte Street and St. Paul's Boulevard. The **Virginia Opera** (ⓒ **866/673-7282;** www.vaopera.org) sings at the **Harrison Opera House,** 160 E. Virginia Beach Blvd. at Llewellyn Avenue (ⓒ **757/623-1223**).

The futuristic **Norfolk SCOPE Arena,** Brambleton Avenue and St. Paul's Boulevard, seats 12,000 for the circus, ice shows, sports, concerts, and other events. It's home between October and April to the American Hockey League's **Norfolk Admirals** (ⓒ **757/640-1212;** www.norfolkadmirals.com).

The best time to be entertained in Norfolk—or anywhere in Hampton Roads, for that matter—is during the **Virginia Arts Festival ★★★** from mid-April through mid-May. That's when the likes of Itzhak Perlman, the Martha Graham Dance Company, and the Tokyo String Quartet appear at venues from Williamsburg to Virginia Beach. Go to **www.virginiaartsfest.com** or call ℂ **877/741-2787** or 757/282-2800 for information, 757/671-8100 for tickets. Adding to the fun, the arts festival coincides with the Norfolk NATO Festival (www.azaleafestival.org).

The restored **Attucks Theatre,** on Church Street at Virginia Beach Boulevard (ℂ **757/664-6464;** www.attuckstheatre.org), was built by African-American entrepreneurs in 1919 and named for Crispus Attucks, a black man who was the first American patriot to die in the Revolutionary War. Duke Ellington, Cab Calloway, Count Basie, and many other famous musicians performed here from the 1920s through the early 1950s, when it was the hub of one of the liveliest African-American neighborhoods in the segregated South. Today it's part of the Crispus Attucks Cultural Center.

Town Point Park, between the Waterside and NAUTICUS on the Elizabeth River, is the scene of constant outdoor entertainment in warm months, most sponsored by **Norfolk Festevents** (ℂ **757/441-2345;** www.festeventsva.org). These include Friday night concerts, the annual Norfolk Harborfest in June, the Cingular Norfolk Jazz Festival in July, and the Cingular Town Point Virginia Wine Festival in October.

The one-stop center for information and tickets is **Seven Venues** (ℂ **800/745-3000** or 757/664-6464; www.sevenvenues.com), which manages Chrysler Hall, Harrison Opera House, Norfolk SCOPE Area, Attucks Theatre, and Town Point Park.

THE BAR & CLUB SCENE

Most grown-up club action these days is found along Granby Street between Main and Charlotte streets, where some of the many restaurants and bars have live music (see "Where to Eat," above). Take a stroll any night, especially on weekends, and you're bound to hear tunes to your liking. Check out **Scotty Quixx,** 436 Granby St. (ℂ **757/625-0008;** www.scottyquixx.com), and **Hell's Kitchen,** 124 Granby St. (ℂ **757/624-1906;** www.hknorfolk.com). Because the scene changes significantly from night to night depending on which bands are playing where, pick up a copy of the local alternative newspaper, *Veer Magazine* (www.veermag.com), which will give a good rundown of what's going on when you're here.

In the heart of the restaurant district, the **Granby Theater,** 421 Granby St. (ℂ **757/961-7208;** www.granbytheater.com), becomes a dance hall Friday and Saturday nights. Expect to pay a $10 cover charge after 10pm.

Opposite the MacArthur Center, the **Norva Theater,** 317 Monticello Ave. (ℂ **757/627-4547;** www.thenorva.com), hosts rock, reggae, and other bands. With lounges overlooking the stage from three levels, it's more a big club than a theater these days.

11 | VIRGINIA BEACH ★

20 miles E of Norfolk; 110 miles SE of Richmond; 207 miles S of Washington, D.C.

With Atlantic Ocean surf stroking its long stretch of soft sand, Virginia Beach attracts thousands of vacationers from the nearby region and a few from as far away as Europe. Although hotels stand shoulder to shoulder in the city's congested resort area, state parks and a marvelous national wildlife refuge preserve much of Virginia Beach in its natural state, making it attractive to lovers of nature. This is also a great place to see dolphins and whales, thanks to Virginia's official aquarium.

Beaches   Most people spend their summer days playing in the surf and soaking up the rays on the 20 miles of unbroken beach extending from Cape Henry south to the North Carolina line. Most of the action is along the 39 blocks of the **Boardwalk** fronting the city's **oceanfront** resort district. About 12 miles south, beyond the U.S. Navy's amphibious training station, less-developed, family-oriented **Sandbridge Beach** is more like North Carolina's nearby Outer Banks.

Things to Do   As with any big beach resort, you'll find plenty to do in the water: Surfing, bodysurfing, fishing, wave running, and parasailing, to name a few. The flat terrain and winding, protected backwaters of **First Landing State Park** are perfect for bicycling and kayaking. On land, it's one of the state's prime golfing destinations, with the **Virginia Beach National Golf Club,** one of the U.S.'s top courses.

Eating and Drinking   With the Atlantic Ocean and the Chesapeake Bay next door, this is the place to eat seafood, especially blue crabs harvested from the bay during summer months. The rich back fin meat is turned into delicious crab cakes at **Waterman's Surfside Grille,** just steps from the ocean. It also is used with shrimp to fill fresh flounder at the charming **Tautog's Restaurant at Winston's Cottage,** one of the few restaurants locals frequent during the crowded summer season.

Nature   Nature lovers can explore the magnificent **Back Bay National Wildlife Refuge,** which attracts migrating birds and protects several miles of beach and marshlands from development. Then walk or take a tram to the deserted beaches of **False Cape State Park** down by the North Carolina border. Here also is the **Virginia Aquarium & Marine Science Center,** an educational place to take the kids even if it isn't raining, and the base for dolphin- and whale-watching cruises.

Essentials

VISITOR INFORMATION

For information on planning your trip or assistance while you're here, contact the **Visitor Information Center,** 2100 Parks Ave., Virginia Beach, VA 23451 (© 800/ 822-3224; www.visitvirginiabeach.com). A large board has phones connected to the reservations desks of major hotels and resorts. Particularly helpful are the center's annual *Vacation Guide* and a free **map** showing public restrooms and municipal parking lots in the resort area. The center is at the eastern end of I-264. It's open daily 9am to 5pm and to 7pm mid-June through Labor Day weekend.

A satellite office is in First Landing State Park's **Chesapeake Bay Center,** 2500 Shore Dr. (U.S. 60; © 757/412-2316). It's open March to November daily 9am to 5pm and from December to February Monday to Friday 9am to 5pm.

There are **information kiosks** at the beach on Atlantic Avenue at 17th and 24th streets during June, July, and August. *Note:* These are the only official visitor information booths at the beach; most others with TOURIST INFORMATION signs are come-ons for the many timeshare sales operations here.

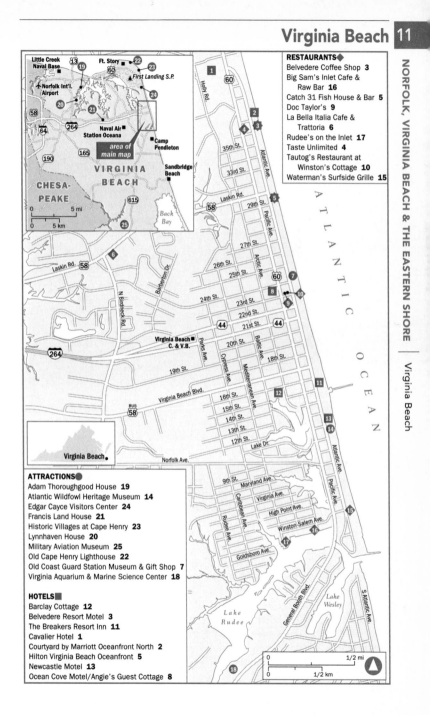

NORFOLK, VIRGINIA BEACH & THE EASTERN SHORE | Virginia Beach

RESTAURANTS◆
Belvedere Coffee Shop **3**
Big Sam's Inlet Cafe & Raw Bar **16**
Catch 31 Fish House & Bar **5**
Doc Taylor's **9**
La Bella Italia Cafe & Trattoria **6**
Rudee's on the Inlet **17**
Taste Unlimited **4**
Tautog's Restaurant at Winston's Cottage **10**
Waterman's Surfside Grille **15**

ATTRACTIONS●
Adam Thoroughgood House **19**
Atlantic Wildfowl Heritage Museum **14**
Edgar Cayce Visitors Center **24**
Francis Land House **21**
Historic Villages at Cape Henry **23**
Lynnhaven House **20**
Military Aviation Museum **25**
Old Cape Henry Lighthouse **22**
Old Coast Guard Station Museum & Gift Shop **7**
Virginia Aquarium & Marine Science Center **18**

HOTELS■
Barclay Cottage **12**
Belvedere Resort Motel **3**
The Breakers Resort Inn **11**
Cavalier Hotel **1**
Courtyard by Marriott Oceanfront North **2**
Hilton Virginia Beach Oceanfront **5**
Newcastle Motel **13**
Ocean Cove Motel/Angie's Guest Cottage **8**

Racks at the visitor information center and elsewhere contain several slick give-away tourist publications packed with information and money-saving coupons.

GETTING THERE

BY PLANE   Virginia Beach is served by **Norfolk International Airport (ORF),** about 15 miles west of the oceanfront resort area (see "Essentials" under "Norfolk," earlier in this chapter).

BY CAR   Follow I-64 to I-264 East. I-264 ends near the heart of the oceanfront resort area. Also from the west, U.S. 60 becomes the scenic Shore Drive, which dead ends at Pacific Avenue on the northern end of the ocean beach; a right turn takes you along this main north-south drag through the resort area. From the north or south, U.S. 13 and U.S. 17 will take you to I-64.

Between mid-June and Labor Day, especially on weekends, on-street parking spaces near the beach can be as scarce as hen's teeth, and you are limited to 3 hours even if you can find one. Try the municipal **parking garages** on Atlantic Avenue at 9th and 31st streets or the city's **parking lots** on Pacific Avenue at Rudee Inlet and 2nd, 4th, 9th, 19th, and 25th streets. For more information call © **757/385-4800** or go to www.vbgov.com/parking.

CITY LAYOUT

The municipality of Virginia Beach covers a huge geographic area between the Chesapeake Bay and the North Carolina line, from Norfolk to the Atlantic Ocean. There's no downtown; instead, it's one giant suburb. The largest commercial district is known as **Pembroke,** off I-64 at the intersection of Independence and Virginia Beach boulevards, where a planned area known as the **Town Center of Virginia Beach** (www.vabeachtowncenter.com) is home to national chain hotels, restaurants, retailers, and the Sandler Center for the Performing Arts (see "Virginia Beach After Dark," later in this chapter).

You can forget all that sprawl if you're here on vacation, for the fun is at the **ocean-front,** or officially the "resort area," where you will find a solid line of big hotels, restaurants, beachwear and souvenir shops, video-game arcades, and other business whose sole goal is to extract money from our pockets between Memorial Day and Labor Day. Although hotels line the beachfront and obscure ocean views from every-where except their own rooms, the 39-block-long **Boardwalk** (it's actually concrete) boasts immaculate landscaping, wood benches, small parks, a bike-skating path, public restrooms, and attractive white Colonial-style street lamps. And during the summer, the Boardwalk hosts free live entertainment most evenings.

The Boardwalk and its adjacent bike/skating path run along the beach from 1st Street at Rudee Inlet north to 39th Street. Behind the beachfront hotels, **Atlantic Avenue** takes you north-south from Rudee Inlet all the way north to Cape Henry. A block inland, the four-lane **Pacific Avenue** goes from the inlet north to 42nd Street (it's a much speedier way through the resort area than Atlantic Ave.).

To the north, Chesapeake Bay and the Atlantic Ocean meet at Cape Henry, once the site of Fort Story. The fort itself is long gone but the land remains a U.S. Navy base—or in navyspeak, the Joint Expeditionary Base Little Creek—Fort Story. What-ever its official moniker, Fort Story is home to **Cape Henry Lighthouse** and the **Historic Villages at Cape Henry.** Nearby is **First Landing State Park.**

At Rudee Inlet, Pacific Avenue gives way to **General Booth Boulevard,** which takes you southwest past the Virginia Aquarium & Marine Science Center some 12 miles south to **Sandbridge Beach,** an oceanfront enclave of cottages and two ghastly condo developments. Sandbridge is aptly named, for it constitutes a "sand bridge" connecting the Virginia mainland to North Carolina's magnificent Outer Banks chain of barrier islands, which stretch for hundreds of miles to the south of here. You can't drive to there from here, however, because **Back Bay National Wildlife Refuge** and **False Cape State Park** protect the peninsula and offer undisturbed beach and marshland for hikers, bikers, bird-watchers, and sun worshipers. A maze of "back bay" marshes and waterways makes this a natural jewel comparable to Assateague Island on the Eastern Shore (see "Chincoteague & Assateague Islands," later in this chapter).

GETTING AROUND

I usually leave my car at my hotel and get around on the bus system known as **VB Wave** (www.vbwave.com). **Route 30** runs from May through September about every 15 minutes 8am to 2am along Atlantic Avenue between Rudee Inlet and 42nd Street. You can transfer at 40th Street to the regular **Route 33** bus for First Landing State Park and other points to the north.

Also during summer, the **Aquarium & Campground Shuttle** (Rte. 31) runs daily, about every 20 minutes from 8am to 2am between Atlantic Avenue at 40th Street and the Virginia Aquarium & Marine Science Center on General Booth Boulevard. And the **Shoppers Shuttle** (Rte. 32) goes from Atlantic Avenue to Laskin Road past the Hilltop Shopping Center to Lynnhaven Mall.

Fare on any VB Wave trolley is $2 for adults, 50¢ for seniors and persons with disabilities, and free for children shorter than 38 inches tall. It may be more economical to buy a 1-day **GO Shuttle** pass ($2 per adult), which permits unlimited rides. Buy them at the automated blue-and-yellow dispensing machines at the trolley stops or at the transit kiosk on Atlantic Avenue at 24th Street.

The trolleys are operated by **Hampton Roads Transit** (**HRT**; ✆ 757/222-6100; www.gohrt.com), which also provides public bus service in the region. HRT's **oceanfront terminal** is on Pacific Avenue between 19th and 20th streets. From there, the Route 20 bus goes to downtown Norfolk (it takes up to 2 hr. each way). Regular bus fares are $1.50 for adults, $1 for children ages 18 and under, and free for kids shorter than 38 inches tall. Exact change is required.

For a taxi, call **Andy's Cab Co.** (✆ 757/495-3300).

Outdoor Activities

Virginia Beach offers a wonderful variety of watersports, starting, of course, with its fine-sand beach for swimming. *Note:* Between Memorial Day and Labor Day, no ball playing, fishing, or other sports are allowed on the beach between 2nd Street and 42nd Street from 10am to 5pm.

BIKING, JOGGING & SKATING   You can walk, jog, or run on the Boardwalk, or bike or skate on its adjoining bike path. The city publishes a map of bikeways and bike trails, available at the visitor center and at www.vbgov.com/parks.

There are biking and hiking trails in **First Landing State Park** (which rents bikes) and in **Back Bay National Wildlife Refuge** (see "Parks & Wildlife Refuges," below).

You can rent wheels from early March to October from **Cherie's Bicycle & Blade Rental** (✆ 757/437-8888) and from **Bonnie's Beach Bikes** (✆ 757/460-9051), which have stations every couple of blocks along the Boardwalk. Rentals start at $6 an hour and $59 a week.

Good Golf Packages

You don't have to be Tiger Woods to take advantage of golf packages organized by **Virginia Beach Golf Getaways** (℗ **866/482-4653**; www.vbgolf.com).

Check the website or ask the visitor center for a copy of its annual golf guide.

FISHING   Deep-sea fishing aboard a party boat can be an exciting day's entertainment for novices and dedicated fishermen alike. Headquarters for both party and private charter boats is on Rudee Inlet at the **Virginia Beach Fishing Center,** 200 Winston-Salem Ave. (℗ **757/422-5700**; www.virginiafishing.com). Make reservations at the center at least a day in advance.

You can also drop a line from the **Virginia Beach Fishing Pier,** between 14th and 15th streets, oceanfront (℗ **757/428-2333**), open April through October. It has bait for sale and rods for rent. On the Chesapeake Bay, **Lynnhaven Fishing Pier,** Starfish Road off Shore Drive (℗ **757/481-7071**; www.lynnhavenpier.com), is open 24 hours a day in summer, rents rods and reels, and sells crab cages.

GOLF   Next to Williamsburg, Virginia Beach offers more golf holes per capita than any other Virginia destination. Sand, water, and wind make up for the area's flat terrain to provide plenty of challenges at the **Virginia Beach National Golf Club** (℗ **877/484-3872** or 757/563-9440; www.vbnational.com), designed by Pete Dye and Curtis Strange and formerly known as the Tournament Players Club of Virginia Beach.

Elevated tees and strategically placed water and bunkers pose problems at **Heron Ridge Golf Club** (℗ **757/426-3800**; www.heronridge.com), designed by Fred Couples and Gene Bates. Sharp fairway angles at the Rees Jones–designed **Hell's Point Golf Course** (℗ **757/721-3400**; www.hellspoint.com) have been described as both "devilish" and "Satanic." Another Rees Jones project, **Honey Bee Golf Course** (℗ **757/471-2768**), is shorter (par 70) but presents challenges for beginners and experts alike. The city has several public links, including **Red Wing Lake Municipal Golf Course** (℗ **757/437-4845**; www.redwinglakegolf.com).

Call the courses for greens fees, tee times, and directions.

KAYAKING   Even if you've never settled your stern into a kayak, you're sure to enjoy a paddling excursion in this area's quiet backwaters or a dolphin-watching adventure on the high seas. As the popularity of kayaking has increased, so has the number of operators here. The local convention and visitor bureau (see "Essentials," above) publishes a *Virginia Beach Adventure Getaways* brochure listing all of them and some hotels that have outdoor packages.

Kayak Nature Tours (℗ **888/669-8368** or 757/480-1999; www.tidewater adventures.com) has been around the longest and is still one of the best. It has 2½-hour dolphin-watching trips from May through October. The guides also lead tours of the Back Bay National Wildlife Refuge and to other nearby locations. Tour prices range from $50 to $110, with a 25% discount for children accompanied by an adult. Reservations are required. The company also rents kayaks.

If Kayak Adventures doesn't have space, contact **Wild River Outfitters** (℗ **877/431-8566** or 757/431-8566; www.wildriveroutfitters.com), **Back Bay Getaways** (℗ **757/721-4484**; www.backbaygetaways.com), or **Ocean Rentals Ltd.**

(© **800/695-4212** or 757/721-6210; www.oceanrentalsltd.com). The latter two are in Sandbridge and specialize in touring the nearby Back Bay National Wildlife Refuge.

SCUBA DIVING   The Atlantic Ocean off Virginia Beach is colder and less clear than it is below Cape Hatteras, North Carolina, but that's not to say you can't dive here. **Lynnhaven Dive Center** (© **757/481-7949;** www.ldcscuba.com) sends its two dive boats out to more than 20 nearby wrecks and other sites year-round, and it has trips to warmer waters in North Carolina. It also teaches diving and rents equipment.

SURFING   Unlike the huge breakers on the north shore of Oahu, the waves here are usually gentle enough during summer for novices to learn to stay up on a surfboard—and probably not break a leg in the process. If you've never been on a board and would like to test your balance, take a 2-hour lesson from **Ocean Rentals Ltd.** (© **800/695-4212** or 757/721-6210; www.oceanrentalsltd.com) in Sandbridge for $45 per person. Reservations are required.

SWIMMING   During the summer season, lifeguards are on duty along the resort strip from 2nd to 42nd streets; they also handle raft, umbrella, and beach-chair rentals. Be careful when swimming in the surf, particularly if a northeast wind is kicking up a dangerous undertow. When in doubt, ask the lifeguard.

You can get away from the summer crowds—and the lifeguards—by driving across Rudee Inlet, turning east on Croatan Road, and going through a residential neighborhood to **Croatan Beach,** where there's a parking lot and changing facilities. Another 12 miles south leads to **Little Island City Park** in **Sandbridge Beach.** To really escape the crowds, take the tram from there to **False Cape State Park** (see "Parks & Wildlife Refuges," below).

WAVE RUNNING & PARASAILING   You can go parasailing and rent exciting WaveRunners from **Rudee Inlet Jet Ski Rentals** next to the Virginia Beach Fishing Center at Rudee Inlet (© **757/428-4614;** www.beachparasail.com).

Parks & Wildlife Refuges

One of the best things about Virginia Beach is that you don't have to go far from the busy resort to find open spaces for hiking, biking, camping, and bird-watching.

BACK BAY & FALSE CAPE ★★★

Especially inviting for bird-watchers, canoeists, and kayakers is **Back Bay National Wildlife Refuge,** in the southeastern corner of Virginia. Actually on the northern end of North Carolina's Outer Banks, its 9,200 acres of beaches, dunes, marshes, and backwaters are typical of the barrier island environment. It is also on the main Atlantic Flyway for migratory birds, and a wide range of wildlife lives here all year. No swimming, surfing, or sunbathing is allowed on the pristine beach, but you can collect shells, surf cast for fish, and bird-watch. There are also nature trails and a canoe launching spot with marked trails through the marshes. Daily admission April through October is $5 per vehicle and $2 per pedestrian or biker; it's free November through March. The refuge is open daily from sunrise to sunset all year. The **visitor contact station** (© **757/721-2412**) is open Monday to Friday 8am to 4pm and Saturday to Sunday 9am to 4pm (closed Sat Dec–Mar). It offers nature and environmental education programs by reservation only. *Note:* Pets are permitted, on leashes, October through March only. From Rudee Inlet, go south on General Booth Boulevard and follow the signs 12 miles to Sandbridge and the refuge. For more information, contact the **Refuge Manager,** 4005 Sandpiper Rd., Virginia Beach, VA 23456 (© **757/721-2412;** www.fws.gov/backbay).

The kayak outfitters mentioned under "Outdoor Activities," above, will take you paddling in the refuge.

Swimming and sunbathing are permitted on the beach in **False Cape State Park,** 4 miles south of the Back Bay visitor contact station via a hiking and biking trail. You'll find 6 miles of beachfront (to the North Carolina line), an interpretive trail, and more than 3 miles of hiking trails. Primitive camping is by permit only, which you can get by calling © **800/933-7275.** The park has no other visitor facilities, so bring everything you will need, including drinking water. It's open daily sunrise to sunset.

You can't park in the national wildlife refuge lot while visiting False Cape State Park, so leave your vehicle at Little Island City Park in Sandbridge. From there, you can either hike or bike the 6 miles to False Cape or take the **Blue Goose Tram** that runs daily from Memorial Day through Labor Day weekend and Friday to Sunday in April, May, September, and October. It departs at 9am and returns at 1pm and stops for about 2 hours at the False Cape. It's first-come, first-served, but call © **757/721-2412** or 757/426-7128 to make sure it's running. Fares are $8 for adults and $6 for seniors and children 11 and under.

For more information, contact the park at 4001 Sandpiper Rd., Virginia Beach, VA 23456 (© **757/426-7128;** www.dcr.state.va.us/parks/falscape.htm).

FIRST LANDING STATE PARK ★★

The Virginia Company, which went on to settle Jamestown, made its first landing in the New World on April 16, 1607, in what is now this fine state park, whose 2,888 preserved acres run between the Lynnhaven River and the Chesapeake Bay to within 2 blocks of the oceanfront. Rabbits, squirrels, and raccoons are among the many species in this urban park with 19 miles of hiking trails. The main entrance is on Shore Drive (U.S. 60), where the visitor information center is open daily 9am to 5pm. The grounds and trails are open daily 8am to sunset. The 64th Street entry, off Atlantic Avenue, leads to a quiet-water beach on Broad Bay. Admission to the park is $4 per vehicle on weekdays and $5 on weekends. Bikes are prohibited except on the gravel, 6-mile Cape Henry Trail, which runs between the 64th Street entrance and the trail center.

There are 20 two-bedroom cabins that can be rented here. Rates vary by season, and bookings are essential, so call the state park reservations center (© **800/933-7275**). Open from March through November, a bayside campground in a wooded area beside a fine beach has 222 sites for tents and RVs for $24 to $30 a night plus tax. The park store (© **757/412-2302**) rents bicycles and beach equipment and supplies.

For more information, contact the park at 2500 Shore Dr., Virginia Beach, VA 23451 (© **757/412-2320;** www.dcr.state.va.us/parks/1stland.htm).

Next to the campground, the **Chesapeake Bay Center** (© **727/412-2316**) has an exhibit about the Jamestown colonists' landing here in 1607. It also shows a short video and has an exhibit about the local ecology, both put together by the Virginia Aquarium & Marine Science Center; it's interesting but not as good as the main museum (p. 297). There's a visitor information desk here. A beachside amphitheater hosts concerts during the summer (call for a schedule). The center is open daily 9am to 5pm.

Segway Tours of Hampton Roads (🕾 757/412-9734; www.segwayofhampton roads.us) will guide you through the park on its two-wheel machines for $75 per person. Call for reservations, which are essential.

The Top Attractions

Atlantic Wildfowl Heritage Museum ★★   This small but excellent museum displays a collection of carved decoys—some of them more than a century old—and decorative wildlife, plus paintings of ducks, geese, and other wildfowl. It occupies the white-brick-and-clapboard DeWitt beach cottage built in 1895 by Virginia Beach's first mayor. The oldest structure on the waterfront, the cottage alone is worth a stop as you stroll along the Boardwalk. It's operated by the Back Bay Wildfowl Guild, which applies the donations and profits from the gift shop (which carries excellent decoys) to its conservation efforts.

1113 Atlantic Ave. (at 12th St.). 🕾 **757/437-8432.** www.awhm.org. Free admission; donations encouraged. Summer Mon–Sat 10am–5pm, Sun noon–5pm; off season Tues–Sat 10am–5pm, Sun noon–5pm. Closed New Year's Day, Easter, Thanksgiving, Christmas, and Dec 31.

Edgar Cayce Visitors Center   You don't have to be the least bit psychic to visit this center carrying on the work of the late Edgar Cayce, who settled in Virginia Beach and built his Psychic Hospital here in 1928. Cayce's own psychic talent manifested itself when he found he could enter into an altered state of consciousness and answer questions on any topic. His answers, or "discourses," now called "readings," number some 14,305. If you don't know about Cayce, show up at 2pm for a 30-minute movie about his life, followed by a 30-minute guided tour. The Meditation Room on the third floor of the visitor center offers a spectacular view of the ocean and is painted with colors chosen because Cayce's readings suggested they can help attain higher consciousness. In the Psychic Hospital building, the health center and spa offer steam baths, facials, and massages to the public.

215 67th St. (at Atlantic Ave.). 🕾 **757/428-3588.** www.edgarcayce.org. Free admission. Mon–Sat 10am–8pm; Sun noon–6pm. 30-min. film daily 2pm. 30-min. tours depart daily 2:30pm. Closed Thanksgiving and Christmas.

Historic Villages at Cape Henry   Beside the beach in Fort Story, these reconstructed villages interpret how the Powhatan tribes lived at the time the English colonists arrived on their shores in 1607. If possible, take a tour led by an American Indian of the local tribes. A round stage is the setting for a 1-hour outdoor drama, *1607: First Landing,* which tells of a young American Indian man who develops a friendship with an Englishman. The villages are open only in summer and the schedule changes from year to year (check the website or call ahead). **Note:** Everyone 16 and over will need a photo ID to access the U.S. Navy's Fort Story, and your car may be searched.

108 Atlantic Ave. (in Fort Story). 🕾 **757/417-7012.** www.firstlandingfoundation.org. Admission $8 adults, $5 children 6–15, free for children 5 and under. Admission including play $15 adults, $10 children 6–15, free for children 5 and under; $40 families. June Sat 2–6pm; July 4th to Labor Day weekends Thurs–Sat 2–6pm. Performances 6pm.

Military Aviation Museum ★   Located in a hangar beside a small airstrip in the strawberry fields south of the rural crossroads of Pungo, this surprisingly good museum houses a fine collection of historic military aircraft, all in mint condition and all but three of which can still fly. If you are lucky, someone will roll out a World War II–vintage P51 Mustang, P40 Flying Tiger, or RAF Spitfire and take off. When they're

The **Naval Air Station Oceana** is home to those low-flying U.S. Navy F/A-18 Hornet fighter planes whose thundering jets disturb the peace over the beach. That's the "sound of freedom" to patriotic locals; the "sound of money" to wags who emphasize that Oceana is the city's largest employer. Other than when they roar over at a 600-foot altitude, the best way for us civilians to see them up close is on a **Naval Air Station Oceana Base Tour** offered in cooperation with the Military Aviation Museum (see below).The tours depart from the visitor information kiosk at Atlantic Avenue and 24th Street from Memorial Day through Labor Day weekend, Monday to Friday at 11am. Fares are $13 for adults; $10 for seniors and children 5 to 12, and free for kids 4 and under. Lunch at the officers' club is $9. Anyone 16 years or older needs a picture ID to get on the base. Do not bring backpacks.

not flying them, staffers and volunteers stay busy restoring other craft. Rather than drive here, you can ride the museum's double-decker bus from the oceanfront from May through October. Call for bus reservations.

1341 Princess Anne Rd. ☎ **757/721-PROP** [7767]. www.militaryaviationmuseum.org. Admission $10 adults, $9 seniors and military, $5 children 6–18, free for children 5 and under. Daily 9am–5pm. Closed Thanksgiving and Christmas. Museum is 14 miles south of Rudee Inlet. From the Oceanfront take Gen. Booth Blvd. south, turn left on Princess Anne Rd. (the traffic light after Nimmo Rd.) to museum on right.

Old Cape Henry Lighthouse ★★   Built in 1791–92, this picturesque brick structure was the first lighthouse authorized by the U.S. Congress. It marked the southern entrance to Chesapeake Bay until 1881, when a "new" lighthouse across the road took over. If you're in shape, you can climb the 191 steps to the top for a spectacular view over Cape Henry, the bay, and the ocean. The gift shop carries a plethora of lighthouse-themed items. Also across the road, the Jamestown colonists' **First Landing Site** is marked by a cross and plaque where they "set up a Crosse at Chesapeake Bay and named that place Cape Henry" for Henry, Prince of Wales. Also here are a monumental relief map showing the French and British naval engagement off Cape Henry during the Revolutionary War and a statue of the French commander. Now known as the **Battle Off the Capes,** this decisive battle effectively trapped Cornwallis at Yorktown and helped end British dominion in America.

  Note: You must be more than 4 feet tall to climb the lighthouse. Everyone 16 and over will need a photo ID to access Fort Story, and your car may be searched.

583 Atlantic Ave. (in Fort Story). ☎ **757/422-9421.** www.apva.org/CapeHenryLighthouse. Admission $5 adults, $3 children 3–12, free for children 2 and under. Mar 16–Oct 31 daily 10am–5pm; Nov 1–Mar 15 daily 10am–4pm. Closed Thanksgiving and Dec 5–Jan 4.

Old Coast Guard Station Museum and Gift Shop ★   In the heart of the oceanfront resort area, this small museum is housed in the white-clapboard building constructed in 1903 as a lifesaving station. Its exhibits recall rescue missions and shipwrecks along the coast. Not all is old here, for you can manipulate a video cam atop the building to get a bird's-eye view of the beach. You can see it all in 45 minutes. An excellent gift shop carries clocks, drawings, books, and other things nautical.

24th St. and Atlantic Ave. ☎ **757/422-1587.** www.oldcoastguardstation.com. Admission $4 adults, $3 seniors and military, $2 children 6–18, free for children 5 and under. Summer Mon–Sat

Provided you're not overly prone to sea-sickness, one of the most interesting things to do here is to take an offshore **dolphin-watching cruise ★★★** given by the Virginia Aquarium & Marine Science Center (daily June–Sept; Sat–Sun Oct–May). The center also has **whale-watching cruises** in winter (also offshore) and **sea life–collecting trips** in summer. The trips cost $21 to $28 for adults and $15 to $24 for children 11 and under. The boats leave from Rudee Inlet. Call the aquarium or check its website for schedules (𝄐 **757/425-3474;** www. virginiaaquarium.com). To make reservations, which are required, call (𝄐 **757/385-3474**).

Another marvelous experience at the center, especially for children 8 and over, is its **Harbor Seal Splash ★★★**. Accompanied by an animal-care specialist, you actually get into a pool and splash around with the resident harbor seals and participate in a training session. The 2-hour sessions take place April through September. If you can afford it, the $175 per person fee is worth it. Call 𝄐 **757/385-0300** for reservations, which are required.

10am–5pm, Sun noon–5pm; off season Tues–Sat 10am–5pm, Sun noon–5pm. Closed New Year's Day, Thanksgiving, Christmas, and Dec 31.

Virginia Aquarium & Marine Science Center ★★★ ☺ This entertaining, educational facility focusing on Virginia's marine environment is a wonderful place to take the kids. Its 45 acres are beside Owl Creek salt marsh, a wildlife habitat. You can easily spend half a day here, a full day to see—and learn—it all. Plan to spend at least half of your time in the main building, where touch tanks will fascinate you and the kids, who also will love playing with the switches and dials in a dark room designed like a submarine, complete with sonar "pings." The sub looks out into one of several room-size aquariums holding a myriad of sea turtles, sharks, rays, and other species found in Virginia waters. Movies in the center's 3-D IMAX theater feature animals leaping off the screen at you.

As you leave the main building, take a look at the salt marsh room, which will prepare you for a .3-mile nature hike along the creek and for an informative 35-minute cruise in a 50-passenger pontoon boat on Owl Creek and through Virginia Beach's last undeveloped salt marsh. There's an observation tower from which you might see some of the wild animals living on an island across the creek. The boardwalk nature trail leads to the smaller Owl Creek Marsh Pavilion, were river otters play in an outdoor tank and more than 50 species of birds fly about an aviary. It also houses the fascinating "*Macro Marsh*" display in which everything is enlarged 10 times normal size to give you a crab's eye view of the world.

717 General Booth Blvd. (southwest of Rudee Inlet). 𝄐 **757/385-3474.** www.virginiaaquarium. com. Admission $21 adults, $20 seniors, $15 children 4–11, free for children 3 and under. IMAX tickets $9 adults, $8.50 seniors, $8 children 3–11, free for children 2 and under. Owl Creek cruise $7 per person. Combination tickets (admission to museum and IMAX movie) $27 adults, $26 seniors, $21 children 3–11, free for children 2 and under; (admission to museum and Owl Creek cruise) $17 adults, $16 seniors, $13 children 3–11, free for children 2 and under. Memorial Day to Labor Day daily 9am–7pm; rest of year daily 9am–5pm. Owl Creek cruises Apr–Sept. Closed Thanksgiving and Christmas.

Historic Homes

After touring Williamsburg, I am seldom in the mood to traipse through more old houses. Nevertheless, Virginia Beach has three, two of which are somewhat different than those in Williamsburg. Dating to around 1680 and 1725, respectively, the Adam Thoroughgood and Lynnhaven houses are interesting because they were both built in the fashion of English farm cottages of Elizabethan times, years before Georgian architecture became prevalent elsewhere in Colonial Virginia.

Adam Thoroughgood House ★   One of the oldest homes in Virginia and the most interesting, this medieval English-style cottage sits on 4½ acres of lawn and garden overlooking the Lynnhaven River. It was built around 1680 by one of Adam Thoroughgood's grandsons (historians believe its namesake didn't live in the house). The interior has exposed wood beams and whitewashed walls, and though the furnishings did not belong to the Thoroughgoods, they are original to the period and reflect the family's English ancestry.

1636 Parish Rd. (at Thoroughgood Lane). Ⓒ **757/460-7588.** www.virginiabeachhistory.org/ thoroughgoodhouse.html. Admission $4 adults, $3 seniors and children 13–18, $2 children 6–12, free for children 5 and under. Tues–Sat 9am–5pm; Sun 11am–5pm. Guided 30-min. tours available on request (last tour 4:30pm). From oceanfront, take I-264 W. to Exit 3, go north on Independence Blvd. (Va. 225), turn right on Pleasure House Rd., right on Thoroughgood Sq., left on Thoroughgood Dr., and follow the very small signs to the house.

Francis Land House   Built as a plantation manor in the mid–18th century (now beside one of the region's busiest highways), this Georgian-style brick house is a restoration work in progress. Some rooms are furnished with antiques and reproductions. The highlights here are 7 acres of herb, vegetable, and pleasure gardens and a .1-mile wetlands nature trail.

3131 Virginia Beach Blvd. (just west of Kings Grant Rd.). Ⓒ **757/385-5100.** www.virginiabeachhistory. org/land.html. Admission $4 adults, $3 seniors and children 13–18, $2 children 6–12, free for children 5 and under. Tues–Sat 9am–5pm; Sun 11am–5pm. Guided 30-min. house tours available on request (last tour 4:30pm).

Lynnhaven House   Built in 1725, this medieval-style cottage still doesn't have running water or electricity. When the Association for the Preservation of Virginia Antiquities took the house over in 1971, it stripped away plaster and discovered the Champford ceiling beams in their original condition (note the chalk marks carpenters made in 1725). Tours led by costumed docents explain the house and interpret Colonial lifestyles. We moderns won't find Lynnhaven oysters as gigantic as the shells excavated from the trash pit and displayed in the kitchen.

4405 Wishart Rd. (off Independence Blvd.). Ⓒ **757/460-7109.** www.virginiabeachhistory.org/ lynnhouse.html. Admission $4 adults, $3 seniors, $2 children 5–16, free for children 4 and under. Tues–Sat 10am–4pm; Sun noon–4pm. Guided 45-min. tours available on request. From the beach, take I-264 W. to Exit 3, head north on Independence Blvd. (Va. 225), take a right, and drive ⅓ mile on Wishart Rd.

Where to Stay

The hotels and B&Bs listed below are just some of the more than 11,000 hotel rooms in Virginia Beach. Even with that many places to stay, you should reserve as far in advance as possible from mid-June through Labor Day, and especially on weekends when room rates are at their highest and minimum stays are required. The lowest rates given below are for winter, highest are for the peak summer season. Spring and fall are somewhere in between. Late spring and early fall are good times to visit; both have warm weather and lower rates.

With so many hotels offering so many rooms, choosing the right one can be a daunting task. The Virginia Beach visitor information center's annual *Vacation Guide* lists all the local hotels and their current rates (see "Essentials" under "Virginia Beach," earlier in this chapter). It also distributes an annual accommodations directory published by the **Virginia Beach Hotel/Motel Association** (www.va-beach-hotels.com). The association's website has links to many of the hotels, most of which give their current room rates.

The Belvedere Beach Resort ★★ ⬧ This five-story building is the crown jewel of the few less-expensive, family-operated oceanfront hotels left on the oceanfront here. It justifiably attracts lots of repeat guests, so book early. Like the nearby Courtyard Virginia Beach Oceanfront/North (see below), it's far enough north to avoid the rowdy crowds. The motel-style rooms have screen doors that swing open to balconies facing the ocean. The combo tub/shower bathrooms are small but compensate with separate sinks and vanities. A few rooms have king-size beds (most have two doubles). The 10 units on the ends of the building are somewhat larger and have cooking facilities. There's a small swimming pool, sun deck, and the **Belvedere Coffee Shop** (see "Where to Eat," below). Guests also get free use of bicycles.

Oceanfront at 36th St. (PO Box 451), Virginia Beach, VA 23458. www.belvederebeachresort.com. ℂ **800/425-0612** or 757/425-0612. Fax 757/425-1397. 50 units. $84–$166 double. AE, MC, V. Free parking. Closed mid-Oct to Apr. **Amenities:** Restaurant (breakfast and lunch); bikes; pool; Wi-Fi (in lobby). *In room:* A/C, TV, fridge, kitchen (in efficiencies).

The Breakers Resort Inn Another reasonably priced, family-operated oceanfront hotel, the Breakers occupies a yellow boxlike nine-story building. Its rooms are comfortably furnished with contemporary pieces. All have oceanfront balconies; some rooms with king-size beds contain hot tubs. Efficiency apartments have a bedroom with two queen-size beds, a living room with a Murphy bed, and kitchenette with two-burner stove (but no oven). Additional amenities include free bicycles. The on-site cafe serves breakfast and lunch.

1503 Atlantic Ave. (oceanfront at 16th St.), Virginia Beach, VA 23451. www.breakersresort.com. ℂ **800/237-7532** or 757/428-1821. Fax 757/422-9602. 56 units. $50–$310 double. Packages available. AE, DISC, MC, V. Free parking. **Amenities:** Restaurant (breakfast and lunch); bikes; pool; Wi-Fi (in public areas). *In room:* A/C, TV, fridge, hair dryer, Internet, kitchen (in efficiencies).

Cavalier Hotel ★★ Virginia Beach's best-equipped resort actually consists of two hotels—the original Cavalier on the Hill, built in 1927 across Atlantic Avenue from the beach, and the Cavalier on the Ocean, which has been kept up-to-date since it opened in 1973. Although it's not directly on the beach and is open only during the summer for overflow guests, the original building has all the charm. Its enclosed veranda with white-wicker furnishings, potted plants, and great ocean views evoke images of the days when F. Scott and Zelda Fitzgerald danced here. Some of the guest rooms have Chippendale reproductions, Colonial-print fabrics, gilt-framed artwork, and museum-quality decorative objects. The heated indoor Olympic-size pool is magnificently tiled and illuminated by a skylight. Open all year, the newer beachside building has nicely decorated contemporary-style rooms, all with oceanfront balconies. A shuttle connects the two wings when both are open. The boardwalk stops just short of the Cavalier, so unlike all other hotels here, its lawn fronts directly on the beach.

11 Oceanfront at 42nd St., Virginia Beach, VA 23451. www.cavalierhotel.com. © **800/446-8199** or 757/425-8555. Fax 757/428-7957. 400 units. $99–$309 double. Packages available. AE, DC, DISC, MC, V. Parking $7.50. **Amenities:** 4 restaurants; 2 bars; bikes; children's programs; concierge; health club; Jacuzzi; 2 pools; room service; 3 tennis courts; watersports equipment. *In room:* A/C, TV, fridge (in suites and oceanfront rooms), hair dryer, Wi-Fi (in beach wing).

Courtyard Virginia Beach Oceanfront/North ★ 🍴 This 11-story ocean-front hotel was one of the first Courtyards designed as much as a resort as for business travelers. Making this a good family choice is the oceanfront's largest and best outdoor pool, with waterfalls, bridges, a lifeguard on duty, and its own bar. Here the beach substitutes for an actual courtyard, and big window walls look out to the Boardwalk from the plush lobby and bright, casual bistro, which provides breakfast and dinner (plus lunch in summer, when you can dine outside). Marriott's standard furniture prevails in the spacious guest quarters, all of which have balconies overlooking the ocean. Ten units have whirlpool tubs. The eight huge suites have bedrooms and living rooms, which come equipped with wet bars, microwave ovens, and refrigerators. A small indoor pool and a fitness room look out to the beach.

Its slightly older sister, the **Courtyard Virginia Beach Oceanfront/South,** 2501 Atlantic Ave., at 25th Street (www.courtyardoceanfront.com; © **800/321-2211** or 757/491-6222), lacks an outdoor pool, but otherwise is identical.

3737 Atlantic Ave. (oceanfront at 37th St.), Virginia Beach, VA 23451. www.courtyardvirginiabeach north.com. © **800/321-2211** or 757/437-0098. Fax 757/437-4272. 160 units. $99–$329 double. AE, DC, DISC, MC, V. Free valet parking in summer. **Amenities:** Restaurant; bar; health club; Jacuzzi; outdoor & indoor pools. *In room:* A/C, TV, fridge, hair dryer, Wi-Fi.

Hilton Virginia Beach Oceanfront ★★ This 21-story tower opened on the oceanfront in 2005 and immediately raised the stakes for all other hotels here. You'll see what I mean upon entering the grand lobby, where a huge water wall shaped like a Neptune's shell changes its colors every few minutes. The hotel's most unique feature is its rooftop recreation area, featuring a heated indoor pool, snack restaurant, bar, and an outdoor pool whose horizon seemingly meets the sea. You can see all the way to Norfolk from up here on a clear day. On the ground level, the casual but sophisticated **Catch 31** fish house is one of the beach's better restaurants (p. 301), and part of it becomes the fine-dining **Salacia** at night. Parlor suites have Murphy beds and kitchenettes. Empyrean Club units on the top three floors have the best views and their own 24-hour concierge lounge serving continental breakfast, evening hors d'oeuvres, and cocktails. All units except the City View rooms have balconies. This Hilton and the Cavalier (see above) are the two best resorts here.

3001 Atlantic Ave., Virginia Beach, VA 23451. www.hiltonvb.com. © **800/445-8667** or 757/213-3001. Fax 757/213-3019. 289 units. $139–$429 double; $270–$1,250 suite. AE, DC, DISC, MC, V. Valet parking $14; self-parking $7. **Amenities:** 3 restaurants; 2 bars; babysitting; concierge; concierge-level rooms; health club; pool; room service; spa; watersports equipment. *In room:* A/C, TV, hair dryer, kitchen (in parlor suites), Wi-Fi ($10 per 24hr.).

Newcastle Hotel Situated beside the Atlantic Wildfowl Heritage Museum (p. 295), the 10-story, family-operated Newcastle offers the most unusual mix of rooms on the beach, ranging from standard motel units to romantic deluxe models with canopy beds, gas fireplaces, his-and-her shower heads, and wooden Venetian blinds to keep passersby from watching you frolic in big whirlpool tubs. All units have balconies, refrigerators, microwave ovens, and spa tubs. Guests get free access to bicycles in summer. The seasonal **Lighthouse Beachside Grille** to one side offers reasonably priced meals under a big, beachside awning.

1201 Atlantic Ave. (oceanfront at 12th St.), Virginia Beach, VA 23451. www.newcastlehotelvb.com. ℰ **800/346-3176** or 757/428-3981. Fax 757/491-4394. 84 units. $49–$229 double. Packages available. AE, DC, DISC, MC, V. Free parking. **Amenities:** Restaurant; bar; bikes; health club; indoor pool; room service. *In room:* A/C, TV, fridge, hair dryer, kitchen (in some), Wi-Fi.

Ocean Cove Motel/Angie's Guest Cottage ★ 𝄃 This eclectic establishment houses one of Virginia's few hostels, offering men's, women's, and coed dorm rooms plus a communal kitchen. Consequently, you'll find a delightful mix of American and international folks here. The original cottage, built in 1918 as family housing for the nearby lifesaving station (now the Old Coast Guard Station Museum and Gift Shop; p. 296), houses two simple but comfortable units with kitchens. Next door are two kitchen-equipped apartments, each with porch and deck. Across the yard are three one-story cottages, each with three bedrooms, two bathrooms, and full kitchens; they are rented by the week and are the only units here with telephones.

302 24th St. (btw. Pacific and Arctic aves.), Virginia Beach, VA 23451. www.oceancovemotel.com or www.angiescottage.com. ℰ **757/491-1830.** 43 units (all with private bathroom), 34 are dorm beds. $50–$150 double room; $1,000–$2,000 per week cottage; $15–$20 dorm bed. MC, V. *In room:* A/C, TV, fridge, kitchen (in duplexes and cottages), Wi-Fi (in some).

A BED & BREAKFAST NEAR THE BEACH

Barclay Cottage ★ 𝄃 This two-story, white-clapboard Victorian with wraparound verandas is *very* coastal Southern, with rocking chairs on the porches and green shutters trimming tall windows hung with lace curtains. It was used as a boardinghouse and school for many years before being converted into this charming B&B. The guest rooms are adorned with Victorian pieces, including feather beds, and the two downstairs rooms have jetted bathtubs. Innkeepers Steve and Marie-Louise LaFond serve a full family-style breakfast in the lounge promptly at 9am. They also provide beach buggies to haul your complimentary umbrellas, chairs, and boogie boards to the beach, a 2-block walk away. Their "business center" is a computer in an armoire in the hallway, and their "fitness center" consists of a basket full of barbells.

400 16th St. (at Arctic Ave.), Virginia Beach, VA 23451. www.barclaycottage.com. ℰ **866/466-1895** or 757/422-1956. 5 units, 3 with private bathroom. $95–$250 double. Rates include full breakfast. AE, DISC, MC, V. Free parking. **Amenities:** Bikes. *In room:* A/C, Wi-Fi.

Where to Eat

My favorite spot for a beachside breakfast is the **Belvedere Coffee Shop,** an old-fashioned diner at the Belvedere Motel, oceanfront at 36th Street (ℰ **757/425-1397**). It's worth waiting a few extra minutes to get the two-person booth with one bench facing the ocean. Prices range from $3 to $10. It's open daily 7am to 2:30pm.

The relatively inexpensive **Big Sam's Inlet Cafe & Raw Bar,** 300 Winston-Salem Ave. (ℰ **757/428-4858;** www.bigsamsrawbar.com), overlooking the Wave-Runner docks on Rudee Inlet, is another good early-morning choice with a view. It's open daily 7am to 2am, making it a good place for a late-night snack, too.

For picnic fare, head to the beach branch of **Taste Unlimited,** 213 36th St. (ℰ **757/243-3011;** www.tasteunlimited.com), at Pacific Avenue. This gourmet market has excellent sandwiches and salads to eat in or carry out, and you can order a box lunch to eat at the beach. It's open Monday to Saturday 10am to 7pm and Sunday 11am to 5pm.

Catch 31 Fish House and Bar ★★ INTERNATIONAL This modernistic restaurant serves seafood almost as good as its spectacular setting on the ground floor of the Hilton Virginia Beach Oceanfront. Floor-to-ceiling windows look out on the ocean in one direction and to the city's lively Neptune Park on the other. Reserve an outdoor table in summer to be treated to the park's nightly live entertainment. You can fill up at the raw bar with steamed shellfish or with a "seafood tower," Catch 31's signature dish—two or three plates stacked high with chilled crabmeat, Maine lobster, Chesapeake Bay crab legs, and a few other items with accompanying sauces. The menu changes as soon as fresh catch is delivered, so keep your eye on the ever-changing specials board for the latest arrivals. Meat lovers can opt for high-quality steaks, ribs, and chops, and there's a nightly pasta for vegetarians. At night part of the restaurant becomes the expensive, fine-dining **Salacia** (www.salaciavb.com).

In Hilton Virginia Beach Oceanfront, 3001 Atlantic Ave. ⓒ **757/213-3472.** www.catch31.com. Reservations highly recommended. Main courses $17–$34. AE, DC, DISC, MC, V. Mon–Fri 6:30am–11pm; Sat–Sun 7am–11pm (to 10pm daily off season). Bar daily 11am–2am.

Doc Taylor's ★ 🍴 AMERICAN   Occupying its own vintage beach cottage, this is the breakfast and lunch operation of Tautog's Restaurant at Winston's Cottage (see below), with which it shares owners and a parking lot. It's really a charming version of a diner, with a kitchen with counter seating in the old living room. The choice seats are on the enclosed porch. Breakfast provides the usual grilled items plus toasted bagels and my favorite, the "Deep South," with diced country ham and eggs over cheese grits. You can wash it down with an excellent and inexpensive bloody Mary. Look for a space in the parking lot in the rear (take the alley btw. here and Tautog's; see below).

207 23rd St. (btw. Atlantic and Pacific aves.). ⓒ **757/425-1960.** www.doctaylors.com. Reservations not accepted. Breakfast $5–$11; lunch $5–$8.50. AE, DISC, MC, V. Daily 7am–3pm.

La Bella Italia Cafe & Trattoria 🍴 ITALIAN   This restaurant and deli is an excellent place to pick up sandwiches or Italian breads, pastries, and cookies for a day at the beach. After dark, you had best reserve a table, for a mesquite-fired oven produces the area's best thin-crust pizzas, and locals flock here for bowls of homemade pasta. You'll recognize a few southern Italian favorites such as spaghetti Bolognese, but others are more creative. For starters, try the bruschetta, fried calamari, or in summer when the tomatoes are ripe and sweet, the *caprese* salad with homemade mozzarella. Check the specials board for today's fresh catch.

In Laskin Center, 1065 Laskin Rd. (1 block east of Birdneck Rd.). ⓒ **757/422-8536.** www.labella italia.com. Reservations highly recommended for dinner. Main courses $17–$23; pizza $13–$15. AE, DISC, MC, V. Restaurant Mon–Sat 11:30am–10pm, Sun 4–10pm. Deli Mon–Sat 9am–10pm, Sun 2–8pm.

Rudee's on the Inlet SEAFOOD/STEAKS   This popular restaurant, occupying a replica of an old Coast Guard station, is dark and cozy on the inside, with big louvered windows overlooking Rudee Inlet. But that's not where you want to dine in good weather. Instead, walk across the parking lot to the marina-side sun deck and grab one of the gliding booths (that's right: you, the booth, and its green canopy actually slide back and forth). They serve a full menu out here. The deck is one of the most popular after-work watering holes for the locals. Although steaks and other fare are offered, seafood is the highlight. Everything is prepared to order, so kick back and enjoy the waterside setting while the chef fries or broils your fish, shrimp, scallops, above-average crab cakes, or oysters (best when they are being harvested during months spelled with an "r": Sept–Apr). Many fresh-off-the-boat items are market price. Valet parking is available.

277 Mediterranean Ave. (at Rudee Inlet). © **757/425-1777.** www.rudees.com. Reservations not accepted, but call ahead for preferred seating. Sandwiches $9–$15; main courses $16–$30. AE, DC, DISC, MC, V. Mon–Sat 11am–10pm; Sun 9am–10pm. Bar open later depending on business.

Tautog's Restaurant at Winston's Cottage ★★ 🐟 SEAFOOD Occupying one of the few remaining Victorian-era beach cottages still standing in the heart of the resort area, this is the most charming restaurant here and one of the most popular with locals, many of whom ride their bikes here in summer to avoid the beach's parking nightmare. You can dine inside, but opt instead for a table under ceiling fans out on the front porch. Seafood predominates, with Wesley's World-Famous Crab Cakes leading the list. Another winner is the flounder with crab-and-shrimp filling poached in parchment. It's all very good value. Look for a space in the parking lot in the rear (take the alley btw. here and Doc Taylor's).

205 23rd St. (btw. Atlantic and Pacific aves.). © **757/422-0081.** www.tautogs.com. Reservations recommended. Sandwiches $8–$10; main courses $14–$20. AE, DISC, MC, V. Sun–Wed 5:30–11:30pm; Thurs–Sat 5:30pm–1:30am.

Waterman's Surfside Grille 🐟 SEAFOOD Many hotels have dining rooms beside the Boardwalk here, but this big coastal-style building is the last stand-alone, family-owned restaurant right on the beach. Surfers started the business as a hot dog stand in the 1960s, although the present full-service restaurant—now a certified city landmark—dates to 1982, with a thorough renovation in 2006. Traditional Chesapeake-style seafood stars here and all of it is fresh, not frozen. I think the crab cakes are the best on the oceanfront, and you can order one of them as a money-saving sandwich. During summer you can wander into the beachside patio without a reservation. Given the higher prices you pay for inferior quality elsewhere, the value for the money is good here.

415 Atlantic Ave. (at 5th St.). ©**757/428-3644.** www.watermans.com. Reservations recommended. Sandwiches and burgers $8–$14; main courses $15–$24. AE, DISC, MC, V. Daily 11am–11pm. Bar open later.

Virginia Beach After Dark

The visitor center can tell you what's on, or go to **www.beachstreetusa.com**, the city's official entertainment site where you can buy tickets for most events.

As in Norfolk, *Veer Magazine* (www.veermag.com), and the "Daily Break" section in the local rag, the *Virginian-Pilot* (www.pilotonline.com), are good sources of entertainment information.

The prime performing arts venue is the 20,000-seat, open-air **Farm Bureau Live at Virginia Beach,** inland at Princess Anne and Dam Neck roads (© **877/686-5366;** www.virginiabeachamphitheatre.net). Big-name singers and bands appear here as well as more highbrow acts like the Virginia Symphony. About 7,500 seats are under cover, with some 12,500 spaces out on the lawn. Big TV screens and a state-of-the-art sound system let everyone see and hear what's going on. The season runs April to October.

Famous entertainers appear all year at the **Sandler Center for the Performing Arts,** 201 Market St. (© **757/385-2787;** www.sandlercenter.org), in the Town Center of Virginia Beach, off I-64 at Independence and Virginia Beach boulevards.

During summer, there is nightly entertainment in **Neptune Park,** on the oceanfront at 30th Street, and frequent outdoor concerts on stages at 7th, 17th, and 24th streets along the Boardwalk (the visitor information center can tell you when and where). The biggest is the annual **Verizon Wireless American Music Festival** (℃ **757/425-3111**) over Labor Day weekend on the beach at 5th Street. You might catch KC & the Sunshine Band on one stage, the Steve Miller Band on another.

Hotels and restaurants all along the beach have live music for nighttime dancing during the summer. Just follow your ears along the Boardwalk. Bear in mind that some pubs along Atlantic Avenue can get rough late at night; in fact, from time to time the city imposes curfews to prevent rowdiness on weekends.

CHINCOTEAGUE & ASSATEAGUE ISLANDS ★★★

83 miles N of Virginia Beach and Norfolk; 185 miles SE of Washington, D.C.

Beside the Atlantic Ocean in Virginia's northeastern corner, **Chincoteague Island** and its uninhabited neighbor, **Assateague Island,** are unique. Surrounded by bays and marshes, Chincoteague was a remote fishing community until Marguerite Henry's children's book, *Misty of Chincoteague,* made famous the **wild horses** which graze on both islands. While condos have replaced all but one of its waterside bars, Chincoteague retains much of its scruffy fishing-village charm. Except for busy summer weekends, watermen in work boats still outnumber tourists on jet skis.

Beaches   Most of the shoreline here comes under the aegis of **Assateague Island National Seashore,** which prevents any development on the island and keeps 37 miles of beach—14 of them in Virginia, 23 in Maryland—in their pristine, all-natural condition. You will see lots of sand, surf, and sea oats but not a single hotel or condo as you laze away your days on Assateague's long, remarkably undisturbed beach.

Things to Do   Playing on Assateague's beach is only one of many things to do. Nature lovers should take **wildlife tours** both on land and in the shallow bays and marshes surrounding Chincoteague. You're almost guaranteed to see the wild horses including Misty herself, now preserved at the **Museum of Chincoteague Island.** Children will enjoy **pony rides,** and everyone will enjoy **biking** around the flat islands. The winding waterways through the marshes are great for **kayaking and canoeing.**

Eating & Drinking   You won't find fine dining here but you will be served **seafood** fresh from the boat and prepared in traditional Chesapeake Bay styles. From the beds in surrounding shallow bays come the famous **Chincoteague oysters,** harvested September to March. **Blue crabs** are trapped during the summer months, steamed with Old Bay spice, turned into **crab cakes,** or consumed in their soft shell state. Every menu features **flounder** year-round and often **tuna** caught offshore by local watermen.

Nature   Both islands are heaven for nature lovers. In addition to the famed herds of wild horses, **Chincoteague National Wildlife Refuge** is on the main Atlantic Flyway for migratory waterfowl, and its population of both migratory and resident birds is simply astounding. Indeed, it's one of the top places in Virginia to bird watch. You may see dolphins frolicking offshore and in the backwaters, and a whale may swim by during winter.

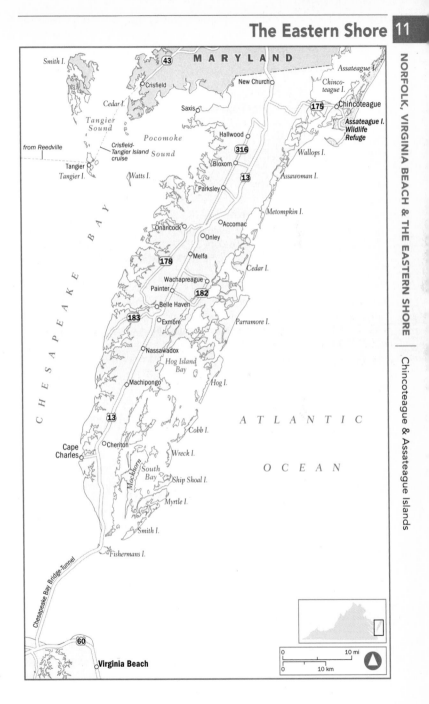

Be sure to stop and take in the view from the restaurant, gift shop, and tourist information kiosk on the southernmost of the four man-made islands making up the 18-mile-long **Chesapeake Bay Bridge-Tunnel** (www.cbbt.com), on U.S. 13. One of Virginia's most scenic drives, it's like crossing the ocean on wheels. Water completely surrounds you: to the east, the Atlantic Ocean; to the west, the Chesapeake Bay. Because of the earth's curvature, you cannot see land from one side to the other. The toll is $12 per car.

Essentials

VISITOR INFORMATION

The **Chincoteague Chamber of Commerce,** 6733 Maddox Blvd., Chincoteague Island, VA 23336 (Ⓒ **757/336-6161;** fax 757/336-1242; www.chincoteaguechamber. com), operates a visitor center in the traffic circle on Maddox Blvd. It is open Monday to Saturday 9am to 4:30pm.

For general information, contact **Virginia's Eastern Shore Tourism Commission,** PO Box 72, Tasley, VA 23441 (Ⓒ **757/787-8268;** www.esvatourism.org).

The Virginia Tourism Corporation (see "Visitor Information" under "Fast Facts: Virginia," in chapter 12) operates a **Virginia Welcome Center** (Ⓒ **757/824-5000**) on U.S. 13 just south of the Maryland state line.

GETTING THERE

There are no airports or public transportation on the Eastern Shore, so you'll need a **car.** From Norfolk and Virginia Beach, U.S. 13 runs north-south down the center of the Eastern Shore. To reach Chincoteague, turn east on Va. 175, about 65 miles north of the Chesapeake Bay and 5 miles south of the Maryland line.

AREA LAYOUT

Va. 175 crosses several miles of salt marshes and the Chincoteague Channel before crossing a curving bridge onto the island at the intersection of **Main Street,** which runs north-south along the western shore, and **Maddox Boulevard,** which heads east to Assateague Island. Maddox Boulevard is Chincoteague's prime commercial strip, with an abundance of shops, restaurants, and motels. Turn right at the stoplight to reach the motels, marinas, and bait shops along Main Street south of the bridge. **Church Street** goes east 2 blocks from the village and turns into **East Side Drive,** which runs along the island's Eastern shore. **Ridge Road** and **Chicken City Road** (yes, it's really named Chicken City) together run north-south down the middle of the island. On Assateague, there's only one road other than a wildlife drive, and it goes directly to the beach.

GETTING AROUND

These flat islands are great for biking. Although there are no bike paths per se on Chincoteague, there are lanes set aside on some of the streets, particularly Maddox Boulevard as it approaches the Assateague Bridge. Bikes are allowed on the trails and paths on Assateague, so you can ride all the way to the beach. Several shops on Maddox Boulevard rent bikes of various sizes. Closest to Assateague are **Bike Depot & Beach Outfitters,** at the Refuge Inn (Ⓒ **757/336-5511;** p. 313), and **Spoke**

The famous **wild ponies**—they're actually small horses—have lived on Assateague Island since the 1600s. Legend says their ancestors swam ashore from a shipwrecked Spanish galleon bound for the gold mines of Peru, but most likely English settlers put the first horses on Assateague, which was a natural corral. A diet of sea oats wasn't enough to sustain large animals, so only pony-size horses thrived and survived. They are a bit larger these days since regular horses have been introduced to improve the gene pool.

Misty, the most famous of the ponies, was born in 1946 not wild but at the **Beebe Ranch,** 3062 Ridge Rd. (© **757/ 336-6520;** http://beeberanch.vpweb. com). Author Marguerite Henry visited the island that year, met Misty as a foal, and made her the star of her children's book, *Misty of Chincoteague.* Henry later purchased Misty, took her to Illinois, and brought her back to Chincoteague in 1957 to give birth to her three foals, Phantom Wings, Wisp O'Mist, and Stormy. More than 100 of Misty's descendants are traced through Stormy. Misty died in 1972; Stormy in 1993. Both are "artfully preserved" at the **Museum of Chincoteague Island** (p. 311), where they are on loan while Beebe Ranch's owner serves in Afghanistan.

The Chincoteague Volunteer Fire Department rounds up the horses on the Virginia end of Assateague, swims them across the channel to Chincoteague, and sells the foals at auction during its famous 3-day **Pony Penning and Carnival** that begins on the last Wednesday in July. Make your hotel reservations well in advance of this extremely popular event.

You can't bring a child here without letting him or her ride a pony at the **Chincoteague Pony Centre,** 6417 Carriage Dr. (© **757/336-2776;** www. chincoteague.com/ponycentre), off Chicken City Road south of Maddox Blvd. This museum, gift shop, and equestrian center is open daily 9am to 10pm from Memorial Day weekend through Labor Day, with pony rides ($6) 9am to 1pm and 4 to 8pm, and a pony show at 8pm. It's open spring and fall Friday to Saturday 9am to 6pm, with the pony show Saturday at 8pm. Admission is $10 for adults and $5 for children. The center also has 30-minute riding lessons for anyone who weighs less than 150 pounds ($40) and a three-morning "pony camp" ($100). You can buy a pony, perhaps one of Misty's descendants.

Learn more about the horses and the book from the **Misty of Chincoteague Foundation** (www.mistyofchincoteague. org).

Depot, at the Best Western Plus Chincoteague Island (© **757/336-6557;** p. 312). Rates at both are $3 an hour and $14 a day.

Another easy way to get around during summer is on the **Pony Express Trolley** (© **757/336-6519**), which circles Chincoteague Island every 30 minutes Sunday to Thursday 5 to 11pm and Friday to Saturday 5pm to midnight. The fare is 25¢ per ride, exact change required. The trolley also has summertime narrated **tours** of Chincoteague, usually on Tuesday and Thursday at 2:45 and 3:45pm, but call ahead for a current schedule. Tickets go on sale the same day for these first-come, first-served tours, which depart from the Chincoteague Community Center, 6155 Community Dr., off Deep Hole near Maddox Boulevard. Fares are $3 for adults and $2 for children ages 12 and under. Get a route map and a schedule at www.chincoteague chamber.com.

11 Assateague Island ★★★

The American people own all of Assateague Island, which is completely occupied by the **Chincoteague National Wildlife Refuge** and the **Assateague Island National Seashore,** and thus jointly administered by the U.S. Fish and Wildlife Service and the U.S. National Park Service. Of the island's 37 miles, 14 are in Virginia. Wildlife in Virginia is afforded a higher degree of protection than in Maryland, where public access is less restricted. In fact, a fence at the state line keeps Maryland's wild horses and other critters away from the Virginia side.

Bird-watchers know Assateague Island as a prime Atlantic Flyway habitat where sightings of peregrine falcons, snow geese, great blue herons, and snowy egrets have been made. The annual Waterfowl Week, generally held around Thanksgiving, takes place when a large number of migratory birds use the refuge.

THE WILDLIFE REFUGE

You first enter the **Chincoteague National Wildlife Refuge,** which is open May through September daily 5am to 10pm, April and October daily 6am to 8pm, and November through March daily 6am to 6pm. The refuge accepts InterAgency entrance passes; otherwise, admission is $8 per vehicle for 1 day, $15 per vehicle for 1 week, and free for pedestrians and bikers.

Unless you're here exclusively for the beach, start your visit at the refuge's **Herbert H. Bateman Education and Administrative Center** (✆ **757/336-3696**), on the left, ¼-mile east of the bridge, where you can watch a video about the refuge and its wildlife. It has wildlife and birding programs, which are great for kids. The center is open daily 9am to 5pm from May through September and to 4pm in the off season (closed New Year's Day and Christmas).

You may see some of the wild ponies while driving to the beach, but the best place to see them—your chance is greatest at dawn—is on the paved **Wildlife Drive,** which runs for 3¼ miles through the marshes. This one-lane, one-way road is open to pedestrians and bicyclists all day, to motorized vehicles after 3pm. The **Woodland Trail,** a 1.6-mile hiking loop, is another good place to spot wild ponies in the marshes. But be advised: This area is infested with mosquitoes, so bring and use insect repellent.

The most informative way to see the multitudinous wildlife is on a **Wildlife Tour** (✆ **757/336-3696**) in an air-conditioned bus. The 1¼-hour narrated rides depart the visitor center at 10am and 4pm daily Memorial Day weekend through Labor Day, and on weekends in March, April, September, and October. The tour costs $12 for adults and $6 for children 12 and under. Buy your tickets at the visitor center.

If your heart's up to it, you can climb the 198 steps for a terrific view from atop **Assateague Island Lighthouse,** built in 1867 to warn ships of the shoals offshore. It is open to the public from 9am to 3pm Thursday through Monday from mid-June through September and on weekends from mid-April to mid-June and in October and November. Admission is $5 for adults and $3 for children 12 and under.

For **information** about the refuge and visitor-center seasons and programs, contact the Refuge Manager, Chincoteague National Wildlife Refuge, PO Box 62, Chincoteague Island, VA 23336 (✆ **757/336-6122;** www.fws.gov/northeast/chinco).

THE NATIONAL SEASHORE

The beach itself is in the **Assateague Island National Seashore,** operated by the National Park Service. You'll find a visitor center, bathhouses, and summertime lifeguards. In addition to swimming and sunning, activities at the beach include shell collecting (most productive at the tip of the Tom's Cove spit of land, on the island's

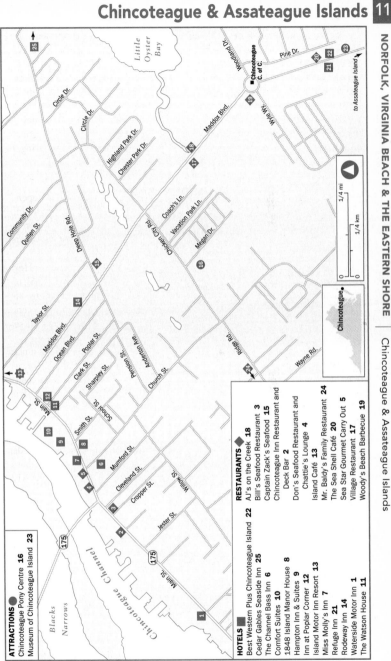

ATTRACTIONS ●
Chincoteague Pony Centre **16**
Museum of Chincoteague Island **23**

HOTELS ■
Best Western Plus Chincoteague Island **22**
Cedar Gables Seaside Inn **25**
The Channel Bass Inn **6**
Comfort Suites **10**
1848 Island Manor House **8**
Hampton Inn & Suites **9**
Inn at Poplar Corner **12**
Island Motor Inn Resort **13**
Miss Molly's Inn **7**
Refuge Inn **21**
Rodeway Inn **14**
Waterside Motor Inn **1**
The Watson House **11**

RESTAURANTS ◆
AJ's on the Creek **18**
Bill's Seafood Restaurant **3**
Captain Zack's Seafood **15**
Chincoteague Inn Restaurant and
    Deck Bar **2**
Don's Seafood Restaurant and
    Chattie's Lounge **4**
Island Café **13**
Mr. Baldy's Family Restaurant **24**
The Sea Shell Café **20**
Sea Star Gourmet Carry Out **5**
Village Restaurant **17**
Woody's Beach Barbecue **19**

I grew up in coastal North Carolina and thus am accustomed to fighting off my share of mosquitoes, but Chincoteague, Assateague, and Tangier islands set a new standard for slapping, itching, and scratching. The Chincoteague mosquitoes seem more prone to make meals of my blood at dawn and dusk, but the Assateague variety is not nearly so finicky. Neither are the biting horse flies on Assateague, which don't care what time of day they attack. Consequently, I go nowhere here—including the beach—before applying ample insect repellent.

southern tip) and hiking. You can ride a bike here from Chincoteague on the paved bike path beside the main road (or make a detour along Wildlife Dr.) to the **Tom's Cove Visitor Center,** which has a splendid view over the marshes. Rangers give programs such as wildlife viewing, aquarium talks, nighttime hikes, and campfires. The seashore is open daily 6am to 8pm March through April, 5am to 10pm May through September, 6am to 8pm in October, and 6am to 6pm November and December. The visitor center is open daily 9am to 5pm in summer and 9am to 4pm in the off season. Both are closed Thanksgiving and Christmas.

Several **regulations** apply. Pets and alcoholic beverages are prohibited, even in your vehicle. In-line skating is not allowed, nor are off-road vehicles. Surf fishing with a Virginia state license is allowed except on the lifeguard beach at Tom's Cove. Climbing and digging in the sand dunes is illegal. No overnight sleeping is allowed anywhere (backcountry camping is permitted on the Maryland end, a 12½-mile hike from the Virginia-side visitor centers). And finally, thou shalt not feed the horses.

For **information** about the national seashore, contact the Superintendent, Assateague Island National Seashore, 8586 Beach Rd. (PO Box 38), Chincoteague Island, VA 23336 (© **757/336-6577;** www.nps.gov/asis).

Outdoor Activities

CRUISES While most visitors head for the beach on Assateague, don't overlook the broad bays and creeks that surround Chincoteague. A good way to get out on them is with **Captain Barry's Back Bay Cruises ★★** (© **757/336-6508;** www.captain barry.net). Barry Frishman moved from New York to Chincoteague and set about learning everything he could about the water and what's in it. Now he shares his knowledge by taking guests out on his pontoon boat for 1½-hour early-morning bird-watching expeditions ($25 per person); 2-hour morning and afternoon "Sea Life Expeditions" ($35 for adults, $30 for children 10 and under); a 4-hour morning "Coastal Encounter" in search of crabs, fish, shells, and clams ($50 for adults, $45 for children 10 and under); and champagne sunset cruises ($40 per person). Call for Barry's schedule and reservations, which are required.

FISHING Before it became a tourist mecca, Chincoteague was a fishing and oystering village for centuries—and it still is. Both work and pleasure boats prowl the back bays and ocean for flounder, croaker, spot, kingfish, drum, striped bass, bluefish, and sharks, to name a few species.

You can get to it yourself, either from a rented boat or by throwing your line from a dock. For charter boats, equipment, supplies, free tide tables, and advice, check in at **Barnacle Bill's Bait & Tackle** (© **757/336-5188**) or **Capt. Bob's** (© **757/336-6654**), both on South Main Street.

Plan to look around **Onancock** (www.onancock.com), a creekside town about 20 miles south of Chincoteague. Dating to 1680, genteel Onancock has always made its living from farming and trading rather than fishing, and even today its immaculate lawns, gourmet market, boutiques, and art galleries stand in marked contrast to Chincoteague's fishing-town image.

From U.S. 13 at Onley, take Va. 179 west through town to the docks and **Hopkins & Bro. General Store,** 2 Market St., built in 1842 and now home to **Mallards at the Wharf** (✆ 757/787-8558; www.mallardsllc.com), guitar-picking chef Johnny "Mo" Morrison's worthy restaurant with water-view tables in warm weather (daily 11:30am–9pm). Brochures and other visitor information are on the wall in the store.

Also worth a peek is **Ker Place,** 69 Market St. (Va. 179), a stately Federal mansion built about 1800 and now home to the Eastern Shore of Virginia Historical Society (✆ 757/787-8012; www.kerplace.org). Admission is $5 for adults and $2 for children. It's open March to December, Tuesday to Saturday 11am to 4pm.

The best place to stay is the **Charlotte Hotel & Restaurant,** 7 North St. (www.thecharlottehotel.com; ✆ 757/787-7400), which has eight rooms upstairs over a very good restaurant serving breakfast and dinner.

Bed-and-breakfasts include **Spinning Wheel B&B,** 51 North St. (www.1890spinningwheel.com; ✆ 888/787-7311) and the **Inn at Onancock,** 30 North St. (www.innatonancock.com; ✆ 757/789-7711).

At night take in a drama or musical at the **North Street Playhouse** (✆ 866/703-7262 or 757/787-2050; www.northstreetplayhouse.com).

KAYAKING The winding waterways surrounding Chincoteague are great for kayaking, although you must be aware of the tidal currents which can rip through the narrow passages. **Assateague Explorer** (✆ 866/766-9794 or 757/336-5956; www.assateagueisland.com) rents kayaks and has guided tours on the marshes off Assateague Island. Tours cost $55 for a half-day and $95 for a full day. **SouthEast Expeditions** (✆ 757/525-2925 or 757/331-2680; www.southeastexpeditions.net), offers instruction and a wide range of guided paddling trips both here and at Onancock (see "A Side Trip to Onancock," below). Reservations are essential at both.

Museums

The large airstrip you pass on the way to Chincoteague on Va. 175 is part of NASA's **Wallops Flight Facility,** a research and testing center for rockets, balloons, and aircraft. The facility also tracks NASA's spacecraft and satellites. Across the highway is the **NASA Visitor Center** (✆ 757/824-2298; http://sites.wff.nasa.gov/VC), one of the best places to park the kids on a rainy day. They will get kicks out of seeing a practice spacesuit from *Apollo 9* and watching videos—mysteriously projected onto a sphere—about the moon and the planets. Admission is free. The visitor center is open July 4th through Labor Day daily 10am to 4pm, March to June and September to November Thursday to Monday 10am to 4pm, and December to February Monday to Friday 10am to 4pm. The center is 5 miles west of Chincoteague.

The **Museum of Chincoteague Island,** 7125 Maddox Blvd. (✆ 757/336-6117; www.chincoteaguemuseum.com), explains the area's people, culture, heritage, and especially the role played by the vital seafood industry from the 1600s to the present. You may see the "artfully preserved" Misty of Chincoteague and her foal, Stormy, here if they haven't returned to their regular home, the Beebe Ranch (see *"Misty of Chincoteague,"* above). One highlight is the original lens from the Assateague Lighthouse, which mariners could see 23 miles offshore from 1865 to 1961. The museum is open Memorial Day through Labor Day Tuesday to Sunday 11am to 5pm and spring and fall Friday to Sunday 11am to 5pm. Admission is $3 per person.

Where to Stay

My friends and I used to rent a cottage when we came to Chincoteague, as it was more economical than a hotel for four or more of us, and we liked having our own kitchen and room to roam around. Among several companies handling cottage rentals are **Chincoteague Resort Realty,** 6378A Church St., Chincoteague Island, VA 23336 (**☎ 800/668-7836** or 757/336-3100; www.chincoteagueresort.com), and **Chincoteague Vacation Rentals,** 7038 Maddox Blvd., Chincoteague Island, Virginia 23336 (**☎ 757/336-1236**).

Most of Chincoteague's accommodations are small, family-run motels and bed-and-breakfasts—including the Best Western Plus Chincoteague Island (see below).

The island's modern, built-to-order chain motels are the **Comfort Suites,** 4195 Main St. (**☎ 800/228-5150** or 757/336-3700; fax 757/336-5452), and the **Hampton Inn & Suites,** 4179 Main St. (www.chincoteaguecomfortsuites.com; **☎ 800/426-7866** or 757/336-1616). They stand next to each other beside Chincoteague Channel in town. Both have heated indoor pools but neither has a restaurant. The budget priced **Rodeway Inn,** 6273 Maddox Blvd. (www.rodewsayinn.com; **☎ 877/291-9816** or 757/336-6565), has an outdoor pool surrounded by its parking lot.

As with any summertime beach destination, you will pay the highest rates from mid-June through Labor Day weekend in September, with spikes on July 4th and during the last week in July for the annual pony penning. Consequently, the lowest rates given below are for winter, highest are for the peak summer season. Spring and fall are somewhere in between. Be sure to reserve as early as possible for the pony penning.

Best Western Plus Chincoteague Island   Between the traffic circle and the bridge to Assateague Island, this motel and the Refuge Inn (see below) are Chincoteague's closest accommodations to the wildlife refuge and national seashore. Entered from the rear, the guest rooms in the gray, three-story, shingle-look building all have balconies facing the road (those on the third floor overlook the marshes). Most contain two double beds, tables and chairs, and full tiled bathrooms. The two suites have two bedrooms, one or two bathrooms, whirlpool tubs, and kitchenettes. Owners Scot and Lisa Chesson make this seem more like a family-operated hotel than a national chain.

7105 Maddox Blvd. (PO Box 575), Chincoteague Island, VA 23336. www.bestwestern.com/chincoteagueisland. **☎** **800/553-6117** or 757/336-6557. Fax 757/336-6558. 52 units. $70–$250 double. Rates include full breakfast. AE, DC, DISC, MC, V. From the bridge, turn left on Main St., right on Maddox Blvd. **Amenities:** Bikes. *In room:* A/C, TV, fridge, hair dryer, kitchen (in suites), Wi-Fi.

Island Motor Inn Resort ★★   The best-equipped motel here, this inn sits on Chincoteague Channel just north of the business district, giving its spacious rooms great views across the bay to the mainland. Reception is in a three-story building whose rooms are better appointed than the standard units in the older, two- and three-story motel blocks adjoining. Rooms on the ends of this new building have bay windows, giving them two-way views. Many units have balconies facing the bay, which sets this motel apart from the Comfort Inn and the Hampton Inn & Suites. On the water side of the property, you'll find a 600-foot-long boardwalk and boat

As I said in chapter 5 (p. 101), remote Tangier Island, 14 miles out in the Chesapeake Bay, is one of my favorite places to escape from civilization. The scenic way to get there is via **Tangier-Onancock Ferry** (📞 **757/891-2505;** www.tangierferry.com), which departs Onancock Tuesday to Sunday at 10am from mid-May through October. About half the 90-minute voyage is spent on the winding, picturesque creek between Onancock and the Chesapeake Bay. The vessel is not actually a ferry, but a 36-foot fiberglass lobster boat, the *Joyce Marie II*, which can carry up to 25 passengers. The return trip departs Tangier at 3:30pm, giving you about 2 hours on the island. Round-trip fare is $25 for adults, $12 for children 6 to 11, and $5 for kids 5 and under. It's first-come,

first-served but I would call in advance to be sure it's operating.

Larger boats depart from Crisfield, Maryland, a fishing town about 25 miles north of Chincoteague. **Tangier Island Cruises** (📞 **800/979-3370** or 410/968-2338; www.tangierislandcruises.com) leaves at 12:30pm daily May 15 to October 15. The return voyages depart Tangier at 4pm. Round-trip same-day fare is $25 for adults and $12 for children 7 to 12. Add $10 per adult if you stay overnight. Fares are the same on the **Courtney Thomas** (📞 **757/891-2240**), also known as "The Mail Boat" because it hauls the U.S. mail. It leaves Tangier at 8am and returns from Crisfield at 12:30pm Monday to Saturday year-round. Try to buy tickets in advance.

dock, a covered barbecue area with hammock for lounging, an outdoor pool, a glass-enclosed indoor pool, and a fitness center (with a trainer on duty year-round). On the road side, owners Reggie and Anna Stubbs have built a landscaped garden with lily ponds and benches for relaxing. The **Island Cafe** only serves breakfast, but it's exceptionally good. The minisuites are reserved for adults only.

4391 N. Main St., Chincoteague Island, VA 23336. www.islandmotorinn.com. 📞 **757/336-3141.** Fax 757/336-1483. 60 units. $78–$195 double. AE, DISC, MC, V. From the bridge, turn left on Main St. to motel on left. **Amenities:** Restaurant (breakfast only); health club; Jacuzzi; pool; room service. *In room:* A/C, TV, fridge, hair dryer, Wi-Fi.

Refuge Inn ★★ ☺ This charming motel is, like the Best Western Plus Chincoteague Island across the street (see above), as close to Assateague Island as you can stay. You can see the ponies here, too, for several live in a small corral on the grounds. Some rooms have country inn–style Colonial pieces. First-floor rooms facing the back have sliding doors to private patios where guests can use outdoor grills. One of the two suites is a one-bedroom apartment with a fully equipped kitchen, a screened porch across the front, a bathroom with whirlpool tub, and a spiral staircase leading to a sleeping loft (the unit can sleep up to six). The suites are rented on a weekly basis in summer. Other facilities include an observation sun deck on the roof, an enclosed pool and whirlpool, and a children's playground. Guests are treated to a continental breakfast with hot waffles.

7058 Maddox Blvd., Chincoteague Island, VA 23336. www.refugeinn.com. 📞 **888/868-6400** or 757/336-5511. Fax 757/336-6134. 72 units. $89–$190 double; $179–$320 suite. AE, DC, DISC, MC, V. **Amenities:** Bikes; children's playground; Jacuzzi; pool. *In room:* A/C, TV, fridge, hair dryer, kitchen (in suites), Wi-Fi.

Chincoteague and Assateague are but two of Virginia's 23 barrier islands, those long slivers of sand separating the Atlantic Ocean from the bays, backwaters, and marshes along the eastern seaboard. A map of the Peninsula may lead you to think that innumerable beaches wait to be explored out there. Yes, there are beaches on the islands, but most of them are privately owned or preserved in their natural state by the government, the Nature Conservancy, and other organizations, which keep them off-limits to members of the general public. People once lived on the islands, and rich and famous folk like President Grover Cleveland came out to hunt and fish. But no more.

The former residents and their water-oriented lifestyle are fondly remembered at the **Barrier Islands Center ★★**, on U.S. 13 just north of Machipongo (✆ **757/678-5550;** www.barrierisland scenter.com). That's 20 miles north of the Chesapeake Bay Bridge-Tunnel, about 55 miles south of Chincoteague. The white-clapboard building looks like a farmhouse standing in the fields beside the highway, but in fact it was built by Northampton County as the Almshouse Farm at Machipongo—a place for poor people to live, in other words. The barrier island residents and their descendants donated the many artifacts on display. Admission is free, with donations encouraged. Open Tuesday to Saturday 10am to 4pm and Sunday 1 to 5pm, it's worth a brief stop.

You can cruise through the narrow channels and take a walk on a deserted barrier island beach with Capt. Buddy Vaughn of **Eastern Shore Adventures** (✆ **757/615-2598;** www.easternshore adventures.com), whose wife, Laura Vaughn, is director of the Barrier Islands Center. Call Buddy well in advance to make arrangements.

Waterside Motor Inn ★ All the accommodations at Tommy and Donna Mason's three-story motel feature private wooden balconies overlooking Chincoteague Channel, guaranteeing some breathtaking sunset views, especially on the end units directly facing the water. (They're worth requesting.) Shingle-look siding gives the property a Victorian appearance. The spacious units are decorated in comfortable contemporary style, and some have a king- or queen-size bed and a pullout sofa bed. Four suites in a nearby Victorian house have two bedrooms and kitchens. The Waterside has an outdoor pool with a deck and its own fishing and crabbing pier. The complimentary continental breakfast includes made-to-order waffles.

3761 Main St. (PO Box 347), Chincoteague Island, VA 23336. www.watersidemotorinn.com. ✆ **877/ 870-3434** or 757/336-3434. Fax 757/336-1878. 49 units. $82–$210 double. Rates include breakfast. AE, DC, DISC, MC, V. At the bridge entering Chincoteague, turn right; the motel is on the right, about ½ mile from the bridge. **Amenities:** Health club; Jacuzzi; pool; tennis court. *In room:* A/C, TV, fridge, hair dryer, Wi-Fi.

BED & BREAKFASTS

Chincoteague has several bed-and-breakfasts, including **Cedar Gables Seaside Inn,** 6905 Hopkins Lane (www.cedargable.com; ✆ **888/491-2944** or 757/336-1096), with a screened outdoor swimming pool and a master suite with climb-up cupola rendering a 360-degree view of the marshes north of town.

In the village are the **Inn at Poplar Corner,** 4248 Main St. (www.innatpoplar corner.com; ✆ 877/336-6111 or 757/336-6115), where I'm especially fond of the Main View room and its balcony overlooking Main Street and Chincoteague Channel; **1848**

Island Manor House, 4160 Main St. (www.islandmanor.com; ℂ 800/852-1505 or 757/336-5436), which consists of two houses joined by a charming guest lounge; the Watson House, 4240 Main St. (www.watsonhouse.com; ℂ 800/336-6787 or 757/336-1564); the Channel Bass Inn, 6228 Church St. (www.channelbassinn.com; ℂ 800/249-0818 or 757/336-6148); and Miss Molly's Inn, 4141 Main St. (www.missmollys-inn.com; ℂ 800/221-5620 or 757/336-6686), where Marguerite Henry stayed.

Where to Eat

You won't find fine dining here but you will be served seafood fresh from the boat. The famous Chincoteague oysters are harvested September to March. The area is also known for flounder, caught year-round. Most Chincoteague restaurants, however, are seasonal operations and close from October until Easter weekend the following spring. It's best to call ahead during the cold months.

Open year-round in town are the venerable Bill's Seafood Restaurant, 4040 Main St. (ℂ 757/336-5831; www.billsseafoodrestaurant.com), which is a bit more formal than Don's Seafood Restaurant and Chattie's Lounge, 4113 Main St. (ℂ 747/336-5715; www.donsseafood.com), which has live or DJ music on weekend nights.

Although it's primarily a fish market, Captain Zack's Seafood, 4422 Deep Hole Rd. (ℂ 757/336-3788), also turns fresh fish, shrimp, clams, and oysters into sandwiches and platters, and it will cook your choices from the chiller.

Under pine trees at the circle on Maddox Blvd., Woody's Beach Barbecue (ℂ 757/336-5531; www.woodysbeachbbq.com) is not so much restaurant as an outdoor beach party, albeit not at the beach. Two shacks and a large smoker provide barbecued pork and chicken to be eaten at outdoor tables. Finish with the old-fashioned banana pudding. Woody's cooks from Memorial Day to Labor Day.

AJ's on the Creek ★ SEAFOOD/STEAKS   The island's most romantic restaurant, AJ's offers dining either on a screened-in patio beside a narrow creek or inside, where candles and dried-flower arrangements adorn a mix of tables and booths. Most romantic is table no. 20 in a private corner; it's worth a wait. The menu offers a mix of Italian-style pastas—Chincoteague oysters in a champagne cream sauce is a house specialty—and traditional dishes such as fried or steamed shrimp and oysters, plus chargrilled steaks. A popular local hangout, the friendly bar offers TVs and its own snack menu (with money-saving half sizes of regular menu main courses). It has live music on weekends.

6585 Maddox Blvd. ℂ 757/336-5888. www.ajsonthecreek.com. Reservations recommended, especially for table no. 20. Main courses $16–$29. AE, MC, V. Summer Mon–Sat 11:30am–9pm (lounge until 1am); winter Mon–Sat 11:30am–2pm and 5–9pm.

Chincoteague Inn Restaurant and Deck Bar SEAFOOD   Sitting beside the channel, the Chincoteague Inn has been a mainstay here for generations, offering traditional preparations and fine water views from big window walls. The delicately seasoned crab cakes with large lumps of back fin meat are the best meal here. But the fun part of this establishment is outside at the rustic and funky deck bar beside Chincoteague Channel. I hang out here because it's the only place in town to sip a cold drink while watching the sun set over the marshes and mainland. The all-day bar menu features burgers, crab cake sandwiches, soft-shell crabs, steamed or raw oysters and clams on the half shell, and shrimp and crab salads. It can be noisy out here on summer weekend nights when bands make music for dancing.

6262 Marlin St. (off Main St., south of village). ℂ 757/336-6110. Reservations not accepted. Sandwiches and salads $6–$10; main courses $16–$28. DISC, MC, V. March to mid-Dec, deck bar daily 11am–10pm, dining room daily 4–9pm. Closed mid-Dec to Feb.

The best breakfast place in town is the **Island Cafe,** a cottage in front of the Island Motor Inn, 4391 Main St. (© **757/336-3141**). The front porch is ideal for enjoying eggs Benedict, lox and bagels, croissants, whole grain cereal, or the chef's specialty, French toast laced with Grand Marnier, Amaretto, and Bailey's Irish Cream (terrific when combined with a fresh fruit plate). Prices range from $6 to $12. It is open daily 6:30am to noon April to October and 6:30 to 11am November to March.

Mr. Baldy's Family Restaurant 🍴 SEAFOOD   This lively family-style restaurant serves a variety of fare, most of it made from fresh ingredients. The day begins with traditional breakfasts and moves on to a variety of salads and sandwiches, including soft-shell crabs and very good crab cakes made the traditional Chesapeake way with back fin meat and a touch of Old Bay seasoning. Main courses also include soft shells and crab cakes plus oysters, shrimp, flounder, steaks, and a few pastas. All in all, it's a very good value. No alcoholic beverages are served.

3441 Ridge Rd. (in middle of the island). © **757/336-1198.** Reservations not accepted. Breakfast $4–$7; sandwiches and salads $5–$9; main courses $7–$28. MC, V. Sun–Thurs 5:30am–9pm, Fri–Sat 5:30am–10pm.

The Sea Shell Cafe AMERICAN/MEDITERREAN   When I've had my fill of traditional Chesapeake Bay seafood preparations at other restaurants, I head here for chef Jonathan Stone's mandarin orange chicken salad, steamed clams Bordelaise, *osso bucco* (with pork shank instead of lamb), and cioppino, a seafood stew from Portugal and Italy. I'm impressed with his coleslaw, made with a light ginger sauce instead of mayonnaise; it was much more like a French cabbage salad.

7085 Maddox Blvd. © **757/336-6005.** www.theseashellcafe.com. Reservations recommended in summer. Sandwiches $8–$10; main courses $15–$23. AE, DISC, MC, V. Daily 11:30am–9pm.

Sea Star Gourmet Carry Out ★ 🍴 LIGHT FARE   I've never had fresher or tastier food on Chincoteague than the tabbouleh wrap I devoured at a picnic table at this little takeaway, in a parking lot on Main Street. There are no indoor tables; in fact, the tiny building has just enough room for the two cooks to work their magic without bumping into each other. Written on a board nailed to the outside wall, the menu depends on what those cooks found at the market or farms over on the mainland. Whatever sandwiches or salads they offer, they will be crispy and very good. Vegetarians and vegans will have their taste buds tingled here, too.

4121 Main St. © **757/336-5442.** Reservations not accepted. Most items $6–$7.50. No credit cards. Memorial Day to Labor Day Mon–Sat 11am–6pm; Mid-Mar to day before Memorial Day and day after Labor Day to Nov Thurs–Mon 11am–6pm. Closed Dec to mid-Mar.

Village Restaurant SEAFOOD   Across Maddox Boulevard from AJ's on the Creek, the gardenlike Village Restaurant enjoys a fine view over a creek and a marsh. The specialties are traditionally prepared seafood such as fried or broiled oysters, flounder, and shrimp. The house seafood platter is piled with fish filet, shrimp, scallops, oysters, clams, and lobster tail. Nonseafood main dishes include veal or chicken Parmesan, fried chicken, and filet mignon.

6576 Maddox Blvd. © **757/336-5120.** Reservations recommended. Main courses $13–$30. AE, DISC, MC, V. Apr–Oct daily 5–9pm; Nov–Mar Thurs–Sun 5–9pm.

PLANNING YOUR TRIP TO VIRGINIA

Whether you plan to spend a day, a week, 2 weeks, or longer in Virginia, you will need to make many "where," "when," and "how" choices before you leave home. This chapter provides basic trip-planning information as well as insider advice based on years of traveling in the Old Dominion.

The travel industry in Virginia is highly developed and modern, and overall the state is adept at welcoming visitors. As we say, there are no "snakes in the bushes" waiting to bite you, meaning you should encounter few unforeseen difficulties if you have carefully planned your trip.

GETTING THERE

By Plane

The major international gateway to Virginia is **Washington Dulles International Airport** in Chantilly, Virginia (IAD; ☎ **703/661-2700;** www.mwaa.com), 26 miles west of Washington, D.C. Dulles is also a regional hub for domestic flights, and fares can be less to fly in and out of here than other airports in Virginia.

Also serving Virginia is **Ronald Reagan Washington National Airport** in Arlington (DCA; ☎ **703/685-8000;** www.mwaa.com). It is located alongside the Potomac River 2 miles north of Alexandria.

Most major domestic and international airlines service Dulles and Reagan. See the destination chapters for details about Virginia's other airports:

- **Charlottesville Albemarle Airport** (CHO; ☎ 804/973-8341; www.gocho.com).
- **Newport News/Williamsburg International Airport** (PHF; ☎ 757/877-0221; www.nnwairport.com).
- **Norfolk International Airport** (ORF; ☎ 757/857-3351; www.norfolkairport.com).
- **Richmond International Airport** (RIC; ☎ 804/226-3000; www.flyrichmond.com).
- **Roanoke Regional Airport** (ROA; ☎ 540/362-1999; www.roanokeairport.com).
- **Shenandoah Valley Regional Airport** (SHD; ☎ 540/234-8304; www.flyshd.com).

Many flights to these regional airports are of the "commuter" variety, and you likely will pay higher fares to fly into them than into Dulles.

By Car

Interstate highway **I-95** runs north-south through Virginia between Alexandria and Emporia. From western Maryland and eastern Tennessee, the major highway is **I-81,** which runs north-south the entire length of the state through the Shenandoah Valley and Southwest Highlands.

Major western entrance points are from West Virginia via **I-77** and **I-64.** The latter runs east-west across the state between Covington and Norfolk. In northern Virginia, **I-66** traverses the state east-west between Arlington and I-81 at Strasburg. I-66 can slow to a snail's pace during rush hour in northern Virginia.

For information on car rentals and gasoline (petrol), see "Getting Around," below.

By Train

Amtrak (© **800/872-7245;** www.amtrak.com) has train service to Alexandria, Fredericksburg, Richmond, Williamsburg, Newport News, Charlottesville, Lynchburg, Staunton, and Clifton Forge. Amtrak's bus service connects Newport News to Norfolk, and Lynchburg to Roanoke.

The high-speed Acela, Metroliner service, and other northeast corridor trains connect New York to Union Station in Washington, D.C., from where the Metrorail subway runs to Alexandria. See "Getting There," under "Alexandria" in chapter 4.

Amtrak offers multiride and multicity tickets as well as the **USA Rail Pass,** good for 15, 30, or 45 days of unlimited travel on **Amtrak.** The pass is available online and through many overseas travel agents. See Amtrak's website for schedules and prices. Reservations are generally required and should be made as early as possible.

GETTING AROUND

By Car

Traveling in your own vehicle is by far the best way to see Virginia. Interstate highways link all the major cities and many towns (see "Getting There," above), but the prime advantage of driving is that you can explore on your own and drive our scenic routes. Many key attractions are in rural areas and not easily visited without your own wheels.

Maximum speed limits are 70 mph on the interstate highways (less in congested areas), 55 mph on state highways, and 35 mph or less in towns and cities.

Accidents are common on both I-95 and I-81, which are heavy-duty truck routes, so be especially careful on them. (So many trucks slow down as they creep side

---

Driving the Civil War Trails

One benefit of touring by car is that you can follow the state's Civil War Trails. These sign-posted driving tours follow the Shenandoah battles, the Peninsula Campaign of 1862, the battles from Manassas to Fredericksburg, Lee versus Grant as the Union marched south to Richmond in 1864, and Lee's retreat from Petersburg to Appomattox in 1865. Check out **www.civilwartrails.org**.

This book doesn't have enough pages to cover all of Virginia's picturesque hamlets, villages, and towns. Don't hesitate to park your car and look around when a charmer catches your attention. My fellow Virginians will ensure that you are richly rewarded.

by side uphill and then race down the other side that it's hard to use cruise control on I-81.)

The Virginia Tourism Corporation (see "Visitor Information" under "Fast Facts: Virginia," below) distributes a detailed **state road map** as well as one that highlights the scenic drives.

The **Virginia Department of Transportation (VDOT),** 1401 E. Broad St., Richmond, VA 23219 (© **804/786-5731;** www.virginiadot.org), publishes a free list of road construction projects, and it maintains a 24-hour **Highway Helpline** (© **800/367-7623**), which you can use to get information about road conditions and to report emergencies. It has live webcams of key northern Virginia and Hampton Roads highways and posts road condition maps online.

Tune your car radio to AM 610 or call © **800/792-2800** to check on conditions in Hampton Roads' often-congested tunnels.

Dial © **#77** on your cellphone to report an accident or other emergency to the state highway patrol.

CAR RENTALS All major rental car companies have agencies at the state's airports. **Enterprise (www.enterprise.com)** also is present in many small towns.

Visitors from abroad who plan to rent a car in the United States should keep in mind that insurance and taxes are almost never included in quoted rental car rates in the U.S. Be sure to ask your rental agency about additional fees for these. They can add a significant cost to your car rental. Most agencies rent only to persons age 25 and older.

Foreign driver's licenses are usually recognized in the U.S., but you may want to consider obtaining an international driver's license, especially if your home license is not written in English.

GASOLINE Petrol is known as gasoline (or simply "gas"), and petrol stations are known as both gas stations and service stations. Like elsewhere in the world, gasoline prices have fluctuated widely in the United States in the past few years. It was around $3.50 a gallon in Virginia at press time. Whatever the price here, it still costs about half as much in the U.S. as it does in Europe. Taxes are already included in the printed price. One U.S. gallon equals 3.8 liters or .85 imperial gallons. All but a few stations have self-service gas pumps.

AUTOMOBILE CLUBS Motor clubs will supply maps, suggested routes, guidebooks, accident and bail-bond insurance, and emergency road service. The **American Automobile Association (AAA)** is the major auto club in the United States. If you belong to a motor club in your home country, inquire about AAA reciprocity before you leave. You may be able to join AAA even if you're not a member of a reciprocal club; to inquire, contact AAA (© **800/222-4357;** www.aaa.com). AAA has a nationwide emergency road service telephone number (© 800/AAA-HELP [222-4357]).

By Plane

You can get around Virginia by flying from one of its airports to another (see "Getting There," above), but you are likely to change planes along the way. For example, you may have to fly through Washington Dulles International Airport, Ronald Reagan Washington National Airport, or Charlotte, North Carolina, to get from Roanoke to Richmond. As a result, flying around the state can be more time-consuming than driving, and more expensive, too. Check with the airlines or your travel agent for the most-efficient, cost-effective routing.

Some large airlines offer transatlantic or transpacific passengers special discount tickets under the name **Visit USA,** which allows mostly one-way travel from one U.S. destination to another at very low prices. Unavailable in the U.S., these discount tickets must be purchased abroad in conjunction with your international fare. This system is the easiest, fastest, and cheapest way to see the country.

By Train

Amtrak trains (© **800/872-7245;** www.amtrak.com) are better for getting to and from Virginia than for getting around the state. All Amtrak trains between New York and Florida stop at Washington, D.C., and Richmond; some stop at Alexandria and Fredericksburg. Another train follows this route from New York to Richmond, and then heads east to Newport News via Williamsburg. From Newport News, Amtrak's Thruway bus service connects to Norfolk and Virginia Beach. Some east- and west-bound trains to and from D.C. stop at Charlottesville, Lynchburg, Staunton, and Clifton Forge. From Lynchburg, a Thruway bus connects to Roanoke via Bedford.

See "Getting There," above, for information about Amtrak's USA Rail Pass.

By Bus

Greyhound (© **800/231-2222;** www.greyhound.com) is the sole nationwide bus line. While you can travel from one major Virginia city to another by bus, service is not available to many small towns, including those in the Shenandoah Valley. Taking the bus may be the least expensive way to travel around Virginia, but it also is the least convenient and the least comfortable.

International visitors who insist on traveling by bus may wish to consider getting the **Greyhound North American Discovery Pass.** The pass, which offers unlimited travel and stopovers in the U.S. and Canada, can be obtained from foreign travel agents or on **www.discoverypass.com**.

TIPS ON ACCOMMODATIONS

Virginia has a vast array of accommodations, from rock-bottom roadside motels to some of the nation's finest resorts. Every national chain is present here in all price categories. So whether you spend a pittance or a bundle depends on your budget and tastes. You can enjoy "champagne tastes on a beer budget"—if you plan carefully and possess a little knowledge of how the hotel industry works.

The Virginia Tourism Corporation publishes a directory of all the state's lodgings (see "Visitor Information" under "Fast Facts: Virginia" later in this chapter).

Bed & Breakfasts

Virginia is home to more than 200 bed-and-breakfasts, and so this book covers only the standouts. Most of them are excellent properties adorned with antiques or quality reproductions, luxurious touches like fresh flowers and top-drawer linens and toiletries, and near-gourmet breakfasts. Some even have whirlpool tubs in their bathrooms. All these niceties come with a price, so most bed-and-breakfasts aren't inexpensive. Nor are they for everyone, since you'll be sharing a home with strangers—with whom you might have to make small talk over breakfast. On the other hand, you don't have to go out for breakfast, and the hosts are usually fonts of current local information. In fact, B&B owners initially recommended many of the restaurants reviewed in this book.

With a few exceptions, the recommended properties in this guide are members of the **Bed & Breakfast Association of Virginia (BBAV; ℂ 888/660-2228** or 540/672-6700; www.innvirginia.com). The BBAV inspects and approves the establishments it promotes, so you are unlikely to stay in a dump. Membership also indicates that the owners are serious about their business and are not operating a B&B merely to take advantage of tax breaks. BBAV publishes an annual directory of its members and lists them on its website.

Most local visitor centers include bed-and-breakfasts on their websites. Regional associations with useful websites include those listed below.

- **Alexandria & Arlington Bed & Breakfast Networks** (www.aabbn.com; ℂ **888/549-3415** or 703/549-3415)
- The Hunt Country's **Loudoun County Bed & Breakfast Guild** (www.loudoun bandb.com; ℂ **866/771-2597**)
- Charlottesville's **Guesthouses Reservation Services** (www.va-guesthouses. com; ℂ **434/979-7264**)
- **Bed and Breakfasts of the Historic Shenandoah Valley** (www.bbhsv.org; no phone)
- **Williamsburg Bed & Breakfast Network** (www.bandbwilliamsburg.com; no phone)

[Fast FACTS] VIRGINIA

Area Codes   Virginia has several area codes. The **703** and **571** codes are both in northern Virginia and eastern Hunt Country, where you must dial both the area code and the local number even when calling locally. The **540** code runs from Fredericksburg west to Winchester and south to Roanoke. The **804** code is in Richmond, Petersburg, and the Northern Neck. The **757** code covers Williamsburg, Hampton Roads, and Eastern Shore. The **434** code is in Charlottesville. And the **276** code is in Southwest Highlands.

Business Hours   Offices are usually open weekdays 9am to 5pm. Banks are open weekdays 9am to 3pm or later and sometimes Saturday mornings. Stores typically open between 9 and 10am and close between 5 and 6pm Monday through Saturday. Stores in shopping malls tend to stay open late on these days—until about 9pm—and many malls and large department stores are open until 6pm on Sunday.

Car Rental   See "Getting Around," above.

Cellphones   See "Mobile Phones," below.

Crime   See "Safety," later in this section.

Customs   Every visitor 21 years of age or older may bring in, free of duty, the following: (1) 1 liter of wine or hard liquor; (2) 200 cigarettes, 100 cigars (but not from Cuba), or 3 pounds of smoking tobacco; and (3) $100 worth of gifts. These exemptions are offered to travelers who spend at least 72 hours in the United States and who have not claimed them within the preceding 6 months. It is forbidden to bring into the country almost any meat products (including canned, fresh, and dried meat products, such as bouillon, soup mixes, and so forth). Generally, condiments, including vinegars, oils, and spices; coffee; tea; and some cheeses and baked goods are permitted. Avoid rice products, as rice can often harbor insects. Bringing fruits and vegetables is not advised, though not prohibited. Customs will allow produce depending on where you got it and where you're going after you arrive in the U.S. International visitors may carry in or out up to $10,000 in U.S. or foreign currency with no formalities; larger sums must be declared to U.S. Customs upon entering or leaving, which includes filing form CM 4790. For details regarding U.S. Customs and Border Protection, consult your nearest U.S. embassy or consulate, or **U.S. Customs** (www.customs.gov).

For details on what you can take home, contact one of the following agencies:

Canadian Citizens: Canada Border Services Agency at © **800/461-9999** in Canada, or 204/983-3500, or go to www.cbsa-asfc.gc.ca.

U.K. Citizens: HM Revenue & Customs at © **0845/010-9000** or 020/8929-0152 from outside the U.K., or consult the website at **www.hmce.gov.uk**.

Australian Citizens: Australian Customs Service at © **1300/363-263,** or log on to **www.customs.gov.au**.

New Zealand Citizens: New Zealand Customs (© **04/473-6099** or 0800/428-786; www.customs.govt.nz).

Doctors See "Health," below.

Drinking Laws The legal age for purchasing and consuming alcoholic beverages is 21; proof of age is required and often requested at bars, nightclubs, and restaurants, so carry ID when you go out. In Virginia, many grocery and convenience stores sell beer and wine, but only state-licensed Alcoholic Beverage Control (ABC) stores sell bottles of hard liquor. All but a few localities allow licensed establishments (restaurants or bars) to sell drinks by the glass. Bars must close by 2am. Do not carry open containers of alcohol in your car or any public area that isn't zoned for alcohol consumption. The police can fine you on the spot. And nothing will ruin your trip faster than getting a citation for DUI ("driving under the influence"), so don't even think about driving while intoxicated.

Driving Rules See "Getting Around," above.

Electricity Like Canada, the United States uses 110 to 120 volts AC (60 cycles), compared to 220 to 240 volts AC (50 cycles) in most of Europe, Australia, and New Zealand. Downward converters that change 220 to 240 volts to 110 to 120 volts are difficult to find in the United States, so bring one with you.

Embassies & Consulates All embassies are located in Washington, D.C. Some consulates are located in major U.S. cities, and most nations have a mission to the United Nations in New York City. If your country isn't listed below, call for directory information in Washington, D.C. (© **202/555-1212**) or check **www.embassy.org/embassies**.

Australia: 1601 Massachusetts Ave. NW, Washington, DC 20036 (© **202/797-3000;** www.usa.embassy.gov.au).

Canada: 501 Pennsylvania Ave. NW, Washington, DC 20001 (© **202/682-1740;** www.canadianembassy.org). Other Canadian consulates are in Buffalo, Detroit, Los Angeles, New York City, and Seattle.

Ireland: 2234 Massachusetts Ave. NW, Washington, DC 20008 (© **202/462-3939;** www.embassyofireland.org). Irish consulates are in Boston, Chicago, New York City, San Francisco, and other cities. See the website for a complete listing.

New Zealand: 37 Observatory Circle NW, Washington, DC 20008 (© **202/328-4800;** www.nzembassy.com). New Zealand consulates are in Los Angeles, Salt Lake City, San Francisco, and Seattle.

United Kingdom: 3100 Massachusetts Ave. NW, Washington, DC 20008 (© **202/588-7800;** http://ukinusa.fco.gov.uk). Other British consulates are in Atlanta, Boston, Chicago, Cleveland, Houston, Los Angeles, New York City, San Francisco, and Seattle.

FAMILY TRAVEL—VIRGINIA IS FOR KIDS, TOO

Virginia will bring history to life for your kids (and you, too) with a myriad of associations involving America's first heroes—Washington, Jefferson, Madison, Monroe, and Patrick Henry among them. Walking through old houses can bring on a case of the fidgets, but children are likely to be entertained by the living history demonstrations at **Jamestown Settlement, Yorktown Victory Center,** and the **Frontier Culture Museum** at Staunton.

Theme parks offer thrills and chills, not to mention food, fun, and entertainment, at **Kings Dominion, Busch Gardens Williamsburg,** and **Water Country USA.**

Virginia's family favorite is the **Virginia Aquarium & Marine Science Center** in Virginia Beach, where computers, exhibits, touch tanks, and the museum's waterside setting help people of all ages understand the marine environment. Nearby in Norfolk, the **NAUTICUS** has interactive and "virtual adventures," featuring make-believe U.S. Navy ships. Across the harbor in Hampton, kids can see spaceships and watch IMAX movies at the **Virginia Air & Space Center.** They also will get a kick out of the **Steven F. Udvar-Hazy Center** in the Hunt Country of northern Virginia, where the National Air and Space Museum displays 200 planes, 135 spacecraft, and the spaceship model that starred in *Close Encounters of the Third Kind.*

Roanoke's **Virginia Museum of Transportation** has a playground full of railroad cars. Richmond's **Children's Museum** and the **Science Museum of Virginia** offer activities and "touch me" exhibits.

It's not a museum, but after reading the story of *Misty of Chincoteague,* kids will adore a chance to ride a pony and see the action themselves at the **wild ponies' swim across Assateague Channel.**

Emergencies   Dial © **911** to report a fire, call the police, or get an ambulance anywhere in the United States. This is a toll-free call (no coins are required at public telephones). Dial © **#77** on your cellphone to reach the state highway patrol.

Gasoline (Petrol)   See "Getting Around," earlier in this chapter.

Health   Malaria may have been a curse for the colonists who settled Virginia in the 17th century, but today the state poses no unusual health threats.

Although Virginia mosquitoes don't carry malaria, they are still rampant in the Tidewater in summer, especially in the marshes around Chincoteague, Assateague, and Tangier islands, so use plenty of insect repellent on the Eastern Shore.

Hospitals and emergency care facilities are widespread in Virginia, so unless you're deep in the backcountry, help is close at hand. See "Emergencies," above.

In case of illness, consider asking your hotel concierge or staff to recommend a local doctor—even his or her own. Most Virginia cities and towns have hospitals, and you can try their emergency rooms for assistance. Many have walk-in clinics for cases that are not life threatening. You may not get immediate attention, but you won't pay the high price of an emergency room visit (about $300 just for signing your name).

If you have a chronic illness, consult your doctor before your departure. Pack **prescription medications** in your carry-on luggage, and carry them in their original containers, with pharmacy labels—or they won't make it through airport security. Visitors from outside the U.S. should carry generic names of prescription drugs.

Insurance   For U.S. travelers, most reliable health-insurance plans provide coverage if you get sick away from home. Unlike many European countries, however, the United States does not usually offer free or low-cost medical care to its citizens or visitors. Doctors and hospitals are expensive, and in most cases will require advance payment or proof of insurance before they render their services. Foreign visitors may have to pay all medical costs upfront and be reimbursed later. Accordingly, you should consider buying travel insurance. Good policies will cover the costs of an accident, repatriation, or death.

Packages such as **Europ Assistance's "Worldwide Healthcare Plan"** are sold by European automobile clubs and travel agencies at attractive rates. **Worldwide Assistance Services, Inc. (© 800/777-8710;** www.worldwideassistance.com) is the agent for Europ Assistance in the United States.

Canadians should check with their provincial health plan offices or call **Health Canada** (© **866/225-0709;** www.hc-sc.gc.ca) to find out the extent of their coverage and what documentation and receipts they must take home in case they are treated in the United States.

Internet & Wi-Fi   Most **public libraries** offer Internet access for free or for a small charge. **Hotel business centers** have access too, but often charge exorbitant rates.

To find cybercafes in your destination, check **www.cybercafe.com**. Most major airports have **Internet kiosks** that provide basic Web access for a per-minute fee that's usually higher than cybercafe prices. Check out copy shops like **FedEx Office** which offers computer stations with fully loaded software (as well as Wi-Fi).

I remember when hotels competed by equipping their rooms with hair dryers and coffeemakers, which are pretty much de rigueur today. Now they try to one-up each other by providing high-speed Internet access for their guests' laptops. In fact, most hotels and motels in Virginia, regardless of price, offer Wi-Fi, and some also have high-speed dataport connections for laptops, the latter using an Ethernet network cable (bring one). The service is free at most hotels and B&Bs, but others—especially large chains such as Marriott and Hilton—charge about $10 a night.

Many airports, cafes, and especially coffee shops are Wi-Fi hot spots, offering free or low-cost high-speed access. Wi-Fi is even found in some campgrounds, RV parks, and entire neighborhoods, such as King Street in Old Town Alexandria. To find public Wi-Fi hot spots, go to **www.jiwire.com**; its Global Wi-Fi Finder holds the world's largest directory of public wireless hot spots.

If you have Web access while traveling, broadband-based telephone services (in technical terms, **Voice-over Internet Protocol,** or **VoIP**), such as **Skype** (www.skype.com) or **Vonage** (www.vonage.com) allow you to make free international calls if you use their services from your laptop or in a cybercafe, and the person you're calling also uses the service. Skype also has a "Skype Out," which lets you make calls from your computer to land lines for a small per-minute fee (depending on which country you are calling into, not the country you are calling from). Calling mobile phones is more expensive. Check the sites for details.

Language   English is the common language in the U.S., but millions of Spanish-speaking immigrants from South and Central America have settled in Virginia.

Legal Aid   If you are "pulled over" for a minor infraction (such as speeding), never attempt to pay the fine directly to a police officer; this could be construed as attempted bribery, a much more serious crime. Pay fines by mail, or directly into the hands of the clerk of the court. If accused of a more serious offense, say and do nothing before consulting a lawyer. Here the burden is on the state to prove a person's guilt beyond a reasonable doubt, and everyone has the right to remain silent, whether suspected of a crime or actually arrested. Once arrested, a person can make one telephone call to a party of his or her choice. International visitors should call their embassy or consulate.

LGBT Travelers Virginia has its intolerant contingent, particularly in rural areas, and the conservative Republicans in our state legislature are not about to legalize gay marriage. (Although seldom enforced, fornication is still technically a crime in Virginia regardless of gender.) But by and large, the state is a safe, comfortable place for gay and lesbian travelers. There are gay and lesbian communities in most cities here.

Mail Domestic postage rates are 32¢ for a postcard and 45¢ for a letter. For international mail, a first-class letter of up to 1 ounce costs 98¢ (85¢ to Canada and Mexico); a first-class postcard costs the same as a letter. For more information go to **www.usps.com**.

If you aren't sure what your address will be in the United States, mail can be sent to you, in your name, c/o General Delivery at the main post office of the city or region where you expect to be. (Call ✆ **800/275-8777** for information on the nearest post office.) The addressee must pick up mail in person and produce proof of identity (driver's license, passport). Most post offices will hold your mail for up to 1 month, and are open Monday to Friday from 8am to 6pm, and Saturday from 9am to 3pm.

Always include a zip code when mailing items in the U.S. If you don't know the zip code for the destination address, visit www.usps.com/zip4.

Medical Requirements Unless you're arriving from an area known to be suffering from an epidemic (particularly cholera or yellow fever), inoculations or vaccinations are not required for entry into the United States.

Mobile Phones Just because your mobile phone works at home doesn't mean it'll work everywhere in Virginia, thanks to our nation's fragmented cellphone system. One of my phones using GSM (Global System for Mobiles), which is used by much of the rest of the world, can go dead out in the country, while my CDMA (Code Division Multiple Access) model works perfectly well. It's a good bet that your phone will work in major cities whatever system it uses, and you will have near-statewide coverage with Verizon Wireless, which uses CDMA. On the other hand, the GSM-based AT&T, T-Mobile, and Sprint can be weak or disappear altogether in rural areas. Take a look at your wireless company's coverage map on its website before heading out.

Also ask how much it charges for roaming calls. It may be much less expensive to buy a prepaid "throwaway" mobile, such as from **Tracfone** (www.tracfone.com) or its subsidiary **Net10** (www.net10.com). You can order from the websites in advance, or pick up a Tracfone and a prepaid card at national drugstore chains, such as CVS and Rite Aid, or at the ubiquitous Dollar General outlets (rare is the Virginia town that doesn't have a cheapo Dollar General). Walmart, Target, Kmart, and Safeway are Tracfone and Net10 retailers.

Tracfone models cost as little as $10, with prepaid cards beginning at $20 for 60 minutes of nationwide airtime good for 60 days. Net10 phones start at $30 and include 300 minutes of nationwide airtime good for 60 days. Neither charges extra for domestic long distance.

Money & Costs Virginia is not a particularly expensive destination, and is much less costly than London, New York, and other major metropolitan areas. It is most expensive in its larger cities and in the Washington, D.C., suburbs of northern Virginia. It's also hard to find bargains at the beach in the summer or in the Shenandoah during the October "leaf season." While there are plenty of high-end restaurants, luxury hotels, and bed-and-breakfasts, smaller independent hotels and motels abound, as well as multitudinous representatives of all the major budget chains. It's possible to eat and stay well in Virginia without spending a fortune, and should you decide to splurge, you can find a lot of luxury for your money.

THE VALUE OF THE U.S. DOLLAR VS. OTHER POPULAR CURRENCIES

US$	A$	C$	€	NZ$	£
1.00	1.00	1.00	0.78	1.25	0.63

WHAT THINGS COST IN VIRGINIA	US$
Taxi from the airport to Old Town Alexandria	15.00
Double room, moderate	120.00
Double room, inexpensive	90.00
Three-course dinner for one without wine, moderate	15.00–25.00
Bottle of beer	2.50
Cup of coffee	1.50
1 gallon/1 liter of premium gas	3.50/0.92
Admission to most museums	10.00
Admission to most national parks	10.00

However much you plan to spend, it's always advisable to bring money in a variety of forms on a vacation: a mix of cash, credit cards, and traveler's checks. If you are an international visitor, you should also exchange enough petty cash to cover airport incidentals, tipping, and transportation to your hotel before you leave home, or withdraw money upon arrival at an airport ATM (automated teller machine, sometimes referred to as a "cash machine" or "cashpoint").

In fact, the easiest and best way to get cash in Virginia is from an ATM. The **Cirrus** (© **800/424-7787;** www.mastercard.com) and **PLUS** (© **800/843-7587;** www.visa.com) networks span the country; you can find them even in remote regions. Go to your bank card's website to find ATM locations at your destination. Be sure you know your daily withdrawal limit before you depart.

Don't forget your personal identification number (PIN) since all ATMs in Virginia require them to withdraw cash. American cards use **4-digit PINs,** so check with your bank before leaving home if yours is longer.

Credit cards are the most widely used form of payment in the United States: The most commonly accepted are **Visa** (Barclaycard in Britain), **MasterCard** (EuroCard in Europe), **American Express, Diners Club,** and **Discover.** They also provide a convenient record of all your expenses, and offer relatively good exchange rates. You can withdraw cash advances using your credit cards at banks or ATMs, but high fees make these advances a pricey way to get cash.

Note: Beware of hidden credit-card fees while traveling. Check with your credit or debit card issuer to see what fees, if any, will be charged for overseas transactions. Recent reform legislation in the U.S., for example, has curbed some exploitative lending practices. But many banks have responded by increasing fees in other areas, including fees for customers who use credit and debit cards while out of the country—even if those charges were made in U.S. dollars. Fees can amount to 3% or more of the purchase price. Check with your bank before departing to avoid surprise charges.

For help with currency conversions, tip calculations, and more, download Frommer's convenient Travel Tools app for your mobile device. Go to www.frommers.com/go/mobile and click on the Travel Tools icon.

Though credit cards and debit cards are more often used, **traveler's checks** are still widely accepted in the U.S. Foreign visitors should make sure that traveler's checks are in U.S. dollars; foreign-currency checks are difficult to exchange.

You can buy traveler's checks at most banks. Most are offered in denominations of $20, $50, $100, $500, and sometimes $1,000. Generally, you'll pay a service charge ranging from 1% to 4%.

The most popular traveler's checks are offered by **American Express** (📞 **800/807-6233** or 800/221-7282 for cardholders; www.americanexpress.com); **Visa** (📞 **800/732-1322;** www.visa.com), and **MasterCard** (📞 **800/223-9920;** www.mastercard.com).

Keep a copy of the traveler's checks serial numbers separate from your checks in case they are stolen or lost. You'll get a refund faster if you know the numbers.

Newspapers & Magazines Each major city in Virginia has its own daily newspaper. The *Richmond Times-Dispatch* (www.timesdispatch.com), the *Roanoke Times* (www. roanoke.com), and the Norfolk *Virginian-Pilot* (www.pilotonline.com) are the largest. The *Washington Post* (www.washingtonpost.com) and *USA Today* (www.usatoday.com) are sold at newsstands and coin boxes throughout the state.

Passports Virtually every air traveler entering the U.S. is required to show a passport. All persons, including U.S. citizens, traveling by air between the United States and Canada, Mexico, Central and South America, the Caribbean, and Bermuda are required to present a valid passport. *Note:* U.S. and Canadian citizens entering the U.S. at land and sea ports of entry from within the Western Hemisphere must now also present a passport or other documents compliant with the Western Hemisphere Travel Initiative (WHTI; see www.get youhome.gov for details). Children 15 and under may enter with only a U.S. birth certificate, or other proof of U.S. citizenship.

Australia: Australian Passport Information Service (📞 131-232; www.passports.gov.au).

Canada: Passport Office, Department of Foreign Affairs and International Trade, Ottawa, ON K1A 0G3 (📞 800/567-6868; www.ppt.gc.ca).

Ireland: Passport Office, Setanta Centre, Molesworth Street, Dublin 2 (📞 01/671-1633; www.foreignaffairs.gov.ie).

New Zealand: Passports Office, Department of Internal Affairs, 47 Boulcott St., Wellington, 6011 (📞 0800/225-050 in New Zealand or 04/474-8100; www.passports.govt.nz).

United Kingdom: Visit your nearest passport office, major post office, or travel agency or contact the Identity and Passport Service (IPS), 89 Eccleston Sq., London, SW1V 1PN (📞 0300/222-0000; www.ips.gov.uk).

United States: To find your regional passport office, check the U.S. State Department website (www.travel.state.gov/passport) or call the National Passport Information Center (📞 877/487-2778) for automated information.

See "Embassies & Consulates," earlier in this chapter, for whom to contact if you lose your passport while traveling in the U.S.

Petrol See "Getting Around by Car," earlier in this chapter.

Police To reach the police in an emergency, dial 📞 **911** from any phone (free).

Safety Most areas of Virginia are relatively free of street crime, but it's still a good idea to use caution in some parts of Alexandria, Richmond, Norfolk, Roanoke, and other cities. Ask your hotel staff or the local visitor information office whether neighborhoods you intend to visit are safe. Avoid deserted streets and alleys, and always be especially alert at night. Never leave anything of value visible in your parked car; it's an invitation to theft.

When heading outdoors, keep in mind that injuries often occur when people fail to follow instructions. Believe the experts who tell you to stay on the established trails. Hike in designated areas, follow the marine charts if piloting your own boat, carry rain gear, and wear a life jacket when boating, canoeing or rafting. Watch for summer thunderstorms that can leave you drenched, send bolts of lightning your way, and suddenly flood peaceful streams. Mountain weather can be fickle any season.

Senior Travelers Mention the fact that you're a senior when you make your reservations. All major airlines, car-rental firms, and most Virginia hotels offer discounts for seniors, especially members of **AARP,** 601 E St. NW, Washington, DC 20049 (📞 **800/424-3410** or 202/434-2277; www.aarp.org). AARP offers members a wide range of benefits, including *AARP The Magazine* and a monthly newsletter. Anyone age 50 or over can join.

The **Interagency Senior Pass** (formerly known as the Golden Age Passport, which is still honored) gives American citizens and permanent residents 62 years or older—and passengers in their noncommercial vehicle or up to three additional adults where per person fees apply—free admission to national parks, monuments, and historic sites, plus national recreation areas and wildlife refuges. The pass costs a one-time fee of $10 ($20 if purchased by mail), lasts for a lifetime, and must be purchased by mail (applications are available from the NPS website; see below) or in person at any national park, recreation area, or wildlife refuge that charges an entrance fee (there are several of them in Virginia, so it can result in big savings). Besides free entry, it also offers a 50% discount on some federal-use fees such as those charged for camping, swimming, parking, boat launching, and tours—but not on fees charged by concessionaires. For more information, go to www.nps.gov/fees_passes.htm or call ☏ **888/467-2757.**

Student Travelers   If you are a student, it's worthwhile to bring along your valid high school or college ID, since many museums and other Virginia attractions have discounted admissions for students.

For comprehensive travel services information and details on how to get an **International Student Identity Card (ISIC),** which qualifies students for substantial savings on rail passes, plane tickets, entrance fees, and more, check out the website of the **International Student Travel Confederation** (www.aboutistc.org). It also offers basic health and life insurance and a 24-hour help line. The card is valid for a maximum of 18 months.

Smoking   Virginia has come a long way since the days when tobacco was the backbone of its economy, and its legislators steadfastly refused to enact antismoking laws. It is now illegal to smoke in public buildings in Virginia, and in restaurants and bars unless there is a smoking room with its own ventilation system. As is true throughout the U.S., you must be at least 18 years old to purchase tobacco products.

Taxes   The Virginia state sales tax is 5% for most purchases plus 2% on hotel rooms. Local hotel taxes vary; in most communities it's 5%, which makes the total tax on your hotel bill at least 12%. Most local jurisdictions also add a restaurant tax, which jacks up the price of food and drink by 10% or more.

The United States has no value-added tax (VAT) or other indirect tax at the national level. Each state, county, and city may levy its own local tax on all purchases, including hotel and restaurant checks and airline tickets. These taxes do not appear on price tags.

Telephones   Hotel surcharges on long-distance and local calls can be astronomical, so you're better off using your **mobile phone** or a **public pay telephone.**

If you don't have a cellphone, you can buy **prepaid calling cards** in denominations up to $50 at many convenience groceries and packaging services. For international visitors these can be the least expensive way to call home. Many public pay phones at airports and elsewhere now accept American Express, MasterCard, and Visa credit cards. However you pay, **local calls** made from pay phones in Virginia cost 35¢ (no pennies, please).

Most long-distance and international calls can be dialed directly from any phone.

For calls within the United States and to Canada, dial 1 followed by the area code and the seven-digit number.

For other international calls, dial 011 followed by the country code, the city code, and the number you are calling.

Calls to area codes **800, 888, 877,** and **866** are toll free. However, calls to area codes **700** and **900** (chat lines, bulletin boards, "dating" services, and so on) can be very expensive—usually a charge of 95¢ to $3 or more per minute, and they sometimes have minimum charges that can run as high as $15 or more.

For **reversed-charge or collect calls,** and for person-to-person calls, dial the number 0 and then the area code and the number; an operator will come on the line, and you should specify whether you are calling collect, person to person, or both. If your operator-assisted call is international, ask for the overseas operator.

For **local directory assistance** ("information"), dial 411; for long-distance information, dial 1, then the appropriate area code and 555-1212.

Time   The continental United States is divided into **four time zones:** Eastern Standard Time (EST), Central Standard Time (CST), Mountain Standard Time (MST), and Pacific Standard Time (PST). Alaska and Hawaii have their own zones.

Virginia is on Eastern Standard Time, the same as New York City and other East Coast cities. For example, when it's noon in Richmond, it's 11am in Chicago (CST), 10am in Denver (MST), 9am in Los Angeles (PST), 7am in Honolulu (Honolulu Standard Time), 5pm in London (Greenwich Mean Time), and 4am the next day in Sydney (Eastern Daylight Time).

Daylight saving time is in effect from 1am on the second Sunday in March to 1am on the first Sunday in November, except in Arizona, Hawaii, the U.S. Virgin Islands, Puerto Rico, and several islands in the Pacific. Daylight saving time moves the clock 1 hour ahead of standard time.

Tipping   Tips are a very important part of certain workers' income, and gratuities are the standard way of showing appreciation for services provided. (Tipping is certainly not compulsory if the service is poor.)

In hotels, tip **bellhops** at least $1 per bag ($2–$3 if you have a lot of luggage) and tip the **chamber staff** $1 to $2 per day (more if you've left a disaster area for him or her to clean up). Tip the **doorman** or **concierge** only if he or she has provided you with some specific service (for example, calling a cab for you or obtaining difficult-to-get theater tickets). Tip the **valet-parking attendant** $1 every time you get your car.

In restaurants, bars, and nightclubs, tip **service staff** and **bartenders** 15% to 20% of the check, tip **checkroom attendants** $1 per garment, and tip **valet-parking attendants** $1 per vehicle.

As for other service personnel, tip **cab drivers** 15% of the fare; tip **skycaps** at airports at least $1 per bag ($2–$3 if you have a lot of luggage); and tip **hairdressers** and **barbers** 15% to 20%.

Toilets   You won't find public toilets or "restrooms" on the streets in most U.S. cities, but they can be found in hotel lobbies, bars, restaurants, museums, department stores, railway and bus stations, and service stations. Large hotels and fast-food restaurants are often the best bet for clean facilities. Restaurants and bars in resorts or heavily visited areas may reserve their restrooms for patrons.

Travelers with Disabilities   Most disabilities shouldn't stop anyone from traveling in Virginia, where most establishments are required to comply with the Americans with Disabilities Act. That means they have ramps for wheelchairs and at least one room equipped for travelers with disabilities.

The federal government's **Interagency Access Pass** (formerly the Golden Access Pass) gives visually impaired persons or persons with permanent disabilities (regardless of age) free admission for life to national parks, monuments, historic sites, national forest recreation areas, and national wildlife refuges. The pass can be obtained in person at any U.S. National Park Service facility that charges an entrance fee. You need to show proof of citizenship and medically determined disability. Besides free entry, the pass also offers a 50% discount on some federal-use fees such as those charged for camping, swimming, parking, boat launching, and tours. For more information, go to www.nps.gov/fees_passes.htm or call ⓒ **888/467-2757.**

Traveling with Pets   The **Virginia Tourism Corporation** website (www.virginia.org) provides information about pet-friendly events around the state and hotels and motels that accept pets. Policies vary from hotel to hotel, so call ahead to find out the rules. Many pet-friendly hotels charge an additional fee to guests who bring along their furry friends. Most B&Bs do not accept pets, but some of their owners have them, so ask before booking if you're allergic to animals.

Pets are allowed on short leashes in Virginia state parks but restricted in national parks (there are a few trails in Shenandoah National Park on which you can walk Fido). Check with each park's ranger station before setting out.

Visas The U.S. State Department has a **Visa Waiver Program (VWP)** allowing citizens of the following countries to enter the United States without a visa for stays of up to 90 days: Andorra, Australia, Austria, Belgium, Brunei, Czech Republic, Denmark, Estonia, Finland, France, Germany, Greece, Hungary, Iceland, Ireland, Italy, Japan, Latvia, Liechtenstein, Lithuania, Luxembourg, Malta, Monaco, Netherlands, New Zealand, Norway, Portugal, San Marino, Singapore, Slovakia, Slovenia, South Korea, Spain, Sweden, Switzerland, and the United Kingdom. (**Note:** This list was accurate at press time; for the most up-to-date list of countries in the VWP, consult http://travel.state.gov/visa.)

Even though a visa isn't necessary, in an effort to help U.S. officials check travelers against terror watch lists before they arrive at U.S. borders, visitors from VWP countries must register online through the Electronic System for Travel Authorization (ESTA) before boarding a plane or a boat to the U.S. Travelers must complete an electronic application providing basic personal and travel eligibility information. The Department of Homeland Security recommends submitting the application at least 3 days before traveling. Authorizations will be valid for up to 2 years or until the traveler's passport expires. Currently, there is a $14 fee for the online application. Existing ESTA registrations remain valid through their expiration dates.

Note: Any passport issued on or after October 26, 2006, by a VWP country must be an **e-Passport** for VWP travelers to be eligible to enter the U.S. without a visa. Citizens of these nations also need to present a round-trip air or cruise ticket upon arrival. E-Passports contain computer chips capable of storing biometric information, such as the required digital photograph of the holder. If your passport doesn't have this feature, you can still travel without a visa if the passport was issued before October 26, 2005, and includes a machine-readable zone; or if the passport was issued between October 26, 2005, and October 25, 2006, and includes a digital photograph.

Canadian citizens may enter the United States without visas, but need to show passports and proof of residence.

Citizens of all other countries must have (1) a valid passport that expires at least 6 months later than the scheduled end of their visit to the U.S.; and (2) a tourist visa.

For information about U.S. visas go to **http://travel.state.gov/visa**, or go to one of the following websites:

Australian citizens can obtain up-to-date visa information from the **U.S. Embassy Canberra,** Moonah Place, Yarralumla, ACT 2600 (✆ **02/6214-5600**) or the U.S. Diplomatic Mission's website at **http://canberra.usembassy.gov/visas.html**.

British subjects can obtain up-to-date visa information by calling the **U.S. Embassy Visa Information Line** (✆ **09042-450-100** from within the U.K. at £1.20 per minute, or ✆ **866/382-3589** from within the U.S. at a flat rate of $16, payable by credit card only) or by visiting the "Visas" section of the American Embassy London's website at **http://london.usembassy.gov.**

Irish citizens can obtain up-to-date visa information through the **U.S. Embassy Dublin,** 42 Elgin Rd., Ballsbridge, Dublin 4 (✆ 1580-47-VISA [8472] from within the Republic of Ireland at €2.40 per minute; **http://dublin.usembassy.gov**).

Citizens of **New Zealand** can obtain up-to-date visa information by contacting the **U.S. Embassy New Zealand,** 29 Fitzherbert Terrace, Thorndon, Wellington (✆ **644/462-6000; http://newzealand.usembassy.gov**).

Visitor Information   Each city and town has a visitor information office. I list contact information for these offices in the destination chapters.

The best source for statewide information is the **Virginia Tourism Corporation,** 901 E. Byrd St. (PO Box 798), Richmond, VA 23219 (*©* **800/847-4882** or 804/786-2051; fax 804/786-1919; **www.virginia.org**). It distributes a host of information, including a statewide travel planner; official state highway maps (including the state's "Civil War Trails" map and a very useful "scenic byways" map highlighting the state's many beautiful routes); lists of hotels, motels, country inns, and bed-and-breakfasts; an outdoor guide to the state; a golf directory; a biking guide; a state park directory; a list of Virginia wineries and wine festivals; and a guide for travelers with disabilities. Most are available on, or can be ordered from, its website, where you can also download its free "Virginia Is for Lovers" iPhone app.

A good regional source is **www.visithamptonroads.com**, a site posted by the Virginia Tourism Corporation and maintained by the Hampton Roads Partnership, a cooperative effort of the local tourism information offices. It covers Norfolk, Portsmouth, Virginia Beach, Hampton, Newport News, the Williamsburg area, and other localities in southeastern Virginia.

Dial 511 for Info

You can dial *©* **511** from anywhere in Virginia and receive up-to-date travel, traffic, and weather information.

Another is the **Shenandoah Valley Travel Association,** PO Box 1040, New Market, VA 22844 (*©* **877/847-4878** or 540/740-3131; **www.visitshenandoah. org**), which covers the valley from Winchester to Lexington.

The **National Geographic Society** (www.nationalgeographic.com/maps) publishes excellent maps of Shenandoah National Park (map no. 228) and of Mount Rogers National Recreation Area (no. 786). I'm an ardent reader of **Virginia Living** (www.virginialiving.com), a slick lifestyle magazine published bimonthly in Richmond. Its compilation of festivals and events is comprehensive.

Wi-Fi   See "Internet & Wi-Fi," earlier in this section.

Index